GERMANY: THE LONG ROAD WEST

Heinrich August Winkler

Germany: The Long Road West

Volume 1: 1789–1933

Translated by
ALEXANDER J. SAGER

OXFORD
UNIVERSITY PRESS

OXFORD
UNIVERSITY PRESS

Great Clarendon Street, Oxford, OX2 6DP,
United Kingdom

Oxford University Press is a department of the University of Oxford.
It furthers the University's objective of excellence in research, scholarship,
and education by publishing worldwide. Oxford is a registered trade mark of
Oxford University Press in the UK and in certain other countries

First published in English by Oxford University Press 2006
First published in English in paperback
by Oxford University Press, 2023

Published in the United States of America by Oxford University Press
198 Madison Avenue, New York, NY 10016, United States of America

British Library Cataloguing in Publication Data
Data available

Library of Congress Cataloging in Publication Data
Data available

ISBN 978-0-19-926597-8 (Hbk.)
ISBN 978-0-19-288461-9 (Pbk.)

Preface

I would like to thank Ms Teresa Löwe and Mr Sebastian Ullrich, who worked on the titles for the subsections of the individual chapters, corrected the proofs, and compiled the index of names. Ms Gretchen Klein transformed my handwritten pages into a manuscript ready for the press. This volume owes a great deal to her care and patience. The book's main editor at C. H. Beck, Dr Ernst-Peter Wieckenburg, was an admirably thorough and critical reader of the manuscript, as with earlier books of mine with this publisher. My warm thanks to them both.

I dedicate this volume to my wife. It took shape in conversation with her, from first outlines to final form. Without her support it would not have been written.

H.A.W.

Berlin
November 1999

Contents

Abbreviations

Abl.	*Abendblatt* (evening edition of *NZ*)
ADGB	Allgemeiner Deutscher Gewerkschaftsbund (General German Trade Union Association)
AdR	*Akten der Reichskanzlei*
AfS	*Archiv für Sozialgeschichte*
APZ	*Aus Politik und Zeitgeschichte*
AStA	Allgemeiner Studentenausschuss
BVG	Berliner Verkehrs-Gesellschaft
BVP	Bayerische Volkspartei (Bavarian People's Party)
CEH	*Central European History*
DDP	Deutsche Demokratische Partei (German Democratic Party)
DNVP	Deutschnationale Volkspartei (German National People's Party)
DuM	*Dokumente und Materialien zur Geschichte der deutschen Arbeiterbewegung*
DVP	Deutsche Volkspartei (German People's Party)
GG	*Geschichte und Gesellschaft*
GWU	*Geschichte in Wissenschaft und Unterricht*
HPB	*Historische-politische Blätter für das katholische Deutschland*
HZ	*Historische Zeitschrift*
Inprekorr	*Internationale Pressekorrespondenz*
JMH	*Journal of Modern History*
KPD	Kommunistische Partei Deutschlands (Communist Party of Germany)
Mbl.	*Morgenblatt* (midday edition of *NZ*)
MECW	Karl Marx and Friedrich Engels, *Complete Works* (New York: International Publishers, 1975–2004)
MEW	Karl Marx and Friedrich Engels, *Werke* (Berlin: Institute for Marxism/Leninism, Central Committee of the SED, 1956–)
MGH	Monumenta Germaniae Historica
MGM	*Militärgeschichtliche Mitteilungen*
MSPD	Mehrheitssozialdemokratische Partei Deutschlands (Majority Social Democratic Party of Germany)
NEKZ	*Neue Evangelische Kirchenzeitung*
NF	Neue Folge (new series)
NPL	*Neue Politische Literatur*
NSDAP	Nationalsozialistische Deutsche Arbeiterpartei (National Socialist German Workers' Party)
NZ	*National-Zeitung* (Berlin)
OHL	Oberste Heeresleitung (Army High Command)
PVS	*Politische Vierteljahresschrift*
SA	Sturmabteilungen (Storm Troopers)
SPD	Sozialdemokratische Partei Deutschlands (Social Democratic Party of Germany)

SS	Schutzstaffeln (Security Force)
Sten. Ber.	*Stenographischer Bericht über die Verhandlungen des Deutschen Reichstags*
Sten. Ber., LT	*Stenographischer Bericht über die Verhandlungen des Preussischen Abgeordnetenhauses*
USPD	Unabhängige Sozialdemokratische Partei Deutschlands (Independent Social Democratic Party of Germany)
VfZ	*Vierteljahrshefte für Zeitgeschichte*
VSWG	*Vierteljahrsschrift für Sozial- und Wirtschaftsgeschichte*
VZ	*Volkszeitung (Berlin)*

Introduction

Was there or was there not a German *Sonderweg*? Did Germany develop along its own 'unique path' through history? This is one of the most controversial questions in German historical scholarship. For a long time, educated Germans answered it in the positive, initially by laying claim to a special German mission, then, after the collapse of 1945, by criticizing Germany's deviation from the West. Today, the negative view is predominant. Germany did not, according to the now prevailing opinion, differ from the great European nations to an extent that would justify speaking of a 'unique German path'. And, in any case, no country on earth ever took what can be described as the 'normal' path.

The question of whether the peculiarities of German history justify speaking of a 'unique German path'—or perhaps of several 'unique German paths'—is the starting point of this two-volume study. Consequently, the attempt to provide an answer can only be made at the end, and this answer must reflect the problems discussed along the way. I present here not a 'total history', but a 'problem history'. At the centre of *this* history of Germany in the nineteenth and twentieth centuries stands the relationship between democracy and nation. On the one hand, I enquire how it happened that Germany was politically so far behind England and France, developing a nation state only after 1866 and a democracy later still, in the wake of Germany's defeat in the First World War and the revolution of 1918–19. On the other hand, I investigate the consequences of this twofold historical belatedness, consequences which are still with us today.

This is a political history, but not of the traditional kind. Affairs of high diplomacy are treated mostly in passing, battles virtually ignored. Events play an important role, but less for their own sake than for the significance ascribed to them by contemporaries and by those who came later. I focus special attention on interpretations of history, how they influenced people, and how they informed political decision-making. Such interpretations were and still are controversial, the objects of discourses. Accordingly, my study is also a discourse history.

To draw is to omit, as the painter Max Liebermann once said. I will omit many things and concentrate on what seems important to me in the light of the central question. It goes without saying that a different central question would elicit a different set of problems and a different evaluation of facts and opinions.

Historical narratives require a vanishing point. Vanishing points change in the course of time. The years 1933 and 1945 are the vanishing points towards which histories of modern Germany have been written after the Second World War. There is now a new vanishing point—the year 1990. We will not reach it until the second volume, which deals with the period between the 'Third Reich' and the reunification of Germany. Nonetheless, the vanishing point of '1990' is already at work in the first volume, which takes us to the downfall of the first German democracy, known as the Weimar Republic, and to the threshold of the 'Third Reich'.

How it happened that Hitler came to power is still the most important question of nineteenth- and twentieth-century German history, if not of all German history. Ever since 1990, however, it has been joined by a new question: why did the German question find its answer in reunification? Or, in other words, why is there no longer a German question after 1990, and why only after this particular year?

In selecting the year 1990 as our latest vanishing point, we will be investigating many interpretations German history has undergone between 1945 and 1990. Since there is now a German nation state once again (albeit not a 'classical' nation state, but rather a 'post-classical' one, firmly integrated into Europe), German history can no longer be understood as the refutation of a German nation state, or indeed of the nation state as such. The first German national state, which came into being in 1871, belongs not only to the prehistory of 1933, but also of 1990. It bears within itself both the causes of its failure in the 'German catastrophe' of the years 1933–45 and, at the same time, much that went into the founding of the second German nation state. Here I will name only the key words: rule of law, constitutional state, federal state, social welfare state, general suffrage, and parliamentary culture. And another point, only seldom mentioned: the Two-Plus-Four Treaty of 1990 was a confirmation of Bismarck's 'Little Germany solution', at least to the extent that the latter rejected the 'Greater Germany solution' of the German problem, the solution *with* Austria.

Towards the end of the first volume it will become clear that, by the eve of Hitler's accession to power, the German people were not only weary of the democracy of 1918–19, but also dissatisfied with the 'Little German' national state of 1871. Educated Germans were fascinated with the idea of an empire that included Austria and controlled central Europe, a polity that sought to be different and more than the typical nation state. The origins of the myth of the 'Reich' lie deep in the German past. The first chapter of the first volume of this German history from the end of the old empire to the reunification begins with an enquiry into the medieval antecedents of this myth. In the second volume, I will discuss the question of what replaced the mythology of the empire after it vanished along with the German Reich in 1945. Was it a particular 'post-national' idea of Europe? Was it, in other words, the idea of a new German mission—the supersession of the nation and the nation state, as an example to all of Europe?

In the prologue to his book *Die Geschichten der romanischen und germanischen Völker von 1494 bis 1535**, Leopold von Ranke wrote that the historian should 'merely tell how it really was'. After Hitler, this kind of history probably can no longer be written. For us, the question should be: Why did it happen the way it

* Ranke, *History of the Romance and Germanic Peoples.*

did? The readers I have in mind for this and the second volume are not only other historians, but all those who would like to know the answer to this question.

I have recourse to historical sources as much as possible (and that is not the only respect in which Ranke is not yet obsolete). I consider narrative not the opposite of explanation, but rather its commensurate form. My notes at the end of the volume contain, in addition to source citations for the quotes, references to selected secondary literature. I include more of these for the central questions of this study, but nowhere is my goal the utopian one of providing an exhaustive list. Footnotes, added for this translation, explain specialized terms and give translations for German poems, titles, and quotations.

1

Legacy of a Millennium

THE REICH AND ITS MYTHOLOGY

In the beginning was the Reich. Everything that divides German history from the history of the great European nations had its origin in the Holy Roman Empire. The parting of ways began in the Middle Ages, when nation-states began to develop in England and France, while in Germany the formation of the modern state proceeded along lower, territorial lines. At the same time, a political construct endured in Germany that claimed to be more than simply one kingdom among many: the Holy Roman Empire. We must go far back in history to understand why Germany became a nation-state later than England and France—and a democracy later still.[1]

Accordingly, the first part of this study concerns the old Reich and the mythology that grew up around it. This is the first of three basic phenomena that shaped the character of German history throughout many centuries. The second is the confessional schism of the sixteenth century, which contributed decisively to making Germany the theatre of a thirty-year European war the century following. The third phenomenon is the opposition between Austria and Prussia. If in the second half of the eighteenth century the Reich seemed to many people no more than an empty shell, the Austro-Prussian antinomy was the reason.

The Reich had always been a myth. Medieval writers expended a great deal of effort attempting to prove that the Roman *imperium* had never actually ceased to exist. To be sure, it had been divided in 395 into eastern and western halves; yet even after 476, when the western empire had collapsed in the tumults of the tribal migrations, the eastern empire still endured with its capital Constantinople, formerly Greek Byzantium. However, the claim of the eastern basileus to be *the* Roman Emperor was recognized ever less in the west, especially after the accession of a woman, the empress-widow Irene, to the throne at the end of the eighth century. Then, in 800, Pope Leo III placed the imperial crown on the head of Charlemagne, the king of the Franks and Lombards and protector of the ecclesiastic state created by his father, Pippin. The Romans rejoiced. Thereafter the imperial mantle passed from the Greeks to the Franks (or, as it later came to be said, to the Germans).

This was, at any rate, how the proponents of the medieval theory of the *translatio imperii*, the transfer or 'translation' of Roman imperial power, viewed things.

Indeed, they had every reason to emphasize the continuity of the empire. Following early Christian tradition, which drew on the prophet Daniel, they considered the Roman empire the fourth and last of the great world empires, preceded by those of Babylon, Medea-Persia, and Macedonia. This succession also implied a shift in geopolitical focus from east to west, from the orient to the occident, with the *imperium Romanum* (from the fourth century AD onwards referred to as the *imperium Christianum*) the westernmost of them all. It was generally believed that the Antichrist would not arise as long as the Roman empire endured. According to the Book of Revelation, in its medieval interpretation based on St Jerome, the Antichrist was a tyrant, false prophet, Jew, and chief of heretics. The New Testament prophecy considered his rule to represent the end of world history. Thereafter Christ would return, destroy the self-proclaimed 'god', and initiate the Heavenly Kingdom. The Roman empire was to play the role of the *catechon*, the power holding back the enemy of Christ and thus delaying the end of the world. It was not until the era of modern theological scholarship that the Pauline authorship of 2 Thessalonians, the source text (chapter 2) of the *catechon* idea, was called into question. It is now generally considered a fictitious ascription.[2]

The theory of imperial continuity played an important role in the coronation of the Saxon king Otto the Great by Pope John XII in 962. This event represented—or was made to represent—not the foundation of a new empire, but the return of the *imperium Romanum*. To be sure, the Treaty of Verdun had divided the Frankish empire in 843, and there had been no emperor in the west for nearly four decades, ever since the murder of the last emperor from the imperial Frankish nobility in 924. However, the East Franks had had a decisive voice in the royal election of Otto's father, Heinrich I, in 919. Looking back on Otto's coronation in 962 from his vantage point in the mid-twelfth century, Bishop Otto of Freising, the uncle and counsellor of the Hohenstaufen emperor Frederick Barbarossa, spoke of a 'retranslation': after the Franks and the Lombards, the Empire of the Romans was now being 'transferred back' (*retranslatum est*) to the Germans (*ad teutonicos*) or, as others saw it, to the Franks, who had before 'let it slip,' so to speak.[3]

In Otto's day there was, as yet, no mention of '*die Deutschen*'. Latinized terms such as *teutonici* and *teutones* only became common around the turn of the millennium. By this time, of course, they no longer referred to the old Teutonic tribes, but to the contemporaneous 'Germans': people who spoke the same language (*deutsch*) despite various tribal ancestry. Thus it makes little sense to speak of 'the German nation' much before 1000. The second half of the eleventh century witnessed the politicization of the concept *deutsch*. During the struggle over the investiture of imperial bishoprics, the first large-scale conflict between secular and ecclesiastical powers, Pope Gregory VII referred to his opponent, Emperor Henry IV of the Salian Frankish dynasty, as *rex Teutonicorum*, 'king of the Germans'. He wanted to make clear that a German king who had not been vetted and crowned by the pope could be, at most, a ruler over *his own* people, but not the Roman emperor. The term was intended as a humiliation, and as such it was fully in keeping with

Gregory's attitude at Canossa, the fortress on the northern slopes of the Apennines in front of which, in January 1077, the pope compelled the emperor to wait three days in the habiliments of a penitent before lifting the papal interdiction against him. North of the Alps, however, the term *regnum Teutonicorum* ('kingdom of the Germans') soon came to be used in a more positive manner, signalling the developing sense of community and growing self-awareness of the Germans.[4]

Nonetheless, the German kings were not going to rest content with a mere kingdom. The concept *regnum Teutonicorum* referred only to the German part of their sovereign territories. It did not apply to Burgundy, which had belonged to the Reich since 1034, nor to the Italian lands under imperial control. The German kings needed the imperial title in order to rule the Reich in its entirety effectively. The terms *imperium* and *imperator* did not necessarily imply a claim to suzerainty over polities that did not belong to the Reich. However, the medieval emperors certainly did insist upon a special *dignitas* and ceremonial pre-eminence over other occidental kings. As long as they restricted themselves to this, they were not challenged, not even in France and England. As protector of the Christian church, the emperor merited a higher rank than other sovereigns. But only in *this* capacity.[5]

During the reign of the Hohenstaufen dynasty, western observers gained the impression that the German emperors were indeed out for more that the prestige of the position of first among equals. In 1160, at a church synod dominated by the imperial episcopate, and thus in no way representative of the church as a whole, Frederick I acknowledged as pope (or rather antipope) a candidate whom, in the prior deliberations of the College of Cardinals, only the minority fraction loyal to Frederick had supported. One of the most famous churchmen of the age, John of Salisbury, the bishop of Chartres, rose in protest: 'Who is he that subjugates the Universal Church to a particular church? Who has appointed the Germans the judge of nations? [*Quis Teutonicos constituit iudices nationum?*] Who has granted to such coarse and violent folk the power to install a prince above the heads of humanity?'[6]

The English critique from Chartres was a response to what we might call Hohenstaufen 'imperial ideology', to use a modern expression. In 1157, the chancery of Frederick I began to employ the term *Sacrum Imperium*, 'Holy Empire'. Hohenstaufen political propagandists referred to the rulers of other kingdoms condescendingly as 'little kings', *reguli*. Certain poems by the Archpoet, a writer belonging to the circle of the imperial chancellor Reinald von Dassel, and the *Spiel vom Antichrist**, written in 1160 in the monastery at Tegernsee, went so far as to thematize a German 'world empire'. The anonymous author of the latter text considered this pretension justified by the special vocation of the Germans within the course of sacred history: as the nucleus of the people of God, the Germans would be the last to resist the Antichrist, the enemy of the fatherland.[7]

* Anon., *The Plays of the Antichrist.*

Such ideas played virtually no role in the practical politics of Frederick I. Still, there is little doubt that his high-handed brinkmanship vis-à-vis the papacy, indeed his entire Italian policy, was unrealistic and catastrophic. And considering the achievements and plans of his son, Emperor Henry VI (1190–7), one is perfectly justified in talking about Hohenstaufen 'world policy'. This prince, having obtained a claim to rule Sicily through marriage, enforced it with military power. He compelled the English king, Richard Lionheart, whom he had taken prisoner after the latter's return from the Third Crusade, to receive England as an imperial fief. He secured suzerainty over Armenia, Tunis, and Tripoli, obtained a Hohenstaufen claim to the succession in Byzantium, and probably contemplated the conquest of the whole eastern empire. He did not succeed in subjecting France to imperial domination, but it is quite possible that he would have extended his plans of conquest to the west, once he had secured the east. In the event, his early death consigns these matters to the realm of speculation. Had he lived longer, he might also have realized yet another of his ambitious goals: to establish the Reich as the hereditary princedom of the Hohenstaufens. This question, too, must remain open.[8]

The short reign of Henry VI marks the turning point in the history of the medieval Reich. Henry had tried to subjugate all of Europe; now, after a seventeen-year interval plagued by competing claims to the throne and civil war, it was left to the other European powers to decide the issue of Henry's succession by his son, Frederick II. The dice fell in 1214 on the field of Bouvines in a battle between the forces of English and French chivalry. The military defeat of the English spelled the final political defeat of their German ally, the Guelf emperor Otto IV, son of Frederick Barbarossa's inveterate enemy, Henry the Lion.

Frederick II of Hohenstaufen was crowned German king in 1215 at Aachen. The imperial coronation took place five years later in Rome. But Frederick was much more a Sicilian than a German prince. For Germany, the most important event of his rule was his renunciation of royal authority in the German lands and his cession of the rights to levy tolls and mint coins to the ecclesiastic and secular princes. These statutes were codified in the *Confoederatio cum principibus ecclesiasticis* (1220) and the *Statutum in favorem principum* (1232). The latter document was directed primarily against the cities and the urban bourgeoisie, who claimed independence from feudal princes under the motto *Stadtluft macht frei*, 'city air liberates'.

The territorial princes had already gained considerably in power during the struggle over lay investiture, during which they had temporarily sided with the pope against the German king. They now emerged as the true winners from the crisis of the high medieval Reich. The documents of 1220 and 1232 consolidated the development of Germany along the lines of the territorial state. This development had actually begun in the previous century, not so much through the transfer of royal privileges, but as a consequence of the local princes' efforts to settle and develop their land and concentrate their power. This happened not only in the old German territories of the west, south, and north, but also in the regions east of the Elbe that had been 'Germanized' in the wake of conquest, missionary activity among the Slavic peoples, and colonization. In terms of general constitutional development, the Battle of Bouvines, which had made Frederick II's rule possible, was merely one turning point among several.[9]

The battle had a greater impact on France and England. In France, the defeat of the English and their ally Otto strengthened the domestic position of the victorious French king. The hitherto powerful vassals of the crown suffered a loss of influence vis-à-vis a strongly centralizing monarchy. On the other side of the English Channel the situation was much different. Magna Carta of 1215 forced the weakened English monarch to concede extensive rights and privileges both to the nobility and to the bourgeoisie. Furthermore, he had to submit monarchical authority to a certain degree of review and control by a committee elected from among the barons. These concessions laid the basis for the development of England into a constitutional state.[10]

The later thirteenth century witnessed the zenith of medieval imperial ideology, even though by this time the power of the German emperors had long since begun to wane. In his influential and widely read treatise *Memoriale der prerogativa Romani imperii* (1289), Alexander von Roes, a canon lawyer from Cologne, outlined the structure of what he considered a sensible and necessary societal order in the following way: the Romans, being the older people, ought to receive the office of the papacy (*sacerdotium*) as their own; the imperial office (*imperium*) rightly falls to the Germans or Franks (*Germani vel Franci*) as the younger people; to the French or Gauls, noted for their mental acumen, accrues the study of the sciences (*studium*).[11] The author intended this scheme of a division of labour among the nations as a defensive manoeuvre against French attempts to establish a claim to the emperorship. However, the idea found no resonance in France. In a document for Philip the Fair from 1296, an anonymous French lawyer repeated a claim that had already been made the previous century on behalf of the French monarch: namely that in *his* kingdom, *he* is emperor. 'And because there was a king in France before there was an emperor, the king may be counted the worthier.' This statement can almost be interpreted as a direct response to the project of Alexander von Roes.[12]

In one area, however, there was agreement between the secular rulers of the west, at least in theory: they all rejected the 'papal revolution', to use the expression of Eugen Rosenstock-Huessey, one of the last German universal historians of the twentieth century, in his 1931 book about the revolutions in Europe. The 'papal revolution' found its manifesto in Pope Gregory VII's 1075 bull *Dictatus Papae*. Gregory's claim that the pope could depose the emperor reversed only the practice of the emperors. His assertion that only the pope could remove or relocate bishops, however, was just as much a declaration of war against the kings of France and England as against the emperor. If the pope had had his will in the matter, the political system of all three lands would have collapsed, since bishops not only exercised spiritual offices, but were also, in personal union, the highest administrative officials of the crown. As it happened, the curia achieved at best partial success. From the early twelfth century onward (first in France, then in

England, then in Germany with the Concordat of Worms in 1122), bishops were elected to their offices according to canon law, but in the presence of the secular ruler, allowing the latter to continue to exert his influence.

The Investiture Contest was only one stage in the struggle between spiritual and secular authority. In 1302 Pope Boniface VIII reasserted the curia's stance that the papacy was above all other rulers. The bull *Unam Sanctam*, directed at the French king Philip the Fair, claimed that two swords lay in the hand of the pope, a spiritual sword and a secular sword. Both were thus under the power of the church, the only difference being that the spiritual sword was wielded *by* the church, the secular sword *for* the church.[13]

The developing nation states of France and England answered the papal challenge by nationalizing their churches to a great extent, beginning with a rigorous restriction of papal taxes from church property. The Roman-German emperors could not go the national route without calling into question their own universal aspirations and provoking the German princes, many of whom were striving to become 'pope' in their own territories by consolidating their regional churches.[14] The reaction of the emperor's 'party' to the secular pretensions of the church (and to the instrumentalization of the church by France during the Avignon papacy from 1309 to 1377) was initially ideological in nature. Two literary advocates of Emperor Ludwig the Bavarian (1314–47), the Italian political intellectual Marsilius of Padua and the English Franciscan William of Ockham, argued that the transmission of the Roman imperial mantle 'from the Greeks to the Germans' in the year 800 derived from the will of the Roman people. Thus, they placed a democratic doctrine against the curial interpretation of the *translatio imperii* by means of the papal office, which had been articulated 'ex cathedra' in 1202 by Innocent III in the bull *Venerabilem*. Yet the reality of the *Sacrum Imperium* contradicted the idea of the sovereignty of the people so radically that the construct had little impact.[15]

The secularization of the church also provoked a response from the German mystics, beginning with Eckhart (*c*.1250–1327). Unlike the efforts of Ludwig's political theorists, the 'inward turn' of the mystics had a great impact on the development of the church in Germany. In his 1929 book on the *Sacrum Imperium*, Alois Dempf interpreted the struggle to deepen and enliven religious devotion in Germany as the counterpart to the 'political reformation' in France and England. Transforming 'piety without priests into a widespread pietistic movement', German mysticism prepared the way for a development of world-historical consequence: the Reformation. The young Luther knew in what traditions he stood.[16]

The estrangement from Rome, implicit in mysticism but restricted to the religious sphere, intensified to an early form of German national consciousness in the course of the fifteenth century. Both the emperor and the imperial estates could agree in their rejection of the papacy's financial demands. *Gravamina nationis Germanicae*, the title of the document into which their complaints were formally gathered (beginning *c*.1440), gives expression to the consciousness of their commonality. The name *Römisches Reich Deutscher Nation* was used for the first time in 1486 in an imperial law; the complete title *Heiliges Römisches Reich Deutscher Nation* first appears in the recess of the Imperial Diet of Cologne from 1512. The addendum 'of the German Nation' was not at first intended to establish equivalence between the Roman empire and Germany, but rather as a restriction indicating the 'German territories' of the Reich in contrast to the territories of the *welsch*— that is, Italian—nation.

Yet even in the original spirit of the title, the German lands were considered the core of the empire, and by means of this usage the term 'nation' acquired a new significance. Whereas before it had served as a practical means of distinguishing and organizing national-ethnic groups at universities, church councils, and among the foreign merchants in west European trading centres, in the fifteenth century it broadened to a general way of looking at the world. The defining factor in the German concept of 'nation' was the commonality of language (*Gezunge*). It probably could not have been otherwise, since, as we recall, the 'German nation' had no political-administrative reality of any kind at this time. In France and England, in contrast, the formation of the nation proceeded from the monarchy, which lent a statist orientation to the idea of the 'nation' that was not possible in Germany.

The emperor made use of the word 'nation' whenever he desired the support of the imperial estates (*Reichsstände*) and their leaders, the imperial electors, in matters of common interest. The seven electors, however (the archbishops of Trier, Cologne, and Mainz, the king of Bohemia, the count of the Rhenish Palatinate, the duke of Saxony, and the count of Brandenburg) had reason to believe that not everything the elected 'Roman king' considered necessary was in the interest of the Reich and nation. The dynastic interests of the Habsburgs, who had stood at the apex of the Reich since 1438, were by no means automatically the same as the interests of the empire or the German nation.[17]

Conversely, the agenda of the electors—to the extent that they could agree, which happened rarely enough—was also not necessarily in harmony with the common good of the Reich. While they were recognized as the co-bearers of imperial authority by the *Golden Bull*, the foundational law of the Reich from 1356, the seven electors did not alone constitute the 'nation'. It also included the princes and the other imperial estates, who had far less influence on imperial policy and legislation, not to mention the cities, which were most burdened by imperial taxation but had no voice in the Imperial Diet (*Reichstag*) in the fifteenth century. Even at the beginning of the 1400s, it was clear to many that the empire needed to be thoroughly reorganized. The steps taken under Emperors Frederick III (1440–93) and Maximilian I (1493–1519), however, hardly merited the name of 'imperial reform'. In Germany, the real institutional development of the state took place not at the level of the Reich, but in the territories, whose princes increasingly took advantage of Roman law and employed the services of well-educated officials trained in its application. The princes of the larger territories were especially energetic in this kind of regional reform and consolidation, and it was they who, in their corresponding lack of interest in centralizing measures, stood in the way of effective imperial reform.[18]

It was this rather dismal reality of the Reich that prompted the German humanists, both before and after 1500, to call for the restoration of the old imperial glory. The source of their hope and inspiration was the remembrance of a distant past, the age of *Germania Magna*, in which the nations of Germanic origin were still undivided. Invoking Tacitus, whose *Germania* had been rediscovered in 1455, the humanists drew an idealizing picture of German virtue that contrasted advantageously with its distorted counterpart: the Romans, who had long since lapsed into decadence and debauchery. Republican Rome, not the Rome of the Caesars, could teach the Germans the love of the fatherland. After all, the Germans had inherited the succession to the Roman empire. The greatness and dignity of the Reich derived from this legacy, which was earned and legitimate. This belief did not, however, prevent the humanists from appealing to Pope Innocent III's bull *Venerabilem* in order to prove that the empire had been transferred from the Greeks to the Germans in the person of Charlemagne in 800. The aspirations arising from this view of things assumed, in the writings of several authors, Hohenstaufen-like dimensions.[19] In his *Narrenschiff**, Sebastian Brant, a member of the upper Rhenish humanist circle, appeals to God to make the Roman empire so large

> daz im all erd sy underthon
> als es von recht und gsatz solt han.†

In this respect, too, Martin Luther was certainly no humanist. According to his letter *An den christlichen Adel deutscher Nation von des christlichen Standes Besserung*‡ (1520), the first Roman empire had been destroyed by the Goths. And the Roman empire over which the emperor presided at Constantinople should, by rights, never have been transferred by the pope to the Germans. That the pope did so was 'violence and lawlessness', and it turned the Germans into the 'knaves of the pope'. Still, even Luther recognized the cunning of reason and the normative power of factual reality. He regarded it as certain 'that God used the papal wickedness in this matter in order to give the German nation such an Empire, and allowed them to build up another after the fall of the first Roman empire, one that still stands today'. Thus, even Luther was unwilling to recommend that

> the same be renounced, but rather it ought to be ruled honestly in the fear of God as long as it please Him. For as I have said, it matters not to Him whence an Empire comes, he nonetheless wishes to have it ruled. If the popes have dishonestly taken it from others, still we have won it not dishonestly . . . It is all God's order, that came to pass too early for us to know about.[20]

* Brant, *The Ship of Fools.*

† that all of earth its vassal be, | as it should be by right and law.

‡ Luther, *To the Christian Nobility of the German Nation Concerning the Reform of the Christian Estate.*

THE CONFESSIONAL DIVIDE

We have arrived at the second of the basic phenomena that have shaped German history, the Reformation. As Hegel wrote in his *Vorlesungen zur Philosophie der Geschichte** in 1830, 'The old, thoroughly tried and tested inwardness of the German people must bring about this break with the past out of the simple, ingenuous heart.' For Hegel, the Reformation was the 'sun that transfigures everything'; the event through which the 'subjective spirit in Truth' became 'free' and 'Christian freedom' became 'real'. Freedom was, in Hegel's view, the 'essential content of the Reformation; man is in his very nature destined to be free'.[21]

A radically different evaluation of the Reformation was undertaken by Marx in his 'Einleitung zur Kritik der Hegelischen Rechtsphilosophie',† written at the end of 1843 and the beginning of 1844. As Marx saw it, Luther

> destroyed faith in authority because he had restored the authority of faith. He changed the priests into laymen because he had changed the laymen into priests. He liberated man from external religiosity because he made religiosity into the inner man. He emancipated the body from its chains because he chained the heart.[22]

Possibly even more radical was Nietzsche's rejection of Hegel's interpretation in *Der Antichrist*‡ (1888): 'The Germans have taken from Europe the last great cultural harvest that Europe could have gathered—the Renaissance.' Cesare Borgia as pope: for Nietzsche, this would have meant 'victory', the end of Christianity. Luther, on the other hand, 'this monk, with all of the failed priest's instincts for vengeance, rebelled in Rome against the Renaissance . . . And Luther restored the Church. He attacked it . . . the Renaissance—an event with no meaning, a grandiose futility.'[23]

The German Reformation was *both*: the liberation from ecclesiastical coercion increasingly perceived as foreign rule *and* the establishment of a new, interiorized, state-supporting regime of coercion. Liberating and repressing at the same time, the Reformation, as Marx noted, could only partially supersede the Middle Ages. Engels was fundamentally in error when he called it the 'revolution no. 1 of the bourgeoisie'.[24] In terms of social history, especially in Switzerland and upper and middle Germany, the Reformation represented the uprising of the 'common man' in the country and city. The Peasants' War of 1524–5 was the culmination of this movement.[25]

In its political consequences, the Reformation is best described as what Rosenstock-Huessey called a 'princes' revolution':

> The grand hierarchy of the Church Visible has lost its pathos. The human soul is no longer where the clergy seeks it. The educational efforts of the church can thus confidently be left to the bishops of each locality and territory, and this bishop is the worldly authority. Luther's imperial elector replaces the supreme bishop . . . Probably in no other country in

* Hegel, *Lectures on the Philosophy of History.*
† Marx, *Critique of the Hegelian Philosophy of Right. Introduction.*
‡ Nietzsche, *The Antichrist.*

the world did two such different fields of vision overlap as they did here. Above, prince and statesman fight for their right and freedom of authority. Below, burghers and peasants live and learn the pure doctrine as well as obedience to authority within the narrow circle of their bondsman's understanding . . . the 'unpolitical' nature of the average German is already implicit in the voluntary division of labour between Luther and his sovereign.[26]

Territorial institutions of ecclesiastical authority had already developed in pre-Reformation times, and Luther did not initiate his movement in order to make (according to a venerable cliché) the territorial prince 'pope in his own country'. Rather, his starting point was the idea of a general 'lay priesthood', both individualistic and egalitarian. In the belief that the end of the world was near and that the Antichrist had already arisen in Rome in the person of the pope, Luther considered spiritual awakening to have priority over the institutional consolidation of the new faith. After all, the new faith was, correctly understood, the old faith. After the German imperial electors had chosen Maximilian's grandson Charles V (and not the French king Francis I, who enjoyed the support of the pope) in 1519, Luther, too, briefly hoped for large-scale reforms through a national council. But these hopes were soon dashed. Under Charles V, Germany was no longer the focus of the Habsburg universal monarchy. Additionally, the new faith was undermined by the activities of the iconoclasts and free sectarians (*Schwärmer*), which Luther regarded as diabolic attacks on the gospel. Faced with these problems, the movement shifted its priorities. Now the goal was to gather the faithful together and to strengthen the faith, which meant, above all, establishing new pastoral communities and reforming schools and universities.

In all their efforts, Luther and the Lutherans needed the support of the secular authorities, who had been ordained by God and who wielded the sword and rod to punish the wicked and protect the devout. Many princes had not merely a religious but also a material interest in promoting the new faith. By means of the Reformation, they gained access to church property, thereby increasing their government revenue and reinforcing their lordship. For Luther, the efforts the states and cities directed toward providing a lawful order for the new faith represented a labour of love. In making Luther's cause their own, secular rulers *could*, but were not *obligated to*, adopt his rationale.[27]

The development of the Evangelical church system in the territories began in 1527 with the visitations of Luther's territorial sovereign, Elector John of Saxony, to church communities and schools. The other princes who professed the new faith soon followed the example of the Saxon elector. The result was a coercive ecclesiastical system in which, in the words of the Evangelical theologian and philosopher of religion Ernst Troeltsch, the human element, hitherto of secondary importance, became the main focus:

The territorial princes unified theology and streamlined dogma, giving the symbolic books compulsory authority. With the help and participation of the theologians, they created an ecclesiastical-state bureaucracy that assumed the functions of the administration and the ecclesiastical courts. They imposed the principles of Christian faith and morals on the secular legal system and mandated civil-legal consequences for spiritual punishments and measures. In theory, the community was ruled by Christ and Holy Scripture; in practice, it was ruled by the territorial sovereigns and the theologians.[28]

Regardless of how sharply the former Augustinian monk Luther distinguished, in the tradition of St Augustine, between the 'two kingdoms', the earthy kingdom and the kingdom of God, in fact he so narrowed the gap between secular and spiritual power, throne and altar, that the state acquired 'a certain quasi-divine quality', to use Troeltsch's expression. Accordingly, the political consequences of Lutheranism in Germany (and here only) were radically different from those of the other main movement of the Reformation outside of Germany, Calvinism. In Geneva, where Calvin lived and taught, the imbrication of the community church with the republican government favoured the eventual development of democratic communities. In Germany, the alliance between territorial sovereignty and episcopate fostered the development of absolutism.[29]

To the Rome–Wittenberg antinomy was thus added the contrast between German Lutheranism and the Calvinist-influenced north-west, the strongest bastions of which were England and the Netherlands. In consequence of the Reformation, Germany became more 'eastern'. In a study of Luther first published in English in 1944, then in a revised edition in German in 1947, Franz Borkenau (an intellectual of wide erudition who had broken with party communism in 1929 and was later driven into exile by Hitler) argued that the Lutheran movement articulated in terms of dogma a number of differences between the eastern church and the western church that were only latent in the antagonism between the two great ecclesiastical systems.

> The Lutheran doctrine of justification, founded exclusively upon Christology, distinguishing sharply between morality and religion, dualistic in nature, and emphasizing a passive inner experience of faith and salvation, was essentially that of the eastern church as it came to be articulated in polemic confrontation with the western church. Lutheranism appears here as a branch of the eastern style of religious observance, grown up in protest against the religious reform movement of the west. Behind the doctrinal opposition to Rome yawns the cultural opposition to the occident.[30]

There is, to be sure, something problematic about such an exact comparison of Lutheranism to Greek-Russian Orthodoxy. Nonetheless, in Luther's religious inwardness there *was* an element that separated the Lutheran movement from the west and linked it to the east. Luther's inner distance from the political world makes his vehement condemnation of the Peasants' War and his dependence on the princes seem logical. The 'summepiscopate' in the Lutheran territories of Germany, the appropriation of the functions of the regional bishopric by the territorial prince, nearly eliminated one of the features of the historical occident distinguishing it from the 'caesaropapism' of the orient: the separation of powers between *imperium* (or *regnum*) and *sacerdotium*, a theme that had pitted the popes against the emperors and kings in a struggle that lasted centuries. Wherever this separation was maintained, or could establish itself again, an environment conducive to ideas of freedom was fostered. The Anglican state church, introduced in England by Henry VIII in 1534, was from the beginning closely linked to the estates; in the second half of the seventeenth century it was parliamentarized and finally, in the nineteenth century, liberalized. In Germany, on the other hand, the summepiscopate had, until 1918, an authoritarian and governmental or—to put it in somewhat exaggerated terms—caesaropapist orientation. Politically speaking, German Lutheranism represented a step backward.

'Lutheranism purchased spiritual liberation at the price of earthly subjection.' Borkenau's verdict summarizes the contradictory legacy of Martin Luther's Reformation. Both sides, the cultural and the political, must be seen in context.

> The German spirit could unfold its wings by leaving practical considerations behind, considerations that can never be set aside whenever every action must be justified in this world [as in Calvinism (H.A.W.)]. German music and German metaphysics could never have arisen in a culture shaped by Calvinism. Of course, a terrible danger lay in this soaring flight over the practical . . . The political is the place where spirit and world, morality and egotism, individualism and solidarity are brought together. The Lutheran attitude lacks the essence of the political and thus is partly responsible for making us into a people that always failed politically, a people tossed about between the equally false extremes of world-shy, good-natured inwardness and the most brutal kind of megalomania.[31]

Even with Luther, only one step separated inwardness from brutality. This is evident in the increasingly unbridled intensity of his attacks on the pope, the Anabaptists, and the Jews. Luther's enmity towards the Jews is *the* aspect of his life and work that confirms with especial forcefulness Marx's verdict that the Reformation only partially managed to overcome the Middle Ages. In Luther's later life, his earlier disappointment over the fact that the Jews could not be converted to the Evangelical faith gave way to a blind hatred. He saw only a malevolent stubbornness in the refusal of the Jews, the blood relatives of Christ, to hearken to the Good News. Expecting the end of the world in the near future, Luther came to see the Jews as yet another manifestation of the Antichrist, as he had done before with the pope and the Turks. His 1543 pamphlet *Von den Juden und ihren Lügen** repeated old charges, ones he knew full well could not be proven: the Jews poison wells and abduct Christian children for ritual killing. He exhorted the political authorities to burn the synagogues; to destroy Jews' houses; to forbid the rabbis to teach under pain of corporal punishment or death; to take away the right of the Jews to safe-conduct; to forbid them to use the streets or practice usury; to compel them to perform manual labour; and, if necessary, to expel them from the country. His advice to Christians was that they cross themselves whenever they saw a real Jew and speak openly and firmly the phrase: 'There walks a devil in the flesh.' This was, indeed, the 'darkness of the Middle Ages',

* Luther, *On the Jews and Their Lies.*

which not only continued to live *in* Luther, but also in no small measure *through* him.[32]

The Reformation forms one of the deepest epochal divisions in German history. In the preface to his *Deutsche Geschichte im Zeitalter der Reformation** (1839), Leopold von Ranke spoke of 'the most important event of our fatherland'. The Reformation did not simply divide the German nation; in certain respects it structured it anew. The emperor himself, belonging as he did to one of the competing religious parties, was less able to represent the whole of the Reich. Not even the curia of the electors could claim to stand for the whole, since it, too, was split into confessional factions. The same was true of the Imperial Diet. The religious parties themselves, however, were supra-territorial, indeed 'national' associations. From the point of view of the followers of the new faith, the German nation was the entity that came closest to embodying the ideal entirety of the Protestant imperial estates, most—but not all—of which had joined together in the Thuringian town of Schmalkalden in 1531, forming a defensive alliance against the ecclesiastical-political aspirations of Charles V. The common bond was not political, but rather cultural: the Evangelical faith in the sense of the 'Augsburg Confession', as it had been worked out in doctrinally binding terms by Philip Melanchthon in consultation with Luther (and not always to the satisfaction of the latter) at the Imperial Diet of Augsburg in 1530. This was the first step toward the 'confessionalization' of the new faith.

One of the most important factors for the spirit of solidarity and community among German Protestants was Luther's Bible translation. This text created the supra-regional German standard language, which in turn became the most important 'national' medium of communication and, as such, the prerequisite for the possibility that even two centuries later, when there was still no unified German state, educated Germans could consider themselves members of a German cultural nation. The Evangelical segment played such a crucial role in the formation of German national identity that one must speak of a Protestant cultural hegemony. For all that, however, Luther's *Volk* remained surprisingly mute, as Eugen Rosenstock-Huessey remarked. 'The nation he awoke to life became a nation of princes, professors, and pastors, and remained so for a long time, all the way to the professors' parliament at the Paulskirche in 1848. This role of the German universities in shaping the German nation develops in the fifteenth century.'[33]

Catholic Germany found little succour in the support of the emperor. The wars between Charles V and Francis I of France, as well as the Turkish danger, forced the emperor and the Catholic estates repeatedly to compromise with the supporters of the new faith, delaying the ultimate confrontation. This happened for the first time at the Imperial Diet held at Speyer in 1526, which left it for each imperial estate to decide whether or not to follow the Edict of Worms, the ostracism of

* Ranke, *German History in the Age of the Reformation.*

Luther and the condemnation of his teachings in 1521. The second instance was the 'Nuremberg Standstill' of 1532, which allowed Protestants the free exercise of their religion for the time being. Only after the year of Luther's death in 1546, when Charles was no longer hampered by involvement in foreign wars and had brought one of the most important Protestant princes, Duke Moritz of Saxony, over to his side (by promising him the electoral dignity, which was in the hands of his cousin from another branch of the Saxon house, John Frederick), could the emperor dare to strike against the Schmalkaldic League.

However, the emperor did not manage to convert his military triumph in the Schmalkaldic War (1546–7) into a political success, since Moritz of Saxony, now an elector, allied himself to the princely opposition, made common cause with the French king Henry II(to whom he conceded the imperial curacy over Metz, Toul, and Verdun), and took up arms against Charles V. The Treaty of Passau, which the emperor found himself forced to conclude in 1552, again granted the Protestants freedom of worship until the convention of a new Imperial Diet. This assembly, held in 1555 in Augsburg, marks both the end of the age of the Reformation and the conclusion of the struggle over imperial reform. From this moment forward, all parties acknowledged the principle *cuius regio, eius religio* ('He who rules the land determines the religion'), formulated later by a jurist. The Augsburg Confession (not the 'reformed' confession of Calvin and of Ulrich Zwingli, the popular priest of Zurich) was now legally recognized in the Reich. The Religious Peace of Augsburg did not consider the individual believer; only the prince had the right to decide between the old and new faiths. Dissidents had only the right to leave the country. Imperial cities with mixed confessions were to be guided by the principle of parity, and in ecclesiastically ruled territories a controversial 'clerical reservation' was to apply: a bishop or abbot of the Reich who converted from Catholicism to the Lutheran faith was supposed to relinquish his office immediately; the cathedral or cathedral chapter had the right to elect a Catholic successor. But the Religious Peace of Augsburg did not compel this to be done.

The recess of the Augsburg Diet spelled the failure of two competing solutions for a universal resolution to the crisis: on the one hand, the restoration of Reich and church through the emperor and in terms of the old faith, and, on the other hand, the restoration of a unified church in terms of the new faith. The possibility of a Reich ruled by the estates (*Stände*), a project pursued in the early sixteenth century by a circle of reformers under the patronage of Berthold of Henneberg, the elector of Mainz and arch-chancellor of the Reich, also ultimately came to nothing. In 1555, as Heinz Schilling wrote, the 'estates and the crown finally agreed that, in Germany, the princes and their territories would be the bearers of a new conception of the state and that the Reich would remain a pre-governmental, political union.'[34]

The Holy Roman empire was thus preserved. In fact, its institutions grew even stronger. A great civil war, a war among the princes, which as things stood would perforce have become a pan-European war, was once again avoided. The compromise of 1555 sanctioned the right of the German territorial states to religious particularity, though it did not yet permit the final consequence of the increase in territorial liberty, namely full political sovereignty. Yet even in 1555 it was clear that the government of princes would have a greater chance than the emperor of claiming the loyalties of the subjects in the event of conflict. Even if the Reich could offer an ultimate organizational support and repeatedly managed, especially in the face of external threats, to call forth waves of 'imperial patriotism', nonetheless a much stronger sense of allegiance and solidarity developed at the territorial level. The idea of a German nation remained an alternative empire, an empire of faith and spirit, and one that required no emperor.

The Religious Peace of Augsburg was one of the main reasons Protestant Germany was able to shield itself for over half a century from the effects of the Catholic Counter-Reformation, which began at the Council of Trent (1545–63). Countries in which the Counter-Reformation triumphed were economically and intellectually so lastingly set back that the effects persist to the present day. Spain, at one time the great Catholic power due to its colonial possessions in Latin America, succumbed to England, its most dangerous enemy, in the second half of the sixteenth century. The defeat was not merely military, that is, the destruction of the Armada in 1588. Within a few decades, the Calvinist-spirited maritime trading power of England had also economically eclipsed the countries of the Iberian peninsula, Spain and Portugal. France, on the other hand, successfully resisted the Counter-Reformation, remaining true to its national ecclesiastical tradition after the bloody Huguenot Wars of 1562–98. The conversion of King Henry IV (of Navarre) from the Calvinist to the Catholic faith in 1593 was not the prelude to a comprehensive re-Catholization of France; rather, it ushered in the policy of religious tolerance that found its classic expression in the Edict of Nantes of 1598.

Wherever it was rigorously implemented, the Counter-Reformation almost completely destroyed any structures of modern capitalism that had existed in the regions that remained Catholic. In comparison, the Calvinist spirit of terrestrial asceticism and merit promoted a dynamic spirit of enterprise in those lands where it prevailed. An impulse of this kind was lacking in Lutheran regions, which persisted in the traditional corporative order and its correspondingly conservative economic practices. The principles of traditional economic life were based not upon notions of individual risk, enterprise, and continually increasing profit margins, but upon the satisfaction of habitual, class-oriented needs and a just price. In this respect, Lutherans differed less from the Catholics than from the Calvinists.[35]

In questions of internal political order in Germany, the confessional differences were rather minor. The governments of the Calvinistic territories were as authoritarian as those of the Lutheran and Catholic lands. However, the fact that the Religious Peace of Augsburg did not recognize the Calvinists as a confession meant that German Calvinism as a whole differed markedly in its political profile from that of English or Dutch Calvinism. It was thus no coincidence that the impulse to alter the confessional status quo for the benefit of the Evangelicals in the first decades after 1555 proceeded not from a Lutheran, but from a Calvinist princedom, the Palatine electorate. The Palatinate thus advanced to the position of adversary against the most energetic of the Catholic imperial estates, Bavaria, where the Counter-Reformation held sway.

The Calvinists began to gain ground when they were joined by a few smaller territories and one larger one, Hesse-Kassel, in the course of the so-called 'Second Reformation'. The balance of power in Protestant Germany shifted even more significantly in 1613, when the elector of Brandenburg, John Sigismund, converted from the Lutheran to the Reformed confession. This was an event with long-term consequences to which we shall devote more attention below. The Catholic imperial estates rallied around the duke of Bavaria, the Protestant estates around the elector of the Palatinate. A Protestant defensive alliance, the 'Union', was founded in 1608, in the next year the counter-alliance of the 'Catholic League'. The opposition of the confessions could turn into a new military conflict at any time. When Emperor Matthias prepared to rescind the religious freedom his brother and predecessor, Rudolf II, had granted to the primarily Protestant estates of Bohemia and Moravia, that time had come. The Thirty Years War began in Prague in May of 1618.[36]

This war was never simply a religious war, whether in its first phases, the 'Bohemian-Palatine War' of 1618–23 and the 'Danish-Lower Saxon War' of 1625–9, or later during the 'Swedish War' of 1630–5 or the 'Swedish-French War' of 1635–48. The marked participation of foreign powers aroused a imperial-patriotic reaction of protest in the empire, a reaction directed at first primarily against Habsburg-ruled Spain, the military ally of the Habsburg emperor, Ferdinand II, and the Catholic League. A pamphlet of 1620, invoking the old doctrine of the four world empires, charged the Spanish with seeking to erect a fifth monarchy, one that would cover the earth. This was an offence against the divine order, according to which the Holy Roman Empire of the German Nation was the fourth and last of the world empires. Imperial patriotism reached its high point in 1635 at the time of the Peace of Prague, which the emperor concluded first with electoral Saxony, then with most of the other Protestant estates, primarily in northern Germany. Yet the attempt to establish a 'German peace' came to nothing. Already that same year, Catholic France intervened in the conflict on the side of Lutheran Sweden, that is, on the confessionally 'wrong' side. Power politics won a decisive victory over the religious controversy.[37]

The Thirty Years War lived on in the collective memory of the Germans for a long time. It was considered *the* national catastrophe, a standing that was not contested until the period of the two world wars of the twentieth century, especially the second. It was a catastrophe primarily in its demographic, economic, social, and moral consequences. Large areas of Germany would not recover from its three decades of murder and pillage until the following century; some took even longer, others never recovered at all. The peasants were impoverished; in the east of Germany, many of them fell into subjection under the manorial lords. The destruction of countless cities ended the rise of the bourgeoisie for a long time to come. From a sociological point of view, the victors of the war were the landed aristocracy; the part of the nobility close to the government; state-supported merchants, entrepreneurs, and bankers; the military, and the governmental officials—all pillars of the emerging absolutist system. The horrors of war, mass mortality, and deprivation prompted the survivors to retreat into inwardness and brought about a renewal of lay piety that prepared the way for the Pietist movement of the late seventeenth and the eighteenth centuries in Evangelical Germany.

If one can speak of any positive effect of the Thirty Years War, it would be an insight into the absolute necessity of religious tolerance—a tolerance that could only be enforced by a strong state willing to secularize itself within certain limits and thereby to become neutral in religious matters. Not least among the causes of princely absolutism was an absolutist attitude in matters of faith: the subjects paid for their greater freedom in the inner realm with an increase in political subjection to the secular authorities. The latter found the most dependable support for their power in the profound, traumatic fear that must be considered the lasting effect of the Thirty Years War: the fear of chaos and the collapse of societal order, of foreign bands of soldiers, of civil and fratricidal war—the fear of the Apocalypse.[38]

The Peace of Westphalia of 1648 (concluded in Münster between the Reich and France, in Osnabrück between the Reich and Sweden) restored the Religious Peace of Augsburg of 1555, extending it to those of the Reformed confession, which was now granted equal rights as a Protestant observance. The geographic boundaries between the confessions, as well as their membership, were fixed according to the state of things in the year 1624. From this date forward, subjects were no longer required to convert to a new confession in the event that their ruling sovereign decided to do so. The northern part of the Netherlands and the Swiss confederates left the Reich for good. France took over the sovereign jurisdiction of Alsace from Austria, definitively weakening the position of the Habsburgs in Germany. The treaty confirmed Bavaria's entitlement to the Palatine electorate (acquired in 1623) and the Upper Palatinate. A new, eighth electoral title was created for the Rhenish Palatinate. The peace treaty recognized the imperial estates' right to co-determination in all affairs of the Reich, full territorial sovereignty in secular and religious matters, and the right to enter into alliances with foreign powers—restricted only by a clause forbidding such alliances to be directed against the emperor or the Reich, a proviso difficult to enforce. In order to prevent the formation of an adversarial quorum, the Evangelical and Catholic estates formed separate deliberative bodies (the *Corpus evangelicorum* and *Corpus catholicorum*) at the Imperial Diet, which in 1663 was transformed into a permanent congress of delegates convening in Regensburg. Decisions could be made only when this *itio in partes* reached an agreement.[39]

On the international stage, France and Sweden emerged as victors from the Thirty Years War. Both countries guaranteed the peace treaty, which was declared the basic law of the Reich. Both were able to extend their territory at the expense of the Reich; Sweden, in fact, which acquired West Pomerania and Rügen among other territories, advanced to the status of an imperial estate (*Reichsstand*). Inside Germany, the winners were the imperial estates. In consequence of the Peace of Westphalia, they were able to take the decisive step to full sovereignty. After 1648, the Holy Roman Empire was no longer a factor in European power politics. Because it helped to stabilize the status quo, its preservation lay in the interest both of the European powers and the smaller imperial estates. As an unwieldy, archaic, and outmoded structure, however, the Reich bore no comparison with the states of France or England, Spain or Sweden. It *was* the 'irregular and monster-like body' (*irregulare aliquod corpus et monstro simile*) described in 1667 by Samuel Pufendorf in his famous work about the constitution of the German empire.[40]

THE AUSTRO-PRUSSIAN ANTAGONISM

We turn now to the third of the basic factors shaping German history, the opposition between Austria and Prussia. That Austria and Prussia, the two most important states to emerge from the medieval German colonization of middle and eastern Europe, were able to advance to the status of European great powers was due to the fact that both of them included significant territories not belonging to the Reich. The Austrian Habsburgs, who had assumed the emperorship for the first time in 1273 and held it from 1438 onwards without interruption, acquired the Netherlands and the Free Margravate of Burgundy through marriage in the second half of the fifteenth century. The lordship over Spain and its border territories, along with Naples and the American colonies, were added at the beginning of the sixteenth century. The dynastic link with Spain was preserved after the abdication of Charles V in 1556, when the title of Emperor was transferred to his brother, Ferdinand I, the lordship over Spain, the Free Margravate of Burgundy, and the Netherlands to his son, King Philip II.

In the long view, the acquisition of the Bohemian and Hungarian crowns in 1526 was even more important. To be sure, under Ferdinand I most of Hungary was lost to the Turks, who had continued to advance through the Balkan peninsula after their conquest of Constantinople (and thus the Byzantine Empire) in 1453. Nonetheless, the Turkish threat was also ideologically and materially profitable for the Austrians. After the first Turkish siege of Vienna in 1529, Austria could claim to be defending the Reich—indeed, the whole of the occident—against the Ottomans and Islam. After the second siege of Vienna in 1683, the tide turned: Hungary was taken from the Turks, falling in 1699 to the House of Habsburg along with Transylvania and large parts of Slovenia and Croatia. Austria had become a great power.

It was able to maintain this status even after the outbreak of the War of the Spanish Succession in 1700, occasioned by the extinction of the Spanish line of the Habsburgs. Although Louis XIV of France managed to break open the Habsburg encirclement and place his grandson, Philip of Anjou, on the Spanish throne, the Peace of Utrecht (1713) precluded the unification of Spain with France. In the same year, Emperor Charles VI determined his own succession in the Pragmatic Sanction: his oldest daughter, Maria Theresa, was to inherit the Habsburg possessions undivided. After long and difficult negotiations, the emperor's resolution was eventually recognized by the Habsburg hereditary lands, Hungary, and finally by the other great powers of Europe. In October 1740, Maria Theresa assumed the throne—almost at the same time as her great rival, King Frederick II, came to power in Prussia.

'Prussia' (*Preussen* or *Pruzzen*) was originally the name of a Baltic tribe that lived in the territory of later East Prussia during the early and high Middle Ages. German colonization of this area began under the auspices of the Teutonic Order, whose help the Polish duke Conrad of Masovia solicited in 1225 against the heathen Prussians. After its military decline in the fifteenth century, the Teutonic Order was able to maintain only a part of its territory as a Polish fief. Polish sovereignty was preserved when Albert of Brandenburg, Grand Master of the Teutonic Order and follower of Luther, negotiated with Poland to transform the Teutonic state into the Grand Duchy of Prussia, which occurred in 1525. The duchy was bequeathed in 1618 to Brandenburg, where the Hohenzollerns had been ruling as margraves and electors since 1415. In 1660 the Great Elector, Frederick William (1640–88), successfully asserted his right to the sovereignty of the Duchy of Prussia, which nonetheless remained outside the Holy Roman Empire. On 18 January 1701, Frederick III, son of the Great Elector, had himself crowned Frederick I, 'King in Prussia', in Königsberg with the assent of Emperor Leopold I. This did not yet make Brandenburg-Prussia into a great power, but it was a significant step along the way to this goal.

Unlike those of the Habsburgs, the subjects of the Hohenzollerns were almost exclusively German-speaking (the Masurians, who spoke a Polish dialect, were Evangelical, and for this reason alone did not consider themselves Poles). The other major difference between Austria and Prussia was confessional: the Habsburgs and most of their subjects were Catholic, the Hohenzollerns Protestant. The rulers of Brandenburg, however, represented a special case. In 1613 Elector John Sigismund converted from the Lutheran to the Reformed confession. Since his subjects (with the exception of the Calvinists and the Catholics on the lower Rhine) remained Lutheran, the Hohenzollerns were compelled to adopt a tolerant attitude in questions of religious observance.

But that was not the only effect of the elector's conversion. In his *Geschichte der preussischen Politik**, Johann Gustav Droysen noted in 1870 that while John Sigismund's conversion to Calvinism was certainly sincere, his new confession was 'not only of religious significance'.[41] Otto Hintze went even further in his 1931 essay 'Kalvinismus und Staatsräson in Brandenburg zu Beginn des 17. Jahrhunderts'.† Taking up ideas from Max Weber's famous study of the links between Calvinism and

* Droysen, *History of Prussian Politics*.

† Hintze, *Calvinism and Reasons of State in Brandenburg at the Beginning of the Seventeenth Century*.

the 'spirit of capitalism', Hintze enquired about the 'elective affinity' between Calvinism and *Staatsräson*, 'reasons of state'. His answer was that Calvinism was 'the midwife that brought the *Staatsräson* of Brandenburg politics into the world'. It served as a 'bridge, over which the *Staatsräson* of western Europe was introduced into Brandenburg', the long-term effects of which was 'a basic political orientation towards the west', primarily towards the Netherlands and France.

The result was paradoxical. According to Hintze, Calvinism served

> to strengthen the power of the monarchy—in contrast to its usual function in world history, that of arousing the estates to a spirit of rebellion against heterodox princes. This function was in no way lacking; but in order to recognize it, one must consider the other front of the territorial power of the princes, that facing the imperial power. In this respect, German Calvinism, too, aroused and led the opposition of the imperial estates against the Catholic emperor.

Frederick II also stood in this tradition, in Hintze's view:

> It is true that Frederick the Great exchanged the religious attitude for a purely secular *Realpolitik* in his political testaments. Nonetheless, upon closer examination it is clear that the impulses of this enlightened sovereign—his categorical imperative of duty, his ascetic devotion to his profession, and his transcendental interpretation of the majesty of the state as an entity standing above its ruler—all came from a soul in which the religious motivations of his predecessors had been secularized, transformed, as it were, into a worldly form, without being merely derivative of, or completely explainable in terms of, the rationalism of the Enlightenment.[42]

It was only short step from the astute perceptions of the historian Hintze to an even bolder thesis proposed by the economist Alfred Müller-Armack. In his 1941 book *Genealogie der Wirtschaftsstile** (hardly a line of which intimates the period in which it was written), the creator of the concept of the 'social market economy' wrote that the importance of the year 1613 lay in the fact that, at that time, Brandenburg-Prussia imposed 'a Reformed upper class upon a Lutheran lower class'.

> Normally Calvinism had a liberalizing effect in a purely Calvinist environment. However, as the example of Brandenburg governmental and economic policy shows, the alliance between the Lutheran lower classes and an ascetically-minded upper class fortified Lutheran state ideology with a governmental discipline from above. This combination of Lutheranism and Calvinism, unique in world history, determined the structure of the Prussian administration and economic policy in the seventeenth century and played a major role in shaping the Prussian state style. A Lutheran country with a Calvinist apex—here was a distinctly new state structure, one that was neither Calvinist nor Lutheran. In a process of mutual assimilation, Calvinism from above and Lutheranism from below, something incomparably new came into being.[43]

Both Hintze's and Müller-Armack's theses have given rise to criticism on points of detail. Nonetheless, they place the paradoxical phenomenon of Prussia in the

* Müller-Armack, *Genealogy of Economic Styles*.

greater historical context in which we must view it. With regard to Brandenburg's pretensions to the succession of the extinct ducal house of Jülich and of the Duchy of Prussia, Hintze himself spoke of the 'fateful question' of whether Brandenburg should orient itself toward the west or toward the east. 'In the east, it was better served by Lutheranism, in the west by Calvinism.' The conversion of 1613 can be interpreted as a decision for the west, but only in terms of the greater European political context and the organization of the government. The sovereign's Calvinist turn facilitated the integration of the new, mostly Reformed estates and subjects in Cleves, Mark, and Ravensburg, the territories of the Duchy of Jülich granted to Brandenburg by the Treaty of Xanten in 1614. In the Margravate of Brandenburg and the Duchy of Prussia, in comparison, the loyalty of the estates and subjects could only be assured at the price of abandoning any denominational coercion. An attempt to introduce the Reformed confession into these regions would have failed, in Hintze's words, 'by dint of the socio-economic structure of these East Elbian territories with their manorial estates. Lutheranism was well-suited to this structure, Calvinism not in the slightest'.[44]

Thus the east–west dichotomy within Prussia that shaped the nineteenth century—the disjuncture between the economically advanced, already partly industrialized, 'bourgeois' west and the manorial, 'feudal' east—was already emerging at the beginning of the seventeenth century. With regard to German-speaking countries as a whole, the manorial system (*Gutsherrschaft*) was a distinctly East Elbian phenomenon, one that had been developing since the late Middle Ages. A formerly free peasantry was not only compelled to do socage for the aristocratic lord, as in the other parts of feudal Germany; they were also reduced to a particular form of serfdom, inherited servitude (*Erbuntertänigkeit*). This was only possible because the manorial lords, the Junkers, were able to appropriate wide-ranging legal competencies from the territorial sovereign, giving them powers of jurisdiction and law enforcement well beyond those of the manorial police. The result was a transformation of the manor into a self-enclosed political entity, its lord into a sovereign authority in his own right. For Lutherans, it was self-evident that this authority had no less a claim to their obedience than the territorial lord. The proximity of throne and altar at the apex of the state found its parallel at a lower level in the relationship between the manorial lord and 'his' parson.[45]

The intensification of manorial authority went hand in hand with the extension of manorial boundaries. After the Junkers succeeded in wresting the grain trade from the cities, permanently weakening the East Elbian bourgeoisie, they also sought to increase their cultivable lands at the expense of the peasantry. Even in the sixteenth century, the eviction of peasants and appropriation of their lands, a phenomenon known as *Bauernlegen*, was widespread in eastern Germany; it increased in the wake of the Thirty Years War. East of the Elbe, practically the only peasants left after the great conflict were those reduced to a permanent and hereditary bondage to the soil. This serfdom made the agrarian society of East Elbia more 'eastern' in character, that is, more like eastern Europe. This process was the converse of the westernization of Brandenburg-Prussia in the seventeenth and eighteenth centuries. In the latter case, the transformation involved completely different aspects of society: the governmental administration and the judicial system were modernized according to west European models. Trade, artisan industry, and science were fostered and promoted, and religious tolerance was secured.[46]

The social power of the Junkers did not always translate into political power. The Great Elector, creator of the standing army, had fought fiercely against the estates and thus against the political aspirations of the manorial lords. His grandson, the 'Soldier-King' Frederick William I (1713–40), transferred the holdings of the nobility into the possession of the state whenever he could. In 1733 he divided the country into levying districts or cantons firmly delimited from each other, and built the army upon this structure. The Junkers formed the officer corps; the soldiers were peasants. In compensation for their duties to the state, the peasantry was granted a certain amount of protection from the Junkers. The manorial lords were no longer permitted to take away the lands of 'their' peasants.

Frederick II (1740–86) adopted a radically different policy with regard to the nobility. Whereas his ancestors, beginning with the Great Elector, had curtailed the power of the manorial lords, under Frederick a process of re-feudalization took place. The Junkers were granted sweeping privileges: the middle classes were no longer allowed to purchase noble estates, and the government granted credit to economically struggling manors.

These material benefits were only one part of the historical compromise with the nobility that supported the rule of Frederick II. Politically, too, the Junkers gained influence on all levels. Their increase in power has been aptly described by Otto Büsch:

> The Junker's secure position on the landed estate and in the officers' corps was the guarantee of his political power. His control over the peasants and the local administration as manorial lord, his position as head of the district [*Landrat*], his influence on the government through the *Landschaften* [The district credit institutes (H.A.W.)], were the guarantee of his political security. They qualified him for a leading role in the military system. As an officer, he controlled the canton and the garrison, enjoyed a societal status higher than that of every civilian, and was appointed not only head of the district, but also to higher—indeed the highest—offices in the civil administration. Called to the dominant positions in government and society, the Prussian aristocrat enjoyed almost unlimited power in both spheres—that is, as long as he continued to perform his duties within the military system. The service of the Junker was the state's stipulation for the guarantee of his power, the guarantee, in turn, necessary for the Junker's fulfilment of his service. The Junker used the levers of power in the state, and the state used the Junker. The old Prussian military system was a comprehensive social system with a basic political character.[47]

This social militarization of Prussia so fittingly characterized by Büsch did not originate in the personal predilections of the electors and kings. It was primarily a consequence of the extreme geographical division of the Prussian territories and their resulting military vulnerability. The spirit of discipline and subordination, the very condition of Prussia's rise, was the answer to a challenge. This answer was one-sided and required correction. By dint of its origins, Prussia was forced to a greater extent than other powers to become a soldier-state. Yet it could only assert itself successfully in the long term by overcoming the hardness and harshness that resulted from the internalization of external coercion.

The internalization of 'Prussiandom' was, to a great degree, the achievement of Pietism. The roots of this devotional movement reached back to the period of the Thirty Years War. With their appeal for a renewal of the church from within, the Pietists were reacting against the orthodox petrifaction within Lutheranism, indeed against every kind of fixation on the external aspects of dogma. In Brandenburg-Prussia, the separation from official Lutheranism formed a bridge between the Pietists and the Calvinist authorities. This relationship was further supported by the Prussian Pietists' great interest in the reform of the schools and higher institutions of learning, efforts that found their classic expression in the *Franckeschen Stiftungen*, a series of educational foundations established in Halle by August Hermann Francke, and in the founding of a Reform-oriented university in the same city in 1694. Never were the 'quiet people of the land' so near to the throne as they were under the Soldier-King. A Pietistically informed ethos of the state outlasted the reign of Frederick William I, a territorial patriotism that raised the subjects' devotion and love towards the sovereign to the status of a religious duty.[48]

Religion was also the ultimate source of the economic prosperity Brandenburg-Prussia experienced in the eighteenth century thanks to the Huguenots. Immediately after Louis IV rescinded the Edict of Nantes in 1685, the Great Elector promulgated the Edict of Potsdam, which invited the persecuted French Calvinists to Brandenburg. Approximately 20,000 followed this call. More than a quarter of them settled in Berlin, where French immigrants formed almost a fifth of the population in 1700. In artisan crafts, trade, and manufactures, the Huguenots introduced into Prussia the dynamic economic ethos that so often went hand in hand with the Calvinist religion. Yet Calvinists also excelled in academic professions. Indeed, wherever they became active, they contributed decisively to the very thing the naturally poor country of Brandenburg, the 'sandbox of the Holy Roman Empire', needed above all else: modernization.[49]

Systematic government support of trade, crafts, and industry; extension of roads and highways; cultivation and settlement of moorlands and wastelands; fostering of the sciences, and religious tolerance—these were the achievements by virtue of which eighteenth-century Brandenburg earned the reputation of marching in the avant-garde of progress. These things were only possible because the energetic rulers of the house of Hohenzollern had an army of disciplined officials at their service. Frederick William I had created the institutional framework, a rationally organized apparatus of governmental offices with the *General-Ober-Finanz-Kriegs- und Domänendirektorium* (commonly known as the General Directory) at the top. The central administration, organized partly along departmental, partly along geographic lines, performed with such effectiveness that by the middle of the eighteenth century the absolutist Hohenzollern state came to be considered the model of efficient government throughout all of Europe.[50]

The same could hardly be said of Austria at that time. The Reich's most powerful estate contrasted sharply with Brandenburg-Prussia in a number of areas. The religious compromise set down in the Peace of Westphalia was not recognized in the Habsburg crown lands. In the course of a forceful re-Catholization, initiated long before 1648, far more that 100,000 Protestants fled from Habsburg-ruled territories, an intellectual and economic loss from which Austria never recovered. The Hohenzollerns did not merely promulgate religious pluralism, they also practised it; the Habsburgs, in contrast, imposed confessional homogeneity. Part and parcel of the Catholic absolutism of Austria was a rigorous system of censorship, in comparison to which Brandenburg-Prussia seemed like a haven of intellectual freedom. Although under Maria Theresa (1740–80) the administration of censorship was removed from the hands of the church, it was also bureaucratically systematized in the process. The spirit of the Enlightenment, which found a home in the Prussian universities, found in Austria only barricades raised against its entry.

But Prussia and Austria also shared structural similarities. Austria, too, can be called a military state. As under the Hohenzollerns, the army became the most important agent in the process of state centralization. And like the Hohenzollerns, if somewhat later, the Habsburgs suppressed the influence of the estates. This was necessary in order to avoid permanently falling behind other states, especially Brandenburg-Prussia. Even under Charles VI, the Habsburg territorial mass represented more an alliance of corporative states (*Ständestaaten*) with a monarchical tip than a modern state entity. When Maria Theresa and her ministers undertook a comprehensive reform of the government administration in the early 1740s, they consciously oriented themselves on the model of Prussia. The result was an absolutist state with highly concentrated apparatus of power, less centralized than Prussia but no less bureaucratic.[51]

The antagonism between the Catholic Habsburgs and the Evangelical Hohenzollerns had long since ceased to be a religious conflict when war began between the two countries in 1740, a few months after Frederick II came to power and a few weeks after Maria Theresa assumed the throne. The first war, over Silesia, was begun by Frederick II, for both reasons of personal ambition and reasons of state. Exploiting the weakness of Vienna after the death of Charles VI, Frederick sought by the conquest of Austrian Silesia to expand the territory, fortify the economy, and elevate the political status of Prussia to that of a European great power. Silesia *did* become Prussian, and Prussia in turn a great power. By the time these results were sanctioned by the Peace of Hubertusberg in 1763, however, Frederick's state had already experienced two wars, the latter of which—the Seven Years War—might just as easily have ended with Prussia's downfall.

With respect to method, Frederick's style of power politics hardly differed from that of other sovereigns like Louis XIV of France or Charles XII of Sweden. The same can even be said of the most reprehensible of his deeds, his cooperation in the first dismembering of Poland in 1772. What set the Prussian king apart was the glaring discrepancy between his resources and his risks. In 1740 Brandenburg-Prussia was still a geographically fragmented and fragile entity. Again and again, Frederick was willing to risk everything, and was ultimately saved only by pure chance, an incident that went down in history as the 'miracle of the House of Brandenburg'—the death of Frederick's most dangerous enemy, Elisabeth, Empress of Russia, in January 1762. The ultimate success of his radical brinkmanship turned Frederick into a legend. His example, however, also promised disaster.[52]

Frederick could not have earned the nickname 'the Great' had he been nothing more than a successful military leader. In the Europe of his day, he was rightly considered the representative—indeed the very embodiment—of a new type of government, enlightened absolutism. His programme of rationalism imposed from the top down differed fundamentally from the typical narrow self-interest of other absolutist rulers. Even during Frederick's lifetime, the phrase *travailler pour le roi de Prusse* ('to work for the King of Prussia') meant to do something for its own sake. However, the thing done had to be *reasonable*, and that meant in the interest of the state. And the ruler-philosopher of Sanssouci, who considered himself the first servant of the state, seemed to guarantee that this was indeed the case.

Frederick opened his country to western ideas and prompted a kind of cultural revolution. At the same time, he restored privileges to the aristocracy, whom he could not otherwise lastingly integrate into his military machine. In so doing, he again pushed Prussian society a stretch towards the east, in the direction of an autocracy supporting itself upon nobility and serfdom. Prussia under Frederick I was more bourgeois in character than Russia, but in comparison with France, which was such an intellectual model for Frederick, it seemed almost a country without a middle class. A comparison within the Reich leads to similar findings: Frederick's Prussia was far less bourgeois than most other states, above all in the western and southern parts of Germany, although it was not as feudal in character as the two duchies in Mecklenburg.

According to a saying widely attributed to Mirabeau, but actually from an eighteenth-century German military historian, Georg Heinrich von Behrenhorst, 'The Prussian monarchy is not a country with an army, but an army with a country, in which it is only quartered, so to speak.' Although it is true that all absolutist states were also military states, Prussia was especially militarized. In mid-eighteenth-century Austria, for example, one inhabitant in sixty was a soldier; in Prussia, the ratio was one out of every thirteen. In the hierarchy of public interests and needs, those of the military stood just as high under the reign of Frederick II as under his father, the Soldier-King.[53]

The primacy of the military, as well as the entitlement of the nobility to which it was intimately linked, prevented the full realization of the rule of law within the government. Nonetheless, Prussia under Frederick continually strove in this direction. Great progress was made in the standardization of the legal system. The administration of justice through governmental offices was restricted, and a new code of procedure, the *Codex Fridericianus*, streamlined legal proceedings and made them more transparent. The crowning achievement was the *Allgemeines Landrecht für die Preussischen Staaten* (General Law for the Prussian States or 'Prussian Code'), which was completed in 1791, five years after Frederick's death. As Reinhart Koselleck observes, the Prussian Code was Janus-faced:

> In theory, it aimed at a legal system that was far in advance of the reality of the day, while in practice it codified this reality in a plenitude of statutes that ultimately stood in the way of the planned system, if they did not contradict it outright. The Prussian Code represented a compromise between tradition-informed reality and future-oriented objective.[54]

The French political thinker Alexis de Tocqueville argued much the same way in 1856 in the appendix to his work *L'Ancien Régime et la Révolution**. Concerning the Prussian Code, Tocqueville wrote: 'Beneath this completely modern head we will see a totally gothic body appear; Frederick had only eliminated from it whatever could hinder the action of his own power; and the whole forms a monstrous being which seems to be in transition between one shape and another.'[55]

Although enlightened absolutism was not unique to Prussia, in certain respects it was unique to the German-speaking lands of Europe. Its other classic representative was Maria Theresa's son Joseph II. From 1765 to 1780 co-regent with his mother, then, after her death in 1780, alone determining the fortunes of the Austrian and Habsburg lands until 1790, Joseph went much further than his model Frederick in many ways. He ended serfdom in Bohemia, Moravia, and the south-west tip of Silesia remaining to Austria; he reformed both civil and criminal law in the spirit of the Enlightenment; he placed the school system completely under the auspices of the state; and he granted to non-Catholics full rights of citizenship as well as the right to exercise their religion in private.

However, Joseph faced stiff resistance from the Hungarians when, in his continuing effort to unify and standardize the administration of Habsburg lands, he tried to replace Latin with German as the official language of government and business in Hungary. His attempt to incorporate the church completely into the service of the state, which involved the dissolution of many monasteries, provoked internal unrest. Shortly before his death, Joseph was compelled to revoke a number of his own measures. Other of his reforms were rescinded by his brother and successor, Leopold II (1790–2).[56]

Although certain aspects of 'Josephinism' survived, all in all the 'revolution from above' failed in Austria. Together with the clergy, with whom it sympathized, the Catholic population rejected enlightened absolutism. Here was a major difference vis-à-vis Prussia. There, the Calvinism of the upper classes had cleared the way for the development of enlightened absolutist rule. Frederick's reforms provoked no Lutheran reaction from below. In contrast to Joseph, who remained a committed Catholic, the free-thinking Frederick did not even attempt to challenge the religious feelings of his subjects. In contrast to 'Old Fritz', who was extremely popular due to his military exploits, Joseph never found his way into

* Tocqueville, *The Old Regime and the Revolution.*

the hearts of his people. And the sentiments inside each ruler's country were also mirrored abroad. This brings us to the question of how the Prussian–Austrian antinomy affected the way the Germans saw themselves.

COSMOPOLITANS AND PATRIOTS

'And so I, too, was a fan of Prussia, or, actually, of Fritz*—for what did we care about Prussia?' Thus wrote Goethe in *Dichtung und Wahrheit*†, looking back on his childhood memories from the time of the Seven Years War. To be *fritzisch* meant to take sides against 'outmoded ways' and for an enlightened government. Such an attitude was certainly more common among the middle classes of an Evangelical free imperial city like Frankfurt am Main, Goethe's birthplace, than among Catholic peasants in Bavaria, for example. Yet even in Goethe's family there were proponents of Austria. The poet's grandfather, Johann Wolfgang Textor, took part in the imperial crowning ceremony of Francis I, the husband of Maria Theresa, in Frankfurt in 1745, where he helped carry the baldachin of the coronation. As a rule, the older, conservative generation supported Maria Theresa, the younger, more progressive folk endorsing Frederick.[57]

However, the two monarchs' strongest support was in their respective countries, of course. The wars that took place in 1740–63 represented an important factor in shaping political identity. They fostered feelings of belonging and allegiance—feelings in which, since they were primarily directed at the state, the patriarch or matriarch of the country played a central yet supra-personal role. The King of Prussia (Frederick was the first to use this title, and under him Prussia first became the name of the whole state) stood at the head of subjects who began to consider themselves Prussians. In 1761 the Enlightenment thinker Thomas Abbt, a 'Prussian by choice' from the free imperial city of Ulm, spoke of Prussia as a 'nation' in his work *Vom Tode für das Vaterland.*‡ According to Abbt, the answer to the question 'What is one's native country?' was not necessarily answered by the simple fact of one's birthplace. Rather, citizenship was a matter of free decision. 'But when birth or my free resolution unify me with a country, to whose holy laws I place myself in subjection, laws that take from me no more of my freedom than is necessary for the good of the whole country—at this moment do I call this country my Fatherland.'[58]

For Austria, on the other hand, the word 'nation' could not be used; the term connoted a commonality of language that did not exist in the multi-ethnic Habsburg empire. The rule of the Habsburgs had long since extended beyond the borders of German-speaking Europe. It included territories in which Hungarian, Czech, Slovak, Slovenian, Croatian, Serbian, Romanian, Italian, French, and Dutch were spoken, as well as Polish, Ukrainian, and Yiddish after 1772. This was

* [Translator's note: *fritzisch gesinnt*, 'Fritz-minded'.]

† Goethe, *Poetry and Truth.*

‡ Abbt, *On Death for the Fatherland.*

a great difference vis-à-vis Prussia, which was always considered a German state, the annexation of Polish territory from 1772 to 1795 notwithstanding. To a far greater extent than in Prussia, the active bearers of Austrian state patriotism were Enlightenment-influenced civil servants. Prussian state patriotism could claim a far broader societal basis, reaching all the way down to the hereditary peasantry. For this reason, it had an appeal that extended much further beyond its national borders than was the case with Habsburg Austria.[59]

In the second half of the eighteenth century, however, the concepts *Vaterland* and 'nation' did not only apply to the territorial state in Prussia. Goethe and the conservative writer Justus Möser used the word *Vaterland* for their respective native cities of Frankfurt and Osnabrück. The Berlin publisher, writer, and Enlightenment philosopher Friedrich Nikolai spoke of a 'Bavarian nation' as well as 'Bavarian patriots' and even 'patriots of Nuremberg'. In 1773 the poet Christoph Martin Wieland, the Pietist-educated son of a pastor from the village environs of the free imperial city of Biberach, came to the conclusion: 'The German nation is actually not one nation, but an aggregation of many nations.'[60]

With this observation, Wieland drew the balance of a process of development that had begun with the Reformation and been invigorated by the Peace of Westphalia. Looking back on the period from 1000 to 1500, we might speak of a gradual formation of German national identity. A consciousness of community, supported primarily by commonality of language, slowly emerged north of the Alps. Two phases are conspicuous, the first around the turn of the millennium, the second in the decades around 1500 with the end of the Middle Ages and the beginning of the Early Modern period. After the Reformation, however, the opposition between the religious confessions brought discord and division to the fore. From that point onward, the strongest feelings of supra-territorial community were shared by Germans of the same denomination. To be sure, the Holy Roman Empire continued to exist, providing an ultimate institutional support for the German nation. And imperially oriented publicists of the seventeenth and eighteenth centuries never grew weary of emphasizing that the Roman empire was ruled by the Germans. Nonetheless, after the Peace of Westphalia, the importance of the Reich for the nation decreased so considerably that, as early as 1667, a sober scholar of constitutional law like Pufendorf could pronounce a final judgement: 'For the rest, it is obvious that Germany not only has no advantage from her title "Roman empire", but in fact has had great harm and unpleasantness from it.'[61]

Pufendorf's assessment anticipated the critique of the eighteenth-century *kleindeutsch* historians like Heinrich von Sybel, who spoke of the great wealth Germany wasted on its Italian campaigns, undertaken only to gain the imperial crown. Like Luther earlier, Sybel rejected the theory of a transmission of imperial authority from the Greeks to the Germans, insisting that the Roman empire had long since fallen into ruin—as a consequence of the West Gothic invasion—by the time of Charlemagne's coronation. Therefore, the present-day Reich could not be equated with the Roman empire. Only one short step led from this

Protestant view of history to Wieland's rhetorical question of 1793: 'But the German patriots, who love the whole German Empire as their Fatherland, love it above all else . . . —where are they?'[62]

The tendency to apply the terms *Vaterland* and 'nation' only to an individual state was more characteristic of Protestant than Catholic authors. Nowhere was it more pronounced than in Prussia in the second half of the eighteenth century, during which Frederick's kingdom rose up to become the most decided opponent of the Habsburgs and thus of the entire obsolete majesty of the Reich and emperor. The acclaim with which Frederick's victories were hailed outside of Prussia attested to the Reich's loss of prestige. This was no surprise, given the powerlessness it demonstrated time after time. The French encroachments in Alsace and occupation of Strasbourg in 1681 had provoked neither reaction nor defence on the part of the emperor and the Reich. The fact that the 'Imperial Army' fought on the side of the French during the Seven Years War (and earned no military glory whatsoever) only further increased Prussia's prestige; for the Reich, the debacle produced only derision and mockery.

For all that, however, imperial patriotism was still very much alive in the eighteenth century. Especially the smaller and middle-sized imperial estates retained the conviction that it was necessary to reform the imperial constitution, all the while remaining faithful to emperor and Reich. This view was expressed with particular urgency by the jurist and Pietist Johann Jakob Moser, one of the foremost authorities on imperial law. From his Württemberg homeland, Moser waged a war against absolutism in the name of the 'old law' of the territorial estates, an activity that earned him a five-year prison term (an illegal sentence) on the Hohentwiel in 1759. Moser's proposals for the restoration of the Reich formed only a small part of his enormous scholarly output. They amounted to bringing Prussia into close alliance with Austria, whereby the former would be elevated so far above the other imperial estates that it would act as a kind of co-regent of the Reich.

The wars between 1740 and 1763 reveal how far from reality such fantasies were. Not that the imperial patriots allowed themselves to be deterred by such realizations. One of them, Moser's son, the publicist Friedrich Carl von Moser, wrote a very popular pamphlet entitled *Von dem deutschen Nationalgeiste** (1765), in which he contradicted the 'false and pernicious doctrine of a *double Fatherland*, a Catholic and an Evangelical Germany', which was deeply ingrained in the minds of contemporaries. 'When a Bohemian count sincerely believes that the German fatherland is to be found in Vienna, a Brandenburg nobleman can only press his hat to his forehead and desire to hear nothing further about any German fatherland.' Moser did not, however, see fit to propose any practical suggestions as to how such 'separatist ways of thinking' might be overcome. He contented himself with the appeal 'to move the lords and heads of our fatherland *to want what they should want*', that is, to place the general good of the Reich above the selfish interests of the imperial estates, especially the more powerful among them.[63]

In addition to imperial patriotism, another kind of pan-German sentiment persisted: a consciousness of a common culture, expressed primarily through the

* Moster, *On the German National Spirit.*

cultivation of the German language. In the half-century between 1720 and 1770, the 'German societies' (*Deutsche Gesellschaften*) inspired by Johann Christoph Gottsched spread over all of Germany, most notably in Evangelical university towns such as Leipzig, where the movement first began. Against the French-inspired culture of the aristocratic courts, the German societies set a bourgeois German culture dedicated to the study of grammar and lexicology, the art of speaking and translation, and the memories of great figures and events in German history (above all Luther and the Reformation). These societies also placed great emphasis on the celebration of public events (the birthday of the territorial sovereign, the anniversary of the city founding, etc.) with due pomp and circumstance. In one of his academic addresses, Gottsched described the ideal member of the German societies as the 'very model of an upright burgher, sincere patriot, and, not least, honest and conscientious speaker'.

For Gottsched, there was only *one* ideal of form, and it was French. In the next generation, the criticism of aristocratic court culture prompted a more radical critique of the French model. In 1770 the *Hainbund* of Göttingen sought to oppose French immorality with German virtues, which were thoroughly bourgeois in character and generally informed with Christian piety. 'The German', as Wolfgang Hardtwig synoptically puts it, 'is upright, noble, good, cultivates "good strict morals", and avoids pomp.' This was hardly more than the literary stylization of national stereotypes that can be traced back beyond the baroque language societies and the humanist movement all the way to the high Middle Ages. In these stereotypes, German self-praise could not easily be distinguished from self-pity and a sense of inferiority. Like the imperial patriots, the literary patriots lamented the fact that, throughout the centuries, Germany had fallen more and more behind France. This was indeed the case. After 1648 the hegemony had passed to the neighbour in the west—not only politically, but also culturally.[64]

A few French intellectuals, first and foremost the historian Jean Baptiste Du Bos and the philosopher Voltaire, went so far as to speak of a migration of cultural leadership from one people to another. Here they had recourse to the ancient idea of *translatio artium*, which, like analogous doctrine of the *translatio imperii*, consisted of four golden ages. In the new interpretation, the Greece of Philip of Macedon and Alexander the Great was followed first by the Rome of Caesar and Augustus, then by the Italian Renaissance under Popes Julius II and Leo X. The last age, the 'great century' that, according to Voltaire, came closest to perfection, was the age of France under Louis XIV. The cult of Greece in German classicism was, in part, an answer to this French challenge. As Conrad Wiedemann notes, the one-sided emphasis on classical Hellas implied not only a rejection of classical Rome, but also classical France.[65]

If Germany wished to catch up to and surpass France, it was clear that it could not do so in the political arena. The French already possessed a nation state, one with a venerable history. Some of the greatest German thinkers doubted whether the Germans would ever become a nation. In his *Hamburgische Dramaturgie** (1763),

* Lessing, *Hamburg Dramaturgy*.

Lessing poured scorn on the Germans, who were 'still the sworn imitators of all that is foreign, and above all still the subservient admirers of the never sufficiently admired French'. He explicitly rejected 'the good-hearted gesture of giving the Germans a national theatre, since we Germans are not even a nation yet!' For Goethe and Schiller, this should remain the case even in the future.[66] As late as 1796 they warned in the *Xenien*:

> Zur Nation euch zu bilden, ihr hoffet es,
> Deutsche, vergebens;
> Bildet, ihr könnt es, dafür freier zu
> Menschen euch aus!*

German poets and thinkers of the last three decades of the eighteenth century envisaged a particular kind of cosmopolitanism or *Weltbürgertum*: an imagined, invented community, not one achieved through personal observation and concrete experience. Of those who advised Germans against going the route of the national state, at least politically, virtually nobody posed the question of whether this sense of a direct, unmediated relationship to the world did not imply a kind of national presumptuousness. But what Goethe and Schiller regarded as an alternative, other thinkers of the classical period considered a false dichotomy. For Herder, differences among peoples were a natural fact, indeed a 'barricade against the presumptuous joining together of peoples, a dam against foreign inundation'. At the same time, however, reasonable Nature also sought the progressive ennoblement of humankind and its consummation in true humanity. As Herder wrote in the third part of his *Ideen zur Philosophie der Geschichte der Menschheit*,† which appeared in 1787, 'Humanity is the purpose of man. Thus Nature and God have put the fate of our kind into our own hands.' 'The course of history reveals that the destructive demons of humankind have truly diminished with the burgeoning of true humanity, and this has happened according to the inner natural laws of an enlightened reason and art of government.'[67]

Immanuel Kant was of the same opinion as his East Prussian countryman. Since providence would have it that peoples did not join together, but rather were in conflict with one another, 'thus national pride and national animosity are necessary for the separation of nations' (from Kant's posthumous manuscripts to the *Anthropologie*). Nonetheless, such blind instincts must be replaced by the 'maxims of reason'. 'Therefore, this national delirium must be rooted out and replaced by patriotism and cosmopolitanism.'[68]

Whether citizens of the world, literary or imperial patriots: German poets and thinkers spoke only for a well-educated minority. And yet, though often divided among themselves, the members of this audience represented nothing less than the public sphere of their day. In comparison, the patriotism of the separate territorial states enjoyed a much broader social basis. In Evangelical Germany, especially in Prussia, the Pietist movement was one of the most influential factors in

* To make yourself a nation—for this you hope, | Germans, in vain; | make yourselves instead—you can do it! | into men the more free.

† Herder, *Ideas on the Philosophy of Human History*.

the formation of territorial identity. Like the enlightened patriotism of a later period, Pietism demonstrated a highly practical interest in the promotion of local community projects. In any case, there was no necessary conflict between the allegiance to an individual territorial state and a partiality to some idea of Germany as a whole. This was just as true of the *Volk* as it was of the representatives of 'Germany of the mind'. The Reich, meanwhile, had come to be regarded in large sections of the population with rather more disdain than reverence. 'The dear old Holy Roman empire, how does it stay together?' Frosch's question in Auerbach's cellar might have been posed by any sober-minded imperial subject.[69]

Given the lack of a common German state, the most important bond uniting Germans was still that of language, and it was with good reason that Herder wrote that the simple people preserved the mother tongue much better than the nobility and the educated classes. To the latter he directed an appeal that has nothing to do with 'linguistic nationalism':

> Whoever disdains the language of his nation dishonors its most noble public, becoming the most dangerous murderer of its spirit, its inner and outer prestige, its creations and inventions, its fine morality and industry. Whoever elevates the language of a people, forming it to the most powerful expression of every feeling, every clear and noble thought, helps to extend that most worthy and most beautiful public, or else unite it and establish it more firmly.[70]

The concept of 'nation' was thus without a real home in Germany. It applied ever less to the Reich, but neither did it find fulfilment in any one territorial state. In such an era, the question of German identity *had* to be posed anew. The outcome of the Prussian–Austrian wars was *one* of the factors initiating a new debate over 'Germany' in the middle of the 1760s. In the 1770s, this debate gave way to a 'poetic and philosophical movement in Germany' that the philosopher Wilhelm Dilthey was the first to identify as 'a self-enclosed and continuous whole, beginning with Lessing and ending with the death of Schleiermacher [1834] and Hegel [1831]'. This more than sixty-year period formed the third phase of rapid development—after those of the years around 1000 and 1500—in the process of national formation that preceded the founding of a German national state.[71]

The German famine of 1770, one of the last great famines of pre-industrial Europe, probably sharpened the general sense of crisis and increased the urgency of the search for understanding and meaning in society. And, of course, Germans were not blind to developments abroad: the great economic and societal transformations the Industrial Revolution was bringing to England, the intensifying political crises in France and America. The widespread consciousness of a new secular era was no respecter of national borders. All aspects of tradition were summoned before the judgement seat of Reason. The *Sattelzeit*,* the period of transition from the estates and fixed corporative structures of old Europe to a new form of society characterized by a desire for freedom and equality, had begun.[72]

* [Translator's note: literally, 'saddle-era', from the secondary meaning of German *Sattel* = 'bridge', 'mountain pass'.]

2

Hampered by Progress 1789–1830

THE FRENCH REVOLUTION AND THE END OF THE OLD REICH

In his Berlin *Vorlesungen zur Philosophie der Geschichte*, Hegel referred to the French Revolution as a 'glorious sunrise'. 'All thinking creatures celebrated this era together. A sublime elation ruled the day, an enthusiasm of spirit shivered through the world, as if the reconciliation of the Divine with the world had finally come about.'

In these passages, written during the last decade of his life, Hegel was invoking for his audience the emotions he and his friends Hölderlin and Schelling had experienced as students at the seminary in Tübingen when they learned of the storming of the Bastille, the great event of 14 July 1789.

A constitution has now been erected according to the principle of Right, and henceforth everything shall be based on this foundation. The like has not been seen as long as the sun has stood in the firmament with the planets circling round—that man has set himself upon his head, that is, upon his Thought, and constructs reality according to the latter. Anaxagoras was the first to say that the νοῦς rules the world [*nous*: 'spirit', 'thought', 'reason' (H.A.W.)]; yet only now has humanity come to understand that spiritual reality should be ruled by Thought.[1]

The ideas that came to power in France were well known in Germany. Montesquieu and Rousseau were among the most read and celebrated authors in Germany during the second half of the eighteenth century. To be 'enlightened' meant to hate despotism and to swear by the doctrines of the separation of powers and the social contract upon which all government power was based. According to general opinion, since France of the *Ancien Régime* was ruled by an unenlightened absolutism, that is, by despotism, the country was justified in its rebellion. The declaration of human and civil rights by the French National Assembly on 26 August 1789 was received with great enthusiasm in Germany, as in nearly all of Europe. Nonetheless, very few German observers considered the events in France a model for what should happen on the right side of the Rhine. The absolutism governing the most important German states was too enlightened to require a violent popular uprising to bring about improvement. The way of peaceful reform (or 'reformation', as was commonly said) was considered the German path towards the goals the French sought to achieve through revolution.[2]

Another factor speaking for reform in the view of enlightened Germans was the particular course taken by the revolution in France. Long before the Jacobin reign of terror, German public opinion had swung around; admiration for the western neighbour gave way to criticism of the manner in which he sought to impose political progress. In October 1789 Christoph Martin Wieland, one of the most astute and influential publicists of the day and an early supporter of the revolution, condemned the deposing of the French king as an act disrupting the proper balance between the legislative, judicial, and executive powers.

Wieland put to his audience, as well as to himself, a question he thought could only be answered in the course of time:

> Will the new order arising from this chaos—when finally *Deus et melior Natura* ['God and better Nature' (H.A.W.)] gain the upper hand—heal the numberless wounds inflicted by the democratic cacodaemon [from *kakós*, the Greek word for 'bad', 'evil' (H.A.W.)] of this nation drunk on freedom, heal them quickly and completely enough to be judged a redress for so much evil?

In May 1790 Wieland saw occasion to note the ever increasing numbers of people throughout Germany who believed that the French National Assembly

> is going much too far in its presumption, is behaving unjustly and tyrannically, is setting up a democratic despotism in place of an absolutist and monarchical one, and, by means of hasty and unwise proclamations on the one hand and factious rabble-rousing on the other, is stirring up the purblind populace, drunk from the delirious chalice of freedom, to the most horrible excesses.

When in June 1790 the National Assembly abolished the hereditary aristocracy along with all its titles and privileges, Wieland went over to public protest. To be sure, the 'efforts undertaken to liberate a great nation from the ironclad despotism of a monarchic government degenerated into the most intolerable aristocracy' were, in Wieland's eyes, 'the most praiseworthy of all enterprises'; yet he could never call it praiseworthy 'to set up a monstrous, endlessly convoluted, awkward and unstable democracy instead of a monarchy restricted to its true limits (after the example of the English constitution) through sufficiently secured rights of the people'. The French solution was reprehensible to Wieland, who was convinced that another path could have been taken in that country, too. 'Without a doubt a reformation—both necessary and unavoidable—should have been undertaken with the nobility, just as with the court and the clergy.'

By January 1793, the month in which the National Convention condemned Louis XVI to death with a majority of one vote and sent him to the guillotine, all Wieland's remaining doubts had been removed.

> I, too, see just as well as anybody that things are not as they should be, and do not work as they ought to work, whether in Germany or in the rest of Europe; and I am very convinced

that the evils about which we have cause to complain can only be addressed by a thorough reformation of the legislative power and the constitution as it stands today. Yet I maintain that neither the new theory of the French demagogues nor insurrections and the overthrow of the existing order of things can bring this about, or should even be be attempted. What has happened in France cannot and should not serve as a model for us, but rather as a warning to princes.[3]

Large numbers of academically educated Germans thought as Wieland did. At first they hailed the revolution as an act of liberation, then turned away to the extent that radical political forces and with them the urban lower classes gained influence and the country threatened to sink into a bloody civil war. Herder, also an impassioned defender of the watershed events of 1789, wrote three years later that he knew nothing more repugnant 'than a populace agitated to madness, and the rule of a mad populace'. What had France accomplished with its revolution, seeing that 'it languishes in the most fearful disorder of things'? How could one hope for a better education from a revolution

that provokes such scenes of inhumanity, deception, and disorder, the impressions of which will perhaps eradicate all traces of humanity from the hearts and minds of several generations? What effects might, indeed *must*, this vertiginous spirit of freedom, and the bloody wars that will in likelihood arise from it, have upon peoples and rulers, but above all on the *organs* of *humanity*, the sciences and arts?

The only thing that the Germans could do was learn from the French experience. 'We can witness the French revolution as a shipwreck on the open sea observed from a safe shore, unless we, too, are pulled by our evil genius into the sea against our will.'[4]

Only a very small number of German publicists had a certain understanding for the Jacobins. Even the majority of the 'German Jacobins' (the term is of questionable legitimacy) clearly rejected the idea of emulating revolutionary France. The travelling scholar and writer Johann Georg Forster, member of the Club of German Friends of Liberty in French-occupied Mainz in 1792, wrote in 1793 that the 'the physical, moral, and political conditions' in Germany were such that the only sensible path to change was a process of 'slow, stepwise perfection and maturity'. Germany should 'learn from the errors and sufferings of its neighbours and perhaps receive gradually bestowed from above the freedom that others have had to seize violently and all at once from below.' The radical writer Georg Friedrich Rebmann admitted in 1796 that he never 'seriously considered a German revolution after the model of the French. That would be absolutely impossible in Protestant lands, and in our Catholic territories nearly so.'

The idea that the reformation of the church had obviated the need for a political revolution was a widespread article of faith in Protestant Germany of the late Enlightenment. According to this view, the religious renewal introduced by Luther held a general promise of freedom, a promise to be redeemed gradually. Thus, historically speaking, Germany was further along than France. It *could* reform itself politically, since it had already been reformed ecclesiastically. In the opinion of late Enlightenment thinkers, Germany *had* to proceed along this path if it wished to avoid the fate of France. After all, a German revolution was by no means an impossibility. 'It will and must happen,' Rebmann warned in 1796, 'if a reformation is not brought about first.'[5]

This insight was not foreign to a few of those who exercised political power in Germany. In 1799 the Prussian minister Karl Gustav von Struensee remarked to a Frenchman: 'The revolution that you have made from the bottom up will take place in Prussia slowly from the top down . . . In a few years, there no longer will be any privileged class in Prussia.' Those were more than mere words. In its own domains, where the Prussian state had a free hand, it pushed through a significant reform between 1777 and 1805, the liberation of the peasants from the obligatory manual and draught services (*Hand- und Spanndienste*) they owed to the manorial lords. This was a prelude to the general 'peasant liberation' of 1808. The sponsors of this revolution from above were the educated civil servants from both the bourgeoisie and the nobility. This group played the part of the 'general estate' that the 'third estate', the bourgeoisie, ascribed to itself in France. An enlightened bureaucracy legitimated (not only in Prussia, but with particular effectiveness there) the claim of the enlightened ruler to unify the executive and the legislative powers in his person. Where justice and reason combined so harmoniously, there could be no need of an elected body of legislators.[6]

Even before the French Revolution, German theorists of the state had interpreted Montesquieu, the classical formulator of the doctrine of the separation of powers, in this sense. After the experience of mass violence and revolutionary terror, the idea of a 'free monarchy' found even greater resonance among the educated German public. But the greatest living philosopher saw things differently. In his *Zum ewigen Frieden** (1795), Immanuel Kant defined despotism as the governmental principle of 'the autonomous execution by the state of laws it has itself decreed'. Accordingly, despotism is 'the public will, to the extent that it is treated by the regent as his personal will'. Against despotism Kant placed republicanism, the form of government in which executive power was separated from the legislative. For Kant, such a republicanism was perfectly compatible with a monarchy at the head of the state. It was not, however, compatible with a democracy in the sense of unmediated popular sovereignty, that is, one of the badly organized 'democracies without a representational system'. Thus, direct rule of the people was perforce a form of despotism.

Kant maintained his publicly announced sympathy for the ideas of the French Revolution through the period of the Terror. 'Such a phenomenon in human history *can no longer be forgotten*,' he wrote in the *Streit der Fakultäten*† in 1798, 'for it has awakened within human nature a predisposition and an ability for improvement, such as no politician could have devised from the course of things hitherto.' By appealing in *Zum ewigen Frieden* for a 'representative system' and, in the *Rechtslehre* of the *Metaphysik der Sitten*‡ (1797), explicitly invoking a 'representative system of the people', the Königsberg philosopher took a decisive step beyond

* Kant, *Perpetual Peace.*
† Kant, *The Conflict of the Faculties.*
‡ Kant, *Doctrine of Right of Metaphysics of Morality.*

enlightened absolutism. The same was true of his advocacy of a constitution 'in which Law is autonomous and depends upon no particular individual'. Yet because Kant insisted upon legal reforms and sought to avoid a violent revolution, the actual addressee of his ideas was the same as that of the other German late Enlightenment thinkers: the enlightened absolutist state.[7]

'Not the German reaction, but rather German progress was the thing that set Germany back behind the west.' With this trenchant paradox, the historian Rudolf Stadelmann attempted in 1948 to express the variety of reasons a successful revolution never took place in Germany.

> The theory of a revolution from above and the practice of the enlightened bureaucratic state, the example of rulers who enjoyed an international reputation as friends of the people, especially the lower classes—these ideas were the only ones strong enough to compete with the declaration of human rights. The ideal of the revolution from above made the German believe he needed no foreign import to keep his house in order. And it was not the princes and their officials who cultivated this notion of the state, but rather the enlightened, literary bourgeoisie.[8]

To Stadelmann's pithy thesis we must add one qualification. The more the revolutionary terror in France repulsed educated Germans, the more the latter felt themselves attracted to Britain, which many considered the embodiment of a liberal, constitutionally limited monarchy. With his *Reflections on the Revolution in France* (1790), a critique of the theory and practice of the French Revolution drawn from the British experience, the originally liberal, later conservative politician and writer Edmund Burke found nearly as much resonance in Germany as in his homeland. This reception was due in part to the brilliant 1793 translation by Friedrich Gentz, a student of Kant, who was later to become one of the closest advisers to the chancellor of Austria, Metternich. Of course, the England so admired by the Germans possessed not only king and upper house, but also a representative legislature in the form of a House of Commons. Thus England was far ahead of Germany, as it had been ahead of the *Ancien Régime* in France. Moreover, the English had acquired their freedoms and rights of political participation not only in a peaceful manner, but also through revolutionary means. Finally, the friendly reception Burke's critique of the French Revolution found in Germany was not least due to the fact that the author's reference to resistance and revolution as the 'extreme medicine of the constitution' was typically overlooked.[9]

The violence of its self-emancipation was not the only phenomenon that alienated educated Germans from revolutionary France. The rallying cry of the 'single and indivisible nation' also met with irritated dismissal in Germany. Long before 1789, indeed even before the appearance of Montesquieu's *De l'espirit des lois** in 1748, German authors had interpreted the dualism between the emperor and the imperial estates as a specifically German version of the limitation of monarchical

* Montesquieu, *Sprit of the Laws.*

power. France was an absolutist and comparatively centralized state. The Reich was neither the one nor the other; in fact, it was not a state at all.

Wieland was among those who attempted to make a virtue out of the necessity of German particularism and political-territorial multiplicity. As he wrote at the beginning of the 1780s, the Germans, by dint of their constitution, would never 'think and act as a single people, never possess what can be called in the moral sense ' "National-Uniform" '. Yet all the disadvantages of the German political situation were

outweighed by the one great, priceless advantage: that, as long as we maintain it, no great policed [i.e. civilized (H.A.W.)] people on this earth enjoys a higher degree of human and civil freedom, no people will be better guarded against general foreign, domestic, political, and ecclesiastical enslavement and subjugation, than we Germans.

Wieland's conclusion is probably the earliest evidence for what is known today as German 'constitutional patriotism'.

If our present-day lawful constitution is the only thing making us Germans into one nation, and if it is manifestly the reason for our most significant advantages, then what else can German patriotism be than love of the present constitution of the community, and the sincere effort to do everything to preserve and perfect the same on the part of everybody, each according to his estate, his abilities, and his relationship to the whole?

When the French revolutionaries undertook to finish the work of unification already begun by the French monarchs, Wieland returned to this thought. 'The present day German imperial constitution', he wrote in 1793, 'is, despite its undeniable faults and failures, on the whole infinitely more congenial to the inner peace and prosperity of the nation, more appropriate to its character and to the level of culture upon which it stands, than the French democracy . . .' The 'apostles of the new religion' had only the most tentative and confused grasp of the real state of things in Germany. Yet it required only the most basic common sense to know

that the German Reich consists of a large number of self-governing [*unmittelbar*] estates, each one of which, within itself independent of every other, has above it the imperial laws, or the emperor and the Reich, to the extent only that these latter are empowered to administer and execute those laws; and that, from its own elected head of state down to the mayor, master, city council, and community of the imperial city of Zell on the Hammersbach, there is no regent in Germany whose greater or lesser authority is not restricted by laws, traditions, and in many other ways, and from all sides; and against whom, if he permits himself any illegal act upon the property, honour, or personal liberty of the least of his subjects, the imperial constitution will not provide protection and remedy to the aggrieved party.[10]

The German rejection of the French project of the *nation une et indivisible* could not have been more decisive. What was proclaimed in Paris was, indeed, a 'new religion': nationalism as a political credo. The secular national sentiments articulated during the Renaissance in France, Italy, and Germany remained confined to humanist circles. Although Britain after the Puritan revolution of the seventeenth century was the first nation to witness the spread of national pride to large segments of the populace, the sentiment was consciously affiliated with a sense of mission nourished from the Old Testament and thus rooted to a far greater degree in a pre-modern world view than was the contemporaneous absolutism of the Continent. The French Revolution was the first to break completely with the old religious basis of national self-evaluation. There were *two* characteristics that distinguished French national feeling of the years after 1789 from the sentiments of past ages: it was purely secular, and it was both the expression as well as the instrument of a mobilization of the masses.

In light of these innovations, it is advisable to reserve the term 'nationalism' (or at least 'modern nationalism') for the period during and after the turning point in world history defined by the French Revolution. One of the more radical consequences provoked by the dethronement of Christian universalism, entering a new phase in 1789, was the development of nationalist sentiment into a substitute religion, in which loyalty to the nation was given priority over every other commitment. And indeed, the nation became in the post-revolutionary era what the church had been before: a binding ethical-moral system giving meaning to the lives of individuals and justifying supra-personal authority. This new character of the nation separated modern nationalism from traditional patriotism, which was an emotional tie, nearly always religious in quality, limited in scope to an individual's home country, its sovereign, and the sovereign's 'house', the dynasty. Patriotism also traditionally lacked the reciprocity between the claims of the individual upon the nation and those of the nation upon the individual, a relation without which modern nationalism could not have become a mass movement.

Yet, as we shall see, nowhere in Europe did old-style patriotism simply die out after 1789. It was able to modernize, absorbing certain elements of modern nationalism. There was also continuity in the other direction: the new republican nationalism of the French, in invoking such ideas as human liberty, equality, and fraternity, had precursors and models in the community spirit that had developed among the citizens of the northern Italian republican city states or confederate Geneva, the home of Jean-Jaques Rousseau, creator of the theories of the *contrat social* and the *volonté général*. Nonetheless, nationalism as the unifying bond of a large nation, recognizing nothing higher than itself on earth—this was something that had not existed in Europe before the French Revolution.

Only the United States of America could lay claim to a small chronological edge when it came to determining the birthright to the new ideology of human community. By no means, however, did the North American subjects of the British break with their traditional religious understanding of the just order when they rebelled against the crown. On the contrary, their revolt and declaration of independence were informed and sustained by religious ideals. The American Revolution was a conservative revolution, something that cannot in any way be said of the events in France. American nationalism, in contrast to the French, was both modern *and* traditional.[11]

Whoever looks for 'modern' forms of national feeling in Germany during the latter half of the eighteenth century will have the best chance of finding them in Frederick II's Prussia. In his above-mentioned work *Vom Tode für das Vaterland* (1761), written during the Seven Years War, Thomas Abbt, the 'Prussian by choice' from Ulm, explained the duty of the individual subject to sacrifice his life for his country in case of necessity. The love of the *Vaterland* sets up the subject's 'nation as an eternal model for other nations'. It assures everlasting fame and the gratitude of posterity to those who give up their lives for their country. The author even attempted to prove that 'the love of the Fatherland (provided one does not have the support of faith in a revealed religion) is the best means to overcome fear of death.' Why, asks Abbt, should we not say that love of one's king is stronger than death? 'The love for the Fatherland convinces us that no pleasure may figure in the face of the pleasure to have served one's country, and that such a death adds more to the sum of our pleasures than we ever would receive in the course of a longer life.'[12]

The love of the *Vaterland* as a correlation to the belief in God—here Abbt, who had commenced his studies with theology before switching to enlightened philosophy, the fine arts, and mathematics, comes very close to nationalism as a political religion. Yet however eager he was to demonstrate that a selfless patriotic love was possible not only in a republic, but also in an enlightened monarchy, Abbt's patriotism exhausted itself in the claims of the *Vaterland* upon the individual. He had nothing to say concerning the voice of the citizen in the politics of his country. In recompense for their duty of self-sacrifice, the Prussian state held out to its subjects only the prospect of honour, which was to be considered the highest reward the nation could bestow. Rights of political participation, such as the French *citoyen* possessed—such things were not to be deduced from the Prussian subject's duty to serve his country to the utmost. He had to content himself with the fact that the laws of the enlightened state did not restrict his liberties even more than they did.

Only in comparison to imperial patriotism could Prussian state patriotism be called 'modern'. The Reich, for its part, could not lay claim to any subjects willing to give up their lives out of patriotic devotion. Its only real support lay with a few smaller and middle-sized estates, flanked by jurists and publicists. When the war waged by Prussia and Austria against revolutionary France after April 1792 was officially designated by the Reich as 'general war of the Empire' in March 1793, its popularity was in no way increased. Even the most virulent German critics of the Jacobins generally rejected military intervention on behalf of the older powers.

Still, when Prussia concluded the Treaty of Basel with France in April 1795 (the treaty that prompted Kant to write *Zum ewigen Frieden*), the indignation in the rest of Germany was great. The anger was not due to Prussia's withdrawal from the War of the First Coalition (1792–7), but rather to its consent in this 'Separate Treaty' to the transfer of the territories on the left bank of the Rhine to the French Republic. This was a betrayal of the Reich and was denounced as such by Austria and the imperial patriots. Then, in the Treaty of Campo Formio in October 1797, Austria itself agreed to the cession of most of the territory in question, including

Mainz, as well as to the renunciation of Belgium, a gesture France honoured by turning over the French-occupied Republic of Venice to Austria, to whom it also held out the prospect of acquiring the Archbishopric of Salzburg and parts of Bavaria. Thus Austria, too, abandoned the integrity of the Reich and sank morally more or less to the level of Prussia.

When the arrangements of Campo Formio were confirmed by the Treaty of Lunéville nearly four years later (February 1801), Napoleon Bonaparte had already long been reigning as First Consul in France. After their defeat in the War of the Second Coalition (1799–1802), the Austrians, as well as the other imperial estates, were compelled to accept the fact that the First Man of France had become the judge of Germany. The Final Recess of the Imperial Deputation of 1803 introduced into Germany radical territorial reforms, the purpose of which was to compensate the estates adversely affected by the loss of territories on the left bank of the Rhine. In the course of the 'secularization', nearly all the ecclesiastical princes were stripped of their landed property. These losses drastically curtailed the power of the Catholic Church and German Catholicism. Through the 'mediatization', numerous small princes and counts, as well as all but six imperial cities, were forced to renounce their status as self-governing subjects of the Reich (their *Reichsunmittelbarkeit*). Prussia, Bavaria, Württemberg, and Baden were able to increase their domains substantially. Altogether, the number of imperial estates was reduced by 112 from about 300. About 3 million people found themselves under new rulership.

In the year after the Final Recess, Napoleon subjected the Reich to yet another provocation. In May 1804, by means of a senate resolution, confirmed by a plebiscite the following November, he initiated the transformation of France into a hereditary empire. On 2 December 1804 he crowned himself Emperor of the French in Notre Dame in Paris, after being anointed by Pope Pius VII. Vienna, expecting the dissolution of the Reich in the wake of the senate's resolution, responded in August 1804 by proclaiming an Empire of Austria for all the lands of the Habsburg monarchy, an act that once again violated the imperial constitution. In August of the following year, Austria joined together with Russia, Britain, and Sweden for the Third Coalition against France. Prussia and Prussian-led northern Germany remained neutral, as they had done during the War of the Second Coalition. The southern German states of Bavaria, Baden, and Württemberg allied themselves with France. Four months later, Austria and its allies were defeated. The Battle of the Three Emperors at Austerlitz on 2 December 1805 was followed by the Treaty of Pressburg on 26 December. The Habsburg empire had to renounce its 'anterior Austrian' lands to Baden and Württemberg, Vorarlberg and Tyrol to Bavaria, and Venice to the Kingdom of Italy, ruled by Napoleon himself in personal union. The duchies of Bavaria and Württemberg were elevated to the status of monarchies.

The victory over Austria allowed Napoleon to extend his influence over Germany. In July 1806 in Paris, sixteen German princes, including the new kings of Bavaria and Württemberg and the Margrave of Baden (who now became a grand duke), formally withdrew from the Reich and formed the Rhenish Confederation, the *Rheinbund*. This organization became part of Napoleon's federal system, enjoying his protection and obliged to provide him with military support in future Continental wars. Thus the Reich was already in shambles by the time Emperor Francis II, submitting to Napoleon's ultimatum, gave up the imperial crown and released all the estates from their duties on 6 August 1806. Although he retained the title of Emperor of Austria (as Francis I), the Holy Roman Empire ceased to exist on that day.[13]

Two eulogies had already been composed before the event. 'German Reich and German Nation are two different things,' wrote Schiller in his fragmentary text *Deutsche Grösse,** written probably in 1801 after the Treaty of Lunéville.

> The majesty of the German never rested on the heads of his princes. Set apart from all that is political, the German has established for himself his own value, and even if the Empire were to collapse, German worth would remain uncontested. It is a moral greatness, one that lives in the culture and character of the nation, a nation independent of its political fate . . . While the political Reich falters, the spiritual Reich has become ever stronger and more perfect a structure.[14]

'Germany is no longer a state.' With this sober observation Hegel begins *Die Verfassung Deutschlands,*† written in 1802 but never published in Hegel's lifetime. The statelessness of Germany, he wrote, had already been designed into in the Peace of Westphalia.

> There is no longer any argument about what term best describes the German constitution. If Germany is a state, then the present condition of the state's dissolution could be called, following a foreign scholar of constitutional law, nothing other than anarchy—that is, if the individual parts had not formed themselves into states once more, to whom not so much a still existing bond as rather its memory grants an appearance of unity . . . [The resolution of the problem of] how it could be possible that Germany is not a state and yet is a state, is very easily discovered: Germany is a state in our thoughts and not a state in reality; formality and reality diverge, empty formality belonging to the state, reality belonging to the non-existence of the state.

While Schiller looked upon the imminent downfall of the Reich with equanimity, Hegel considered it possible that Germany would again organize itself into a state. He did not believe the agent of unification would be Prussia, which as 'an independent, sovereign, powerful state' was no longer in a position to 'enter into association with other estates on equal terms'. Rather, he expected the imperial cities and territorial estates to collaborate with the emperor and his hereditary lands, which, in contrast to Prussia, themselves formed a state based on the principle of representation and in which the populace had rights. Thus only from the emperor may 'we expect support for that which the world presently understands by the term "German liberty" '.[15]

Hegel's hopes were unfounded, and they were shared by only a few. Emperor Francis II, on the throne since 1792, had never been interested in the Reich. Little mourning or consternation was seen in Germany upon his renunciation of the

* Schiller, *German Greatness.*

† Hegel, *The Constitution of Germany.*

crown. The dissolution of the Holy Roman Empire made an impression like that of an official obituary written for someone who had taken a very long time to die. The Reich had been a mere shadow of its former self for decades, ever since—at the very latest—Prussia emerged from the Seven Years War as a great power.

This state of affairs did not, however, prevent the imperial patriots from clinging to the idea of the Reich and believing in its restoration. The Reich had many posthumous devotees, especially among the 'mediatized princes'—the counts, lords, and imperial barons, who in 1803 had lost their self-governing status under the old Reich—as well as among the middle-sized and smaller imperial estates. Many publicists of the Rhenish Confederation looked to the federative unification of a 'third Germany' (*drittes Deutschland*), that is, a Germany without Austria and Prussia, but nonetheless consciously taking up the legacy of the old Reich. This was also the line adopted by Napoleon's 'Prince Primate' at the head of the Rhenish Confederation, Karl Theodor von Dalberg, Elector and Archbishop of Mainz and previous Arch-Chancellor of the Reich, elevated to the title of Grand Duke of Frankfurt in 1810. Ironically, however, the more important princes of the new confederation, above all the kings of Bavaria and Württemberg, stubbornly resisted granting a new central authority any more rights than the old Reich had possessed. Since the imperial patriotism of the Rhenish Confederation could not alter these realities, it remained mere doctrine and political wishful thinking.[16]

In terms of societal development, the territories of the Rhenish Confederation experienced a powerful burst of modernization during the short time the alliance lasted. Napoleon pressed the member states to adopt 'his' civil legislation, the Napoleonic Code, and was at least partly successful in his efforts. The fact that, outside of Baden, the Code was only partially implemented was due, in the words of Elisabeth Fehrenbach, to the 'confrontation between a revolutionary legal code and a pre-revolutionary legal and societal order'.

In contrast to France, the states of the Rhenish Confederation possessed no bourgeoisie that would have supported agrarian reforms out of their own interests. Furthermore, there were few noble landowners who stood to benefit from the transformation of peasant feudal dues into money payments, and few discontented peasants who might have collaborated with the 'Third Estate' against the feudal order. In Germany west of the Elbe, peasants were directly subject to manorial legal jurisdiction far more often than in France. The vast majority of them also exercised personal control of their production, were often part owners of their lands, and were generally less encumbered by feudal burdens than their counterparts in France under the last Bourbon kings. The German nobility, for its part, was no 'court nobility', as in France since the time of Louis XIV. While the wealthy French aristocrats controlled their estates only indirectly through tenant administrators, the noble landowners in western Germany leased nearly all of their holdings directly to the peasants. Accordingly, as Eberhard Weis has remarked, the west German nobility was less alienated from their peasants and soil than the French nobility.

The social development experienced by the states of the Rhenish Confederation was due not least to the necessity of integrating new territories whose populations often had a different confession than the country to which they were annexed. This was especially the case in Bavaria, which acquired Evangelical areas, and Württemberg, which acquired Catholic regions. In Baden, too, the annexations from the anterior Austrian provinces strongly increased the percentage of Catholics in the population. These large-scale geographical redivisions led to a sort of delayed revolution from above, pushed through, as in Prussia and Austria, by an enlightened bureaucracy. Events took a comparatively mild course in Bavaria and Baden under the ministers Montgelas and Reitzenstein. In Württemberg, however, King Frederick autocratically disregarded the 'good old laws' of a country that was, until that point, co-ruled by the estates. This challenge was answered ten years later, after Napoleon's final downfall, when Frederick attempted to impose a constitution, leading to Germany's first constitutional conflict.[17]

Far more radical than in the Rhenish Confederation were the transformations affecting the regions on the left bank of the Rhine annexed to Napoleonic France. Here, the Napoleonic Code was imposed in its totality (and remained in force until the introduction of the Civil Code on 1 January 1900). To this was added the adoption of the French legal procedure and court system, as well as French governmental administration, including the division into *départements*. The areas of Germany ruled by members of the Bonaparte family (the Grand Duchy of Berg, established in 1806 on the lower Rhine under Napoleon's brother-in-law Murat, and the Kingdom of Westphalia under Napoleon's youngest brother Jerome, formed in 1807 after the defeat of Prussia) also experienced profound changes. Ironically, however, these showcases of direct Napoleonic rule in Germany were also prime examples of a dilemma. The measures Napoleon had to take in order to consolidate his rule fundamentally contradicted the political-societal goals he proclaimed. On the one hand, if they wished to gain the lasting loyalty of the bourgeoisie and the peasants, the 'Napoleonists' were compelled to destroy the traditional feudal, manorial, or seigneurial structures after the model of revolutionary France. On the other hand, however, Napoleon needed the expropriated property and estates to give to his victorious commanders and provide a material basis for the new 'imperial nobility'. The second of the two goals won out over the first, thus stripping considerable appeal from the 'ideas of 1789'.[18]

A half-century later, in his *Geschichte der sozialen Bewegung in Frankreich** (1850), the Hegelian Lorenz von Stein looked upon Napoleon as a great bridge-builder. By establishing the Empire, restoring the nobility, and negotiating the Concordat with the Roman Church, Napoleon aspired to build bridges into the past, between revolutionary France and a not yet revolutionized Europe. In this view, Napoleon embodies a new era in the conflict between revolution and traditional society.

In a first phase, which Stein dates from 1789 until the end of the War of the Second Coalition in 1802 with the Anglo-French Treaty of Amiens, Europe's goal was 'simple expulsion' of the foreign body of revolution.

* Stein, *History of the Social Movement in France.*

With the entrance of Napoleon, this first stage of the battle is over. The French movement has been victorious against the attack from the rest of the organism; the new France has become a *recognized* power . . . The state of things set up by the Treaty of Amiens recognized a feudal Europe and a civil France, a part significantly different from its whole, and thus acknowledged an absolute contradiction as the basis of a European peace . . . In consequence, the state of war was not brought to an end with that treaty, and the real question was not answered. The struggle had to begin again, now with a new character. Instead of acting purely on the defensive, France began to intervene positively in the organism of states. Up to this moment it had been the element that set the others in motion; it now became the constitutive element for the European powers.'[19]

The positive echo Napoleon found in Germany was, in truth, based on the hope that he would help the original ideas of 1789—that is, a progressive agenda purified of Jacobin terror—to achieve success in all of Europe along a course of evolutionary development obviating the necessity of a radical break with the past. The fact that in Germany, too, Napoleon's relatives were more interested in power than in social change contributed much toward the disappointment of these high expectations.

Yet even if Napoleon had acted rigorously in the political and social reform of Germany, he would still not, in the eyes of most Germans, have been freed from the stigma of being the ruler of a foreign universal monarchy. *Deutschland in seiner tiefsten Erniedrigung** was the title of an anonymous anti-Napoleonic pamphlet disseminated by the Nuremberg bookseller Johann Philipp Palm in 1806. The price for the patriotic deed was high. At Napoleon's command, Palm was condemned to death by a French military tribunal and shot on 26 August 1806 in Braunau on the Inn. The cause of German nationalism had its first martyr.[20]

THE BEGINNINGS OF GERMAN NATIONALISM

It is highly doubtful whether we can speak of German nationalism as a political movement before Napoleon, or, to be more exact, before the downfall of the Holy Roman Empire that Napoleon brought about. In any case, the German national sentiment articulated after 1806 contrasted strongly with the patriotism of the latter part of the eighteenth century, in both its literary and imperial varieties. Several of these differences appear already in *Fragmente zu einer Geschichte des europäischen Gleichgewichts*, written in Dresden (published in Leipzig) in 1806 by Friedrich Gentz, the translator of Burke and one of Napoleon's staunchest opponents. 'Europe has fallen because of Germany, and through Germany it must arise again,' Gentz writes.

Our ill-fated inner conflict, the fragmentation of our glorious powers, the mutual jealousy of our princes, the alienation of our peoples from each other, the extinguishing of every authentic feeling for the common interest of the nation, the enervation of the patriotic

* Anon., *Germany in its Deepest Humiliation.*

spirit—these things have been our conquerors, the destroyers of our liberty, our mortal enemies and the enemies of Europe. If we can come together, if we can forget our families, if, in the hour of danger and common necessity, we can resolve to be Germans, then we can defy any tempest. Never so much as a foot of German territory ever became the booty of the arrogant foreigner, when we were so united in the past . . . Divided, we have been conquered; only united can we rise again. Of course, to enter upon this one path to salvation is far more difficult now than in the past. But so much is absolutely certain: if the state-powers of Germany are ever to be one, the national will must be one first.

Gentz, who had become a publicist in the service of the Austrian government in 1802, spoke of a 'German nation', not a Prussian nation. With the term 'patriotic spirit' (*vaterländischer Geist*) he meant a German national outlook, not a patriotism limited to an individual German state. He avoided invoking the old Reich in his appeal for the unity of the Germans. He thought, rather, of a new kind of union among the individual German 'state-powers' (*Staatskräfte*). In his view, the German princes, who had continued to style themselves the guardians of 'German liberty', were among the 'destroyers of our liberty'. The liberty he had in mind, however, was different from that of 1789. It was not to be a democratic liberty, but a liberty of the individual estates, the precise nature of which he did not describe. The antagonism to the French usurper was of fundamental significance in Gentz's national outlook, but he did not take the next logical step: his text was not an *appel au peuple*, summoning the German people to battle against Napoleon. Instead, he turned to the educated classes. Gentz was 'modern' to the extent that he viewed the German nation no longer as merely a cultural unity, but rather as a political organization, one that had the potential to form a state. Nonetheless, he was not a representative of modern nationalism. To inspire a mass movement could not have been further from his intentions. He remained a 'European', one who thought in terms of a European balance of power. No longer imperial-patriotic or 'culturally national', not yet nationalistic in the sense of a secular religion—Gentz's 1806 text documented a transition.[21]

The year 1806 marks a caesura in German history for yet another reason. In this year, Prussia renounced the policy of neutrality it had maintained since 1795, declaring war on France on 9 October after entering an alliance with Russia. Five days later it suffered its first severe defeat. The double battle of Jena-Auerstädt cleared Napoleon's path to Berlin, which he entered on 27 October. There followed the victory over the Russians at Friedland in 1807 and the French occupation of Königsberg. In the Treaty of Tilsit, concluded in July 1807, Prussia lost its possessions west of the Elbe as well as most of the territories it had gained from the three partitions of Poland after 1772. Of Frederick the Great's Prussia only a fragment now remained. The defeat was, to be sure, a catastrophe, yet the experience was clearly necessary in order to release the forces within the Prussian state that were capable of and resolved upon reform.

The moral reserve army that took up the work of inner reform after 1806 consisted largely of non-native 'Prussians by choice'. Baron Karl Stein, leading minister in 1807 and 1808, was the son of an imperial-knightly house in Nassau; Karl

August von Hardenburg, the politically more significant, long-time chancellor of Prussia, was a Hanoverian; Gerhard Scharnhorst, the reformer of the military, came from a family of peasants and soldiers in Lower Saxony; Field Marshal Neidhardt von Gneisenau was born in Saxon Schildau. The Prussian reformers intended, and effected, the fundamental modernization of state and society. They abolished the inherited servitude of the peasantry and established the right—thereafter anchored in law—of communal self-governance for the urban middle classes (that is, for those who met a certain minimal income); they placed Jews on a fundamentally equal legal footing with the other Prussian subjects (without, however, giving them access to civil and military positions within the government); they introduced universal conscription and freedom of trade (thus abolishing compulsory guild membership); they instituted a state ministry divided into departments and a reformed system of education throughout the country, the crowning achievement of which was the founding of the University of Berlin in 1810—an institute dedicated to the new humanistic ideal of a general education, which abandoned the old model of learning by rote hitherto dominant in Prussia, as in the rest of Europe.

Did the Prussian reforms really add up to that 'revolution from above' announced in 1799 by Struensee? This question can only be answered when one considers what the reforms did *not* achieve. The 'peasant liberation' was a major watershed in German social history, but its outcome was just the opposite of Struensee's expectation that there would be no privileged class in Prussia within a few years. The manorial system emerged from the agrarian reforms, which the Junkers contested bitterly, even stronger than before. The property concessions, through which the peasants owing draught labour services could buy their way out of their duties to the lord, extended the holdings of the big landowners at the expense of peasant land. Agrarian capitalism was introduced into the Prussian manorial system; the free exchange of goods permitted wealthy bourgeois to purchase landed estates. After hard-fought battles, however, the nobility was able to retain most of its privileges. Patrimonial jurisdiction remained in force until 1848, manorial exemption from property taxes until 1861, and manorial police authority until 1872. The thoroughly authoritarian *Gesindeordnung*, the system of rules governing relations between masters and servants, was not abolished until 1918; the manorial district (*Gutsbezirk*) remained as a unit of state administration until 1927, and even the manorial lord's authority as patron of the church outlasted the Wilhelmine empire.

The Edict of Peasant Liberation from 9 October 1807 granted the peasants freedom in a legal sense. The poorest among them, however, the *Kossäten*, previously exempt from obligatory draught labour, were unaffected by the edict and compelled to continue rendering their services and payments. Even the small farmers who were able to pay off their manual and draught obligations by relinquishing land continued to belong to the manorial association. Unlike in post-revolutionary France, where an independent class of farmers with small parcels of land was recruited from among the agricultural workers and landless peasants, in Prussia this class became, to a great extent in any case, the 'industrial reserve army' of Marx: a reservoir of labour that made the industrial revolution possible in Germany. Prussia's peasant liberation thus contributed *both* to the preservation of a pre-modern ruling class, the East Elbian Junkers, *and* to the modernization of German society. Of course, this modernization was quite different from the one envisioned by the reformers of 1808.

A national system of representation was also one of the goals of the Prussian reformers in Stein's and Hardenberg's circles. This was not to be a system of direct representation through general elections, but rather an advisory council in which indirectly elected agents of the propertied and educated classes should have a voice. 'Political consultation as political participation on a short leash, but no active co-determination and sharing of power'—such was, in the judgement of the historian Hans-Ulrich Wehler, the vision of the reformers. Yet a national representation did not come to fruition even in this diluted, non-parliamentary form. The plan encountered massive resistance, first from a conservative faction of the nobility around Friedrich August Ludwig von der Marwitz, then even from the enlightened bureaucrats themselves. Two congresses of notables (the first convened in 1811 by King Frederick William III, the second an indirectly elected group, composed almost exclusively of nobles and empowered to handle very few issues, convened the following year) were enough to convince reform-minded bureaucrats that a representative body along estate lines would do more to hamper than to help the renewal of Prussia. Consequently, the promise of a constitution, which Frederick William had made in the Edict of Finance of 27 October 1810, was never redeemed. It was not to be the last such pledge to suffer that fate.

If we count the revolution of industry among the consequences of the Prussian reforms, the concept of 'revolution from above' is nonetheless justified. In any case, Prussia made a great leap forward in the years after 1807. Even if Bavaria, Baden, and Württemberg developed into constitutional states much sooner than Prussia, the latter acquired the leadership in the modernization of government and society for a long time to come. With the exception of the Kingdom of Westphalia, no other German state pushed the emancipation of the Jews as far as Prussia, where it was secured in law in 1812. Freedom of trade, proclaimed through edicts in 1810 and 1811, was introduced in Austria only in 1859, in the other larger German states not until the 1860s. Freedom of commerce, the economic counterpart of freedom of trade, was cultivated earlier and more actively in Prussia than in any other German state with the exception of Baden. Greater co-determination in Prussian society would have meant less social change: such was the view of the enlightened bureaucracy, which claimed to be the only authentic general estate. In his *Rechtsphilosophie*,* Hegel, the Prussian by choice from Stuttgart, teaching at the University of Berlin from 1818 onwards, provided the theoretical basis for a Prussian self-image that had long become political practice. The state as the 'reality of a moral idea'—whoever had the privilege of serving Prussia in a high position could recognize himself in this precept.[22]

* Hegel, *Philosophy of Right.*

If Hegel laid the foundations for a new kind of Prussian-German ideology of the state, it was Johann Gottlieb Fichte who founded German nationalism proper. Fichte, too, was no Prussian native; he came from the upper Lusatian region of Saxony, where he was the son of a weaver. In 1793 Fichte stepped into the public eye with a defence of the French Revolution. Somewhat later he gained notoriety with a series of theses identifying God with a moral world order, an effort that also earned him accusations of atheism and cost him his professorship in the city of Jena in Saxon-Weimar. In 1800 he published *Der geschlossene Handelsstaat,** which he dedicated to Struensee. This text makes the case for an isolationist polity founded upon public property and comprehensive guild membership; a state that, in order to secure its economic independence, is justified in expanding to its 'natural borders'—or limiting itself to these, as the case may be. In the 1806 work *Grundzüge des gegenwärtigen Zeitalters,*† Fichte professed an adherence to a republican state based on the principles of reason—a place in which, on the one hand, civil liberty is guaranteed to all, and on the other hand every citizen is obligated to subordinate himself unreservedly to the power of the government.

The greatest sensation was caused by the *Reden an die deutsche Nation,*‡ which Fichte delivered in Berlin during the winter of 1807–8 and published as a book in 1808. These lectures were an early document of German nationalism—*modern* nationalism, with its characteristic secularization, the systematic transposition of religious into national loyalties. As we have seen, Gentz's *Fragmente* of 1806 did not go this far. Like Gentz, Fichte addressed the 'educated estates of Germany' in particular, but unlike Gentz he did so with the express intention of reaching, through them, the *Volk*, from whom 'all human progress made in the German nation has thus far proceeded'.

Fichte elevated the Germans to the status of 'primal' or 'first people' (*Urvolk*), the German language to the position of 'primal language' (*Ursprache*). In order to substantiate these claims, he asserted that the Germans, unlike the Romanized peoples in western and southern Europe, had remained in the original homelands of their ancestors, successfully defending their language against incursion from Latin and themselves against the world domination of the Romans. In the German cities of the Middle Ages Fichte saw 'excellent civil'—indeed 'republican'—constitutions at work. In Martin Luther he viewed the German man who had opened the eyes 'of all the people in the world' to the 'damnable deception' of the Roman papacy. Consequently, the Reformation was for Fichte 'the German people's last great—and in a sense perfected—deed for the world'. More than any other people, the German *Urvolk* was a receptacle of 'divine' revelations, such as were to be 'eternal'. As 'bearer and pledge of earthly eternity', *Volk* and *Vaterland* were justified in demanding absolute devotion from the Germans, even the sacrifice of their lives. 'For this very reason, the love of the Fatherland must rule the state itself, as absolutely the highest, last, and independent authority; and it must

* Fichte, *The Closed Commercial State.*
† Fichte, *Characteristics of the Present Age.*
‡ Fichte, *Addresses to the German Nation.*

do this primarily by limiting the state in the means selected for its most important goal, domestic tranquillity.'

Fichte was able to invoke many phenomena that had been regarded for centuries as German achievements and central aspects of German character. The German humanists of the fifteenth and sixteenth centuries, as well as many an eighteenth-century poet (like Klopstock), had celebrated the battles the Germanic tribes had fought to preserve their liberty from decadent Rome. Luther had been acclaimed the spiritual liberator of Germany from Roman foreign domination ever since the Reformation; towards the end of the eighteenth century he was also regarded as the harbinger of the Enlightenment. The prejudice against abundant use of foreign words (*Ausländerei)*, especially French, could be traced back to the Middle Ages, when the commonality of language was the most important characteristic of German self-awareness. Fichte was also not the first to ascribe a particular 'cosmopolitanism' (*Weltbürgerlichkeit*) to the Germans. Goethe and Schiller had both done so, each in their own way. What Fichte accomplished was to politicize and reinterpret in terms of the state what the Weimar classicists considered to be a German cultural vocation. The 'cosmopolitanism' informing Fichte's idea of the German nation meant nothing less than the spiritual-intellectual world domination of the Germans.

'Re-creation of the human race . . . from earthly and sensual creatures to pure and noble spirits': such was the task Fichte assigned to the Germans as the morally highest people. In the voice of the ancestors who had fallen in the 'holy battle for freedom of religion and faith', Fichte declared to the Germans of his time: 'So that this spirit may gain the freedom to develop itself and grow up to an independent existence—for this reason our blood has been spilt. It is for you to give meaning and justification to the sacrifice by elevating this spirit to the world domination for which it has been appointed.'[23]

Fichte repeatedly invoked the age of the religious wars, and for good reason. In the Reformation he saw *the* analogy of the present. Luther was not only the 'model for all future ages', but also Fichte's personal model. Just as Luther had fought against the clerical world domination of the Roman church, so Fichte fought against the rising secular world monarchy of Napoleon. The German Protestants who willingly shed their blood for eternal blessedness in heaven also achieved, in the opinion of the philosopher, a profoundly secular aim: 'through their sacrifice, more of Heaven on this side of the grave, a more courageous and joyful gaze up from the earth, and a freer stirring of the spirit came into all life that followed.'

If one followed Fichte, the existence or non-existence of a fatherland in heaven was almost immaterial. The terrestrial *Vaterland*, too, promised life after death in the form of patriotic commemoration. The prospect of earthly immortality was, in fact, the only thing that justified the obligation of the subject to place his life at the disposal of the *Vaterland*. Patriotic love gave the state a higher purpose, higher than the 'typical one of preserving domestic tranquillity, property, personal liberty, the lives and well-being of all'. Only when this purpose informed the life of the state could the government avail itself of its 'true sovereign right', 'like God to hazard lower life for the sake of higher life'.

Here, the love of the *Vaterland* stepped into the place occupied by the Christian faith, the community of the nation replacing the community of the church. God was still necessary; without the appeal to him, the new gospel would have reached only a minority of the educated, and the *Volk* not at all. The 'God' Fichte claimed for the service of the German nation was, however, an entirely secular divinity, similar to the 'highest being' of the Jacobins. Like the French revolutionaries, the republican Fichte regarded love of the *Vaterland* as the true religion. To the *German* nation alone did he grant the right to demand the highest sacrifice, not to the Prussian nation, as Thomas Abbt had done four and a half decades earlier in his *Vom Tode für das Vaterland.* Since the German nation did not yet even exist as a state, particular effort was required to make it the object of sentiments of loyalty. Indeed, the sense of belonging to a German nation was experienced by growing number of educated Germans, who maintained contact with each other across the borders of the individual states and who read the same poets and thinkers in the German language. To the imagination of the simple *Volk*, however, the territorial state with its sovereign at the top was much closer than Fichte's German nation, which had lost all semblance of concrete reality with the downfall of the Holy Roman Empire.

The lack of a real German state and the humiliation at the hands of Napoleon conspired to create the national inferiority complex out of which Fichte's compensatory nationalism was designed to lead the Germans. The *Reden an die deutsche Nation* do not enter into the question of how, exactly, the German state was to be organized. Fichte certainly did not have the restoration of the old Reich in mind, nor the union of Germany through *one* of its princes, for example the Prussian king. Five years later, however, his *Entwurf zu einer politischen Schrift im Frühlinge 1813** went a decisive step further. He justified excluding Austria as candidate for leadership on the grounds that its emperor would use German power only for the interests of his own country. Prussia, however, was different:

> It is an authentic *German* state; as emperor it has absolutely no interest in subjugating or being unjust—provided that in a future peace it gains back the provinces belonging to it and bound to it by Protestantism. The spirit of Prussia's history compels it to stride forward along its path to the Reich. Only thus may it continue to exist; otherwise it will crumble.

In calling upon the Prussian king to accept the role of an 'imposer of Germanness' (*Zwingherr zur Deutschheit*), Fichte did not cease striving for a German republic. After the death of the crowned founder of the proposed Reich, power over the German state was to be held by a senate. The philosopher believed the use of force justified; otherwise civil liberty could not be secured for all Germans. That King Frederick William III would take up the challenge seemed, in the spring of 1813, no longer fully implausible. On 28 February of that year, Prussia and Russia formed an alliance in Kalish. The proclamation of the alliance, written by Stein's colleague Karl Niklas von Rehdiger and promulgated by Kotusov, the

* Fichte, *Outline of a Political Writing in the Spring of 1813.*

Russian commander-in-chief, promised the 'princes and peoples of Germany' the return to liberty and independence and the 'revival of the venerable Reich'. The text even referred to a constitution for the new Germany, a work 'out of the deep-rooted and distinctive spirit of the German people', over which the 'Emperor of all the Russias' promised to hold his sheltering hand. Approximately two weeks after the Kalish manifesto, on 17 March 1813, King Frederick William delivered his appeal 'An Mein Volk', which became the immediate impetus for Fichte's *Entwurf*.[24]

Lorenz von Stein ascribed nearly epoch-making significance to the Kalish proclamation.

> The great act, by means of which the German states renounced the old society and recognized the new, was the *Proclamation of Kalish*. This proclamation has almost the same meaning for Germany as the *Déclaration des droits* [the Declaration of Human Rights (H.A.W.)] has for France. Napoleon was defeated in name of the constitution. Through this hope, the German people withdrew from the cause of Napoleon. The battle against Napoleon became the battle of a developing civil society against despotism.

The announcement at Kalish thus assumed a position alongside of the French *Charte constitutionelle* of June 1814, the constitution of the restored Bourbon monarchy proclaimed by Louis XVIII. Both documents, in Stein's view, stood for the historic compromise between feudal and civil powers within the state, the event bringing the revolutionary age to a close. Only after 1813–14 were the 'prerequisites for a general peace, the similarity of general social and political conditions, really in place'.[25]

Were declarations of intent the same as deeds, the Hegelian Stein would have been correct in his historical characterization of the events at Kalish. However, as Hegel puts it in his *Phänomenologie des Geistes*,* 'Only the deed itself is the truth of the intention.'[26] The promises made in the Kalish proclamation were never carried out, whether with respect to the constitution or in terms of German unification. The claim that the late date represents the most remarkable thing about the proclamation can be taken with a grain of salt. When Austria took up the battle against Napoleon in 1809, Prussia did not come to its aid, thus contributing significantly to the victory of the French emperor. Only after the *Grande Armée* was forced to withdraw in defeat from Russia in the autumn of 1812 did the Prussian reformers manage to assert their long-postponed agenda of arming the people and liberating Germany.

Besides Fichte, who died in 1814, two other classical theorists of German nationalism belong among the spiritual pioneers of the military action: the 'Father of Gymnastics' (*Turnvater*), Friedrich Ludwig Jahn, son of an Evangelical minister from the vicinity of Wittenberge in Brandenburg, and Ernst Moritz Arndt, son of a peasant from Rügen (which belonged, as did all of Pomerania, to Sweden until 1815). Jahn, who in 1800 anonymously published a short text entitled 'Über die Beförderung des Patriotismus im Preussischen Reiche',† turned a short time

* Hegel, *Phenomenology of Spirit*.

† Jahn, *'On the Promotion of Patriotism in the Prussian Empire'.*

afterwards to the promotion of 'German folk culture' (*deutsches Volkstum*), a concept he was the first to use. By this time, Jahn was willing to recognize only two peoples who had taken up the 'holy idea of humanity' within themselves: the Greeks of classical Hellas and the Germans. In his 1810 book *Deutsches Volkstum*,* Jahn, like Fichte, assigned the Germans the task of humanity's salvation. 'Hard to learn, still more difficult to exercise is the holy office of the benefactor of the world—yet it is a sensual delight of virtue, a divine human thing to bless the earth as savior and to plant into its peoples the seeds of human becoming.'

Models for the present age were 'Hermann', that is, Arminius, the leader of the Cheruscans, whom Jahn called a 'savior of the people' (*Volksheiland*); the Saxon king Henry I, and Martin Luther. Frederick I, on the other hand, whom Jahn called 'Frederick the Only' (*Friedrich der Einzige*), was to be a model in a strictly limited fashion. The great Prussian king certainly understood very well how to create a state, but not how to create a people. Without a people, a state can only be a 'soulless work of art', just as without a state a people is nothing more than a 'disembodied, airy spectre, like the world-shy gypsies or the Jews'.

Nonetheless, when it came to the unification and leadership of Germany, Prussia alone came under consideration. In contrast to the multinational empire of the Austrians (to whom Jahn sought to make clear that their historical mission lay in the domination of the entire south-east European Danube region all the way to the Black Sea), Prussia, this 'youngest, fastest-growing shoot from the old root of the Reich', was predominantly German in ancestry and population. The Father of Gymnastics discovered in the Prussian state, as he professed in the introduction to his book, 'a force driving toward perfection' that promised great things for the future. 'Thus I imagined, *in* and *through* Prussia, the timely rejuvenation of the venerable old German Reich, and in the Reich a great people who would walk in humanity the noble path to immortality in the history of the world.' If Prussia chose the path predestined for it, a golden age would dawn, and not only for Germany: 'If Germany, at one with itself as the German community, can develop its immense powers, powers it has never yet used, then one day it may be the founder of perpetual peace in Europe and the guardian angel of humanity.'[27]

In Jahn's view, the inner constitution of unified Germany was to be liberal. The imperial congress of the estates, an elected body of representatives selected from all of society, must be a *Sprechgemeinde* ('speaking community', Jahn's folkish Germanziation of 'parliament'), not a 'deaf-mute institution of yes-men and sycophants, or a collection of conformists, brought together to make the best of a bad thing. No people can be ruled more easily and securely than one that has a firmly founded popular [*volkstümlich*] constitution.'

In order to promote the love of their own *Volk*, Jahn recommended to the Germans a wide range of activities and events: *Wandern* in the German

* Jahn, *German Folk Culture*.

countryside, folk festivals, the dedication of popular monuments and memorials, a general German traditional costume, a publishing industry oriented towards the people, and above all the cultivation of the mother tongue. Yet even with the Father of Gymnastics, it was only a short step from the appreciation of one's own *Volk* to a contempt for other peoples and cultures. Jahn did not believe that Germans should learn foreign languages too early in life, if at all. For those who only cultivate them as a hobby or out of love of prattle, foreign tongues contain hidden poison. This was especially true of French, which language, in Jahn's view, was enthralling Germany's men, seducing its youth, and dishonouring its women. Readers who agreed with Jahn in this evaluation would also have agreed with his advice: 'Germans, know again with manly pride the value of your own noble *living* language; draw from its never-failing wellsprings, uncover the old sources and leave Lutetia's [the name of Paris in classical antiquity (H.A.W.)] *cesspool* alone.'[28]

Jahn's sacralization of Germandom and demonization of everything French, extreme as it was, was surpassed in the writings of Ernst Moritz Arndt. Originally an Evangelical theologian, Arndt expressed the pseudo-religious character of his German nationalism in classic fashion at the beginning of 1807:

> To be *one* people, to have *one* feeling for *one* cause, to run together with the bloody sword of vengeance—this is the religion of our time. Through this belief you must be united in harmony and strong, conquering hell and the devil . . . This is the highest religion: to conquer and die for justice and truth, to conquer or die for the holy cause of humanity, which is being destroyed by tyranny in vice and disgrace. This is the highest religion: to love the Fatherland more than lords and princes, fathers and mothers, women and children. This is the highest religion: to leave behind for our grandchildren an honest name, a free country, and a sense of self-worth. This is the highest religion: to protect with our most precious blood what our fathers have gained with their most precious, freest blood. This holy cross of the salvation of the world, this eternal religion of community and glory, preached by Christ himself—make it your banner, and after vengeance and liberation bring the joyful sacrifice under green oaks to the altar of the Fatherland for the God who protects you.

The God who protects and punishes was no longer a supranational God. He was the 'dear old German God', whom Arndt first invoked in 1810 in the poem 'Gebet'.* In the year 1813, with the war of liberation against Napoleon under way, Arndt wrote a 'Katechismus für den deutschen Kriegs- und Wehrmann'.† In antiquated language imitating Luther's translation of the Book of Revelation, he called out to the participants in the campaign:

> And a monster has been born and a bloodstained horror has arisen. And his name is Napoleon Bonaparte, a name of woe . . . Arise, you peoples! Slay him, for he is accursed of me; destroy him, for he is a destroyer of freedom and right . . . And you must recognize in concord and peacefulness that you have one God, the old, faithful God, and that you have one Fatherland, old, faithful Germany.

* Arndt, 'Prayer'.

† Arndt, 'Catechism for the German Soldier and Militiaman'.

The battle against Napoleonic foreign domination as a battle for the unity of Germany—several other of Arndt's writings from 1813 seek to enlist support for this goal. In his appeal 'An die Preussen',* he wrote: 'Only a bloody hatred of the French can unify German power, restore German glory, bring out all the noble instincts of the people and submerge the base ones.' The following passage is taken from an article entitled 'Was bedeuten Landsturm und Landwehr?'†

We are now looking at just such a people's war, one for all Germans. Only in a general rebellion against the enemy, only through a fraternal and faithful unification of all German powers can Europe and the Fatherland be rescued and the hideous might that threatens the freedom and happiness of the world be torn down.

The task of uniting a militant message with the Christian command to 'love your neighbour' caused little difficulty for Arndt. In an essay entitled 'Über Volkshass',‡ also from 1813, he wrote that a person with the right kind of love must necessarily feel a mortal hatred of evil. God desires such hatred, indeed he commands it. The French must be hated for what they have done to Germany not merely in the last twenty years, but for more than three centuries.

I want a hatred of the French. I don't want it simply for this war, but for a long time. I want it forever . . . Let this hatred burn as the religion of the German people, as a holy madness in all hearts, and let it preserve us forever in our faithfulness, uprightness, and courage. Let it make Germany into an unpleasant land for the French in the future, as England is an unpleasant land for them.[29]

The holy madness of hatred against the French had, in Arndt's view, a protective function. It was to serve as a wall of separation between the two peoples. It could not, however, replace a secure geographic boundary. For this reason, Arndt demanded in 1813 the return of Alsace and German-speaking Lorraine to Germany, making the linguistic into the political border between the two countries. 'Through the ancestry and language of the people, this ancient border is fixed, for all time and clear for all to see, in the Vosges, Jura, and Ardennes. Nothing French shall ever be desired by the Germans, to whom it would only bring harm.' This demand was repeated in 'Der Rhein, Deutschlands Strom, aber nicht Deutschlands Grenze'¶ of the same year. Language represents the only valid natural boundary. 'Therefore, language is what makes the right boundary between peoples . . . Whoever dwells together speaking the same language, belongs together, as God and Nature have intended it.'

Arndt interpreted the victory of Prussian arms in the battle against Napoleon as a revelation of the divine will.

There are now, and have been for years, a thousand signs showing that God has great things in store for humanity and for the German people . . . Thus the Prussian people and army

* Arndt, 'To the Prussians'.
† Arndt, 'What do *Landsturm* and *Landwehr* mean?'.
‡ Arndt, 'On Ethnic Hatred'.
¶ Arndt, 'The Rhine, Germany's River, but not Germany's Border'.

have revealed their true colours . . . thus have God and God's might and an enthusiasm, which we cannot understand, appeared also among us. God is with the Prussians, God is with the Germans, God has come among us, God has wrought the great deeds through which the path of freedom has been opened—God, and not we.

Prior to the wars of liberation, Arndt did not advocate the unification of Germany through Prussia. After 1814 he did so. At the end of that year, with the Bourbons again in power in Paris, Napoleon in exile on Elba, and the peace conference beginning in Vienna, Arndt for the first time gave expression—though still in somewhat cryptic form—to his hope for an emperorship of the Hohenzollerns. At the beginning of 1815, he attempted to justify a Prussian claim to the Rhineland, including Mainz and Luxembourg, as the Prussian 'western marches'. Just as Prussia has always defended Germany on the east, it must from now on do the same on the west against France. Germany needs a 'leader and purifier'. 'This great and good spirit, whose highest position in Germany nobody can and will contest, I wish to name here for all to see and mark: its name is Prussia.' Austria has burdened itself, to its own misfortune, with foreign peoples, and is not even a match for them. 'Prussia, on the other hand, stands with all its advantages and aspirations firmly rooted and enclosed in Germany; with Germany it must henceforth stand or fall.'[30]

Like Fichte and Jahn, Arndt was a vehement critic of the German princes, especially those of middling and lower rank. In 1808 he was still invoking the ideals of the French Revolution, whence he believed the 'third great era of Christianity' (after the early Christian church and the Reformation) would proceed. In 1813 he supported a two-house system for the future German parliament, one representing 'the people as a whole or the commons'. By the next year he was professing a commitment to democracy, though not in the French sense. To be sure, the concepts 'democrat, democratic, and democracy' had become in the last twenty years a kind of 'rat-poison for the hearts and ears of all good folk', but in the words themselves lay nothing repugnant. 'The people are as holy as the mob is unholy. A democrat is one who wants government for the people and by the people. Someone who wants mob rule is called an "ochlocrat".'[from *ochlos*, Greek for 'mass', 'mob' (H.A.W.)] The three estates, the nobility, peasantry, and bourgeoisie, must have advisory and co-determinative political power in all issues and requirements of the country; the princes are to exercise executive authority 'within boundaries established by the general laws of Germany'.[31]

For Arndt, Jahn, and Fichte, there existed not only no contradiction between unity and liberty; the appeals for the unity of Germany and for human rights anchored in law were the two sides of the same coin. If unity and liberty had been realized as these authors envisioned, the existing order of things in Germany and Europe would have been revolutionized. The intellectual pioneers of German unification under Prussia rejected traditional notions of the European balance of power. In 1808 Fichte labelled the 'artificially maintained balance of power' a 'thoroughly foreign creation' that should 'never have taken root in the soul of a German'. Arndt spoke of the 'balance of power' in 1815 as the 'bloody puppet theatre' on whose stage the 'German idiot' gets jerked around as the 'buffoon of Europe'. The German nationalists of the early nineteenth century were radical reformers in matters both domestic and international. They stood on the left in the political spectrum of their day, closer to the ideas of 1789 than their anti-French agitation made it seem.[32]

Nonetheless, their differences with the French Revolution were many and fundamental. Since there was, as yet, no German national state, early German nationalism was not able to orient itself according to a political order of its own that it subjectively felt to be ideal. As an alternative, it invoked supposedly objective entities like *Volk*, *Sprache*, and *Kultur*, as if these phenomena preconditioned any political will or choice. It did not occur to Arndt to actually ask the inhabitants of Alsace and Lorraine if they wished to be Germans. In order to incorporate them into Germany, it was enough that they spoke German and had once belonged to the Reich. The Swiss were to be forced by a commercial war to turn to Germany and to feel themselves to be German. The Dutch and Flemish were to be granted limited autonomy, as long as they were prepared to adhere closely to Germany. To be sure, Arndt no longer considered Scandinavia part of Greater Germany, as he did in his youth. Nonetheless, his writings from 1814 to 1815 indisputably bear witness to an idea that goes back to the humanists of the fifteenth century: the concept of *Germania magna*, which included all Germanic nations and whose natural leader was Germany.

Even the idea of racial purity was not foreign to Arndt. He took pains to assert that he did not simply hate 'the Jews as Jews' or consider them a naturally bad people, nor did he question the equal civil rights of Jews born in Germany, even if he did strongly urge them finally to convert to Christianity. Foreign Jews, on the other hand, especially those from Poland and eastern Europe, should never be received into Germany, which was threatened more than any other country by a Jewish inundation. The admission of foreign Jews is 'a disaster and plague of our people'; the 'peoples' frequent mingling with foreign substances' spells ruin and destruction of character. 'The Jews as Jews do not fit into this world and into these nations, and therefore I do not wish their numbers to be unduly increased in Germany. I also do not desire it because they are a totally foreign people and I would like to preserve the Germanic race [*Stamm*] free of any foreign elements.'

Concerning the traditional otherness of the Jews, Fichte expressed views even more radical than those of Arndt. In his 1793 book about the French Revolution, the philosopher wrote that Jewry is 'a powerful, hostile state, at permanent war with all the others', a kind of 'state within the state'. The obstacles preventing the Jews from achieving 'love of justice, humanity, and truth' seemed to Fichte insurmountable, namely their morality of double standards and their belief in a misanthropic God. The Jews ought not to be denied human rights,

> even though they begrudge us the same . . . Nonetheless, I see no means of granting them civil rights other than cutting off all their heads in one night and replacing them with ones not containing any Jewish ideas. Further, in order to protect us from them, I see no alternative but to conquer their beloved homeland for them and send them all there.

According to the early German nationalists, to be German meant to be of German ancestry. To desire to be German was not sufficient; nor, however, was it necessary in order to be treated as a German for purposes of service to the *Vaterland*. The early nineteenth-century German concept of the nation was a case of circular reasoning. It was far more 'deterministic' than the nation of the French Revolution. For all their self-proclaimed esteem for and closeness to 'humanity', the early German nationalists had no universal values like liberty, equality, and fraternity to offer, but only the proposition that humanity recognize the superiority of the German spirit and agree to find its salvation through Germany. Since the world gave no indication that it would do so, God had to step into the breach. The experience of powerlessness created fantasies of power that only the Almighty could bring about.[33]

The self-overestimation characteristic of Fichte, Jahn, and Arndt are reminiscent of the Hohenstaufen aspirations to world empire during the Middle Ages. At that time, of course, the Holy Roman Empire was a powerful force in international politics. By the time the classical texts of early German nationalism were written, it was nothing more than a memory. Nonetheless, there were German intellectuals for whom the universal aspirations of the old Reich had been transformed into the pretensions of the Germans to be models of humanity. The *Sacrum Imperium* had no chance of being resurrected. Still, even a new Reich, in order to bear comparison with the past, would need a kind of sacralization. This was the task of the early nineteenth-century German nationalists. They did not 'invent' a tradition, but rather reconstructed traditions already in existence. Above all, they transformed into secular language and argumentation older religious beliefs about a German mission in the world. From this recasting emerged the phenomenon we call German nationalism.[34]

This nationalism was 'modern' because it aimed at a fundamental renovation of society and strove to break with the past. The revolutionary aspect of early German nationalism is especially clear in comparison with representatives of political romanticism like Novalis, Friedrich Schlegel, and Adam Müller. While the two movements have much in common in their idealization of Germanness, the differences are more significant. The political romantics praised the virtues of the nobility and of a society structured according to traditional *Stände*. They felt an affinity with the Christian universalism of the Middle Ages, developing a strong inclination towards Catholicism, to which several of them, like Müller and Schlegel, converted. The early nationalists wanted to abolish the privileges of the nobility. They were anti-universalists and 'cultural Protestants' (in a wider sense than contained in the term as it was used in the Wilhelmine era). Prussia as antagonist of Austria, as contender for the crown of a new German Reich—such thoughts were sacrilege to the political romantics. The early nationalists made them into a political agenda.[35]

The political leaders in Prussia during the early nineteenth century were themselves still unable to adopt such a programme without undermining the basis of their own rule. The founding fathers of German nationalism were certainly not *Kleindeutsche*, that is, proponents of a 'Little Germany' who wished to exclude Austria (there is room for doubt only in Jahn's case). Yet to advocate, as Arndt did,

'Germany as a whole', a German state 'as far as the German tongue is heard', a Germany 'from the North Sea to the Carpathians, from the Baltic to the Alps and the Vistula'—this was equivalent to breaking up the Habsburg monarchy. An anti-dynastic revolution of this kind could only be endorsed by 'ideologues', a term Napoleon used to brand intellectuals who engaged in politics.

The Prussian king and his ministers were neither ideologues nor revolutionaries. The thoughts concerning Germany's future that Baron Stein committed to paper between 1807 and 1815 were contradictory, but closer in spirit to political romanticism than to German nationalism. It was never Stein's intention to demote Austria to second place behind Prussia. He desired a good understanding between the two German great powers and a curtailment of the influence wielded by the other German princes. 'The firm, constant, uninterrupted accord and friendship of Austria and Prussia' as the keystone of a German 'union of states', a voluntary and coequal affiliation of sovereign princes—such was also the vision expounded by Wilhelm von Humboldt in his 'Denkschrift zur deutschen Verfassung'* of 1813. Hardenberg imagined a German federation led by Austria, Prussia, and Bavaria. A German national state was *not* among the goals of Prussia's ruling reformers.[36]

Thus the early German nationalists were lacking in firm support from the state. The support they found from within society as a whole, on the other hand, can be fairly clearly identified. Fichte, Arndt, and Jahn appealed above all to educated young people—often still at university—of the Evangelical confession. This audience was far more numerous in northern Germany than in the Catholic and multi-confessional south and west, which had strong reservations concerning Prussia and a certain amount of sympathy for Napoleon. By no means, however, were all Evangelicals necessarily apostles of German nationalism. The patriotism preached in Prussian churches during the wars of liberation did not generally refer to 'Germany', but only to Prussia. Love of the Prussian, not German *Vaterland* was the sentiment that brought women together at that time in societies for the public welfare and in numerous associations for the care of the poor, sick, and wounded, the nuclei of the women's charity organizations in the Evangelical church. Prussian soldiers went to war 'with God for King and Fatherland'. The *Vaterland* was embodied in King Frederick William III (who had invented the soldiers' rallying cry himself) and Queen Louise (who died in 1810), as well as in the Great Elector and Frederick the Great—not in 'Hermann the Cheruscan' or in the symbolic female figure of 'Germania', who began at that time her career as a symbol of the unity of the German people.

Such was, at any rate, the case in the countryside and the smaller cities, where the influence of Pietism had been strongest. In Berlin and the other large (especially university) cities, the appeal to 'religious patriotism' (a concept that first appeared in June 1816 in an edict of the Royal Consistory of the Province of Brandenburg concerning the 'religious solemnities for the remembrance of

* Humboldt, 'Memorandum on the German Constitution'.

soldiers fallen in battle') was not always sufficient. Friedrich Schleiermacher, pastor at Holy Trinity Church in Berlin and professor at the capital's newly founded university, brought Prussian and German patriotism together. Nonetheless his patriotism, though religiously informed, was no political religion after the manner of Fichte, Jahn, and Arndt. Only in a limited way can Schleiermacher be numbered among the early German nationalists, despite his support for a unification of Germany through Prussia.[37]

Between the downfall of the old Reich and the Congress of Vienna, an organized polity called 'Germany' did not exist. But neither was Germany merely an imagined community. It existed as a network of language, culture, and communication sharing a common memory of the Holy Roman Empire. In the years before 1815, only an intellectually powerful and eloquent minority of educated Germans looked to the founding of a German national state. The German cultural nation was a product of education, and education was required in order for Germans to take the further mental step from cultural to actual nation. The educated bourgeoisie sponsored and embodied the force that united all Germans—*Kultur*. The dynasties and the landed aristocracy stood for the phenomenon that kept them apart—particularism. If the *Volk* could be convinced that its own best interests lay in subduing and transcending the petty princedoms, as well as every other form of particularism, then the spokesmen of the educated middle classes had a good chance of exercising far more influence in a unified Germany than they did at the present.

This gave rise to a paradox. As described above, early German nationalism can be seen as an expression of the emancipatory aspirations of the bourgeoisie, making it akin to French nationalism. Simultaneously, however, German nationalism had to set itself in opposition to France, since it owed its most powerful impetus, if not its very existence, to the battle against foreign domination by Napoleon. The victors of the battles from 1813 to 1815 were not, however, the German nationalists, but the two German great powers, Austria and Prussia, whose prestige the defeat of Napoleon increased considerably. Whoever sought both national unity *and* civil liberty at the same time continued, in consequence, to have a much more difficult time than the French revolutionaries of 1789. In France, the goal was the liberation of the 'third estate' in an already existing national state. In Germany, the national state had first to be created, a state the early German nationalists could only imagine as liberal.

The challenge was very great. A firm political belief system was necessary to maintain a commitment to both unity and liberty. On the other hand, this belief system was a source of strength and support for those devoted to the cause. Herein lay in Germany, as elsewhere, nationalism's great chance: it was able to fill the emotional vacuum left in the wake of the Enlightenment, when the old religious beliefs and commitments were summoned before the judgement seat of Reason. The resulting spiritual crisis was felt primarily by the educated classes. From their ranks came—not only in Germany—the prophets and the first apostles of the new creed of nationalism.[38]

THE ERA OF THE RESTORATION

The peace settlement reached by the Congress of Vienna was like a declaration of war against German nationalism. And it was intended to be. After the old powers had survived collapse and emerged strengthened from the battle against Napoleon, they had no intention of ceding any power to a fanciful construct called 'the German nation', thereby making it a reality. After Napoleon's defeat, it was again possible to lord it over peoples and territories in the traditional style of absolutist power politics, and since it was possible, it was done. The Poles had to suffer a fourth partition. The Habsburg empire was no less a multinational state after the end of the Napoleonic era than before its defeat in 1809. Saxony, as a punishment for its king's loyalty to Napoleon in the decisive 'Battle of the Nations' at Leipzig in mid-October 1813, was forced to relinquish its northern half to Prussia. That country also gained West Pomerania (hitherto controlled by Sweden), as well as the far more important territories of Westphalia and the northern Rhineland, bringing the Hohenzollern state into the possession of the most advanced German centres of industry and making it more 'western' than before. Bavaria, which had withdrawn from the Rhenish Confederation before the Battle of the Nations, joining the alliance against Napoleon, increased its territories in Franconia, and received back the left Rhenish part of the Palatinate. The right Rhenish area was given to Baden. Hanover, now a kingdom, returned to the personal union with England that had existed since 1714.

The restoration of the Holy Roman Empire was not on the agenda at the Congress of Vienna. For the German great powers and the larger German states, the *Mittelstaaten*, reasons of state dictated that no superior imperial authority could be tolerated. In public opinion, the old Reich had virtually no remaining support. Nonetheless, the representatives of the German states did not consider it advisable to simply ignore the many calls for a new and more effective form of German unity. The German Confederation (*Deutscher Bund*) was the result of the efforts to bring the forty-one German states together that had survived the Napoleonic era or were resurrected after 1815. The German Confederation was not a federal state, but a federation of states: a union of sovereign nations with a single common institution, the Federal Diet (*Bundestag*), a congress of legates meeting permanently in Frankfurt am Main.

The German Confederation also had three non-German members, all monarchs: the King of England as King of Hanover, the King of the Netherlands as the Grand Duke of Luxembourg, and the King of Denmark as the Duke of Holstein and Lauenburg. The two most important members belonged to the Confederation only with the parts of their territory that had formerly belonged to the Reich: Austria (which held the presidency) with Bohemia and Moravia, all of Styria, Carniola with Trieste, and Italian Tyrol around Trent, but without Hungary and most of the Italian possessions; and Prussia, the real winner of 1815, without East Prussia, West Prussia, and the Grand Duchy of Posen (created in 1815). The recursion to the old imperial borders had significant consequences.

Since their domains extended beyond those of the German Confederation, Austria and Prussia were permitted to maintain larger armed forces than the *Bundeskriegsverfassung* of 1821, the statutes of the Confederation applying to military matters, otherwise allowed. They availed themselves of this privilege. As European great powers, both Prussia and Austria had to emphasize the fact that they were more than mere members of the German Confederation.

In principle, the Confederation could defend itself from outside attack. However, it was 'structurally offence-incapable', to use a newer term. This lay in the interest of all European powers participating in the Congress of Vienna, especially the five great powers, England, Russia, France, Austria, and Prussia. As signatories of the Final Act of the Congress of Vienna (9 June 1815), these countries also approved the Federal Act (*Bundesakte*), given final form the previous day. Although this charter granted the non-German great powers no formal right of intervention in the affairs of the Confederation or any of its member states, it did entitle Europe to expect that the status quo fundamentally be maintained in Germany. The German Confederation as the pledge of a European balance of power—on this matter there was consensus among all the great powers in 1815, including both the German ones.

Domestic military intervention by the Confederation was permitted (granted the necessary majorities in the Federal Diet) if a member state acted in a manner inimical to the Confederation or if its leadership saw itself threatened by rebellion or overthrow. Furthermore, according to Article 13 of the Federal Act, the participating states were required to introduce 'constitutions of the territorial estates' (*landständische Verfassungen*). When and how they chose to do so was their affair, and the actual meaning of the term *landständische Verfassung* was uncertain. It could mean a traditional corporative constitution, in which each *Stand* spoke and made decisions only for itself. Equally, it could describe a modern constitution representing the whole of the population. Of the first German constitutions, the second type was represented by those of Bavaria and Baden in 1818, that of Württemberg in 1819, and that of Hesse-Damstadt in 1821, while the constitutions of several small states in middle Germany, such as Saxony-Weimar (from the year 1816), corresponded to the first type. The plan of Chancellor Metternich of Austria, who wanted to limit the member states to traditional corporative constitutions, failed. Nonetheless, the Final Act of 1820 saw to it that the rights of the representatives of the *Landstände* were restricted in favour of the 'monarchic principle', that is, the concentration of political power in the highest office of the state. This measure contributed in great measure toward blocking any further progress within the constitutional movement until 1830. The two German great powers, for their part, would submit to no constraint (except perhaps by their own people) when it came to introducing a constitution.[39]

All those who had striven for a liberal, unified Germany during the time of the Napoleonic Wars were bitterly disappointed by the results of the Congress of Vienna. In April 1815 Joseph Görres, at one time a Coblenz 'Jacobin', later one of the most passionate and effective of Napoleon's literary enemies and an admirer of Prussia, wrote in his newspaper the *Rheinische Merkur* that the post-war German order then emerging was a 'miserable, misshapen, deformed constitution, defective at birth . . . four-headed like an Indian idol, without strength, without unity and cohesion', 'the mockery of future centuries', 'plaything of all the neighboring peoples'. In this verdict, the Catholic publicist could be assured of the agreement of those who went even further than he, hoping for a German emperor from the House of Hohenzollern. The outrage was especially great among the students, many of whom had enlisted and fought voluntarily against Napoleon in the wars of liberation. The most famous volunteer corps, that of Major von Lützow, was the first to use the colours black, red, and gold, which the newly founded 'Fraternity of Jena', at Jahn's suggestion, established as their symbol of union in 1815. The fraternities (*Burschenschaften*), spreading rapidly over all of Germany, were at first national—that is, all-German—and mostly democratic in spirit, qualities through which they consciously distinguished themselves from the regional student associations, the *Landsmannschaften*.

The first large public demonstration of the fraternities was the Festival of Wartburg on 18 October 1817, which was held to commemorate the 300th anniversary of Martin Luther's Reformation as well as the fourth anniversary of the Battle of the Nations at Leipzig. The official ceremony proceeded without incident; patriotic and liberal speeches elicited the applause of the participants, who numbered about 500. Then, in the evening, the gymnasts provoked a sensation, burning 'un-German' books including the *Code Napoléon*, Samuel Ascher's sarcastic polemic *Germanomania*, and the southern German particularist journal *Allemania*, as well as several hated symbols of absolutism: a Hessian military pigtail, a corset of the Prussian uhlans, and the stick of an Austrian corporal. Jahn's followers, whether gymnasts or fraternity members, also gave vent to their anti-Jewish and anti-French feeling. In order to feel secure in their 'Germanness', they apparently needed to differentiate themselves as sharply as possible from everything they felt to be 'un-German'.

The conservative powers, led by Metternich, were alarmed. Revolution again seemed about to rear its head, this time in Germany. Two years after the Festival of Wartburg, the governments struck. The occasion was the murder in March 1819 of August von Kotzebue, Russian counsellor of state and German comedic playwright, by Karl Ludwig Sand, a theology student at Jena and member of a fraternity, as well as the failed attempt by another fraternity member on the life of a councillor of Nassau, Karl von Ibell, at the beginning of July. In the Teplitz Accord of 1 August 1819, Austria and Prussia agreed to harsh measures for the control of universities, press, and parliaments. Later that same month, the most prominent members of the Confederation adopted the Karlsbad Decrees, which were approved in the Federal Diet in September. They contained the legal titles for the dismissal of professors disseminating ideas critical of the status quo, the 'suppression of demagoguery' throughout Germany, a ban on the fraternities, and the censorship of newspapers, journals, and printed matter less than twenty pages in length. Among the victims of the 'suppression of demagoguery' was Jahn, who was imprisoned from 1819 to 1825, as well as Arndt, who lost his professorship in Bonn in 1820 and was only rehabilitated after 1840 when Frederick William IV came to the Prussian throne. Teplitz and Karlsbad signal the real beginning of the system of 'restoration' in Germany. The German Confederation now assumed the role that has impressed itself upon historical memory, that of an instrument of suppression aimed at all liberal and national aspirations.[40]

The years 1815–19 have great historical significance for the German unification movement. Between the end of the old Reich and the overthrow of Napoleon, German nationalism was mainly confined to educated circles. Between the Congress of Vienna and the promulgation of the Karlsbad Decrees, it began to spread among the *Volk* and become publicly organized (in contrast to the clandestine organizations of the years after 1808). While the members of the fraternities, as well as the students as a whole, came predominantly from the educated middle classes, many tradesmen—masters as well as journeymen—became active among the gymnasts. The same was true of the men's choral societies founded in the 1820s. By 1819, when the Federal Diet declared war on it, the national idea was strong enough to defy the system of repression, even though it did not yet enjoy the support of the masses.

However, the meaning of the concept 'national' was subject to considerable change in the atmosphere of Restoration politics, especially in their Prussian version. The prestige of Prussia had increased so greatly during the wars of liberation that even Germans outside the Hohenzollern state, especially members of the newly founded German Societies, began to entreat Prussia to take up the work of German national unification. The manner in which Prussia developed and represented itself after 1815, however, was not calculated to win the hearts and minds of liberal forces in other German states. On 22 May 1815 King Frederick William III once again promised his subjects a constitution, and once again the promise came to nothing. This time not only backward-looking nobles opposed the move, as in the years before, but also the bureaucratic elite itself, who wished to push forward the economic modernization of Prussia without being hampered by conflict with corporative and regional interests. In the 1819 Teplitz Accord, Prussia resolved not to introduce general popular representation, but only a central committee of representatives from provincial congresses of the territorial estates. The year after the death of Chancellor Hardenberg, 1823, saw the enacting of a law introducing provincial estates (*Provinzialstände*), which granted the nobles and large landowners a secure predominance over the urban bourgeoisie. Thus the Prussians saw their hopes of national representation and a written constitution disappointed yet again.

The struggle for national representation in Prussia between 1815 and 1823 was described by Friedrich Meineke as the first phase in the battle between the 'common state' or 'state as community' (*Gemeinschaftsstaat*) and the 'authoritarian and militaristic principle'. For the bourgeoisie, the outcome of this first test of strength was as negative as were to be those of the second, the revolution of 1848–9, and the third, the Prussian constitutional conflict of 1862–6. It is true that, through its bureaucratic reform from above, Prussia, which after 1815 extended from Memel to Saarbrücken (though not in one continuous land mass), was able to make great and lasting progress in its economic development and inner unification. In the years after the Congress of Vienna, Prussia became the leading industrial power on the Continent. At the same time, however, the express denial of the right of its citizens to have a voice in its politics made Prussia seem retrograde, lagging behind the southern German constitutional states of Baden, Württemberg, and Bavaria—which, in their turn, made far slower economic progress than did Prussia.

As long as it had neither constitution nor parliament, the Hohenzollern state could not be the adversary of Austria, which as a multinational polity was the born enemy of every national movement. Since both German great powers had other agendas than that of German unification, the national idea lacked a clear state-oriented political profile during the Restoration era. In other words, whoever invoked the idea of German unity in the decade after Karlsbad scarcely thought in terms of a national state, and certainly not one led by Prussia. The goal of the nationally minded was now more modest: they sought to consolidate the Germans' consciousness of belonging to *one* nation despite the existence of many German states. The liberal idea, narrowly linked with the national, found even less of a home in Restoration Prussia than before; liberals now gravitated towards the southern German states. While these, too, were pillars of the Restoration system, at least they remained 'constitutional'. They kept their constitutions, which, with the exception of Württemberg's of 1819, were all imposed (*oktroyiert*) by the ruling prince in a one-sided manner. The southern German constitutions all possessed a two-chamber system: the first chamber a kind of upper house or house of lords, the second chamber representing the populace as a whole. In this and other ways they were modelled upon the French *Charte* of 1814.[41]

In Germany, however, this paradigmatic structure of a constitutional monarchy was understood differently than in France. For most French liberals (the concept 'liberal', originating in Spain, spread throughout Europe after 1812), the strict separation of royal authority and parliament—executive and legislative, in other words—was a transitional stage on the way to a parliamentary system in which the legislative body (or, to be more exact, its second chamber) was to be the politically decisive organ of government. This is also the way Benjamin Constant, one of the representative thinkers of early political liberalism much read in Germany, saw things. In comparison, the German liberals of the early Restoration era generally considered the dualism of parliament and administration a permanent and indispensable fixture of government. To think of oneself as 'liberal' in Germany meant to support the strengthening of basic individual rights, above all freedom of the press and of association, and to advocate the exclusive right of the parliament to approve taxes and ratify laws.

Early German liberalism was simultaneously national and international in scope. The goal of close cooperation between German friends of liberty did not exclude solidarity with the emancipatory efforts of other peoples. When the Greeks began to rebel against Turkish rule at the beginning of the 1820s, they found active and enthusiastic support among liberals in western and middle Europe. In Germany, the philhellenic movement became a symposium for liberal and democratic opposition against the politics of the Restoration—an opposition all but muted in its parliamentary form since the promulgation of the Karlsbad Decrees. Moreover, within a short period of time, the friends of Greece built a network of communications that traversed the boundaries of the particular states and showed signs of becoming a truly national organization of liberalism. The early nineteenth-century Greek shepherds and small farmers had virtually nothing in common with the heroes of classical Hellas. Nonetheless, the German philhellenes consciously invoked the myth of Greece in order to mobilize public opinion for a cause that was not primarily Greek, but German in aim: the creation of a liberal society in all of Germany.[42]

A completely different kind of mobilization took place in Germany in the summer of 1819. Beginning in Würzburg, anti-Jewish rioting, the so-called 'Hep-Hep Riots', took place in many cities, including Frankfurt am Main, Hamburg, and Heidelberg, as well as in a number of villages. Jewish houses were attacked and destroyed, and Jews were mocked wherever they went with the call 'hep! hep!' and subject to physical aggression if they defended themselves. The initiators of the riots came mainly from the ranks of the small tradesmen and merchants. The primary motive was the desire to eliminate Jewish competition. Indeed, the legal and economic position of the German Jews had much improved since the French Revolution. In a sense, the 1819 riots can be interpreted as a protest against the beginning Jewish emancipation. The dominant sentiment was no longer the Christian prejudice against the supposed 'murderers of God', but rather a resentment against the Jews as the beneficiaries of the process of modernization. While already chiefly secular in nature, however, the anti-Jewishness of the Restoration era was, in general, not yet 'racist' in expression. In a word, it was no longer religious anti-Judaism and not yet 'modern' anti-Semitism. The new orientation of the prejudice did not, in any case, mean that the old image of the Jews no longer applied. The tradition lived on in conjunction with the latter-day resentments.

For the conservative opponents of liberalism, the anti-Jewish hatred of artisans, merchants, and peasants was perfectly expedient. At the beginning of 1811, the Brandenburg landowner Friedrich August Ludwig von der Marwitz conjured up the danger of 'our venerable old Brandenburg-Prussia' becoming 'a new-fangled Jew state' in the wake of Jewish legal emancipation. For the anti-liberal propagandists, the emancipation of the Jews, freedom of trade, and the free movement of labour were practically all of a piece, and the figure of the Jew served as symbol for all the forces that threatened custom and tradition.

But liberals, too, were in no way unanimously in support of the civil equality of the Jews. Many of them considered the Jews inveterate enemies of progress, a view that even enlightened authors like Voltaire had held. For many liberals, it made sense to postpone emancipation until the Jews could be re-educated and elevated to the cultural level of the present age. In 1833 Carl von Rotteck spoke for the majority of liberals and their constituents in Baden when he urged delaying the Jewish civil emancipation until a time

> when the Jews cease being Jews in the strict and fixed sense of the word, for the Jewish religion is a religion that contains and promotes a fundamental enmity, or at least strong reservations, against all other peoples, whereas it is the nature of the Christian religion to strive to make brothers out of all nations of the earth.[43]

'The hatred of Jews is one of those Pontine swamps fouling the beautiful spring landscape of our liberty,' wrote Ludwig Börne in 1821, three years after his conversion from Judaism to Christianity. 'The German spirit lives on Alpine heights, while the German character wheezes away in sticky marshlands.' Nonetheless, the writer was not able to imagine that the sentiments coming to the surface during the 1819 riots would last very long. 'The new persecution the Jews have suffered in ignorant Germany is not one in the spring of its youth. It has simply risen for one last struggle to the death. The flames of hatred blazed up one last time before being extinguished forever.'[44]

In the cold light of day, there was little indication that Germany would be able to overcome its medieval past so quickly and completely. Thanks to the Romantic movement, the Middle Ages were held in high regard throughout all of Europe, and their vitality was nowhere so great as in Germany. In France and Britain, too, Romanticism was a powerful force challenging the Enlightenment, but it was far more successful in Germany. Inspired by Herder, the Romantics had discovered the 'spirit of the people' (*Volksgeist*) everywhere in Europe, but nowhere did they shape this spirit so lastingly as in Germany. The 'other' and the 'foreign', from which the German *Volksgeist* sought to differentiate itself, had many faces, but none so sharply defined as that of the Jew.

It is true that hatred of the Jews was a pan-European phenomenon. In 1792 revolutionary France became the first country to introduce Jewish civil equality—a measure for which a German author, Christian Wilhelm Dohm, was among the first to make a case in 1781. Restoration France, too, witnessed broad-based opposition to the social advancement of the Jews, an advancement that continued there, as in Germany, despite all resistance. The main difference between the two countries lay in the fact that a countervailing force against the prejudices of the anti-Semites was present west of the Rhine that was lacking to the east: the proud memory of self-empowered liberation in the form of a revolution.[45]

The memories of 1789 were still very much alive when, on 27 July 1830, petty bourgeois and workers, led by journalists and lawyers, rose up to overthrow the restored Bourbon monarchy. The immediate cause of the revolt was a series of ordinances by King Charles X abolishing freedom of the press and curtailing voting rights. The old regime was brought down after a three-day battle in the streets of Paris. From the July Revolution emerged the July Monarchy, the 'civic kingship' of Louis Philippe, formerly duke of Orléans. The Restoration era had come to an end in France, a circumstance that had consequences far beyond the French borders. Once again, a French revolution had become a turning point in European history.

3

Liberalism in Crisis 1830–1850

THE IMPACT OF THE JULY REVOLUTION

'With the July Revolution we enter completely new territory.' Thus begins the second volume of Lorenz von Stein's three-volume *Geschichte der sozialen Bewegung in Frankreich*, published in 1850. From the point of view of this Hegelian, the July Revolution is the event that established the dominance of industrial society once and for all. The year 1830 is 'the actual conclusion of the first revolution', the Revolution of 1789, and the 'starting point of the social movement as such'. In Stein's interpretation, a ruling class of plutocrats seized power under the Orleanist July Monarchy, forcing the subjugated classes, the proletariat, to resort to violence in their turn. 'Society splits into two large camps, the philosophy of human society into two absolutely opposing systems, social development into two large-scale, mutually exclusive movements that await the moment they can fight it out in the open.'[1]

In analysing the development of French society two decades after the July Revolution, Stein had the advantage of being able to look back on the fall of the July Monarchy in yet a third French revolution, that of 1848. The contemporaries of 1830 did not yet know how the social question would play out. Nonetheless, even then it could be predicted that the ranks of the proletariat and the sufferings of the working class would increase as industrialization took hold of the Continent. That much could be observed in Britain, the motherland of the Industrial Revolution.

For the time being, however, the political consequences of the new French revolution claimed the lion's share of attention. The events in Paris in July 1830 divided Europe into a liberal west and a conservative east. To the one camp belonged Britain and France, to the other Russia, Austria, and Prussia, the three states that had inaugurated the 'Holy Alliance' at the Congress of Vienna in 1815 for the defence of Christianity and the old order. The signal that went out from Paris alarmed the ruling classes, especially in the absolutist monarchies, and gave heart to their subjects, to the extent that their political consciousness had already been awakened. The first in the series of national revolutions that followed the French took place in the autumn of 1830 in Belgium, under Dutch rule since 1815. The result was a new state, founded with the assent of the European great powers: the Kingdom of Belgium, which straightaway became the very model of the liberal European state.

Completely different was the outcome of the second revolution in the series, the Polish Revolution, which began in November 1830. In the wake of bloody battles, 'Congress Poland', the main part of the country, after 1815 again allied with Russia, lost what independence it had been granted by Tzar Alexander I. The 1815 constitution was abolished, and Congress Poland sank to the status of a Russian province. In the winter of 1831–2 began the 'Great Emigration': between four and six thousand Poles crossed through Germany into France. There, as in other countries in Europe, the Polish emigrants became very active in the cause of liberalism and democracy. In the early 1830s the call to support the Polish patriots had a galvanizing effect similar to the enthusiasm generated by the Greek war of independence a decade earlier.[2]

In Germany the July Revolution had an effect similar to the breaking of a spell. A wave of political and social unrest shook many cities, among them Hamburg, Cologne, Elberfeld, Aachen, Munich, Berlin, and Vienna. In the *Mittelstaaten* Brunswick and Saxony, two of the politically most backward countries in Germany, the protest against the status quo quickly escalated into open revolution. In both cases, the sovereign (in Brunswick the duke, in Saxony the king) were compelled to give up the throne to another member of the ruling family. The unrest also spread to Hanover and the Electorate of Hesse, which underwent a change of government in consequence. All four states saw the introduction of representative constitutions (leading in the Electorate of Hesse to a constitutional conflict lasting several years). In southern Germany, the July Revolution ushered in the era of 'chamber liberalism' (*Kammerliberalismus*), the stronghold of which was Baden, where the liberals took control of the newly elected second chamber at the beginning of 1831.[3]

If we look for a pithy expression that sums up the liberal agenda of the *Vormärz*, the 'Pre-March' period between the French July Revolution of 1830 and the March 1848 revolutions in Germany, it would be the formula 'liberty and unity'. Liberty was the cause of the Baden liberals when they made a stand against the censorship system of Karlsbad, forcing the government in December 1831 to pass progressive legislation concerning the freedom of the press—legislation that contradicted the statutes of the German Confederation and was revoked several months later (July 1832) by the grand duke at the behest of the Federal Diet. German unity was the aim of a petition lodged in the state parliament of Baden in October 1831 by the author of the press law, the Freiburg teacher of constitutional law Carl Theodor Welcker, together with Carl von Rotteck, editor of the well-known *Staatslexikon*. In this 'motion' the liberal representative exhorted the government in the name of the German people and German liberalism to support the cause of national parliamentary representation. In order to reach the goal of an 'organic development of the German Confederation to the best possible support of German national unity and German civil liberty', an elected People's House ought to take its place at the side of the delegate congress, the Federal Diet.

Another famous liberal declaration of German national unity was made that same year. In his *Briefwechsel zweier Deutschen,** Paul Pfizer, jurist and deputy in the second chamber of the Württemberg government, made an appeal for the 'spiritual unity' of the German nation through the pen of one of the fictive correspondents, 'Friedrich'. In the second edition of the book, published the following year, the same character endorsed the peaceful development of the German Confederation to a federally organized constitutional state. The other correspondent, 'Wilhelm', advocated a Prussian protectorate over Germany. While Catholic Austria had become ever more alienated from Germany in the course of the previous three centuries, a more open-minded development of its own system was to be expected from Protestant Prussia. Yet 'Wilhelm' (whom many contemporaries considered to be the actual mouthpiece of the author, for good reason) went even further. The Germans must learn from the French, he wrote in the second edition of the *Briefwechsel*, 'that national independence must precede even civil liberty and is more sacred than the latter'.[4]

Other south-west German liberals were convinced that both paths were doomed to failure. Neither in a limited reform of the Confederation's constitution nor in a Prussian hegemony lay Germany's salvation, but rather in the German people themselves. Among the most eloquent advocates of this school were the political writers Philipp Jacob Siebenpfeiffer from Lahr in Baden and Johann Georg August Wirth from Franconian Hof. In January 1832 these two men founded the German Patriotic Press Association (*Deutscher Press- und Vaterlandsverein*) in Palatine Zweibrücken.

It was no accident that this initiative came from the Bavarian Palatinate. The particularist mentality was much weaker there than in the rest of the German south-west. Very few inhabitants of the Palatinate had developed emotional ties to the Wittelsbach dynasty after its rule was re-established in 1815, whereas many preserved vivid memories of the civil freedoms of the 'days of the French'. When King Ludwig I dissolved the very self-assured Bavarian parliament, convened the year before, in December 1831, the protest was loudest in the left Rhenish Palatinate. The founding of the Press Association—a party-like union of like-minded spirits that rapidly spread beyond the Palatinate—was the first organizational fruits of the uprising. The second was the largest demonstration of German patriots and friends of liberty that had ever yet been held: the Hambach Festival, convoked by Siebenpfeiffer, Wirth, and others at the end of May 1832.

By the time the 20,000–30,000 participants (among them students, tradesmen, and vintners, predominantly from south-west Germany and above all from the Palatinate itself) gathered in the ruins of Hambach Castle, the Press Association, as well as Siebenpfeiffer's and Wirth's two newspapers, had already been banned, the former by the Bavarian government, the latter by the Federal Diet at Frankfurt. The

* Pfizer, *Correspondence between Two Germans.*

All-German Festival (*Allerdeutschenfest*), however, could not be stopped in time. On 27 May 1832, under banners of black, red, and gold (the official colours of the German unification movement from that day forward), the speakers declared to a jubilant audience their belief in a free and democratic Germany, to be established as a unified republic against all the resistance of the princes.

In Siebenpfeiffer's words, the new Germany was to be a country where

> the German woman, serving maid of the ruling man no longer, but now the *free companion of the free citizen*, shall nurse our sons and daughters as babbling infants upon the milk of liberty and nourish the meaning of true citizenship in the seeds of edifying language; where the German maiden will recognize as most worthy the youth who burns with the purest zeal for the Fatherland . . . where noble Germania shall stand on the pedestal of liberty and right, in one hand the torch of enlightenment shedding the light of civilization to the farthest corner of the earth, in the other the scales of judgement, granting the sought-after law of liberty to warring peoples—the very peoples who gave us the law of brute force and kicked us with scornful contempt.

The German patriots at Hambach affirmed their sympathy with France and Poland, as well as with all nations who loved liberty. Nothing concrete was resolved, however, and it remained unclear until the end through what means the national and democratic goals would be achieved, as well as what, exactly, Wirth intended with his demand for a 'lawful revolution'. At a smaller gathering at Neustadt on 28 May, Siebenpfeiffer failed to find a majority for his petition that a committee of representatives be formed on the spot as a provisional national government confronting the Federal Diet. Self-doubts about their own 'competence' were considerably stronger than the patriots' will to revolution in Germany.

The national sentiment of the Hambach patriots was of a completely different kind from that embraced by the Prussophiles Fichte, Jahn, and Arndt during the Napoleonic era. With the exception of Wirth (who cautioned France against making a new grab for the Rhineland, demanded the reunification of Alsace and Lorraine with liberated Germany, and opposed every attempt to purchase liberty 'at the price of our territorial integrity'), no speaker at the May 1832 festival displayed any sign of anti-French feeling. The German national state envisioned there was not supposed to come into being at the expense of Europe, but as part of a European federation of nations. The goals of liberty and unity were considered inseparable, and by 'liberty' the Hambach orators meant nothing significantly different than radical democrats in other countries when they used the term.

The moderate liberals of Germany, who backed reforms within the existing German states, were repelled by the republican rhetoric of the Hambach Festival. Here were the first signs of the parting of the ways between 'democrats' and 'liberals' in the narrower sense. And the liberal opposition to the national aspirations of the All-German Festival was not restricted to the question of the form of government. For Rotteck, whom the Baden government had forbidden to travel to Hambach (as it did all state employees), the push for German unity constituted a real threat to the goal of liberty. At a festival of Baden liberals in Badenweiler a few weeks after Hambach, Rotteck clearly stated his priorities:

I desire unity only with liberty, and I would prefer liberty without unity to unity without liberty. I want no unity under the pinions of the Prussian or Austrian eagle, nor under a strengthened Federal Diet, as long as it retains the present form of organization. I do not even desire unity under a general German republic, because the way leading thither would be terrible, and the success or fruit of its achievment seems highly uncertain in character . . . In effect, I desire no German unity sharply defined in its external form. As history is my witness, a federation of nations is better able to safeguard liberty than the undivided mass of a large empire.[5]

If Hambach had this effect on moderate liberals, the alarm it caused in many governments is not difficult to imagine. At the end of June 1832, four weeks after the event, the Federal Diet, in response to an initiative from Austria and Prussia, agreed to a more severe interpretation of the Karlsbad Decrees of 1819, the so-called 'Six Articles'. When, in April 1833, a group of fraternity members failed in a putsch-like attack against the Diet in Frankfurt (called the *Frankfurter Wachensturm*, 'the Storming of the Frankfurt Bastions'), the latter deployed federal troops to secure the city. The sweeping investigations, trials, and sentences that followed were far more draconian than those to which some few of the main participants at Hambach had been subjected. Despite these circumstances, however, the 'general subversion party of Europe' Metternich saw at work in both Frankfurt and Hambach did not yet exist in Germany, except in the wishful thinking of a few radicals or in the nightmares of the ruling classes.

It was not until 1834, the year after the events as Frankfurt, that the secret society 'Young Germany' (*Junges Deutschland*) was founded in Switzerland by German emigrants, mostly academics and journeymen in the craft trades. After a short time, the organization joined 'Young Europe', the revolutionary international founded during the same period, and in the same country, by Guiseppe Mazzini. Young Germany shared its name, its radical critique of political repression in Gemany, and its endorsement of a German republic with a literary circle founded in 1830 around the writers Ludwig Börne, Heinrich Heine, and Karl Gutzkow. In contrast to these men of letters, however, the members of the secret political society actively set about preparing for revolution. In the years following, a diffuse network of contacts, affiliated groups, and points of support was developed between the Black Forest and the Odenwald. Nonetheless, only a tiny minority of Germans were engaged in revolutionary activities of this sort. An overthrow of the existing order was not to be expected from this quarter for the time being.

Nor was there a great deal at stake politically when, at the end of 1837, liberal Germany showed its solidarity with the 'Göttingen Seven', a group of university professors, including the Grimm brothers and the historians Dahlmann and Gervinius, who had been relieved of their posts and exiled from the country by the new king, Ernst August (the first 'German' Guelf to sit on the throne of Hanover after the end of the personal union with England), after they had publicly declared the continuing validity of their oath of allegiance to the 1833 state constitution abolished by the king. Although the Göttingen Seven were far from being revolutionaries, their resistance to Ernst August's coup made them into heroes among all liberals in Germany. And more than that: in the fourth volume of his *Deutsche Geschichte im Neunzehnten Jahrhundert*,* Heinrich von Treitschke wrote in 1889 that the exile of the Seven 'established the political power of the German professorate', a public acclaim that aided many university faculty when, a decade later, they sought admittance to the Frankfurt parliament as representatives of the people.[6]

The system of political repression, such as it was exhaustively codified yet again in Vienna in the secret 'Sixty Articles' during 1834–5, bore the stamp of two men, the Austrian chancellor, Metternich, and the Prussian foreign minister, Ancillon. With the exception of Hesse-Darmstadt, the constitutional states of Germany participated only reluctantly in the strengthening of the system of surveillance and persecution. Although the two German great powers saw eye to eye when it came to the suppression of liberal and national forces, nonetheless there was a fundamental difference between Austria and Prussia. While the policies of the former were always utterly conservative in aim, those of the latter could be decidedly innovative. Prussia liberalized its economic life and endorsed industrialization. And it cannot be doubted that the great pace of economic and social transformation was partly due to the absence of a Prussian parliament in which the adversaries of change might have balanced, braked, or blocked the power of the enlightened bureaucracy.

The path taken by Prussia thus contrasted not only with that of Austria, but in other respects also with that of the southern German constitutional states, especially Baden, the paradigmatic liberal country. The main concern of the Prussian innovators was to make their country competitive with the most advanced industrial nation of the era, Britain. The guiding vision of the Baden liberals was a society of small urban and rural property owners, like the post-feudal, yet still pre-industrial society that emerged in France after the Revolution of 1789. The Baden approach prioritized political participation over societal modernization. The Prussian approach did the exact opposite. The Baden liberals paid attention to public opinion and were especially solicitous of the interests of the broad bourgeois and peasant strata whose trustees they considered themselves to be. This was the reason they exercised such restraint when it came to demands for freedom of trade and the free movement of labour. This was also the reason—or, more accurately, among the reasons—many of them, Rotteck for example, opposed a swift legal emancipation of the Jews. The reform-minded bureaucrats in Prussia had no such concerns and reservations. For them, societal transformation was paramount. For the south-west German liberals, the most important concern was individual rights—or, at any rate, the rights important to their constituents. The advantages and disadvantages of each path were equally plain to see.[7]

* Treitschke, *German History in the Nineteenth Century*

The most ambitious part of Prussia's modernization programme of the 1820s and 1830s was the merging of northern and southern Germany into a single customs union. This goal was all but realized on 1 January 1834. The newly founded German Customs Union (*Deutscher Zollverein*) included eighteen states with a territory of 425,000 square kilometers and over 23 million inhabitants, 15 million of them Prussian. Most of Germany outside of Austria belonged to this Prussian-dominated organization, including Bavaria, Württemberg, Saxony, Hesse-Darmstadt, and Thuringia. More states joined during the first eight years (the term of the Union's original contract), among them Baden, Hesse-Nassau, the Free City of Frankfurt, and Brunswick. Hanover followed in 1854, the two Mecklenburgs in 1868. The Hanseatic cities of Hamburg and Bremen only joined after the foundation of the new Reich, in 1888.

It was more or less self-evident that the Habsburg monarchy would not participate in the German Customs Union. Economic development was on widely disparate levels in the various Austrian domains, precluding for the Vienna government even the moderate policy of free trade promoted by Prussia and the Union membership. In establishing the German Customs Union, Prussia secured its position as the leading economic power in non-Austrian Germany once and for all. This in no way implied that the German question was now resolved in the direction of a *klein-deutsch* national state under the aegis of Prussia. Yet the economic interests of the industrial bourgeoisie (especially in the Rhineland and Westphalia) were now linked with Prussia more closely than ever. Prussia stood for the development and expansion of the national market and thus for improved commercial potential. Liberals in Prussia's Rhenish provinces had a strong material interest in a progressive unification of Germany, an interest much less frequently encountered among the liberals of the largely still pre-industrial German south.[8]

PRE-MARCH GERMANY

The year 1840 witnessed two events of signal importance in German history: the Prussian succession and the Rhine Crisis. The accession of Frederick William IV to the Prussian throne in July awakened great expectations, both at home and far abroad. While not considered liberal, the new king had a reputation for being national in outlook and much more open-minded about inner reform than his father, Frederick William III. Shortly after his accession, Frederick William IV reinstated Ernst Moritz Arndt, a victim of the Karlsbad Decrees, in his professorship in Bonn, a move that found as much applause in liberal circles as the rehabilitation of Friedrich Ludwig Jahn (another 'demagogue' in the Karlsbad sense), and the appointment of three of the Göttingen Seven, Friedrich Christoph Dahlmann, and Jacob and Wilhelm Grimm, to the Academy of Sciences in Berlin. Despite these positive signs, however, the younger Frederick William demonstrated within a few months of the coronation ceremonies and obeisances in Königsberg that his understanding of the concept of liberty had nothing to do with a constitution, but rather was grounded in the old order of the *Stände*. He had no intention of giving in to demands—especially loud in East Prussia—for a representative constitution. 'I feel I am king solely by the grace of God, and with His help I will continue to feel the same until the end,' he wrote on 26 December 1840 to the liberal Theodor von Schön, chief administrator of East and West Prussia. 'I leave without envy all the glory and trickery to the so-called "constitutional" princes, who have become a pure fiction for the people, an abstract concept, by dint of a piece of paper. A paternal governance is the way of true German princes.'[9]

The Rhine Crisis, the other great event of 1840, had its origins in the Near East. Through its support for Muhammad Ali, the belligerent viceroy of Egypt fighting against Turkish sovereignty, France had made enemies out of England and Russia. The latter found allies in Austria and Prussia. The London Treaty of July 1840, in which the four powers committed themselves to preserving the Ottoman empire, was deeply humiliating to France, which demanded immediate retribution. As compensation, Germany was called upon to surrender its territories on the left bank of the Rhine—a goal that could only be achieved, if at all, through war.

The French demand for Rhineland territory was greeted in Germany by a national outcry.

> Sie sollen ihn nicht haben,
> Den freien deutschen Rhein,
> Ob sie wie gier'ge Raben
> Sich heiser danach schrei'n.*

wrote Nikolaus Becker, a legal clerk from Geilenkirchen near Aachen, in his 'Rheinlied',† which was sung in all of Germany and earned the author accolades from the kings of Prussia and Bavaria. In the 'Wacht am Rhein'‡ the young poet Max Schneckenburger exclaims:

> Es braust ein Ruf wie Donnerhall,
> Wie Schwertgeklirr und Wogenprall:
> 'Zum Rhein, zum Rhein, zum Deutschen Rhein!'
> Wer will des Stromes Hüter sein?§

The 'Deutschlandlied'¶ by Heinrich Hoffmann von Fallersleben, written on Heligoland in 1841, also belongs among the echoes of the previous year's patriotic

* They shall not have it, | the free German Rhine, | though like greedy ravens, | they caw themselves hoarse for it.

† Becker, 'Song of the Rhine'.

‡ Schneckenburger, 'The Guard on the Rhine'.

§ A call goes out like a thunder-echo, | like clash of swords and crash of waves, | 'To the Rhine, to the Rhine, the German Rhine!' | Who will the stream's protector be?

¶ Fallersleben, 'Song of Germany'.

excitement. No Franco-German war came about; the rapid defeat of Muhammad Ali by the English, Austrian, and Turkish navies was followed by a change of government in Paris. In contrast to the former prime minister, Adolphe Thiers, the strong man of the new cabinet, Guillaume Guizot, favoured the reconciliation between France and Europe.

The year 1840 was a turning point in the history of German nationalist sentiment. Never before had pan-German nationalism taken possession of the masses to such an extent as during that year. The anti-French animus of the wars of liberation, considerably faded since 1815 (though it had never entirely disappeared), was suddenly alive again, this time for the long term and without the north–south difference of the Napoleonic era. The Rhine Crisis gave rise to a sense of external threat through France in all political camps, among the lower classes no less than their rulers. This feeling outlasted the event itself, causing many liberals to reconsider seriously whether unity might not, after all, be more important than liberty. The leader of the liberals in Hesse-Darmstadt, the jurist Heinrich von Gagern, son of a free imperial baron, had come to this conclusion in 1832. At the beginning of 1843, he observed that many liberals in Baden, after learning the hard lessons of political defeat, had begun to rethink their priorities.

> What we usually think of as the view of only a minority now turns out to be the majority view: unity, positive unity, and not some mystical union, is the nearly unmuted rallying cry of all the leaders of opinion. Particularism no longer has any voice. That is a great step forward, albeit still only a preliminary one.[10]

In the 1830s, Rotteck's vote for the precedence of liberty over unity had all but acquired the status of dogma among the liberals of south-west Germany. But Rotteck died in 1840, and few of the moderate liberals of the decade following abided by his maxim. The Rhine Crisis had revealed the emptiness of the hope that the combined strength of a constitutional 'third Germany,' the 'Trias', could, if necessary, advance the goals of liberty and unity even in the face of opposition from Austria and Prussia. The German–French confrontation of 1840 taught moderate liberals that the German question was above all a question of power, one that could only be resolved in cooperation with the indisputably German great power, Prussia.

The Saxon Karl Biedermann, publicist and professor of history in Leipzig, set the new tone in 1842 when he initiated the founding of a new 'National Party' with the goal 'to establish the unity, power, and indivisibility of the German nation on a lasting basis'. The liberal party, too, must realize that, 'in order for a free nation to be built, there must first be a nation, and that this nation will never come into existence if all we ever do is fight over the kind of constitution it must have.' In 1844 the Brunswick liberal Karl Steinacker argued for the expansion of the Prussian-led Customs Union to a German national state. He contested the danger of a 'universal Prussian monarchy in Germany': even if Prussia has ambitious plans, these can 'only ever be fulfilled if they have the sympathy and full understanding of the German people'. During the 1840s, Paul Pfizer from Württemberg definitively joined the camp of those who pushed for the unification of non-Austrian Germany under Prussian leadership. By 1842 he believed, like Jahn long before, that Austria, to whom he recommended a close 'federal and internationally recognized' relationship with Germany, should extend its influence in the Danube region, a task in which immigrants from Germany could assist. In the rest of Germany, Pfizer anticipated and endorsed the increasing importance of the national principle 'the closer we approach the real ascendancy of the law of reason. The national state is the normal state in the sense of law [*der rechtliche Normalstaat*], the reasonable state.'

Like his compatriot Pfizer, the economist Friedrich List, who came from Reutlingen, advocated German and Austrian dominance of central Europe, in which the countries of the lower Danube and the Black Sea region, as well as the whole of Turkey, were defined as German hinterland. Yet even List could only conceive the national unification of Germany in terms of the extension of the Customs Union of 1834. In 1845, one year before he took his own life in Kufstein, he expressed his belief in the German nation in classic fashion, suggestively recasting a passage of the Bible:

> The Customs Union should unite Germans economically and materially into a nation. It should, in this capacity, represent the whole of the nation to the outside world, increasing its material strength by looking to its collective foreign interests and protecting its collective domestic forces of production. By merging the different interests of the provinces together into a national interest, the Customs Union should awaken and enhance national feeling. It should have not only the present, but also the future of the nation in mind. The separate German provinces should always be mindful of the maxim: 'What does it profit you to gain the world and lose your—nationality?'

German nationalism of the 1840s was by no means entirely defensive in nature, concerned only with warding off external threat. Already during the Rhine Crisis, the demand for the return of Alsace and Lorraine was raised again, this time more loudly than during the wars of liberation. In the course of industrialization, the educated and wealthy bourgeoisie increasingly favoured a powerful Germany capable of dominating the Continent. Opinions were divided on the issue of protectionism, that is, whether a future German state should shield itself from the competition of industrially more powerful Britain by means of protective tariffs (as List and most of the Württemberg and many of the Rhenish-Westphalian industrialists thought), or whether German interests would be better served by the Prussian practice of moderate free trade. Moderate liberals were united, however, in their belief that German particularism had no future in an age that saw the development of steamship travel and an increasingly dense rail network stretching across the country. From the liberal point of view, the dictates of progress called for national unification. Yet without the active participation of Prussia, the economically most powerful state, the project would inevitably fail. What is more, in order to fulfil its German mission, Prussia had first to enter the ranks of the constitutional states, something it showed no indication of doing under Frederick William IV, to the increasing chagrin and disquiet of the impatient liberals.[11]

The Prussian king's frequent assertions of national and Christian sentiment failed to compensate for his neglect in matters of constitutional policy. In September 1842, he arranged a celebration to mark the commencement of work to complete the great medieval cathedral of Cologne as a declaration of German greatness and a symbolic reconciliation of the confessions under the auspices of a common cultural heritage. Cologne was an opportune location for a demonstration of this kind. In the last decade of Frederick William III's reign, the city had witnessed a fierce battle between the Prussian state and the Catholic Church over the law concerning the upbringing of children in confessionally mixed marriages, a battle culminating in the arrest and incarceration of Archbishop von Droste-Vischering. When Frederick William IV, in order to settle the conflict, adopted a very accommodating policy vis-à-vis the church, liberal suspicions were necessarily aroused. The notion of the 'Christian state', in which the denominations would be reconciled (as promoted, with the applause of the king and his conservative camarilla, by the constitutional scholar and Lutheran convert Friedrich Julius Stahl, a son of Jewish parents), came straight from the imagination of the political romantics. It was absolutely incompatible with enlightened ideas concerning the relationship between state and society.

The view of Germany cultivated by the Prussian king and his advisers also diverged sharply from that of the liberals. For Frederick William IV, Germany was first and foremost the community of its princes, led by the Austrian emperor. The romantics saw things similarly. The champions of the liberal unification movement of the 1840s strongly disagreed. They wanted to create a modern nation-state of civic character, which meant curtailing the power of the princes and particular states. They did concur with the romantics on the importance of the German language; liberals, too, believed that language was the best way to determine whether a territory and its inhabitants belonged to Germany and the Germans. 'A *Volk* is the very embodiment of a people speaking the same language,' Jacob Grimm declared at the first congress of Germanists in Frankfurt am Main in 1846. This was a formula upon which both liberals and conservatives could agree. Moreover, periods of threat from abroad, like the Rhine Crisis of 1840, were conducive to at least one shared political conviction—that the danger must be warded off. But when the external threat disappeared, the differences grew again and the visions of Germany remained incompatible.[12]

The conflict between liberals and conservatives also emerged inside the oppositional movement of the *Vormärz* itself. During the 1840s, the antinomy between moderate liberals and radical democrats grew sharper, and a socialist movement composed of intellectuals, journeymen in the craft trades, and workers began to form to the left of the bourgeois democrats. Liberals in the narrower sense had no desire to overturn the existing order through revolution; they sought to alter it through reform, working together with the princes and governments as much as possible. Moderate liberals had no intention of mobilizing the masses; they wanted to keep the representation of the *Volk* in the hands of the educated and propertied bourgeoisie. Thus they espoused a socially gradated voting system, oriented on tax rates determined through the census. The democrats advocated popular sovereignty and—more or less openly—a German republic; they wanted universal suffrage for men, general elections, and the right of every citizen in good standing with the law to exercise the office of juror.

One of the sources nourishing the democratic movement of the late *Vormärz* period was religious in nature. After 1815, under the reign of Frederick William III, the Lutheran and Reformed Churches had merged together into the Old Prussian Union (*Altpreußische Union*). The resulting ossification of Protestantism into a new official state church aroused dissent, on the 'right' from old-style Lutherans and a new Pietist revival movement (with some of its most important centres among the aristocratic estates in Pomerania), on the 'left' from the Illuminati or Friends of the Light (*Lichtfreunde*), a movement that started in 1841 in Saxony, thereafter spreading to all of Prussia. As disciples of 'Theological Rationalism', the Illuminati (as well as the Free Congregations emerging from their ranks after 1846) opposed not only church orthodoxy, but also the doctrine of the Christian state promoted by Frederick William IV. This brought them into contact with the dissident intellectual circle around the Young Hegelian Arnold Ruge and his *Hallische Jahrbücher* (founded 1838), a journal dedicated primarily to the critique of religion and the church.

The Catholic counterpart to the Protestant Illuminati was German Catholicism (*Deutschkatholizismus*), a broad movement based primarily in the petty bourgeoisie. In the beginning, the strength of the movement lay entirely in its protest against the exposition of the 'Holy Coat' in Trier in 1844. This mass pilgrimage, condemned by the critics as a regression into the medieval cult of relics, was organized by the church in conscious protest against liberalism, democracy, and socialism. The success of the ecclesiastical offensive was considerable: some 500,000 people took part in the pilgrimage to Trier. But in many places (Silesia and predominantly Evangelical Saxony, for example), the *deutschkatholisch* opposition took on the same character of a partly religious, partly political mass movement seen in the Illuminati. The *Deutschkatholiken* considered themselves the avant-garde of a unified German national church independent of Rome, and like the Illuminati, whose membership was also mainly petty bourgeois, they inclined politically toward the left wing of liberalism, toward the democrats.[13]

In Prussia, religious and philosophical issues gave the initial impulse to the formation of a party, which then turned to actual politics only when a favourable economic situation permitted the expansion long since anticipated in social conditions. Thus in our country, the party system gradually came down from heaven to earth.

This observation, made by the historian Gustav Meyer in his classic 1913 essay 'Die Anfänge des politischen Radikalismus im vormärzlichen Preussen',* has been confirmed by more recent research.

It was not by chance that this politicization began in the extreme east and west of the Hohenzollern state. In East Prussia, the ideas of Kant and the national economist Christian Jakob Kraus from Königsberg, one of the early German disciples of Adam Smith's economic liberalism, continued to exercise influence. To the intellectual ferment were added more material interests in a liberal and national Prussian politics. Large landowners and merchants naturally wanted to see East Prussian grain sold in all of Germany and exported to other European countries. Thus the resonance was great when East Prussia demanded a constitution and a Prussian national representation. Theodor Schön did exactly that in 1840, immediately after the accession of Frederick William IV to the throne. In consequence, he lost his position as *Oberpräsident.* The Jewish doctor Johann Jacoby, also from Königsberg, reiterated the same demands in 1841 in his anonymously published polemic *Vier Fragen, beantwortet von einem Ostpreussen,*† which the Federal Diet immediately banned at Prussia's request. But the censorship, as well as Jacoby's acquittal of the charges of attempted high treason and lese-majesty, only increased the effect of the pamphlet. The call for the redemption of the royal promise for a constitution, made in 1815, could no longer be silenced.

The western part of the monarchy, the Rhine province, possessed something that barely existed in the rest of Germany: a modern economic bourgeoisie, the natural sponsor of a liberalism that differed markedly from the liberalism of both East Prussia and south-western Germany. Hermann von Beckerath, Ludolf Camphausen, David Hansemann, Friedrich Harkort, and Gustav Mevissen—the leading Rhenish liberals were bankers, merchants, or industrialists. They were also members of the Rhenish or Westphalian provincial parliament at various times. If nothing else, their economic interests alone dictated strong support for a Prussian parliament, a Prussian constitution, and Prussian initiative in the unification of Germany. For these men, the liberalization of the industrially most developed German state and the unification of Germany were the two sides of the same coin of progress. Prussia had to become a constitutional state so that its king could take his place at the head of a united Germany; Germany had to become a national state because, as such, it could promote the interests of the German economy worldwide far more effectively that any particular state, including Prussia.

Rhenish liberalism was more 'bourgeois' or *bürgerlich* than the East Prussian variety. At the same time, it was less *bildungsbürgerlich*, less oriented towards culture and education, and thus less 'idealistic' than the liberalism of south-west Germany. It shared with the somewhat aristocratic East Prussian liberalism a proximity to the government: according to its leading representatives, neither the

* Meyer, 'The Origins of Political Radicalism in Pre-March Prussia'.

† Jacoby, *Four Questions, Answered by an East Prussian.*

parliamentarization of Prussian nor the unification of Germany could be effected against the will of the king. This attitude still remained after Frederick William IV convened a representative assembly of the eight provincial parliaments as United Committees (*Vereinigte Ausschüsse*) in Berlin in October 1842, but then accorded this body only an advisory function, far less than what liberals of all stripes had demanded.

Prussian liberals further to the left saw things differently. To the extent that they had placed any hopes in the new king, they soon learned their lesson. Up to 1838 Arnold Ruge, the publisher of the Young Hegelian *Hallische Jahrbücher*, was still declaring that the 'Protestant principle' or 'principle of Reformation' was the 'principle of Prussia', one that made any revolution superfluous, if not impossible. By 1841, however, he had found it advisable to flee from the Prussian censors into neighbouring Saxony, where he continued to publish his journal under the title *Deutsche Jahrbücher*. At the beginning of 1843, Ruge published his essay 'Selbstkritik des Liberalismus',* in which he proposed that liberalism disband and become part of the democratic movement. The Saxon government promptly banned the *Jahrbücher*, and Ruge left Germany for Paris, the refuge of so many German democrats and radicals.[14]

Another even more radical Young Hegelian took the same step the same year for similar reasons: Karl Marx from Trier, the son of a lawyer who had converted from Judaism to Protestantism. Marx was a doctor of philosophy and part-time editor (1842–3) of the *Rheinische Zeitung*, a radical-liberal newspaper founded by Gustav Mevissen and banned by the Prussian government in spring 1843. In November of that year, Marx moved to Paris, where he published the *Deutsch-Französische Jahrbücher* together with Ruge before falling out with him shortly thereafter. In the only double edition of this journal ever to appear (February 1844), Marx made an open declaration of his final break with the philosophy of Hegel. But the essay 'Kritik der Hegelschen Rechtsphilosophie. Einleitung' represents far more than a settling of accounts with the consummate representative of German Idealism. In this text, Marx announced the most radical of all revolutions: the proletarian revolution, which could only be a German revolution.

The basis of this bold prophecy was a thesis concerning the 'anachronistic nature' of political, economic, and social conditions in Germany, which Marx compared to the situation in France on the eve of the 1789 revolution: 'Negating the situation in Germany in 1843 barely puts me in the year 1789 according to the French calendar, much less at the focal point of the present age.' For Marx, Germany's backwardness was so radical that only a radical revolution could avail against it, a revolution so fundamental that the emancipation of the Germans would be tantamount to the emancipation of humankind in general. 'The *head* of this revolution is *philosophy*, its *heart* the *proletariat*.' The role of philosophy

* Ruge, 'Liberalism: A Self-Critique'.

was predetermined by German history. 'For Germany's *revolutionary* past is theoretical; it is the *Reformation.* Back then it was the *monk,* in whose mind the revolution began—now it is the *philosopher.*' This philosopher seeking simultaneously to replace and transcend Luther had a name: Karl Marx.

The ideas Marx put into writing in Paris in 1843–4 suggest the medieval doctrine of the *translatio imperii* transformed into contemporary terms, a *translatio revolutionis,* so to speak. Just as in the Christian interpretation the Roman empire was transferred in 800 from the east to the west, from the Greeks to the Franks or Germans, so now the Revolution migrated from the west to the east, from the French to the Germans. To be sure, its character was changed in the process. What the French achieved in 1789 was the classic bourgeois revolution; but society had moved forward in the meantime, so that when the 'Gallic rooster' crowed again, he would herald a different revolution—the revolution of the proletariat. Once again, France would be the starting point. The decisive battle, however, could be fought in only *one* country, Germany. Since German society was so retrograde, any bourgeois revolution there could 'only be the direct prelude to a proletarian revolution'. Although this insight first appears explicitly in the *Communist Manifesto* of 1847–8, Marx and his friend Friedrich Engels simply repeat here the main thrust of the 'Einleitung zur Kritik der Hegelschen Rechtsphilosophie'.

This correlation between the 'proletarian' and 'bourgeois' revolutions, the cornerstone of Marx's theory of revolution, was audacious. What had happened in France in 1789 was that an obsolete ruling class, the feudal nobility, was stripped of power by a rising class, the bourgeoisie, which was at least partially justified in its claim to represent the entirety of non-privileged society and to be qualified in every respect for the exercise of political power. It was questionable whether the proletariat would ever find itself in a parallel situation with respect to the bourgeoisie. For Marx, however, such a development was historically inevitable. No less bold was the inferential link he posited between the German Reformation and the coming revolution of the German proletariat. No German author since Fichte had identified so completely with Luther. In demanding for himself the leadership role, Marx was acting, as he saw it, in the name of, if not under actual commission from, the revolutionary intelligentsia. Like the early German nationalists, the early German socialists, those possessed of the 'correct consciousness' in Marx's sense, wanted to be regarded in society as the avant-garde. The most daring corollary of all, however, was the third: the mental leap from Germany to the rest of the world. In this, Marx took Fichte's thinking to its logical conclusion. The Germans as the people who would save humanity by means of their revolution—one had to feel very intimate with the World Spirit in order to assume the world would welcome such a fate.[15]

The industrial proletariat in whom Marx placed such hopes was, in *Vormärz* Germany, still too weak to be a revolutionary subject. The social misery of the early factory workers was more conducive to passive acceptance than to active resistance. Of the minority of workers and journeymen who found the will to protest, many had come into contact with early socialist ideas while they were abroad, especially in

France, Britain, and Switzerland. Many of them were drawn to the utopian-religious communism of the tailor-journeyman Wilhelm Weitling. Somewhat later, in 1848, the Workers' Brotherhood (*Arbeiterverbrüderung*) of the printer-journeyman Stephan Born (one of the first to use the term 'social democracy') attracted many others. In comparison, the Communist League founded in 1847 in London with active assistance from Marx and Engels drew very few numbers, and was destined to play no very considerable role in the Revolution of 1848–9.

The 'social question' of the *Vormärz* concerned not only the early industrial proletariat, but also the rural lower classes who could find employment no longer in agriculture but not yet in the factories. The revolt of the Silesian weavers in 1844 made the decline of the 'proto-industrial' cottage industries unmistakably clear. In the years 1845–7, an 'old-style' crisis in agriculture combined with a 'new-style' industrial crisis. A potato famine and large-scale crop failure provoked a general elevation of prices for essential foodstuffs in 1845–6, leading to bloody riots by starving mobs throughout most of Europe. At the same time a cyclical crisis of overproduction, beginning in England, shook large parts of the Continent, with the result that large numbers of banks collapsed and many factories were forced to close. For the workers, the years 1846–7 brought extremely low wages, high prices, and altogether one of the worst periods of early industrial pauperism. In the meantime, industrial development had entered a new phase. In 1845 the 'Industrial Revolution' began, the 'Great Leap Forward,' the industrial 'take-off'. And there was no doubt that the single biggest factor contributing to the acceleration of the pace of industrialization was construction of rail networks. The locomotive of economic development was—the locomotive.[16]

The railroad was also one of the reasons King Frederick William IV summoned the United Diet (*Vereinigter Landtag*) to Berlin in February 1847. This assembly consisted of a curia of lords along with three other curiae, one each from among the manorial landowners, other rural landowners, and specially qualified urban property owners, each body formed by delegates from the respective curiae in the provincial parliaments. The United Diet was supposed to have the right to approve new taxes and government loans, but not the right of 'periodicity'. That is, it was not permitted to convene of its own accord, but only at the behest of the king. In the speech that opened the Diet on 11 April 1847, Frederick William wasted no time in making it abundantly clear that he categorically rejected a Prussian constitution. Never would he allow, he announced, 'a piece of paper with writing on it to interpose itself like a second providence between our Lord God in Heaven and this country'.

The United Diet did not wish to acquiesce in the stunted version of a parliament proposed by the king. Both sides remained stubborn, with the result that the intention for which Frederick had summoned the pseudo-parliament in the first place came to nothing. The United Diet refused to underwrite state loans of 25 million thalers for the construction of the planned eastern railline to Königsberg. Despite this project's great economic attraction for both western industry and East Prussian agriculture, the political interest of both parties in a Prussian constitution and parliament was greater still. This rejection of the government's agenda marks the end of Prussia's renewal from 'above', led by the enlightened bureaucracy. If the Hohenzollern state wished to continue the process of modernization, it would no longer be able to avoid granting Prussian society a considerable portion of political co-determination.

Although the moderate liberals did not want to capitulate to the king, at no time did they contemplate resolving the power struggle through revolutionary means. Even after the experience with the United Diet, the anti-revolutionary credo of liberalism held true, such as it was formulated by the Marburg historian Heinrich von Sybel (originally from Düsseldorf) in his essay *Die politischen Parteien der Rheinprovinz in ihrem Verhältnis zur preussischen Verfassung** written at the beginning of 1847: 'The revolution awakens unbridled lust for power on all sides, a desire that can be called the grave of the constitution as well as of all true liberty.' If the socialist and communist tendencies especially prevalent among the youth and the working classes continued to spread as they had during the previous ten years, they would soon terminate any influence the government or the bourgeoisie might still have over the fourth estate, that is, the proletariat.

> For this there is only one remedy: tie the bourgeoisie firmly to the power of the state by granting it political rights. This is the way, and it is the only way, to restore the natural opposition it [i.e. the bourgeoisie (H. A. W.)] feels, down to its least member, for the aforementioned tendencies, the only way to create the spiritual energy necessary to anchor public opinion in a salutary contemplation of societal conditions.[17]

The other German great power, Austria, was also without a constitution, but otherwise had little in common with Prussia. Although the *Vormärz* witnessed a few reforms in the Habsburg monarchy (such as in the judicial system), as a whole the Austrian bureaucracy was far less effective, press censorship more complete, and the surveillance system more extensive than their counterparts in Prussia. In addition, the industrialization of the empire had hardly even begun. In the 1840s Metternich rapidly distanced himself from the goal of putting the government's finances in order. This led to growing debts and increasing dependence on the banks, above all the Jewish Rothschilds. However well-disposed the liberal Vienna bourgeoisie was towards demands for a liberal constitution including the whole of the state, the actual addressee of such demands, the crown and the government, were not. German-speaking Austrians of all political camps continued to consider themselves culturally part of the German nation. At the same time, however, they looked upon themselves as the natural rulers of the multi-ethnic Habsburg empire.

The non-German nations thought differently, of course. Yet wherever resistance formed against the foreign rulers, as in the Polish rebellion in Galicia in 1846, Vienna struck ruthlessly. Cracow lost the independence it had gained in 1815 by treaty agreement and, with the assent of Russia and Prussia, the other powers involved in the partition, was annexed to Austria over the protests of Britain, France, and all European liberals. In Hungary, which enjoyed wide independence and

* Sybel, *The Political Parties of the Rhenish Province in their Relation to the Prussian Constitution.*

whose king was the emperor of Austria, Magyar nationalism turned against the majority of the non-Magyar nationalities, including Croats, Romanians, Slovaks, and even Germans. In Bohemia, a bourgeois Czech nationalism began to take shape, and in much-partitioned Italy, where (beginning in the 1820s and continuing after the 1830 July Revolution in Paris) regional revolutions had given vent to the widespread dissatisfaction with the status quo, Mazzini's secret society *Giovane Italia* competed with other, more moderate groups over the leadership role in preparing for the battle of national independence.

Metternich responded to the national aspirations of the non-German and non-Magyar nationalities in the same way as he answered the demands of the liberals—with repressive measures. One of the unintended consequences of the 'Metternich system' was the psychological alienation of Austria from the rest of Germany, a result of the continuing effort to keep all oppositional currents and influences originating in the other members of the German Confederation out of the Habsburg empire. The psychological estrangement was accompanied by a lack of interest in the common transportation network. Rail connections between Austria and the rest of the federal territory were not high on the Vienna government's list of priorities. Only in 1849, after years of negotiations, was the first line opened linking Austria with Prussia. By the end of the *Vormärz*, it took a great deal of imagination to believe that Austria, if faced with the choice between the preservation of its empire and the unification of Germany, would opt for the latter.[18]

In the southern German constitutional states, the separation of the democrats from the moderate liberals continued to assume more distinct organizational form in the period preceding the Revolution of 1848. The Baden democrats initiated the process. On 12 September 1847, called together by the Mannheim lawyers Gustav von Struve and Friedrich Hecker, the 'Wholes' (*die Ganzen*) who sought to differentiate themselves from the moderate liberal 'Halves' (*die Halben*) met in Offenburg. The Offenburg platform included the classical liberal basic rights with the freedom of the press at the top of list, the election of a German parliament on the basis of equal suffrage, military service in the form of a people's militia, a progressive income tax, and 'redress of the imbalance between capital and labor'. There was no mention of a republic, but this was the result of tactical caution rather than a renunciation of the goal.

The response of the 'Halves' followed on 10 October 1847, ironically in the 'Hotel of the Half-Moon' in Heppenheim. Here, representatives of the moderate parliamentary 'chamber' opposition met from Baden, Württemberg, Hesse-Darmstadt, and the Electorate of Hesse. Several of the most famous participants were Heinrich von Gagern from Hesse-Darmstadt, Friedrich Römer from Württemberg, Carl Theodor Welcker, Friedrich Bassermann, and Karl Mathy from Baden, as well as David Hansemann as honorary guest from the Prussian Rhenish province. It was the same circle whose common voice had been expressed in the *Deutsche Zeitung*, published in Heidelberg, from 1846 onward. Instead of a platform, the Heppenheim circle drafted a protocol. It advocated the expansion of the German Customs Union, which was to be supplemented with a representative body. Though it could not participate in its entirety, Austria might join the Customs Union through its territories belonging to the German Confederation and thus contribute to German national unity. The protocol further included demands for civil liberties and legal reforms very much resembling those of the Offenburg circle, as well as a declaration of support for a 'just distribution of the public burdens to relieve the smaller *Mittelstand* and workers'.*

The governments of the German Confederation were alarmed by the announcements of both camps. The Baden government was the least prone to agitation. In Austria and Prussia, on the other hand, fear of a new wave of revolutions was great, and it grew still greater when, at the end of November 1847, the 'radicals' controlling the Swiss government managed to decide the issue of the war against the separatist union of seven Catholic cantons (known as the *Sonderbund*) in their favour. Signs of approaching turmoil increased during the first two months of 1848. At a large public gathering in Stuttgart, demands for universal suffrage, the general arming of the populace, and a German customs parliament were announced. Anti-government demonstrations took place around the same time in Munich.

A wave of unrest also shook the extreme north of Germany at the beginning of the new year. On 20 January 1848 King Christian VIII of Denmark died. In July 1846 he had announced in an 'open letter', in which he appealed to the Danish law of succession, the future incorporation of Schleswig into the Kingdom of Denmark (i.e. the separation of Schleswig from Holstein). This proclamation provoked a national protest movement in Germany, joined by democrats and liberals with equal fervour. Christian's successor Frederick VII immediately convened a commission to consult over the already existing draft of a constitution for the new integrated Denmark. The nationalist party of the 'Eider-Danes' promptly demanded that the government make the annexation official and extend the national borders southward to the Eider river. The breach of old historical law was obvious. The Treaty of Ripen of 1460 had declared that the duchies should remain united and undivided in perpetuity. Energetic opposition immediately arose in both territories, but was unable to prevent the new government, controlled by the 'Eider-Danes', from proclaiming the annexation on 21 March in Copenhagen. War was in the air, and at a time when Germany had just crossed the threshold to open revolution.

Two months previously, on 23 January 1848, Friedrich Engels, writing in the *Deutsche Brüsseler Zeitung*, had once again taken stock of the 'movements of 1847' and arrived at a highly favourable judgement concerning the situation of the European proletariat.

> Go on fighting bravely, you lords of capital! We need you for the present. Indeed, we even need you to be in control in this or that place, for you must sweep away the remains of the

* [Translator's note: the word *Mittelstand*, though often simply translated as 'middle class(es)', is an economic term meaning small and medium-sized tradesmen and business owners.]

Middle Ages and absolutist monarchy, you must destroy patriarchy, you must centralize, you must transform all the more or less propertyless classes into real proletarians, into recruits for our cause; you must create with your factories and commercial connections the material foundation the proletariat needs for its emancipation. Your reward for all this is to rule for a short space. May you dictate laws, may you sun yourselves in the glory of the majesty you have created, may you banquet in the royal hall and court the lovely princess! But forget not—'the executioner is at the door.'[19]

THE REVOLUTION OF 1848

'When all the internal conditions have been fulfilled, the *German day of resurrection* shall be announced by the *crowing of the Gallic rooster.*' This had been Marx's prediction in February 1844 in the *Deutsch-Französische Jahrbücher.* Four years later the time had come. In Paris, the republican opposition to the July Monarchy called for demonstrations for universal suffrage. The first barricades were built on 22 February 1848. The next day, the 'National Guard' went over to the side of demonstrators. On 24 February, King Louis Philippe abdicated in favour of his grandson and went into exile in England. But the masses were not satisfied with a simple change of regent. They desired, and achieved, the proclamation of the republic. On 25 February, the provisional government passed a law guaranteeing workers the right to work. Universal male suffrage followed on 4 March.[20]

The spark of revolution leaped quickly across the Rhine. On 27 February a public gathering in Mannheim, attended by the leading Baden liberals and democrats, petitioned the Karlsruhe government for freedom of the press, trial by jury, introduction of constitutions in all German states, and a German parliament. The following day, the delegate Heinrich von Gagern placed before the Hesse parliament an official request for the convocation of a national assembly and the 'renewal of the federal presidency'. In this, he was repeating demands made two weeks before (12 February) by the Baden liberal Friedrich Bassermann in a speech to the Baden parliament. The liberal agenda was thus staked out: political liberty and national unity formed the core of the 'March demands', soon made in all of Germany.

Moderate liberals had not turned into revolutionaries overnight. What happened in February and March 1848 was that leading liberals simply placed themselves at the forefront of a movement that might easily have fallen into the hands of more radical forces if left without the moderating influence of the educated and propertied bourgeoisie. The threat was already evident by 1 March in Karlsruhe, where a large band of armed men forced its way into the plenary hall of the parliamentary chamber during the official submission of the Mannheim petition. Only a few days later, a peasant uprising began in large parts of south-west Germany, from the Bodensee over the Kraichgau to the Odenwald. The revolt was directed not only against the nobles and their officials, but also against the Jews, in their capacity as creditors. Jewish houses were destroyed in numerous locations, their inhabitants driven out of the community. The catalyst for the pogrom was the decision of the second chamber of the Baden parliament to grant the Jews political and legal equality, which many communities opposed. Equal civil status for the Jewish minority meant that the communal governments would be responsible for the social welfare of a large number of destitute Jews, something they felt they could not afford. Thus, at the beginning of 1848, traditional Jew-hatred combined with the rejection of feudal and fiscal burdens in an explosive combination. The rural protest was sparked by the revolution and expressed itself in a revolutionary manner. But its goals were the opposite. It took aim at everything emancipatory, liberal, and modern the revolution had to offer.

March 1848 was the month of new cabinets in the administrations of most German states. The 'March governments' saw the entrance of many moderate liberals into office: Heinrich von Gagern in Hesse, Friedrich Römer and Paul Pfizer in Württemberg, Carl Stüve in Hanover. Only in Bavaria was a monarch forced to renounce the throne. In consequence of his affair with the dancer Lola Montez, King Ludwig I had so damaged his reputation that he had no choice but to abdicate in favour of his son, Maximilian II, after a violent uproar on 20 March. Only with the two German great powers, however, would the fate of the German revolution be decided. Both Prussia and Austria saw new governments take power in March 1848. In Vienna, revolutionary students together with bourgeois and workers created an agitation that was finally too much for Chancellor Metternich. On 13 March the man who embodied the system of censorship, surveillance, and repression, like no other, stepped down. Not that the members of the new government could be called 'liberal'; almost all of them had already occupied important positions under the former chancellor.

The only possibly 'liberal' aspect of the new government was the contents of the Austrian imperial constitution of 25 April 1848, which was modelled after the Belgian constitution of 1831. Yet because Emperor Ferdinand imposed it without any consultation with representatives of the bourgeoisie, it suffered from a considerable deficit in legitimacy. In mid-May the student and proletarian left reacted against the imperial dictate with armed violence, causing an ostensible reversal on the part of the court: the April constitution was now to be revised by a newly formed Imperial Parliament (*Reichstag*) elected by universal suffrage. In reality, the 'court party' had by this time already resolved to defy the revolution. The imperial family betook itself via Salzburg to Innsbruck, from where it set about organizing resistance to the Vienna radicals.

After another wave of revolutionary violence on 26 May, a sort of dual government assumed power in the capital. The weak administration of Franz von Pillersdorf was confronted with a Security Committee controlled by the radicals. Tensions were only eased somewhat when Archduke Johann, to whom the emperor had granted full authority on 15 June during the period of his absence from Vienna, fulfilled the demand of the Security Committee for a reorganization of the administration. On 22 July the newly elected Imperial Parliament convened in Vienna, representing all territories of the Habsburg monarchy except Hungary and the Lombardo-Venetian kingdom. The German delegates were in the minority, and the radicals were forced to accept defeat even in the capital, the centre of their power. The distribution of parliamentary seats allowed the administration to decide the most important issue in favour of the executive: the Imperial Parliament recognized the emperor's power of absolute veto over decisions of the legislature.

The revolutionary movement was foiled on other fronts as well during the summer of 1848. The Czech national movement was suppressed by the middle of June. The troops of the Kingdom of Sardinia-Piedmont, supporting the battle for liberation in Lombardo-Venetia, suffered a series of serious defeats at the end of July and beginning of August. Supported by Austria, a Croatian opposition under 'Banus' Joseph von Jelačić formed against Lajos Kossuth's Hungarian revolution.

Because of these developments, Emperor Ferdinand did not have a difficult time returning to Vienna on 12 August at the request of the parliament. The court party did not have to fear that a majority of its imperial subjects would turn on it when it came time to settle accounts with the radicals.[21]

The events unfolding in Austria also had an effect in Prussia. In Berlin the first disturbances occurred on 14 March. News of Metternich's resignation, reaching the Prussian capital two days later, increased the agitation of the general populace. On 18 March (a Saturday), King Frederick William IV drafted two proclamations, the first lifting censorship, the second hastening the convocation of the United Diet and demanding the reorganization of the German Confederation to include federal representation. This representation 'necessarily requires a constitutional structure [*konstitutionelle Verfassung*] of all German states', which could only mean that Prussia, too, was to become a constitutional state.

The rumour that great changes were imminent brought crowds of thousands to the royal palace in the early afternoon. If the king had not posted great numbers of soldiers in the square, the crowd would probably only have demonstrated their gratitude for his proclamations. In the event, the ostentatious display of military power acted as a provocation and the mood of the demonstrators changed. As the troops were clearing the square, two shots were fired. The crowd, believing itself betrayed by the king, responded by erecting barricades in the streets.

Civil war raged in Berlin until the next morning. The king, whose disposition was about as far from that of a 'soldier-king' as could be imagined, was deeply shaken. That night, he wrote an appeal to his 'dear Berlin subjects', in which he promised, in exchange for the dismantling of the barricades, to withdraw the troops from the streets and public squares and to station them only in a few select locations such as the palace and the armoury. And in fact, the removal of the barricades had hardly commenced when the troops began to withdraw. They left the city almost entirely, which was much more than what the king had promised. Victory appeared to belong to the insurgents, and this impression was reinforced that afternoon when the king, with bared head, bowed over the bodies of the more than 200 dead the rebels had transported into the palace courtyard. The events of

March 1848 in Berlin—with the sovereign publicly humiliated and now protected by nothing more than the newly formed revolutionary civil guard, and the heir to the throne, Frederick William's brother William, champion of an unyielding anti-revolutionary course, in flight to England—were for conservative officers and landowners, among them the young Otto von Bismarck from Schönhausen in the Altmark, a deep disgrace to old Prussia, one that would have to be set to rights as quickly and effectively as possible.

Frederick William, on the other hand, sought to save himself by taking the bull by the horns. Together with the princes of the royal house, as well as several generals and ministers of the government newly constituted two days previously (and which was to remain in power only ten days), the king made a ceremonial tour through Berlin, during which he and his entourage wore armbands sporting the black, red, and gold of the German unification movement. Addressing students of the University of Berlin, he not only proclaimed his support for German unification, but declared it his personal mission to lead the princes and people of Germany to the realization of this goal. On the evening of the same day he issued an 'Appeal to My People and to the German Nation', in which he expressed his wish that the second United Diet, which would convene on 2 April, be transformed into a temporary congress of German estates by including delegates from other estate assemblies. In the decisive final sentences of the proclamation, he went so far as to pay tribute to the myth that black, red, and gold originally had been the colours of the old Reich: 'Today I have assumed the old German colours, placing myself and my people under the venerable banner of the German Empire. From now on Prussia will merge into Germany.'

The king's message met with a certain measure of sympathy from well-meaning Prussian liberals, but not with unconditional agreement. The assimilation of Prussia into Germany was not on the liberal agenda. For the conservative faction, which began to form in March 1848, the words and deeds of Frederick William IV on 21 March represented yet another attempt to curry favour with the revolution, if not moral high treason against the state. The resolute left, for its part, divided over the question of Prussian assimilation into Germany, saw no occasion to trust in the king's change of heart. Outside Prussia, the reaction to Frederick William's German initiative was uniformly negative. The events of 18 March in Berlin severely damaged the reputation of the Hohenzollern king in the 'third Germany'. The other German governments had no intention of entrusting national unification to *this* monarch, and none of the leading liberals of the 'Trias' in spring 1848 was able to envision an expanded Prussian parliament as *the* German national assembly.

And yet it was clear that the Hohenzollern state and its king would continue to play a major part in German politics. Old Prussia was as far from collapse in March 1848 as the Habsburg monarchy. Their early successes deceived many liberals into thinking they had already won the decisive battle. In reality, the aristocratic, bureaucratic, and military foundations of the Prussian state survived largely intact. While the dissatisfaction with the state of things was strong enough to express itself in revolutionary form, only a revolutionary minority sought a radical break with the past. Moderate liberals still believed Prussia capable of reform, and considered it intellectually and economically the most progressive part of Germany. They knew they needed the Prussian state to protect a unified Germany from external threat. Internally, too, Prussia might still prove a valuable partner—when the moment came to prevent the revolution, which no liberal had truly wanted, from straying into political and social radicalism. In spring 1848 most of the Prussian liberals and their fellow travellers in the 'third Germany' were convinced that they could change Prussia's government enough to serve their purposes—thus serving Germany—within a reasonably short period of time. To dismantle the Prussian state or destroy its military power was not part of their programme.

On 31 March 1848, two days after a liberal 'March ministry' led by Ludolf Camphausen as prime minister and David Hansemann as minister of finance (both from the Rhineland) took office in Berlin, the Preparliament (*Vorparlament*) convened in Frankfurt am Main. This assembly of notables, composed of more than 500 liberal and democratic delegates from all of Germany (though only two Austrians attended), deliberated the political future of Germany for four days in the old coronation city of the Holy Roman Empire. The leftist minority around Hecker and Struve, if it could have had its way, would have changed the Preparliament into a revolutionary executive and made Germany into a federal republic like the United States. But the majority, led by Heinrich von Gagern, was able to block any move in this direction. Most of the delegates did not want to continue the revolution, but rather to channel it as quickly as possible into a process of peaceful evolution on the foundations of monarchy. The epicentre of power was to be a German parliament functioning as the representative of the sovereign *Volk* and elected by general direct suffrage of all adult German males. Schleswig, East Prussia, and West Prussia would become members of the German Confederation and send delegates to the German parliament. The status of the Grand Duchy of Posen, inhabited primarily by Poles, remained uncertain for the time being. Until the German parliament could convene, a 'Committee of Fifty' appointed by the Preparliament was to cooperate with the Federal Diet, where representatives of the 'March governments' were setting the tone at the present. The collaboration functioned smoothly. The Preparliament and subsequently the Committee of Fifty placed proposals before the Diet, which generally sanctioned them.

The radical leaders, Hecker and Struve, were not elected into the Committee of Fifty, and there were consequences. The extreme left wing of the revolutionary movement came to the conclusion that the counter-revolution was now in full swing and that the moderate liberals had betrayed the revolution. They took aim especially at the liberals dominating the government of the Grand Duchy of Baden, who, for their part, entertained no illusions about the radicals' subversive intentions. On 13 April, starting from Constance, Hecker and about fifty supporters began a march that was to culminate in the proclamation of the German republic. Within very few days, the number of participants grew to over a thousand. For the Committee of Fifty in Frankfurt, Hecker's putsch represented an attack on the elections for the national assembly planned in May. Moderate democrats failed in their attempts to mediate. Troops from Baden and the German Confederation inflicted several severe defeats on the rebels. On 24 April, the Tuesday after Easter, Freiburg was occupied by government forces. Three days later, the last battle was fought near Dosenbach on the Rhine, ending in a debacle for the revolutionaries under the leadership of the poet Georg Herwegh. Hecker and Struve had already fled to Switzerland. For the left as a whole, the political consequences of their enterprise were fatal. The idea of a German republic fell into discredit for a long time to come. Among the bourgeoisie the tendency grew to draw a sharp line of division between themselves and the supporters of radical positions, and to look upon a rapprochement with the existing powers as the only viable path.

It was no fluke that the attempted coup from the left took place in a region where, at the same time, peasants rioted against the Jews. In the south of Baden, a poor region of small-scale agriculture and domestic trades virtually untouched by industrialization, economic backwardness provided fertile ground for many different varieties of political radicalism. Thanks to the relative liberality of the grand duchy, hard-line democrats enjoyed a latitude they found nowhere else in Germany. The geographic proximity of two progressive neighbour states was also an important factor; without the active support of German emigrants living in Switzerland and France, the disciples of Hecker and Struve would hardly have been in a position to arm themselves and inflict heavy casualties on the regular military forces of their opponents. The extreme bourgeois left considered resistance to be a natural right and rarely failed to invoke the laws of reason to justify their actions. Nothing was more foreign to these 'men of the people' than to think in the categories of historical development and national individuality, as was natural for the moderate liberals representing the educated and propertied bourgeoisie. The leaders of the bourgeois democrats also rejected the tendency of liberals further to the right to invoke German national interests in order to justify cooperating with the princes, above all the king. They considered such a partnership incompatible with the cause of democracy.

On 21 March the Kingdom of Denmark announced the annexation of Schleswig, which it promptly effectuated by military occupation. Here was a national interest upon which all Germans, right and left, could agree. The provisional government of Schleswig and Holstein, formed three days later in Kiel, demanded the incorporation of Schleswig into the German Confederation. On the same day, the duke of Augustenburg (the German heir to the throne of Schleswig and Holstein), who had gone to Berlin, requested Prussia's military protection for the 'eternally indivisible' (*up ewig ungedeelte*) duchies. With the approval of the king, the new Prussian foreign minister, Heinrich von Arnim, agreed, and Prussian troops crossed the Eider on 10 April. On 12 April the Federal Diet in Frankfurt resolved to make the Danish evacuation of Schleswig a matter of Confederation policy. While it avoided formal incorporation of Schleswig into the German Confederation (in contrast to the Preparliament, which had taken this step already, on 31 March), it nonetheless officially recognized the provisional government in Kiel. On 3 May federal troops, under the command of the Prussian General von Wrangel, crossed the border of Denmark and advanced to Jutland. All German patriots were elated. But Russia and Britain, both signatories of the Final Act of the Congress of Vienna in 1815, perceived a threat to their interests in the Baltic and North Sea. They made it clear that they would not tolerate a German annexation of Schleswig. An international conflict seemed to be in the making, one that Prussian's difficult relationship with Germany could also quickly turn into a major domestic crisis.

What it eschewed in the case of Schleswig on 12 April, the Federal Diet had already done the day before with regard to another territory. In response to a petition from the Preparliament, it accepted East and West Prussia into the German Confederation, thereby making Prussia the largest German state. Since the inhabitants of the annexed province (with the exception of parts of West Prussia) considered themselves German or (like the Evangelical Masurians and the Lithuanian-speaking Evangelical inhabitants of the territory on the Neman* river) at least Prussian, the expansion of the Confederation into these areas caused virtually no controversy.

This was not true of the decisions taken in the matter of Posen. On 31 March the Preparliament had spoken of the 'disgraceful injustice' of the Polish partition and acknowledged the 'sacred duty of the German people' to join in the restoration of Poland. But the assembly refrained from committing itself to recognizing the borders *prior* to the first partition of Poland in 1772. The question of whether Posen should send delegates to the National Assembly remained unresolved. On 22 April the Diet, at the behest of Prussia, accepted the predominantly German territories of the Grand Duchy of Posen into the German Confederation; the city of Posen (Poznań) and the district of Santer followed on 2 May. In the months following, the German National Assembly was responsible for two further eastward shifts of the federal boundary into Polish territory. The Poles, whose protests availed nothing, saw the expansion for what it was: yet another partition of their historical territory and the beginning of the attempt to transform the Polish subjects of the Prussian king into 'Germans' against their will.

The Moravian and Bohemian Czech subjects of the Austrian emperor were spared such a fate. It was true that the electoral law passed by the Federal Diet on 7 April applied to the entire population of the German Confederation, including the Czechs. Yet when the Committee of Fifty invited the famous Czech historian František Palacký to participate in its deliberations, the latter refused. Palacký declared his allegiance to the supranational Austrian state, which he considered necessary for the defense of Europe against a universal Russian monarchy. In the interest of Europe, indeed for the sake of humanity itself, Palacký said, the Austrian empire would have to be invented if it did not already exist. This 'Bohemian of

* [Translator's note: the Neman is the Memel in German.]

Slavic descent' had no desire to be a 'German', and, since his compatriots either felt the same or else sought an even more radical break with the Germans in the form of a Czech national state, the May 1848 elections to the German National Assembly did not take place in the Czech territories of Bohemia and Moravia. It was no different in the Slovenian districts of Carinthia, Carniola, and Styria. With the exception of Italian Tyrol and Trieste, only the German-speaking provinces of Austria sent delegates to Frankfurt.[22]

Thus the German National Assembly, which held its constituent session in the Church of St Paul—the Paulskirche*—in Frankfurt on 18 May 1848, was a *German* parliament in a much stricter sense than its founders had envisioned. In terms of social composition, it was not a 'parliament of professors', as one often hears. Nonetheless, it was more than anything else an assembly of the educated bourgeoisie. Of the 585 members who took up their mandates, 550 were in academic professions. As in the Preparliament, the left, divided against itself, was in the minority, but it was still considerably stronger than the conservative right. The dominant tone was that of a moderate liberalism of various shades.

The delegates considered their primary task to formulate a constitution, especially the 'fundamental rights of the German people'. The 'Draft of the Seventeen' (*Siebzehnerentwurf*), an outline drawn up by a committee appointed by the Federal Diet, was largely ignored. Considering the delegates' experience with governmental repression in the three decades since the Congress of Vienna, their decision to prioritize the constitution was understandable. But it was unrealistic. The most important questions thrown open by the German revolution were questions of power, the resolution of which could not be postponed with impunity. First, there was the matter of the relationship between the future German national state and the supranational Habsburg empire. Secondly, there was the relationship between the Frankfurt parliament and the other German great power, the Kingdom of Prussia, whose own freely elected National Assembly was inaugurated on 22 May 1848 (four days after the convocation of the German parliament) by Frederick William IV in a speech proclaiming the king's commitment to German unity.

On 28 July 1848 the German National Assembly made what, four days previously, its president Heinrich von Gagern had called a 'bold move': it passed a resolution setting up a provisional central authority to replace the Federal Diet. The next day it elected the Austrian archduke, Johann, to the office of imperial regent, thereby expressing the wish of the Frankfurt parliament to include Austria in the founding of the German national state. This act gravely affronted Prussia and its king, albeit inadvertently. On 15 July Prince Karl von Leiningen, a noble from the Odenwald and half-brother of Queen Victoria, was appointed to head the imperial ministry. But the new central government had no real power and authority, a fact that became clear when the president of the imperial ministry officially entered

* [Translator's note: the German National Assembly/Frankfurt parliament is often called 'the Paulskirche'.]

office on 6 August. The two German great powers and several *Mittelstaaten* refused to permit their troops to pay homage to the imperial regent, as the Prussian General von Peucker, the imperial minister of war, had ordered them to do.

The moment of truth for the provisional central government and the German National Assembly came at the end of the Schleswig-Holstein crisis. The parliamentarians themselves had helped to make the international conflict worse by inviting the delegates elected in Schleswig into the National Assembly, thereby accepting—de facto if not de jure—the duchy into the German Confederation. The protest from London and St Petersburg was loud. On 26 August Prussia, under pressure from Russia and Britain and ignoring the stipulations of the imperial ministry, signed an armistice with Denmark in Malmö. The agreement called for the evacuation of both Danish and Confederation troops from Schleswig and Holstein as well as the replacement of the provisional government in Kiel with a new joint administration appointed by the Danish and Prussian sovereigns, the latter acting as a sort of trustee of the German Confederation.

A storm of national protest shook Germany. When the imperial ministry, which did not have the means to compel Prussia to continue the hostilities, resigned itself to the inevitable and expressed its willingness to accept the armistice despite all protest, the National Assembly broke out in rebellion. The Bonn historian Friedrich Christoph Dahlmann, member of the right-liberal 'Casino' and correspondent for the committees of international affairs and the central authority, emphasized that not only Schleswig was at issue, but also the very unity of Germany.

> To nip . . . the new German authority . . . in the bud: that is the intent here. It must be torn apart from all sides and finally smashed! In this first test that is approaching, let us throw ourselves at the feet of the foreign powers . . . then, gentlemen, you will *never* again be able to hold up your proud heads! Consider these my words: *never*!

On 5 September, after an impassioned debate lasting two days, Dahlmann's petition calling a halt to the implementation of the armistice was accepted by a narrow majority of 238 to 221 votes. This was tantamount to a continuation of the war between the Confederation and Denmark. The imperial ministry under Leiningen resigned later that same day.

The logical next step for the parliament would have been to constitute a second government supported by the majority voting against the armistice. At the behest of the imperial regent, Dahlmann tried for several days to form a new cabinet. But it was ultimately beyond his abilities to transform the negative majority, carried mainly by the left, into a positive governmental majority. Two further days of tumultuous parliamentary debate followed on 14 and 15 September. Jacob Venedy of the left-moderate 'Westendhall', the so-called 'tail coat left', sought in vain to draw the attention of the delegates to the many dispatches exhorting the parliament 'to create a new German Reich, even at the risk of waging war against the whole world to become a united Germany'. In vain he expressed his conviction 'that the sons of the men who shed their German blood at Fehrbellin,

Rossbach, and on the Katzbach would also now stand up for Germany if we wage war with Denmark, indeed with all of Europe.' But on 16 September, the National Assembly voted 257 to 236 that the fulfilment of the armistice should no longer be hindered. The Austrian Anton von Schmerling, hitherto minister of the interior, became the new prime minister.

The Frankfurt parliament had only itself to blame for its defeat. Since it was clear from the start that Prussia would not revoke the armistice of Malmö, the resolution of 5 September was little more than an attempt to save face before the German public. Had the German states, led by Prussia, complied with the demands of the German National Assembly, a European war would have been the result. If the National Assembly had not reversed itself, the German governments would have been forced to break all ties with it.

But the self-correction came at a high price, drawing down upon the parliament a great wave of popular anger and resentment. On 17 September an assembly of the Frankfurt radicals accused the delegates who had voted in favour of the armistice of treason against the German people and declared their mandates invalid. At Schmerling's request, the city senate ordered Prussian and Austrian troops to march from the Confederation garrison in Mainz. Barricades sprang up and furious street fighting began. Before nightfall, however, the military had the situation under control. Among the victims of the Frankfurt uprising were two conservative delegates from Prussia, Prince Friedrich Lichnowsky and General Hans von Auerswald, who had voted for the armistice of Malmö. They were seized and murdered by insurgents during a scouting patrol in the northern part of Frankfurt.

There was a warning sign in the fact that the leader of the mob that killed the two delegates carried a red banner. Would the proletariat now attempt in Germany, as in France the previous June, to turn the political into a social revolution? The workers' uprising had been brutally suppressed in the French capital. In Frankfurt, too, the official forces won the day. But Frankfurt was not Germany. On 21 September Struve left Basel, crossed the border to Baden, and proclaimed the German republic from the town of Lörrach. Among the active participants of the second Baden rebellion was Wilhelm Liebknecht, later to become one of the leaders of the German social democratic movement. The red armbands of the insurgents caused a stir among both friends and foes of the uprising. The same was true of their attitude toward private property. The family of a wealthy Mühlheim vintner was forced to pay a poll tax, and a ransom of a sort was extorted from the Jews of Sulzburg. After four days, the putsch was at an end. Baden troops won a clear victory at Staufen on 25 September, and Struve and Liebknecht were soon arrested.

On the same 25 September Cologne, the city in which Marx had been editing the *Neue Rheinische Zeitung* since 1 June and where the Communist League had more supporters than anywhere else in Germany, also appeared to be on the brink of a second revolution. At the rumour of the approaching Prussian military, barricades were erected, upon which red flags were flown during the whole night. The next day, after soldiers failed to materialize, the defenders left their posts. Order was restored, a state of emergency declared, the civil defense dissolved, and the *Neue Rheinische Zeitung* temporarily banned.

The cathedral city on the Rhine had made no serious preparations for becoming the staging ground of the red revolution. The chances were minimal to begin with. Only a small minority of workers stood behind the Communist League. Much stronger was the following of Stephan Born and his 'General German Workers' Brotherhood,' which did not preach social revolution, but the reform of the existing social order. Radical sloganeering enjoyed even less support among the independent tradesmen, many of whom had welcomed the revolution in the spring of 1848. In the middle of July, a General Congress of Tradesmen and Craftsmen in Frankfurt spoke out against the republic, freedom of trade, socialism, and communism. Its positive demands included cooperation between the bourgeoisie and the monarchy as well as the restoration of the guild system. Although the Congress did not speak for all the craft trades in Germany, its platform nonetheless reflected the beliefs and wishes of a large part of the *Mittelstand*. This state of affairs was far more satisfying to conservatives than liberals.

Among the peasantry, too, there was a shift from 'left' to 'right'. In spring 1848 the peasants of south-west Germany had rebelled against landowners and government officials. After their most important demands (above all the abolition of feudal obligations) had been met, they rejoined the ranks of those who wished to safeguard the traditional order. Although the social protest of the peasants and agricultural workers was generally less radical in the manorial system of the *Gutswirtschaft* predominant east of the Elbe than on the estates—*Grundherrschaft*—of the large western landowners, even in the east there were changes. The abolition of patrimonial jurisdiction and other concessions cleared the way for a reconciliation between the agricultural lower classes and the manorial lords. In Austria, too, timely reforms took the wind out of the sails of peasant rebellion by September 1848. Throughout the autumn of that year, with the exception of Silesia and Saxony, revolution was all but forgotten in rural Germany. To the east of the Elbe, the main tendency was more conservative than radical.

Of the conservative ruling classes, the Prussian landowners were politically the most active in the revolutionary year of 1848. By July, the core of a political party had taken shape from among their ranks, the Association for the Protection of Property and the Promotion of the General Welfare of All Classes of the People. At its first general meeting, the organization gave itself a more honest name, Association for the Protection of the Interests of the Landowners, which, however, maintained the claim 'Promotion of the General Welfare of All Classes of the People' in an addendum to the new title. Much broader and more *volkstümlich* in character was the societal catchment area of the more than 400 Catholic Pius Associations, which could claim about 100,000 members by the autumn of 1848. The petitions sent by these organizations to the German National Assembly aimed at the complete emancipation of the Church from the State as well as the preservation and support of Catholic schools. Such demands were not strictly 'conservative', but still less were they 'revolutionary'. The political Catholic movement, which began to form at this time, was conscious of the fact that its ecclesiastical-political agenda would sooner find sympathy among conservative Protestants than among the emphatically secular liberals. The Evangelical churches remained what they had been before 1848—pillars of the throne. Their resolutely anti-revolutionary credo deepened the chasm separating them from many of their politically active flock.

For the moderate liberals, the events of September 1848 were a bitter lesson. The cooperation of some of their number with the left during the protest against the armistice of Malmö had caused a debacle. One demonstration of political impotence led to another as the original opposition was retracted, further damaging the reputation of the Frankfurt parliament and provoking the radicalization of extra-parliamentary elements that led to street fighting in Frankfurt and the carnage of the second Baden rebellion. Their radicalization under the symbol of the red flag isolated the extreme parliamentary left, the ultra-left 'Donnersberg' fraction (to which Arnold Ruge belonged) most of all, the more moderate 'Deutscher Hof' of the Leipzig bookseller Robert Blum somewhat less so. The liberal centre moved noticeably to the right, a development that had started with the June Days in Paris and gained ground among broad sections of the German populace, including even the educated and propertied bourgeoisie, at the signs of an approaching 'second revolution' in September 1848.[23]

The more the majority of the German National Assembly tried to marginalize the radical minority, the more tense grew its relationship to the Prussian National Assembly, where from the start the left had been more strongly represented than in Frankfurt. In July 1848 resolute democrats like Johann Jacoby from East Prussia and Benedikt Waldeck from Westphalia lodged a protest against the election of an imperial regent not responsible to the German parliament, in which office they suspected the future hereditary Habsburg emperor. 'We desire to place the sword we have so long wielded in victory for Germany in the lap of the National Assembly. We gladly hand it over to the head of the centralized German state,' proclaimed Waldeck on 11 July. 'But to an imperial regent who could declare war on his own we will not entrust the sword of Frederick the Great.'

When at the beginning of August the Prussian government, with the approval of public opinion, refused to allow Prussian troops to pay homage to the imperial regent as the imperial minister of war had ordered, the opposition from the left was weak. Against the armistice of Malmö, too, the democrats were reserved in their criticism. But the September unrest in Frankfurt was a different story. When the Frankfurt central authority, seeking to protect the members of the National Assembly from insult and injury, took measures restricting the freedom of association and assembly in Frankfurt and vicinity, the protest from the staunch left was loud, and not only in Prussia. The Frankfurt policies were compared to the repressive system under the German Confederation. On 24 October Waldeck lodged a petition demanding that decrees from the central authority touching upon matters of domestic policy in the individual states be approved by the Prussian representative assembly before entering into effect in that country. The democrat Jodocus Temme accused the Frankfurt parliament of entering upon a path that would lead back to the Vienna and Karlsbad Decrees. To this accusation he added, with the applause of the left: 'We have not fought and earned our liberty only to throw it away on a parliament in Frankfurt am Main.' The vote to grant Waldeck's petition priority in the parliamentary protocol failed by only one vote.[24]

The hostility of the Prussian left to the German National Assembly in October 1848 was caused in part by a major political development: the counter-revolution was gaining ground in Austria, and the Frankfurt central authority was doing little to counteract it. It began with the decision of the Vienna government (supported by the majority of the Imperial Parliament) to assist the Croatians in their struggle against the revolution in Hungary. The response of the Austrian radicals was another Vienna rebellion (the third of that name), in the course of which the minister of war, Count Latour, was murdered. After the city had fallen into the hands of the extreme left, the emperor and his court made their escape to Olmütz in Bohemia. It was the monarch's second flight from Vienna within half a year.

From Bohemia, beginning on 11 October, Prince Alfred Windischgrätz prepared for the coming battle with revolutionary Vienna, assisted by political counsel from Prince Felix Schwarzenberg. Emissaries from the German central authority, attempting to mediate between the revolution and the counter-revolution, were shown the door both at Windischgrätz's headquarters and in Olmütz. At the same time, representatives of the parliamentary left, including Robert Blum, went to Vienna to support the insurgents—not on behalf of the German National Assembly, which rejected their activities, but only in the name of the minority. On 26 October, imperial troops under Windischgrätz and Jellačić, the governor of Croatia, commenced their attack on the capital of the empire. Vienna fell on 31 October. Blum, who had taken part in the fighting, was condemned to death and put before the firing squad on 9 November.

By executing the German delegate, a flagrant violation of parliamentary immunity, the Habsburg monarchy challenged the German National Assembly in a way approaching an open declaration of war. Once again, the Frankfurt parliament and the German central authority, possessing no real power of their own, had no recourse but to protest on paper, which availed nothing. The new Austrian government, whose leadership Schwarzenberg assumed on 21 November, *wanted* to break with Frankfurt, seeking to return to the pre-revolutionary order both in the Habsburg empire and in the non-Austrian part of the former German Confederation. This aspiration was now supported by a large part of the Slavic nationalities, namely the Czechs, Croatians, and Slovenians.

The most radical among the revolutionaries reacted with bitterness and hatred to what they considered the treason of the Slavs. Only the Poles were excepted from this verdict. Writing in the *Neue Rheinische Zeitung* in January 1849, Friedrich Engels wrote of 'nationlets' (*Natiönchen*), 'ruined fragments of peoples', and 'residual wastes of peoples' representing the counter-revolution, and he threatened: 'The next world war will not only wipe reactionary classes and dynasties from the face of the earth, but also entire reactionary peoples. This, too, is progress.' Against a 'Slavdom that has betrayed the revolution', the same author proclaimed one month later, 'ruthless warfare and terrorism—not only in the interest of Germany, but also in the interest of the revolution'.

The term 'world war' was borrowed from Karl Marx. In his new year's article for the *Neue Rheinische Zeitung*, Marx had come to the conclusion that the revolution would only succeed if it assumed the form of a European war, indeed a world war—a war that must begin with the overthrow of the French bourgeoisie and then spread both to capitalist Britain and to Russia, the pre-eminent representative of eastern barbarism. '*Revolutionary uprising of the French working class, world war*—this is the table of contents for the year 1849.'[25]

By the time these articles appeared, the central European counter-revolution had succeeded not only in Austria, but also in Prussia. In Berlin, the key events took place in October. On 12 October the Prussian National Assembly struck the words 'by the grace of God' from the royal title during the deliberations over a draft for the constitution. Outraged, Frederick William IV swung round to the course urged upon him by the ultra-conservative camarilla of the brothers Leopold and Ludwig von Gerlach: he decided to take up the struggle against the National Assembly and to reject a liberal constitution of the kind taking shape in the parliamentary deliberations.

In the middle of October, unrest broke out among the Berlin workers, and barricades went up in the streets of the Prussian capital. The civil defense forces soon had the situation in hand, but when on 31 October the Prussian National Assembly rejected Waldeck's petition demanding Prussia's intervention on behalf of the revolution in Vienna, the radical democrats vented their fury in a new round of tumults. The prime minister, the politically moderate General Ernst von Pfuel (successor to the moderate liberal Rudolf von Auerswald, who had resigned in September), was not prepared to take responsibility for the declaration of a state of siege the king had been demanding since 16 October, whereupon he resigned. His successor, Count Frederick William of Brandenburg, received a pronouncement of no confidence from the National Assembly on 2 November. But neither this, nor the wish of a delegation of representatives that he appoint a popular cabinet, nor Johann Jacoby's famous words to him on the occasion ('It is the misfortune of kings that they never want to hear the truth') could impress the king of Prussia.

On 9 November Frederick William ordered the Prussian National Assembly to be moved to Brandenburg and adjourned until 27 November. When a majority of the parliament refused to comply with the behest, which looked very much like a *coup d'état*, and continued their deliberations on 10 November in the Berlin Schauspielhaus, troops under General von Wrangel forced an end to the meeting. The next session, in which a majority of the delegates called for a general tax strike, experienced the same fate. The Frankfurt central authority and the president of the German National Assembly, Heinrich von Gagern, attempted to mediate, but in vain. On 5 December 1848, the king dissolved the National Assembly and, against the will of the camarilla, proclaimed a constitution. Many, though certainly not all, of its significant provisions followed the 'Charte Waldeck', the draft of the constitutional commission of the National Assembly. It even included general male suffrage for elections to the second chamber. One of the main differences was in the king's power of veto: the constitution of 5 December granted the sovereign an absolute veto, whereas the commission's draft contained only a suspensive veto, that is, the power to postpone legislative resolutions of the chambers. The next day, on 6 December, the government announced elections for both chambers of the new parliament for January 1849. The most important task of the assembly was to be the revision of the imposed constitution.

Frederick William's coup, which in many ways can be considered a 'revolution from above', brought the March Revolution to an end in Prussia, at least for the time being. The power of the old state had triumphed over the new understanding of rights that had emerged from the revolution. It was a quick victory, due mostly to the fact that large portions of the population, in the cities as well as the country, had come to see the consolidation of royal power as an effective antidote to political and social radicalism. In any case, the call for a tax strike, itself a violation of current law, found little resonance, and most moderate liberals seem to have shared Gustav Mevissen's analysis of the situation. In a letter of 8 December 1848 the Rhenish businessman, a member of the Casino fraction in the Frankfurt parliament, spoke of a 'bold move by the king' and believed that the moment had arrived 'in which all men of political influence and political courage must place themselves on the basis of the new legal order and fight the impending anarchy'. Mevissen's political colleague, the historian Dahlmann, thought no differently when he spoke of the 'the deed of deliverance, which is its own justification' (*Recht der rettenden Tat*) in the plenum assembly of the Frankfurt parliament on 15 December, arguing for the right of the future German head of state to have absolute and not merely suspensive veto power over the decisions of parliament.[26]

'GROSSDEUTSCHLAND' AND *'KLEINDEUTSCHLAND'*

By the close of 1848, the revolution had been defeated or was in retreat nearly everywhere in Europe. In France, where it had begun, Louis Napoleon, the nephew of the Corsican, won the presidential elections on 10 December. His triumph did not yet mean the restoration of the Empire, but there could be no doubt that this was his goal. In Austria, the success of the counter-revolution preserved the integrity of the Habsburg empire, a polity irreconcilable with the plan of the Frankfurt parliament to found a German national state. Prussia, on the other hand, remained the focus of German liberalism's national aspirations even after the coup of its king. The German National Assembly had disapproved of the Prussian parliament's forced adjournment and relocation to Brandenburg. But it had also looked askance at the tax boycott approved by the majority of the Prussian representatives. Considering the tensions between the two bodies, it was not very surprising that the news of the coup on 5 December was received in Frankfurt with a certain measure of relief. Prussia was, after all, now a constitutional state, and the expectation that the climate between the Frankfurt and Berlin parliaments would improve after the January 1849 elections did not seem far-fetched.

On 27 October 1848, shortly before the victory of the counter-revolution in Austria, the German National Assembly had clarified the conditions for a *gross-deutsch* ('Great German' or 'Greater German') solution, that is, a national state including Austria. The great majority of the delegates approved the draft of the constitutional commission for the first articles of the imperial constitution. According to Article 1, the new Reich was composed of the territory of the former German Confederation, with the status of the Duchy of Schleswig and the borders of the Grand Duchy of Posen 'deferred until definitive ordinance'. Article 2 proclaimed that no part of the Reich was to be united in statehood with non-German lands. When a German and a non-German country shared the same head of state, Article 3 determined that the relationship between the two was to be structured along the lines of a purely personal union, that is, as a dynastic arrangement and not a matter of national law.

Thus the *grossdeutsch* solution advocated by most of the delegates at that time was tantamount to the dissolution of the Habsburg monarchy. Several of the speakers in the debate, however, made no secret of the fact that they neither believed the plan could be effected nor even desired it to be. The Vienna jurist Eugen von Mühlfeld, member of the moderate conservative fraction 'Café Milani', supported the idea of an alliance between a German federal state and a federative Austrian state, with which position he—consciously or unconsciously—took up Paul Pfizer's thoughts from the early 1840s. His Prussian party colleague, the Westphalian Georg von Vincke, articulated very similar sentiments: 'We want a confederation with all of Austria, and a federal state for ourselves without Austria.' Finally, Heinrich von Gagern, president of the National Assembly and member of the right-liberal Casino, spoke out for Austria remaining 'in permanent and indissoluble confederation with the rest of Germany, in view of its constitutional conjoinment with non-German lands and provinces'. The precise nature of this confederate relationship was to be set down in a special federal act.

Those who argued like Gagern or Vincke advocated the *kleindeutsch* ('Little German') solution, that is, the unification of Germany under Prussian leadership and excluding Austria. Neither speaker could imagine any other way a German national state might be established. Mühlfeld came essentially to the same conclusion, although he was less interested in a German national state than in the integrity of the Austrian empire. In order to mitigate the inevitable separation, the narrower federation of non-Austrian Germany was to be supplemented with a broader federation between Germany and the Habsburg monarchy. In this point, too, members of the *kleindeutsch* 'party' agreed with parliamentary defenders of the multinational Austrian state like Mühlfeld. Advocates of Little Germany were typically Evangelical, belonging to the moderate liberals or, less frequently, to the moderate conservatives. They came from the educated or propertied bourgeoisie, generally showed a good deal of sympathy for and confidence in Prussia, and could be found much more frequently north of the Main than in the German south.

The *grossdeutsch* 'party', in contrast, came from a variety of backgrounds. For Catholics, the thought of having to live in a *kleindeutsch* national state dominated by Prussia and Protestants was difficult to bear. This fact alone predisposed many Catholics to the *grossdeutsch* idea. German democrats had no intention of subordinating their conception of the German *Volk* to dynastic interests and of renouncing German-speaking Austria simply because it shared a monarch with other peoples. The poet Ludwig Uhland, professor of German in Tübingen and member of the left-moderate Deutscher Hof, designated Austria an 'artery of the German heart'. Speaking before the National Assembly on 26 October, he said that Austria had mixed its blood into the mortar of the new edifice of German liberty. 'Austria must be with us and remain with us in the new political Church of St Paul.'

At the end of October 1848, many moderate liberals still thought as Uhland did; otherwise there would not have been a majority to support the commission's draft. The *grossdeutsch* vision did not confine itself to the annexation of German-speaking Austria, however. Italian Tyrol and Trieste, which gave Germany access to the Mediterranean, were also included. On 20 June the Frankfurt parliament had warned the Piedmont-Lombard-Venetian associations blockading the Adriatic, including the harbour of Trieste, that an attack on the latter would be considered a declaration of war on Germany. Bohemia and Moravia, too, were parts of Germany, such as the constitutional commission defined it. With regard to these territories, one of the founding fathers of German nationalism, Ernst Moritz Arndt (elected, like Friedrich Ludwig Jahn, to the Frankfurt parliament and a member of the right-liberal Casino), exhorted the Germans, with a quote from Klopstock, not to be 'too just'. Germany must hold firm to the principle 'that whatever has belonged to us for a millenium and has been a part of us, must continue to belong to us'.

The Czechs in Bohemia and Moravia were not, of course, linguistically German, nor did they desire to become German in any sense. For all his linguistic nationalism, Arndt dismissed these realities with sovereign indifference. Yet he was articulating a conviction held by a majority of the German National Assembly: when push came to shove, the right to self-determination of Czechs, Slovenians, and Italians must—like the political will of the Danes in northern Schleswig—take second place to the historically justified national interest of the Germans. 'Germany ought rather to die than to give in and renounce any of the Fatherland.' This pronouncement of the leftist Karl Vogt during the debate over the status of Italian Tyrol on 12 August 1848 was greeted with a storm of applause from nearly the whole house. The only concession the National Assembly was prepared to set down in the imperial constitution was a tolerance clause guaranteeing the 'non-German-speaking peoples of Germany' the right to their 'native development' (*volkstümliche Entwicklung*) as well as 'equality of language' in religious practice, schools, local governmental administration, and local law. In the case of Posen, too, the Frankfurt parliament (with the exception of the extreme left, eloquently led by Arnold Ruge) rejected any compromise of the 'healthy egoism of the people', to use a term coined on 24 July 1848 by the East Prussian Wilhelm Jordan, delegate for Berlin (originally a member of the democratic Deutscher Hof, then the centre fraction 'Landsberg').

Among the 90 representatives who rejected the third article of the draft, and with it the dissolution of the Habsburg monarchy spelled out there, were 41 of the 115 delegates from Austria. The non-Austrians of this group were mostly conservatives and Catholics. Speaking for a number of the Catholic delegates on 24 October, the Rhineland native August Reichensperger (who soon left the right-liberal Casino for the *grossdeutsch* 'Pariser Hof') warned that when the ring that held the whole Austrian monarchy together was broken, Germany would lose its 'bulwark against the east' and hence be guilty of 'Russian-style politics'. The Vienna historian Alfred von Arneth (who at the end of 1848 made the same change of party membership as Reichensperger) argued in very similar fashion: by preserving Austria, 'empires on the eastern border of Germany, be they Slavic or Hungarian, would be prevented.' In the logic of *this* justification of the Austrian empire lay a '*mitteleuropäisch*' solution to the German question, one that could no longer be called national, since it included the whole of the Austrian empire along with non-Austrian Germany. Count Friedrich von Deym, a non-aligned representative from Bohemia, spoke of 'a giant empire of seventy, possibly eighty million souls'.

Neither the *kleindeutsch* nor the *grossdeutsch* camp had any intention of giving up the possibility of a German national state, but the former had an easier time coming to terms with the strategic arguments of the *Grossösterreich* ('Greater Austria') party. Explaining his conception of a narrower and a wider federation, Gagern emphasized that a close relationship between a unified Germany and the Austrian empire would consolidate the German influence in south-east Europe. If unified Germany were to support Austria's mission of 'spreading German culture, language, and customs along the Danube to the Black Sea', then the German emigrants presently headed for the west, for America, would instead turn to these regions. As a 'great world-commanding people', it is the vocation of the Germans 'to bring those peoples along the Danube who have neither call nor claim to independence like satellites into our solar system'. Clearly, the *kleindeutsch* solution was no platform of national self-moderation. Gagern and his political associates entertained as little doubt about Germany's and Austria's joint mission to rule south-east Europe as before them Friedrich List, Paul Pfizer, and other *Vormärz* liberals had done.[27]

The idea of a narrower and a wider federation initially found so little support in the Frankfurt parliament that Gagern withdrew his petition at the end of October 1848. A month later, however, the situation changed drastically. On 27 November Schwarzenberg responded to the resolutions of the German National Assembly from 27 October. Speaking before the Austrian Imperial Parliament, which at the behest of the emperor convened in the Moravian town of Kremsier from that month onward, Schwarzenberg described the preservation of the Austrian empire as a German and European necessity. Only when a renewed Austria and a renewed Germany had taken solid form would it be possible to officially determine their mutual relationship. Until that time, Austria would continue to fulfil the duties incumbent upon it by virtue of its alliances.

Soberly considered, Schwarzenberg's categoric rejection of *Grossdeutschland* only left room for a *kleindeutsch* solution. Thus the position of Schmerling, the president of the imperial ministry, was now untenable, and he resigned on 15 December 1848. His office was assumed by Gagern, and the presidency of the National Assembly was taken over by Eduard Simson from Königsberg, a professor of Roman law, baptized Jew, and, like Gagern, member of the Casino. The new president immediately became active on behalf of his interpretation of the narrower and wider federation, but Schwarzenberg, at the urging of Schmerling, dismissed the idea.

In the German National Assembly, there had never been a majority for the project of a confederation between Germany and the whole of the Austrian empire, Schwarzenberg's ultimate goal. On 13 January 1849 the Greifswald delegate and Casino member Georg Beseler, who came from Schleswig-Holstein, called the 'middle kingdom [*Reich der Mitte*], controlling Europe with seventy million,' a 'political monster'. 'We do not accept this middle kingdom. Europe would not allow it, and it would not satisfy Germany.' However, a *kleindeutsch* solution without Austria, among the most decided supporters of which were the delegates from Schleswig-Holstein under the leadership of Beseler, was at this time—the beginning of 1849—supported only by a relatively narrow majority. A strong minority, joined by many who had recently defended the Austrian cause, would in no way accept a break with Austria, even though important constitutional questions continued to divide the proponents of *Grossdeutschland* into democrats, republicans, and conservatives. There were, to be sure, similar contrasts of opinion among those who were now, for the time being, prepared to be satisfied with a German national state without Austria. Supporters of an elective emperorship stood at loggerheads with proponents of the hereditary principle. Consequently, Gagern could not be certain of success in canvassing a sufficient majority for his core programme, the creation of a *kleindeutsch* national state under a hereditary Prussian emperor, by making concessions to the moderate left in constitutional matters.

Once again, the unresolved questions were cleared up by Austria. At the urging of Schwarzenberg, Emperor Francis Joseph, acceding to the throne at the beginning of December 1848 after the abdication of Ferdinand I, dissolved the parliament at Kremsier on 7 March 1849 and imposed a constitution proclaiming the national unity of the Habsburg empire. Two days later, Schwarzenberg demanded that the imperial ministry in Frankfurt accept the whole of the Austrian state into a renewed German Confederation and establish both a centralized German authority in the form of a directory, to be dominated by Austria and Prussia, and a House of States (*Staatenhaus*) composed of representatives from the separate national parliaments. As the Austrian prime minister saw it, the majority of seats in this body would be occupied by delegates from the Habsburg monarchy.

The Vienna ultimatum broke up the *grossdeutsch* party. One of its leaders, Carl Theodor Welcker from Baden, went over to the camp advocating a *kleindeutsch* solution with a hereditary emperorship. Welcker did not succeed in obtaining a majority for his motion of 12 March calling for the wholesale acceptance of the draft of the imperial constitution in its second reading and the conferral of the hereditary emperorship on the king of Prussia. However, the representatives of the liberal centre, led by Heinrich von Gagern, agreed to support the moderate democrats under Heinrich Simon in voting for a restricted, suspensive veto on the part of the head of state, as well as for universal suffrage for the populace. After this, on 27 March, a diluted version of the first articles (originally presented by the constitutional committee in October 1848) succeeded in finding a majority. According to the revised version, German countries sharing a head of state with a non-German country were required to have their own separate constitution, government, and administration. Since it was clear from the start that Vienna would reject these terms, the resolution of 27 March was a tacit vote for *Kleindeutschland*, that is, for separation from Austria.

During the debates leading up to this vote, several speakers warned the assembly against the dangers of civil war in the event of a break with Austria. Among these were Joseph Maria von Radowitz, a conservative delegate of Hungarian descent, committed Catholic, general in the Prussian army, and personal friend of Frederick William IV, as well as Moriz von Mohl, a moderate democrat from Stuttgart, Protestant, ardent federalist, and member of the Westendhall. At the end of his speech on 17 March, in words greeted with applause from the left and the gallery, Mohl invoked the likelihood of a new thirty years war:

> It seems to me that the terrible consequences for all of Germany that must attend upon the creation of a hereditary emperorship have not been considered. It has not been considered that war lies hidden in such a resolution, indeed three separate wars: war between the north and the south of Germany, war between Protestantism and Catholicism, and war between the ruling nationality and the other nationalities. Each one of these struggles would alone be enough for a thirty years war. I beseech you, gentlemen, do not cast the burning brand of civil war into our German Fatherland!

The left did not seem much disturbed by the prospect of a large European war. The zoologist Karl Vogt, member of the Deutscher Hof and proponent of a federation between the German and Austrian empires in their entirety, gave a speech on 17 March in which he proclaimed that the time had come to fight, along with Poland and Hungary, the decisive battle between west and east: 'Gentlemen, do not denigrate and poison this holy war of Western culture against the barbarism of the East with a duel between the House of Habsburg and the House of Hohenzollern . . . No, gentlemen, you must be resolved to let this war be what it should be—a battle of nationalities.' This speech was greeted with a storm of applause from the delegates on the left.

The leftist call for a 'holy war' against the 'military despotism' of Russia and Austria was, however, as little able to impress the majority of the Frankfurt parliament as had been the similar messages of Marx and Engels in the *Neue Rheinische Zeitung*. On 27 March the assembly voted with a narrow majority to confer the imperial mantle on a reigning German prince and to make the office hereditary. On the next day, King Frederick William IV of Prussia was elected emperor. Of the 590 delegates 290 voted for him; 248 abstained. The imperial constitution, proclaimed and issued by President Simson, went into effect that same day, 28 March 1849.

When the parliamentary delegation under Simson met with Frederick William IV in Berlin on 3 April 1849 to offer him the emperorship, the Prussian sovereign had long since made his decision. He had no intention of exchanging the office of king by the grace of God for an imperial throne by the grace of the people. What bothered him was not merely the fact that the new constitution offered only suspensive, not absolute, power of veto against decisions of both chambers of the imperial parliament, the People's House and the House of States; this alone was tantamount to the introduction of a bona fide parliamentary system. He was also repulsed by the 'fictitious crown, baked from mud and clay' because it exuded the 'sordid stench of revolution'—because, in other words, the democratic legitimization of the imperial office would have separated him from his equals, the emperors in Vienna and Russia and the kings in the capitals of Europe. It was easily foreseeable that the Austrian emperor would have interpreted Frederick William's acquiescence as a hostile act. It was probable, too, that in the event of war with Prussia and Germany, the Russian tzar would have supported the Habsburgs as actively as he had done in the summer of 1849 against the Hungarian revolution. Consequently, Frederick William's thinly disguised refusal on 3 April 1849 came as no surprise to anybody who knew him well. The final rejection on 28 April also included the constitution, which by that point had been recognized by twenty-eight governments, though not by the larger *Mittelstaaten* of Bavaria, Württemberg, Hanover, or Saxony.

The Prussian rejection spelled the end of the German National Assembly, which followed shortly after. The imperial ministry under Gagern, which had been acting in a purely caretaker capacity since 22 March, stepped down on 10 May. Austria had already withdrawn its delegates on 5 April. Prussia, Saxony, and Hanover followed suit in May, Baden in June. Most of the moderate liberal representatives resigned of their own accord between 20 and 26 May. In their own justification, a group of sixty-five delegates, including Dahlmann, Gagern, Simson, Droysen, and Beseler, announced on 20 May that the decision not to put the constitution into effect was a lesser evil than the propagation of a civil war that had already begun. A rump parliament of about one hundred members, dominated by the left, removed to Stuttgart on 30 May, where it was forcefully dispersed by Württemberg troops on 18 June.[28]

THE ROAD TO OLMÜTZ

While the parliament in the Paulskirche was falling apart, a last wave of revolutionary activity, the 'campaign for the imperial constitution' (*Reichsverfassungskampagne*) shook parts of Germany. In the Rhineland and in Westphalia, the Prussian national guard mutinied. Dresden saw fierce street fighting, in which the Russian anarchist Mikhail Bakunin and the German composer Richard Wagner also took part. In the Palatinate, the republicans rose up against their Bavarian overlords. Peasants, too, were active in many places. It was in Baden that the 'May revolution', the third uprising in that state, was most successful and where it had the broadest social base, including not only famous figures like Friedrich Engels, Gottfried Kinkel, and Carl Schurz, but also—and to a far greater extent than in the Palatinate—regular troops of the army. A revolutionary government was set up in Karlsruhe; the grand duke fled first to Alsace, then to Mainz, whence he appealed to Prussia for assistance. Prussian troops occupied Saxony, the Palatinate, and Baden. Supported by groups from the still-existing central authority, they managed to restore 'order', though with extreme harshness. In the Palatinate and in Baden, the Prussian forces stood under the supreme command of Frederick William's brother William, the 'Kartätschenprinz',* who would become emperor of Germany somewhat more than two decades later.

Engels expressed the paradoxical nature of the *Reichsverfassungskampagne* in a polemically exaggerated formulation: 'Those who were serious about the movement were not serious about the constitution, and those who were serious about the constitution were not serious about the movement.' On the one hand, the revolutionaries condemned the Prussian king for letting the constitution fail; on the other hand, the republicans in their ranks rejected one of its core provisions, the hereditary emperorship. In 1849, the military balance of power was such that the rebellion stood no chance of success. And outside of Baden, its civil support was too weak. While the liberal bourgeoisie was disappointed with the Prussian king's attitude, only a small minority decided to make common cause with the radicals against the state. Ultimately, the movement lacked a centre. It pursued national goals, but possessed no national organization, without which these goals were unattainable.

On the heels of this revolutionary epilogue from 'below' followed a diplomatic coda from 'above'. On 3 April 1849, the day the Frankfurt delegation was received in Berlin, the Prussian foreign minister, Count Arnim-Heinrichsdorff, had announced to the governments of Germany that Frederick William IV was prepared to assume leadership of a confederation of willing participants. In a memorandum of 9 May, the Prussian government once again took up Gagern's idea of a narrower and a broader federation (it had first done so in a circular on 23 January). This initiative was rejected by Schwarzenberg that same month. Among the other German governments, Saxony and Hanover associated themselves with

* [Translator's note: 'the canister prince' (he ordered canister shot to be fired on the demonstrators during the uprising).]

the Prussian proposals and signed a 'Three Kings' Alliance' (*Dreikönigsbündnis*) on 26 May in Berlin. The three states accepted the constitution proposed by Radowitz for a new German 'Union' (the so-called *Unionsverfassung*), a document that differed from the Frankfurt constitution in two significant respects: the emperor was to receive absolute veto power over parliamentary decisions, and the lower house of the parliament was to be elected not according to universal, direct, and equal suffrage, but rather by the three-class system favouring the wealthy introduced in Prussia in May 1849.

The democratic left rejected the Prussian project of a German Union. Moderate liberal proponents of the heredity principle (the so-called *Erbkaiserlichen*), on the other hand, declared their support at a meeting in Gotha at the end of June 1849. In the months following, most of the German states joined the Three Kings' Alliance, though Bavaria and Württemberg declined. In mid-October, after Prussian influence in the new Union's 'administrative council' carried the decision to set lower-house elections for January 1850, Hanover and Saxony withdrew again from the alliance, under pressure from Schwarzenberg. Austria had long been pushing for a restoration of the German Confederation. It now threatened war if the parliament of the Union should compromise peace and order in Germany. The parliament was duly elected in January 1850. It met in Erfurt in March and passed the now completed draft of the constitution. However, without the participation of the kingdoms of Bavaria, Württemberg, Saxony, and Hanover (which had in their turn formed a 'Four King's Alliance' in February), the new union remained a pale reflection of Prussia's original plan.

Shortly after these events, in July 1850, Prussia was also forced to suffer a painful reverse on the wider European political stage. In April of the previous year, when Denmark renounced the Malmö armistice, Prussian troops had once again entered Jutland. A second armistice with Copenhagen in July 1849 was followed in July 1850 by the Treaty of Berlin and the First London Protocol, which restored the duchies of Schleswig and Holstein to Danish rule. Prussia, under massive pressure from Tzar Nicholas I, bowed to these arrangements. Ever since the summer of 1849, when it had come to the aid of Austria against the Hungarian revolution, Russia had advanced to become the greatest protector of all conservative forces in Europe. A Prussian king who risked war with the autocratic tzarist regime would automatically hazard his support among the nobility and military. Frederick William IV had no intention of purchasing the approval of the German patriots at such a price.

The tension between Germany and Austria also entered a new phase about this time. The catalyst of the crisis was Hesse-Kassel, where the prince elector came into conflict with the estates over the constitution. In May 1850 the government of Elector Frederick William had renounced membership in the new Prussian-led Union. At the beginning of September, he dissolved the chamber, decreed unconstitutional emergency taxation measures, and placed the land in a state of siege. Austria, which had reconvened the Federal Diet in Frankfurt on 2 September with the backing of most of the German *Mittelstaaten*, took the side of the elector. Prussia backed the estates, claiming among other reasons that Electoral Hesse was still a member of the Union.

When the Federal Diet proclaimed the federal execution in Electoral Hesse on 16 October, war between Prussia and Austria seemed only days away. Once again, Russian pressure was brought to bear, and Prussia backed down. On 28 November 1850 Schwarzenberg and Otto von Manteuffel, the Prussian foreign minister, signed the Punctation of Olmütz. The core of this treaty was the agreement to resolve the crisis in Electoral Hesse in harmony with all the German states and to join together against Holstein, which had gone to war on its own against Denmark after the conclusion of the Treaty of Berlin. The reform of the Confederation was to be negotiated immediately at a conference of ministers in Dresden. In a secret addendum, Manteuffel agreed to reduce the Prussian military to peacetime status at once.

Schwarzenberg was able to achieve few of his aims during the negotiations, neither the acceptance of the entire Habsburg empire into the German Confederation nor the recognition of the rump Federal Diet as successor to the former parliament at Frankfurt. To this extent, Olmütz was not the Prussian 'disgrace' the liberals would long continue to decry. Yet Manteuffel, for his part, failed to secure the principle of equal partnership between Austria and Prussia for the proposed renewal of the Confederation, a status offered by Schwarzenberg as late as May 1850. Prussia had been compelled to make more concessions than Austria, and it was correspondingly more difficult for the Prussian government to find support for its policies in the Second Chamber of parliament.

Among the most eloquent defenders of the Olmütz treaty was a conservative delegate in the Prussian parliament, Otto von Bismarck. On 3 December 1850, in a speech to the second chamber, Bismarck declared that 'the only healthy foundation for a great state is national egotism, not romanticism.' While he conceded that a Prussian rejection of the Austrian demands would have been popular, he found no plausible case for war:

> It is easy for a statesman, whether in the cabinet or in the chamber, to let sound the clarions of war with the winds of populism, all the while warming himself at his hearth, or to hold thunderous speeches from this same tribunal, and to leave the business of achieving victory and acclaim for his system to the musketeer bleeding to death in the snow. Nothing could be easier than that. Yet woe to the statesman who does not seek in these times a case for war that still holds up after the war is over.

Bismarck in no way sought to subordinate Prussia to Austria. However, in order to assert itself successfully against the latter, Prussia would require a more propitious starting point than the constellation at the end of 1850. For Bismarck's own political career, however, the situation was considerably more propitious after the speech on 3 December 1850. Henceforth, it was clear that Prussia and Germany would have to come to terms with the man who had the courage to declare war on public opinion in the name of Prussian national interest.[29]

THE REVOLUTION OF 1848–1849 IN PERSPECTIVE

A belligerent left and a peaceable right. Such a formula, applied to German history between 1848 and 1850, would be too summary, but less inaccurate than the reverse. From Karl Marx to Karl Vogt, the left saw in tzarist Russia—and quite correctly—the mortal enemy of the European revolution. Thus it was quite logical to make a successful war against Russia the first condition of revolutionary victory, or to claim, as Arnold Ruge of the Donnersburg fraction had put it during the parliamentary debate over the Posen question on 22 July 1848, that such a war would be 'the last war, the war against war, the war against the barbarism that is war'. Benedikt Waldeck pursued goals only seemingly less ambitious when, at the end of October 1848, he appealed to Prussia to intervene against the Weimar counterrevolution. If the Prussian government had allowed itself to be guided by the demands of the parliamentary left in Berlin, the German war would inevitably have broadened into a pan-European conflict. Even during the parliamentary uproar over the Malmö armistice a month earlier, revolution in Germany might easily have given way to European war—in the event that Prussia had bowed to the will of the momentary majority in the Frankfurt parliament.

The conservative forces, for their part, were by no means as inclined to peace as Bismarck's defense of the Olmütz agreement made them out to be. After all, the military suppression of the revolution in Austria, in parts of Germany and Italy, and finally in Hungary was a kind of warfare. It was, to be sure, a warfare within existing political borders, not for the purpose of their radical revision, and for the defense of the traditional order, not for its overthrow. Nonetheless, the traditional order can itself be described as a kind of structural violence. Not least among the factors contributing to the success of the conservatives was the fact that the forces desiring a complete break with the past were never more than minorities. The political, economic, and social consequences of such a break were unforeseeable in scope. For a vast majority of Germans, the familiar way of things was more bearable than the unknown in the form of a German republic, a social revolution, a civil war, or even a world war. This was not only true for the educated and propertied bourgeoisie, but also for the great majority of the lower middle classes and peasants. Moderate liberals, who had never wanted revolution, moved to the right in the same measure that the left became radicalized. Nothing contributed more to this radicalization than the suspicion that the moderates were prepared to yield unconditionally to the old powers. This was the dialectic of the German—and not only of the German—Revolution of 1848–9.

Gustav Rümelin, former Württemberg representative and member first of the 'Württemberger Hof', the left-centre fraction in Frankfurt, then of the *kleindeutsch* 'Augsburger Hof', expressed the dilemma of moderate liberalism in classic fashion several times throughout 1849. 'German unity cannot, and ought not, be realized along the path of civil war,' he wrote in the *Schwäbische Merkur* at the beginning of May. In September 1849, in an essay for the same newspaper, he wrote that the 'way to salvation and deliverance' still lay in the 'Gagern program', the cooperation of a narrower and a broader federation, an alliance between Germany and Austria for mutual protection. After all, this programme had enjoyed majority support in the National Assembly. Rümelin warned against two other paths. If Prussia were once again to join the troika of absolutist eastern powers, the 'restoration of the old system, both domestically and abroad', would be the result. If, on the other hand, Prussia maintained its independent course, which for Rümelin meant the execution of the *kleindeutsch* solution in open confrontation with Austria, there would loom 'a battle between northern and southern Germany, a civil war that, like the Thirty Years War, will summon foreign armies over the borders and once again make Germany the battlefield of Europe.'

The utopian view of a great war for the liberation of peoples, the militant side of the dream of the 'springtime of nations', lent considerable political plausibility to the convergence of liberal and conservative forces. On no account did this convergence proceed in only *one* direction, the assimilation of liberalism to conservatism. Prussia *was* a constitutional state by the end of 1848, and unlike Austria not in name only. Thus the Hohenzollern state had already accommodated to liberalism in no small measure. If before 1848 it could be called a comparatively progressive German country only in terms of economic and social developments, the imposed constitution of December 1848 reduced the political gap between Prussia and the southern German states. Many features of Prussian absolutism outlasted the revolution, especially in the military. But as a whole, post-revolutionary Prussia was, without question, an absolutist state no longer.

The constitutionalization of Prussia is one of the reasons the typical assessment of the German revolution of 1848—namely, that it failed on all fronts—falls short of the mark. According to its twin goals of political liberty and German unity, the revolution certainly did fail. Germany did not became a liberal national state, nor could liberalism successfully assert itself in the individual German states. And yet, after 1848, the political and geographic meaning of 'Germany' was much clearer than before. It was now much more manifest who 'Germania' really stood for, that goddess with the black, red, and golden banner in her left hand, sword and freely rendered olive branch in her right, whose giant image had presided for nearly a year over the meetings of the delegates in the Paulskirche. The *kleindeutsch* party, a small minority before 1848, had gained considerable ground. 'Waiting for Austria is the death of German unity.' At the time it was uttered during the parliamentary sitting on 12 January 1849, many liberals disagreed with this phrase of Hermann von Beckerath, a representative of the Casino. Yet it expressed a fact that sober consideration was now no longer able to deny.

The experiences of the 1848 Revolution were necessary in order to impress upon moderate liberalism a sufficiently realistic idea of the boundaries of a German national state. This happened only gradually. Before realism could triumph over wishful liberal thinking, the counter-revolution had won the day, both in the two German great powers and in Europe as a whole. The chances of unifying non-Austrian Germany without military conflict with the European great powers of Austria and Russia were now much smaller than in the spring of 1848. In short: when the *kleindeutsch* solution was politically feasible, the Germans did not yet desire it, and when they finally did desire it, it was no longer politically feasible.

The revolution did much to weld together the forces that, in future, would never again relinquish the goal of a liberal and unified Germany. Liberals and democrats throughout all of Germany developed closer associations than they had ever had before. Their rapprochement also influenced their respective political programmes. The common labour over the imperial constitution, especially the sections treating of basic rights, had established pan-German standards for the things to be achieved in order to assure the victory of progress, both in the separate German states and in a future unified nation. Equality before the law was one of these basic German rights. A second was full freedom of religion and conscience. A third would have ended the privileged status of one religious community over another and abolished a national church. Discrimination of the Jews would have thus come to an end—if the fathers of the constitution of 1848–9 had had their way.

The main reason the revolution failed was because German liberalism had to deal with too many political desires and demands within too short a space of time. It proved impossible to achieve both unity and freedom simultaneously. In the older national states of the European west, especially Britain and France, national unification was achieved gradually, in the course of centuries, through the agency of monarchs and assemblies of the estates. Those desiring more freedom were able to work within the existing political framework. In Germany, a framework for liberal and democratic projects had to be created. The German liberals (in the narrower political sense) labouring on these structures were fully aware that they needed the power of the larger German states, led by Prussia, in order to protect the work of national unification from outside threat. For that very reason, and not only because they feared social revolution, they sought to avoid a policy of confrontation with the older powers—a policy promoted and prosecuted by the left.

The left was correct when it claimed that the moderate liberals' willingness to compromise had helped the forces of the old regime recover quickly from the storms of March 1848. But to the question of how Germany could be liberalized and unified at the same time, the democrats and socialists had no answer. The leftist call to a pan-European war of national liberation was an expression of German intellectual wishful thinking, uninformed by any consideration of the true balance of power, both domestically within the individual states and between the states on the international stage. Consequently, it was blind to the human costs of the desperado politics it espoused. If the war clamoured for by the left had indeed broken out, the counter-revolution would no doubt still have won, but the victory would have been far more sanguinary than the events that actually took place between autumn 1848 and the closing months of 1850.

German political culture paid a disastrously heavy price for the failure of the liberals and democrats to achieve their goals of unity and liberty by their own power. The authoritarian deformities of German political consciousness persisted and were reinforced. Yet the fact remains that the ambitious twin goals of 1848 were objectively unattainable. That they were was not entirely a misfortune. For if the radical revolutionaries had gained the opportunity of putting their programme into practice, the consequences would probably have been a European catastrophe.[30]

4

Unity before Liberty 1850–1871

THE ERA OF REACTION AND THE CRIMEAN WAR

In the 1850s Germany seemed to wear a Janus face. Politically speaking, the decade following the revolution went down in history as the 'era of reaction'. On the economic front, the same time period witnessed the triumph of the Industrial Revolution. External circumstances favoured this development. After the discovery of rich gold and silver deposits in the mountains of California, Mexico, and Australia in 1849–50, the worldwide circulation of money suddenly increased. Banking, mining, industrial production, and rail construction and transport all experienced a powerful surge in growth. With the accumulation of capital through joint-stock companies, the 'spirit of capitalism' spread ever further. During the world economic crisis of 1857–9, Germany, too, was affected by one of the cyclic slumps that characterized the capitalist system. But the pace of economic and societal change did not slow. In 1859 the economy began to recover, and by 1866 the boom had come again.

The economic revolution was accompanied by a profound transformation of consciousness. The 'idealism' of the *Vormärz* and the revolutionary period was now considered obsolete. To be up to date meant to be a 'realist', a 'positivist', or even a 'materialist'. In 1856 the liberal Berlin *National-Zeitung* enthusiastically described the new way of thinking:

> Amid the general sentiment of dissatisfaction over failed ideals and causes, in the despair over noble efforts come to naught, the intellectual and material forces of the people now concentrate themselves within the confines of human industry, and the present age is witness to what the concentrated power of the nations may achieve when intelligence and physical labor unite in common purpose. What the idealist sought after in vain, the materialist has accomplished in a few short months, completely transforming the existing order, shifting the power relations and the focal points into the organism of societal life, and disciplining the efforts and aspirations of nearly all minds. Never before has such an energy been harnessed, a veritable craving for restless activity in all nerves, muscles, and sinews.[1]

The daring entrepreneur and the audacious stockbroker have little in common with the stolid burgher of the *Biedermeier*, who, for all the aggressive imagery of the new developments, was no less characteristic of the age. Both types, 'capitalist' and 'philistine', supported the political system of the reaction in their own way, primarily by virtue of not getting involved in 'high politics' in the first place. Politics was first and foremost the business of the governments of the German states and, as between 1815 and 1848, their common institution was the Federal Diet in Frankfurt.

From May 1851 onwards, Prussia and the former members of the Erfurt Union once again participated in the Diet, thus restoring the pre-revolutionary political order without any constitutional reform. The eastern provinces of Prussia were still considered outside Confederation territory, as they were before 1848. In the preceding conferences in Dresden in spring 1851, Prussia had sought in vain to win Austrian approval for the principle of parity in the form of a rotating presidency in the Federal Diet. Austria remained what it had been since 1815, the presidential power of the German Confederation.

On 31 December 1851 Austria abolished its imposed constitution of 1849, becoming an absolutist state once again. Prussia kept its constitution. However, when the second chamber, elected in January 1849, recognized the imperial constitution on 21 April, it overstepped the king's and cabinet's notion of parliamentary authority, whereupon Frederick William IV dissolved the assembly in May. That same month, the system of general suffrage was abolished by emergency decree, replaced with a three-class system, the *Dreiklassenwahlrecht*. As a gesture of protest, the democratic left refused to vote in the elections of July 1849, as well as in the two following elections of 1852 and 1855.

The new chambers revised the constitution, but almost entirely in favour of the monarchical authority. The king returned to being a sovereign 'by the grace of God'. The administration depended solely on the confidence of the king, not of the parliament. Nor did the latter have any control over the army, bureaucracy, or foreign affairs. While royal decrees still needed to be countersigned by the ministry, the power to command military operations was explicitly exempted from this requirement. And yet, despite all these restrictions, Prussia continued to be a fundamentally constitutional state after 1849–50. On 6 February 1850 the king swore to uphold the constitution firmly and unswervingly, and to rule in accordance with it. His power was great, but not limitless.

Among those who had advised Frederick William to swear this oath was Friedrich Julius Stahl, the intellectual leader of the conservative '*Kreuzzeitung* party', founded in 1848 and named after its leading newspaper. Stahl had also written a defence of the 'monarchic principle' in 1845. The revised Prussian constitution was, in Stahl's view, in harmony with this principle, and his example allowed—indeed, compelled—his conservative colleagues and followers to endorse constitutional monarchy. For Stahl, the law existed exclusively through the state, and the state exclusively through the law. The conservative commitment to the 'inviolability of the order of law' made by Stahl in spring 1849 contained the insight that this very order 'is, at the present, a barrier against the arbitrary will of the people, as it has been hitherto against the arbitrary will of the prince'. Thus the *Rechtsstaat*, the state under the rule of law, was an answer to the 'permanent revolution', the constitution a bulwark against democracy. When it came to adapting old agendas to new conditions, a not inconsiderable number of post-revolutionary conservatives, led by Stahl and Ernst Ludwig Gerlach, the president of the Magdeburg appeals court, demonstrated a willingness to learn.

Prussian politics in the *Reaktionszeit* were part bureaucratic, part feudal in expression. The main goal of the conservative bureaucracy, which had its most influential representative in Otto von Manetuffel, the prime minister from 1850 to 1858, was to reverse the expansion of the individual and societal rights and liberties gained during the course of the revolutionary period. To this end, political and press offences were withdrawn from trial by jury, and the freedoms of assembly and association were curtailed. The Junkers succeeded in restoring the manorial police, the right to guarantee the integrity of their estates through entailment (*Fideikommissen*), and the old system of district and provincial diets that guaranteed a strong predominance of the manorial class.

Many conservatives, including the king himself, would gladly have gone even further. Frederick William and several of his closest advisers contemplated a radical redrafting of the constitution to reflect corporative principles. But the king was cautious enough to make all alterations of the constitution dependent on the approval of both parliamentary houses, thus eschewing another *coup d'état*. The first chamber, in any case, was amenable to his wishes. After the House of Representatives had sanctioned a constitutional amendment granting him the right to determine the composition of the first chamber, the king created a House of Lords (*Herrenhaus*). Its membership consisted exclusively of men of 'birth', no longer elected, but proposed for nomination by certain privileged bodies and then personally selected by the king. The restructuring of the first chamber as a House of Lords was the high point of the reaction in Prussia. Yet the new upper house was no guarantee that the system would last, no more than the highly developed surveillance apparatus and the numerous political trials the Prussian state used to combat democrats and other opponents.[2]

Compared to Austrian neo-absolutism, Prussian constitutionalism of 1850–8 could almost be called a 'mild' reaction. In this the Hohenzollern state resembled the German *Mittelstaaten*, which also retained their constitutions (the Grand Duchy of Baden was the only one that did not take a reactionary turn in the 1850s, or did so in a very limited fashion) and with whom Prussia continued to share economic interests in the framework of the German Customs Union. When in 1849 the Austrian minister of trade, Karl Ludwig von Bruck, began to build upon Schwarzenberg's central European plans by promoting the project of a central European customs and economic union (i.e. a merger between the *Zollverein* and the Habsburg monarchy), Prussia necessarily saw this as a challenge. The contest for the patronage of the other German states was decided in favour of the northern power. In February 1853 Prussia concluded a separate trade agreement with Austria, which was to last twelve years. In April of the following year, the German Customs Union was extended another twelve years. A few months earlier, on 1 January 1854, Hanover, which hitherto had lead a separate north German customs union, the *Steuerverein*, joined the *Zollverein*. To be sure, the battle to determine the relationship between the German Customs Union and Austria was not decided at this time, but only postponed until 1860, when a new round of discussions over customs agreements would take place. Still, the contours of *Kleindeutschland* had become much clearer in the course of 1853–4, at least in terms of customs and trade policy.

In matters of foreign policy, too, Prussia was no longer content to remain in the shadow of the Habsburg empire. The events in the Crimea offered an opportunity to demonstrate initiative. Originally (beginning in November 1853) a conflict between Russia and Turkey, by March 1854 the Crimean War had drawn Britain and France in on the side of the latter. Britain was primarily interested in defending the security of its interests in the eastern Mediterranean. Napoleon III, the new 'Emperor of the French' by virtue of a plebiscite at the end of 1852, was primarily concerned with gaining prestige through military and foreign policy successes.

In Prussia, opinions were extremely divided over the position the country should take. A moderate conservative faction, the '*Wochenblatt* party' around Moritz August von Bethmann-Hollweg, wanted Prussia to join the western powers in order to gain their support for a return to the policies of the Erfurt Union. Victory in the war on the Black Sea could help Prussia to unify Germany at the expense of Austria. The old-conservatives decisively rejected a break with Russia, Prussia's old ally. In their view, the real enemy was still the revolution, embodied by Bonapartist France. The prime minister, Manteuffel, held yet a third position, wanting to keep Prussia neutral as long as possible. As it transpired, that was not entirely possible. In April 1854 Prussia and Austria concluded a defensive alliance, an 'addendum' to which demanded that Russia clear out of the Danube princedoms it had occupied, Moldavia and Wallachia.

Vienna had insisted upon this clause as a means of consolidating Austria's position in the Balkans. When, at the instigation of Count Buol, the foreign minister, it went a step further and concluded a treaty of alliance with France and Britain, but without renouncing its neutrality, Prussia refused to go along. Otto von Bismarck, Prussian ambassador to the Federal Diet in Frankfurt since 1851, canvassed the relevant committees and brought a majority together that took the anti-Russian sting out of the Austrian motion to mobilize federal troops, thus neutralizing its intended effect. This, the first major foreign policy success of the Junker from Mark Brandenburg, was also one of the turning points in the history of the relationship between the two German great powers.

The Crimean War ended in the defeat of Russia. In the Peace of Paris (late March 1856), the tzarist regime was forced to agree to a demilitarization of the

Black Sea region, among other things. The era of the 'Holy Alliance', the pact proclaimed in 1815 by the three eastern powers for the defence of the old order, had finally come to an end. For the foreseeable future, Russia was no longer in a position to prosecute its conservative interventionist politics, the high point of which had been the suppression of the Hungarian revolution in summer 1849. The formerly good relationship between Russia and Austria suffered lasting damage. Prussia, on the other hand, which had thwarted Vienna's anti-Russian diplomatic offensive, could hope that the Russians might one day, when occasion arose, show their gratitude for services rendered. Austria suffered an additional setback that weakened its position: the Kingdom of Sardinia-Piedmont, which had entered the war in 1855 on the side of Britain and France, succeeded in making the Italian question part of the agenda at the peace conference in Paris. The war changed the balance of power in Europe. The west had won, the east had lost, and if one could speak of a hegemonic power on the Continent, it was no longer Russia, but France.

There were winners and losers in Germany, too. The old Prussian conservatives rightly considered the eclipse of autocratic Russia and the strengthening of Bonapartist France as a personal defeat. The plight of the liberals, in contrast, who were no less anti-Bonapartist than the conservatives, improved to the extent that the reactionary forces could no longer count on the tzarist empire. Yet Bismarck was also among the winners. The Prussian ambassador to the Federal Diet saw no occasion to regret what he considered the most important result of the conflict: thanks to its neutrality, Prussia now had more options and a greater scope of action than before. It had liberated itself from the one-sided dependence on Russia and Austria. Its status as a European great power had increased, and along with it the status of Otto von Bismarck.

The distinctly non-ideological attitude Bismarck showed during the Crimean War earned him the criticism of a staunch legitimist, General Leopold von Gerlach, the older brother of the conservative party leader Ernst Ludwig von Gerlach. But Bismarck knew how to defend himself. 'Sympathies and antipathies with regard to foreign powers', he wrote on 2 May 1857 to Gerlach,

> are feelings I find myself quite unable to reconcile with my sense of duty in the diplomatic service of my country . . . To subordinate the interests of the Fatherland to personal sentiments towards foreigners, be they love or hate—not even the king has the right to do that, in my view . . . Or do you find the principle I have sacrificed to reside in the precept that a *Prussian must always be an enemy of France?*

Four weeks later, Bismarck became even more categorical:

> The principle of war against the revolution I, too, recognize as my own. Yet I do not consider it correct to make Louis Napoleon out to be the only representative, or even the representative κατ'ἐξοχήν [*kat' exochén*: 'pre-eminently' (H.A.W.)] of the revolution . . . How many entities still exist in the political world of today without roots in revolutionary soil? Take Spain, Portugal, Brazil, all the American republics, Belgium, Holland, Switzerland, Greece, Sweden, and England, which even today is consciously grounded in

the 'glorious revolution' of 1688 . . . Bonapartism is not the father of the revolution; it is, like every other kind of absolutism, only a fertile field for its seed. I am by no means seeking here to place Bonapartism outside the purview of revolutionary phenomena; I only wish to reveal it for what it is, without all the accretions not necessarily intrinsic to its nature.

Bonapartist France as Prussia's ally in a future confrontation with Austria—for Leopold von Gerlach the idea was sacrilege, but for Bismarck it was something reasons of state could conceivably render plausible, if not imperative. The Prussian ambassador to the Federal Diet did not cease to be a conservative when he confronted conservative party ideology with the conservative interest in an increase of Prussia's power. 'We must deal with realities and not with fictions.' The verdict of his letter to Gerlach of 2 May 1857 reflected his years of experience with Austria in the Federal Diet. Before the Crimean War he would hardly have spoken so explicitly about the long-term exigencies of Prussian foreign policy. Although the Crimean War was not, as Heraclitus said of war in general, the 'father of all things', it was an extremely effective tutor in a discipline that first received its name during this era: realpolitik.[3]

THE LESSONS OF 1848

*Grundsätze der Realpolitik. Angwendet auf die staatlichen Zustände Deutschlands** was the title of a study published in 1853 in Stuttgart by the liberal publicist Ludwig August von Rochau, a jurist from Wolfenbüttel. Rochau had been active in a Göttingen fraternity, had participated in the storming of the Frankfurt bastions in 1833, had fled to France after being condemned to life in prison, and had returned to Germany in 1848, where he worked as a publicist in the cause of moderate liberalism. Though it is not known whether he invented the term realpolitik or simply borrowed it from elsewhere, it was through Rochau that the term became a political buzzword, not only in Germany, but also abroad.

'To rule means to exercise power, and power can only be exercised by one who possesses it. The direct connection between power and rule is the fundamental truth of all politics and the key to all of history.' In these two sentences lay the core of Rochau's German liberal self-criticism, written so that the failure of the 1848 revolution might provide political lessons for the present and future. Although, in the opinion of the author, German liberals had fairly clear ideas about the kinds of domestic reforms necessary in the separate German states, about their one truly revolutionary demand, the unification of Germany, they did not. 'This lack of clarity thwarted the main purpose of the movement of 1848.' When it came to the antinomy between the imperial interests of Austria and the national interests of Germany, the liberals had been labouring under an illusion. They were unable to

* Rochau, *Principles of Realpolitik. Applied to the Political Conditions in Germany.*

recognize the inner necessity of antithesis between Austrian and Prussian politics. 'Prussia must grow in order to survive, and Austria must not allow Prussia to grow, lest she herself be destroyed. That is the reality that gives the interrelationship between the two countries its true character.'

Accordingly, realpolitik meant above all recognizing the interests of the German states, especially the two great powers, as clearly as the interests of the German nation.

If one wishes to enlist the power of the Austrian or Prussian state in the service of the German national cause, then the earnest that must be offered is nothing less than Germany herself. Once we realize this, then we can see that it is impossible to gain the support of both powers for the national project. And by extension, each great power has a vital interest in preventing the other from making common cause with the nation. Thus the first task of the national project must be to decide which, if either, of the two great powers is in a position to serve the cause in an effective manner.[4]

Rochau did not disclose in this text what necessarily followed from his other statements about the German question: namely, that Austria could not be the power to lead Germany to nationhood, since its ultimate interests were irreconcilable with those of a unified Germany. Nor did he say explicitly that only Prussia was a viable candidate for the task. Yet he left no doubt about the fact that, as a country still divided into two unequal parts, Prussia suffered a deficit in power that made expansion necessary, both in the north of Germany and beyond:

Let us assume that all of northern Germany goes to Prussia. Even if that were to happen, her power and security would still not be fully adequate. If we imagine her borders stretching all the way to the borders of Austria, then we cannot but see even more vividly that such a Prussia would not rest until she had finished the job by annexing the German lands of Austria. Even if the ambition of the Berlin cabinet were completely satisfied with the control of non-Austrian Germany, the ambition of the nation would compel it to decide the competition with Austria in a final either-or showdown.

Thus in Rochau's realpolitik, Little Germany was only a transitional stage on the way to Greater Germany. Another reason he considered only Prussia fit for German leadership was the fact that Prussia was a constitutional state and Austria was not. Rochau was, to be sure, under no illusions about the inner weakness of German and Prussian constitutionalism. The integrity of the constitution, he wrote, depended 'on indulgence from above, which may cease at any moment or at least be made subject to other conditions'. Nonetheless, constitutionalism had become 'the political school of Germany'.

The significance of constitutionalism as a political tumbling ground has dwindled somewhat of late, but it has not ceased. We may deem this importance to be great or little, and we may look to the future effects of this political gymnastics with concern or hope. Nonetheless, the constitutional process has become indispensable and unavoidable. However exhausted it may seem to some people, however contemptible to others, however repulsive to yet a third party, the constitution continues to exist with the agreement of all.

Even after defeating it, historical sovereignty has restored to the constitutional movement at least a portion of its rights, and has thereby sown the seeds of new battles.

For the liberal Rochau, it was far better to hold on to constitutionalism and develop it further than to follow the radical ideas of the democrats or the even more extreme socialists, who ultimately only played into the hands of the reaction.

The most energetic companion of conservative politics is revolutionary socialism. To threaten and endanger property is to drive not only the propertied classes, but also the intellectuals into the arms of the authority that promises protection against such attacks. And the authority that has the propertied classes and the intellectuals on its side is guaranteed the power to rule.

The recent developments in France—the February Revolution, the June Days, the election of Louis Napoleon to the presidency in December 1848—provided a warning example. 'France, terrified by socialism, has fallen victim to a kind of regime that seemed to have been left behind generations ago.' Although Germany managed to avoid such developments, here, too, the fear of revolutionary socialism had become 'a conservative power of the first order'. 'The German national movement has no worse enemy than revolutionary socialism—an enemy who cannot be bought off with concessions, nor weakened through compromises, nor bribed with gifts, but who must be crushed in open, merciless war.'

For liberal realpolitik, this war was to be a pre-emptive strike preventing revolutionary socialism from ever having the chance to pave the way for a dictatorship from the right. Rochau was perfectly conscious of the fact that the social question could only be solved by policies of social reform, and not by suppressing socialism. Yet the policies he proposed remained completely within the boundaries of liberal notions of 'helping people to help themselves', including 'the greatest possible scope for the spirit of association', namely labour union activity.

'Help yourself, and God will help you': thus goes one of the wisest sayings that passes from mouth to mouth among the people. And vice versa: he who does not help himself cannot be helped by either God or the state. 'Help yourselves' is the watchword of the North American spirit of enterprise and the North American worker, the magic formula that has created on the other side of the ocean an economic power of the first order within two lifetimes and a common prosperity that history has never yet known.[5]

Lorenz von Stein, who can best be described as a 'reform conservative', derived completely different lessons from the course of the latest French revolution. If this theorist of the state (who came from Eckernförde in Schleswig) had a political ideal, it was not America, but Prussia. In the third volume of his 1850 *Geschichte der sozialen Bewegung in Frankreich*, Stein attempted to demonstrate that the July monarchy, which he characterized as a system of 'sham constitutionalism' (*Scheinkonstitutionalismus*) had failed of inner necessity. It had tried to control the ruling class of industrial society, the capitalists, through corruption, but had sacrificed its own higher principles in the process and prepared the ground for a broad opposition against the monarchy.

The consequences were now plain to see. In the republic that emerged from the February revolution in Paris, the opposition between capital and labour was transformed into a broader antagonism between property and poverty, between haves and have-nots. The defenders of property closed ranks behind the industrial reaction. Although Louis Napoleon owed his victory in the presidential elections of December 1848 primarily to the rural populace, he immediately went over to the side of the propertied classes. The industrial reaction thus had the power of the state in its hands, an autonomous power independent of the parties. The contradictions inherent in industrialized society were not thereby resolved, however. Far from it. Now a new battle commenced, the issue of which was not yet decided. This was no longer simply the old conflict between capital and labour, but 'the battle between social democracy and the industrial reaction'. If the latter emerged as the victor, 'then the result will be the definitive rule of capital and the subjugation of labour, even in a legal sense. If social democracy wins, then it will impose its own contrasting order upon society—perhaps only after a very bloody interval.'[6]

It was still possible to avert a development of this kind in Germany, including the 'bloody interval' that went along with it. But in order for that to happen, the monarchy would have to recall its historical task of embodying an idea of the state 'elevated above all societal interests' and, for that very reason, standing for the principle of liberty. Since the king was the representative of the independent idea of the state, it followed 'in a natural manner that the part of society subject to rule will turn—now out of immediate instinct, now consciously and intentionally—to the monarchy as its natural protector'. In complying with this expectation, the monarchy would simultaneously be fulfilling its own need for independent action. It lay in the nature of this need 'that the monarchy, to whom the highest power of the state has been entrusted, should use it in an independent manner, promoting against the will and the natural inclination of the ruling class the elevation of the lower class, hitherto subjugated in state and society.'

In Stein's view, the reward of such autonomy lay not only in the possibility of gaining for the king the support of the entire lower class. More importantly, the sovereign would link his very existence with 'the happiness of the state, the love and trust of the genuine people'. In doing so, the monarchy would 'identify the throne itself with the idea of liberty, lending it the most secure support humanly possible to achieve . . . By thus fulfilling its truly divine mission within its people, the monarchy shall wear a double crown!'

This, then, was the lesson Germany and Prussia could learn from the developments in France since 1848: in order to pre-empt the dangers of industrial reaction and social revolution, the monarchy must do everything it can to gain 'an infinitely great social power to complement its power of state'.

It is a certain truth that the monarchy is never more powerful than when it enjoys the support of the people, in the narrower sense of the word . . . The true, the mightiest, the most lasting and most popular monarchy is the monarchy of social reform . . . If it does not have the high moral courage to become a monarchy of social reform, then monarchy will, here and everywhere, henceforth become either an empty shadow or a despotism, or else sink into republic.

The Right Hegelian Lorenz von Stein resolved the antinomies of society on the same level as had Hegel, on the level of the state. He sought to give the monarchy a new social legitimacy in order to overcome the antithesis between monarchy and popular sovereignty. The idea of the 'double crown', however, could also be interpreted in another way, though Stein himself could hardly have been conscious of it in 1850.

In an essay (appearing in 1852 in the *Deutsche Vierteljahrs Schrift*) concerning the constitutional question in Prussia, Stein denied Prussia's 'constitutional capacity'. In the Hohenzollern state, 'the actual state-forming element in the historical process of state development' was to be found in the princes, not the provincial estates, as had been the case in France, Britain, Switzerland, and the Netherlands. Furthermore, Prussia was 'still without a completely ordered, closed and fixed territorial area' and lacking 'the harmonious measure and proportions of a body, the basis of lasting power'. For these reasons, the centre of gravity in the constitutional life of the country could only be the monarchy, not the political representation of the people. In 'states of this kind, assembled patchworks of different masses unstructured according to a uniform societal order', popular representation was

of course not impossible, if we mean that one could not impose it from the outside, gather representatives into a hall, and commence debate. But that such an institution could be considered the central focus of politics, the thing holding together, ruling, mediating and balancing the life of the state—in this sense it is indeed impossible.

Here, Stein rationalizes the very system he had called 'sham constitutionalism' two years before. But he does not stop here. Once again, he resolves the antagonism—the conflict between government and popular representation, between state and society—on a higher level, this time that of the nation. The need for popular representation in Prussia is

basically only a particular form of the need for a *German* popular representation. The contradictions on display in Prussia disappear as soon as we look upon the Prussian constitution as a great and solemn preparation for the representation of all of Germany. The particular historical foundation, the special national inwardness, the commonality of interests and of social development—it is perfectly clear that all these unique phenomena, traversing and touching state and society on all sides of Prussia and hampering the firm crystallization of a Prussian constitution, belong to the *German* people, and that this state of things ceases to be as soon as we imagine a representation of this people.

The inadequacy of the Prussian constitution as proof of the necessity of German unification—Stein's dialectics were more than mere speculation. If we connect his two trains of thought, one derived from French, the other from Prussian history, we find a political programme based on a dual synthesis. The Prussian state was confronted with the necessity of legitimating itself anew, internally through social reforms, externally through the unification of Germany. If it was successful, then the idea of the 'double crown' was doubly meaningful. The Prussian state would be a monarchy by both the grace of God and the will of the people, and to the crown of the king of Prussia would be joined the crown of the German emperor. Stein did not expand any further upon this scenario, but the contours of his ultimate aspirations were plain to see.[7]

The basic difference between Rochau and Stein was obvious. The liberal publicist depended upon the reasoned insight of the bourgeoisie and the self-help of the working class to solve the social question. The conservative theorist of the state, in contrast, expected the monarchy to do everything, and thus, unlike Rochau, had no interest in increasing the influence of bourgeois-controlled parliaments at the expense of governments. In one matter, however, the two did agree. Both wanted to avoid social revolution and considered social reform as the means of doing so. This was what fundamentally differentiated Rochau and Stein from a radical socialist like Karl Marx, who was motivated by the failure of the 1848 revolutions to undertake a critical review of his ideas concerning the conditions for a successful proletarian revolution.

The result of these reflections was *Die Klassenkämpfe in Frankreich*,* written in London, where Marx was living after his exile from Prussia and after a brief sojourn in Paris in the late summer of 1849 (the text appeared in 1850 in instalments in the *Neue Rheinische Zeitung. Politisch-ökonomische Revue*, at that time published in Hamburg). Marx's historical and theoretical reappraisal of the experiences of 1848 did not lead him to revise, but to radicalize his ideas concerning the revolution of the working class. Systematic suppression of the class enemy was going to be the only way the proletariat could hold onto any power it would gain—this was, for Marx, the most important lesson of 1848. His view is reflected in his synopsis of the programme of 'revolutionary socialism' or 'communism':

> This socialism is the proclamation of permanent revolution, the class dictatorship of the proletariat as a necessary stage of transition to the abolition of all class differences, to the abolition of all relations of production upon which they rest, to the abolition of all societal relations corresponding to these relations of production, and to the overturning of all ideas emerging from these societal relations.

Marx did not refer in this text to the historical example of the Jacobin *terreur* of 1793, although it was continually present in his thoughts. In 1847 he had written that 'the reign of terror, by its mighty hammer blows, could only serve to spirit away, as it were, the ruins of feudalism from the soil of France. The anxious and considerate bourgeoisie could not have accomplished this task in decades. The bloody acts of the people simply cleared its path.' At the beginning of November 1848, after the victory of the counter-revolution in Vienna, Marx gave expression (in the *Neue Rheinische Zeitung*) to his hope that 'the cannibalism of

* Marx, *Class Struggles in France*.

the counter-revolution' would convince the people that there was only one way 'to *shorten* the murderous death-throes of the old society and the bloody birth-pangs of the new, to simplify them, to *concentrate* them', namely through '*revolutionary terrorism*'. The idea of the 'dictatorship of the proletariat' as a proletarian reign of terror was not a secondary element in Marx's attempt to draw conclusions from the course of the 1848 revolutions, especially the revolution in France. In a letter to his friend Joseph Weydemeyer on 5 March 1852, Marx counted the realization 'that the class struggle necessarily leads to the dictatorship of the proletariat' among the core elements of his theory.[8]

Marx's momentous correlation between the 'bourgeois' and the 'proletarian' revolutions did not escape the criticism of his contemporaries. In 1853 Rochau drew attention to a significant difference between the 'third' and the 'fourth estate'. 'It is a meaningless platitude,' he wrote,

> to speak of a fourth estate that will take the place of the middle class, just as the middle class once took the place of the aristocracy. There is no inner connection between the two ideas; the former is prophecy, the latter actual historical process. The middle class wrested power from the nobility not because it was more numerous (indeed, the number of abused peasants was far greater still, and it availed them nothing), but because it was intellectually and morally superior, as well as more prosperous. These were the qualities that gave the middle class both the claim to greater political importance and the power to obtain it. The very lack of such qualities, in comparison, is what best characterizes the so-called fourth estate. However much sympathy ignorance, uncouthness, and poverty deserve, only a complete fool could accord to them the vocation of political leadership and rule. If we strip away those negative qualities and educate it, then the so-called fourth estate will simply blend together with the middle class, and the only possible antagonism remaining will be the one between the middle and the upper classes.

Such criticism had no effect on Marx, who retained an unshakable belief that '1789' and '1793' would repeat themselves in the next stage of the great historical class struggle, albeit in somewhat different form. Marx, too, saw differences between the 'bourgeois' and the 'proletarian' revolutions. But they were other differences than the ones pointed out by Rochau. In 1851–2 Marx commenced work on what was to be one of his most brilliant historical studies, *Der achzehnte Brumaire des Louis Bonaparte*,* an analysis of the coup d'état on 2 December 1851 by means of which President Louis Napoleon, following the example of his uncle on 9 November 1799 (the 18 Brumaire of the revolutionary calendar), had united all powers of state in his own person.

The usurper's triumph gave Marx occasion to compare the new revolution with the old. 'Bourgeois revolutions, like those of the eighteenth century,' he wrote,

> rush more swiftly from success to success, their dramatic effects continually eclipsing each other. Men and things seem to be outlined in a brilliant light, and ecstasy is the spirit of the

* Marx, *The Eighteenth Brumaire of Louis Bonaparte.*

day. But they are short-lived, their zenith soon come and gone, and a long hangover takes hold of society before it can assimilate the results of its storm-and-stress period soberly. Proletarian revolutions, on the other hand, like those of the nineteenth century, continually critique themselves, continually interrupt their own course and return to what seemed already accomplished in order to begin it anew. They deride with cruel thoroughness the half-measures, weaknesses, and pitiful inadequacies of their first attempts. They seem to hurl down their enemy only to let him draw new power from the earth and rise up once again, even more colossal than before. They quail again and again in the face of the indefinite monstrousness of their own purposes, until a situation is created that makes all turning back impossible, and the very conditions themselves cry out:

Hic Rhodus, hic salta!
Here is the rose, here dance!

A figure like Louis Napoleon should never have existed in the first place; as long as his reign lasted, it abrogated fundamental presuppositions of Marx's theory. The state, as Marx and Engels had proclaimed in the *Communist Manifesto* of 1848, is 'only a committee that administers the common affairs of the whole bourgeois class.' Louis Napoleon, however, was what Marx called the 'executive power that had made itself independent', and Bonapartism was nothing more than the admission of the bourgeoisie 'that its political power must be broken so that its societal power might be preserved intact'. The emancipated power of the Bonapartist executive could thus no longer be described as the organized collective interest of the ruling class in society. But then who ruled in its place, and in whose interest did Napoleon III rule? After the military successes of the second French Empire in the Crimean War, Marx began to take the political role of the army seriously. In 1859 he spoke of the 'establishment of the rule *of* the army in place of rule *through* the army', and shortly afterwards even of the 'fundamental antagonism between bourgeois society and the *coup d'état*'. The materialist interpretation of history seemed to be at the end of its rope. The societal basis, no longer capable of determining the political superstructure, was now at the mercy of the latter. Napoleon III had made the impossible possible.

The theoretical untenability of the prevailing conditions fostered in Marx, and even more in his friend Friedrich Engels, an intense longing for crisis, and, when crisis came, the inclination to concentrate revolutionary hopes upon it. When the world economic crisis broke out in 1857, Engels rejoiced: 'The crisis will do me good physically, as good as a swim in the sea, that I can already tell. In 1848 we said, "Now our time has come," and it came in a certain sense. But this time it is coming fully and utterly. This time it is life or death.'

Although the economic crisis did not fulfil its promise, signs of danger soon increased on the political front, not least of all in Prussia. In October 1858 Prince William assumed the regency on behalf of his mentally ill brother, King Frederick William IV, and within a short period of time formed a liberal-conservative ministry under Prince Karl Anton von Hohenzollern-Sigmaringen. At first, Marx cautioned against exaggerated expectations. After the victory of the moderate liberals in the lower-house elections in November, however, Engels was convinced of Prussia's 'political reawakening', a development he compared with similar events in other countries and thus saw as part of a pan-European watershed. Ten years after the revolution, the bourgeoisie seemed no longer prepared to accept the consequences of its political self-incapacitation, its subjugation under military and political despotism. Its societal power had increased with its wealth, and now the bourgeoisie began once again to feel the political fetters laid upon it.

Engels's conclusion was simultaneously a prediction:

> The present movement in Europe is the natural consequence and expression of emotion, paired with a regained confidence in its own power over the workers, regained in ten years of undisturbed industrial activity. The year 1858 bears a striking resemblance to the year 1846, which likewise ushered in a political reawakening in most of Europe and which also featured a number of reform-oriented princes, princes who, two years later, were helplessly swept away by the rush of the revolutionary flood they had unleashed.[9]

FROM THE NEW ERA TO THE CONSTITUTIONAL CONFLICT

Like the socialist émigrés Marx and Engels in London and Manchester, Germans of all political stripes watched with great anticipation the events unfolding in Prussia beginning in autumn 1858. Prince William, the 'Kartätschenprinz' of 1849, was no liberal. Neither, however, did he want anything to do with his brother's arch-conservative 'camarilla', fully intending, in fact, to reign in a constitutional manner. Consequently, when he assumed the regency on 9 October 1858, William disregarded the last wish of the king, now quite deranged, that he refuse to take the oath upon the constitution. The swearing of the oath before both chambers on 26 October 1858 was followed on 8 November by a sensational speech before the state ministry, composed of moderate conservatives and 'old-liberals' in equal proportion. The most famous passage spoke of the 'moral conquests' Prussia must make in Germany. This revealed William's intention of breaking with his brother's realpolitik and moving the unification of Germany forward.

Another part of the speech received somewhat less attention—William's reference to changes in the armed forces, necessary in order to give Prussia real clout in European power politics. The 'New Era', talk of which commenced immediately both within Prussia and abroad, began amid great hopes, and these contributed decisively to the overwhelming victory of the moderate liberals in the Prussian parliamentary elections of November 1858, where they gained an absolute majority of seats in the second chamber.

Many supporters of the democrats also returned to the polls for the first time since 1849. Nonetheless, the staunch left was not yet prepared to enter its own candidates, contenting itself for the time being with recognizing the legality of the revised constitution and announcing its willingness to support the government under certain conditions. These conditions were spelled out in the Königsberg 'Wahlaufruf der preussischen Demokratie',* written by Johann Jacoby: the left expected the state ministry under the prince of Hohenzollern-Sigmaringen and his representative, the old-liberal Rudolf von Auerswald, to 'conscientiously observe the constitution of the land and to further develop it in a liberal sense on the basis of the law'.

The exaltation of autumn 1858 did not last long. The government was slow to introduce reforms of the inner administration, and, when it did so, it met with resistance and delaying tactics from conservative ministers and provincial governors. The House of Lords, too, was defiant, blocking liberal bills in civil law as well as tax reform measures aimed at the privileges of the Junker estates. Yet the old-liberals refrained from using their parliamentary strength against the ministry and the first chamber. The watchword of the leading fraction, led by and named after Georg von Vincke, former delegate to the German National Assembly, was 'Let us not be pushy.' Governmental liberals adhered to this philosophy throughout all of 1859, to the increasing discomfort of the democrats and many younger liberals. In consequence of a major foreign event, the Italian war of independence, the year 1859 was to mark a caesura in the history of the liberal and national movement in Germany.[10]

In July 1858 Napoleon III and the prime minister of the Kingdom of Sardinia-Piedmont, Count Camillo di Cavour, came to an agreement that France would aid Sardinia in the conquest of Lombardy and Venetia—that is, in a war with Austria—and, in turn, receive from its ally the provinces of Nice and Savoy. This secret agreement was completely in keeping with the policy of close cooperation Cavour had begun with France in 1855, when he led his country to war in the Crimea on the side of Britain and France. At the end of April 1859, after Cavour ignored an ultimatum from Vienna, Austrian troops invaded Sardinia-Piedmont. The war for the unification of Italy had begun, and it was only natural that this conflict would stir public opinion in Germany to a far greater extent than the Crimean War a few years previously.

The debate over the question of which side Prussia and Germany should take in a war pitting Austria against Italy and France prompted the emergence of completely new political 'camps' in 1859. The most unified of these was a group advocating Prussian support for Austria in return for the latter's recognition of Prussia's political and military leadership in non-Austrian Germany. To this group belonged most of the *kleindeutsch* liberals of 1848, including the historians Johann Gustav Droysen, Heinrich von Sybel, and Georg Waitz. Far more mixed were the groups of unconditional supporters and unconditional opponents of Prussian intervention on behalf of the Habsburgs.

* Jacoby, 'Election Appeal for the Prussian Democrats'.

The group of unconditional supporters included old Prussian conservatives like the Gerlachs, the *grossdeutsch* democrat Waldeck, the socialists Marx and Engels, and, far more surprisingly, the anti-Habsburg liberal Rochau and the former president of the German National Assembly, Heinrich von Gagern, who went over from the *kleindeutsch* to the *grossdeutsch* party at this juncture. Among those who favoured a break with Austria, even in alliance with France, were the socialist Ferdinand Lassalle, the 'Forty-Eighter' democrats Arnold Ruge and Ludwig Bamberger, the liberal publicist Konstantin Rössler, and the conservative political realist Otto von Bismarck. The latter, upon Prince William's assuming the regency, had been compelled to give up his post as Prussian representative at the Federal Diet; now, as Prussian envoy in St Petersburg, he had been, as he saw it, 'put on ice' on the Neva.

As he wrote in a confidential letter to the general adjutant of the Prince of Prussia on 5 May 1859, Bismarck would have preferred to send the Prussian army to the south—with boundary posts in their knapsacks, to be pounded in 'either at Lake Constance, or wherever the Protestant confession is no longer dominant'. The Germans, once taken 'into possession' by Prussia, would gladly fight 'for us', 'especially if the prince regent does them the favour of renaming the Kingdom of Prussia the Kingdom of Germany'.

Ferdinand Lassalle saw things similarly. Born in Breslau in 1825, son of a Jewish merchant, Lassalle was strongly influenced by both Fichte and Hegel. He became an active follower of Marx during the revolution; then, after serving a prison term for inciting resistance against state authorities, he turned to political theory and writing. In his pamphlet *Der italienische Krieg und die Aufgabe Preussens. Eine Stimme aus der Demokratie*,* Lassalle considered Austria the very embodiment of the 'reactionary principle' and consequently a more dangerous enemy than Napoleon III, who was, after all, compelled to base his rule on democratic principles like general suffrage. Although a politics in the style of Frederick the Great—like the conquest of Austria's German territories and the proclamation of the German Reich—was out of reach for Prussia at the moment, nonetheless it could still lay claim to glory. 'If Napoleon reworks the map of Europe in the south according to the national principle, so much the better; we shall do the same in the north. If Napoleon liberates Italy, so much the better; we will take Schleswig-Holstein!'

Marx and Engels, for their part, remained faithful in 1859 to their belief that no regime stood more in the way of the revolution than that Bonapartist government. Therefore it was in the revolutionary interest to defeat or at least weaken Napoleon. For that reason alone, Germany was obligated to 'defend the *Po on the Rhine*.' In his pamphlet *Po und Rhein*,† written at the beginning of the year and published in April, Engels urged the Germans to cause whatever harm they

* Lassalle, *The Italian War and the Mission of Prussia: A Democratic Voice.*

† Engels, *Po and Rhine.*

could to France and to avoid moral reflections about 'whether such behaviour is in keeping with absolute standards of justice and the national principle. One must save one's own skin.' Once Germany achieved unity, then it would still be able to forgo 'all the Italian rubbish'.

The policy the Hohenzollern state actually pursued in the early summer of 1859 disappointed *all* parties: it remained neutral. In late June, after the Austrian debacle at Solferino, Prussia declared itself willing to attempt an 'armed mediation' at the side of Britain and Russia. But this proved superfluous when, in early July, Emperor Francis Joseph and Napoleon III agreed to a compromise peace. In the provisions to the treaty of Villafranca, Austria renounced claims to the greater part of Lombardy, but was able to retain Venetia, Mantua, and Peschiera. Thus the Italian national state that emerged from the war and the ensuing revolutionary popular movement was still incomplete (Venetia was not taken until 1866, Rome four years later). Yet the Vienna system of 1815, already shaken by the Crimean War, had lost one important buttress, and that gave heart to all forces in other parts of Europe fighting against the hegemony of monarchist legitimacy in the name of the national principle.[11]

The leaders of Austria were aware of the possibility that the Italian example might find imitators. In the year following the 1859 defeat, the Habsburg monarchy made another attempt to become a constitutional state. The October Diploma of 1860 granted the nobility of both German and non-German crown lands considerable autonomy within a federal structure. Yet this solution provoked so much hostility among the Hungarians and the German-Austrian liberals that it was replaced four months later by a new constitution, the February Diploma.

The constitution of 1861, the work of the former imperial prime minister and now newly appointed minister of state, Anton von Schmerling, created an 'Imperial Council' (*Reichsrat*) as a centralized legislature for the entire monarchy. Hungary was partially excepted; all questions pertaining only to Cisleithan—that is, non-Hungarian—territories of the empire were the province of a 'smaller council' (*engerer Reichsrat*). But the Hungarians, Czechs, Poles, and Croats sent no delegates to the assembly out of protest against the new system, and the Imperial Council had to begin as a primarily German rump parliament. This was clearly not going to be the way to fortify the cohesion of the empire. Still, the February Diploma had one advantage: a 'German' and 'liberal' Imperial Council in Vienna might well impress public opinion in Germany, especially if Prussia continued to disappoint liberal expectations.

Prussia was still inspiring hopes as late as the autumn of 1859. What had long been obvious to *kleindeutsch* liberals now came to be accepted by many who had hitherto inclined in the *grossdeutsch* direction: namely that after the defeat of the Habsburg empire, only the Hohenzollern state could protect the Germans against France. The organizational expression of this national-political rapprochement between liberals and democrats was the German National Union (*Deutscher Nationalverein*), founded in September 1859 in Frankfurt am Main after the example of the Italian *Società Nazionale* of 1856. The leading personalities behind this organization were the Hanover jurist Rudolf von Bennigsen on the liberal side, and on the side of the moderate democrats the district judge Hermann Schulze-Delitzsch, who in 1848–9 had been a member of the Prussian National Assembly on the left centre.

For the new association, the only remaining solution to the German question was the *kleindeutsch* project, a unification of Germany under Prussian leadership. The promise to keep membership in a German federal state open to Austria's German territories was little more than a tactical concession to southern German predilections and animosities. The founding of the National Union sent out a signal impossible not to hear. Liberals and democrats put aside their remaining differences (for example on the question of suffrage), since both parties were now convinced that the creation of a liberal national state was more important than everything else and would tolerate no further delay. The Italian example began to catch on in Germany, too.

In terms of social composition and ideology, the new association was dominated by the educated and propertied bourgeoisie, the *Bildungsbürgertum*. Confessionally speaking, its orientation was Protestant. With soon more than 25,000 members, however, the National Union was far more than an assembly of dignitaries. It stood in close contact with various other groups, including organizations for the education of workers, gymnastics associations, defensive alliances, and shooting clubs. Still, most of these managed to retain their independence from the Union's aspiration to leadership, and many of them remained essentially *grossdeutsch* in sentiment even throughout the 1860s. The National Union was only one expression of the national idea, and certainly not the one closest to the *Volk*. It played virtually no organizational role in the celebrations in honour of the centenary of Friedrich Schiller's birth in November. Although it did take part in the gymnastics and shooting festivals in Coburg, Gotha, and Berlin in 1860 and 1861, as well as the German Shooting Festival in Frankfurt am Main in July 1862 and the German Gymnastics Festival in Leipzig in August 1863, the Union did not succeed in taking control of these events. It also failed, despite great efforts, in its attempt to constrain the German gymnastics movement to cultivate the practice of military gymnastics (*Wehrturnen*).

Nonetheless, on many occasions the German National Union was able to set the tone. These included numerous celebrations in honour of the centenary of Fichte's birth in May 1862, as well as the events within the framework of a *Reichsverfassungskampagne* in the spring of 1863. It also played a significant role in the collection of contributions for the reconstruction of the German fleet, first created in 1848 by the provisional central authority, then broken up in 1852 by the Federal Diet and ultimately sold in public auction. The recipient of the donations was the Prussian ministry of the navy, until internal developments in the Hohenzollern state brought the campaign to a sudden end in spring 1862.

It was within the German academy that the Union was perhaps most influential. Its organizational structures traversed all political boundaries, and its major publication, the *Wochenschrift* (edited by Rochau), provided a firm base for all varieties of *kleindeutsch* nationalism. The Union was the organizational anticipation of an all-German party, something not yet possible in reality. And indeed, the National Union provided the impetus for the founding of a new political party very soon after it came into existence.[12]

Nonetheless, a different kind of impetus was going to be necessary before the system of political parties in Prussia would experience a profound transformation. This catalyst was the reform of the army. Upon assuming the regency, Prince William gave the reorganization of the armed forces highest priority. That such reform was necessary was uncontroversial. The last reform, the Scharnhorst-inspired *Heeresgesetz* of 1814, now lay a half-century in the past, and despite the fact that Prussia's population had grown from 11 to 18 million in the intervening years, the numerical strength of the army had not changed since Frederick William III fixed it in 1817. Of the 180, 000 annually eligible for military service, only about 40, 000 were drafted.

But the increase in the number of recruits (by about 23,000) was only one of the goals set at William's behest by the new Prussian minister of war, Albrecht von Roon, appointed in December 1859. The reform plans also included a restructuring of the relationship between the national guard (*Landwehr*) and the regular troops. The three younger annual levies of the national guard would, in future, be shifted to the reserves and thus incorporated into the army. This was tantamount to a weakening of the 'bourgeois' element in the Prussian military system. This effect was no less evident with respect to another measure: Roon wanted to retain the three-year term of military service, even though, from a purely military point of view, the two-year period of training in effect since the revolutionary era was perfectly adequate. From the point of view of William and the generals, however, the issue had as much to do with politics as with the military. Another year of training and discipline would better serve to turn the recruit into a dependable pillar of the Prussian soldier-state, a system that was to be defended not only against external enemies, but also internally, against overthrow and revolution.

The conflict with the bourgeoisie and its political representatives was thus clear from the outset. Strictly speaking, the Prussian House of Representatives was only authorized to decide upon the reform's budgetary dimension, not upon matters pertaining to military organization. In effect, the budget was the lever Roon's opponents were constrained to use in their effort to block the reform. This opposition was by no means particularly resolute. On the contrary: despite its reservations, the parliament approved a 'provisorium' permitting the government to move ahead with the reorganization, despite the fact that the latter was not clearly defined. Just less than a year later (18 January 1861, a few weeks after the death of Frederick William IV),

William had himself crowned king in Königsberg. It was clear to all observers that, as king, he would pursue the reform even more emphatically than before. Nonetheless, in spring 1861, the parliament once again approved 'provisional' funding—a designation the government rejected on the quite appropriate grounds that the increase in the armed forces was already a matter of established fact.

The liberal majority of the chamber committed a great mistake in letting slip the opportunity to tie the hands of the state ministry in its use of the approved funds. The error was costly. On 6 June 1861, shortly after the passing of the second provisional finance measure and the end of the parliamentary session, the German Progressive Party (*Deutsche Fortschrittspartei*) was founded in Berlin. This was an alliance of younger liberals who had long opposed the all too compliant attitude of the 'Vincke fraction', as well as democrats who had cut their political teeth in 1848. The regional focal point of the opposition was in East and West Prussia, a fact that earned the liberal rebels the mocking title 'Young Lithuanians'. The most active representatives of the group were the East Prussian Junker Leopold von Hoverbeck and the Elbing lawyer Max von Forckenbeck (originally from Westphalia). The party soon found numerous supporters in the most eastern Prussian province, not least among free-trade-oriented noblemen and merchants. Much better known were several democrats who joined the Progressive Party, foremost among them Johann Jacoby from Königsberg and two other former members of the Prussian National Assembly of 1848, Benedikt Waldeck from Westphalia and Hermann Schulze-Delitzsch from the province of Saxony, both of whom had recently been elected to the lower chamber.

In the close cooperation of liberals and democrats, the Progressives were following the footsteps of the National Union from two years earlier. Indeed, the new party considered itself a kind of executive of the latter. But it was more than that. The German Progressive Party was Germany's first really 'modern' political party. In terms of organization it went far beyond the typical election committees, developing a firm party infrastructure from the local to the national level. It put forward a binding party platform emphasizing the common ground between liberals and democrats, their mutual commitment to liberal reforms in Prussia, and German national unification. Differences, though de-emphasized, remained. On the controversial question of suffrage, the democrats retained their commitment to the universal franchise, whereas the liberals (in a narrower sense) preferred a census that gave the propertied classes more political influence than the propertyless masses. With new lower-house elections set for December, however, the party's foremost concern was the battle for the consolidation of the constitutional state and thus against a reorganization of the army that would effect the very opposite.

The parliamentary elections were a landslide victory for the Progressives, who received over 100 seats and immediately became the strongest fraction. Together with the left centre, the other group of 'resolute liberals', they controlled more than half the seats. In awareness of its strength, the Progressive Party put forward the 'Hagen motion' at the beginning of 1862 in direct challenge to the government. In this motion, the deputies furthest to the left demanded more stringent itemization (the term used was 'specialization') of the state budget, including for the current year. The purpose was clear: to prevent the state ministry from covering the surplus costs of the army reform out of other budgetary titles, as was the customary practice. The old-liberal finance minister, Robert von Patow, spoke of a 'vote of no confidence', but could not prevent the parliament from taking up the Hagen motion with 177 votes against 143. Five days later, on 11 March 1862, King William I dissolved the lower chamber. On 14 March he dismissed the ministry he had appointed in November 1858, at the beginning of the New Era. The new cabinet, under the nominal leadership of Prince Adolf von Hohenlohe-Ingelfingen and the actual leadership of the finance minister, August von der Heydt, was now exclusively conservative in composition.

The voters responded on 6 May 1862. The losers in the parliamentary elections were the conservatives, the Catholic fraction, and the old-liberals, the victors once again the staunch liberals. The Progressive Party gained a further twenty seats. Together, the liberal fractions controlled about four-fifths of the seats. In the middle of September, the delegates Friedrich von Stavenhagen and Heinrich von Sybel, both from the Left Centre Party along with Karl Twesten of the Progressive Party, proposed a last compromise measure on the basis of the two-year period of military service. Although Roon himself and the entire ministry regarded the compromise as a solution, the obstinacy of the king spelled its doom. William briefly considered abdication, then allowed Bismarck to talk him out of it. Bismarck, Prussian ambassador in Paris since May 1862, had been summoned to Berlin by Roon from his vacation in Biarritz. In long conversations in the palace and gardens of Babelsberg on 22 September, Bismarck managed to win the king over to a policy of confrontation with the parliament. That same day, William conferred on Bismarck provisional leadership of the state ministry.

In his *Gedanken und Erinnerungen*,* Bismarck wrote that he had succeeded in convincing the king that for him 'it was not an issue of "conservative" or "liberal" in this or that nuance, but rather a matter of monarchical vs. parliamentary rule,' and that the latter 'must unconditionally be averted, even at the price of a period of dictatorship'. In speaking of a choice between monarchical and parliamentary rule, as well as with the term 'dictatorship', Bismarck was obviously referring to the British revolution of the seventeenth century. Just as obvious was his rejection of the liberal understanding of constitutionalism. From 1862 to 1866, when Bismarck ruled without a budget approved by the parliament, the Prussian government could no longer be described even in terms of 'sham constitutionalism'. It was non-constitutionalism, pure and simple.

In calling for clarification of the budget, the lower house had brought up the question of power. The response of the Prussian soldier-state was the 'gap theory'

* Bismarck, *Thoughts and Recollections.*

(*Lückentheorie*) as practised and justified by Bismarck: whenever one of the two chambers upset the balance between the three legislative powers (king, House of Lords, House of Representatives) by withholding necessary budgetary funds (a scenario for which the constitution made no provision), then, according to the monarchic principle, it was the duty of the royally appointed state ministry to rule without budgetary legislation until the chamber in question retrospectively approved the expenditures made in the interim.

On 23 September the House of Representatives pronounced its final rejection of the army reform budget. A week later, on 30 September, Bismarck declared before the budget commission a later oft-quoted maxim of his political philosophy:

It is not Prussia's liberalism that Germany sees, but its power. Bavaria, Württemberg, and Baden may indulge liberalism, but nobody expects them to play Prussia's role. Prussia must gather her forces and hold them ready for the most propitious moment, a moment that has slipped away several times already. Prussia's borders according to the Vienna treaties are not conducive to a viable political existence. The great questions of the day will not be settled by speeches and majority decisions—that was the great mistake of 1848–9—but by iron and blood.

The public reaction to this statement was so negative that Bismarck found it necessary to travel to Jüterborg on 4 October to meet the king (who was on his way back to Berlin from Baden-Baden by rail) and explain his point of view to him. When William, in a black mood, evoked the probability of a bloody end to the conflict ('first Bismarck's, then his own head would roll on the Opernplatz in Berlin'), the prime minister responded with lessons from the history of the European revolution: the king should not take the weak-willed Louis XVI of France as an example, but rather the noble historical image of Charles I of Britain, who, 'after he had drawn his sword for his royal principles and had lost the battle, confirmed them unbowed with his own blood.'

The allusion to the execution of 1649 had its intended effect. The king's fighting spirit returned and with it his resolution to see the showdown with parliament through to the end with Bismarck. Blow after blow followed. On 3 October the House of Representatives accepted the state budget *excluding* the military allocations. Eight days later the House of Lords took the side of the monarch, approving the budget in its entirety. On 13 October the king terminated the parliamentary session. In his proclamation, read by Bismarck, the delegates were told that the administration could not roll back the reorganization of the army and must now conduct the governmental budget in the absence of a basis in the constitution. It was promised, however, that the non-budgetary regime would not be extended beyond the fiscal limits set by law, and the government was optimistic that, in due course, the chambers would retroactively approve whatever expenditures had proved necessary in the intervening period.[13]

BISMARCK AND THE LIBERAL DILEMMA

The breach of the constitution by king and ministry did not provoke a revolutionary response. At no time did Prussia's liberals and democrats consider fighting the Bismarck administration with other than legal means. They did not even call for demonstrations, apparently fearing that either the masses would not follow them or that the situation would soon escalate beyond control if they did. A repeat of 1848 was to be avoided.

The only Progressive politician to speak openly in autumn 1862 of a conflict between king and people was Johann Jacoby, who exhorted the latter to the 'legal resistance' of refusing to pay taxes. But this appeal found no echo. 'Resolute liberalism' seemed resolved not to let itself be provoked by the 'Napoleonic ideas' of the new prime minister. At a banquet given by the second Berlin electoral district to its Progressive delegate at the end of October, the main speaker, Rudolf Löwenstein, modified Bismarck's words before the budget commission in an instructive manner: 'the unification of Germany will be brought about as surely as a law of nature is fulfilled—not, however, by iron and blood, but rather by iron and coal.'

Through all liberal factions ran the belief that the constitutional conflict was ultimately rooted in a societal conflict, the 'battle between the bourgeoisie and the Junkers in alliance with absolutist tendencies' of which the *Preussischen Jahrbücher* spoke in 1862. Karl Twesten (originally from Holstein), an official in the Berlin city court and one of the most astute Progressives, had written in 1859—citing the sociologist Auguste Comte, founder of scientific positivism—that the 'dominant social classes' must necessarily become the 'political ruling classes'. On 22 February, in one of his last speeches before the chamber during the constitutional conflict, Twesten called the struggle 'between the Junkers and the people' the 'true conflict'. 'The liberal majority of the House of Representatives is not, as the conservatives claim, the *bourgeoisie* as a small, particular class, living from large enterprises and filled only with material interests'; but rather the *Bürgertum*, which 'represents both the material and the ideal interests that fill the working people and the thinkers, classes that have been steadily rising since the end of the Middle Ages and that have the moral authority always in hand and, sooner or later, will have the political authority of our state in hand as well.'[14]

When in their own company, however, Prussian liberals often expressed themselves more sceptically. The 'whole opinion concerning our moral successes' is certainly only 'a chimera', wrote Leopold von Hoverbeck to a friend at the end of June 1865.

> The circles of society that read newspapers and occupy themselves somewhat with politics formed their views on these questions long ago and remain true to them to this day . . . But upon the great mass of the people, the third and even partly the second electoral class, our debates have no influence, since they learn nothing of them—if the official provincial press doesn't make them even more absolutistic than they are already, by virtue of their whole education.

A month later, Hoverbeck summarized his assessment of the situation in one sentence: 'We who are working for the liberation of the people have no solid societal base upon which to stand.'

The reactionary inclinations of the provincial population east of the Elbe represented only one of the dangers by which liberals saw themselves threatened. Another came from 'the left', from the industrial workers. Ferdinand Lassalle's agitation for state-supported 'production cooperatives' (*Produktivgenossenschaften*) found increasing support among the working class. His General German Workers' Association (*Allgemeiner Deutscher Arbeiterverein*), founded in 1863, competed with the liberal cooperative movement, a system of self-help organizations for craftsmen and workers initiated by Schulze-Delitzsch. And that was not all it did. The new association cast fundamental doubts on the liberals' claim to represent the whole of the *Volk*. Lassalle made a demand the Progressive Party was unable to make, being itself divided on the issue between democrats and liberals: the demand for universal equal suffrage. As yet, the liberals knew nothing—or almost nothing—about the secret interviews between Lassalle and Bismarck in 1863 and the beginning of 1864. If they had, they would have been able to claim with greater justification that the socialist agitator was stabbing the liberal opposition in the back in its confrontation with the ministry. On the other hand, however, the Progressives themselves were hardly in a position to deny the accusation Lassalle made against them in the progressive-liberal district association of Friedrichstadt in Berlin during the election campaign in the spring of 1862—namely, that the liberals 'do not dare to admit openly that constitutional questions arise not from questions of law, but from questions of power'.[15]

The liberal publicist Heinrich Bernhard Oppenheim contradicted Lassalle's critique in the *Deutsche Jahrbücher* (which Oppenheim edited) in 1864, arguing that, alongside the real relations of power, the 'public consciousness of the law' was also a 'power that must be dealt with if lasting conditions are to be achieved. From the conflict between such opposites proceeds the *mediating* character of most constitutional documents.' Hereafter, however, the author expressed such strong doubts about the political maturity of the bourgeoisie that critical readers were forced to wonder if Oppenheim's assertion concerning the power of consciousness of the law even applied to Prussia.

> The bourgeois classes still generally consider the field of politics tedious and unfamiliar. They stand gaping in front of it as in front of a theater, taking, as it were, more of a dramatic than a personal interest in the business. Seldom enough does the individual feel that sua res agitur ['it concerns his own affair' (H.A.W.)].

For the Berlin *National-Zeitung*, it was established fact that the weakness of the Prussian bourgeoisie had its roots in the specific character and traditions of the Hohenzollern state. 'In vain has the Prussian bourgeoisie waited fifty years for institutions to be cleared away that keep its political status below the measure it has been granted in all other neighbouring states—with the exception of those in the Slavic east,' lamented the liberal newspaper in April 1862.

The gap separating our conditions in this respect from those of the other German states has already become so wide as to threaten the closer community in the most worrying manner. What is called the 'Junker state' appears so strange and repulsive there that every sympathy immediately freezes at the mere mention of the name.

The Prussian liberals did not blame only their own bourgeoisie for the fact that the old Prussian soldier-state and Junkerdom had survived to the present day. In their opinion, the rest of Germany shared responsibility for the conditions in Prussia by continuing to accept the *Bundeskriegsverfassung* of 1821. In keeping with Article VIII, which disallowed 'even the appearance of the supremacy of one federal state over another', only three Prussian army corps were permitted in the federal army. Despite the fact that three-quarters of its territory belonged to the Confederation, however, as a European great power Prussia maintained six further army corps for reasons of security. As much as they despised Prussian militarism, the other German states were not unhappy with this arrangement. Ever since the wars of liberation, they believed they could depend on Prussia in a crisis, and were able to restrict their own military spending accordingly.

The consequences of this state of affairs for Prussian liberalism were elucidated in the *Deutsche Jahrbücher* in 1861 by Wilhelm Löwe-Calbe (democratic delegate to the German National Assembly in 1848–9, last president of the Stuttgart rump parliament, and Progressive Party delegate to the Prussian lower house since 1863). The Prussian government, he wrote, needs the army 'not so much for Prussian purposes, but rather to fulfil her external obligations as a German great power. Yet only from Prussia does the government demand the means for these obligations as German great power, whereas its duty is to demand them from Germany and to provide only for Prussia's own share.' The high military expenditures in Prussia were causing a 'withering away and restriction of prosperity and consequently of the available energies of the people'. The most important goal was thus the creation of a German army as the material guarantor of German unity.

Max von Forckenbeck expressed the same thought in a pithy formulation: 'Unless the German situation is given another form, then in my opinion the existence of a reasonable and liberal constitution is also, in the long term, an impossibility,' he wrote in a letter to Hoverbeck of 21 August 1859. 'If the German situation remains as it is, then only the military state will and must be further developed in Prussia.'[16]

Under Bismarck's rule, it became even more difficult for Prussia's 'resolute liberals' to gain an audience for such demands in the rest of Germany. To be sure, the other liberal parties, which also felt a close solidarity with the National Union, initially applauded the Progressives in their parliamentary battle with the non-budgetary regime of the new prime minister after October 1862. They also hailed the great victory of the Progressive and Left Centre parties in the provincial elections at the end of October 1863, after the lower chamber had been dissolved once again. But already in May 1863 the committee of the National Union was expressing the wish that the House of Representatives would adopt a more 'resolute attitude' toward the 'insulting behaviour of the government'. In the words of a resolution drafted by Karl Brater, a liberal delegate in the Bavarian parliament, and edited by Hoverbeck, Prussia had proved itself to be 'the most dangerous adversary of the national interests'. If its political leaders should attempt to seize the 'leadership of Germany', then they would 'find the National Union among the first ranks of those to fight against such temerity'.

Prussia suffered a dramatic loss of prestige in liberal Germany after the autumn of 1862, at the same time the reputation of Austria was on the rise again as a consequence of Schmerling's liberal policies. In addition, at the end October 1862, the National Union had to deal with organized competition from the *grossdeutsch* party. The German Reform Union (*Deutscher Reformverein*) united Catholics and Protestants, conservatives, liberals, and democrats who rejected Prussian hegemony. Among the founders of the new *grossdeutsch* association were Julius Fröbel, the leftist delegate of the Frankfurt parliament who in 1848 had hastened with Robert Blum to embattled Vienna, where he barely escaped execution; the Catholic historian Julius Ficker, the adversary of Heinrich von Sybel in the debate over whether the medieval emperors would have been better served by pursuing a nationalist policy instead of Christian universalism; and finally the erstwhile leader of the *kleindeutsch* party of 1848, Heinrich von Gagern, who had gone over to the *grossdeutsch* camp in 1859 during the Italian war. Even though the new organization was as unsuccessful as the National Union in overcoming its internal antitheses, its founding in autumn 1862 was nonetheless a symptom. *Kleindeutschland* was now on the defensive. Its situation worsened still further in summer 1863, when Bismarck's government, under the direction of the arch-conservative interior minister, Count Eulenburg, began to use a new press decree to shut down oppositional newspapers, some temporarily, others permanently.

Austria tried to exploit this opportunity. At an assembly of the German princes convened by Francis Joseph in Frankfurt, which Bismarck induced King William I not to attend, the renewal of the German Confederation was resolved in a reform act on 1 September 1863. The new constitutional draft proposed the creation of a six-member directory with three permanent members—Austria, Prussia, and Bavaria—flanked by a Federal Council (*Bundesrat*) as a permanent congress of princely envoys as well as an assembly of elected delegates from the parliaments of the member states. But Prussian rejection doomed the project. Bismarck insisted on veto powers for the two leading members in matters of war, a presidency representing Prussia and Austria equally, and a directly elected German national assembly.

In terms of the last two points, parity and direct elections, the Prussian demands accorded with the resolutions of another body convening at the same time and in the same place as the meeting of the princes: the German Delegate

Congress (*deutscher Abgeordnetentag*), a congress of parliamentarians from non-Austrian Germany. In mid-October the National Union rejected the Austrian proposal as completely inadequate, but at the same time called into question the credibility of the Prussian initiative. The Reform Union supported Austria, but that was of little help to the Vienna government; the German question could not be resolved against the will of Prussia and a great part of German public opinion. Nor, for that matter, could Prussia hope to achieve its version of the national project as long as the government found itself in conflict with the representatives of the people and with German liberalism.[17]

After Bismarck's nomination, there remained only one issue on which Prussian liberals saw eye to eye with the administration: trade policy. At the end of March 1862, the ministry under Prince Hohenlohe-Ingelfingen and Count Bernstorff, the foreign minister, concluded a liberal trade agreement with France, radically reducing the tariffs between the two countries. Two years previously, in the 'Cobden Treaty', France had largely dismantled its customs barriers against trade with Britain. Thus the Franco-Prussian agreement was tantamount to a fundamental decision *for* economic integration in the free trade system of western Europe and *against* the Austrian project of a central European customs union built upon protective tariffs. With this decision, Prussia all but put a stop to the negotiations between the German Customs Union and Austria to coordinate or unify their respective tariff policies. (Agreed upon in 1853, the negotiations were originally planned for 1860, but then delayed in the face of Prussian resistance.) The members of the Customs Union now had to make a decision—between free trade and protectionism, between Prussia and Austria, between west and east.

The liberal position was clear from the outset. 'By means of the French treaties', it was announced in the report of the parliamentary committees dealing with finance, tariffs, trade and industry,

> Europe is dividing in two: into a western group of nations opening itself up to world trade, and an eastern group closing itself off from the same. The choice that lies before the Customs Union is not subject to doubt. The Union owes it to the high educational and cultural level of the German people to join the progressive nations. This is the only way to secure a position worthy of the German nation among the peoples of the world, as well as its full participation in the development of a world culture.

The German proponents of free trade, who had formed the Congress of German Economists (*Kongress Deutscher Volkswirte*) in 1858, argued much like the Prussian liberals, as did the German National Union and the governments of the *Mittelstaaten* Saxony and Baden. The opposing standpoint was adopted by the protectionists, who controlled the German Chamber of Commerce (*Deutscher Handelstag*, founded in 1861), by the German Reform Union, and by the governments of Bavaria, Württemberg, Hesse-Darmstadt, and Nassau. Only when Prussia withdrew from the treaty of the Customs Union in 1863 and, a half-year later, signed a renewed customs treaty with Saxony, did the resistance of the protectionist states collapse. In October 1864 the erstwhile members agreed to a new customs treaty of twelve years' duration. A trade agreement with Austria was concluded in April 1865. In terms of economic policy, the battle for the leadership of Germany was decided in favour of Prussia.

The domestic repercussions of Bismarck's successful trade policy were great. The leaders of business and industry began to regard the government in an increasingly positive light. For the liberals, at that moment waging an embittered war against the prime minister, this was hardly a good thing, since it meant that they were now deprived of the active support of the very members of the bourgeoisie for whose material interests they were so tenaciously fighting. After the end of the constitutional conflict, the *Preussische Jahrbücher* summed up:

> Unlike the interests of practical politics and the doctrines of national law, the interests of the national economy have never found themselves in such a fundamental opposition to Bismarck. After all, it owes its most important advance in trade policy in the last ten years, the conclusion of the Franco-Prussian trade agreement and the a renewal of the Customs Union on the basis of a liberal tariff, to the steadfastness of the prime minister.[18]

FROM DÜPPEL TO KÖNIGGRÄTZ

At the end of 1863, Austria let it be known that it was not interested in further aggravating the customs conflict with Prussia. The reason was a new crisis in Schleswig-Holstein, which necessitated German–Austrian cooperation. In May 1852 the five European great powers, along with Sweden and Denmark, had recognized (Second London Protocol) the integrity of the Danish state and the right of Prince Christian of Schleswig-Holstein-Sonderburg-Glücksburg to the throne of Denmark and its neighbouring territories. Christian's claim was through the female line; through the male line, which was recognized in Schleswig and Holstein, the rightful heir would have been Duke Christian August von Augustenburg—who, however, renounced all claim to the throne for himself and his descendants after a financial settlement. Prussian and Austrian acquiescence in the London treaty was made conditional upon the promise of the Danish king to respect the special status of Schleswig and Holstein.

On 30 March 1863 King Frederick VII of Denmark issued letters patent contesting this agreement. In July the Federal Diet demanded their retraction and, when Denmark refused, proclaimed the federal execution against Holstein on 1 October. Copenhagen was unimpressed. On 13 November 1863 the government, a cabinet controlled by the nationalistic Eider-Danes, presented the parliament with a new constitution ordering the annexation of Schleswig. Two days later Frederick VII died. He was succeeded by Prince Christian, who became King Christian IX. One of the new sovereign's first acts was to sign the new constitution (18 November 1863). In doing so, he exploited the London Protocol's succession clause while simultaneously negating the whole basis of the agreement.

The oldest son of Augustenburg, Frederick, who had already attained his majority in 1852, had never accepted his father's renunciation of the throne. On 16 November 1863, the same day Christian IX assumed the throne in Copenhagen, Duke Christian conferred his right to succession in Schleswig and Holstein on his son, who immediately proclaimed himself Duke Frederick VIII and claimed the rulership of both duchies. All German nationalists, *kleindeutsch* and *grossdeutsch* alike, applauded him. At the end of December 1863 an assembly of almost 500 delegates from all parts of Germany convened in Frankfurt, proclaimed the Augustenburg cause the cause of the German nation, and set up a committee of thirty-six representatives to coordinate their activities. Schleswig-Holstein associations sprang up over all of Germany, organizing demonstrations, proclamations, and collecting contributions for the young duke.

The governments of the *Mittelstaaten* were also among Frederick VIII's supporters. Not so the two German great powers, who insisted upon the renewal of the 1852 agreement, in light of which Augustenburg's position was untenable. Considering where the other European great powers stood, this policy, developed by Bismarck and accepted by the Austrian foreign minister, Count Rechberg, was the only realistic one. Nevertheless, the Austro-Prussian motion to proceed with the (thus far delayed) federal execution against Holstein was not endorsed by the German national movement, and most of the *Mittelstaaten* voted against it. The measure was carried in the Diet on 7 December 1863, but by an exceedingly narrow majority.

This tacit rejection of Frederick VIII enraged the supporters of the National Union no less than those of the Reform Union. Austria's behaviour 'has destroyed the Greater German party', lamented Gustav von Lerchenfeld, the president of the German Reform Union and leader of the liberal chamber majority, in a letter to the former 'March minister' of Saxony-Weimar, Oskar von Wydenbrugk, on 25 December 1863. 'If Prussia understands its own advantage, it can now drive Austria out of Germany without so much as a cock crowing afterwards.'

Federal troops entered Holstein on 16 January 1864, whereupon the two German great powers issued an ultimatum: if Denmark did not withdraw its new constitution, Schleswig would be taken as security. When Copenhagen refused, war began—war for the return to the London Protocol, not, as the southern German states and the nationalists demanded, for the rights of Duke Frederick VIII. On 18 April Prussian troops took the Düppel entrenchments in the north of Denmark, sealing the country's fate. One week later, a European conference began in London, but it was unable to come to an agreement on any of the proposed solutions to the Danish problem, including a simple personal union between Denmark and the 'Elbe duchies' and a division of Schleswig along national lines. The failure of the conference, which ended on 25 June, effectively destroyed whatever political significance the London Protocol had retained.

The ceasefire, effective since May, expired the next day. Austria and Prussia immediately went on the offensive again, conquering all of Jutland and the island of Alsen. Denmark was forced to sue for a ceasefire and peace. On 1 August a preliminary peace agreement was concluded, the final treaty on 30 October. The Danish king renounced all rights in Schleswig, Holstein, and Lauenburg to the emperor of Austria and the king of Prussia, promising to abide by their decisions concerning the future of the Elbe duchies.

The Vienna treaty made no mention of the hereditary claims of Frederick VIII. To be sure, the foreign minister of Saxony, Friedrich von Beust, had backed them at the London conference in the name of the German Confederation, gaining the support of Austria and, finally, of Prussia. But then, in an interview on 1 June, the heir apparent learned the conditions under which Bismarck would be willing to accept Schleswig-Holstein as an independent *Mittelstaat*. They were terms calculated to make the Elbe duchies into a Prussian protectorate: a Prussian naval base in Kiel, a federal fortress in Rendsburg to be occupied by Prussian troops, military and naval conventions with Prussia, shared construction of a canal between the North Sea and the Baltic, and the separation of the prince from liberal advisers. When Frederick VIII did not prove immediately compliant, Bismarck dropped him. The Treaty of Vienna left the final status of Schleswig-Holstein unresolved, creating a construction that could, by its very nature, only be temporary: an Austro-Prussian condominium over the Elbe duchies.[19]

The controversy over Schleswig-Holstein's future, which grew especially heated in the summer of 1864, plunged the Prussian parliamentary opposition into a violent conflict. From the beginning of the Schleswig-Holstein crisis, the Prussian liberals were in a more difficult position than their like-minded colleagues in the other German states. While they hoped for military success in the war against Denmark, the liberal delegates of the House of Representatives also felt bound by their vow 'not to grant this ministry one cent'. They stuck to their clear budgetary standpoint, despite the fact that one of the most outspoken of them, Karl Twesten, had announced that if it were up to him to make a choice between 'whether the tenure of the Bismarck ministry should be extended for a period or whether the duchies of Schleswig and Holstein should be given up forever, I would not delay one moment in choosing the former.'

While the great majority of 'resolute liberals' supported Frederick VIII, a minority, under the leadership of the democrat Waldeck, had no desire to aid in the accession of a new dynast. They preferred the wholesale annexation of Schleswig-Holstein to Prussia, which they considered the only 'democratic monarchy' in Germany, the non-constitutional nature of the Bismarck regime notwithstanding—a view Waldeck habitually justified with reference to Frederick the Great's 'enlightened liberalism'. When a opportunity to annex all of Schleswig-Holstein (including the north of Schleswig with its predominantly Danish population) actually did arise in summer 1864, however, the right wing of the Progressive Party began to rethink its position.

At the end of May 1864 the *National-Zeitung*, the mouthpiece of this faction of 'resolute liberalism', declared that 'a Prussian admission that she cannot liberate all of Schleswig would be preferable to a war with several great powers.' On 11 August, while the negotiations over peace with Denmark were being conducted in Vienna, the same newspaper published an article under the title 'Glück und Macht'* delineating its fundamental stance: 'To turn our country into a barracks while making Schleswig-Holstein into a peaceful farmstead—that is, for us, too one-sided, a too unequal distribution of pleasure and pain.'

An appeal was sent out to the 'friends of peace' to no longer look upon the Prussians as the 'Spartans of Germany'.

> Against their own interests, the small German states sometimes expect the impossible from Prussia, that we should always be clad in the armor of war and ready to act for Germany's sake . . . But the eighteen million Germans united in the Prussian state cannot forever defend thirty-five million against all the turns of chance, cannot alone represent the interests of all of Germany.

Every German must realize and admit

> that Germany cannot, and will never be able to, continue her liberal development if Prussia regards herself as fundamentally a military state, and is regarded as such by others . . . For the exertion of a country's entire energies for the purpose of war is very rarely a means of advancing the cause of domestic liberty at the same time . . . Neither the Prussian people nor their representatives gain in liberty when the state's military duties are always seen as the highest and most pressing. In this case, the highest taxes must be paid according to the demands of the military offices, the highest military expenditures must be defrayed while continually strengthening the armed forces, and we know all too well what then happens to the business of parliament. It has come to the point where all those who recall the civic duties of the state receive the honorary title of 'wind-bag', and only the accomplishments and obedience of the soldier are seen as useful to the state.

At this time, the newspaper of the Progressive right wing was still only concerned with Schleswig-Holstein's military-political integration with Prussia; it was not yet a question of annexation. But the same arguments might have been used to justify the more radical solution. Hitherto, the argument that the unequal distribution of military expenditures as a result of the 1821 *Bundeskriegsverfassung* was preventing the liberal development of Prussia had been more a matter of theoretical Progressive doctrine. The victory over Denmark provided the first chance to examine its practical consequences. Hitherto, Progressives had taken it for granted that only a liberally minded Prussian government could advance the cause of German unification. Now, a number of the party conceded that a conservative ministry—indeed, even a ministry in direct violation of the constitution—could take up this task with equal success. If that was the case, then the relationship between unity and liberty would have to be worked out anew. The maxim with which the *National-Zeitung* brought its reflections over the inadequacies of the *Bundeskriegsverfassung* to a close on 12 August 1864 was not merely a

* 'Luck and Power'.

vote in the struggle over Schleswig-Holstein's future, but pointed far beyond the immediate occasion: 'Yet every step forward in the attainment of the necessary German power is, at the same time, a step forward for liberty. Conversely, the prolonged neglect of power—power that must be seen as indispensable for the attainment of nationhood—leads only further into bondage.'

For the Progressive left wing, regardless of whether they were 'Augustenburg' advocates like Schulze-Delitzsch or supporters of 'Greater Prussia' like Waldeck, all such second thoughts about the Bismarck administration were sacrilege. As long as the government ruled without a budget approved by the parliament, it was to be fought without any ifs and buts. In the spring and summer of 1864 the Berlin *Volkszeitung*, published by the democratic delegate Franz Duncker and close in spirit to the viewpoint of Schulze-Delitzsch, had declared as emphatically as the *National-Zeitung* against the partition of Schleswig-Holstein according to the nationality principle and on the basis of popular referendum. In contrast to the Progressive right-wing newspaper, however, the democratic *Volkszeitung* demanded that the citizens of the Elbe duchies be guaranteed the right to determine their own domestic affairs. Prussia was to impose nothing upon Schleswig-Holstein, but seek a mutual agreement on liberal terms that took the duchies' legitimate military, economic, and political interests into consideration.

'Unity and Liberty' was the title of the democratic newspaper's response to the *National-Zeitung* on 16 August:

> The German-national party has not a few enthusiasts who declare: 'We are prepared to sacrifice ten years of liberty for German unity!' We would certainly respect this statement, if such an enthusiast would only guarantee that we would indeed have our liberty in the eleventh year of unity . . . Ten years of reaction—during which, for the sake of the ideal of unity, we should cease all opposition—would, if they were at all possible, either fundamentally corrupt the basic character of the nation and render the people incapable of dealing with their liberty in the eleventh year, or else so intensify their craving for liberty that they would rather dissolve their unity than do without it any longer.

The conclusion to which the *Volkszeitung* came was no less unambiguous than that of the *National-Zeitung*: 'Germany's unity will only become possible through Germany's liberty.'

The Austro-Prussian condominium over Schleswig-Holstein proved to be so contentious that war seemed imminent in spring 1865. Under the leadership of Bavaria, the *Mittelstaaten*, themselves under pressure from the German National Union, the thirty-six representatives of the Delegate Congress, and the Schleswig-Holstein associations, urged the Federal Diet to recognize the rights of the duke of Augustenburg. Prussia responded with the 'February demands', which went even further than the conditions Bismarck had placed before Frederick VIII on 1 June 1864. Berlin now required full military authority over the Elbe duchies, the integration of their economies and transportation infrastructures with Prussia, and the cession of territories around the mouths of the planned North Sea–Baltic canal. On 6 April 1865 Austria, seeking to counter the Prussian challenge, concurred with a federal petition from the *Mittelstaaten* exhorting the two German great powers to grant the duke of Augustenburg his rights. When at the end of May King William I, with the support of the minister of war, Count Roon, and the chief of the general staff, Helmuth von Moltke, proclaimed his intention of annexing Schleswig-Holstein, the outbreak of war between Austria and Prussia seemed only a matter of days.

But it was Bismarck's more flexible approach that prevailed in the end. After lengthy negotiations in Bad Gastein from the end of July to mid-August 1865, the Prussian prime minister came to an agreement with Austria concerning the division and administration of the duchies: Holstein fell to Austria, Schleswig to Prussia; Kiel was to be a federal military port, though with Prussian administration and police; Prussia was to construct fortifications in the harbour and was granted the right to establish its own naval station in the city. The duchy of Lauenburg was ceded to the king of Prussia, who took it over in personal union.

The Gastein Convention of 14 August 1865—the event to which Bismarck owed his elevation to the title of count—was as much a provisional solution as the condominium it replaced, and explicitly so. Yet Bismarck considered the time not yet ripe for war with Austria, if indeed such a war was even necessary. There is much evidence to suggest that, after the defeat of Denmark, the Prussian prime minister was prepared to be satisfied for some time with a Hohenzollern hegemony north of the Main. Such a solution to the German problem might well have found the support of Austria, provided it received compensation in northern Italy. However, the German national movement would never, under any circumstances, have consented to such a division of Germany, a *grosspreussisch* alternative to *Kleindeutschland*, as it were. For that reason alone, the much-debated 'dualistic' solutions of 1864–5 never had a chance in the long term.[20]

As the 1865 crisis between Prussia and Austria was passing, the schism within Prussian liberalism was deepening. In April Theodor Mommsen, a historian from Garding in Schleswig-Holstein who had been elected to the Prussian House of Representatives in 1863, became the first right-wing Progressive parliamentarian to call for the complete annexation of Schleswig-Holstein. The duchies' right to self-determination was in and of itself perfectly legitimate, Mommsen explained in a circular letter to the delegates of the city of Halle and the Saale district, 'but it is not an absolute right. It is limited by the general interests of the German nation. For there is no distinct people in Schleswig-Holstein, only Germans, and when the latter speak, the former must obey.' Although Prussia, which Mommsen considered a sort of trustee of the German nation, was only justified in demanding partial—that is, military and maritime—integration of the duchies, the people of Schleswig-Holstein were well advised to assent to complete annexation.

Mommsen nonetheless rejected the naval bill presented to the parliament in April 1865 requesting approval of funds for the construction projects in the Kiel harbour.

It is one thing to approve of the policy pursued by the government in this matter. It is a completely different thing to approve the funds for its completion by the present ministry. Since the budgetary competence of the parliament has been suspended by the administration, it has been completely suspended, even in cases where the administration and the government materially agree.

In the debate conducted over the government's naval bill in the lower chamber at the beginning of July 1865, the Progressive delegate Otto Michaelis, economics editor of the *National-Zeitung*, made a remarkable connection between domestic and foreign policy. If Prussia were to set its sights on 'great goals', then the end of non-constitutional rule would soon sound.

If, however, we ourselves begin . . . to pursue the policies of a small state; if we, for whatever reason, fail to seize the banner of Prussia and Germany against Austria, then things will go downhill. We will become increasingly habituated to the actions and considerations of small statehood, and one day we will find ourselves once again under the hegemony of Austria. We will discover that the population of Prussia, without an ideal goal, has lost the energy necessary to fight the constitutional conflict with us to the end.

The *National-Zeitung*, of the same mind as Michaelis and Mommsen, came at this same time to the realization that, even in the worst of times, Prussia had 'always been the champion of a fundamentally inconsistent reaction, a reaction at odds with the highest purposes of the state, whereas the reaction sponsored by Austria is fundamentally consistent, since its very existence and cohesion rests upon it.' At the beginning of August 1865, the liberal paper gave its *grosspreussisch* manifesto a pointed conclusion: 'History is also familiar with peoples and states that have become more free by growing larger.' The roots of bondage lay in the princes' alliance of 1815. The individual states could not gain liberty by their own initiative; a German National Assembly was necessary. 'Therefore, from unity to liberty: that is the way and the means of our party.'

The democratic *Volkszeitung* responded in ironic tones that the *National-Zeitung* was endeavouring 'to present the goddess of liberty a debenture, due on the day of German unity'. But the heedlessness prevailing at the creation of Germany unity would also dig the grave of liberty. 'Unity through blood and iron, even if it were possible, would eradicate the last traces of liberty.'

All liberal factions protested against the Gastein agreement, though not all for the same reasons. The Augustenburg party deplored the disregard for Schleswig-Holstein's right to self-determination. The German Delegate Congress, convening on 1 October in Frankfurt, considered the entire lawful order and public security in Germany fundamentally violated by Austria's and Prussia's 'breach of the law'. According to a statement by the German National Union from the end of October, Schleswig-Holstein had been liberated from arbitrary Danish rule only to be 'raped' by the German Confederation. Even the Prussian advocates of annexation found fault with the convention. The *National-Zeitung* complained that Prussia's 'ineradicable entitlement to both Holstein and Schleswig' was not reflected in the agreement. 'No, this treaty is not the work we have in mind; this solution has nothing in common with our just demands.'

Only a few members of the Prussian parliamentary left took part in the Delegate Congress in Frankfurt. The right wing of the Progressive Party did not attend at all, wishing to pre-emptively refute the expected proclamations of an anti-Prussian 'particularism'. Mommsen and Twesten justified this decision in open letters to the president of the Delegate Congress: 'The bankruptcy of particularism', wrote Mommsen,

> must reveal itself to each and every German with far more grievous blows before a majority of the population of the middle and smaller powers will cease only to be inspired by a nebulous idea of German unity, a unity reserved for some distant future, and will stop making every excuse—at the present moment, for example, by draping their opposition to Prussia's burgeoning power in the more fashionable garments of opposition to Herr Bismarck's carryings-on—every excuse to run away from the beginnings of this unification, wherever they present themselves in great earnest, and perhaps under unpleasant and onerous conditions.

Twesten's language was even sharper. The majority of the Prussian House of Representatives had to recognize not only the right of the German people to self-determination, but also 'the power interests of our state'. Therefore, 'every alternative' was preferable to a 'defeat of the Prussian state'. The liberal response from the *Mittelstaaten*, as well as from Prussia itself, was no less biting. A declaration by the Westphalian entrepreneur Friedrich Harkort, a member of the parliamentary Left Centre, drew the greatest attention. Harkort recognized Schleswig-Holstein's right to self-determination and emphasized his point with Kant's maxim: 'To disregard another's right to self-determination is to undermine one's own liberty.'

Like the controversy over the armistice of Malmö seventeen years earlier, the Schleswig-Holstein crisis caused a deep rift in the liberal party. And in both cases, for the Prussian constitutional conflict no less than for the Revolution of 1848, the struggle over the Elbe duchies represented a turning point. In 1848 the Paulskirche had been unable to force the Prussian government to continue the war against Denmark, thus revealing the powerlessness of the liberal movement in the face of the traditional political authorities. Likewise, in 1864 the liberals did not succeed in compelling the German great powers to wage the *particular* war against Denmark *they* considered necessary, the war for the self-determination of Schleswig-Holstein. Afterwards, they had to come to terms with a victory over Denmark that revealed the unbroken power of the historical state. In both cases, in 1848 as well as in 1864, the Schleswig-Holstein question led to a 'moment of truth', to which 'left' and 'right' liberals reacted in opposite ways. Whether humiliating defeat as in 1848 or triumphant victory as in 1864, the war with Denmark resulted in a polarization within the liberal movement.[21]

In 1864–5 this crisis was not confined to Prussian liberalism. After the victory over Denmark, the extreme right wing of the National Union under the Göttingen attorney Johannes Miquel, who had been a supporter of Marx in 1848, went over to the annexationist line of Mommsen and Twesten, while most democrats withdrew from the association after 1865. The adamantly *grossdeutsch* democrats, the greater part of whom belonged neither to the National nor to the Reform Union, remained hostile to Prussia. When in April 1864 the *Volkszeitung* maintained that Prussia needed only a firm national program to assume the leadership of Germany, the Stuttgart *Beobachter*, the mouthpiece of the Württemberg left, responded: 'Derided, beaten, and kicked as these Prussians are, they nonetheless want to conquer Germany. Why don't you conquer your own liberty instead? But if you are slaves, do not demand that others share your lot!'

The *Beobachter* was speaking for the radically federalist ('particularist' in the view of their opponents) faction of the democratic movement in the smaller and medium-sized German states when it announced on 10 February 1864 that wherever nationality and liberty came into conflict, one must choose liberty. The slogan that Germany's future lay in a 'confederation of free states, a German *Eidgenossenschaft*', derived from the same way of thinking, influenced by the philosophy of natural law. When Ludwig Pfau, one of leaders of the Württemberg left in both parliament and press, sharply rejected the idea of a Prussian empire in an article in the *Beobachter* at the end of April 1864, his thoughts, paraphrasing the elder Cato, proceeded with a kind of inner logic from the idea of a confederation: 'Without the dissolution of Prussia into its constituent peoples, it will be absolutely impossible to form a unified and free Germany. *Ceterum censeo Borussiam esse delendam* ['Furthermore I think Prussia must be destroyed'(H.A.W.)].'

The declarations of the *Beobachter* in spring 1864 were a kind of platform, the founding documents of the 'People's party' that began at that time to detach itself from the Württemberg Progressive Party, formed at the end of 1859. The political mobilization brought about by the Schleswig-Holstein associations redounded to the benefit of the democrats, who took advantage of the widespread German anger at the Prussian and Austrian disregard for Schleswig-Holstein's right to self-determination. The old *Vormärz* idea of the 'Trias'—that the 'third Germany' of the smaller and medium-sized states represented the authentic nation—was once again revived in the language of the democratic movement, a language that found fertile ground especially among the petty bourgeoisie. With this vision, the democrats challenged moderate Württemberg liberals—men like the Stuttgart attorney Julius Hölder—who, despite their open criticism of the Bismarck administration, held fast to the belief that Germany could not be united without or against the will of Prussia. The views of the moderates, who exercised strong influence over the second chamber, were echoed by the industrialists and the educated bourgeoisie, though not yet by the broad masses. In Württemberg (and not only there), a politician could win considerable popularity by attacking the two German great powers, especially if he criticized Prussia more than Austria.[22]

Württemberg was the starting point of the German democratic movement, which in 1865 began to organize itself throughout Germany. The driving forces were not, however, natives of Württemberg, but nationalist democrats from other south-west German states, first and foremost the literary historian Ludwig Eckardt from Baden and the physician and author of the much-read materialist study *Kraft und Stoff*,* Ludwig Büchner from Hesse-Darmstadt. It was in Darmstadt that the Democratic People's Party (*Demokratische Volkspartei*) was officially founded in September 1865—against considerable resistance from the Württemberg democrats, who considered the new party insufficiently federalist in outlook.

Eckardt and Büchner were the 'liberal' democrats who made the greatest effort to include the workers in the People's Party. Their efforts were rebuffed by the General German Workers' Association, which had been plagued by leadership crises ever since its founder, Lassalle, had died in August 1864 from wounds incurred in a duel. The rival Union of German Workers' Associations (*Verband Deutscher Arbeitervereine*, founded in 1863 with the substantial participation of Leopold Sonnemann, owner and editor of the *Neue Frankfurter Zeitung*), on the other hand, joined the democratic movement at its Stuttgart convention in September 1865. One of the delegates at this congress was the man who shortly thereafter would advance to become the leader of the German workers' movement: August Bebel, a turner from Cologne, at that time president of the workers' education association in Leipzig.[23]

The founding of the People's Party seemed to herald a shift to the left, away from the alliance between liberals and democrats and towards a greater left transcending class boundaries; away from endeavours to reach a compromise with the government and towards a resolutely oppositional course; away from realpolitik and towards a politics of principle. However, the 'third Germany' also saw developments tending in the opposite direction at the same time, proceeding primarily from Baden. In Karlsruhe, the liberals had been in power since 1860–1. Under August Lamey as minister of the interior and Franz von Roggenbach as foreign minister, the cabinet reformed the judiciary and bureaucracy, introduced freedom of trade in 1862 (the same year as Württemberg, following Saxony the year before), and removed the school system from the controlling influence of the church. The latter reform incited a bitter conflict with the ecclesiastic establishment that lasted years and, while strengthening the cohesion of the liberal party, also subjected it to growing pressure from a popular religious movement.

In the first half of the 1860s, liberal Baden became the political antipode to authoritarian Prussia and, paradoxical though it seems, the latter's partner of choice among the southern German *Mittelstaaten*. On the issue of free trade, and thus on the basic questions of customs union policy, the grand duchy and the Hohenzollern state saw eye to eye. Yet the ruling liberals of Baden advocated

* Büchner, *Force and Matter*.

German unity under Prussian leadership not merely for economic, but also for foreign policy reasons. The geographic proximity to France created a need for security best served by cooperation with Prussia. When it finally came to conflict between the two German great powers, the decision to join the presidential power of the German Confederation was, of all the middle powers, the most difficult for Baden.

Among the governments of the other *Mittelstaaten*, sympathy for Prussia was hardly to be found. Although Saxony acted in concert with the north German hegemon on trade policy, in questions of 'grand politics' the foreign minister, Friedrich von Beust, tended to side more with Vienna than Berlin. The Bavarian government, led (since December 1864) by Ludwig von der Pfordten, a moderate *grossdeutsch* liberal, wished to avoid a break with Austria at all costs. The same was true of the foreign minister of Württemberg, Karl von Varnbüler. Likewise, most of the other *Mittelstaaten* had as yet given no grounds for the assumption that they would, if necessary, support Prussia against Austria. Thus the Hohenzollern state was forced to conclude that it would have the majority of the Confederation members against it in any war with the Habsburg empire. This was the state of things, as both powers saw it, at the beginning of 1866, when the conflict over Schleswig-Holstein entered a new phase.[24]

The Gastein convention already contained sufficient grounds for dispute. The mere fact that Prussia had to pass through Austrian-administered Holstein in order to reach Schleswig, its own protectorate, caused great difficulties. The Austrian governor in Holstein was manifestly uninterested in a good relationship with Prussia; otherwise he would not have given the impression that he approved of the pro-Augustenburg agitation in the south of the Elbe duchies. The moment of crisis came at a demonstration in Altona on 23 January 1866, which demanded the convention of an assembly of all the estates in the duchies. Berlin protested, Vienna refused to tolerate any Prussian interference in the administration of Holstein, and the cooperation between the two powers came to an end.

From that moment, politicians and military leaders in both Prussia and Austria began to prepare for war. Prussia had good reason to hope that Russia would not attack it from the rear in case of armed conflict with Austria. The relationship between Vienna and St Petersburg had not significantly improved since the Crimean War, whereas the understanding between Russia and Prussia could generally be considered good—especially since Bismarck, by means of the 'Alvensleben Convention', had come to the aid of the tzar in suppressing a new Polish rebellion at the beginning of 1863. Likewise with the Bonapartist regime: Prussia could count on France not supporting Austria as long as the latter held Venetia. With the Kingdom of Italy, which sought to liberate this territory from Habsburg control, Prussia concluded a secret offensive and defensive alliance of three months' duration on 8 April 1866. This treaty violated the current statutes of the German Confederation, as did the secret Franco-Austrian treaty of 12 June 1866, with which Vienna assured itself of French neutrality in the event of war with Prussia. This assurance came at a high price: if Austria was victorious in Germany, Venetia was to be given up; in the event of victory in Italy, the pre-war status quo was to be preserved. In addition, Vienna agreed to the transformation of Prussia's Rhenish provinces into a new state, formally independent, but de facto dependent on France.

The two German great powers were also active within Germany itself. In mid-February Bismarck attempted to gain the support of the Bavarian foreign minister, Ludwig von der Pfordten, for a conjoint Prussian–Bavarian initiative in the Federal Diet calling for the establishment of a German parliament to be elected by general, equal, and direct suffrage, a voting system the Prussian prime minister was convinced would actually strengthen the old powers. 'Direct elections and general suffrage, however, I consider greater guarantors of a conservative outlook than any artificial voting law calculated to win ready-made majorities.' Yet since the Bavarian foreign minister wanted to preserve his country's place at the head of the 'Trias' as mediator between the two German great powers, he rejected a common initiative.

The result was that Prussia was compelled to present its constitutional reform motion alone to the Federal Diet, which it did on 9 April 1866. Bismarck's hope that his demand for a German parliament and democratic suffrage would win public opinion for Prussia went unfulfilled. Both within and without the Hohenzollern state, the verdict was nearly unanimous: the Prussian government ought first to look to the constitutional and parliamentary process inside its own state before stepping onto the German stage with progressive sounding language that, in the mouth of Otto von Bismarck, made rather a caesarist, Bonapartist impression.

Even among the right wing of the Progressive Party, Bismarck's new course met with little approbation. To be sure, the *National-Zeitung* began at the beginning of April to prepare its readership for the possibility of war between Prussia and Austria. Such a war, it wrote, must not perforce be called a 'fratricidal war' simply because both states belong to the German Confederation. Prussia and Austria only ever stood together in times of greatest peril, 'in conditions, under which two completely different and heterogeneous peoples likewise tend to cooperate'. Thus it would be a mistake to believe that Prussia 'is bound with the holy bonds of kinship and political community' to the Austrian polity in its present constitutional form. Nevertheless, the Berlin newspaper did not trust the Bismarck ministry, at odds with the Prussian parliament, to gain the sympathy of the rest of Germany, without which no war could waged against Austria.

Bismarck's constitutional reform proposal was commented on by the *National-Zeitung* with a rhetorical question: 'General and equal suffrage, direct elections, a German parliament—these are, for us, great and worthy goals. But what concern are they of Counts Bismarck and Eulenburg? What concern are they of the Federal Diet?' Karl Twesten was of the same opinion. 'Bismarck is not the man who can rule with a true parliament,' the liberal politician announced on 17 April in a speech before the delegates and primary electors of the first Berlin electoral district. 'German unification can only be brought about under Prussian leadership, but this leadership must be in liberal hands.'

Notwithstanding the failure of its spring diplomatic offensive, Prussia repeated the motion for Confederation reform on 10 June 1866. Yet despite the greater subtlety and more polished form of the proposal, it found even less support this time. Immediately before introducing the measure in the Federal Diet, Prussia had itself flagrantly violated Confederation statutes. On 7 June Prussian troops had entered Holstein. The occupation of the duchy was Berlin's response to a spectacular move by Vienna on 1 June: the Austrian governor of Holstein was ordered to convene an assembly of the estates, and Austria formally requested that the Federal Diet decide the issue of the Elbe duchies' future, since all efforts to come to an understanding with Prussia had come to naught. This manoeuvre breached the Gastein convention, yet for that very reason was calculated to gain Austria a great deal of support in the 'third Germany'.

On 9 June Austria countered the Prussian deployment in Holstein with a petition to mobilize the federal army (excluding the Prussian contingents). Although Prussia rejected the motion as contrary to federal law, the vote nevertheless took place on 14 June. All the *Mittelstaaten* approved the motion, with one exception: Baden first abstained, then gave in to public pressure shortly thereafter and went over to the side of Austria. A few of the smaller states sided with Prussia against the mobilization, including Brunswick and the two grand duchies of Mecklenburg. Prussia itself did not participate in the vote, but responded by declaring that the decision rendered the Confederation accord null and void.

Since both Prussia and Austria had already commenced mobilization in April, the military operations needed no further preparation. On 16 June, after the expiration of ultimata that had gone out to the governments in Dresden, Hanover, and Kassel two days before, Prussian troops marched into Saxony, Hanover, and Electoral Hesse. On 20 June Italy declared war on Austria. Prussia followed suit the next day, immediately sending troops across the border into Bohemia.[25]

Austrian liberals saw the war as an act of deliverance. 'That for which Austria is now to strike a blow', wrote the Vienna *Neue Freie Presse* on 19 June in a commentary to the imperial declaration of war, 'is the idea of liberty in the federation; that against which its blows are aimed is detestable caesarism, the plague of our times, poisoning all that is right and lawful.' The right wing of Prussian liberalism saw the situation in diametrically opposite terms. When the war began, the *National-Zeitung* had no further recourse to its earlier position that the domestic deficiencies of the Bismarck ministry would prevent the successful prosecution of an Austrian war. The north German population, the Berlin paper wrote on 30 June, would doubtless decide that the highest national purposes were being defended in the Prussian ranks.

Even if the ministry currently at the helm is not one friendly to the people, nonetheless, in her confrontation with Austria, Prussia represents the cause of German liberty, just like the stubborn Lutherans and Reformed represented and rescued the freedom of the spirit during the Thirty Years War.

On the same day, the Berlin city attorney, Duncker, speaking before the delegates of that city's first electoral district, employed the same rhetoric of a 'clash of cultures': if the war should lead to a national parliament, he declared, it would be a victory for constitutional liberty. 'In a war against Austria, a Prussian victory surely means the victory of civil and religious liberty. It means the preservation of northern Germany—in spiritual terms from the Jesuits, in material terms from financial and economic ruin.'

Southern German Catholics and democrats naturally had a different attitude. In Catholic upper Swabia, as Adolf Rapp wrote in his 1910 study *Die Württemberger und die nationale Frage*,* the people were galvanized by the feeling that their church, too, was under attack in the war.

The Little Germany party had themselves given cause for this reaction. How often could it be heard from them that a Protestant Germany was the goal and that Austria must abide by the Peace of Westphalia, by means of which it had explicitly excluded itself from Germany. The Catholic clergy did not fail to point this out to their communities.

In the capital of Württemberg, on the other hand, Protestant democrats set the tone, which was no less pugnacious: 'Give the troops the black, red, and gold!' demanded the *Beobachter* (24 June), the newspaper of the People's Party, which in the prior months had advocated a policy of armed neutrality in the 'third Germany' in the case of a 'fratricidal war' between Austria and Prussia. According to the mouthpiece of the Swabian democrats, the German colours would make an overwhelming impression upon the enemy, the Prussian 'separatists': 'That the German banner must triumph on German soil—this realization will strike the spiked helmets like a flash of lightning, and the irresistible force of the idea will once again make itself manifest in history.'

Things turned out much differently. On 3 July, the Prussians inflicted a decisive defeat on the Austrian army at Königgrätz in Bohemia. The allies of the Habsburg empire—those that had intervened in the conflict (Baden was able to avoid doing so at the last minute)—were defeated in short measure in a number of lesser battles. Even prior to Königgrätz, Emperor Francis Joseph, despite the fact that his troops were victorious in the Italian theatre, had offered to cede Venetia to France and requested Napoleon III's arbitration with Italy, a step that immediately cost Austria the sympathy of the 'third Germany' and encouraged the latter's readiness to cooperate with Prussia in mutual defence against the expansionist intentions of France. On 5 July the French emperor agreed to Francis Joseph's request, but extended the mediation to include Prussia.

* Rapp, *The National Question in Württemberg.*

Since Napoleon promised to accept an increase in Prussian power north of the Main, Bismarck acquiesced. He was also prepared, in the interest of the European balance of power (such as Napoleon understood it), to accede to a number of French demands, including the independence of a federation of southern German states, the preservation of Austria's territorial integrity excluding Venetia, a referendum in northern Schleswig, and the preservation of Saxony. France's demand for the cession of left Rhenish territory, however, met with Bismarck's staunch rejection. Instead, he directed Napoleon to Luxembourg, which was tied to the Netherlands in personal union, and to Belgium. Yet for France to go in this direction meant conflict with Britain.

The Prussian prime minister also had to skirmish with his own king in the weeks following Königgrätz. William I wanted to impose harsh peace terms on Austria. His leading minister, in contrast, sought with mild terms to create the basis for future cooperation. It was Bismarck who prevailed in the end. On 21 July Prussia and Austria agreed to a provisional ceasefire of five days' duration. On 26 July the 'preliminary peace' was signed in Nikolsburg, becoming effective two days later. This agreement accorded with the assurances the Prussian prime minister had already given to Napoleon's envoy, Vincent Benedetti. Bismarck managed to deter the convention of a European peace conference, such as Russia wanted. The final peace treaty could thus be concluded with little delay, and was signed on 23 August in Prague.

The Habsburg empire acquiesced in the dissolution of the German Confederation and in the reshaping of Germany without the participation of Austria. Vienna recognized the planned North German Confederation, which included Prussia and fifteen northern German states (seventeen after the two duchies of Mecklenburg joined on 21 August). It also recognized the confederation of southern German states, designed to have an independent international existence, but permitted to have closer ties with the North German Confederation. The southern alliance, however, ultimately came to nothing. Article V of the peace treaty granted the inhabitants of northern Schleswig the right to join Denmark, provided that they expressed this wish in an open referendum.

The victorious state grew through annexation. Hanover, Electoral Hesse, Nassau, and the Free City of Frankfurt, all of which had stood with Austria in the war, were integrated into Prussia, along with Schleswig-Holstein. Saxony became a member of the North German Confederation, as did Hesse-Darmstadt, though only with its territory situated north of the Main. With the southern German states Prussia concluded not only the official peace treaties, but also secret defensive alliances. These stipulated that, in the case of war, the undersigned would place their armies under Prussian supreme command and organize them according to the Prussian model. Through these agreements, northern and southern Germany became more closely linked than they had been before. Nonetheless, the German war did not produce a German national state, but rather a new kind of

German dualism, now between Greater Prussia on the one hand and southern Germany on the other. Many contemporaries trusted in the finality of the border along the Main, but most of them did not, though how and when it would be set aside was uncertain. Only one thing could be ruled out with near-total certainty: that the Germans would be able to solve the German question, which was still very much open, with as little outside intervention as the 1866 war had occasioned.[26]

BISMARCK'S 1866 'REVOLUTION FROM ABOVE'

The German war of 1866 was *not* a civil war. It was a war between German states, fought by regular armies, not by guerrillas or irregulars fighting in the streets. The Prussians and Austrians who met at Königgrätz were fighting for king and country; they fought against enemy soldiers, not against German brothers. The situation of the soldiers from the *Mittelstaaten* who entered the war was very little different. In the public opinion of the 'third Germany', however, the feeling was widespread, among *kleindeutsch* and *grossdeutsch* advocates alike, that the war was a 'war between brothers' that might easily lead to the partition of Germany. In the smaller and middle powers, state patriotism and German patriotism blended together less problematically than in Prussia—not to mention in Austria, which had been growing apart from Germany for centuries.

Regardless of what politicians, publicists, and pastors wrote and said, the conflict was also not a religious war. Rather, religion had given rise to ideology, and to a far greater extent on the Protestant and liberal side than among Catholics and conservatives. The ideologization of religion was highly effective. When Prussian liberals invoked the legacy of the Reformation, when they went so far as to place the war with Austria in a 'Schmalkaldic' perspective or in relation to the Thirty Years War, they were not making arbitrary comparisons, but calculated arguments. They were appealing to one of the fundamental existential and emotional factors of Prussian identity, but which at the same time transcended Prussia. The Evangelical 'life-feeling' embraced a particular conception of Germany, one that excluded another, no less particular conception—the Catholic idea of Germany, which was oriented towards the old Reich and its succession in Austria.

The multinational Habsburg empire had been far less 'German' than the Hohenzollern state for a long time. When Count Belcredi, the leader of the Vienna government since 1865, suspended the February patent, the brief 'German' and liberal interlude of the Schmerling era was at an end. Austria began to seek a compromise with Hungary, leading in December 1867 to the establishment of Austria-Hungary as an 'imperial and royal' (*kaiserlich und königlich*) double monarchy. A compromise with Prussia, on the other hand, had never stood on the agenda. As powerful as Prussia had become after 1815, Austria refused to recognize its equal status until the end of the German Confederation. However the course of German history might have run if Vienna had not clung so adamantly to its role as presidential power and agreed to an authentic reform of the German Confederation, Austria's policy vis-à-vis Prussia must be considered one of the significant factors contributing to the war of 1866—indeed, one of its immediate causes. In Vienna no less than in Berlin, there was a 'war party' in 1865–6 that clamoured for the Gordian knot of German dualism to be cut through with the sword.

A German national state could not be formed with Austria. *Grossdeutschland* would have meant the end of the Austrian empire. Nor could a national state have arisen from any conceivable renovation of the German Confederation. Consequently, the German national movement was not to be satisfied with Confederation reform. The nationalists wanted both unity and liberty. Unity was only possible with Prussia—that was one of the lessons of the German war. In the *Mittelstaaten*, liberty was possible without German unity, but for the liberals in these countries, to renounce the cause of unity was unthinkable, for both ideological and material reasons. By definition, therefore, an arrangement with Prussia was going to be necessary.

In Baden, a number of liberals had already come to this conclusion before 1866. After Königgrätz, this group prevailed. Under the new government, led by Karl Mathy, the grand duchy consolidated its status as Prussia's closest ally south of the Main. In Württemberg moderate liberals, led by Julius Hölder, founded the German Party (*Deutsche Partei*) in August 1866, thereby drawing a clear line of separation between Prussia-friendly 'realists' and democratic 'particularists'. In Bavaria, the liberal Progressive Party declared for the first time its unanimous support of the *kleindeutsch* solution. In an announcement on 28 August, the Progressive delegates of the second chamber demanded the establishment of a close federation with Prussia, the political enlargement of the German Customs Union, and Bavaria's earliest possible entry into the North German Confederation. Foreign intervention was, from now on, to be met collectively. 'Should a foreign power threaten German territory, we demand that Bavaria immediately join the leading northern German power for the purpose of common defence under Prussian leadership.'

The man who took over leadership of the Bavarian government at the end of 1866, Prince Chlodwig zu Hohenlohe-Schillingsfürst, did not think much differently, although he expressed himself more cautiously in public. 'I look upon the present catastrophe with great peace of mind,' wrote the Prussia-friendly, liberal-conservative Catholic on 13 July 1866, ten days after Königgrätz, in his journal.

It was unavoidable. The antagonism between Prussia and Austria had to be dealt with and settled, and it was better to do it now than ten years hence. But the catastrophe is also an occasion for healing, for it clears out much that is rotten in Germany and, to the small and middle states especially, demonstrates very clearly *ad hominem* ['very personally' (H.A.W.)] their nullity and paltriness. This is a misfortune for the dynasties, I admit, but a boon for the German people.[27]

Prussian liberals had long entertained doubts that liberty was at all possible without unity. The war with Denmark strengthened those doubts, and the war with Austria changed them into certainties, at least on the right wing of the Progressive Party. The new attitude resembled an insight of Lorenz von Stein in 1852: not in the Prussian military state, but only in the German national state would liberty find her true home.

Thus seen, the Prussian annexations in northern Germany were virtually an anticipation of the liberty of all Germany. To be sure, the prospect of integration with Prussia was greeted with 'antipathy to the Prussian character, a feeling that has, unfortunately, been fed and amplified by the present administration, and with fears that greater burdens will have to be borne,' conceded the *National-Zeitung on* 17 July, four days before the signing of the ceasefire.

However, the stringent, disagreeable bureaucratic-military system that tends to take over wherever political necessity has created a strong centralization, as well as the disproportionately large military expenditures, will all be mitigated and alleviated as soon as a greater material basis renders the unnatural exertion of energies superfluous, and when the integration of new living elements overcomes the old Prussian one-sidedness.

The liberal Berlin newspaper celebrated the 'complete elimination of Austria from Germany' as a great event.

Only with this step have the Middle Ages and the feudalism of our nation been overcome and left behind, finally and completely. By separating ourselves from the House of Habsburg, which could not divest itself of the ideas and pretensions of the Roman-German empire—only through this separation are we now able to become an independent nation and establish a German national state. We can be more German than our ancestors were permitted to be.

To see only political advantage in the break with Austria was to overlook the cultural loss that accompanied it. The viewpoint of the victors—among whom many Prussian liberals counted themselves—was historically conditioned. But the Germans defeated in 1866 could appeal to history with equal justification. Foremost among these were the German Catholics, at least those who were not in the liberal camp. In the Prussian-led Germany now emerging, Catholics were definitely a minority. This had never been the case in the old Reich and during the era of the German Confederation, and the unfamiliarity of the experience was accompanied by feelings of alienation and existential threat.

The words of one Catholic writer offer a telling counterpoint to the *klein-deutsch* credo of the Prussian liberals. Edmund Jörg, editor of the *Historisch-politische Blätter für das katholische Deutschland* since 1852 and, after 1866, one of the leaders of the Bavarian Patriots' Party, wrote that the breaking-up of the German

Confederation heralded 'a destruction of the political basis and traditional living conditions' of the German people

> such as has not been seen in a thousand years. The new way has utterly triumphed over the old. But the old way does not date merely from 1815; it goes all the way back to Charlemagne. The idea of the Reich has fallen and been buried. If the German people are ever again united in an empire, then it will be an empire that can no longer look back upon a thousand-year history, but only a history of three hundred years.

The political conclusions of Jörg's article, which bears the date 13 August 1866, were nonetheless pointedly realistic:

> We do not wish, in our misfortune, to throw ourselves away on Prussia in a cowardly and contemptible manner. Nor, however, must we forget for a single moment that it is not France on whom our political existence depends and to whom we are now tied in political community, but rather the one great power that may still call itself 'German'.

For the bishop of Mainz, Wilhelm Emanuel von Ketteler, former member of the German National Assembly, Austria's departure from Germany was, as he wrote to Emperor Francis Joseph on 28 August 1866, 'more painful than words can express. Thus is fulfilled, at least for the time being, the task that has been the leading inspiration of all Prussian statesmen since Frederick the Great. Now everything is destroyed that could still remind us of the German Reich of old.'

A few months later, the bishop turned his gaze to the future. In *Deutschland nach dem Krieg von 1866*,* which appeared in 1867, he invoked Heinrich von Gagern's distinction between a 'narrower' and a 'broader federation'. As painful as it was to renounce the 'unification of the entire German Fatherland', nonetheless the task at hand necessitated conscious reflection upon the 'force of reality' and the 'disconcerting world situation'. 'We need a swift resolution to the German question, and the only way that seems to present itself at the moment is [for the southern states] to join the northern federation and to cultivate a close alliance with Austria.' For it must not be forgotten that the coming 'new federation', Germany unified under Prussian leadership,

> only forms one, albeit the largest part of Germany, and that another large part belongs to Austria. These two parts of the one German nation must not look upon one other as strangers or entertain merely diplomatic relations with each other as foreign peoples, but must found such a indissoluble alliance as two parts of the same nation by right and necessity of nature ought to do.[28]

Among the 'losers' of 1866 were also conservative legitimists of the Lutheran faith, including supporters of the Hanover Guelfs like the *grossdeutsch* historian and publicist Onno Klopp from East Frisia, who followed his dethroned king to Austria in 1866, where he converted to Catholicism seven years later. In Prussia Ernst

* Ketteler, *Germany after the War of 1866.*

Ludwig von Gerlach, the 'Rundschauer'* of the *Kreuz-Zeitung* and one-time mentor of Bismarck, led a small faction of old-conservative critics adamantly opposed to the 'Bonapartist' policies of the prime minister. In May 1866 Gerlach had warned against a 'fundamentally destructive war' between Prussia and Austria. 'It would be a war that would injure Germany, and especially Prussia and Austria, in their vital organs, with perhaps fatal consequences, no matter who emerges the victor.' In the late summer, Gerlach spoke out against the removal of the ruling dynasties in Hanover, Electoral Hesse, and Nassau, against the annexations of their territories, and against Bismarck's policies as a whole. 'Mere violence cannot be the foundation of legitimate right'; 'the planned north German federal parliament means basically a victory for democracy'; 'the beneficiary of the "*tearing apart* and *weakening* of Germany" is none other than Napoleon III himself.' In the ensuing period, Gerlach drew closer to political Catholicism. At the beginning of 1873, he was elected to the Prussian House of Representatives as a delegate for the Catholic Centre, albeit without converting to Catholicism.

Finally, 1866 also meant a defeat for the democrats. In Prussia this was also the case for the representatives of the bourgeois left who approved of the annexations, like Waldeck and now also Schulze-Delitzsch. They remained opponents of Bismarck and thus in the same 'camp' as Franz Duncker, the publisher of the *Volkszeitung*, and Johann Jacoby, who, in the opening debate of the newly elected House of Representatives on 23 August 1866, declared unity without freedom to be the 'unity of slaves', and compared Bismarck to Napoleon III. 'Only in the service of right and of liberty may the banner of the national principle be raised. In the hands of a Louis Napoleon or one of his ilk, it only serves to confound and destroy the peoples.'

The political sentiments of the Württemberg democrats were given eloquent expression by the delegate August Österlen at a public gathering in Schwäbisch Hall on 9 September 1866. 'The victory of violence', declared the lawyer from Stuttgart, 'makes a deplorably strong impression on those whose character is less firm. We, however, will not give up our principles, which are as eternal as the stars. The power that has cast down thrones will not be able to cast down our principles.'

This statement would also have been endorsed by August Bebel and his friend Wilhelm Liebknecht in Leipzig—who were not, however, in agreement with the particularism of the Württemberg People's Party, which had thus far stood in the way of a truly national organization of German democrats. On 19 August 1866 Bebel and Liebknecht inaugurated in Chemnitz a new democratic party, summarizing its national aspirations in the following words: 'The unity of Germany in a democratic form of government. No inherited central authority, no Little Germany under Prussian hegemony, no Prussia expanded through annexations, no Greater Germany under the aegis of Austria.'

This was nothing other that the resurrection of the anti-dynastic pan-Germanism of the 1848 republican left. The Saxon People's Party consciously oriented itself

* [Translator's note: *Rundschauer*: 'one who looks around', 'observer'. The title of Gerlach's column in the *Kreuz-Zeitung* was the 'Rundshau'.]

toward the democratic middle and working classes, thus renouncing a 'proletarian' image. This distinguished it in two ways from the General German Workers' Association, which had founded a new party in its own turn, the Social Democratic Party of Germany (*Sozialdemokratische Partei Deutschlands*), at the end of December 1866. The followers of Lassalle, led after 1867 by the Frankfurt lawyer and writer Johann Baptist von Schweitzer, were, on the one hand, firmly *kleindeutsch* in outlook. On the other hand, they consciously sought to organize only the working classes, distancing themselves from all varieties of bourgeois liberalism.[29]

Marx and Engels had been no less *grossdeutsch* and anti-Prussian during the German war than Bebel and Liebknecht. After Königgrätz, however, they immediately accommodated to the new reality. The most important thing for both was that the proletarian revolution could profit from the suppression of German particularism. 'In my view, we simply have no other choice', wrote Engels from Manchester on 25 July 1866 to Marx in London, 'than to accept the fact, without countenancing it, and then to exploit as well as we can the better opportunities that must now present themselves for the *national* organization and unification of the German proletariat.'

The tactical manoeuvre with the principle of general suffrage in April 1866 had already revealed Bismarck to be an able pupil of Napoleon III. For Engels, this was a confirmation of his argument that Bonapartism was 'the true religion of the modern bourgeoisie'.

> It is becoming ever clearer to me that the bourgeoisie doesn't have what it takes to rule directly, and that therefore a Bonapartist demi-dictatorship is the normal form of government wherever there is no oligarchy—as there is here in England—to take upon itself the well-compensated task of leading state and society in the interests of the bourgeoisie. This dictatorship enforces the great material interests of the bourgeoisie even against the bourgeoisie itself, but allows it no part in actual rule. On the other hand, however, it is itself compelled to adopt these material interests of the bourgeoisie against its own will. Thus we now have monsieur Bismarck, who has adopted the platform of the National Union.

Nearly two decades later, Engels would go so far as to ascribe revolutionary significance to Bismarck's 1866 policies. As he wrote to August Bebel in November 1884, 1866

> was a complete revolution. Just as Prussia only amounted to anything through treason and war against the German Reich, in alliance with foreign powers (1740, 1756, 1795), thus it has brought about the German-Prussian Reich by violent overthrow of the German Confederation and civil war . . . After the victory, it brought down *three thrones 'by the grace of God'* and annexed their territories, along with that of the once Free City of Frankfurt. If that wasn't revolutionary, then I don't know what the word means.

With regard to Bismarck and his policies, many contemporaries were already speaking of 'revolution' and 'revolution from above' in 1866. 'If revolution must be, then we would rather make it than suffer it,' wrote Bismarck himself on 11 August 1866 in a telegram to General Erwin von Manteuffel. On 23 June 1866, the liberal Heidelberg jurist Johann Caspar Bluntschli, a native of Switzerland, considered the German war 'nothing other than the German revolution in the form of war, led from above rather than from below'. The Austrian chief of the general staff, Heinrich von Hess, wrote to the Prussian field marshal, Fredrich von Wrangel, in the autumn of 1866: 'So, revolution from above has now come into fashion through you Prussians. Double woe unto you if, in the deluge of the times, it should someday seize hold of you, too, now that all feelings of justice have been swept away. Then you are lost.'

Prussian liberals saw no cause for such pessimism. When they spoke of 'revolution' in the autumn of 1866, they meant the word in a positive sense, appealing to the revolutionary legitimacy of the 'nation' against two competing notions: the dynastic legitimacy of the rulers Prussia had deposed, and the democratic legitimacy of the annexed populations. In the 20 December debate over the annexation of Schleswig-Holstein, Karl Twesten declared to the House of Representatives that although the 'present revolutionary course of Prussia' violates old positive law, nonetheless 'radical changes in history simply do not conform to the paths of legality. That which is rational is not brought about through reason . . . Prussia represents the victorious whole, to which the individual parts must subordinate themselves.' The events of 1866 had changed Twesten from the self-confessed apostle of August Comte of the late 1850s into a Hegelian. The 'cunning of Reason' was, in any case, not a positivist, but rather a dialectical hypothesis.

On 1 December 1866 Hans Viktor von Unruh—originally a left-centre, later right-centre delegate to the 1848 Prussian National Assembly, in 1859 one of the founders of the German National Union and in 1861 of the German Progressive Party—spoke of the Prussian government's dualism between conservative domestic and revolutionary foreign policy agendas, embodied in ministers Eulenburg and Bismarck, respectively. 'I find the external policy of the Herr Prime Minister, in contrast to the internal policy, to have the same idea of state, the same guiding principle as the policy of Frederick the Great—the goal of creating an independent, powerful, enduring state inside Germany.' Frederick's policies, according to Unruh, had not been conservative, but decidedly revolutionary in character; they had not invoked historical law, but rather the historical requirements of the era. In this sense, too, the policies of Count Bismarck are

> not conservative, but rather, if you will, revolutionary . . . I approve wholeheartedly of this direction in Bismarck's policies . . . I consider it absolutely necessary for the interest of Prussia, for the future of Prussia, and also for the interest of Germany. But 'conservative' such policies are not, gentlemen!

The year 1866 was a 'revolution from above'. It was 'the *great German revolution*' the Swiss historian Jacob Burckhardt spoke about shortly thereafter, a radical overturning of the political order in Germany with the help of the military might of Prussia, whose success assured the northern power the military hegemony in Germany and transformed Austria into non-German power. Thus 1866 was the answer to the Revolution of 1848—a failed revolution, measured by its own goals, for the 'mad year' had brought neither unity nor liberty. The German war, on the other hand, by eliminating the *grossdeutsch* solution to the German question and thus clearing away one of the major obstacles to the *kleindeutsch* solution, had brought Germany at least a considerable step closer to unity.

In bringing the issue to a forceful decision, the Prussian state possessed the power the Paulskirche had never had. What Bismarck achieved in 1866 answered a need of the educated and propertied bourgeoisie, at least those who considered themselves liberal: the desire to advance along the road to a German national state that could hold its own, economically and politically, with the older national states of the west. In principle, this desire was also in accord with the aspirations of the young workers' movement. It was, in fact, an urge that permeated all of society, rendered especially acute by the ongoing process of industrialization. Any government that did not respond to this situation ran the risk of precipitating a new period of revolutionary turmoil. Because he knew this, Bismarck became a 'revolutionary'. Yet he saw in the 'revolution from above' no break with the Prussian tradition, but rather its very essence: 'In Prussia, only the kings make revolutions,' he remarked to Napoleon when the latter warned him of the dangers of revolution during the Prussian constitutional conflict.

The achievements of the battlefield and the negotiating table in 1866 did not contradict the interests of the old Prussian ruling classes from which Bismarck came. These interests, too, found satisfaction in the war's outcome. It is true that the liberals wanted more than the Prague treaty actually spelled out. They wanted to overcome the division between northern and southern Germany, and they wanted to increase their political influence. As far as the first goal was concerned, the liberals could be sure that it corresponded to Bismarck's own ideas. The outcome of the second aspiration depended on the issue of the constitutional conflict. *This* was the question that demanded resolution in Prussia as soon as the German war had come to an end.[30]

THE LIBERALS AND THE END OF THE CONSTITUTIONAL CONFLICT

For Prussian liberals 3 June 1866 had a double meaning. On the same day that Austria was defeated at Königgrätz, the Prussian Progressive Party suffered a decisive setback on the domestic political scene. In the elections to the House of Representatives, the number of seats they controlled fell from 143 to 83. Added together, the seats of the Progressive Party and the Left Centre, the parties of 'resolute liberalism', amounted to only 148, three-fifths of their total of 247 seats after the 1863 elections. The unequivocal victors of the elections were the conservatives, who gained more than 100 seats, controlling now 136 instead of the previous 35. The voters had 'punished' the opposition and 'rewarded' the parties friendly to the government. The election results weakened parliamentary legalism and strengthened Prussian patriotism.

The military victory of the old Prussian order and the political defeat of the liberal opposition placed Bismarck in the agreeable position of now being able to offer his internal adversaries, too, a peace on his own terms. At the official beginning of the constitution conflict on 13 October 1862, the government had announced that it would eventually ask the House of Representatives for retrospective approval of the expenditures made during the non-budgetary period. Nearly four years later, in his speech opening the new parliamentary session on 5 August 1866, King William I gave expression to the hope that the delegates would now grant 'indemnity' to the government. On 14 August the government placed the bill to that effect before the House of Representatives.

The request for indemnity was not an admission of culpability. Far from it: both the monarch and the ministry continued to insist upon the absolute necessity of the non-budgetary regime. The only thing the government was concerned about was obtaining the parliament's blessing for the facts it had created. Without such a sanction, a return to constitutional normality was inconceivable, not to mention the cooperation of the moderate factions of the liberal party Bismarck required for his German agenda.[31]

In terms of constitutional legality, the position of the Bismarck government was just as untenable in August 1866 as it had been in October 1862. The king and his ministers were only permitted to invoke a supra-legal obligation to preserve the essential functions of the state in cases where the parliament was either non-functional or resolved upon an obstructionist course. Neither was the case here. The Prussian representative assembly was simply availing itself of its classic right to approve the yearly budget. It was also within its constitutional rights to demand, as it did on 22 May 1863, a new government from the king, an agreement with the old administration having proved impossible. The appeal to the monarch to reshuffle the ministry was a means of preserving parliamentary rights when a fundamental conflict arose between the legislative and the executive bodies. If he did not wish to accede to such an appeal, the monarch in turn had the right to dissolve parliament and set new elections, thus appealing directly to the people (as William I had done in spring 1862 and again in May 1863). Since the people were in support of the parliamentary majority at the time, the king would have been compelled to come to an understanding with the latter. To rule without an approved budget and against the representative body was not permitted in any constitutional system, not even in Prussia.

Even in the case of a true state of emergency, however, the costs of an army reform à la Roon would not have been covered under the category 'absolutely necessary expenditures'. Bismarck himself, as he openly admitted to Twesten at the beginning of October 1862, considered the three-year term of military service, the main point of the reform conflict, to be completely dispensable, in contrast to the king's view. The prime minister's 'gap theory' was intended to justify what could not lawfully be justified, the break with the constitution. In legal terms, the demand he placed before the House of Representatives after the victory over Austria was a demand for the squaring of the circle: a retrospective enabling act that was annulled the moment it passed.[32]

Thus it seemed only logical when, in the parliamentary debate over the indemnity measure at the beginning of September, Benedikt Waldeck declared that a positive vote was tantamount to a 'disavowal of everything we have fought for'. Most of the Progressive left argued similarly. The right wing of 'resolute liberalism' came to a different conclusion. Several of its best-known speakers, including Unruh, Michaelis, and Twesten, had left the fraction of the Progressive Party in April out of protest against the intransigence of the democrats. They now pressed for the approval of the government's indemnity bill, claiming it represented the only way liberalism would be able to shape the future of Prussia and Germany according to its own ideas.

The jurist Eduard Lasker, first elected to the House of Representatives in 1865 in a by-election, also left the Progressive Party shortly after the indemnity debate, claiming 'inner reasons' had convinced him that 'the public consciousness of justice is satisfied under the current conditions, despite the breach of the constitution.' The most important reason for Lasker was that the unification of northern Germany represented Prussia's first chance to relieve its overstretched military finances. Michaelis exhorted the representatives 'to act as a factor of this state in the spirit of this state' and to make *the* decisions 'that bring about the results we desire'. Twesten, finally, declared that the representatives were not to 'renounce the development of liberty; but the development of the power of our fatherland, the unification of Germany, that is the true, the highest foundation we can create for the development of liberty, and we can now have a hand in this great work.' It was true that the Bismarck administration had, in past years, committed grave sins against the law and the people's consciousness of justice. 'But the history of the past year has granted him indemnity. Let us pronounce it!'

The majority followed these appeals. The government's bill was approved with 230 votes against 75. Most conservatives and moderate liberals voted positively. The negative votes came from the ranks of the Progressive left wing, the Left Centre, and from a few old-conservatives.

The delegates of the right wing of the Progressive Party had no intention of capitulating to Bismarck. They also refused to participate in the 'idolatry of success' that Rudolf Virchow, the famous physician and delegate of the party left wing, had warned against in the 23 August debate in which the assembly considered its response to the king's inaugural speech. These men made no sudden political shift in the late summer and autumn of 1866. They simply attempted to come to terms with a radically altered situation, drawing logical conclusions from the differences of opinion on the national question, differences that had been driving the Progressive Party to the verge of rupture since 1864. By promoting conciliation on the domestic front, they hoped to achieve more for the cause of civil liberty and the consolidation of parliamentary rights than had been accomplished by the stubborn protests of the conflict era. And they remained deeply convinced that national unification would redound to the benefit of liberalism. 'It is completely certain', wrote the *National-Zeitung* on 19 August 1866 in an article on the eightieth anniversary of Frederick the Great's death, 'that the Prussian government must act in accordance with liberal principles, for its daily labour, the unification of Germany, is per se a liberal and progressive goal. But the liberal party, too, must dedicate itself to ideas that build up the state, or else it will be completely left behind.'

Such ideas were not eccentric. Ever since 3 July 1866, the chances that Prussia could transform itself single-handedly into a liberal polity had grown even smaller than they had been before. The politicians and publicists from the Progressive right were quite justified in complaining about the unfair distribution of German military burdens. The smaller German states had been living at Prussia's expense, militarily speaking. Thus it made a certain sense for Prussian liberals to imagine that Germany's unification would help them in their battle against the old Prussia of the Junkers, at least in the long term.

It also made sense to assume that the project of German unification was still a question of power. Germany, as Lasker pointed out in the indemnity debate, was not in the fortunate position of England, which had been able to attain and consolidate its liberty primarily because its insular geography protected it against outside invasion.

> Only when Germany has achieved complete unification, only then will liberty have been won—and not merely for Germany, but for all of Europe. Until that time, we remain subjected to that worst enemy of liberty, armed peace. A secure peace will only come when, from the one side, Italy, and from the other side, Germany form enclosed states, and the unified nations are in a position to suppress French ambitions forever. When that time comes, all countries will have the leisure to reflect and to busy themselves with the tasks that best serve humanity.

'The liberals must not again cast doubts upon the power of the state!' Twesten's declaration before an assembly of the liberal Berlin district association in November 1866 was an expression of liberal self-critique. Outside of Prussia, this self-criticism sometimes went even further. In spring 1866 the historian Hermann Baumgarten, a native of Lower Saxony living and teaching in Karlsruhe, wrote an essay entitled 'Der deutsche Liberalismus. Eine Selbstkritik',* published in the *Preussische Jahrbücher* at the end of the year. Baumgarten did not reproach the liberals for not being resolute enough in their opposition to Bismarck. Rather, their mistake had been to shun an understanding with the government and, over the course of years, to employ the 'strongest language', despite it being perfectly clear that the 'general conditions' of the Prussian state precluded a violent resolution to the conflict. 'A people getting richer by the day does not make revolution.'

* Baumgarten, 'German Liberalism: A Self-Critique'.

This argument was not easy to refute. But Baumgarten did not leave it at that. He more or less denied the ability of the bourgeoisie to engage in effective political action. 'The bourgeois is created to work, not to rule, and the fundamental task of the statesman is to rule.' For the nobility, on the other hand, the author saw a great future.

> Now that we have discovered that the nobility is an indispensable part of a monarchical state, and now that we have seen that these much-despised Junkers know how to die for their country, despite the best liberal, we shall restrain our bourgeois conceit somewhat and content ourselves with taking an honourable place at the side of the nobility.

To be sure, Baumgarten noted on the last page of the essay that 'liberalism must develop the ability to rule.' Nonetheless, his opinion seemed to be that the liberal bourgeoisie could now only acquire this ability in *conjunction* with the nobility, the 'real political class in any monarchical state', and no longer in *opposition* to it.

The Prussian liberals who left the Progressive Party and the Left Centre in August 1866, forming the 'fraction of the national party' in the middle of November, wanted no truck with such bourgeois self-denial. In a manifesto from 24 October 1866, the embryo of the later National Liberal Party, they asserted their full support for the government's foreign policy, justifying this course with their 'confidence' that the efforts of the Bismarck ministry were directed at German unity. On the domestic front, however, they still did not consider fully secure the 'new direction' that would allow them to go along with the government's measures with trust. For that reason Twesten, Michaelis, Unruh, Lasker, and twenty further signatories declared it their task to be a 'vigilant and loyal opposition'. They summarized their domestic political demands in the following statement:

> In addition to armed might and the prestige of arms, a liberal administration is necessary. In the mixture of both elements, in the development of the long-withheld organic laws and in self-government as the basis of the community, we recognize the straight path to the highest meaning of Prussia and to its rule in Germany.

None of the constitutional demands of the Progressive party was renounced in this statement. The 'resolute liberals' had never, in fact, demanded changes in the constitution for the purpose of establishing a parliamentary system. After all, they considered themselves to be the defenders of the constitution. Of course, their goal was a situation in which a government could only maintain itself in power if it succeeded in coming to terms with the popular representation—a de facto rather than *de jure* parliamentary system, in other words. The most important means to the realization of this goal were a law concerning the accountability of the ministers as well as full recognition of the parliament's budgetary authority.

The Prussian National Liberals remained firmly committed to this programme, despite knowing that Bismarck, at least in the near future, would not accommodate them as much as they wished. Therefore, the goal of de facto parliamentary governance was postponed until the unification of Germany was achieved, at which time the constitutional demands of the liberals would be easier to fulfil than at the present. Such expectations were given classic and pithy expression by Ludwig Bamberger from Mainz, who had been a member of the German National Assembly for a few months in 1849, thereafter a participant in the rebellion in the Palatinate and an exile in France, where he had remained until 1866. In an appeal to the voters in Rhenish Hesse during the December 1866 parliamentary elections in the grand duchy of Hesse-Darmstadt, Bamberger asked the rhetorical question: 'Is not unity itself a part of liberty?'

Bamberger gave voice to a hope, one as easy or as difficult to justify as the fear expressed by Friedrich Harkort during the annexation debate in the Prussian House of Representatives on 7 September 1866: 'What the sword has gained only the sword can maintain, and as we were before, so we shall have to remain armed against east and west. Thus it seems that the hoped-for relief in the military burden will not happen, at least for a long time.' In 1866 it was generally expected that the unification of Germany and Italy would liberate and lastingly preserve Europe from the threat of Bonapartist France. But was it not rather presumptuous to add, as Lasker did, that the nationality principle would also help the principle of humanity to victory?

In 1866 Bismarck seemed to many liberals—not merely to Baumgarten—to be a kind of German Cavour, whom one could expect, while acting in the best interests of Prussia, to stride forward toward German unification just as the prime minister of Sardinia-Piedmont had worked for the unity of Italy until his death in 1861. National Liberals now eschewed the comparison to Napoleon III, and for good reason. While Bismarck employed 'Bonapartist' political tactics like general, equal, and direct male suffrage (to be introduced for the elections to the North German Reichstag), he was nonetheless too much the loyal Brandenburg Junker to become a plebiscitary dictator in the style of the French emperor. On the other hand, however, the prime minister had also distanced himself considerably from the expectations of the old Prussian conservatives—so considerably, in fact, that he was now regarded by some of them as an apostate. For the National Liberals, of course, this could only be a further recommendation.

In the view of many conservatives, Bismarck's indemnity bill already represented an unacceptable concession to the liberals. Indeed Bismarck, unlike William I, had *not* stated that he would again act as he had done during the constitutional conflict if a similar situation arose in the future. Although he certainly reserved for himself the right to rule again without a parliament-approved budget, he much preferred to come to an agreement with the elements of the liberal bourgeoisie willing to make a compromise—provided the monarchy could preserve its independence from parliamentary control in the core areas of the military and foreign policy.

Jacob Burckhardt called the 'great German revolution of 1866' a 'curtailed crisis of the first order'. With respect to the resolution of the question of hegemony between Prussia and Austria, this judgement was accurate. The internal question of power in Prussia, however, was not settled once and for all with the passing of the indemnity bill. Since it did not address the crucial problem of whether the monarchical or the parliamentary authority had the priority in cases of budgetary conflict, the political accord of 1866 could only be, in the language of the legal and political theorist Carl Schmitt, an 'inauthentic' peace, a 'dilatory formal compromise'. If the House of Representatives had rejected the bill, the consequence would hardly have been the beginning of a revolution from below. None of the 'nay-sayers' had anything of the kind in mind. Rather, there would probably have been open counter-revolution in the form of a *coup d'état*. The alternative to both scenarios was the revolution from above that actually occurred in 1866.

Bismarck emerged triumphant from the constitutional conflict. Nonetheless, the approval of the indemnity bill was not a defeat for liberalism. Compared with the era of conflict and reaction, liberals had gained in political influence, at least the groups who had agreed to cooperate with Bismarck. To what extent liberalism, thus divided, would be able to make its mark on Prussian and German politics—that was an open question in autumn 1866.[33]

INTERLUDE: THE NORTH GERMAN CONFEDERATION

The year 1866 saw not only a split within Prussian liberalism, but also among Prussian conservatives. At the end of July 1866, approximately twenty conservative delegates who—in contrast to the majority of the Conservative Party—unconditionally supported Bismarck's policies founded the 'Free Conservative Union' (*Freie Konservative Vereinigung*). In addition to high state officials, diplomats, and scholars, the membership of the new group included Rhenish industrialists and Silesian magnates, the latter not infrequently combining large landownership with involvement in heavy industry. However, in the elections to the constituent North German Reichstag on 12 February 1867, in which voting took place according to general, equal, and direct male suffrage, the Free Conservatives did not come off as well as the Conservative party, with 39 and 59 seats respectively.

The actual winners of the elections were the National Liberals, who captured 79 seats, in comparison to the Progressive party, which gained only 19. In its constituent session on 28 February, the fraction gave itself the name 'National Liberal Party' (*Nationalliberale Partei*). The Prussian representatives around Twesten, who had disassociated themselves from the Progressive party after August 1866, were joined by like-minded liberals from the other members states of the North German Confederation, including Rudolf von Bennigsen from Hanover, the president of the German National Union (which had disbanded in the autumn of 1867, since, as Bennigsen explained, other organs had assumed its tasks, most notably the North German Reichstag). Together with the Free Conservatives, the old-liberals and several 'wild' delegates, that is, those belonging to no fraction, the National Liberals formed a parliamentary majority united in the conviction that the most urgent task at hand was the swift adoption of a constitution.

In fact, a constitutional draft already lay before the assembly when it first convened in Berlin on 24 February 1867. This document, formulated by the Prussian government according to Bismarck's guidelines and in accordance with the governments of the northern German states, proposed a Prussian-led federal polity with a presidency to be occupied by the Prussian king. In the Federal Council (*Bundesrat*), the organ of sovereign federal authority composed of plenipotentiaries bound by orders from the individual state governments, Prussia—which contained five-sixths of the population of the North German Confederation—had at its disposal a mere 17 of 43 seats. Nonetheless, the possibility of a two-thirds majority against Prussia was thereby excluded, with the consequence that the constitution could not be amended without the consent of the presidential power. The federal chancellor, appointed by the president, was the sole minister and, in the original version of the draft, would function only as the executive of the Federal Council. A catalogue of basic rights was not part of the text, since, according to Bismarck, it would be incompatible with the federal character of the North German Confederation.

The representatives of the Progressive party around Waldeck were highly dissatisfied with the federal approach. They desired a unitary north German state, indistinguishable from a Greater Prussia. Many National Liberals thought similarly, like the historian Heinrich von Treitschke (who was not a member of parliament). But the majority was prepared to acquiesce in Bismarck's solution. The office of chancellor, however, was—with Bismarck's blessing—accorded considerably more power than in the government's draft. Although Bennigsen, the floor leader of the National Liberals, did not succeed with a motion to create a collegial federal ministry answerable to parliament, the Reichstag did approve his motion to subject the office of chancellor to parliamentary review. This did not mean the introduction of a legally enforceable form of accountability, much less a bona fide parliamentary system. Bismarck would never have consented to such things. The federal chancellor simply assumed political responsibility before parliament, to whom he was to account for his actions. Yet it was by means of this provision that, in the words of the constitutional historian Ernst Rudolf Huber, 'the federal executive was conferred upon the federal chancellor; the Federal Council was reduced to a cooperating and controlling executive organ.'

While the international representation of the Confederation, as well as all decisions concerning war and peace, were the sole province of the president, the Reichstag managed to make the enforcement of international treaties dependent upon its approval, thereby gaining a voice in at least *part* of foreign policy. It also succeeded—following a motion of Karl Twesten—in making the armed forces subject to the legislative authority.

The representatives were unable to obtain unrestricted recognition of the parliament's budgetary competence in military matters, however. Bismarck wanted the federal army to have a peacetime strength of 1 per cent of the 1867 population and a yearly total sum of 225 thalers per soldier, to be adjusted every ten years—in effect, a permanent budgetary enactment or *Äternat.* The Reichstag rejected this proposal. Following a motion by Max von Forckenbeck, it approved Bismarck's peacetime military strength, but restricted it to a period of four years, until 31 December 1871. The resolution of the power question was thus postponed.

Under massive pressure from Bismarck, a majority of the Reichstag, led by National Liberals and Free Conservatives, finally voted through another compromise: the 1867 resolution was to stay in effect after 1872 until the planned federal law went into effect. While the government's military spending was to be constrained by the budgetary law, the legislature, too, was required to observe the legally codified provisions of the army organization when deciding the military budget.

The 'dilatory formal compromise' that settled the Prussian constitutional conflict thus became the cornerstone of the constitution of the North German Confederation. It was a constitution that favoured the executive branch of government, which secured far greater powers than those granted to the imperial government by the imperial constitution of 1849. The military command authority of the Prussian king, the exercise of which required no countersignature in the ministry, represented a portion of absolutism, both in theory and in practice, in the German constitution of 1867. The North German Confederation *was* a constitutional federal state, but it was constitutional and federal only within the limits set by the foreign and domestic successes of old Prussia in the year 1866.

In one respect, however, the North German Confederation was actually far more democratic than the contemporaneous parliamentary monarchies of Europe, even those of Britain and Belgium. General, equal, direct, and secret suffrage gave German males a lawful right to political participation far beyond that granted to the citizens of states with census-based suffrage. It also went further than the moderate liberals in the separate German states and communities approved, though it would have been politically inconceivable for liberals to oppose Bismarck's successful campaign for the suffrage law of 1849. Even as early as 1867, the effects of these democratic achievements proved to have a good deal less effect on government than the Prussian prime minister had expected. But there was no going back on general suffrage, not even for Bismarck. Thus the antithesis between democratic voting law and authoritarian government persisted—an antithesis that was to outlast the short-lived federal state of 1867 by half a century.

On 16 April 1867 the constituent assembly of the Reichstag approved the revised constitutional draft with 230 votes against 53. The nay-sayers consisted of the Progressive party; the Saxon particularists; the Hanover 'Guelfs', including

Ludwig Windthorst, former minister and later leader of the Catholic Centre party, as well as two further prominent Catholics, the Berlin *Obertribunalrat* Peter Reichensperger (originally from Koblenz) and the Westphalian landowner and governmental official Hermann von Mallinckrodt; August Bebel, the only delegate from the Saxon People's party; and the Polish members of the Reichstag. In consequence of the favourable vote, Bismarck's *ultima ratio*, the forceful imposition of the constitution through the member governments, proved unnecessary. It was ratified by the parliaments of the member states in the ensuing weeks and went into effect on 1 July 1867. Two weeks later, on 14 July, King William, as president of the North German Confederation, appointed the prime minister of Prussia, Count Bismarck, to the office of federal chancellor.

The founding of the North German Confederation took place at the same time as a new customs union agreement was being concluded. The new treaty included provisions for a federal customs council (*Zollbundesrat*) and customs parliament (*Zollparlament*)—state-like institutions that seemed, like the defensive alliances made public in March 1867, to anticipate the federal integration of northern and southern Germany. However, the protectionist reservations south of the Main were no less serious than during the controversy over the Franco-Prussian trade agreement several years previously, and the military alignment of the southern states with Prussia did not make the latter any more popular. In Bavaria, the first elections to the customs parliament in February and March 1868 were carried by the candidates from the Catholic-conservative Patriots' party around Edmund Jörg. In Württemberg, the victors were the democrats of the People's party. Two short years after the German war, there was little trace of a broad movement for German unification. The trend seemed, rather, to be going in the opposite direction, towards a hardening of the border along the Main, at least in the view of many southern Germans.

The division between north and south was so deep that Bismarck could not yet risk an open attempt to settle the outstanding issues in the balance of power among the states of Germany. When Napoleon III, with Bismarck's discreet encouragement, took steps in spring 1867 to purchase the grand duchy of Luxembourg—a member of the German Customs Union—from King William III, popular protest was much stronger to the north of the Main than to the south. In view of the anti-Prussian sentiments in the chambers and among the populace, the governments in Munich and Stuttgart could not afford to agree with Bismarck's view that a war between Prussia and France over Luxembourg would necessitate the activation of their defensive alliances with Prussia. Consequently, the Prussian prime minister found himself compelled to agree to a compromise. At the London conference over Luxembourg in May 1867, the Prussian envoy gave his consent to a guarantee of the grand duchy's independence and neutrality by the five great powers, the Netherlands, Belgium, and Italy.[34]

But resolute opposition to Bismarck's policies was not confined to the south. In none of the states annexed by Prussia were the loyalty to the old dynasty and the antipathy to the new masters as strong as in Hanover. Eight 'Guelf' delegates had sat in the new federal parliament's constituent assembly where, as members of the adamantly federalist 'Federal-Constitutional Association' (*Bundesstaatlich-konstitutionelle Vereinigung*) along with the pro-Augustenburg party from Schleswig-Holstein and the Catholic Westphalian Hermann von Mallinckrodt, they had voted in April 1867 against the ratification of the constitution.

Much more effective was the opposition on the left side of the political spectrum, which began in Saxony. In August 1869 August Bebel and Wilhelm Liebknecht, the leaders of the Saxon People's party, joined together with a minority of Lassalle's followers, including Wilhelm Bracke, to found the Social Democratic Workers' Party (*Sozialdemokratische Arbeiterpartei*) in Eisenach. Whereas the Saxon People's party had been half proletarian, half petty bourgeois in membership, the new party, in the spirit of Lassalle, was devoted exclusively to the concerns of the workers. At the same time, the majority of the Union of German Workers' Associations, led by Bebel and Liebknecht, began at the 1868 Nuremberg congress to work towards a rapprochement with the Marx-inspired International Workers' Association, the First International, founded in 1864. Despite the many differences between the 'social' and the 'particularist' wings of the People's parties, however, these developments did not yet represent a rupture in the democratic movement along 'class lines', that is, between the proletarian and the bourgeois democrats.

That split took place a year later, when the new Social Democratic party adopted the Basel resolutions of the International from September 1869, wherein the party of Marx and Engels demanded the immediate abolition of private property and the radical restructuring of society. From this moment forward, the 'proletarian' Social Democrats and the 'bourgeois' democrats parted company. This rift, which was a permanent one, represents one of the most radical caesuras in the history of German political parties.

In their antipathy towards Prussia, the southern German democrats were every bit as uncompromising as Bebel and Liebknecht, and the more the governments in Stuttgart and Karlsruhe adapted themselves to the northern German hegemon, the fiercer the opposition of the People's party became. The differences between the two countries were nonetheless great. In Württemberg, the July 1868 parliamentary elections had been carried by the democrats and the *grossdeutsch* partisans. The new parliament confronted a cautiously manoeuvring ministry, the Varnbüler government, which took pains to prevent its de facto dependence on Prussia from becoming all too evident. The Baden parliament, in comparison, was dominated by moderate liberals, and was just as interested as the government—led by Julius Jolly, the interior minister, after Karl Mathy's death in 1868—in making the grand duchy a member of the North German Confederation as quickly as possible.

The situation in Bavaria, the largest of the southern German states, was different again. Like Baden, the moderate liberal government under

Hohenlohe-Schillingsfürst pursued uncompromisingly anticlerical policies in the schools and a liberal course in economic and judicial matters. Freedom of trade was introduced at the beginning of 1868, followed by liberal municipal ordinances a year later. But the educational reform was successfully opposed by the Catholic protest movement. In two parliamentary elections in 1869, the conservative Bavarian Patriots' party under Edmund Jörg achieved resounding victories. In the second of these, in November, it managed to secure the absolute majority of seats. In January and February 1870, both chambers of parliament voted no confidence in the Hohenlohe administration, and the prime minister stepped down at the beginning of March, against the will of Bismarck. Hohenlohe's successor, Count Bray, hitherto the Bavarian envoy in Vienna, made an effort to compromise with the parliamentary majority. This was a serious setback for the chancellor of the North German Confederation.[35]

After the election of the new Confederation's first 'regular' Reichstag in August 1867, the chancellor and the National Liberals developed, all in all, a fairly close cooperative relationship in matters of domestic policy, far closer than even the optimists had dared to imagine in autumn 1866. Along with the Progressive and Conservative parties, the National Liberals had improved upon their results in the elections of February 1867. They were now more successful in the legislative process than they had been with the constitution. The 1869 law mandating the equality of religious confessions in civil and citizenship affairs, which concluded the legal emancipation of the Jews, bore the mark of liberalism, although it only proved practically necessary in Mecklenburg, where legal discrimination against the Jews was still in effect. The new trade ordinances, also passed in 1869, expanded commercial and mercantile freedoms, though pressure from the Conservatives kept them from allowing agricultural workers and manorial servants the same freedom of association they granted to other workers. The penal code of 1870, on the other hand, could not be counted among the liberals' successes, since they failed to obtain their most important objective, the abolition of the death penalty. The combined strength of the member governments and the Conservatives proved too great on this issue. Still, when one added the 1867 law concerning the free movement of labour and further laws for the standardization of the economy, including the 1868 ordinance on weights and measures, the National Liberals had every reason to be satisfied, on the whole, with the new federal parliament's year of legislative achievement. The interplay between the Reichstag and the ministerial bureaucracy had led to the development of a 'portfolio liberalism' (*Ressortliberalismus*) going far beyond the parliament's original authority in trade policy.

In their most important goal, however, the National Liberals had made no progress since the election of the customs parliament. The unification of Germany had flagged and was now in a phase of stagnation. The liberals began to doubt whether Bismarck was even serious about the issue and, consequently, whether further liberal cooperation with him was justified. 'If things continue like this, then the task of the national party can no longer be only to stand idly at the Herr Chancellor's side,' wrote the *National-Zeitung* on 22 February 1870. Two days later, on the occasion of the third reading of the jurisdiction treaty between the North German Confederation and Baden, the delegate Eduard Lasker presented a petition expressing the disappointment and impatience of the National Liberals with a hitherto unusual candour. The Reichstag, Lasker declared, should thank Baden for its 'unflagging national aspirations' and recognize as the state's main goal the 'most rapid possible accession' to the North German Confederation.

Bismarck was outraged, and for more than one reason. The parliament's interference in matters of foreign policy was bad enough in itself. But he also suspected the Baden government to be behind Lasker's initiative, and he declared this openly in the assembly. From a practical point of view, he thought it a mistake to accept into the federation *the* southern German state most narrowly associated with the national idea, since the north–south unification of Germany would thereby be made more difficult as a whole. In any case, any southern German key to German unity was not, for the federal chancellor, to be found in Karlsruhe, but in Munich.

It was clear to all at the time, without it having to be spoken openly, that the integration of Bavaria into the North German Confederation would lead to war with France. In Bismarck's view, the accession of a single state could not justify such a war. If war with France for the unification of Germany was going to be unavoidable, then all of Germany, both north and south of the Main, would have to share the conviction that it would be a just and necessary war. That conviction did not yet exist in February 1870.

'The policy of the North German Confederation does not require expansion. The situation in the north has not yet been sufficiently consolidated to allow for the increase of fractious elements with impunity.' Such were Bismarck's words to the Württemberg envoy, Baron Spitzemberg, in a confidential conversation on 27 March 1870. This was certainly no pretext. In order to contain the dangers emanating from an 'increase of fractious elements', whether Württemberg democrats or Bavarian Catholics, a national movement of considerable strength was going to be necessary. In spring 1870 nothing of the kind was in evidence. But even as he spoke to Spitzemberg, Bismarck might have suspected that the situation could change rapidly.[36]

THE POPE, KÖNIGGRÄTZ, AND THE DOCTRINE OF INFALLIBILITY

'*Casca il mondo*!' ('The world is crumbling!') was the reputed cry of the papal secretary of state, Cardinal Antonelli, when he heard the news of the Prussian victory at Königgrätz. For militant Protestants and liberals an occasion for triumph, the defeat of Austria was a catastrophe for the curia. For the *Protestantische*

Kirchenzeitung, a newspaper closely associated with the liberal German Protestant Association, the battle of 3 July 1866 had 'finally brought the Thirty Years War to an end' and 'destroyed ultramontanism [from *ultra montes*, 'beyond the mountains' (H.A.W.)] once and for all in Germany. For not only have Austria's power and ambitions been expelled from the land; the papacy, too, has therewith lost its single remaining earthly support in Europe.'

In truth, Austria's defeat was in more than one way a defeat for the papacy. The 'world' that crumbled in the summer of 1866 was, in the words of the historian Georg Franz,

> the Catholic world of *Mitteleuropa*, in the German Confederation, in Italy. The supreme Catholic and legitimist power, Habsburg Austria, had lost its hegemony in central Europe and its prestige as the leading Catholic power. This role was now taken over by France, with its hybrid, half-legitimate and half-revolutionary character.

It was true that Napoleon III continued to exercise the role he had assumed in summer 1849 when he became president of the Republic of France; he remained the protector of the Papal States, in which capacity he even sent troops to Rome at the end of 1867 for the pope's protection—the same troops he had withdrawn a year before in fulfilment of a treaty with the Kingdom of Italy. Yet after hitherto Austrian Venetia had fallen to Italy in the autumn of 1866 (after first being ceded to France), there was no longer any doubt that the liberal Italian national movement would exert all its effort to achieve the last great goal of the *Risorgimento*, the annexation of the Papal States and the relocation of the kingdom's capital from Florence to Rome. The pope's days of worldly rule were numbered.

Pope Pius IX and his advisers had no intention of submitting to the will of the liberals. In 1864, in *Syllabus errorem*, an addendum to the encyclical *Quanta cura*, the pope had castigated as 'modern' errors not only pantheism and rationalism, socialism and communism, but also classic liberal ideas like state authority in education, separation of Church and State, and the legal equality of Catholics and non-Catholics, demanding the unconditional subordination of the state and the sciences under the authority of the Catholic Church. Six years later, the ecclesiastic declaration of war against the modern world was even more radically formulated. The First Vatican Council, which convened in December 1869 and ended in July 1870, promulgated the doctrine of 'infallibility', according to which the pope, when speaking *ex cathedra* upon matters of church teaching, could not err. In both Germany and Austria, most bishops (including Ketteler) were opponents of the new doctrine, but that had no effect upon the final vote on 18 July 1870. The critics submitted to ecclesiastic discipline, thus inadvertently confirming the impression of the absolutist character of the Roman Catholic Church.

The Catholic opposition lost ground outside of the Council, too. Stubborn adversaries like the Munich theologian Ignaz von Döllinger, a former delegate to the German National Assembly, were excommunicated, while only a small majority of firmly liberal 'old-Catholics' (*Altkatholiken*) openly broke with Rome on their own initiative. The governments of several primarily Catholic countries reacted to the new doctrine of infallibility even more vehemently than many Protestant states. Austria repealed the Concordat of 1855; Bavaria hindered the proclamation of the resolutions by withholding official government sanction; Baden, which had come into conflict with the church over school policy even before Bavaria, rejected their legal validity. Prussia and the North German Confederation, for their part, reacted with marked reservation. In March 1870 Bismarck had informed the Prussian ambassador to the Vatican, Harry von Arnim-Suckow, that Prussia considered the doctrine of infallibility primarily a Catholic matter. On 16 July he instructed Arnim to eschew any demonstrative protest.

There was good reason for such cautious manoeuvring. On 19 July 1870, the day after Pius IX proclaimed the new papal doctrine, the Franco-Prussian War broke out—for Bismarck everything but unexpectedly. Solicitude for the feelings of German Catholics was, in such a situation, a simple imperative of Prussian self-interest. The German liberals, who had always been among the most relentless opponents of the Catholic Church and who now, in their turn, felt the massive challenge of the clerical counter-offensive, were forced as of 19 July 1870 to turn their undivided attention to the war with the western neighbor. The historical confrontation between the avant-garde of secular modernism and the guardians of ecclesiastic tradition—the great *Kulturkampf* of which Rudolf Virchow spoke before the Prussian House of Representatives on 17 January 1873—experienced only an interruption. It was already clear in the summer of 1870 that this conflict would be the ruling theme of the post-war period, and not only in Germany.[37]

THE ROAD TO EMPIRE

The immediate prehistory of the Franco-Prussian War of 1870–1 began in 1868 with a Spanish revolution that was part military coup, part popular rebellion. It resulted in the downfall of the Bourbon monarchy. In 1869 a Catholic Hohenzoller, Prince Leopold von Hohenzollern-Sigmaringen, was named as one of the candidates for the succession to Queen Isabella II, who had fled to France. In February 1870 the Spanish prime minister, Marshal Prim, sent an inquiry to the Prussian king to ascertain whether Wilhelm I, as head of the House of Hohenzollern, would approve of the offer of the Spanish throne to Leopold. From the beginning, the most active proponent of the prince's candidacy was Bismarck. The Prussian prime minister could not possibly have been unaware of the foreign policy risk the venture represented. To be surrounded by Hohenzollerns would have been as threatening for Napoleon III as the French predicament after Charles V in the sixteenth and seventeenth centuries, when France was encompassed by Habsburg powers. From the moment Leopold prepared to assume the throne, war was in the air.

Bismarck would not have been Bismarck if he had not recognized the opportunity that lay in Prim's inquiry. A veto from Paris against a Spanish king from the House of Hohenzollern could prove to be the lever needed to set the unification of Germany in motion once again. If Paris acted forcefully in the matter, a wave of patriotic feeling was sure to sweep not only Prussia, but all of Germany. Such a movement was the very thing to weaken not only particularist sentiment in Bavaria and Württemberg, but also the parliamentarism of the North German Confederation. In 1871 the provisional settlement of the military budget, concluded three years before, was set to expire. The National Liberals made no secret of the fact that they would not consent to a further provisorium, but were going to insist upon the yearly approval of the army budget, as well as the strengthening of parliamentary rights as a whole. If the conflict with France came to a head, then there was every reason to believe that the forces sympathetic to the government would once again gain the upper hand in the strongest party. Thus, in the event of war, Bismarck stood a good chance of being able to eliminate not only the French opposition to German unification, but also, within Germany itself, the particularist and parliamentary elements standing in the way of *his* German solution.

In the summer of 1892, two years after his dismissal, Bismarck declared openly that the French war had been 'necessary'. 'Without having defeated France, we were never going to be able to establish a German Reich in the middle of Europe and elevate it to the power it now possesses.' Armed with this insight, the chancellor of the North German Confederation refused to accept Leopold's rejection of the Spanish offer in April 1870, doing everything in his power to change the prince's mind. By June he had succeeded, and King William, too, finally gave his consent to Leopold's decision, at which point—on 2 July—the Spanish prime minister informed the French ambassador of the Hohenzoller's intention. The response from Paris was not long in coming. On 6 July Foreign Minister Gramont, speaking before the chamber, threatened Prussia with war. France, he declared, would not suffer 'a foreign power, by placing one of its princes on the throne of Charles V, to disrupt the present balance of the powers of Europe to our detriment and so to endanger the interests and the honour of France.'

On Gramont's orders, the French ambassador to the North German Confederation, Count Benedetti, twice had an audience (on 9 and 11 July) with Wilhelm I, who was taking the waters at Bad Ems. Pressured by the Prussian king, Leopold formally renounced his candidacy for the Spanish throne on 12 July. But the French government was not satisfied, insisting upon William's official endorsement of Leopold's declaration and his promise to accept no future candidacy on the part of his relative. When Benedetti broached these terms with Wilhelm on the promenade in Bad Ems on 13 July, the king rejected them out of hand. Bismarck, upon receiving the communiqué on this interview from Heinrich Abeken of the foreign office, radically shortened and edited the text in such a way as to make the offensive character of the French diplomacy all too clear. This was the form in which the report reached the courts and the public of Germany. As the leader of Prussia had intended, the 'Ems dispatch' provoked a national outcry. Now, France was subject to the very humiliation it had thought to visit upon Germany. In this situation, Napoleon III had no choice but to do what Bismarck expected him to do. On 19 July, France declared war on Prussia.

With the coup of the Ems dispatch, Bismarck managed to outmanoeuvre Wilhelm I, disregarding all the constitutional stipulations making the Prussian king the bearer of the highest executive power of the North German Confederation. The war, which the dispatch made inevitable, was Bismarck's war. The Prussian prime minister and federal chancellor of the North German Confederation had wanted this war, for it offered the unique opportunity to annul, with the support of all of Germany, the French interdiction on German unity.

Nonetheless, it would be wrong to ascribe the responsibility for the war entirely to Bismarck, Prussia, or Germany. As in Copenhagen and Vienna in 1864 and 1866, there was a war party on the other side, too, in Paris of 1870. Whereas France could only justify its rejection of German unification in terms of power politics, Germany could defend its aspiration to unity by appealing to the fundamental principle of national self-determination—an incipiently democratic principle, and one continually invoked by Napoleon himself, though it had never occurred to the emperor of the French that Germany, too, possessed such a right. By 1870, in any case, Napoleon's own authority inside France was already too far weakened to permit him any room for a compromise with Bismarck. '*Revanche pour Sadowa!*' was a popular rallying cry in France (*Sadowa* was the name for the battle of Königgrätz used on the left side of the Rhine), and the policy to which it corresponded set its sights on repairing the losses of 1866 and putting Prussia in its place. Foreign Minister Gramont, who had been ambassador to Vienna until May 1870, was a proponent of this broad current. To employ foreign policy as a tool to deflect internal unrest had always been a preferred tactic of Bonapartist rule. Thus the war of 1870–1 was *also* Napoleon III's war—his last, as it soon turned out.[38]

The German north was veritably unanimous in the conviction that the war was in defence of a just cause. In the federal Reichstag, the speech of the king and Bismarck's announcement of the declaration of war on 19 July were greeted with storms of applause from members of all parties. Even the followers of Lassalle, as well as one Social Democratic delegate, approved the war credits. Bebel and Liebknecht abstained, believing the war to be a dynastic conflict. In this they found themselves in conflict with their German colleagues from the International Workers' Association, who by this point had come to demand the annexation of Alsace and Lorraine. Marx and Engels, living in England, did not go this far. Yet even they had cause to go over to the side of Prussia and Germany, since the war opened up the possibility of bringing about the downfall of the hated Bonapartist regime. It was true, wrote Marx in the 'Erste Adresse des Generalrats' of the International, that Prussia had first put Germany in the position of having to defend itself against Louis Napoleon. But that did not change the decisive fact: 'On the German side, the war is a war of self-defence.'

South of the Main, the mood changed within a few days of the incidents at Bad Ems. On 8 July the *Reutlinger Neue Bürgerzeitung*, a democratic paper, had written that 'the Frenchman' could not and would not tolerate 'being surrounded by the Prussian satellites of Muscovy; in this matter, the French people see eye to eye with their government, and rightly so.' After Napoleon's declaration of war, the same newspaper wrote that 'the war that France is forcing upon us may be a dynastic war; but since the people are bound to dynasties, it is, in fact, a war of the French nation against the German nation.' During the debate over a war finance bill of the Württemberg government in the second chamber on 21 July, Karl Mayer, one of the leaders of the People's party, declared his support for fraternal allegiance with Prussia and for the victory of the German banners, 'which, at this moment, are the banners of Prussia'. The speech was greeted with storms of applause from the delegates and the listeners in the gallery. At the beginning of August, the colours black, red, and gold were hardly to be met with in Stuttgart any longer, having yielded their place at the side of the Württemberg flag to the black, white, and red banner of the North German Confederation's navy and merchant marine—the flag in which Bismarck united the Prussian black and white with the white and red in the colours of the Hanse cities.

In Bavaria the war drove a powerful wedge into the Patriots' party. Whereas Edmund Jörg wanted Bavaria to pursue a policy of armed neutrality, his erstwhile comrade in arms, Johann Nepomuk Sepp, 'giving free reign to enthusiasm', urged the deputies of the second chamber to approve the war credits sought by the government. The majority followed Sepp. On 19 July the parliament, by 101 votes to 47, recognized the treaty obligation to Prussia and approved the war credits.

The call for the annexation of Alsace and German-speaking Lorraine was heard earlier and, at first, more emphatically in the German south than in the north, uniting not only liberals and democrats, but also, at the end of July 1870, representatives of political Catholicism. The latter were guided, to be sure, not only by the need for security against the western neighbor, but also by the calculation that the inclusion of the Alsace-Lorrainers would shift the confessional balance in Germany to the benefit of the Catholics.

The sharpest sword in the annexationist cause was wielded by a son of Saxony turned Prussian by choice—Heinrich von Treitschke. Quoting Ernst Moritz Arndt, the national-liberal historian wrote in the *Preussische Jahrbücher* that the land claimed by Germany 'is ours by virtue of nature and history'.

> We Germans who know Germany and France know what is good for the Alsatians even better than they do, those unfortunate people, who in the miseducation of their French lives have had no true and faithful knowledge of the new Germany. We desire to give them back their authentic self, even against their will . . . The spirit of a people embraces not only the races [*Geschlechter*] living near them, but also those that come after them. Against the misguided will of those living there, we appeal to the will of those who were there before . . . The Alsatians learned to despise fragmented Germany; they will learn to love us, under the tutelage of Prussia's strong hand.

Bismarck showed as little regard as Treitschke or any other annexationist for the fact that the great majority of Alsatians and Lorrainers did not wish to become

German, but preferred to remain citizens of France. The chancellor's foremost concern was that a defeated France would be out for revenge regardless of whether it had lost territory to Germany. The possession of Alsace and Lorraine promised, in Bismarck's view, a certain security against the repetition of the war. For that reason he agreed, albeit reluctantly, to the annexation of the French territory around Metz requested by the general staff for strategic reasons. The domestic-political motivation for the annexation was also not insignificant. Bismarck found it far more palatable to conciliate the national movement through an expansion of German territory than through the expansion of parliamentary rights.[39]

For this to happen, however, Prussia and its allies had first to win the war. One of the preconditions for victory was already fulfilled: the war was popular. Germans from north and south, who had fought against each other only four years previously, now knew themselves to be united in the goal of vanquishing the historic enemy of German unity. Professors and publicists, pastors and poets repeatedly invoked the memories of the wars of liberation of 1813–15. Just as then Napoleon I, so now his nephew Napoleon III was pilloried, and with him the nation that suffered him as its leader. Whoever listened to Evangelical war sermons or participated in religious services in the field learned that God intended to punish the French through the agency of the Germans, and that Germany was fated to win, since God would not permit the just cause to go down in defeat.

To the French claim to be defending European civilization against the German barbarians, German newspapers and journals responded with articles and caricatures lampooning the 'savages', that is, North African soldiers, fighting in the armies of the *grande nation*. The *Vossische Zeitung*, a liberal Berlin paper, based its assurance of victory on the insight that the Germans went 'to war as a whole nation with one mind, like never before'. On the other hand, perhaps the war against France was the very precondition for making a 'whole nation' of the Germans. The war poem 'Wider Bonaparte'* by Emil Rittershaus, at least, could hardly be interpreted in any other way:

Ein einig Deutschland! Ach wie lang' begehrt,
Wie oft erfleht in uns'rer Träume Dämmern! –
Und es ist da! Nun muss das Frankenschwert
Mit einem Schlage uns zusammenhämmern!
Doch seit der Mutter Schmach geboten ward,
Giebt's keinen Grenzstrich mehr auf uns'rer Karte,
Da kennen wir nur einen Schrei der Wut
Und einen Kampf auf's Messer, bis auf's Blut!
Nur einen Wahlspruch: Nieder Bonaparte!†

* Rittershaus, 'Against Bonaparte'.

† A united Germany! Ah, how long desired, | how often besought in our dreams' gloaming! – | And it is here! Now must the Frankish sword | hammer us together with one blow! | But ever since the Mother was dealt disgrace, | no border on our map we recognize; | we only know one single cry of rage | and battle to the finish, to the death! | One war cry only: Down with Bonaparte!

On 2 September this dream found its fulfilment. The victory at the Battle of Sedan, the master stroke of Helmuth von Moltke, chief of the Prussian general staff, brought about the end of the second French empire. Napoleon III was taken prisoner. Yet the dagger he surrendered to William I after the capitulation of the army of Marshal MacMahon was only the dagger of the emperor, not of France itself. Two days after Sedan, the Bonapartist government in Paris collapsed and Empress Eugénie was forced to flee. A 'government for the national defence' was formed at the Hôtel de Ville with Jules Favre as foreign minister and Léon Gambetta as minister of the interior, and the new government promptly proclaimed the republic. Meanwhile the German armies continued to advance. The siege of Paris began on 18 September. Toul surrendered on 23 September, Strasbourg on 27 September. On 7 October Gambetta famously left the capital by hot air balloon and, from Tours, called upon the nation to resist the German enemy.

In Germany, Sedan was interpreted as a divine judgement and as a turning point in world history. On 3 September a victory celebration took place in the New Theatre in Leipzig. The prologue began with the words:

Gott hat gerichtet! Unser ist der Sieg!
Voll Lorbeern blühen die Gräber unserer Todten.
Der uns gehetzt in diesen heil'gen Krieg,
Er liegt geächtet heut' vor uns am Boden.—
Vier Wochen sind's—nicht Deutschlands bloss, es sind
Der ganzen Weltgeschichte grösste Wochen!*

It was primarily Evangelical Germany that saw Sedan in this way. Already in September 1870, members of the German Protestant Association were suggesting that a patriotic public festival be held every year on 2 and 3 September. But neither William I nor Bismarck had any interest in the proposal. It was not until the Pietist pastor Friedrich von Bodelschwingh, founder of the Bodelschwinghsche Anstalten in Bethel near Bielefeld and army chaplain in the war of 1870–1, began to campaign for a 'Sedan Day' in June 1871 that the idea gained political momentum.

Bodelschwingh consciously invoked a particular historic precedent: Ernst Moritz Arndt's proposals—put into practice in many places in Germany—to commemorate the October 1813 Battle of the Nations at Leipzig in an honourable and simultaneously popular manner. In 1814 Arndt had given voice to his conviction that the German people 'knows no more festive days—apart from those occasions made holy by divine revelation—than the joyful days this autumn past when the Leipzig battle was fought.' Like Arndt, Bodelschwingh wanted to bring together Church and State, throne and altar, uniting in one emotion love of the *Vaterland* and Christian faith on Sedan Day. 'On 2 September, the hand of the

* God has judged! Ours is the victory! | Full of laurels bloom the graves of our dead. | He who hounded us into this holy war | Now lies, outcast, before us on the ground. — | Four weeks in all; not just Germany's, they are | The greatest weeks in all of world history!

living God intervened so visibly and powerfully in history that it will be especially easy on this commemoration day to get the people to reflect upon the great things the Lord has done for us.' Yet 2 September, as—beginning in Prussia in 1872—it came to be celebrated in the predominantly Evangelical regions of Germany, was not the civic-religious festival the liberal Protestants had intended, but a day of military parades and acclamation for the monarchy.

The reaction of the extreme left to the events of early September was radically different. In a letter to the committee of the Social Democratic Workers' party at the end of August, Marx and Engels drew from the German demands for Alsace and Lorraine the conclusion 'that the war of 1870 necessarily bears a *war between Germany and Russia* in its womb, just like the war of 1866 bore the war of 1870.' In his 'Zweite Adresse des Generalrats über den Deutsch-Französischen Krieg' of 9 September, Marx wrote that 'with the surrender of Louis Napoleon, the capitulation of Sedan, and the proclamation of the republic in Paris,' Germany's 'defensive war' was ended.

> Just as the second empire considered the North German Confederation irreconcilable with its own existence, so too must autocratic Russia believe itself threatened by a German Reich under Prussian leadership. Such is the law of the old political system . . . If the fortunes of war, the arrogance of success, and dynastic intrigue entice Germany into the theft of French territory, then only two paths will remain open to it. Either it must become the *avowed* tool of Russian expansion, come what may, or else it must prepare itself after a short reprieve for a new 'defensive war,' not one of those new-fangled 'localized' wars, but a *racial war* against the allied Slavic and the Roman races.

In autumn 1870 there seemed to be little evidence to back up this bold prognostication. The Russian government received the news of the downfall of Napoleon—their adversary in the Crimean War—with manifest relief. At the end of October, with Bismarck's encouragement, it annulled the clause in the Paris treaty of 1856 restricting the tzarist regime's sovereignty in the Black Sea. The Kingdom of Italy, too, exploited the downfall of the French empire in its own way, rescinding its agreement with Napoleon, marching into Rome after the withdrawal of the French occupying forces, annexing the Papal States after a referendum, and relocating its capital from Florence to Rome. Austria-Hungary, certainly no stranger to thoughts of revenge for Königgrätz, was held in check by Russia. Britain, however, whom Bismarck had informed at the start of the war concerning the French plans from 1867 to annex Belgium, urged the Prussian leader to negotiate with the new provisional government in Paris.

Bismarck was not only fundamentally willing to negotiate; on 19 September he actually met twice with Favre. But a positive result was a priori impossible. The chancellor of the North German Confederation insisted upon the cession of Alsace and Lorraine, a condition the French foreign minister was unable to accept. From this point forward Bismarck, in order to forestall further interference from foreign powers and avoid a widening of the war, did everything in his power to see to it that the military operations were brought to an close. To this end he required the capitulation of Paris, and sought to have the city taken under bombardment.

At this point began a protracted and at times dramatic confrontation between Bismarck and Moltke, the prima facie subject of which was whether the bombardment should commence at an earlier or later date. The larger matter at stake was whether political or military goals should have the priority in the conduct of the war. On 31 December German artillery finally opened fire on the French capital. Yet another conflict between Bismarck and Moltke over the conditions of capitulation was decided by the king in favour of the chancellor. An agreement over a ceasefire of three weeks and the surrender of Paris was signed on 28 January. On 26 February, after elections for a national assembly had been held throughout France (even in Alsace and Lorraine), a provisional peace treaty was signed in Versailles. France ceded to the newly founded German empire Alsace and a part of Lorraine, including the territory around Metz. In addition, it agreed to pay reparations of 5 billion francs. The final peace agreement was signed on 10 May 1871 in Frankfurt am Main.

The founding of the Reich was the result of negotiations Bismarck conducted with the representatives of the southern German states in October and November 1870 in Versailles. With regard to Baden and Hesse-Darmstadt, the chancellor prevailed in his view that accession to the North German Confederation had already all but been accomplished in a de facto sense. Both states adopted the constitution without modification. To Württemberg and Bavaria, on the other hand, he had to make far-reaching concessions in terms of special rights (known as *Reservatrechte*), from which Baden, in view of its state regulation of taxes on beer and spirits, also profited in part. The most significant privilege was the maintenance of separate postal and rail administrations in the two states. Bavaria was also able to secure peacetime sovereignty over its military forces and—per secret treaty—the right to be separately represented at peace negotiations. In addition, the constitution was modified in such a way as to strengthen the federal element; federal executions and, within certain limits, declarations of war would henceforth require the assent of the Federal Council, which preserved its name. In this institution, the three non-Prussian monarchies, Bavaria, Württemberg, and Saxony, together possessed 14 out of 58 votes, which nominally represented a political weight nearly as great as that of Prussia, which held 17. According to Article 78, 14 votes were sufficient to prevent amendments to the constitution (and only in the Federal Council was a qualified majority necessary for constitutional amendments). In the newly created Council committee of foreign affairs, the second largest state, Bavaria, held the chairmanship.

Bavaria's special privileges met with sharp criticism from the National Liberal delegates, who were not federalists, but essentially unitarians who would have preferred a homogeneous to a federal state. Nonetheless, they did not seriously consider rejecting any of the 'November treaties', nor the amended constitution as a whole; to have done so would have risked the very national state they sought to establish. For the Catholic fraction, on the other hand, which began to acquire firmer organizational outlines in the summer of 1870, the new constitution was not federal enough, and for the Progressives and the Social Democrats not sufficiently democratic in character. From these three parties, along with the 'Guelfs' (the Poles and the Danes did not participate) came the 32 negative votes in the final ballot over the treaty with Bavaria on 9 December 1870 in the Reichstag. Of the 227 delegates 195 present voted positively, including the National Liberals, the Free Conservatives, and the Conservatives (though the latter had a difficult time overcoming their reservations about the lack of an upper house). On the following day, the Reichstag adopted the first amendment to the constitution, approved by the Federal Council on 9 December. The title German Confederation (*der Deutsche Bund*), still used in the November treaties, was replaced with German Empire (*das Deutsche Reich*). The federal presidency became 'the German Emperor' (*der Deutsche Kaiser*).

It had cost Bismarck a great deal of effort (and the approval of continuous discreet payments from the 'Guelf fund', the assets of the king of Hanover, confiscated in 1866) to convince the Bavarian king, Louis II, that the Prussian king would bear the name German Emperor in the future and that he, Louis, should be the one to propose the new title. William I himself wanted nothing to do with it for a long time, believing that the glory of the Prussian monarchy would thereby be eclipsed. When Bismarck refused to accept his reservations against the 'bogus emperorship', William proposed the title Emperor of Germany (*Kaiser von Deutschland*). This, too, was impossible for Bismarck to accept, since it could be construed to imply a claim to territorial supremacy unacceptable to most of the other German princes. The variant Emperor of the Germans (*Kaiser der Deutschen*), used in the imperial constitution of 1849, was disqualified for other reasons—it sounded to 'democratic' in the ears of the people who mattered. German Emperor was ultimately the least problematic of all the proposed designations. It allowed the Prussian king to stand forth as the first among the princes of Germany, as in truth he was.

Only six Reichstag delegates voted against the terms *Kaiser* and *Reich*—the Social Democrats and Lassalleans. Indeed, apart from socialists, dyed-in-the-wool Great Germans, southern German particularists, and old Prussian legitimists, the two words had something to offer everybody. Germans in the smaller and middle states were given the feeling of living in a community that was more than just a Greater Prussia. Catholics could meditate upon the tradition of the old Reich, democrats upon the legacy of 1848–9. The National Liberals, of whom not a few initially objected to the medieval and *grossdeutsch* connotations of the emperor title, were optimistic that the Hohenzollern national monarchy would finally be able to overcome German particularism. Most Prussian conservatives were proud that their state and ruling house had gained in power and prestige. That Prussia would ever be absorbed into Germany seemed unthinkable to them.

In its last session on 10 December 1870, the North German Reichstag not only approved the constitutional amendments making the 'German Confederation' into the 'German Empire' and the federal presidium into the 'German Emperor'. It also adopted (once again with the opposition of the six Social Democrats and Lassalleans) a resolution brought forward by Eduard Lasker requesting King William I to 'consecrate the work of unification by accepting the German imperial crown'. On 18 December 1870, the imperial deputation of the Reichstag was received by William at Versailles. At the head of the delegates stood the president of the parliament, the National Liberal Eduard Simson, who once before, on 3 April 1849, as president of the German National Assembly, had asked a Prussian king to accept the title of German Emperor.

This time the delegates could be sure that their request would be granted. For already on 2 December, William had received the letter of King Ludwig II of Bavaria (drafted by Bismarck) asking the Prussian king if he would consent to the common wish of the princes of Germany that he bear the title of German Emperor in the exercise of his presidential powers. Since the king had not refused *this* request, which came from his peers, his answer to the parliament's entreaty could only be positive. William was in a much different position than that of his brother Frederick William IV in spring 1849. The commentary of the conservative *Kreuz-Zeitung* hit the mark: 'Today, the "emperor" makes the "constitution", not the constitution the emperor.'

The southern German parliaments had not yet ratified the November treaties by the time the parliamentary deputation received the royal affirmative. They only did so—with a single exception—in the days between 21 and 29 December 1870. The exception was Bavaria. The first chamber in Munich approved the treaty with the North German Confederation by a large majority on 30 December. In the second chamber, however, the resistance was strong enough to cast doubts on the feasibility of the necessary two-thirds majority. On 13 January 1871 the *Bayerisches Vaterland*, the mouthpiece of the extreme wing of the Patriots' party, declared its objections to the founding of a new Reich:

> We want nothing to do with a 'German Empire' born of blood, erected with blood, and forced together with iron. We want nothing to do with a 'German Emperor' whose crown drips with the blood of our sons and grandsons . . . whose sceptre is a scourge of nations, whose imperial power is an endless list of the dead and a catalogue of broken treaties. Why do we need an 'Emperor' when we already have a king?

On 21 January Bavarian particularism was forced to acknowledge defeat. The second chamber ratified the treaty with two votes more than the necessary number.

By this time, the new German Reich was officially already three weeks old. On 1 January 1871 the treaties between the North German Confederation and Hesse-Darmstadt, Baden, and Württemberg entered into effect. The emperorship, however, was not officially proclaimed until 18 January 1871—170 years to the day after the crowning of the first Prussian king in Königsberg. None of the other German kings personally attended the ceremony in the hall of mirrors at Versailles; they were represented by princes of their dynasties. Though emissaries of the parliament were not present, the military was. One of the young officers in attendance was 23-year-old Paul von Benneckendorff und von Hindenburg. The vexed question of title, which plagued William to the end, was solved by Grand Duke Frederick von Baden, who simply circumvented it by exhorting the assembly to hail 'Emperor William'.

The enthusiasm of those who had worked and waited for German unity for decades knew no bounds. On 27 January 1871, the day special editions of the newspapers were reporting the imminent capitulation of Paris, the liberal Bonn historian Heinrich von Sybel, then 53 years old, expressed his tears of joy in a letter to his like-minded colleague, the Karlsruhe historian Hermann Baumgarten:

> How by the grace of God have we earned the privilege of witnessing such great and momentous events? And how will we live afterward? Twenty years of desire and effort now fulfilled in such a boundlessly glorious way! How ought one of my age to find new meaning and purpose for the rest of his days?[40]

5

The Transformation of Nationalism 1871–1890

ON THE ROAD TO A 'LITTLE GERMAN' NATION STATE?

One of the earliest attempts to place the events of 1870–1 in a larger historical context was undertaken by Benjamin Disraeli. The Franco-Prussian War, declared the leader of the Conservative opposition before the British House of Commons on 9 February 1871, was no typical war like the one between Austria and Prussia, the Italian or the Crimean war.

This war represents the German revolution, a greater political event than the French Revolution of last century. I don't say a greater, or as great, a social event . . . but what has really come to pass in Europe? The balance of power has been entirely destroyed, and the country which suffers most, and feels the effects of this great change most, is England.

If in 1871 the German question had found a *grossdeutsch* solution (i.e. one including the German-speaking territories of Austria), the European balance of power would have been even more radically upset—so radically, in fact, that Britain and Russia would probably not have accepted it. As it was, they were just able to tolerate the 'half-hegemonic position of the Bismarck Reich on the continent', as the historian Ludwig Dehio put it in 1951. Events in post-war France made their self-restraint more palatable. While the country was still under German occupation, the French capital undertook to give the world an example of a society in complete political and social chaos in the form of a revolt of the Commune. The shock that went out from Paris at the end of March 1871 was as lasting as it was violent. In the face of the red revolution of the Communards, which was finally and bloodily suppressed at the end of May by troops of the French government, the fear of Bismarck's 'German revolution' rapidly faded. The newly founded Reich was able to present itself to Europe as a custodian of the public order.[1]

Disraeli was not the only one to compare 1871 with 1789. Evangelical theologians and writers in Germany interpreted the military defeat of France as the final defeat of the principles of the French Revolution. 'If we contemplate the forces that struggled against each other in this war,' wrote the *Evangelische Kirchenzeitung* at the beginning of 1871, 'it presents itself as a victory of loyal subservience over the revolution, of the divine order over anarchy, of the forces of morality over the dissoluteness of the flesh, of rule from above over the sovereignty of the people, of Christianity over modern paganism.' Shortly afterwards the same paper observed: 'The revolution is France's chronic illness. Not only has it gone through the most sanguinary revolutions itself; it has also carried the principle of revolution everywhere it has gained a firm foothold.'

During the war, Evangelical theologians compared Paris with sinful Babylon, interpreted the French Revolution and the two Bonapartes as incarnations of the Antichrist, and designated the French 'the most satanic of peoples'. Now they saw in the German triumph proof that God had predestined the Hohenzollerns to do great things for Germany. It goes without saying that 'Germany' meant 'Evangelical Germany', an identification that brought the founding of the Reich into close relation with the Reformation. 'The paths of the Most High with our people are being made straight, His thoughts concerning us are coming to their fulfilment,' announced the *Neue Evangelische Kirchenzeitung* on 7 January 1871. 'The epoch of German history that began in the year 1517 is coming to a divinely appointed end with war and the cry of battle.' 'The holy Evangelical empire of the German Nation is reaching its fulfilment,' rejoiced Adolf Stoecker, future court chaplain, three weeks later, after the proclamation of the emperorship at Versailles; 'in such a way do we recognize the hand of God from 1517 to 1871!' And on 18 March 1871, exactly twenty-three years after the fighting in the streets of Berlin in 1848, the *Neue Evangelische Kirchenzeitung* hailed Emperor William 'as the initiator of a new history, as the founder of the Evangelical empire of the German Nation'.

The expression 'Evangelical empire' (*evangelisches Kaisertum*) quickly caught on. On 6 March 1872 Bismarck, speaking before the Prussian House of Lords, warned against the danger to the confessional peace since the 'Austrian war, after the power that had formed the stronghold of Roman influence in Germany was defeated and the future of an Evangelical empire clearly loomed on the horizon'. The National Liberal party leader Rudolf von Bennigsen took this thought further in the Prussian House of Representatives on 26 January 1881 when he invoked the 'bitter enmity that prevailed and still prevails in Rome at the founding of the Evangelical empire'—which comment drew from the ranks of the Catholic Centre the corrective interjection '*partitätisches Kaisertum!*'* Even after his dismissal, the founder of the new Reich still insisted upon the its Protestant character. 'I am committed to the secular leadership of an Evangelical empire, and to this empire I am faithful,' Bismarck announced on 31 July 1892 in the town square of Jena.[2]

* [Translator's note: '[An] empire of parity!', i.e. representing Evangelicals and Catholics equally.]

The watchword of the 'Evangelical empire' would help create national identity by dramatizing a double difference: between the old Reich and the new, and between the German Reich and Austria. Since the appeal to a common language, culture, and history was not sufficient to legitimate a German national state, an ideological justification was necessary, one that could give Prussian leadership a meaning comprehensible even to non-Prussian Germans. The invocation of the Reformation fulfilled this purpose, but only for some Germans. The attempt to undergird the political hegemony of Prussia with the cultural hegemony of Protestantism united and divided Germany at the same time. The expression 'Evangelical empire' brought together Evangelical liberals and Evangelical conservatives, Evangelical Prussians and Evangelical non-Prussians. But it also drove a wedge between Protestants and Catholics and thus impeded the progress of the national unification it was intended to further.

The formation of the German nation did not begin with the founding of the German national state, nor did it come to an end with the conclusion of the latter. Rather, it entered a new phase. In a larger sense, everything that gave the Germans the consciousness of a community transcending the borders of their territorial states was part of the process of national formation—first and foremost language, culture, and history. Seen in this light, the beginnings of the nation lay in the Middle Ages, regardless of what national-liberal historians wrote and said about the Holy Roman Empire of the German Nation. For the formation of a *kleindeutsch* nation, such a common ground was a necessary but not sufficient condition. The development of a Little German *Staatsnation* out of a German *Kulturnation* was intimately connected with another developmental history—that of Austria, whose centre had long ago shifted from Germany to central Europe. Non-Austrian Germany, in both its predominantly Evangelical and predominantly Catholic territorial states, was marked by a history of confessional conflict. Austria had successfully closed itself off from Protestantism, but in doing so had separated itself from the rest of Germany. This allowed not only the Habsburg empire to submit to the decision of 1866, but also the German states defeated by Prussia as allies of Austria.

A gradual accommodation of the liberals of the 'third Germany' to Prussia can be traced back to the *Vormärz* period. Confessional sympathies were as important as economic interests. In terms of trade policy, the German Customs Union anticipated the *kleindeutsch* solution, though it did not render it inevitable. The Revolution of 1848–9 caused many, but by no means all, German nationalists to realize that a part of the Habsburg empire could not join a German nation without fatally compromising the whole. Austria did everything in its power, both before and after 1848, to keep the German national movement at a distance. After the die had been cast on the fields of Königgrätz, there was still a great deal of popular opposition to a Prussian-led German national state, above all south of the Main. But a realistic alternative no longer existed.

Unlike the National Liberals, the federal chancellor had no intention of waging a frontal war against the individual patriotic movements of the German states outside of Prussia. 'As a rule, German patriotism requires the medium of dynastic loyalties in order to be active and effective,' Bismarck wrote in his memoirs' most famous chapter, entitled 'Dynastien und Stämme'.* He acted according to this maxim when he organized the new Reich along federal lines. His expectation that the war with France would strengthen German national feeling was fulfilled. The National Liberals emerged from the first Reichstag elections in March 1871 as the strongest party by far, gaining fully 30 per cent of the vote. In Bavaria the liberal parties together, and in Württemberg and Baden the National Liberals alone gained the absolute majority. The results did not indicate the decline of particularist sentiment so much as a broad approval of the new German Reich.

The strongest bastion of individual state patriotism continued to be Prussia. There, the Conservative party did only marginally worse than the National Liberals in the federal elections (20.8 and 23.3 per cent of the vote, respectively) and far better that the emphatically empire-friendly Free Conservatives (12.2 per cent). In the conservative view, the unification of Germany was primarily Prussia's achievement, not that of the national movement. In consequence, Germany had every reason to become more Prussian, that is, more military in spirit, but was not in a position to demand the converse, that Prussia become more German, that is, more bourgeois. This credo could be articulated both offensively and defensively. Hans von Kleist-Retzow chose the second option when he declared before the House of Lords on 21 December 1870:

> Just as we wish to grant the other German peoples the right to cultivate their distinctive character, so also do we wish to preserve our distinctive Prussian character, our old, tough north German nature. We have no desire to be absorbed into the German Reich, but wish to remain Prussians and to dedicate to it our essentially Prussian talents and powers.

The conservative Evangelical pastors, bourgeois almost without exception, were well in advance of the primarily aristocratic politicians of the Conservative party in declaring the Prussian cause of 1871 to be one with the German cause and in recognizing the hand of God no less than Prussia's German mission in the course of history after 1415 (the year in which Emperor Sigismund had given the Mark Brandenburg to Frederick of Hohenzollern, burgrave of Nuremberg). Not until 1876, after severe electoral losses, did the Conservative party give itself a consciously national image, renaming itself the German Conservative party (*Deutschkonservative Partei*) and undertaking to organize throughout Germany. For perceptive National Liberals, however, it was already clear in 1871 that their monopoly on nationalist rhetoric was under threat.

Before the founding of the Reich, to be 'national' meant to be against the dynastic principle of the *Partikularstaat* and for the civic principle of the national

* 'Dynasties and Clans'.

state. Seen in this way, 'national' and 'liberal', 'unity' and 'liberty' were conceptually very nearly of a piece. However, after Prussia, the largest *Partikularstaat*, placing itself at the head of the national movement and, at the same time, at the head of the German states, had unified Germany to the enthusiastic applause of the National Liberals, there arose conservative competition to the liberal claim to sole national representation. What we today call 'imperial nationalism', *Reichsnationalismus*, did not yet possess clear outlines in 1871. The only thing that was clear was that the foundation of the German Reich had set off a battle over what the concept 'national' would now signify.[3]

Liberals and conservatives were not the only participants in this struggle. German Catholics, many of whom voted for one of the liberal parties in the first federal elections and not the newly founded (1870) Catholic Centre Party (*Zentrumspartei*), were fundamentally provoked by the Evangelical interpretation of the Franco-Prussian War and the founding of the Reich. *One* of the Catholic interpretations hurled the challenge back to the Protestants. In his new year's article for the first 1871 issue of the *Historisch-politische Blätter für das katholische Deutschland*, Edmund Jörg adapted the medieval doctrine of the *translatio imperii* to describe—or at least suggest—the 'transfer' of the imperial crown from Napoleon III to William I, thus highlighting the illegitimate character of the new Reich, born of 'the politics of revolutionary nationalism'.

'If we are soon to have a German Reich,' wrote Jörg,

> in other words, if Prussia is to rule all countries of the former Confederation as its provinces, with the temporary exception of the Austro-German territories, then the new Bonaparte can boast, if he wishes, that he is the real creator or initiator of this German Empire, the crown of which has been proffered and accepted before besieged Paris, at Versailles. Without his national-liberal offensive against Austria in 1859, no Franco-Prussian trade agreement and not even a Count Bismarck would have been possible. Without his perfidy in the German–Danish conflict, Prussia would not have concocted the war of 1866, which violated the Confederation. Without the Italian ally, Prussia would not have found it so easy to triumph on the Bohemian fields. And if Austria had not been ejected from Germany, then a German war with France really would have brought peace to this exhausted part of the world. In any case, it would not have resulted in a Little German empire.

Jörg, one of the leaders of the Bavarian Patriots' party, spoke only for a small minority of German Catholics. During the war with France, most of his co-religionists acted and thought no less 'nationally' than the Protestants. They rejoiced at the annexation of Alsace and Lorraine, at the founding of the German Reich, and at the proclamation of the emperorship. Nonetheless, the rhetoric of the 'Protestant victory' and the 'Evangelical empire' could not be ignored. It galvanized the elements within German Catholicism pressing for a more cohesive political programme and party organization. In 1873 the Mainz bishop Wilhelm Emanuel von Ketteler, the first leader of the church to come to terms with the *kleindeutsch* solution after the German war of 1866 and who also participated in the founding of the Centre party in 1870, justified the necessity of concerted action in light of the shifted confessional balance.

> If in public life we are seen to lack power and influence, then we have everything to fear from our opponents, all the more now that we have lost ten million Catholics with Austria's departure from the German Reich and only represent a third of the entire population instead of a half, as we did before.

The following year, in August 1874, Ketteler sent an injunction to the clergy of his diocese forbidding any church participation in the celebrations initiated by Friedrich von Bodelschwingh to commemorate the German victory in the Battle of Sedan on 2 September 1870—celebrations lampooned in Catholic newspapers as 'St Sedan' and 'Celebrations of Satan'. Such events, wrote Ketteler, did not proceed from the people, but mainly from one party. The bishop was referring to the National Liberals, the main opponents of the Catholic Church and political Catholicism in the *Kulturkampf.* This party, unjustly claiming to represent the German people as a whole, was the same one currently at the forefront of the battle against Christianity and the Catholic Church.

> If its demand for religious participation in the Sedan celebrations seems especially eager, given that otherwise it shows very little concern for religion, we can be quite sure that the motivation is not religious at all. The Sedan celebrations celebrate not so much the victory of the German people over France as the party's victories over the Catholic Church.[4]

As bad as the Catholic situation after 1871 was or was perceived to be, the political pressure brought to bear on the German Social Democrats was far greater. After the committee of the Social Democratic Workers' Party, on 5 September 1870, had called for demonstrations of the German workers against the annexation of Alsace and Lorraine, the members of this body—those who did not enjoy parliamentary immunity—were arrested and incarcerated. On 28 November, the four Social Democrat and four Lassallean delegates to the Reichstag voted against further war credits. On 17 December, after the closing of the parliament, August Bebel and Wilhelm Liebknecht were arrested on charges of attempting and preparing to commit high treason. They were released on 28 March 1871, after Bebel was elected to the German Reichstag as one of two Social Democrat representatives. On 25 May he spoke before that body against the annexation of Alsace and Lorraine and came out in support of the Paris Commune. His observation 'that the battle in Paris is only a minor outpost skirmish, that the main event in Europe is yet to come' not only sounded like a threat, it was intended as such.

The trial of Bebel and Liebknecht in Leipzig in March 1872 resulted in two convictions for preparation of high treason. Both party leaders were sentenced to two-year prison terms. The Leipzig district court also found Bebel guilty of lese-majesty in July 1872 and gave him nine further months. The verdicts corresponded to the prevailing image of social democracy in the minds of the bourgeoisie. The Evangelical theologian Johann Hinrich Wichern summarized the typical view in October 1871: the battle against France was only the 'preliminary stage' of the even more difficult battle against the spirit of untruth and error, embodied in international social democracy, inside the new Reich. Just as seven years previously, after the battle with Denmark, many Prussian conservatives had clamoured for war against the 'inner Düppel', so now many Germans wanted to vanquish the 'inner France', whether in the form of Catholicism or of social democracy.

It was true that Bebel made it easy for the enemies of the German workers' movement to draw a distorted picture of his party. His declaration of unreserved solidarity with the Paris Commune was indebted to Marx's completely uncritical assessment of the Paris events in 'Der Bürgerkrieg in Frankreich', formally entitled 'Adresse des Generalrats der Internationalen Arbeiter-Assoziation'.* Two decades later, in the preface to the third German edition of the text, Engels summarized this assessment in the exhortation: 'Look at the Paris Commune. That was the dictatorship of the proletariat.' Considering the putsch-like characteristics of the rebellion, the excesses of violence committed *also* by the Communards, the abolition of the traditional separation between legislative, executive, and judicial powers, and the strident contrast between the ideal of this supposedly higher form of democracy and its reality, it is understandable even today why in spring 1871 the great majority of Europeans looked towards the French capital with fear and abhorrence. The German Social Democrats had little in common with the Communards. Yet Bebel gave the impression that his party was well on its way to eclipsing the French example. In doing so, he set consequences in motion that he could not possibly have intended and, in the interests of the German workers' movement, should have avoided.[5]

In their protest against the annexation of Alsace and Lorraine, the Social Democrats stood virtually alone in the new Reich. The only well-known bourgeois democrat to speak out publicly against this violation of the right to self-determination in September 1870 was Johann Jacoby of Königsberg, who was thereafter arrested. In April 1872, shortly after the announcement of the verdicts in the trial of Bebel and Liebknecht in Leipzig, Jacoby joined the Social Democratic Workers' party. Far more representative of the liberal bourgeois attitude was the position taken by David Friedrich Strauss (originally from Ludwigsburg), a scholar of religion and the founder of the historical study of the life of Jesus Christ, in an open correspondence with his no less famous Paris colleague Ernest Renan in 1870–1. Strauss wanted to recover the two 'German provinces' primarily for security reasons. We Germans, he wrote on 29 September 1870, would have to be 'supreme fools, if we do not seek to regain what was ours and what is necessary for our security (but no further than is necessary, of course)'.

* Marx, 'The Civil War in France'; 'Address of the General Council of the International Workers' Association'.

Renan, who saw in the Franco-Prussian War the greatest disaster that could have befallen civilization, answered Strauss's letter on 15 September 1871, nearly a year later.

In terms of language and race, Alsace is German. But it does not desire to be part of the German state. That decides the question . . . Our policy is the policy of the rights of nations. Yours is the policy of races. We believe ours is better. The too greatly emphasized classification of the human race into races—apart from being based upon scientific error, since only very few countries possess a really pure race—can only lead to wars of annihilation, to 'zoological' wars . . . That would be the end of this fruitful mixture called 'humanity,' composed of such numerous and altogether necessary elements. You have raised the banner of ethnographic and anthropologic policy in the world in place of liberalism. This policy will be your undoing . . . How can you believe that the Slavs, who emulate you in all things, will not do the same as you have done to others?

The voice from Paris was the voice of reason. In Renan's view, the nation was a community of will, or, as he expressed it in a lecture at the Sorbonne in 1882, 'a plebiscite repeated daily' (*un plébiscite de tous les jours*). In imperial Germany, this concept of the nation as a political idea based on the subjective decision of the individual found no echo. Since no common German state had existed before 1871, the seemingly objective factors of language, extraction, and culture had always been fundamental to the German conception of nation. It was true that, with the foundation of the Reich, the long-desired national state had finally become reality. But this state could not make membership in the German nation conditional upon the free decision of its citizens—otherwise the Alsace-Lorrainers in the west, the Poles in the east, and the Danes in the north would have dissociated themselves from Germany. On the other hand, there were millions of German-speaking Austrians in the Habsburg monarchy, whom erstwhile *gross-deutsch*-oriented Germans, whether Catholics or Social Democrats, still considered part of the German nation. From their perspective, the new German Reich was an 'unfinished nation state'.

For *kleindeutsch* Protestants, this point of view bordered on spiritual treason. The Evangelical rationalization of the Reich after 1871 had its origins in a dilemma. Since the German nation could be defined neither as a linguistic community nor as a community of the will, it was necessary to look for German imperial identity on another plane. The National Liberals and nationalist conservatives were convinced they had found it: the hegemony of the Protestant principle in German culture, society, and state. From the beginning, this version of imperial nationalism implied *both* the continuing secularization of German Protestantism, making religion ideologically of very flexible utility, *and* the increased theologization of German nationalism, separating the latter from the purely secular nationalism of France.

In a 1935 book, written during his exile, the philosopher and sociologist Helmuth Plessner called the Bismarck Reich a 'great power without an idea of the state' (*Grossmacht ohne Staatsidee*). Plessner discussed the belated nature of

German national politics: by the time Germany had become a nation, the time of the great world-political visions was already at an end. In 1789 the French were still able to link the revolutionary re-founding of their nation with an appeal to the universal validity of 'liberty, equality, fraternity'. Bismarck's 'revolution from above' brought forth a 'power state' (*Machtstaat*) that could no longer justify itself in terms of universal ideas. German pastors, professors, and publicists sensed this deficiency. Regardless of what they did to address it, however, the result could only be compensatory in nature.

Still, this compensation did have a certain tradition. For the early German nationalists after 1800, intellectual world leadership served to make up for the political impotence of Germany. The unwilling revolutionaries in the Frankfurt Paulskirche had created a German-dominated central Europe in their imaginations before their more modest plan for a *kleindeutsch* state foundered on the hard reality of two German great powers. The later National Liberals were ever more inclined during the era of constitutional conflict to consider the expansion of the Hohenzollern state the prerequisite for liberal domestic reforms.

Thinking in categories of the 'power state' as compensation for internal political powerlessness—before 1871, liberal Germany had gone so far along this path that it was very difficult to turn back once the 'power state' had become reality in the form of the German Reich. On the international stage, the founding of the Reich represented the fulfilment of liberalism's national goal. But inside Germany the liberal programme remained in large part unrealized. Since there was no lack of opponents, the great question was now whether the thinkers and visionaries of the 'power state' would seek out a sphere of activity within the newly created nation.[6]

THE BEGINNING OF THE *'KULTURKAMPF'*

By the time the German Reich was established, the conflict between State and Church we refer to as the *Kulturkampf* (from Rudolf Virchow's speech in the Prussian House of Representatives on 17 January 1873) had long since begun. In the 1860s, two primarily Catholic states, Bavaria and Baden, became the first in Germany to initiate policies of educational reform, in response to which they aroused the embittered and protracted opposition of the Catholic clergy. Such battles over the boundaries between Church and State also went on in other countries during the second half of the nineteenth century, and it was not by chance that they were most intense in predominantly Catholic countries, above all France and Italy.

The conflict was inevitable, but the particular form it took was not. From the viewpoint of the church, liberalism, heir of the Enlightenment and embodiment of modernism, was the aggressor, since it sought to abolish vested ecclesiastical rights like the clerical supervision of the schools. For liberals in the broad sense of the term, whether Catholic, Protestant, Jewish, agnostic, or atheist, the papacy was the first to throw down the gauntlet in its quasi-medieval declaration of war against the present age. When the First Vatican Council promulgated the doctrine of infallibility, it seemed to confirm this impression. Clearly, the Catholic Church's will to power was not going to be defeated by human reason alone.

Germany contributed indirectly but decisively to the termination of the pope's worldly rule only a few months later. The Kingdom of Italy was only able to annex the Papal States in October 1870 after the Germans had defeated its protector, Napoleon III, and brought about his downfall. Although an Italian law of May 1871 guaranteed the pope's sovereign rights as well as his possession of the Church of St Peter, the Vatican, and the Lateran palaces, Pope Pius IX rejected the offer and opted for the status of 'Vatican captivity', which lasted nearly six decades, until the Lateran treaties with fascist Italy in February 1929.

The restoration of the pope's worldly rule was the first political demand made by the Centre party after the foundation of the Reich. On 18 February 1871, in the Prussian headquarters at Versailles, Bismarck received from the hands of Bishop von Ketteler a petition from fifty-six Catholic members of the Prussian House of Representatives requesting that Emperor William do everything in his power to make the pope once again the lord of the Papal States. Bismarck angrily rejected the petition, since its acceptance would have meant a rupture with Italy and most certainly war.

The next challenge from the Catholic Centre was a motion by the party fraction in the Reichstag on 27 March 1871 to incorporate (as in Prussia) articles on basic rights into the federal constitution, including freedom of religion and the guarantee of ecclesiastic self-government. The chancellor, whom the emperor had just made a prince for his contribution to the founding of the Reich, saw in the Catholic initiative an attack on the cultural sovereignty of the individual states. For its part, the Reichstag majority had no intention of promoting church affairs, and promptly rejected the proposal. The complete draft of the constitution, presented to the federal parliament by Bismarck on 23 March, represented a version of the North German constitution revised and updated in only a few points. On 14 April 1871 the great majority of the plenum adopted it against only seven negative votes—from the two Social Democrats, four Guelfs, and one Dane. Despite the rejection of its motion on basic rights, the Centre party voted for the constitution.

In his *Gedanken und Erinnerungen*, Bismarck wrote that for him the beginning of the *Kulturkampf* was defined by its Polish aspect. He suspected the 'Catholic section' in the Prussian ministry of education and ecclesiastical affairs of promoting the Polish national movement in Posen and West Prussia through the Catholic clergy. In July 1871, he succeeded in having the ministry dissolved. It was only a short step from the allegation of the Catholic Church's complicity in the Polish cause to the claim that the Catholic Centre was also allied to other 'enemies of the Reich' like the Guelfs and the Alsace-Lorrainers—that is, that the Centre itself was hostile to the Reich. Bismarck considered the attitude of the Centre and the

Catholic clergy a challenge to be met with measures strengthening the authority and unity of the state. He was prepared to accept that a sharply laical policy, which to a certain extent also affected the Evangelical church, was rejected by the majority of old Prussian conservatives, who broke with the chancellor on this occasion. For his agenda in the *Kulturkampf*, Bismarck could depend on a majority gathered from a Conservative splinter group, the Free Conservatives, the National Liberals, the greater part of the Progressives, and the newly founded (but short-lived) Liberal Imperial Party (*Liberale Reichspartei*), whose parliamentary fraction consisted in roughly equal parts of federally minded Protestants and liberal Catholics. (The latter group included Baron Roggenbach, former Baden foreign minister, and Prince Chlodwig von Hohenlohe-Schillingsfürst, former prime minister of Bavaria.)

The first legislation of the *Kulturkampf* derived from a Bavarian initiative. The 'pulpit paragraph' of December 1871 made it a criminal offence for clerics to discuss affairs of state 'in a manner endangering public peace' in the exercise of their offices. A law dealing with the supervision of schools followed in March 1872. Clerical inspection of city and district schools was abolished, and all private schools were placed under state supervision. Four months later, in July 1872, the federal parliament passed the so-called 'Jesuit law' banning all establishments of the Society of Jesus in the Reich and imposing residency restrictions on individual members of the order. This law emerged from the campaigns of the old-Catholics and the German Protestant Association, who sought to outdo each other in the fierceness of their attacks on the Jesuits. The violation of liberal principles was flagrant, but only a few committed liberals like Bamberger and Lasker voted against the measure. The liberal majority found itself entirely of one mind with Bismarck as never before when, on 14 May 1872, the chancellor declared to parliament: 'To Canossa we shall not go—neither in body nor in spirit!' This promise was greeted with storms of applause.

Prussia's next blow fell in spring 1873. Buttressed by a constitutional amendment, one of the so-called 'May laws' made the appointment of any priest or minister to ecclesiastic office conditional upon his getting a certificate from a German gymnasium and passing a 'cultural exam' in the fields of philosophy, history, and German literature. Another law created a royal court of law for ecclesiastic affairs where appeals against church penalties could be heard. In March the Prussian House of Representatives passed a law subsequently adopted (February 1875) by the Reichstag in expanded form: the law concerning obligatory civil marriage, which transferred the documentation of marital status (birth, marriage, and death) from the church to newly created register offices, the *Standesämter*. This law is the only piece of *Kulturkampf* legislation that survives to the present day.

The 'expatriation law' of May 1874, on the other hand, was nothing more than an instrument of repression. Disregarding the most basic principles of the rule of law, it permitted the governments to confine clerics to certain places of residence, or to expatriate and ban them from the Reich. A Prussian law was passed the same month empowering the minister of education and ecclesiastic affairs to appoint a commissioner to temporarily administer bishoprics that fell vacant owing to state action. Two further Prussian laws of spring 1875 were aimed at the material basis of the adversary. The April 'bread basket law' stopped all payments of state funds to the Catholic Church. In May the 'monastery law' dissolved the monasteries of all the orders except those devoted exclusively to the care of the sick. The annulment of the Prussian constitution's article on religion in June 1875 represented a kind of keystone of the *Kulturkampf* legislation—an unwilling admission on the part of parliament and administration that the constitutionality of the foregoing laws was not above all suspicion.[7]

'Germany has taken up the battle against the minions of Rome, who have no fatherland, knowing full well that this battle will be longer and more difficult than the one against our arch-enemy across the Rhine.' In expressing such sentiments in its leading article on 21 October 1876, the national-liberal Berlin *National-Zeitung* had no criticism to fear from its readers. A year later, in an article on 'Sedan Day' in 1877, the same paper compared Catholics to Social Democrats:

> The main enemies of our Reich, the ultramontanists and the socialists, do not threaten us alone; they are the opponents of civil order over all the earth. Both the church and socialism do not so much attack a particular state or a particular constitution; rather, they attack the basis of all states and all societies.

In attacking Catholicism, the National Liberals were fighting a power that contested their claim to be *the* largest party of the people. Their attempt to strip the Centre party of all national credibility derived from a desire to maintain their own power: if they, the National Liberals, wished to maintain their key position as the chancellor's most important support, they were forced to do everything they could to prevent a scenario that, in the longer term, was perfectly plausible: the formation of a majority among conservatives and Catholics. Yet the methods they employed or sanctioned in this battle were also highly dangerous to themselves, severely shaking the liberal credibility of national liberalism.

The result of the *Kulturkampf* legislation was quite different from what Bismarck and the parties supporting him had expected. Although many Catholic parishes fell vacant and most Prussian bishops were imprisoned, removed, or expelled from the country during the mid-1870s, this could hardly be considered a 'success' for the government and the parliamentary majority. The faithful remained loyal to the persecuted bishops and swelled the ranks of the Centre party, which gained twice as many seats in the 1874 elections as in 1871. To be sure, the Catholic party was far more successful among the urban and rural lower classes than among the educated and propertied bourgeoisie, which in many places—Cologne and Bonn, for example—continued to favour liberal candidates over those from the Centre party.

The clergy aided this development by encouraging a movement of popular piety aimed at promoting cohesion among Catholics—which, however, tended to appeal to women far more than to men. Thus, the *Kulturkampf* contributed to Catholicism's anti-intellectual tendencies and to the widening of the chasm separating Catholics from Protestants. And for a great number of Catholics the wounds left by ostracism and repression had not healed even long after most of the legislation had been softened or repealed. They had been accused of national untrustworthiness, even of hostility to the Reich, and they could not give themselves over to the illusion that prejudices were shorter-lived than paragraphs.[8]

THE RISE OF 'MODERN' ANTI-SEMITISM

On 9 May 1873 the Vienna stock market collapsed. The 'great crash' shook Europe like an earthquake. Its effects were especially harsh in Germany, where the French war reparations of 5 billion francs had heated up the national economy. The years 1871–3 had seen a mushrooming of new joint-stock companies, joint-stock banks, railroad companies, construction firms, and coal and steel enterprises, a large number of which rested upon purely speculative economic foundations. After the summer of 1873, numerous bankruptcies and bank closings drastically reduced the average share price; at the end of 1874, it was just over half of what it had been at the end of 1872. But the low point was not reached until 1878–9. The boom of the the new empire's *Gründerzeit*, the 'founders' era', seemed increasingly like a 'founders' fraud', and the long-term economic consequences of the 'great crash' were felt by many contemporaries to be a 'Great Depression'.

The social-psychological impact of the economic collapse has been well described by the historian Hans Rosenberg, who speaks of the 'radical climate change in consciousness and in ways of reacting' throughout the 1870s and 1880s, all the way up to the onset of a new economic upswing in 1896. The characteristics of this 'climate change', according to Rosenberg, were

> a primarily anxious and pessimistic economic mentality, tending towards constant complaint; an intensification of now chronic and increasingly widespread social dissatisfaction and disquiet; an escalation of ideological energy and aggressiveness; a constant, frequently heated conflict over the distribution of the ever more limited real national income—a conflict often fought with political means.

After 1873, liberalism found itself in the dock. According to critics, the deeper cause of the decline in commerce and industry was the policy of laissez-faire, laissez-aller. A part of public opinion, however, began to suspect a single wirepuller behind both liberalism and stock market capitalism—international Jewry. It fitted nicely into the theories of the anti-Jewish agitation that the most spectacular bankruptcy of the crash was that of the 'rail king' Bethel Henry Strousberg, a converted Jew of East Prussian descent. Strousberg owed his influence not to his own capital, but to connections with members of the East Prussian nobility and high bureaucracy, who counted in their turn upon the investments of countless small shareholders—until Strousberg's failed speculations dragged everybody into ruin.

Strousberg was no liberal. He had served in the North German parliament from 1867 to 1870 as a Conservative delegate. It was, in fact, a liberal politician who revealed the 'Strousberg system' in the Prussian House of Representatives on 7 February 1873—Eduard Lasker. Along with Ludwig Bamberger, Lasker was the most prominent Jew among the leading National Liberals. Heine's famous dictum that the baptismal certificate was the 'entry ticket to European culture' had lost its universality; neither Lasker nor Bamberger had been baptized. Nonetheless, they were among the most distinguished and popular politicians of the National Liberal party and two of the most convinced and convincing apostles of the maxim that 'the path of freedom lies through unity.'

One of the blessings of liberty many German Jews believed national unity would bestow was progress along another path, the one leading to authentic, not merely legal, equality between Christians and Jews. In other words, German unity was supposed to lead to the full emancipation of the Jews at the same time as it led to the political emancipation of the bourgeoisie. The German liberals of the new imperial era made the cause of Jewish emancipation their own in a way one can almost call the 'liberalization of liberalism'. There seemed to be little left of the anti-Jewish reservations common among liberal politicians of the *Vormärz*—despite the fact that anti-Jewish clichés could still be found in the much-read novels of liberally minded authors of the 1850s and 1860s, writers like Gustav Freytag, Wilhelm Raabe, and Felix Dahn.

The case of Richard Wagner was different. In May 1849 the composer had fought for the Revolution in the streets of Dresden. In 1850, while in exile in Switzerland, he wrote his essay 'Das Judentum in der Musik',* in which he attacked the 'Jewification of modern art,' professed his 'instinctive antipathy towards Jewishness', and demanded 'emancipation from the Jews'. Fifteen years later, his essay 'Was ist deutsch?'† (1865) went even further. Wagner lamented that after the *Vormärz* period, 'French-Jewish-German democracy' had been well received 'by the misunderstood and wounded spirit of the German people', and sought to explain the failure of the 1848 Revolution by asserting 'that the authentic German suddenly found himself and his name represented by a kind of human being utterly foreign to him'.

The 'great crash' of 1873 brought to a close the short period of general open-mindedness towards Jews that had begun in 1859 with the renaissance of the liberal movement. The National Liberals were unable to preserve their national image in the face of defamatory accusations of their being the henchmen of Jewish-controlled international finance. It was no help to National Liberal Jews that one of their own had been the first to attempt to expose the 'founders' fraud'.

* Wagner, 'Judaism in Music'.

† Wagner, 'What is German?'

In mid-1875, the journalist Franz Perrot initiated with the so-called 'era articles' in the *Kreuz-Zeitung* a campaign vilifying not only liberals and Jews in general, but also Bismarck's banker Gerson Bleichröder, the secret financier of the Prussian war of 1866 and intimate of some of the most powerful European statesmen. Perrot even went so far as to attack the chancellor himself.

If the monetary and economic policies of the German Reich, wrote Perrot, always give the impression of being Jewish policies, that is, policies and legislation by Jews and for Jews, that is

> quite understandable, for the intellectual progenitor of these policies, Herr von Bleichröder, is himself a Jew . . . What is more, our fellow citizens of Semitic race and Mosaic faith have also taken over the intellectual leadership of the legislative activity in our organs of representation—with the exception of the House of Lords, of course. Messrs Lasker and Bamberger, as well as their close friend H. B. Oppenheim, who admittedly has only just taken his seat in parliament, are all Jews, and they make up the actual leadership of the so-called 'national-liberal' majority of the assembly and the Prussian second chamber . . . At the present time we are, in fact, ruled by Jews.

Articles hostile to the Jews appeared in the mid 1870s not only in the mouthpiece of the Prussian conservatives, but also in *Germania*, the Centre party's most important newspaper, and other organs of political Catholicism. Edmund Jörg, at that time also a Centre party delegate to the Reichstag for the Bavarian electoral district of Schwaben, came at the beginning of 1877 to the conclusion that the *Kulturkampf* was a 'prime promotional tactic of the new stock-market era', since it had also drawn well-meaning Protestants into its vortex and thus prevented a 'reconstruction of the conservative elements'. 'In such a way, however, this unbloody war of religion has also been greatly of service in assuring the Mamelukes of money power in the parliamentary bodies their majority and their influence.' Shortly thereafter, Jörg spoke of 'Jewified liberalism in German lands'. The *Historisch-politische Blätter für das katholische Deutschland* equated the Jews with the 'high cosmopolitan powers of finance' and the actual 'enemies of the Reich'. Even Ketteler saw in the *Kulturkampf* a 'Freemason-Jewish-liberal conspiracy' against the Catholic Church.[9]

The anti-Jewishness of the 1870s could no longer be considered religious in motivation. It was 'modern' insofar as it took aim against modern, emancipated Jewry using purely secular discourse. The Jews were portrayed as agents of those aspects of modernism by which various groups in society felt themselves threatened. For many of its opponents, liberalism was nothing more than the world-view of modern Jewry. Those who considered themselves victims of capitalist speculation tended to see things like the publicist Otto Glagau, who in the popular *Gartenlaube* contrasted the Jews as representatives of unproductive, 'grasping' capital with the productive, 'creative' capital of Christians. Many would have echoed Glagau's much-quoted assertion that 'The social question today is, basically, a Jewish question.' Jewish bankers found themselves stigmatized as members of a 'Golden International' (the title of an 1876 text by the Berlin judicial official Carl Wilmanns), which made it easy to suspect them of being nationally untrustworthy and in close contact with the—also putatively Jew-dominated—'red International'.

This was not the first time hostility toward the Jews and anti-liberalism had come together. The origins of their partnership lay back in the era of Prussian reform, when conservatives like Friedrich August Ludwig von der Marwitz, seeking to mobilize peasants and tradesmen, declared war on Jewish emancipation, freedom of trade, and the free movement of labour. Emancipation itself was always accompanied by an anti-Jewish counter-movement. Tracts and pamphlets compared Jews to vampires and disease-causing agents; demands for the expulsion, castration, and even the destruction of the Jews were frequently heard. From the late 1830s, and increasingly during the 1860s, 'ultramontanist' writers denounced the Jews as the beneficiaries and exploiters of the process of secular emancipation threatening everything the Catholic Church considered sacred. Immediately after founding of the Reich, *the* event that sealed the minority position of the German Catholics, this simultaneously anti-Jewish and anti-liberal movement within Catholicism gained new force. After 1873, anti-Jewish rhetoric was employed almost universally against everything considered to be 'modern' and thus an attack on tradition. Liberalism and socialism suffered the same fate, and since Jews played a role in both movements, they were both considered manifestations of the Jewish will to power.

In fact, if one gave credence to the accusations of popular writers like Constantin Frantz and Wilhelm Marr, the Jews had advanced to become the real rulers of Germany in the new imperial era. Under the regime of national liberalism, as Frantz wrote in 1874, the Jews had entered into 'the cynosure of our development', and whatever was called 'progress' was ultimately only the 'progress of Jewification'. 'A *German Empire of the Jewish Nation* is thus rising before our eyes.' 'Who actually rules the new Empire?' the same author asked two years later. 'And to what purpose were the victories of Sadowa and Sedan achieved, to what purpose the billions carried off, to what purpose is the *Kulturkampf*, if not to further the *rule of the Jews*?' In his protest against Jewish emancipation, Frantz did not hesitate to invoke the 'short work' that Fichte had wanted to make of the Jews in his 1793 work on the French Revolution: before giving the Jews civil rights, their heads were all to be cut off in one night and replaced with others containing no Jewish ideas.

For Marr, baptism made absolutely no difference. In his extraordinarily successful book *Der Sieg des Judenthums über das Germanentum. Vom nicht confessionellen Standpunkt aus betrachtet** (1879), the writer fought not against the religion of the Jews, but against the Jews as a race, one that had become a 'world

* Marr, *The Victory of Jewry over Germandom: A Non-confessional Point of View.*

power of the first order' and strove for 'world domination'. Membership in the Jewish community thus became an unalterable fact of nature, one that could not be changed by an act of volition like conversion to a Christian confession. Throughout the 1870s, Jews were increasingly referred to as 'Semites'. The term 'anti-Semitism' first arose in the autumn of 1879 in Marr's circle. The 'League of Anti-Semites' was founded in Berlin at approximately the same time, and by followers of the same writer.[10]

The secularization of anti-Jewish hatred allowed the latter to make pretences to a 'scientific' and 'objective' character. Paradoxically, the 'modernization' of anti-Jewish hatred gave rise to anti-modernism in its most extreme form. The 'great crash' of 1873 was merely the catalyst setting a momentarily retarded protest movement in motion once again—protest not against the founding of the Reich as such, but against everything that linked the new German state to the philosophy and practice of liberalism. Those strata of society who felt themselves threatened by increasing industrialization—above all peasants, tradesmen, and small merchants—proved especially susceptible of anti-liberal mobilization.

Another sworn enemy of liberalism was the Catholic Church, and not only since the *Kulturkampf*. The Catholic adversaries of the Jews expressed the traditional anti-Judaism of the church in a manner frequently indistinguishable from the political, economic, and social discourse of 'modern' anti-Semitism. The reverse was also true: 'worldly' anti-Semites like Wilmanns and Perrot invoked the example of Christian Jew-haters like the Münster Catholic theologian August Rohling, who in 1871 published *Der Talmudjude*,* a classic work of religious anti-Semitism. The old hatred of the 'murderers of God' and 'usurers', as common among Protestants as Catholics, was not simply replaced by 'modern' anti-Semitism. Christian anti-Judaism united with secular anti-Semitism and lent it a historic 'depth' independent of any temporary fluctuations in the state of the economy.

Most Christian anti-Semites, Protestants as well as Catholics, were at pains to deny they countenanced any kind of racial hatred. In his first major speech against 'modern Jewry', held on 19 September 1879 at an assembly of the Christian Social Workers' party (which he founded) in Berlin, Adolf Stoecker, from 1874 chaplain of the royal Prussian court in Berlin, assured his audience that he dedicated himself to the Jewish question 'in full Christian love'. This sentiment did not prevent him from describing 'modern Jewry'—which he sought to differentiate from both traditional-orthodox and enlightened reform-Judaism—as 'a great danger to the life of the German people'. The Jews were and would remain a 'people within a people, a state within a state, a tribe isolated among a foreign race'. Here and there, noted Stoecker, hatred was already flaming up against the Jews, a hatred irreconcilable with the Gospel. 'If modern Jewry continues to use the power of

* Rohling, *The Talmud Jew.*

capital as well as the power of the press to the ruin of the nation, a catastrophe will be unavoidable in the end. Israel must give up its aspiration to become the lord of Germany.'

Among the remedies Stoecker proposed were the 'reintroduction of confessional statistics, in order that the imbalance between Jewish wealth and Christian labour might be ascertained; reduction of the appointment of Jewish judges to the proportion of Jews in the population; removal of Jewish teachers from our public schools.' A week later the court chaplain fulminated against the fact that Jews enjoyed a much greater representation among employers, 'directors and directresses', in commerce, and among the students of higher education—especially in Berlin—than was warranted by the percentage of Jews in the population.

> In itself, such a drive for social preference, for higher education, deserves the highest recognition. However, for us it means a fight for survival of the most intensive kind. If Israel grows even further in this direction, it will be more than we can cope with. For let us harbour no illusions: on this soil, race stands against race and is waging a racial conflict—not in the sense of hatred, but in the sense of competition . . . If Israel is united in social-political activity over the whole earth through the 'Alliance Israelite' [the *Alliance Israélite Universelle*, an international Jewish association (H.A.W.)], that is a state within the state, international within the nation.

Among the industrial workers, Stoecker's actual target audience, whom he sought to draw from social democracy into the conservative camp, neither his Christian-inspired solution to the social question nor his attacks against 'modern Jewry' found any resonance. Among the petty bourgeois of Berlin, on the other hand, who until that point had remained loyal to the National Liberals, his anti-Semitic speeches were very well received. That he distanced himself from fanatical racial hatred helped his brand of anti-Semitism also gain a certain amount of respectability among 'elevated' circles of society.

The other founder of the new anti-Semitic 'Berlin movement' was even more successful in this respect: the historian and Reichstag delegate Heinrich von Treitschke, who left the National Liberal party in 1879, the same year the first volume of his *Deutsche Geschichte im 19. Jahrhundert* came out. In November of that year, a few weeks after Stoecker's first two speeches against 'modern Jewry', Treitschke, writing in the *Preussische Jahrbücher* (which he edited), observed concerning the 'passionate movement against the Jews' that the 'instinct of the masses' had

> indeed correctly perceived a great danger, a deeply disturbing source of harm to the new life of the German people . . . The number of Jews in western Europe is so small that they cannot exercise a perceptible influence on the national mores. But across our eastern border, year after year, out of the inexhaustible cradle of Poland, streams a horde of ambitious, pantaloon-peddling youths, whose children and children's children will one day control the stock markets and newspapers of Germany . . . Let us not deceive ourselves: the movement is very deep and strong, and a few jokes about the sage pronouncements of Christian-social stump-speakers will not suffice to get it under control. Up to and including the best-educated circles of society, among men who would reject with disgust any thought of

religious intolerance or national arrogance, the German people of today speak as if with one voice: the Jews are our misfortune.

To be sure, Treitschke let it be known that, among those who understood the issue, there could be no talk of a 'revocation or even a restriction of the completed emancipation', since that would be a 'clear injustice'; the only thing demanded of the 'Israeli fellow citizens' was that they 'become German and, plainly and simply, feel German, regardless of their religion and their ancient sacred memories'. Yet the Berlin historian had broken a spell. His article made it plain that 'modern anti-Semitism' had penetrated even the liberal educated bourgeoisie. The social advancement of the Jews had been followed by the social advancement of anti-Semitism.

Treitschke's essay initiated a furious controversy, the 'Berlin anti-Semitism conflict'. Declared opponents of the Jews, men like Stoecker, supported the historian. Censure came from Jewish scholars and politicians like the philosopher Hermann Cohen and the Reichstag delegate Ludwig Bamberger, but also from prominent Gentiles. Crown Prince Frederick publicly expressed his outrage over anti-Semitism several times in the years 1879–81. On 12 November 1879 liberal personalities, led by Max von Forckenbeck, the mayor of Berlin and former president of the Reichstag, joined together to protest that in many parts of Germany 'racial hatred and the fanaticism of the Middle Ages has awakened to new life and is being directed against our Jewish fellow citizens.' Treitschke's name was not mentioned, but he, too, was implied in the observation that Lessing's legacy of tolerance between Jews and Christians was being undermined by men 'who should be proclaiming from pulpit and lectern that our culture has overcome the isolation of the tribe that once gave the world the worship of the one God'.

One of the seventy-five signatories of the declaration was the world-famous historian of antiquity Theodor Mommsen, who shortly afterwards wrote a pamphlet aimed directly at his long-time political comrade in arms. Jews of German nationality, wrote Mommsen, were forced to conclude from Treitschke's article that the author 'considered them second-class citizens, a kind of penal battalion that might, at best, be somewhat reformed. That is tantamount to preaching civil war.' The 'feeling of alienation and inequality' with which, even today, many a Christian German confronts the Jewish German, contains a danger for both: 'the civil war of a majority against a minority, even only as a possibility, is a national calamity.'

It was not only in Germany that anti-Semitism proliferated as a consequence of the stock market crash and the economic crisis. It also spread in Austria, Hungary, and France, especially in the 1880s, and in Russia, where anti-Jewish pogroms were frequent throughout the same decade. But when it came to 'modern anti-Semitism', the battle against emancipated Jewry, Germany was the master and its neighbors the pupils. It was, to be sure, a very studious master, who learned what the British natural scientist Charles Darwin had to teach concerning the struggle for survival and absorbed the lessons of the French anthropologist Count Joseph Arthur de Gobineau on the inequality of the human races and the superiority of the 'Aryan' race.

Bamberger, in his response to Treitschke, speculated that the deeper cause of German anti-Jewish sentiment lay in a peculiar interrelationship of attraction and repulsion between Germans and Jews.

A mixture of heterogeneous and related psychological features—exactly from such material are brewed the most bitter enmities. In this case, too. The common ground is the basic spiritualistic character; Jews and Germans are, without a doubt, the two most spiritualistic nations of all times and places. The Christian-Germanic is no mere invention of Teutonizing pietists and professors . . . The speculative philosophy of Spinoza has never been as profoundly understood and honoured as in Germany, and if it is permitted to name names of such disparate value in one breath: in no other land could the two philosophizing socialists Marx and Lassalle have gained such a following.

Bamberger detected another German-Jewish spiritual affinity in the 'cosmopolitan disposition, which is closely allied to the ability to break with the established order'. What separated the two peoples he characterized in the following way: 'A thoughtful, solemn, reverent, serious, obedient character contrasts markedly with a strangely agile, sarcastic, sceptical, undisciplinable spirit.' Heinrich Heine and Eduard Lasker were two figures who, according to Bamberger, had combined the German and Jewish spirit in completely different but equally impressive ways: here the profound poet with a humour verging on frivolity, there the brilliant parliamentarian, who fought for the cause of German idealism 'with the most brilliant weapons of Jewish dialectic' against the great realist Bismarck.[11]

A half-century before, in the year 1834, Heine had speculated in his Paris exile over what would happen if Germany should one day proceed from contemplation to practical action, from the revolution in the realm of thought to revolution in the empire of reality. At the end of his *Geschichte der Religion und Philosophie in Deutschland*,* Heine wrote that Christianity had somewhat moderated the brutal Germanic lust for battle, but had not been able to destroy it,

and when one day the taming talisman, the cross, should crack, then the ferocity of the old warriors will surge forth again, the mindless berserker rage of which the Nordic poets speak and sing so much. That talisman has grown brittle, and the day will come when it shall break wretchedly asunder. The old stone gods will then arise out of their forgotten ruin and rub the dust of a thousand years from their eyes, and Thor with his giant hammer will finally leap forth and pulverize the Gothic cathedrals . . . The thought precedes the deed like the lightning the thunder. Nonetheless German thunder, being German, is not very agile, and comes rolling up somewhat slowly. But come it will, and when you hear it crash like it has never yet crashed in all of world history, know this: the thunder of the Germans

* Heine, *History of Religion and Philosophy in Germany.*

has finally reached its goal. At this sound, eagles will fall dead from the sky, and the lions in the desert of Africa will crawl into their kingly caves with their tails between their legs. In Germany, a drama will be enacted that will make the French revolution seem like a harmless idyll.

Lasker, Bamberger's other star witness for the possibility of a successful mixture of the German and the Jewish, had, by the time his colleagues' pamphlet appeared in 1880, already been made to feel the increase in the number of those who resented his Jewish heritage. In the 1879 elections to the Prussian House of Representatives, he lost the support of his Breslau electoral district, not least of all due to intense anti-Semitic agitation.

The demonstration of liberal solidarity with the Jews had virtually no effect on the anti-Jewish campaigns, which continued unabated. At the end of 1880 appeared the first edition of *Die Judenfrage als Rassen-, Sitten-, und Kulturfrage** from the pen of the positivist popular philosopher Eugen Dühring. In this book, the author sought to draw attention to the 'evil of Jewification and the rule of the Jews for the modern nations' and the possibility of 'de-Jewification' (*Entjudung*). Dühring concluded with an exhortation difficult to misunderstand:

The strength and sustainability of the remedy must correspond to the magnitude and the tenaciousness of the evil . . . Now that the race has been thoroughly understood, we will set ourselves from the beginning a more distant goal, the way to which cannot be cleared by any but the strongest remedies. The Jews are—this will always be the conclusion of those who know the race—an inner Carthage, whose might the modern nations must destroy, lest they themselves be destroyed by it in their moral and material foundations.

During the same period, in the years 1878–81, the first anti-Semitic organizations and parties arose in Berlin and Saxony, among them the German Reform Party (*Deutsche Reformpartei*), established in Dresden in September 1881. The anti-Semitic Association of German Students (*Verein Deutscher Studenten*) was founded the same year in Berlin. On 13 April 1881 the chancellor received an 'anti-Semites' petition' with 255,000 signatures demanding the prohibition of further Jewish immigration, the exclusion of the Jews from all higher political office and from the faculty of the public schools, the restriction of the number of Jews in higher education and the judiciary, and the reintroduction of confessional statistics. Five years later, in January 1886, the *Antisemitische Correspondenz* (published in Leipzig by Theodor Fritsch) stated the movement's ultimate goal: the 'elimination of the Jewish race from international public life'. Finally, in 1887, the famous orientalist Paul de Lagarde (whose real name was Paul Anton Bötticher), despite repeated denial of a belief in racial anti-Semitism, referred to the Jews as 'rampant vermin' (*wucherndes Ungeziefer*) that had to be crushed underfoot. 'One does not negotiate with trichinae and bacilli. Trichinae and bacilli also cannot be educated and improved. They are destroyed, as quickly and completely as possible.'

* Dühring, *The Jewish Question as a Racial, Moral, and Cultural Qusetion.*

Physical destruction was the most radical conceivable solution to the 'Jewish question'. For the extremist anti-Semites of Germany, the idea that there was no more room on earth for the Jews seemed to flow naturally from their conviction that the Jews were at home in the whole world and therefore belonged nowhere. In this view, the Jews were either not a nation or a nation within the nation. Either way, they represented a foreign body. The Germans, for their part, had left behind their own 'cosmopolitanism' with the founding of their national state. Many of them thought the Jews either unwilling or unable to do the same.

A more probable explanation is that the Germans, whom Helmuth Plessner has called a 'belated nation', were profoundly insecure about their national identity after 1871. Once the external 'arch-enemy' had been overcome, many were tempted to create an internal arch-enemy who could help answer the question of what was 'German' and what 'un-German'. 'International Jewry' was especially apt for this role. It could be connected to practically everything by which Germans felt themselves to be threatened—to international finance capital as well as to international socialism. Since Protestants and Catholics, believing and non-believing Christians could agree on this view of the Jews, the latter seemed to afford an even better internal enemy—and thus support for national cohesion—than ultramontanist Rome.

Only a small minority of Germans hearkened to the diatribes of the radical anti-Semites after the mid-1870s. But those who fought against anti-Semitism were a minority, too. The majority was evidently not greatly disturbed by the activities of the anti-Semites and not free of anti-Jewish prejudice. Bamberger declared in 1880 that 'the people generally think in more human and less prejudicial terms than a few academics.' But he also felt that Treitschke had done a service to the Jews

> by making many of them whom the last decades had lulled into illusion once again aware of how things really stand. He who labours under self-deception always labours wrongly, and when he discovers the truth, he falls into dismay, if not despair. It is better for the Jews to acknowledge the feelings of antipathy hidden under the outer reflexes of politeness.[12]

FROM LEFTIST TO RIGHTIST NATIONALISM

The first years of the new German Reich seemed to confirm Bamberger's prediction of December 1866 that unity would help the cause of liberty. In Prussia, the liberal's cooperation with Bismarck brought about notable successes, above all in the reform of county (*Kreis*) administration. The December 1872 *Kreisordnung* for the six eastern Prussian provinces abolished the manorial police and the hereditary office of the village mayor (*Schulze*), opened the office of county administrator (*Landrat*) to officials of the state with the appropriate legal training, and created the basis for a new judicial branch, administrative jurisdiction. In order to break conservative resistance to the reform, however, the king had to appoint new, regime-friendly members to the House of Lords.

On the federal level, the laws for the standardization of currency and coinage, passed between 1871 and 1875, bore the mark of the National Liberals. The *Kulturkampf* legislation was also 'national-liberal' in inspiration, though in a completely different way. So important were these measures to the largest party that it was willing to assure Bismarck's cooperation by accommodating the chancellor in a different, highly controversial area—the military budget. In 1871 the peacetime strength of the army was set at 401,000 troops for three years. In 1874 Bismarck sought a military budget in perpetuum, the so-called *Äternat*. Since this would have removed four-fifths of the federal budget from the control of the Reichstag, the National Liberals could not vote for it without renouncing the core of their political identity. The result of a long process of conflict and negotiation was a compromise worked out between Bismarck and Bennigsen, the *Septennat*, a seven-year military budget. Since the legislative period lasted three years, only every second or third Reichstag would be able to exercise its full budgetary authority.

In the second half of 1877, it seemed for a time as though the chancellor was going to accept a parliamentary governance of sorts in Prussia and the Reich. He offered Bennigsen a ministerial position in the Prussian government and, at the same time, the office of an undersecretary to the imperial chancellor; in effect, he proposed making Bennigsen his representative in both governments. According to Article IX of the imperial constitution, simultaneous membership in the Federal Council and the parliament was prohibited; as a Prussian minister, Bennigsen would have been compelled to give up his seat as a Reichstag delegate. If the leader of the National Liberals, alone of his party, had joined the government, he would have risked isolation, if not a total loss of power. In order to avoid this danger, he proposed to Bismarck that two further National Liberals, Max von Forckenbeck and the Swabian-Bavarian landowner Franz Schenk von Stauffenberg (both members of the party left) also receive governmental offices. If this had happened, Bennigsen's 'ministerial candidacy' would have been transformed into a step towards a real parliamentary monarchy. And that, of course, was precisely what Bismarck wished to avoid.

His offer to Bennigsen had a rather different motivation. In 1875 Bismarck had decided to abandon economic liberalism and free trade for the sake of a protectionist tariff policy. This change of course was, for him, not a matter of doctrine, but primarily a question of financial pragmatism. At that juncture, 'matricular' contributions from the individual states were the main source of federal funds, making the Reich financially dependent on its members. Protective tariffs, state monopolies (for example in tobacco), indirect taxes (for example on beer, liquor, and coffee), and a tax rise on tobacco would have ended or reduced this dependence, and thus they seemed to Bismarck a good means to reach this goal. Most National Liberals, however, fundamentally rejected state-run monopolies and protective tariffs, and they were prepared to approve new federal taxes only if the Reichstag were granted the same yearly budgetary competence over a part of the revenue it already possessed with respect to the allocations from the individual states.

Thus, it was inconceivable that the whole of the National Liberal party would support Bismarck's economic about-face. But the chancellor did not expect them to do so. Rather, his proposal to Bennigsen was calculated to split the party and bring about the formation of a new parliamentary majority, including the conservatives, who, after their re-establishment as the German Conservative party in 1876, had once again been aiming at a role in government. In the event, Bennigsen was not willing to go along with Bismarck's scheme. For his part, the chancellor did not seriously wish to have the leader of the National Liberals as a minister. Thus Bennigsen's 'ministerial candidacy' remained an episode. Parliamentary rule never had a chance in Bismarck's Germany.

Bismarck's 1877 initiative was not least an attempt at a pre-emptive strike, with which the chancellor sought to prevent the left wing of the National Liberal party (which he continually claimed was under the control of Bamberger and Lasker) from gaining more influence under the successor of the aged emperor. Indeed, the political understanding between Crown Prince Frederick and the resolute liberals was very much in evidence. This was one of the main reasons Bismarck favoured any step that could bring the conservatives closer to power. Moreover, when Pope Pius IX died in February 1878 and was succeeded by the relatively 'realistic' Cardinal Pecci as Leo XIII, the opportunity presented itself for a reconciliation between the Reich and the Catholic Church and therewith the chance, sooner or later, to gain the support of the Centre party for the government.

The conservatives and the Centre were opponents of economic liberalism, above all free choice of trade or industry. In the middle of the 1870s, the grain-exporting manorial lords of East Elbia were not yet demanding the end of free trade. The Association of Tax and Economic Reformers (*Vereinigung der Steuer- und Wirtschaftsreformer*), founded in 1876 and closely allied to the German Conservative party, pronounced itself basically in support of free trade and against protective tariffs, though it considered the question of entrance tariffs and consumer taxes open to debate. The most adamant supporters of protective tariffs sat in the rows of the Free Conservatives and in the right wing of the National Liberals. Their strongest backing came from the Rhenish-Westphalian iron and steel industry and the southern German cotton industry—two branches that felt themselves particularly threatened by the British competition. In 1876 they played the decisive role in the founding of the first leading association of German entrepreneurs, the Central Association of German Industrialists (*Centralverband Deutscher Industrieller*), which campaigned openly for protective tariffs.

In February 1878 Bismarck presented to the Reichstag a bill to raise the tax on tobacco. In exchange for their support, the National Liberals demanded guarantees in law for the budgetary rights of the federal parliament and the Prussian

House of Representatives. This was a price Bismarck was unwilling to pay. Moreover, he prevented all possibility of compromise by stating to the Reichstag on 22 February that he considered the tobacco tax merely a stop along the way to state monopoly on tobacco. That destroyed the bill. Bennigsen took the chancellor's speech as an opportunity to declare the negotiations over his joining the government officially at an end (for his part, Bismarck considered them long since closed). Shortly thereafter, the two last representatives of German 'portfolio liberalism,' Minister of Trade von Achenbach and Finance Minister von Camphausen, stepped down, just as the president of the imperial chancellery, Rudolf von Delbrück, had done in June 1876, when it became clear to him that Bismarck was turning away from economic liberalism. 'The system shift is becoming ever more evident'—the balance drawn by Grand Duke Frederick I of Baden in a private letter from the beginning of April 1878 represented the view of most well-informed observers of the empire's inner crisis.[13]

Even if it had not been for the two attempts on the life of Emperor William, which took place in rapid succession in spring 1878, the open break between Bismarck and liberalism would still have occurred. Nonetheless, the attacks fundamentally changed the political situation in Germany and gave the chancellor an earlier opportunity to revise the distribution of parliamentary power more to his taste. On 11 May 1878 Max Hödel, a plumber's journeyman, fired at the emperor on Unter den Linden street without hitting him; on 2 June, very near the first assassination attempt, William was shot and seriously wounded by Dr Karl Eduard Nobiling, an economist by profession. Hödel had earlier belonged to the Socialist Workers' Party (founded in Gotha in May 1875 as successor to the hitherto separated Social Democratic and Lassallean parties), though he had been excluded for embezzling party funds. In Nobiling's case, no connection with the socialists could be proved. Bismarck, however, was not interested in legally compelling evidence of a social-democratic motivation for the assassination attempts; he was resolved to use the attacks as a pretext for settling accounts with both socialism *and* liberalism.

The first draft of an anti-socialist law, presented to the parliament on 20 May, a few days after Hödel's attack, did not outlaw the party, but made provisions for the possibility of banning Social Democratic associations, gatherings, and printed material. The great majority of the deputies rejected the bill, including most of the National Liberals. On 11 June, after the second attack, Bismarck dissolved the Reichstag—an act aimed primarily at the National Liberals, to whom the Bismarck-inspired press ascribed a 'moral complicity' in the assassination attempts. Immediately following the first attack, the *Norddeutsche Allgemeine Zeitung*, Bismarck's house organ, claimed that social democracy had accustomed itself 'to settling into the nests prepared for it by liberalism'. After the second attempt on the emperor's life, the same paper accused the party of 'forcing the second part of its name into the foreground, at the expense of the first', and condemned it for having deserted the nation.

The *Kreuz-Zeitung* went much further, calling socialism the 'logical development of liberalism' and making, once again, 'modern Jewry' responsible for liberalism's errors. ' "Jewification" is making great strides, and it is being pushed along by liberalism . . . The real enemies of the Reich are those who have taken from our people their firm belief and firm support in the eternal Word of God, thus destroying the foundations of a healthy national life.' Several days later, the conservative paper declared that the German people were becoming ever more dependent on money men, and that these were, unfortunately, mostly Jews. 'Liberalism does harm to our people, both spiritually and materially . . . And it cannot be denied that, because of this, the *national power of Germany* suffers harm.'

The appeal to the Germans' conservative and national instincts was successful. The Conservative and Free Conservative parties emerged victorious from the federal elections on 30 July 1878. The National Liberals, the Progressives, and the Social Democrats were the losers. The Centre party managed to hold its own. In the wake of their defeat (they lost 29 of their former 128 mandates), the National Liberals gradually swung around in the very direction Bismarck wished to see them go. The majority under Bennigsen was now basically prepared to vote for the government's draft of a 'Law against the Dangerous Aspirations of Social-Democracy'. The leftist minority around Lasker initially intended to persevere in the rejection of an unlawful emergency measure, but then, after it had pushed though several revisions and a restriction of the law to two and a half years, decided to concur. On 18 October 1878 the Reichstag passed the anti-socialist law (the so-called *Sozialistengesetz*) with 221 against 149 votes from the ranks of the Centre, the Progressive, and the Social Democratic parties.

The prohibition of socialist associations, assemblies, and press; the expulsion of socialist agitators; the possibility of declaring a year-long 'minor state of siege' in 'endangered' districts—all these suppressive measures were rationalized with the unproved and unprovable assertion that the emperor's attackers in May and June 1878 were incited to their deeds by 'social democracy'. The anti-socialist law was an emergency measure, directed against particular ideologies, not only against clearly defined acts. It violated elementary principles of the rule of law, such as liberals interpreted it. That the National Liberals nonetheless voted for it marks a turning point in the history of German liberalism, a partial capitulation before the power embodied by Bismarck.

For Social Democrats the law, continually extended until 1890, meant danger and persecution. In the twelve years it was in effect, some 1,300 writings in periodicals and elsewhere and 332 workers' organizations, including unions, were banned. Approximately 900 individuals were expelled from 'siege areas', more than 500 of whom were breadwinners of families. Some 1,500 persons were imprisoned, the prison sentences reaching a combined total of about 1,000 years.

Yet Bismarck did not manage to destroy social democracy. In fact, his efforts contributed to the spreading of the social-democratic workers' movement in cultural form, as prohibited organizations were replaced by workers' sporting associations, glee clubs, voluntary aid collections, and other similar groups. A further paradoxical effect was a certain 'parliamentarization' of the party: since participation in elections, agitation in the parliaments, and the corresponding reportage were not banned, the actual party leadership migrated from the party executive to the Reichstag fraction. The new party organ, the *Sozialdemokrat*, as well as other social-democratic writings, were published in Switzerland, whence they were illegally brought into Germany and distributed via the 'red army postal service'. And in Wyden, Switzerland, the Socialist Workers' party held a party congress in 1880, at which the 1875 Gotha platform was modified. Instead of aspiring toward its goals 'by all legal means', the statement now read 'by all means'. This was not a affirmation of illegality as a principle, but simply a recognition of the fact that, under the anti-socialist law, nearly everything the Socialist Workers' party did was illegal.

During the anti-socialist years, there developed among the members and supporters of the Social Democrats a consciousness of living in a political ghetto. This experience helped transform socialism into a kind of religion of secular redemption. Consequently, social-democratic workers usually took from the writings of Marx and Engels only as much as served their need to compensate for a repressive reality with the belief in a bright future. The world-view formed during those years was broadly 'deterministic' in nature: the conviction that the historical process, by force of nature, would lead to the overcoming of capitalism by socialism. Before the classless society could be realized, however, it would be necessary to wage the class war of the proletariat and to develop an ever clearer class consciousness. The anti-socialist law demonstrated the reality of class society, the class state, and class justice. It effected one thing above all: a broad absorption of basic Marxist assumptions.[14]

With the anti-socialist law commenced the 'system shift' predicted by the grand duke of Baden, which contemporaries were already referring to as an 'inner founding of the Empire' (*innere Reichsgründung*). Bismarck had never expected the suppression of social democracy to solve the social question. Already in 1871, he had told the Prussian minister of commerce, Heinrich Friedrich August von Itzenplitz, that 'the action of the currently ruling state authority' was, in his view, the only means 'to put a stop to the socialist movement in its present aberration and to lead the same along more salutary paths, notably by realizing what seems justifiable in the socialist demands and what can be accommodated in the framework of the present-day order of state and society.'

This was another reason Bismarck regarded the break with economic liberalism as unavoidable. If he wished to make—precisely as did Lorenz von Stein—the Hohenzollern monarchy into a 'monarchy of social reform', he might depend upon the support of conservatives who were open-minded about social policy, but not upon devotees of the pure doctrine of 'Manchester liberalism'. Initially, however, everything depended on completing the paradigm shift in finance and trade policy, so as to provide the Reich with the material basis without which an active social policy was inconceivable. The elections of 1878 had brought Bismarck significantly closer to this goal. In the autumn, the 'tariff protectionists', at the instigation of the Central Association of German Industrialists, joined together in an inter-fractional 'National Economic Association' (*Volkswirtschaftliche Vereinigung*). Of the total (397), 205 delegates participated, including 27 National Liberals in addition to Conservatives, Free Conservatives, and almost all the members of the Centre.

Before the Reichstag could have its say, however, Bismarck still had to overcome strong resistance to his tariff plans in the Federal Council. The southern German states were against all protective tariffs; Saxony desired duties on iron and textiles, but none on grain. Bismarck, who sought to establish a lasting connection between western heavy industry and the East Elbian manorial system, insisted upon a package deal: no industrial tariffs without agricultural tariffs. At the end of March 1879, the Council agreed to a compromise, accepting the iron and textile tariffs at the level the chancellor wished, but pushing through considerably lower duties on grain than Bismarck's bill envisioned.

In the Reichstag, too, the industrial protectionists were far more numerous than the agrarian. During the second reading of the tariff bill, the attempt by several Conservatives to raise the duties on rye from those decided by the Council failed. But there was another way of obtaining a majority for Bismarck's original tariff project: by linking the question of tariffs to the reform of state finances. This new 'package' brought to prominence a party that had bitterly fought against the chancellor until shortly beforehand—the Centre.

As a federalist party, the Centre wanted to maintain the 'matricular' contributions of the individual states; as a constitutional party, it wanted to preserve the parliament's right to approve the budget. A Bavarian delegate, Georg von Franckenstein, drafted a motion uniting both goals. The 'Franckenstein clause' limited state revenues from tariffs and the tobacco tax to 130 million marks annually; any surplus was to be distributed to the federal states. Since the financial needs of the Reich would not be fully covered by this measure, it would remain dependent on allocations from the states, which now, however, were to be financed by the funds transferred from the federal government. Since surpluses would remain, the states, too, would profit from the protective tariffs and higher tobacco tax. The Reichstag retained the right to approve—together with the Federal Council—the amount of the 'matricular' contributions, thus preserving its budgetary authority.

In agreeing to Franckenstein's motion (and rejecting a second compromise by Bennigsen placing greater emphasis on the budgetary rights of the parliament), Bismarck assured himself of the Centre party's compliance on higher agricultural duties. On 12 July 1879 the Reichstag formally approved the protective tariffs and the increase in the tobacco tax with the votes of the two conservative parties, the Centre, and sixteen National Liberal delegates. This vote was an important turning point. In accepting the 'Franckenstein clause', Bismarck ended his cooperation with the National Liberals, begun twelve years previously, and took a sharp turn to the right, in favour of a party constellation in which a National Liberal party might find a place only if it, too, shifted rightwards and 'liberated' itself from its left wing.

The economic and societal consequences of the shift to protective tariffs in summer 1879 were even more momentous. The East Elbian landowners, now shielded from international competition (more as a result of Bismarck's exertions on their behalf than of their own), found themselves in a singular position, which they exploited to the full: they could lead lives of privilege at the expense of society and, at the same time, fully maintain their societal influence and dominance. Within industry, the protectionist policy benefited the old branches, above all coal and steel, whose long-term competitiveness was open to doubt. The new growth sectors—electricity, chemistry, and mechanics—paid the price. The relation between 'manor and blast furnace' developed into the conservative axis of German politics, an alliance against liberalism and democracy that, despite its inner contradictions and frequent conflicts, always managed to hold together in mutual defence against mutual enemies.[15]

The change from free trade to protectionism was accompanied by a transformation in German nationalism. The opponents of free trade spoke of the 'defence of national labour', employing both a social and a nationalist argument—in this case the preservation of German jobs—in order to isolate the German economy from the effects of international competition. Before 1871, to be 'national' generally meant to be 'anti-feudal', both in a bourgeois-liberal and in a proletarian-socialist sense. In the decade after the founding of the Reich, 'national' and 'anti-international' began to mean the same thing, transforming an originally liberal and leftist expression into a battle cry of the political right.

'National' and 'liberal' were a *contradictio in adjecto*, an oxymoron—thus remarked the formerly liberal *Grenzboten* (financed from 1879 through Bismarck's 'reptile fund' and published by his intimate associate, Moritz Busch) on the crisis occasioned within the National Liberal party by the shift in economic policy:

> We must see the establishment of a national party, as the only one capable of rule, working together on a temporary basis with those parties that are not unconditionally anti-national, but also not only conditionally national—working now to this, and now to that purpose along the path of the national idea.

That the advocates of free trade did not belong to the 'national' camp clearly emerged from the pages of the *Grenzboten* shortly thereafter. 'The Manchester radicalism is like the ultramontane and the social-antinational. Its mania is the cosmopolitan free-trade society, the atomistic world-fog with its nucleus of a sort in the might of English capital, which preserves it from complete evaporation.'

After the transformation on the domestic political front in 1878–9, to be 'national' no longer meant to promote the emancipation of the bourgeoisie or the workers. Rather, it meant to defend the existing order against everybody engaged in the struggle for greater societal openness, greater liberty, and greater equality. Consequently, 'national' discourse, such as it was understood by the right, involved aggressive attacks against those who were not considered 'national' in this sense. The suspicion of 'national unreliability', which the liberals had expressed against Catholics and socialists, was now increasingly turned against them. Anti-Semitism, which was always also a form of anti-liberalism, had prepared the way for this anti-liberal nationalism. Nonetheless, one did not have to be an anti-Semite to be 'national' in the new, post-1879 meaning of the term.

This semantic shift was also accompanied by a transformation in the identity of those who considered themselves 'national'. Ever since the Prussian conservatives had renamed themselves the German Conservative party in 1876, they claimed to be the authentic representatives of the national idea. At the same time, they began increasingly to court the central groups of the urban middle classes, tradesmen and small merchants, who had generally voted liberal up to that time, but were now feeling more and more threatened by liberalism in the shape of freedom of trade and free movement of labour. These were the same groups to whom organized anti-Semites sought to appeal after 1880. In 1888 Ludwig Bamberger subjected the rightward re-orientation of nationalist discourse to an evocative and biting analysis:

> The national banner in the hands of the Prussian ultras and the Saxon guildsmen is the caricature of what it once symbolized, and this caricature has come about quite simply in that the defeated adversaries have donned the discarded garments of the victors and turned them out in their own fashion, freshening up the colours and tailoring them to fit, so as to be able to parade around in them as the cheery heirs of the national movement.

The shift from left and liberal to right and conservative nationalism in the last third of the nineteenth century was as little confined to Germany as the transition from free trade to protectionism. Between 1876 and 1881, Russia, Italy, and France made similar changes in their commerce policies; the United States had already commenced in 1864. What distinguished the rightward swerve in German nationalism from comparable developments in France and the Anglo-Saxon world was, first, its 'feudal' beneficiaries and the role it played in consolidating the influence of an aristocratic ruling class, and, secondly, the weakness of the liberal counter-movement. German liberalism was unable to look back in pride upon a legacy of successful revolution. The liberals had allied themselves with Bismarck's 'revolution from above'. This was the only thing they could do, given the circumstances. Nonetheless, this collusion had made liberalism more dependent on the elites of old Prussia—crown, Junkerdom, and military—than these upon liberalism. Moreover, the liberals had sacrificed a great deal of their credibility by employing or countenancing illiberal measures in their fight against political Catholicism and social democracy. They paid the price in 1879, when they had become too weak to mount effective resistance to Bismarck's swing to the right.

In the course of the 1860s, German liberalism had liberalized itself in many respects, for example with regard to the civil equality of the Jews and the achievement of freedom of trade. The following decade saw a reversal of this process, the de-liberalization of liberalism. In the course of the campaigns for the 'defence of national labour' and a stringent anti-socialist law, press organs close to the National Liberal right began to call for the acquisition of colonies. The arguments used were not only economic, but also 'social'. In the summer of 1878, the *Grenzboten* wrote that the state that considers domestic tranquillity its primary civic duty gains a great deal 'when unquiet spirits, who do no good at home, leave the country . . . A system, similar to the one used to excellent effect with the deported Australians, seems to us the most appropriate when, one day, the question presents itself to the German Reich of getting rid of its wayward sons.' The *Volkswirtschaftliche Correspondenz*, the mouthpiece of the protectionists, summarized the same idea in 1878 in the crisp assessment: 'As a safety valve for the rumbling volcano of the social question, no country on earth is in such need of a nationally organized emigration system as Germany.'

The *National-Zeitung*, at that time still oriented towards free trade, objected: more dependable and useful than enticing pictures of 'flourishing factories in Africa and America' were 'enterprises bringing the colonial chisel to bear on the periphery of our own national territory', so as to make (predominantly Polish) Posen into 'German soil'. But this argument did not convince the protectionists and advocates of colonialism, who saw no essential conflict between the 'Germanization of Posen'—which the *National-Zeitung* claimed would be a blessing for both Germans and Poles—and the acquisition of overseas colonies. In spring 1879 Treitschke's *Preussische Jahrbücher* demanded that the government use direct measures to encourage German farmers to settle in Posen. 'In the west, it is imperative that we protect and secure the state, but we do not need immigration [*wir haben . . . aber nicht volklich zu erwerben*]. The east, on the other hand, has always been the land of promise for us, for as long as there has been German history.'

Treitschke and his friend Wilhelm Wehrenpfennig, co-editor of the *Preussische Jahrbücher*, had left the National Liberal party the day before the vote over the tariff and finance reform. The next day, 12 July 1879, sixteen further protectionists followed their example. The staunch advocates of free trade hesitated to take the same step, but increasingly lost their confidence in Bennigsen's ability or desire to bring the party back to a resolute liberal platform after he had gone so far to accommodate Bismarck on the question of protective tariffs. On 15 March 1880 the first 'leftist,' Eduard Lasker, declared his resignation from the National Liberal parliamentary fraction. In a letter to his constituents, he criticized the assumption 'that a reactionary economic and tax policy, so out of step with the times, can be combined with a progressive policy in other areas'. He believed the parliamentary tactics of the party were guided by the intention of preventing, under all circumstances, the formation of a clerical-conservative majority and instead working towards, at best, a liberal-conservative majority. I, for one, consider such a combination impossible, except at the price of sacrifices that would damage a moderately liberal party in the present and endanger it in the future.

Five and a half months later, on 30 August 1880, an additional twenty-six delegates from the left wing, among them Bamberger, Forckenbeck, Stauffenberg, and Mommsen, announced their departure from the National Liberal party fractions of the Reichstag and the Prussian parliament, joining together to form the Liberal Union (*Liberale Vereinigung*), which for a short time was known as the 'Secession' after the title of a pamphlet by Bamberger. The immediate cause of the break was the willingness of the majority under Bamberger to support Bismarck in relaxing the May laws of 1873, that is, in putting an end to the *Kulturkampf.*

Yet the declaration of the 'secessionists' went far beyond this particular issue. Their manifesto proclaimed 'firm resistance to the backwards course, holding fast to our hard-won political liberties' as 'the common duty of the whole liberal party'. While the split within resolute liberalism was not yet overcome by the secessionists, nonetheless there was now an attempt to reunite all those who still identified themselves as resolute liberals. Fourteen years after the National Liberals had separated themselves from the Progressive party, a number of the 1866 secessionists had come to realize that they could only preserve their identity by means of a new secession, one that meant breaking with Bismarck. Among the 1880 secessionists, the Prussian element was predominant, and not by chance: most of those who now defied Bismarck had already done so once before, in the years of the Prussian constitutional conflict.[16]

BISMARCK'S FOREIGN AND DOMESTIC POLICIES IN THE 1880s

The settlement of the *Kulturkampf* in the 1880s had a spiritual father, Pope Leo XIII, and a secular father, Bismarck. One of the reasons the new pontiff was interested in improving relations with Prussia and the Reich was events in France, where the 1877 electoral victory of the laicizing forces was threatening to open a new front in the battle between Church and State. Another was the pope's investment in the struggle against liberalism and social democracy. Bismarck, who had become convinced that the *Kulturkampf* could not be won, and himself interested in the backing of the church for government measures against social democracy, decided in the summer of 1878 to tread the path of reconciliation with the Catholic Church.

The first mitigating legislation, in July 1880, empowered the Prussian government to reinstate its financial allocations to the Catholic Church and to release bishops from the requirement of swearing to uphold Prussian law. Five vacant bishoprics were promptly filled again, none of whose occupants was compelled to pronounce the aforementioned oath. The restitution of diplomatic relations between Prussia and the Vatican, severed in 1872, followed two years later. In May and July 1882, the second and third mitigating laws entered into effect, permitting a large number of exceptions to the requirement of a 'cultural exam', and allowing the king to pardon bishops who had been removed from their posts. The so-called 'peace laws' of 1886 and 1887, which Bismarck negotiated directly with the curia without any participation from the Centre, formed the conclusion of the revision. The state recognized the disciplinary authority of the pope, abolished the cultural exam, and rehabilitated all religious orders with the exception of the Jesuits. Three 'achievements' of the *Kulturkampf* were preserved: the Jesuit ban (abolished in 1917), the pulpit paragraph (abolished in 1953), and obligatory civil marriage.

The wounds left by the *Kulturkampf* could not be healed as quickly as its laws could be changed or abolished. Most faithful Catholics retained profound feelings of discrimination and humiliation. This was one of the many reasons political Catholicism, unlike Protestantism, remained a solidly unified force even beyond the end of the imperial era. The dense network of Catholic associations for peasants, workers, journeymen, craftsmen, merchants, teachers, academics, and students, which together formed the Catholic 'milieu', was a product of the *Kulturkampf*. Thus, in its effects, the anti-Catholic legislation was much like the anti-socialist law; pressure from the state promoted the formation of a societal 'subculture' that sought to seal itself off from its environment.

Nonetheless, there were considerable differences in the degree and duration of state pressure. Unlike Social Democrats under the anti-socialist law, Catholics were able to publish and engage in politics relatively unhindered during the *Kulturkampf*. Anti-Catholic discrimination was far less comprehensive than the persecution of social democracy. The transformation of political Catholicism into part of the governmental establishment began about a decade after the official end of the anti-Catholic era. The Social Democrats, on the other hand, continued to think of themselves as a fundamental opposition, and continued to be perceived and treated as fundamental adversaries of state and society, well after the expiration of the anti-socialist law in 1890.[17]

In the first Reichstag elections after the 1878–9 transformation of domestic policy, which were held in October 1881, the Social Democrats suffered modest losses, from 7.6% of the previous vote in 1878 down to 6.1%. With 23%, the Centre obtained almost exactly the same amount of support as before. The biggest losers were the National Liberals, who fell from 23.1% to 14.7%, the biggest winners the left-liberals. The secessionists of the Liberal Union straightway received 8.4%; the German Progressive party was nearly able to double its mandate, climbing from 6.7% to 12.7%. Although the conservative camp, as a whole, declined in influence, the losses were confined to the Free Conservatives (called the *Deutsche Reichspartei*, German Empire Party, from 1871), who fell from 13.6% to 7.4%; the German Conservative party climbed from 13% to 16.3%.

Taken as a whole, the election could be interpreted as a referendum against Bismarck's swing to the right, since the chancellor lost his governmental majority. Now, a bill could pass the parliamentary hurdle only when either the Centre or the two left-liberal parties voted with Conservatives, Free Conservatives, and National Liberals. In this assembly, there was no majority for the tobacco monopoly Bismarck had placed at the centre of the electoral campaign.

The two left-liberal parties had so much in common that their reunification seemed inevitable. It duly happened in March 1884: the German Progressive Party and the Liberal Union united under the leadership of the Berlin jurist Eugen Richter, head of the Progressive party, forming the German Liberal party (*Deutsche Freisinnige Partei*). With 110 seats, the new party formed the strongest fraction for the time being. In order to gain as much National Liberal support as possible, it opted for a deliberately 'soft' platform in the controversy over free trade and protectionism, speaking out against a 'tariff and economic policy in the service of special interests'. The demand for legislation to create a responsible governmental ministry, on the other hand, was fully clear: socialism was to be fought 'also in the form of state socialism'.

Around this same time, the southern German National Liberals were turning towards what left-liberals termed 'state socialism'. In their 'Heidelberg declaration' of the end of March 1884, drafted by the Frankfurt mayor Johannes Miquel, they expressly approved 'the aspirations of the Reich Chancellor towards heightened solicitude for the well-being of the working class' and the efforts of the government 'to improve the social situation of the working class'. The rejection of Manchester liberalism was flanked by a statement of support for the customs tariff of 1879, protection of agriculture, renewal of the anti-socialist law, and the maintenance of a strong German armed force. In May 1884 a National Liberal party congress made the 'Heidelberg declaration' the official platform of the entire party.

What the Liberals fought and the National Liberals welcomed was, by this time, already in full swing—the erection of a German system of social insurance. Bismarck had not broken with economic liberalism for reasons of social policy, but without this break, he would never have gone down in history as a socio-political innovator. The ground for policies making it the task of the state to mediate social conflicts had been prepared not only by theoreticians like Lorenz von Stein and the so-called 'lectern' or 'professorial socialists' (*Kathedersozialisten*) around Gustav Schmoller who founded the Association for Social Policy (*Verein für Sozialpolitik*) in 1872, but also by close associates of Bismarck like Theodor Lohmann. The chancellor himself was convinced of the rectitude and necessity of the task. 'It is possible that our policies will one day perish, when I am no longer around,' he said to the writer Moritz Busch on 26 June 1881. 'But we will push state socialism through. Everybody who takes up this thought again will have his chance at the helm.'

At first, Bismarck wanted government allocations to completely replace insurance contributions by the workers, expecting that such a programme would make workers loyal to the state. The anti-parliamentary ulterior motives he pursued with this policy cannot be denied. In the trade associations managing accident insurance he saw the nucleus of a profession-based organization that, according to his plan, was to culminate in a *Reichsvolkswirtschaftsrat*, a corporative chamber competing with the Reichstag. This plan was never realized, hampered partly by the bureaucracy, partly by the Reichstag.

The reform that actually took place in the 1880s was far more progressive than what Bismarck had conceived. The health insurance law of 1883 obligated employees not belonging to a voluntary insurance association to join a local provider. They were responsible for two-thirds, employers for one-third of the costs. The costs of accident insurance, created in 1884, were borne entirely by the companies, organized into associations. The 1889 old-age and disability insurance law divided the contributions evenly among employers, employees, and the federal government.

What distinguished these social insurance programmes from traditional organizations caring for the poor was the fact that they gave the individual worker a lawful claim to social services. The legislation of 1883, 1884, and 1889 laid state and society under the obligation of providing assistance in emergency situations for which the individual was not responsible and which he could not prevent. These laws made Germany into a pioneer in social policy. It achieved this status in the course of an inward political shift that threw the country back in other areas. Protectionist tariffs and progressive social legislation—these were two sides of the same coin, the 'inner founding of the Reich'.[18]

Bismarck did not consider it promising to attempt to win a governmental majority on the strength of social policy alone. The looming federal elections influenced another major policy development in 1884: in this year, Germany became a colonial power. From 1882, colonial acquisitions were on the agenda of the newly founded German Colonial Association (*Deutscher Kolonialverein*), in which, along with industrialists, merchants, and bankers, politicians from the ranks of the National Liberals and the Free Conservative German Empire party set the tone. These men were not only interested in obtaining new markets for German products, but also in the integrating effect the colonial movement would have within Germany itself. At the association's founding congress in Frankfurt in December 1882, Miquel described colonies as a task 'at which the conflict of the confessions, the religious, political, and social antagonisms, do not gnaw'. The president of the association, the Free Conservative Reichstag delegate Hermann von Hohenlohe-Langenburg, declared at the founding of the Berlin branch in 1884 that 'no aspiration is better suited to overcome the social question, presently exercising all spirits, than the aspirations of our association. Everyone who joins is doing his bit for the resolution of the social question.'

Until well into the 1880s, Bismarck wanted nothing to do with German colonies, for reasons of foreign policy as well as of cost. In April 1884, however, he took advantage of British problems with France and Russia, which temporarily distracted the maritime power, to place a territory acquired by the Bremen merchant Adolf Lüderitz on the bay of Angra Pequena in south-west Africa under the protection of the Reich. In July 1884 Germany proclaimed its sovereignty over Togo and Cameroon. In 1885 followed the declaration of protective sovereignty over a large east African territory acquired by the colonial agitator Carl Peters and the founding of the colony of German New Guinea.

The chancellor became a momentary ally of the colonial movement in 1884–5 because it seemed to have found a means of giving Germany a national goal once again. If his countrymen occupied themselves with a national enterprise like colonies, it would be easier for Bismarck to keep them away from activities he considered irreconcilable with the interests of the Reich. These included the overthrow of the existing order, which the Social Democrats were generally thought to be planning; regional and confessional particularism, still very much alive; and, not least, the pressure of the Liberals for parliamentary rule. The demand for colonies, on the other hand, came from parties that assured Bismarck of their support—the Free Conservatives and the National Liberals. Accordingly, the strengthening of these parties lay in the interest of the Reich, such as Bismarck interpreted it.

Their firm negation of colonial policy did the left-liberals as little good as their rejection of the social insurance legislation. In the 1884 Reichstag elections, the German Liberal party lost 39 of their 106 seats. Yet it would be incorrect to speak of a resounding victory for the parties supporting Bismarck in these areas. The Free Conservatives held on to their 28 seats, but suffered minor losses in their percentage of the vote; the National Liberals gained a further 2.9% and 4 seats. The German Conservatives profited from the fact that far fewer votes were necessary to obtain a parliamentary mandate in sparsely settled, agricultural East Elbia than in the densely populated west. They climbed from 50 to 78 seats, even though they lost approximately 1% of the total vote. Among the clear winners were the Social Democrats, who grew from 6.1% to 9.7% and were thus able to double their number of seats from 12 to 24. The Centre party, Guelfs, Alsace-Lorraine independents, Poles, and Danes experienced no significant changes. Since the new Reichstag was hardly any closer to a government-friendly majority than its predecessor, rule with ad hoc majorities continued.

If colonial policy was elevated to a national mission in the years 1884–5, the year 1886 saw a new focus of national attention: the promotion of *Deutschtum* in the eastern part of the Reich. The policy's deeper roots were economic and social. The lack of agricultural jobs caused a continuous decrease in the rural population of Prussia's eastern provinces; many emigrated abroad, many migrated to the 'industrial heart' of Germany, the Ruhr area. Since more Germans left than Poles, the ratio of Poles to Germans increased in the home territories, especially in Posen and West Prussia. The resulting fear of a 'Polonization' of the east led, in 1886, to renewed agitation for the 'Germanization of the soil'. The fact that Polish ownership of land had significantly declined in the years prior to the campaign was deliberately ignored by its authors, the foremost of whom was Christoph von Tiedemann, president of the Bromberg government. In spring 1886, bolstered by a memorandum from Tiedemann, the Prussian government drafted a bill proposing the purchase of Polish-owned land through a fund of 100 million marks under the control of the Royal Settlement Commission. The law went into effect on 26 April 1886.

Bismarck's main goal was to weaken the Polish nobility permanently. He initially weighed the thought of making the purchased territory into domains. It was the National Liberals who proposed giving the land over to peasant settlement, an idea Bismarck quickly appropriated, thus helping to make the 'Germanization of the soil' into an official part of Prussian policy. Between 1886 and 1914, Prussia spent about 1 billion marks in gold bullion for the settlement of German peasants. Considering the expectations, the time duration, and the size of the territory in question, the practical results of the land-settlement law were modest. Despite massive propaganda from the German Eastern Marches Association (founded in 1894), only about 22,000 peasants—including their families some 120,000 Germans—could be settled in Posen and West Prussia by 1914.

The 'Germanization of the soil' was accompanied by the linguistic Germanization of the east. In the mid-1870s two pieces of legislation (Prussia's *Geschäftssprachengesetz* of 1876 and the federal *Gerichtsverfassungsgesetz* of 1877) had made German into the official language of public administration and law. 'In the ensuing decades, this wave of linguistic and national standardization made its way into the most remote legal district,' writes Hans-Ulrich Wehler.

> Under the growing pressure of German imperial nationalism, the Polish language was gradually supplanted in school and religious instruction, in assemblies and courts of law. And at the same time, the bureaucracy of the eastern provinces continually pushed to extend its authority to circumvent laws guaranteed by the constitution.

The laws of 1876 and 1877 not only affected the Poles, but also the Danes of northern Schleswig. The 1877 federal law also affected the French-speaking inhabitants of the territory around Metz. Only in the east, however, could one speak of a 'war between peoples', a *Volkstumskampf* between 'Teutons' and 'Slavs'. Germans did not bring to bear against Danes and Frenchmen the cultural superiority they claimed to have over the Poles. The German relationship to Poland was infused with racial prejudice. In this, it was more akin to anti-Semitism than 'normal' expressions of nationalism. At the same time, however, nobody would have accused the Poles, as they did the Jews, of seeking to control Germany, much less to control the world. Only anti-Semitism contained an admixture of an inferiority complex. In this way, the German hatred of the Jews was again different from 'normal' racism, such as that expressed against the Poles.

The discrimination against the Alsace-Lorrainers was mild in comparison. Some 60,000 of them, availing themselves of the right of 'option', left their homes for France in the first two years of the new German Reich. Those who stayed had fewer civil rights than other Germans. At first, Alsace-Lorraine was administered as an 'imperial territory' (*Reichsland*) by an *Oberpräsident* under the authority of the imperial chancellery. In 1879 it became a federal state, but of a particular kind: its voice in the Federal Council was merely advisory, and the governor in Strasbourg, who headed the administration, was not under the authority of the chancellor, but directly subject to the emperor. Up to 1911 Alsace-Lorraine had no popular representation; the provincial parliament was replaced by a provincial committee of notables. Nonetheless, a certain half-hearted attempt at rapprochement with the other German states could not be overlooked. The autonomists around August Schneegans actively contributed to the imperial law of 1879 reorganizing the relationship between the *Reichsland* and the Reich.[19]

In the year 1887, Alsace-Lorraine became the theme of a federal electoral campaign, if only indirectly. At the beginning of 1886 General Boulanger, the idol of those who wanted a war of vengeance against Germany in order to win back the lost provinces, took over the French ministry of war. At the same time, a serious crisis with Austria-Hungary led to an increase of pan-Slavist influence in Russia. Bismarck feared Germany could quickly plunge into a two-front war. The *cauchemar des coalitions*, the nightmare of hostile alliances against Germany, was never so strong for the German chancellor as in 1886–7.

When in January 1887 he demanded a renewal of the seven-year military budget (the last *Septennat*, approved in 1880, having expired), his main argument was the revanchist mood in France. The rejection of the petition prompted Bismarck to dissolve the Reichstag three-quarters of a year before the legislative term was to come to an end. The ensuing electoral campaign was completely dominated by a national-psychological mobilization against the western neighbor. National Liberals, German Conservatives, and Free Conservatives fought as a political 'cartel' at Bismarck's side for a new *Septennat*, and they were successful. The new parliament, elected on 21 February, had a governmental majority again, composed of the three above-mentioned parties together holding more than 220 of 397 seats. In March 1887, the new 'cartel parliament' passed its first law, the third *Septennat*.

That same year, Bismarck orchestrated the foreign policy coup his posthumous admirers long considered to represent the summit of his diplomatic mastery: the signing of the secret 'Reinsurance Treaty' with Russia. The relationship between Germany and Russia had deteriorated after the Congress of Berlin in 1878; Russia felt that Bismarck had stripped it of the fruits of its victory against the Turks. Germany's response was an alliance with Austria-Hungary in 1879, a secret treaty of mutual assistance in the case of a Russian attack against either partner. Additional security was the goal of the 1882 triple alliance between Germany, Austria-Hungary, and Italy, in which Berlin and Vienna promised to help Rome in the event of an unprovoked French attack. If the attack went against Germany, the latter could, in turn, count on Italian assistance. If one partner went to war with another European power, the other partners committed themselves to a policy of benevolent neutrality. In the event of war with several powers, they were to provide assistance.

In the meantime, Russia and Austria-Hungary had managed to smooth out their differences in the Balkans sufficiently to conclude a secret 'Three Emperors' League' (*Dreikaiservertrag*) in 1881, a three-year agreement in which St Petersburg, Berlin, and Vienna promised to observe a policy of mutual benevolent neutrality in case one of the partners got involved in a war with a fourth party. This treaty was extended another three years in 1884. In 1885, however, a new Balkan war broke out between Serbia and Bulgaria, leading to a serious conflict between Austria and Russia. The Bulgarians won. Without first discussing the matter with Russia, Austria prevented Serbia from ceding territories. Russia interpreted this action as a violation of the 1881 treaty, which required consultations in such cases. The year following, the relationship between Vienna and St Petersburg deteriorated still further. With Russian help the prince of Bulgaria, Alexander von Battenberg, was deposed. His successor—though it was not yet decided who that would be—was to bring the country into closer dependency on the tzarist empire. Under these circumstances, a renewal of the Three Emperors' League in 1887 was inconceivable.

After the coup in Sofia, Bismarck came under strong pressure from the governments of Austria and Britain, who wanted the Reich to commit itself in advance to counteracting any Russian military measures against Bulgaria or on the Bosphorus. If the chancellor had agreed, he would have provoked a complete break with Russia and probably also a Franco-Russian alliance. This would have been tantamount to abandoning the foreign policy axiom he had formulated on 15 June 1877 in the so-called 'Kissinger Diktat', in which he declared that his view of Germany 'has nothing to do with accumulating territories, but concerns a total political situation in which all powers except France need us, and are restrained as much as possible by their relationships with each other from entering into coalitions against us.'

To promote rivalries between foreign powers for the purpose of preventing coalitions against Germany was in keeping with the Kissinger rule. In 1887, too, the chancellor remained faithful to his maxim, endorsing Rome's proposal of a 'Mediterranean entente' between Britain and Italy from February of that year, with Austria-Hungary joining in March. The anti-Russian tenor of the secret treaty was obvious. The three powers obligated themselves to preserve the status quo in the entire Mediterranean and the Black Sea as much as possible, as well as to prevent annexations, occupations, and the erection of protectorates. Germany, the only European great power informed of the agreement, was a kind of secret sharer in the alliance. In Bismarck's view, it was in Germany's interest for London both to cooperate with Vienna and to become a greater adversary of Russia than it had been in the past. What the chancellor could not want, on the other hand, was a war between Russia and Austria-Hungary, Germany's closest ally. Yet with the British now backing the Austrians in the Mediterranean, the danger of such a war grew.

The Reinsurance Treaty with Russia, which Bismarck signed on 18 June 1887, contradicted the Mediterranean entente (and also the Treaty of London of March 1871, which closed the straits between the Bosphorus and the Dardanelles to all military vessels) in one important respect: in an 'extremely secret supplementary protocol', Germany promised to assist the tzarist empire if the latter should decide to defend its interests at the outlet of the Black Sea. The chancellor accepted this contradiction as a price for the advantages contained in the many body of the treaty: Germany committed itself to neutrality in the case of an unprovoked Austrian attack on Russia, and Russia promised to remain neutral in the case of an unprovoked French attack on Germany.

The treaty with St Petersburg lessened the risk of a two-front war—as did the fall of Boulanger in Paris shortly before, in May 1887. Still, Bismarck was not at all convinced that the agreement had forever averted the danger of a Franco-Russian alliance. At the end of December 1887, he remarked to the Prussian minister of war, Bronsart von Schellendorf, that, to judge by the course of European politics, it was likely 'that in the not too distant future we will have to deal with a war against both France and Russia'. Herbert von Bismarck, the son of the chancellor and secretary of the foreign office, noted soberly in June 1887 that the treaty would keep 'the Russians off our backs probably six to eight weeks longer than without it, when push comes to shove'. But European politics was not the only thing keeping the fear of a two-front war alive. Bismarck's tariff policy, too, strained the relationship with Russia. In 1887, the 1879 duties on grain were drastically increased for the second time, which meant virtual economic war with Russia. The consequences of the conservative swing in domestic policy put increasing pressure on the alliance between Germany and the great conservative power in the east.

Bismarck's biographer Lothar Gall has called the chancellor's domestic policy after 1881 a 'system of expedients'. The same can be said for his foreign policy in 1887. The conflicts between the alliances in which Germany was—directly or indirectly—involved were impossible to resolve. Only the relationship with Austria-Hungary was comparatively stable—not unlike, after the 1879 alliance, the 'wider federation' of which Heinrich Gagern had spoken three decades before. Bismarck had entered into the pact in consciousness of the centuries-old common bond between Germany and Austria, but he was not blind to the fact that this alliance, too, had its dangers for Germany.

The Reinsurance Treaty did not violate the letter of the agreement with Austria, but it violated its spirit. In turn, the 'Lombard prohibition' of November 1887, by means of which Bismarck almost completely cut Russia off from German sources of credit, violated the spirit of the Reinsurance Treaty. In the second half of the 1880s, the foreign policy of the Reich founder had reached an impasse, a predicament for which he himself, through his domestic policies, bore no small share of responsibility.[20]

THE ACCESSION OF WILLIAM II AND THE FALL OF BISMARCK

On 9 March 1888 Emperor William I died, shortly before reaching 92 years of age. His successor was already mortally ill by the time he acceded to the throne. Emperor Frederick was no less the Prussian officer than his father, but he was much more liberal. The party closest to his political views was the Liberal party—or, to be more exact, the group of former National Liberals around Bamberger, Forckenbeck, and Stauffenberg. His repeated demonstrative protests as crown prince against the enemies of the Jews during the Berlin anti-Semitism controversy stuck in the memories of many contemporaries. He had clashed with Bismarck again and again, from the time of the Prussian constitutional conflict onwards. He openly admitted his sympathies for parliamentary Britain, feeling a close connection with the native country of his wife Victoria, daughter of the British queen. During the ninety-nine days of his rule, however, he was unable to influence German politics in any significant way. The dismissal of the arch-conservative Prussian minister of the interior, Robert von Puttkamer, was the only example he set. Nonetheless, when he died of throat cancer on 15 June 1888, he left behind a myth that endures to this day, the widespread opinion that Emperor Frederick, had he lived and ruled longer, would have given a different course to German history—a liberal turn on the domestic front, and externally an understanding with England.

Among those who disagreed with this view even at the time was Theodor Fontane. In this writer's last novel, which appeared in 1898, the year of his and Bismarck's death, the eponymous hero, the old Junker Dubslav von Stechlin, a moderate conservative, explains to the rather liberal Count Barby why Emperor Frederick most certainly would have failed:

> Because of his friends, perhaps, but definitely because of his enemies. And those were the Junkers. You always hear that Junkerdom is no longer a powerful force, that the Hohenzollerns have the Junkers eating out of their hands, and that the royal family is simply growing them to have them ready for any contingency. And that was perhaps true for a time. But today it's no longer true, today it's utterly wrong. Junkerdom . . . has gained a massive amount of power in the battle of these years, more power than any other party, hardly excluding even the Social Democrats, and sometimes it seems to me that the old Quitzows are rising from the grave again.

When Barby objected, 'And you believe that Emperor Frederick would have run aground on this sharp Quitzow-reef?' old Stechlin nodded: 'That I do.'

The Quitzows were the embodiment of the robber-barons of Mark Brandenburg. At the beginning of the fifteenth century, they had waged war against the Brandenburg cities, neighbouring princes, and even their own margraves. The Junkers of the late nineteenth century no longer lived from robbery and plunder, but from the proceeds of the grain tariffs that burdened the consumers. By the time Fontane was writing *Der Stechlin*, he was able to look back on the bitter campaign waged by the East Elbian nobility against Bismarck's successor, General von Caprivi, a resolute opponent of high agricultural tariffs. Just as Caprivi had failed not least owing to the resistance of the Junkers, so too would Emperor Frederick have failed, if he had attempted to pursue a policy counter to the central interests of the Prussian manorial lords. That was the upshot of old Stechlin's reflections, and he was probably right.

William II, who succeeded Frederick on 15 June 1888, was just 29 old at the time and the precise opposite of his father in nearly all important respects: no man of liberal convictions, but rather profoundly authoritarian; at times closely allied with leading representatives of the anti-Semitic movement like the court chaplain, Stoecker; widely talented, but superficial; a vain, pomp-loving blusterer, who sought to compensate for inner insecurity and a physical defect—his left arm had been crippled since birth—with tough talk. That he would clash with Bismarck was clear from the outset. In 1887–8, the prince sided with the 'war party' around the emperor's general aide-de-camp, Count Waldersee, which pushed for a swift conquest of Russia and France. Reinforced in his tendency to overestimate his abilities by ambitious favourites like the amateur poet-composer Count Philipp von Eulenburg and enemies of Bismarck like the anti-Semite and Russian-hater Waldersee, William, when he assumed the throne, was determined to step out from behind the shadow of the Reich founder and rule by himself.

The antagonism between the young emperor and the old chancellor was especially marked in the social field. At the beginning of 1890 William sought to undermine social democracy by adopting a number of labour-protection measures, among them a prohibition of Sunday work. Bismarck feared such measures would have the opposite effect and advised the emperor against a proclamation of social policy. When William insisted, Bismarck relented—but only tactically, hoping that the legislative process would thwart William's plans.

The simultaneous conflict over a further renewal of the anti-socialist law was even more serious. The National Liberals would not vote for the bill unless the paragraph authorizing expulsion was eliminated. William was prepared to make this concession in order to salvage the law. When the conservatives demanded that Bismarck condemn this move through an open declaration before parliament, Bismarck refused. On 25 January 1890 the Conservatives, Centre, Liberals, Social Democrats, the Alsace-Lorraine party, and the national minorities voted against the third reading of the amended bill. The 169 negatives were opposed by only 98 positive votes from National Liberals and Free Conservatives. The anti-socialist law thus expired on 30 September 1890, and there could be no doubt about result: the 'cartel' of 1887 was destroyed and the power of the chancellor permanently weakened.

On 20 February 1890 a new Reichstag was elected, with run-off elections on 28 February. The parties of the former 'cartel' suffered a decisive defeat, losing a combined total of 85 seats and therewith the majority. The winners were the Social

Democrats, now the strongest party, climbing from 10.1% of the vote to 19.7% and from 11 to 35 seats; and the Liberals, who gained 16% of the vote, up from 12.9%, won 66 seats, up from 32.

It was impossible for Bismarck to rule with the new parliament. To be sure, he could attempt to break the Centre party out of the oppositional front, and to that purpose held a conversation (mediated by Bleichröder) with his long-time parliamentary adversary, Ludwig Windthorst, on 12 March 1890. But a governmental majority of the former cartel parties—German Conservatives, Free Conservatives, National Liberals, and Centre—was inconceivable. The antagonisms between the parties had become too great, and the small but numerically possible conservative-clerical majority was a long way from being a political majority for the same reason.

Bismarck was resolved upon an even fiercer battle against social democracy, and this now meant battle against the Reichstag—both the one currently sitting and, in all likelihood, against the one soon to be elected anew. In his efforts to paralyse parliament the chancellor, in a meeting of the Prussian ministry on 2 March, went so far as to consider the renunciation of the imperial office by the Prussian king and even the dissolution of the Reich by the princes. At first the emperor seemed willing to attempt the coup, but then refused, intimidated by the consequences.

This spelled the failure of the anti-parliamentary strategy of the chancellor. Yet there can be no doubt about the seriousness of Bismarck's attempt to replace the imperial constitution with a new one more to his taste. His 1890 scheme for a *coup d'état* suddenly revealed the merely provisional nature of the compromise that had brought the Prussian constitutional conflict to an end in 1866. In a power struggle between parliament and executive, one that would come sooner or later, the government was going to have to decide whether it would adapt itself to the representative majority or violate the constitution. In 1890 Bismarck was clearly prepared to take the second path.

The interview with Windthorst (which is occasionally and questionably cited as evidence that Bismarck ultimately preferred a parliamentary and thus constitutional solution to the crisis) contributed significantly to the fall of the first chancellor of the Reich. The emperor was enraged that Bismarck had not sought his permission for the talks. It provoked William still more that, on 4 March, Bismarck sent the Prussian ministers a copy of a cabinet order of Frederick William IV from the year 1852 prohibiting them from consulting directly with the monarch without the approval of the head of government. When William demanded that Bismarck abolish the old order, the latter refused to present a draft for a new one.

As the conflict between emperor and chancellor reached a head, Bismarck sought to negotiate an extension of the Reinsurance Treaty. The Russian ambassador, Count Shuvalov, had received instructions in St Petersburg to conclude the negotiations with Bismarck, and only with him. He came too late. On 17 March 1890, the day Shuvalov met Bismarck, the emperor requested the chancellor's resignation. Bismarck obliged on 18 March. Two days later he was dismissed from the offices of Reich chancellor, prime minister, and foreign minister of Prussia. The Reinsurance Treaty was not extended. The enemies of Bismarck's Russian policy, led by Count Waldersee and the *éminence grise* in the foreign office, the councillor Friedrich von Holstein, had exploited the situation and convinced William that it would be better for Germany to reject the Russian wish.[21]

BISMARCK AND THE CONSEQUENCES

Bismarck's dismissal spared Germany a serious crisis of state. The chancellor's aggressive strategy could not have been realized without a more or less disguised form of military dictatorship. His domestic policy, ultimately even more than his foreign policy, had led the Reich into a dead end. This conclusion is no less true for the fact that his successors, especially those directing the foreign office, renounced the moderate policy Bismarck had generally followed with the other great powers and replaced it with an uninhibited pursuit of power and prestige.

As long as Bismarck held the office of federal chancellor and was subjected to the conflict between the political parties, his admirers and critics largely held each other in check. The cult of Bismarck began practically the same moment the discharged 'iron chancellor', at the end of March 1890, withdrew to Friedrichsruh in the Saxon Forest, the estate William I had awarded him in June 1871 as an expression of gratitude for the founding of the German Reich. This honour had been intended for the man who had created the Reich and elevated Germany to a position of respect among the European great powers. Yet even while the 'Old Man in the Saxon Wood' was still living, an uncritical, simultaneously idealized and distorted picture of Bismarck emerged, persisting as legend and myth for the duration of the empire he had established. The doubts he himself harboured about the perdurability of his creation were foreign to most Germans. They liked to quote a passage from his parliamentary address of 6 February 1888: 'We Germans fear God, but nothing else on earth'. But that was only half of the sentence. The second part, 'and the fear of God is the thing that makes us love and preserve peace,' did not become proverbial.

A particular warning issued by the chancellor in this same speech had even less of an effect on contemporaries and posterity.

> Every great power seeking to constrain, influence, or direct the affairs of other countries outside of its own sphere of interest is hazarding itself outside of the limits God has imposed upon it, pursuing policies of power and prestige, and not of interest. We shall not do that. When oriental crises emerge we shall, before committing ourselves to a stance, first wait and see what stances the more interested powers adopt.

Bismarck had not always followed in practice the guidelines outlined in this speech. In 1875 a newspaper article against France under the title 'Ist der Krieg in

Sicht?'* directly inspired by the chancellor, provoked an international crisis that ended with diplomatic defeat for the Reich and personal defeat for Bismarck. Even if he had no intention of starting a pre-emptive war against Germany's western neighbor, both his policy in the 1875 crisis and his colonial policy of 1884–5 were guided, to a considerable extent, by the desire for national prestige. And yet, at the same time, it was his deep personal conviction—at least after 1875—that Germany was 'sated'. A younger generation of 'nationally-minded' Germans saw things differently. The German desire to draw even with the other world powers, above all Britain, became overpowering only after Bismarck's dismissal.

Bismarck's historical greatness was confined to foreign policy. Virtually no historian would rank Bismarck's achievements on the domestic front in anywhere close to the same category. On 10 July 1879 Albert Hänel, professor of constitutional law in Kiel and delegate of the German Progressive party, expressed what by that time was the common opinion of all critical observers:

> It has turned out that the Herr Chancellor has brought ministerial dictatorship to a hight at which all parliamentary life is indeed illusory . . . With this Chancellor, every constitutional assembly is more or less an ornament. All that is happening is that the Herr Chancellor is using the constitutional system as a way of avoiding to some extent the responsibility for his dictatorial plans.

The accusation of being 'enemies of the Reich', which Bismarck levelled at most opponents of his policies, burdened German public life long after his rule. He himself first came to feel its effects between 1881and 1887, when he was forced to govern with shifting majorities. The Social Democrats would never have supported Bismarck, not even if an anti-socialist law had never existed and the social welfare legislation had begun earlier. Were it not for the *Kulturkampf*, however, the Centre might very well have become a part of the moderate conservative 'governing camp'. Of course, this was precisely the constellation the National Liberals, the force behind the *Kulturkampf*, considered it their most important political goal to impede. Bismarck was not the only reason the parliamentarization of Germany and Prussia never came about. It also failed because of *the* party that supported it in principle, but identified it so completely with its own political hegemony that a 'legitimate' shift in parliamentary power was out of the question.

And yet, despite all that, the nation grew closer together—so much so, in fact, that the founder of the Reich was probably the only German in 1890 to brood over the possibility of its dissolution. The only adversaries of the Reich as a national state were those belonging to it by compulsion, the Poles in the Prussian eastern provinces and the Danes in northern Schleswig, who could no longer look forward to a popular referendum over their nationality after an October 1878 treaty between the German Reich and Austria-Hungary had abolished the

* Newspaer article, 'Is War in Sight?'.

corresponding clause from the 1866 treaty of Prague. Concerning the Alsace-Lorrainers, on the other hand, by 1890 it could no longer be assumed that they were all 'Germans by force'. First the Protestants, then the Catholics of the imperial territory had come to accept their place in the Reich. No more 'protesters' were elected to the parliament after 1890. In the 'old German' areas, nobody seriously questioned the existence of the Reich after 1871. By 1890, hardly anyone still felt a conflict between loyalty to a particular state and loyalty to the Reich. Two decades after the empire's foundation, the feeling of German national community was at least as strong as the sense of individual regional differences. By the time Bismarck was compelled to leave the government, the formation of the German nation state could be regarded as complete.

One and a half years before his dismissal, at the end of September 1888, Bismarck had Heinrich Geffcken, a jurist from Hamburg and university friend of Emperor Frederick, arrested on the charge of disseminating state secrets through the publication of the crown prince's war journal from the years 1870–1. Geffcken was acquitted in January 1889 in a federal court. Fontane, as well as the liberal press, considered Bismarck's behaviour not only damaging to his reputation, but also to the reputation of Germany. 'Perhaps it is only an outraged sense of patriotism, but it gives the impression of a mean personal hatefulness,' Fontane wrote to the court official Georg Friedlaender on 7 January 1889.

The great man was indeed a great hater, and in his hatred was often very ignoble. When Eduard Lasker died in New York on a visit to the United States in January 1884, the chancellor saw to it that no member of government took part in the funeral services in Berlin, and he did not forward a message of condolence from the American House of Representatives to the Reichstag. When he tried to justify his behaviour before the delegates on 13 March 1884, he did not refrain from yet another attack on his deceased opponent.

To be sure, Bismarck also made other, more positive contributions to what we today call 'political culture'. Many of the great speeches he gave in the Prussian House of Representatives and the Reichstag have gone down in the annals of German parliamentary history for their rhetorical brilliance, the clarity of their language, and the keenness of their argumentation. Yet stylistic virtuosity could not counterbalance the political unscrupulousness that was *also* part and parcel of Bismarck's character. Theodor Mommsen, one of the liberals who first fought, then supported, then finally fought Bismarck again, came in 1902—the year before his death—to a deeply pessimistic conclusion about the effects the founder of the Reich had had on Germany. In a letter to the economist Lujo Brentano of 3 January, Mommsen wrote: 'Bismarck broke the back of the nation'.

Some three decades before, in the year 1873, Nietzsche had written in the first of his *Unzeitgemäße Betrachtungen** about the error committed by public opinion and by all those who publicly opined that German culture was one of the victors

* Nietzche, *Untimely Meditations*.

in the war against France. 'This madness is highly pernicious: not because it is madness (for some errors are very salutary and blessed), but because it threatens to turn our victory into a signal defeat: *into the defeat, indeed the extirpation, of the German spirit for the sake of the "German Empire."* '

At about the same time, Jacob Burckhardt in Basel was already predicting that within a few years, thanks to the 'moulting process' taking place within German historical scholarship, 'all of world history from Adam onwards will be given a new coat of German victory paint and oriented towards the years 1870–1.' This goal had not yet been reached by 1890, nor was it the goal of all German historians. But it is true that the dominant schools of German historiography, as well as the writers of school textbooks, made a concerted effort to place the rise and 'German mission of Prussia' in the centre of all modern historical study.

In an academic address given shortly after the outbreak of the Franco-Prussian War, Emil Du Bois Reymond, the famous Berlin physician, referred to his university as the 'intellectual royal guard' (*geistiges Leibregiment*) of the House of Hohenzollern. As it happened, neither Du Bois Reymond's alma mater on Unter den Linden street, nor the German university system as a whole, ever lived up (or rather down) to that distinction. In fact, German higher education experienced a new renaissance during the Wilhelmine empire, gaining prestige and admiration throughout the whole world. Yet the phrase 'intellectual royal guard of the House of Hohenzollern' had been pronounced, and it certainly did apply to a part of public opinion. Professors and politicians, pastors and publicists created the cult and the mythology around Bismarck, Prussia, and the Hohenzollerns, which became inalienable components of German imperial nationalism.

'Rarely has a dynasty ruled so completely over the hearts of its subjects as the Hohenzollerns,' wrote the *National-Zeitung* at the beginning of December 1878, when Emperor William I, recovered from Nobiling's assassination attempt, returned to Berlin. 'Already something of the radiance of myth surrounds the majestic head. Charlemagne and Frederick Barbarossa seem like the only worthy figures of history whom we might compare with him as equals.'

Educated Germany celebrated the country's belatedly achieved national unity. The continuing absence of the political liberties for which the liberals had fought before 1871 was not something the majority of Germans felt to be a lack. German liberalism *had* failed. Mommsen's verdict on Bismarck's twenty-eight years of rule in Prussia and Germany cannot be interpreted in any other way.[22]

6

World Policy and World War 1890–1918

FROM CAPRIVI TO HOHENLOHE

In May 1895 the economist Max Weber, then 31 years old, delivered his inaugural lecture at the Albert-Ludwigs-Universität in Freiburg. The subject, 'Der Nationalstaat und die Volkswirtschaftspolitik',* gave the young scholar occasion to lament the political immaturity of the German bourgeoisie, which, at the very moment of the 'economic death throes of old Prussian Junkerdom', lacked the necessary instinct for power. Weber located the cause of this immaturity in the unpolitical past of the German bourgeoisie, a legacy of Bismarck's rule. The means of overcoming it lay in political education through world politics after the example of older great powers like Britain and France.

> Crucial also for *our* development is the question of whether politics on the grand scale can bring home to us the importance of the great questions of political power. We must learn that the unification of Germany was a youthful prank which the nation pulled off in its old age, and which would better have been avoided if it is to be the end-point of German world power politics and not the starting point.

Three decades before, Otto Michaelis, delegate of the right wing of the German Progressive party, had argued in very similar fashion. Prussia, the liberal delegate declared before the House of Representatives on 13 June 1865, must set itself 'great goals' and seize the 'banner of Prussia and Germany against Austria'; for without such an 'ideal goal', the people would lose the energy necessary 'to fight the constitutional conflict with us to the end'. In 1895 the Freiburg economist and sociologist found himself up against the same inner adversary Michaelis had confronted in 1865, and like the latter Weber believed that the means to supply the power struggle against the Prussian Junkers with new energy lay in foreign policy. Since the national goal of German liberalism had been achieved with German unification, however, the foreign policy objective could not be the same as thirty

* Weber 'The Nation State and National Economic Policy'.

years before. Austria had been replaced with the world—not as a target of attack, but nonetheless as a sphere of activity.

The nationalist thrust of Weber's critique of Prussian Junkerdom lay in his reference to the growing significance of migrant Polish labour. Seasonal, low-cost agricultural workers from Russian Poland were increasingly replacing German day laborers fed up with conditions in the old patriarchal manors. 'Large-scale operations, which can only be maintained at the cost of Germandom, ought, from the point of view of the nation, to go under,' Weber concluded. In other words, they should be left to fend for themselves without their life support of protective tariffs burdening society.

Though condemned to economic decline, politically the Junkers were still the most influential class in society. And more than that. Like his fellow economist Werner Sombart and the constitutional scholar Hugo Preuss, Weber saw that the entrepreneurial class of the German bourgeoisie had gone far in adapting itself to aristocratic values. The desire to acquire noble titles and landed estates, imitate a seigneurial lifestyle, achieve the status of reserve officer, cultivate dueling—there was a plethora of evidence to support the thesis of the *Verjunkerung* or 'feudalization' of the upper German bourgeoisie. Yet the social emulation of the nobility was not confined to Germany, and within Germany was not everywhere as strong as in the old Prussian territories. The 'aristocratization' of parts of the bourgeoisie was accompanied by a *Verbürgerlichung* or 'bourgeoisification' of parts of the nobility, and even when ennobled, a bourgeois—for example an industrialist—could not renounce his heritage. The 'feudalization' was not an invention of bourgeois scholars, but it was also not as profound as its critics imagined. Ultimately the counter-forces, working consciously and unconsciously towards the *Verbürgerlichung* of Wilhelmine Germany, would prove the stronger.[1]

It was no coincidence that the new debate over Prussian Junkerdom began in the last decade of the nineteenth century. It was set off by the manner in which the East Elbian landowners reacted to the about-face in commercial policy by Bismarck's successor. Caprivi had correctly recognized that Germany's transformation from an agricultural to an industrial state was irreversible and that the country's economic future depended on an increase in exports. 'We must export,' he announced to the Reichstag on 10 December 1891. 'Either we export goods, or we export people. Without an industry growing at the same rate as our population, we cannot survive.' The commercial treaties of the Caprivi era (in 1891 with Austria-Hungary, Italy, Belgium, and Switzerland, and in 1893–4 with Spain, Serbia, Romania, and Russia) were guided by this insight. Germany promoted the export of industrial goods and, in exchange, dismantled its tariff barriers, including the duties on grain so important to agriculture east of the Elbe.

The opposition of conservatives and landowners began immediately in 1891, and it grew more intense when the chancellor extended his commercial system to agricultural countries like Romania and Russia. The founding of the Federation of Agriculturalists (*Bund der Landwirte*) in February 1893 gave organizational expression to the protest against the government's policies. Although the great landowners were the driving force behind this association, it sought from the beginning to appeal to all groups who felt threatened by the continuing industrialization of society, especially the peasants and the small and medium-sized tradesmen and business owners, the *Bauernstand* and the *Mittelstand.* The success of this effort was not very great among craftsmen, but among small farmers it was resounding: by the turn of the century, they formed nine-tenths of the organization's more than 200,000 members.

Nonetheless, the leadership of the Federation was dominated by the great Prussian landowners, who did not shrink from promoting their interests with a propagandistic excess hitherto unknown in Germany. An early example of the new style of agitation was the call to establish the Federation, sent out to German agriculturalists in December 1892 by the Silesian *Generalpächter** Alfred Ruprecht-Ransern:

> I am suggesting nothing more and nothing less than that we go out among the Social Democrats and earnestly form a front against the government, show it that we are not willing to allow ourselves to be treated as badly as we have been, let it feel our power . . . Instead of complaining further, we must scream until the whole country hears it; we must scream until it is heard in the halls of parliament and in the ministries—we must scream until it is heard on the steps of the throne.[2]

In fact, it would take some time before the screams were heard. But their opponents in the chancellery, without knowing it, were playing into the hands of the landowners. The commercial treaties and a number of domestic reforms—such as the prohibition of Sunday and child labour, the institution of industrial tribunals (*Gewerbegerichte*, consisting of a state official as chairman and one representative each from among the employers and the workers), and a progressive income tax in Prussia—demonstrated the earnest desire of Caprivi and his colleagues in the federal offices and Prussian ministries to promote the much-discussed 'new direction' in economic and social policy. When it came to turning his plans into practical realities, however, the chancellor made one bad mistake after another. In March 1892, his failure to push through an education reform measure friendly to church interests had led to his resignation as Prussian prime minister. The bill had outraged the Liberals, with whom Caprivi had cooperated well up to that point; its retraction incensed the Catholics. On 6 May 1893, during the hearing of a federal bill to increase the armed forces, the majority of both fractions voted against both the governmental draft and a compromise proposed by the Centre delegate Huene with the government's agreement, thus terminating the project. Caprivi responded by dissolving the Reichstag (which otherwise would not have been re-elected until February 1895, according to the five-year legislative period introduced in March 1888).

* [Translator's note: a *Generalpächter* leased fallow land from landowners and rented it out at higher prices.]

The May 1893 vote had far-reaching consequences for the Liberals. Caprivi's bill had gone far to accommodate them in one important point: the term of military service was reduced from three to two years. Consequently, six Liberal delegates voted for Huene's compromise proposal. When the party leader, Eugen Richter, demanded that the rebels receive a sharp reprimand and canvassed a narrow fractional majority to that purpose, the German Liberal party split. The majority, under Richter, renamed itself the Liberal People's Party (*Freisinnige Volkspartei*); the minority, including the 'secessionists' Bamberger, Mommsen, and Stauffenberg, founded the Liberal Association (*Freisinnige Vereinigung*). The social profiles of the two left-liberal parties differed considerably. The People's party was strongly petty bourgeois in character; in the Union, representatives of the propertied and educated classes set the tone.

In the federal elections of June 1893, the proponents of military enlargement, the former 'cartel' parties, performed well, the opponents of the measure poorly, with the exception of the Social Democrats. The two liberal parties did worst of all, together falling from 66 to 37 seats (24 for the Liberal People's party, 13 for the Liberal Association). The new Reichstag passed the military bill. But the chancellor's victory strengthened his position only temporarily. In the next year, the antagonism between Caprivi and the arch-conservative Prussian prime minister Count Botho zu Eulenburg came to such a head that further cooperation between the two was impossible. The leader of the Prussian government favoured a new emergency law against social democracy, as William II was demanding, as well as the emperor's plans for a *coup d'état*; the chancellor rejected both schemes. The conflict ended in October 1894 when the emperor dismissed the two adversaries and appointed the former Bavarian prime minister and then-governor of the imperial territory of Alsace-Lorraine, Prince Chlodwig von Hohenlohe-Schillingsfürst, to the offices of federal chancellor and Prussian prime minister.

Hohenlohe, 75 years old at the time, was a Catholic and a moderate in the southern German liberal tradition. As chancellor, however, he bowed to the will of the emperor, who intended to exploit Caprivi's dismissal for a sharp change of course to the right. To the extent that this involved more forceful action against social democracy, a particular matter of concern for William II, success continued to elude the government. To the so-called 'subversion bill' (*Umsturzvorlage*) of December 1894, which contained strong punitive measures against inciting class hatred and against insults to the monarchy, religion, marriage, family, and property, a further clause was added, in order to secure the support of the Centre, punishing slander against doctrines of the church. For National Liberals, however, the added clause made the bill completely unacceptable, and the Reichstag rejected it by a large majority in May 1895.

After the attempt to pass a new—albeit disguised—anti-socialist law had failed on the federal level, it was the turn of the individual states. But even in Prussia the government did not manage to find a House majority for a so-called 'little anti-socialist law' granting the police wide authority to disband associations and disperse gatherings. Saxony's efforts met with more success. In March 1896 the Saxon parliament replaced its moderate census-based voting law with a three-class system (*Dreiklassenwahlrecht*) favourable to propertied interests. The consequence was that, at least for the time being, the Social Democrats could send no delegates to the parliament of a state that was a stronghold of social democracy. The Saxon proletariat reacted with bitterness and a marked shift to the left.

Three years later, the Reich leadership undertook a renewed legislative effort against social democracy. The so-called 'penitentiary bill' (*Zuchthausvorlage*) of May 1899 increased the penalties for 'compulsion to coalition' (*Koalitionszwang*), that is, attempting to force workers to participate in a strike or labour union. Except for the two conservative parties, however, no fraction was prepared to vote for the new emergency measure. The 'penitentiary bill' was the last legislative attack on social democracy at the federal level. Nonetheless, legal and de facto discrimination of members of the social-democratic worker's movement continued to be very frequent, for example the Prussian *Lex Arons* of June 1898 (for which also the Centre voted) excluding Social Democrats from all academic teaching positions.[3]

Far-sighted people of all political camps knew that the war against social democracy could not be won with suppressive measures alone. But they also saw that the social policy of the government was unable to stop the rapid growth of the movement. In the federal elections of 1893, the Social Democratic Party of Germany (SPD; *Sozialdemokratische Partei Deutschlands*, as it was called after the 1891 party congress at Erfurt) had increased its share of the vote from 19.7% to 23.3% and its seats in the Reichstag from 35 to 44. This sobering experience was partly responsible for the lack of major social policy initiatives during the 'Hohenlohe era' from 1894 to 1900.

Instead, the containment of social democracy would be attempted by other means—through the 'gathering together' (*Sammlung*) of all forces wishing to uphold the prevailing order of state and society. The actual author of this *Sammlungspolitik* was Johannes von Miquel, Prussian minister of finance from 1890 and in 1897 ennobled by the emperor. A former National Liberal delegate to the Reichstag and mayor first of Osnabrück, then of Frankfurt am Main, Miquel had long since turned his back on economic liberalism, both freedom of commerce and freedom of trade. In 1879 he demanded an end to the neglect of the craft trades by the government and the ruling classes, believing this state of things 'a very dangerous one, especially dangerous in times of revolutionary agitation against the foundations of our societal order'. In the 1884 'Heidelberg declaration' of the southern German National Liberals, which he penned, he advocated the protection of German agriculture. Both groups played an important role in the *Sammlungspolitik* of the 1890s. Miquel aimed at a grand alliance of elites uniting industry and agriculture, liberalism and conservatism, in their entirety. The *Mittelstand* was to form the broad base of society, with the independent craft trades as its solid nucleus.

It was relatively easy to accommodate the craft trades to a certain extent. In 1897 an innovation in the trade ordinances created 'handicraft chambers' (*Handwerkskammern*) as corporations covered by public law, as well as instituting 'elective compulsory guild membership' (*fakultative Zwangsinnung*); that is, when the independent craftsmen of a given trade within a particular handicraft chamber district opted to establish a guild, membership was obligatory. The attempt to reconcile the interests of agriculture and industry proved much more difficult. In September 1897, in accordance with a demand from the Central Association of German Industrialists taken up by Miquel, an Economic Committee was formed in the federal ministry of the interior for the purpose of preparing commercial policy measures. This council, which contained representatives from both agricultural and industrial organizations, was to prepare a new customs tariff for implementation after the commercial treaties from the Caprivi era expired.

Miquel intended the East Elbian agricultural protectionists and the heavy industrialists to have a dominant voice in this body. It was so dominant, however, that the export and finished goods branches (organized in the League of Industrialists after 1895 and the Association for the Protection of the Interests of the Chemical Industry) immediately began to form an anti-protectionist defensive front. In an appeal of March 1898, the free traders confronted the old protectionist shibboleth for the 'protection of national labour'—which Emperor William II, at Miquel's instigation, adopted in June 1897—with the accusation that the 'fulfilment of the demands of the agricultural special interests necessarily causes inflation in the cost of living for the broad strata of society' and represents a 'preference for the few at the expense of the many'. In November 1900 the Commercial Treaty Association (*Handelsvertragsverein*), an anti-agrarianist forum, was founded in Berlin. In terms of customs policy, therefore, Miquel's *Sammlungspolitik* was a failure. Protective tariffs were not going to be a platform upon which all of agriculture and industry could be brought together, at least for the time being.[4]

By the turn of the century, however, a promising solution to the conflict of economic interests had been discovered: the German naval fleet. The 'father' of the German navy, Rear Admiral Alfred von Tirpitz, head of the imperial navy since June 1897, knew that he would have a good chance of convincing the educated and propertied bourgeoisie of the merits of a navy. The memory of the first German fleet, created by the provisional central authority in 1848 only to be auctioned off disgracefully in 1852, was still alive, and ever since the revolutionary era, Germans were widely disposed to regard a German navy as the armed branch of the merchant marine—a 'bourgeois' fighting force, in contrast to the aristocrat-dominated army.

In the Reichstag, however, there were still serious reservations about the kind of large-scale naval expansion envisioned by the emperor and Tirpitz. The modest plan establishing the navy in 1873, which considered the protection of German marine commerce and the German coast the navy's most important task, was still in effect. Since a longer-term programme meant longer-term budgetary decisions, it would be unworkable unless parliament voluntarily restricted its own budgetary powers. Moreover, large-scale fleet construction would require the creation of offensive capabilities, and thus threatened to have a negative impact on Germany's relationship to the leading naval power, Great Britain. In light of such considerations the Reichstag, which had agreed to the construction of three new cruisers in March 1896, rejected the proposal for three more the following year. The immediate consequence of the government's defeat was the resignation of the federal naval secretary, Admiral Hollmann. The indirect consequence was the nomination of Tirpitz as his successor.

The watchword for the new chapter of German naval policy that began with Tirpitz's appointment was pronounced by Baron von Marschall, secretary of the foreign office, in the Reichstag debate over the construction of the cruisers on 18 March: 'The question of whether Germany should pursue a world policy is directly connected to another question: whether or not Germany has world interests. This question has long since been answered'. To pursue a 'world policy' (*Weltpolitik*) meant the desire to compete with England on an equal basis, a goal inconceivable without a strong navy. Thus a German fleet of the dimensions Tirpitz had in mind was necessarily a fleet against Britain. Simultaneously, however, the construction programme was aimed against an inner adversary, social democracy. A letter from Tirpitz to the leader of the imperial admiralty, General von Stosch, written at the end of 1895, makes no secret of this motivation. Germany, wrote Tirpitz, must undertake a world policy 'in no small measure because in the great new national undertaking and the economic boon associated therewith lies a strong palliative against educated and uneducated social democrats'.

Tirpitz's first naval bill, passed by the Reichstag at the end of March against the votes of the Social Democrats, the Liberal People's party, and a minority of the Centre, as well as Guelfs, Alsace-Lorrainers, and Poles, provided for the increase of the naval fleet to nineteen battleships, eight coastal defence ships, twelve heavy and thirty light cruisers. Two years later, in June 1900, the Reichstag—newly elected in June 1898—consented to a new bill from the imperial naval office practically doubling the size of the fleet. At the conclusion of the programme, the strength of the German navy was to be comparable to that of the British in a ratio of two to three. This would mean parity in the North Sea. After 1900, therefore, there could be no doubt that the law of 1898 had been only the first stage of a comprehensive plan.

The parliamentary majorities for the naval bills were not fortuitous. Tirpitz revealed himself to be a master at gaining the necessary public support for his policies. He was aided in this effort by an organization founded in 1898 with his collaboration: the German Navy League (*Deutscher Flottenverein*), a modern 'pressure group' comparable to the Federation of Agriculturalists. Active in the League were the direct and indirect interests of heavy industry, shipyards, wholesale and foreign commerce, and the export branches; a broad spectrum of political parties from the Free Conservatives through the National Liberals to the Liberal Association; and wide strata of the bourgeoisie and petty bourgeoisie, whose support of the fleet construction gave them the feeling of participating in a great national enterprise. By 1900 the association numbered some 270,000 individual members. If we include corporate members (i.e. members of organizations who had joined the League), by 1908 the number had grown to over a million.

With *one* group of the 'power elite', however, Tirpitz's naval policy was not especially popular. From the point of view of the Prussian conservatives and Junkers, everything that had to do with the German navy was suspect. They instinctively regarded it as the competitor of the Prussian army. Its economic beneficiaries could only be industry and commerce and thus the same 'modern' world by which rural East Elbian Germany saw itself threatened. To be sure, the conservatives could not easily vote against the naval bills; to do so would have brought the party of Count Kanitz and Ernst von Heydebrand und der Lasa into close proximity with the party of Eugen Richter and August Bebel. For their assent to the second naval bill (1900), however, the conservatives demanded 'payment': a promise to increase the grain tariff. This promise was fulfilled in December 1902 by Chancellor Bernhard von Bülow (in office from October 1900). The so-called 'Bülow tariff', passed by the Reichstag with a large majority and in effect from 1 March 1906, awarded the landowners higher duties on wheat, rye, and oats (albeit not as high as the conservatives and the Federation of Agriculturalists had demanded). Thus the most important goal of Miquel's *Sammlungspolitik*, an understanding between industry and agriculture over customs policy, was achieved by means of a 'detour' through the naval programme. Miquel himself, who died in September 1901, did not live to see this triumph. The success was above all the work of Bülow—and Tirpitz.

In 1928 Eckart Kehr, author of the first critical study of the societal foundations of German *Sammlungspolitik* and naval policy, summarized the provisional conclusion to the political struggle: 'Industry and agriculture came to an agreement that each would not seek alone to control the state and to exclude the loser from the use of the legislative process; rather, they would together erect an agro-industrial condominium directed against the proletariat.' The first phase of German *Weltpolitik* thus occasioned a result completely different than the one Max Weber had put forward in 1895. Not only had it not broken the political power of the Prussian Junkers, it had actually helped to consolidate their societal base.[5]

THE BEGINNINGS OF GERMAN *WELTPOLITIK*

At the high point of the *Sammlungspolitik*, Germany's position on the international stage seemed stronger than ever before. A new rapprochement with Russia under Hohenlohe in 1897 had helped the Reich gain Chinese Kiaochow with the port of Tsingtao. The following year, Germany purchased the Mariana and Caroline islands in the Pacific from Spain. At the end of 1899, shortly after the beginning of the Boer War in South Africa, Germany was able to convince England to agree to a division of the Samoa islands—also in the Pacific—between the German Reich and the United States of America. These new acquisitions made it clear that the German navy aspired to create a worldwide network of bases. In all three cases, the German imperial naval office was the driving force behind a policy outlined by Bernhard von Bülow (at that time Prussian foreign minister and secretary of the foreign office) in the Reichstag on 6 December 1897 to the effect that Germany did not seek 'to put anyone in the shade, but we do demand our place in the sun'.

When Bismarck temporarily overcame his aversion to colonies in the mid-1880s, Germany was in the middle of a depression. Colonial acquisitions could be seen as a means of leading the nation out of the depths of its economic woe. By the time William II, Bülow, and Tirpitz took up the cause of a German *Weltpolitik*, the country was in the midst of an economic upswing (beginning in 1895 and lasting until about 1900) comparable to the foundation years of the Reich. Conscious of their economic strength, the political leaders of Germany issued demands that aimed at a dramatic change in the international balance of power.

In principle, their actions were no different from the imperialism of other great powers like Britain and France. In terms of its impact on Europe, however, the German bid for overseas acquisitions did indeed have a different quality. For France, a colonial empire was *also* a compensation for the losses in power and prestige the country had experienced in 1870–1. The British empire supported Britain's claim to be the world's leading maritime power. For Germany, already semi-hegemonic on the Continent by virtue of the founding of the Reich, the decision to pursue a 'world policy' could only mean that it was no longer satisfied with its Continental status, that it intended to become a sea power as strong as British (at least in the North Sea)—that it sought, in other words, to advance from semi- to outright hegemony. It was inevitable that the other great powers affected by this policy would attempt to counter it. These included, in addition to Britain and France, Russia, which was just as unwilling to see its world-political status reduced by Germany.

In the autumn of 1900, after the defeat of the Chinese 'Boxer rebellion' by the cooperative efforts of all the European great powers, America, and Japan, the German–British relationship seemed about to take a turn for the better. Both powers came to an agreement that all nations should have unrestricted trade access to all the rivers and coasts of China. However, although an alliance was discussed between London and Berlin in 1901, neither side was truly interested. A return to some version of Bismarck's 'reinsurance' policy with Russia was now also out of the question. A 1893 military convention between Paris and St Petersburg—the Russian reaction to a trade war initiated by Caprivi—had outlasted the

German–Russian rapprochement under Hohenlohe. When Russia, after the conclusion of a British–Japanese alliance at the beginning of 1902, once again showed an interest in a treaty with Germany, the Wilhelmstrasse refused. Berlin suspected that St Petersburg was only interested in German backing for its expansionist plans in the Far East.

The June 1902 renewal of the Triple Alliance with Austria-Hungary and Italy initially seemed to be a foreign policy success for Germany. Five months later, however, Rome concluded a secret agreement with Paris, committing both countries to strict neutrality in the event a third party attacked either. The rapprochement between Italy and France, which undermined the Triple Alliance, was unmistakable. By the end of 1902, Germany had only one remaining ally on whom it could depend, but with which it could also easily find itself drawn into entanglements with unpredictable outcomes: Austria-Hungary. Bülow's 'free hand' policy had manoeuvred Germany into a dangerous isolation. The increased national power German *Weltpolitik* had generated was nothing more than appearance. In reality, Germany was more vulnerable twelve years after Bismarck's dismissal than it had ever been before, and it had only itself to blame.[6]

NATIONALIST ORGANIZATIONS AND NATIONAL SYMBOLS

Around the turn of the century, everything considered 'patriotic', 'national', or contributing to German 'world standing' could count on the support of the greater part of bourgeois and especially Evangelical Germany. The German Navy League was only one of many associations committed to making the augmentation of national power into a cause espoused by broad classes of German society. And it was hardly the most extreme. To the 'right' of the League were situated the Pan-German League (*Alldeutscher Verband*), founded in 1891, and the German Eastern Marches Association (*Deutscher Ostmarkenverein*), established three years later. While these organizations had memberships far smaller than the Navy League (with about 20,000 members each in 1900), both exercised a strong influence on the thinking of the national-liberal through to conservative bourgeoisie. Both were typical representatives of the radical nationalism of the period after 1890.

The Pan-German League, a product of the colonial movement and closely connected with Rhenish-Westphalian heavy industry, declared war on all groups within Germany that opposed 'national development', that is, leftists of every shade. Outside Germany, the League supported the 'German-national aspirations' of Germans living abroad throughout the world. In 1894 the Pan-Germans began calling for a German-controlled *Mitteleuropa* and the conversion of Germany from 'great power status' to 'world power status'. Of the political parties, the National Liberals and Free Conservatives were initially closest to the

Pan-Germans (for a time, in fact, the Pan-German League sought to transform both into one 'National party'). After 1911, when they became advocates of an expansionist German world policy, the German Conservatives, too, drew closer to the Pan-German agenda. At all times, the Pan-German League looked upon itself as the avant-garde of all forces pushing for an aggressive German foreign policy. For this reason, it was careful to maintain its distance from official government policy, which was seldom aggressive enough to find favour in the eyes of the Pan-Germans.

The Eastern Marches Association saw its main task in the 'strengthening and gathering together of Germandom in the Polish-dominated eastern marches of the Reich through the uplifting and consolidation of German national feeling as well as through the increase and economic enhancement of the German population'. In other words, the agenda of the 'Hakatist Association' (the unofficial name, composed from the beginning letters of the names of the organization's founders, Ferdinand von Hansemann, Hermann Kennemann, and Heinrich von Tiedemann-Seeheim) was the rigorous Germanization and de-Polonization of the empire's eastern provinces. Place names and surnames were to be Germanized, and the Poles replaced with German settlers.

Measured by the number of Germans who actually migrated to the east, the success of the Association was modest. Far more significant was its impact on 'informed opinion'. The 'Hakatists' transformed the German prejudice against the allegedly racially inferior Poles into a weapon of ethno-cultural warfare, and their efforts were endorsed by the parties of the political right, the German Conservatives, the Free Conservative Empire party, and the National Liberals. The Hakatist attitude toward the government was more favourable than that of the Pan-Germans. Official government policy was fundamentally no less anti-Polish than the Hakatist agenda; the only real differences were tactical in nature.[7]

In contrast to the Eastern Marches Association and the Pan-German League, the 'warriors' associations' (*Kriegervereine*) formed a veritable mass movement. They were dominated not by members of the educated and propertied bourgeoisie, nor by the 'one-year volunteers' (*Einjährig-Freiwilligen*, holders of a patent of *mittlere Reife* who, after six years in a middle or higher school, served only one year in the military, not two, but in exchange had to pay for their own lodging, board, and equipment). Rather, their membership was predominantly craftsmen, shop owners, peasants, day labourers, lower civil servants, employees, and industrial workers—that is, 'ordinary folk', who cherished the memories of their years of military service and, if they were old enough, of the Franco-Prussian War, thereby holding up an idea of the nation as the community-in-arms of *all* German men, even of the least wealthy and educated. The umbrella organization, the Kyffhäuser Union of German Warrior Associations (*Kyffhäuserbund der Deutschen Landeskriegerverbände*), founded in 1899, had a country-wide membership of 1.8 million at the beginning of 1900, and nearly 2.6 million in 1910. Its name referred to a national symbol, in the cause of which the most important 'warriors' associations' in the individual states had rendered great services in the 1890s: the construction of a monument for William I on Kyffhäuser Mountain.[8]

This monument was built between 1892 and 1896 by Bruno Schmitz, the architect of the 'official' emperors' monuments at the Porta Westfalica and Am Deutschen Eck near Koblenz; it was dedicated by Emperor William II on 18 June 1896. The location was chosen carefully. In the words of the inscription on the foundation stone: 'On Kyffhäuser Mountain, under which, as legend tells, Emperor Frederick Redbeard awaits the renewal of the Empire, Kaiser William Whitebeard shall rise up, having fulfilled the legend.' In his famous 1968 study *Nationalidee und Nationaldenkmal in Deutschland im 19. Jahrhundert*,* Thomas Nipperdey wrote that the Kyffhäuser monument represented a moment of transition from the 'monarchical monument' to the 'monument of national concentration' (*Denkmal der nationalen Sammlung*):

> The isolated event and the individual retreat behind mytho-historical conceptions of ancient German imperial glory. The Reich is situated in the deeps of time and, at the same time, celebrated as the fulfilment of national history . . . It is the nation itself, the monarchical nation, but above all the powerful and closed nation, that celebrates itself here in the fulfilment of a mythic history.

The victorious emperor at the head of the nation-in-arms—in nearly 400 public monuments to William I, the Germans of 'national' sentiment not only celebrated their first common ruler since the downfall of the old Reich, they also celebrated themselves. The Kyffhäuser monument was not an 'official' monument like the equestrian statue William II had erected in his grandfather's honour at the Schlossfreiheit in Berlin (commissioned from Reinhold Begas). Nor was it, like most other emperors' monuments of its day, the result of initiatives among the industrial, commercial, and academically educated bourgeoisie. Rather, in keeping with the social composition of the *Kriegervereine*, the Kyffhäuser monument was the fruit of the financial exertions of broad strata of the population, above all the petty bourgeoisie, and it was to *their* collective memory that the glorious history of the medieval German Reich was united in its stone.

Of similar breadth was the movement that, after the death of the first German chancellor on 30 July 1898, joined together in almost 300 'Bismarck associations' and collected money for the erection of monuments to Bismarck. Along with academics (both independent and state-employed), entrepreneurs, and wealthy merchants, mid-level employees and officials, craftsmen, and shop owners accounted for a considerable part of the membership. More than 700 Bismarck monuments went up in the ensuing period (not including the innumerable 'Bismarck towers' and 'Bismarck columns' erected at the petition of university students). Most showed the founder of the Reich either in the uniform of his cuirassier regiment (in which he had so often appeared before the Reichstag), or, less frequently, in the freely rendered

* Nipperdey, *National Idea and National Monument in Germany in the Nineteenth Century.*

symbolic armour of a knight. The man to whom bourgeois and petty-bourgeois Germany dedicated these monuments was the man of 'blood and iron', not the master of diplomacy. Occasionally Roon and Moltke, representatives of the Prussian soldier-state, appeared in Bismarck's company—not only on the Avenue of Victory in Berlin and in other cities of old Prussia, but elsewhere in the Reich, too, for example at the imperial palace in Goslar and Am Friedensengel in Munich.

These monuments to the emperor and chancellor reflected changes in public consciousness, changes nobody had contributed more to bring about than Bismarck himself. The concepts of 'monarchization' and 'militarization' summarize the essentials. The monuments erected by the Wilhelmine bourgeoisie in honour of the founding hero of the Reich no longer betrayed anything of the bourgeoisie's own liberal origins. It was not within liberalism that the legacy of 1848 lived on, but within social democracy.

The historian Wolfgang Hardtwig speaks in this context of a 'deformation of bourgeois political consciousness' that accompanied the 'bourgeoisification of society, culture, and political culture in the Reich'. Part of this 'deformation' was to be found in the fact that the *Volk*, whom general and equal suffrage in parliamentary elections had made into a political factor of no inconsiderable weight, simply did not appear in the political iconography of the Reich—or, as in the case of the Niederwald monument near Rüdesheim (dedicated in 1883), only in the form of victorious or fallen soldiers. A popular cause from the *Vormärz* period, the construction of the Hermann monument in the Teutoburg Forest, was not completed until 1875, and only after Emperor William I provided the necessary funds. The result was that this national symbol, too, lacked a specific 'bourgeois' character.

When, on 5 December 1894, the keystone was placed in the new Reichstag building (built by Paul Wallot) on the Königsplatz in the presence of William II (who referred to the building as the *Reichsaffenhaus*, 'imperial monkey house', in a personal letter to his friend 'Phili' Eulenburg), the ceremony—just like the laying of the cornerstone ten years previously—took on the character of a military spectacle. True to this spirit, the president of the Reichstag, the conservative delegate Albert von Levetzow, appeared in the uniform of a *Landwehr* major. However, the commentary in the liberal *Vossische Zeitung* made it clear that this kind of demonstration would not necessarily come off without criticism in Wilhelmine Germany. 'The President of the Reichstag is the master of the house,' wrote the '*Vossin*',

> and the highest authority within his chambers. But the major is subservient to every last lieutenant colonel, to whom he must bow. The military uniform symbolizes the relation of service and hierarchical subservience. It has its importance and does honour to the one who wears it. But everything in its proper place. If the army were mobilized tomorrow and Major von Levetzow rushed off to the standards, nobody would take issue with his uniform . . . Yesterday, however, the Major had no business to attend to . . . only the President of the German Reichstag was occupied, the freely elected representative of the people, and therefore we might have wished that he had done justice to this high honor in the attire of a free man.

The emperor did not like new parliament building. The large glass dome bothered him (probably because he saw in it the attempt to outdo the dome of the palace, the official seat of his rule). Nor was he happy with the inscription *Dem deutschen Volke* ('To the German People') that Wallot had chosen for placement over the main entrance (it was not put up until December 1916, in the middle of the First World War). When, on a visit to Rome in spring 1893, William referred to Wallot's building—under construction at the time—as the 'pinnacle of tastelessness'. German architects were not the only ones who were outraged. The verdict of the self-proclaimed expert was one of the many comments that ended up damaging William's reputation.

As an institution, however, the emperor remained a national symbol, not least because the Reich did not have many other symbols. Imperial Germany had no national anthem of its own, but only the monarchical anthem 'Heil dir im Siegerkranz',* sung to the same melody as 'God Save the King'. The black, white, and red flag of the navy and merchant marine was declared the national flag in 1892, but it only achieved a certain popularity in the course of the propaganda campaign for the new naval policy. Germany also had no national holiday like the French 14 July, the day of the storming of the Bastille. The day the emperorship was proclaimed at Versailles, 18 January, remained first and foremost the coronation day of the Prussian kings; 2 September, 'Sedan Day', was a festival of Evangelical Germany, and 27 January, the birthday of William II, was too intimately connected to the person of the reigning sovereign to unite Germany in national celebration.

Nor did the symbols of the Reich overshadow those of the individual German states, but coexisted with them. This was not only true of flags, anthems, and monuments, but also of dynasties. All in all, this hodgepodge of relationships and loyalties was, as Bismarck had correctly recognized, more beneficial than detrimental to the cohesion of the new nation. It was true that the federalism of Bismarck's Reich was not coequal, owing to Prussia's dominance. Yet Bismarck made Prussian hegemony bearable for non-Prussian Germans. And despite the centralization that set in under the first chancellor, the Reich did not cease to be meaningfully federal after 1890. A completely centralized state, such as envisioned by Heinrich von Treitschke and other National Liberals, would no doubt have achieved far less national integration than the federal state created by Bismarck.[9]

DEVELOPMENTS IN THE PARTY SYSTEM

The institutional antipode to the emperor was not found in the other German princes and the Free Cities, but in the democratic organ of the constitution, the

* 'Hail to Thee in Victor's Laurels'.

Reichstag. General, equal, and direct suffrage for men over the age of 25 guaranteed the Germans a voice in government—not, to be sure, in the composition of the administration, but at least in the legislative process. By invoking this right and utilizing its results, *all* parties and associations, regardless of whether or not they considered themselves 'national', were instrumental in bolstering Germans' sense of themselves as a *single* national agent, though one of many voices. This consciousness grew stronger as the activities and competencies of the central government—and with them the importance of the Reichstag—increased. William II's animosity against the House was not unfounded.

Parliamentary power struggles depended on many factors, not least of which was the economy. For example, the fact that the anti-Semitic parties were able to increase their share of the vote in the 1893 federal elections from 0.7% (in 1890) to 3.4% and their number of seats from 5 to 16 was closely connected to the economic depression of the years 1890–5. In the election of 1898, an economically good year, they again managed a modest gain of 0.3%. In the next two elections, 1903 and 1907, which took place during an economic upswing, the anti-Semites fell to 2.6% and 2.2% of the vote, respectively. Party-based anti-Semitism was a social protest movement. It was divided within itself into, on the one hand, a radical, aggressively anti-conservative wing around the former Berlin school director Hermann Ahlwardt, originator of the battle cry 'against Junkers and Jews', and the Hessian archivist and 'peasant king' Otto Boeckel, and, on the other hand, a faction amenable to cooperation with the conservatives and led by Max Liebermann, former Prussian officer and functionary of the Federation of Agriculturalists. Political anti-Semitism found support among peasants, small merchants, craftsmen, and company employees, who felt themselves equally threatened by large-scale capitalism and the Marxist worker's movement. As the economic situation improved, the attractiveness of this kind of anti-Semitism decreased.

However, the decline of the anti-Semitic parties is not to be confused with the extinction of anti-Jewish sentiments. Far from it: anti-Semitism had also been absorbed into the platforms of other parties and associations. These had the advantage of offering their constituents much more than the single-issue focus of the 'pure' anti-Semitic parties. At the same time, they recognized anti-Semitism as legitimate, thereby contributing to its social respectability. For example, in its first official party platform, the openly agrarian-conservative 'Tivoli platform' of 1892, the German Conservative party committed itself to the battle against 'the multiform, obtrusive, and pernicious Jewish influence on the life of our people'. To this statement were linked a number of concrete anti-Semitic demands: 'a Christian leadership for a Christian people and Christian teachers for Christian schools', as well as 'effective governmental intervention against any economic activity harmful to the community and against un-German offences to good faith and credit in business'.

In conservative discourse, declarations of war against modern Jewry were accompanied by disavowals of *Radauantisemitismus*, the violent, rowdy anti-Semitism preached by the likes of Hermann Ahlwardt and all purely anti-Semitic parties. According to the fourth edition of the German Conservative party handbook, which appeared in 1911, these parties, with their 'diatribes against all of Jewry', only cause Jews to unite more closely together, even though there are also 'very many honourable and patriotic Jews—many more than the radical anti-Semites care to admit'. Thus the anti-Semitism of the German Conservatives was not 'racist' in the 'biologistic' sense. But that only contributed to its appeal. With their 'differentiating', seemingly moderate Jew-hatred, with its pretence of cultural scruple, the German Conservatives gave voice to a widespread feeling.

The Federation of Agriculturalists, closely connected to the Conservatives, were far less scrupulous in appealing to the anti-Jewish prejudices of the rural populace and the urban middle classes. In June 1895, for example, the group's main publication described agriculture as the main embodiment of Germandom and, as such, the irreconcilable enemy of the Jews: 'Thus it is a natural fact that agriculture and Jewry must fight against each other, fight to the death, until the one party is lying lifeless, or at least powerless, on the ground.'

The German League of Commercial Employees (*Deutscher Handlungsgehülfen-Verband*; founded in 1893, the same year as the Federation of Agriculturalists), which renamed itself the German National League of Commercial Employees (*Deutschnationaler Handlungsgehilfenverband*) in 1896 and initially maintained close contact with the anti-Semitic German Social Reform Party (*Deutschsoziale Reformpartei*) of Liebermann von Sonnenberg and the Austrian Pan-Germans around Georg Ritter von Schönerer, expressly excluded 'Jews and persons shown to be descended from Jews' from membership. The societal group targeted by the League was mockingly referred to as 'proletarians in stand-up collars' (*Stehkragenproletarier*) by many on the left. For their own part, the majority of commercial, industrial, and bank employees saw themselves as members of a 'new middle class' (*neuer Mittelstand*, a concept first appearing in the 1890s) or, in part, as 'private officials', but in no way as proletarians. As 'brain workers', nothing was more important to them than emphasizing the distance that separated them from those who worked with their hands. Since most 'blue-collar' workers had joined the Marxist and internationalist social democratic movement, it seemed clear to many 'white collar' workers that proletarian internationalism was part of a Jewish conspiracy. Thus, for the early employees' organizations, patriotism and animosity towards 'international Jewry' were first and foremost a means of promoting the claim of their members to a higher social status—through a strict dissociation from a class movement that, for its part, placed great value on not being 'nationally' minded.[10]

Yet anti-Semitism was not necessary for a 'bourgeois' alternative to social democracy in dealing with the social question. The Evangelical minister Friedrich Naumann, originally a follower of Adolf Stoecker and his Christian Social Workers' Party (*Christlichsoziale Arbeiterpartei*, founded in 1879, renamed the *Christlichsoziale Partei* after 1881), finally broke with the latter in 1896 by establishing the National Social Association (*Nationalsozialer Verein*). The anti-Semitism of the former court chaplain (Stoecker had been dismissed from his post by William II at the end of 1890) played a smaller role in the separation than the fact that Stoecker's party had never ceased to form a part of the German Conservative party, which, ever since the 1892 'Tivoli platform', sought to become the political arm of the East Elbian agrarian interests.

Naumann had long been the leading voice of the socially engaged younger members (referred to as *die Jungen*) of the Evangelical-Social Congress (co-founded by Stoecker), and a large number of social reformers followed him when he left. The National Social Association did not aspire to a radical transformation of the existing order of society, but it did express its expectation 'that the representatives of German education in the service of the community support German labor in its political struggle against the predominance of existing vested interests' and, on the other hand, that the 'representatives of German labor be willing to promote patriotism in child-rearing, education, and the arts'. The workers were to receive a greater share in the total production of the German economy; women were to be permitted access to professions, both private and public, in which they could 'effectively demonstrate nurturing and educational abilities for their own sex'. These reform demands were made from 'the soil of the nation', and, as such, were accompanied by a declaration of support for a 'reasonable expansion of the German navy' as well as for the preservation and extension of the German colonies.

The 'basic principles' of the National Social Association, which were drafted by Naumann, made no mention of the restriction of Jewish influence. In fact, the manifesto expressly called for the 'unrestricted preservation of the civil rights of all citizens of the state'. General suffrage was not only not to be interfered with, it was to be extended to the parliaments of the individual German states and organs of communal representation. If there is one phrase that summarizes the Association's platform, it is the appeal for a 'vigorous cooperation between the monarchy and the people's representatives'—a distant reminder of Lorenz von Stein's 'monarchy of social reform'.

Naumann further developed this idea in his book *Demokratie und Kaisertum*,* which appeared in 1900. He had come to set all his hopes on William II, the 'emperor of navy and industry', whom he considered willing and able to prepare the way for the 'social empire' (*soziales Kaisertum*) of the future. 'As Prussian king he has assumed the legacy of the old tradition; as emperor he is the national *imperator*, incarnation of the general will, personal leader out of an old and into a new age.' The emperor as executor of the popular will, overcoming the dominance of agriculture by means of a 'dictatorship of industrialism' and using national power politics to create the basis for a dissolution of class antagonisms—in connecting imperialist world politics to the modernization of society, Naumann showed himself to be an avid pupil of Max Weber. For his part, however, the sociologist did

* Naumann, *Democracy and Empire.*

not share Naumann's belief that the emperor was the one called upon to lead Germany on the path to renewal. For Weber, the democratic proving ground of national leadership was the parliament, and Germany should be parliamentarized. Naumann was not long in joining him in this demand.

Social democratic workers were not won over by Naumann's synthesis of national power politics and Christian socialism. Consequently, they remained deaf to his appeal that social democracy endorse the emperor's military and naval policies and prove 'that Germany can be governed without the East Elbian and clerical parties'. This well-intended product of political wishful thinking resonated strongly with intellectuals, but it found no echo in the electorate. In the federal elections of 1898, the candidates of the National Social Association, which was running as a party for the first time, obtained a mere 27,000 votes. In 1903 only one National Social candidate succeeded in getting into the Reichstag: the former anti-Semite Hellmut von Gerlach, who joined the Liberal Association as an auditor.

These failures prompted Naumann to take radical steps. In August 1903 he caused the National Social Association to be dissolved, urging the active members to join the Liberal Association, which most of them did. The two groups did indeed have a great deal in common. Under the influence of Theodor Barth, the editor of the Berlin weekly *Die Nation*, the former secessionists had abandoned their doctrinaire Manchester liberalism and turned toward social reform and colonialism. Naumann's transformation into one of the leading representatives of German left-liberalism formed the temporary conclusion to a development that had begun with a split in the left wing of the conservatives.[11]

The turn of the century also saw a 'national' turn among the Catholic part of the political centre. Like the Liberal Association, the Catholic party voted for Tirpitz's first navy bill in April 1898. It had already given its support the year before to a bill authorizing 176 million marks to re-equip the artillery; in 1899 it agreed to a further increase in the peacetime strength of the army. The Centre's motives had nothing to do with military policy. Rather, it hoped its cooperation with the government in matters affecting the prestige of the Reich would help bring about the abolition of the remaining *Kulturkampf* statutes and enable the German Catholics to be recognized as a 'national' party. When the first reading of the second navy bill was about to take place at the beginning of February 1900, Cardinal Georg Kopp, prince bishop of Breslau, demanded in a letter to the delegate Carl Bachem that the Centre tell Tirpitz it was prepared 'to treat the bill as favourably as possible', but on the condition that 'the Jesuit law be completely abolished *beforehand*, in order to sooth the spirits of the Catholic voters'.

The cardinal's plan did not come off. The navy bill was passed on 12 June 1900 with the votes of the Centre. The only thing the fraction was able to achieve was a six-year delay in the construction of six cruisers destined for service abroad. When the third navy bill went up for a vote in June 1906, the Navy League exerted such massive public pressure that the Centre, no longer daring to propose its usual package deal (assent to the naval office's bill in exchange for abolition of the Jesuit law), simply voted in unconditional agreement. To have turned its back on the 'national' voting record it had compiled in the previous years would have cost the Centre its political credibility.

This danger loomed over the Centre above all from the right. As far as the bourgeois left and the Social Democrats were concerned, the credibility of the Catholic party had been deeply compromised ever since it had gone over to the side of the government 'with beat of drums and flourish of trumpets', as Bebel remarked in 1897. Mommsen went even further in 1902, rounding off his assessment of the Bismarck years ('Bismarck broke the back of the nation') with the comment: 'the Centre has taken over the inheritance.' And in truth, the political opportunism of the Catholic party was obvious, if not its most characteristic feature. There was no important political question the Centre did not consider primarily in tactical terms, deciding its parliamentary behaviour according to the advantages or disadvantages a given measure would bring for political Catholicism.

The short-term benefits of cooperating with the government were obvious. Under Hohenlohe, and under his successor Bernhard von Bülow until 1906, the Centre party became so powerful that it began to nurture the belief that, without it, Germany could not be governed. From this perspective, it made little sense to campaign for the parliamentarization of the state; a majority government without the participation of the Centre would clearly achieve far less for German Catholics than direct negotiations between the party and the leaders of the Reich, who were appointed by the emperor and not beholden to the Reichstag. The political cost of the Centre's tactics only became evident at a later date, when the threat of war grew as a result of policies it had supported from the late 1890s. The parliamentarization of Germany did not depend on the Catholic party alone, but it was not possible without the Catholic party. The constitutional-authoritarian German state was (at least for the time being) strong and sure of itself, and one of the sources of its security was the fact that the Centre did not question the status quo.

Under the leadership of Ernst Lieber, the successor of Windthorst (who died in 1891), the Centre endorsed German colonialism. Whenever an opportunity presented itself, it emphasized its loyalty to emperor and Reich. Yet political Catholicism was never a driving force behind nationalism and colonialism; it simply helped enable German *Weltpolitik* by supporting the relevant legislation for its own domestic-political reasons. With respect to anti-Semitism, the situation was different and yet similar. The Centre rejected legislation that would have resulted in the reversal of Jewish emancipation. In November 1880, when the Prussian House of Representatives, in response to a motion from the Progressive party, debated the collecting of signatures for the 'anti-Semite petition', Windthorst had committed his party to an unambiguously negative vote on the restriction of Jewish civil rights. However, this did not mean that politicians and publicists of the Centre did not share Catholic prejudices against the Jews. The speeches of Peter Reichensperger and Julius Bachem during the debate left no room for doubt that they did, and during the 1890s, the *Historisch-politische Blätter* demonstrated the same vehemence in the anti-Semitic campaign as they had done two decades before.

The decline of party anti-Semitism at the turn of the century also had an effect on the Centre. To be sure, Catholics continued to hold Jews in great suspicion, and there was a specifically Catholic discourse of anti-Semitism, which included the dictum that the Catholic position represented the only legitimate opposition to the Jews—opposition based on the Christian religion. Yet at no time did the Centre consider making anti-Semitism part of its political platform, as did the emphatically Evangelical German Conservative party. Catholics knew only too well what it felt like to be a disadvantaged minority; their own experiences warned them against active participation in discrimination towards another.

Compared with the *Kulturkampf* era, the Catholic situation at the turn of the century was comfortable. Catholics were politically influential and no longer had to feel like they were living in a fortress under siege. Liberalism was still an enemy, but had lost a good deal of its former menace. The domestic-political détente came at a price, however. The last year the Centre managed to gain more that 20 per cent of the federal vote was 1887. Thereafter it stagnated at about 19 per cent. The 'electoral discipline' of German Catholics was no longer as high as it had been during the era of legislative persecution. The Catholic microcosm had lost some of its cohesive force. Catholic workers, peasants, academics, small tradesmen, entrepreneurs, and landowners all lived in different social worlds, held together by a common faith and by Evangelical anti-Catholicism, which was no less strong—indeed, militant—after the *Kulturkampf* had formally passed. (A defensive nationalist Protestant organization, the Evangelical Union for the Protection of German-Protestant Interests, was founded with the expressed goal of keeping up the anti-Catholic political pressure. Its membership increased from 81,000 in 1891 to 510,000 in 1913.)

It was only in comparison with the fragmented Protestant political landscape that turn-of-the-century German Catholicism represented any kind of unified whole, the so-called 'Catholic milieu'. In terms of social composition, the Centre was more of a 'people's party' than any other. From the 1890s, bourgeois politicians became increasingly dominant in the party leadership, pushing out the nobility. While continuing to support the Catholic workers' associations, after 1894 the Centre began to promote the Christian Trade Unions (*Christliche Gewerkschaften*). These were not exclusively Catholic in membership, but interconfessional, and as such they marked the beginning of a conflict in Catholic political identity. The Centre had to decide if it saw itself as a confessional or supraconfessional party, whether it wished to remain a purely Catholic organization or open itself up to Protestant participation.[12]

In the meantime, social democracy was moving—or at first glance seemed to be moving—in a very different direction. The expiration of the anti-socialist law on 30 September 1890 restored to the party of August Bebel the full range of political activities it had done without for twelve years. However, the vast majority of social democrats had no intention of renouncing their opposition to capitalist society and authoritarian imperial government, just as, for their part, the leaders of the Reich and the federal states did not cease considering social democracy a force of subversion. Nor did the proletarian left abandon its anticipation of what Bebel called the 'great crash-bang-wallop' (*grosser Kladderadatsch*), that is, the approaching collapse of exploitative bourgeois society, and the socialist 'state of the future' that was to replace it. At the 1891 party congress in Erfurt, Bebel went so far as to predict that the 'realization of our last goals is so near that there are few people in this hall who will not live to see it.'

The 1891 Erfurt platform of the Social Democratic Party of Germany, the basic principles of which were drafted by the editor of the theoretical party organ *Neue Zeit*, Karl Kautsky (born in Prague in 1854, active in the socialist movement from his first semester at the University of Vienna), was much more 'Marxist' than its predecessor, the 1875 Gotha platform, which, to Marx's chagrin, had contained a strong residual Lassallean influence. In its very first paragraph, the new platform took up the thesis of the 1848 *Communist Manifesto*, according to which the development of the economy would, 'by necessity of nature', lead to the downfall of small private business, the concentration of the means of production in the hands of a few large capitalists and landowners, and the swelling of the ranks of the propertyless proletariat with former small proprietors. Marxist, too, was the claim that class struggle between bourgeoisie and proletariat would become more bitter, dividing society into two hostile camps. The same was true of the demand to make the means of production the common property of the community at large—a goal that, according to the text, the working class could not achieve 'without first obtaining the requisite political power'.

The pragmatic part of the Erfurt platform, primarily the work of Eduard Bernstein (born in Berlin in 1850, son of a Jewish railway engineer; trained as a bank employee; during the anti-socialist era editor of the weekly *Sozialdemokrat*, which was published first in Zurich, then in London), presented the SPD more as a radical democratic than socialist party. Its demands included general, equal, and direct suffrage in all elections and ballots, 'irrespective of sex'; a 'general legislature of the people by means of the right to propose and reject legislation'; a 'people's army in place of the standing armies'; the 'authority of the people's representatives to decide matters of peace and war'; secular schools; the restriction of religion to the private sphere; the abolition of all laws 'discriminating against women in public and private law'; the abolition of the death penalty; and the guarantee of the freedom of association.

One particular concept that played a key role in the thinking of Marx and Engels did not appear in the Erfurt platform, the 'dictatorship of the proletariat'. So as to provide no pretext for further 'legal' persecution of social democracy, the document's authors also refrained from referring to their goal of the 'democratic republic'. Nor did they adopt the alternative proposed by Engels that they demand the concentration 'of all political power in the hands of the people's representatives'. That the text should contain no mention of 'revolution' went without saying.

Yet it was not merely a tactical move when, two years after Erfurt, Kautsky, who had replaced Wilhelm Liebknecht as party theoretician by this time, sought to liberate the concept of 'revolution' from its connotations of revolt, urban warfare, and bloodshed. In the *Neue Zeit* (December 1893), he described social democracy as 'a revolutionary, but not a revolution-making party'. It had no intention 'of inciting or preparing a revolution. And since we cannot wilfully make one, we also cannot say anything about when, under what conditions, and in what form the revolution will come.'

Kautsky remained firm in his insistence that the radical social changes envisioned by social democracy could only be achieved 'by means of a political revolution, through the conquest of political power by the fighting proletariat'. Unlike its situation in backward Russia, however, the proletariat in the 'modern states', thanks to the freedom of association, freedom of the press, and general suffrage, now had other and better weapons at its disposal than the revolutionary bourgeoisie had in the eighteenth century. When the proletariat availed itself of democratic institutions, it did not cease to be revolutionary.

> Democracy cannot overcome the class differences inherent in capitalist society, and it cannot stand in the way of their necessary final outcome, the overthrow of this society. But one thing it can do: it cannot prevent the Revolution, but it can prevent many a premature, fruitless attempt at revolution and render many a revolutionary uprising superfluous.

The main thrust of Kautsky's argument was that imperial Germany, too, was one of the 'modern states' in which the proletariat could win political power in the democratic way, by means of electoral victory. Radical social change, the social revolution, could follow in a more or less evolutionary manner. As for the 'dictatorship of the proletariat', Kautsky could not, as he wrote in a letter to Franz Mehring on 8 July 1893,

> imagine a form other that that of a vigorous parliament of the English type with a Social Democratic majority and a strong and self-conscious proletariat behind it. In Germany, the struggle for authentic parliamentary rule will, in my view, be the decisive battle of the social revolution, for a parliamentary regime means, for Germany, the political victory of the proletariat. But the reverse is also true.[13]

Marx had considered the peaceful transition from capitalist to post-capitalist society a historical exception. For Kautsky, it was now the European rule. To this extent he *had* distanced himself from Marx, or 'revised' him. Yet he could not admit it. To have done so would have risked the unity of the party and given impetus to 'anarchists' or a new anti-parliamentary opposition like the 'young' fraction (*die Jungen*) thrown out of the party in 1891. This was the reason Kautsky sharply contradicted his friend Eduard Bernstein in 1897 when the latter, writing from

London (where he had moved in 1888 after his expulsion from Switzerland), began to openly criticize the teachings of Marx and Engels.

Inspired by debates in the London Fabian Society, a circle of intellectual social reformers around George Bernard Shaw and Sidney and Beatrice Webb, Bernstein called fundamental premises of Marx's and Engel's 'scientific socialism' into question, first in a series of articles entitled 'Probleme des Sozialismus'* in the *Neue Zeit*, then in a summarizing communication to the Social Democratic party congress in Stuttgart in October 1898. Citing a wide range of evidence, Bernstein argued that the 'catastrophe theory', the prognosis of the inevitable collapse of bourgeois society, as well as the doctrines concerning the deterioration of societal conditions, the end of small business ownership, and the disappearance of the middle classes, had all been disproved. His political conclusions were radical:

> The more . . . the political institutions of the modern nations are democratized, the more the need and opportunity for great political catastrophes are decreased . . . The conquest of political power by the working class and the expropriation of the capitalists are not ultimate ends in themselves, but only a means to the attainment of certain goals and aspirations.

In response to the first objections of Kautsky and other theoreticians, among them Viktor Adler in Vienna, Bernstein, in a letter to the party organ *Vorwärts*, further sharpened his theses:

> Everywhere in advanced countries we see class struggle taking on milder forms, and it would not bode well for the future were it otherwise . . . Reforms that would have required bloody revolution a hundred years ago we achieve today by means of the ballot box, demonstrations, and similar means of political pressure.

At the beginning of 1899, at Kautsky's request, Bernstein presented his comprehensive critique of Marx and Engels, *Die Voraussetzungen des Sozialismus und die Aufgaben der Sozialdemokratie.*† In this book, the author called democracy both 'means and end'. 'It is the means of achieving socialism, and it is the form of socialism realized.' Socialism was the legitimate heir of liberalism, not only chronologically, but also in terms of political-intellectual substance. For social democracy, the guarantee of civil liberty was always more important than the fulfilment of an economic theory. The party's influence would be much greater than it was at the present 'if Social Democracy could find the courage to emancipate itself from a phraseology that is truly obsolete and to represent itself as that which it is in fact today: a democratic-socialist reform party'.

Bernstein repeated his much-criticized statement that what was typically referred to as the 'ultimate goal of socialism' meant nothing to him, 'the movement everything'. He was not seeking to 'overcome Marxism', he emphasized, but to 'expel

* Bernstein, 'Problems of Socialism'.

† Bernstein, *The Preconditions of Socialism and the Tasks of Social Democracy.*

certain residues of utopianism that Marxism is still dragging around with it'. He invoked the spirit of Kant, the critic of pure reason, against the 'comfortable shelter' of Hegelian dialectic. Then, on the final pages of his study, Bernstein once again made clear what, more than anything else, separated him from the left of his party:

As soon as a nation has reached a condition in which the rights of the propertied minority have ceased to be a serious obstacle to social progress, in which the negative tasks of political action take a back seat to the positive, then the appeal to violent revolution becomes a meaningless phrase. A government and a privileged minority can be toppled, but not a people.[14]

Bernstein's book was in large part a response to Rosa Luxemburg's critique of his articles in the *Neue Zeit.* Luxemburg was born in 1871 in Zamosc in Russian Poland, the daughter of an emancipated Jewish merchant. Raised in Warsaw, she became active in the revolutionary socialist movement as a schoolgirl. During her university years in Zurich, she founded the 'Social Democracy of the Kingdom of Poland' together with other emigrants. After receiving her doctorate in economics, Luxemburg moved to Berlin in 1898. In September of that year she published her critique of Bernstein's thesis in series of articles entitled 'Sozialreform oder Revolution'* in the Social Democratic *Leipziger Volkszeitung* (the articles appeared under the same title in pamphlet form in 1900). According to Luxemburg, Bernstein had renounced the materialist interpretation of history, the economic theory of Marx, and class struggle. His claim that the development of capitalism did not proceed to its own destruction meant that socialism was no longer 'objectively necessary'. Bernstein's revisionist theory was a 'theory of socialist stagnation, justified with a vulgar-economic theory of capitalist stagnation'—the '*first*, but also the *last* attempt to provide opportunism with a theoretical basis'.

Luxemburg considered Bernstein's understanding of reform and revolution, democracy and dictatorship of the proletariat completely undialectical.

Legislative reform and revolution are . . . not two different methods of historical progress one can select like hot sausages or cold sausages from the dinner table of history. They are different *moments* in the development of class society, conditioning and completing, yet at the same time excluding each other, like, for example, south pole and north pole, like bourgeoisie and proletariat.

Marx had, to be sure, considered the possibility of a '*peaceful exercise of the proletarian dictatorship*', but

not the replacing of the dictatorship with capitalist social reforms. The necessity of the proletariat's seizure of political power was itself never open to doubt, neither for Marx nor for Engels. And it was reserved for Bernstein to believe the chicken coop of bourgeois parliamentarism to be the appointed organ by means of which the most powerful world-historical revolution, the transformation of society from *capitalist* to *socialist* forms, would be effected.

* Luxemburg, 'Social Reform or Revolution'.

Just as Bernstein viewed the development of the German and international workers' movement through the eyes of the British reformers, Rosa Luxemburg saw them with the eyes of a revolutionary coloured by the experience of tzarist Russia. Bernstein had a tendency to underestimate the resistance faced by parliamentary and democratic reformers in Hohenzollern Germany. Luxemburg overestimated the revolutionary potential in the international and German proletariat, and she underestimated not only the opportunities opened up to social democracy by general suffrage, parliamentary politics, the right to strike, freedom of speech, and freedom of the press, but also the consciousness-transforming power of these achievements.

Karl Kautsky, the third important participant in the great debate over democracy and dictatorship, reform and revolution (a debate that was to have a great influence well into the twentieth century), found himself in a dilemma. On the one hand, he had begun to relativize the revolutionary aspect of Marxism even *before* Bernstein. As far as the possibility and desirability of an evolutionary transition from capitalism to socialism was concerned, he was far closer to 'rightist' Bernstein than 'leftist' Luxemburg. But on the other hand, as the foremost theoretician of the SPD, Kautsky considered it his duty to hold the social democratic movement together as a party. A particular understanding of Marxism had established itself in the party, based, in not inconsiderable part, on the reading of Engels's *Anti-Dühring* and Bebel's *Die Frau und der Sozialismus*,* which had appeared in 1878 and 1879, respectively. Bernstein was now calling the fundamentals of that understanding into question, and Kautsky had to take steps against him. He could do so in good conscience, since Bernstein's account of Marxism was, in many ways, more like a caricature. Kautsky interpreted Marx in a different way than Rosa Luxemburg, but he agreed with her that Marx's theory was still the correct one and that it should therefore still be the intellectual and practical guide for the international workers' movement.

In his 1899 book *Bernstein und das Sozialdemokratische Programm*,† Kautsky accused his colleague of fabricating a Marxist 'theory of collapse' that had little to do with what Marx had actually written; even the 'theory of immiseration' did not appear in the writings of Marx and Engels, but was invented by the opponents of Marxism. Kautsky held firm to the thesis concerning the progressive concentration in industry and agriculture, and, in consequence, to the idea of the long-term inviability of small business. In order to be victorious, therefore, social democracy would have to remain faithful to Marx's clear historical theory and the ultimate goal of social revolution. The alternative was 'muddling through on a case by case basis', which would necessarily result in the proletariat losing the consciousness of its great task. Nonetheless, social revolution and rebellion were to be sharply differentiated: 'Social revolution is a goal we can set by way of principle; rebellion

* Bebel, *Woman under Socialism.*

† Kautsky, *Bernstein and the Social-Democratic Programme.*

is a means to an end, a means we can only ever evaluate according to practical purposes.'

In contrast to Bernstein, Kautsky drew a clear line of distinction between socialism and liberalism. 'A progressive democracy is, in an industrial state, now only possible as a *proletarian democracy*. Hence the decline of progressive bourgeois democracy . . . Today, only a firm belief in the necessity of the rule of the proletariat and in its political maturity can lend power of attraction to the democratic idea.' For the rest, Kautsky exhorted social democracy to have hope: 'What has become the strongest party within three decades can, within another three decades, become the ruling party, maybe even sooner.'[15]

Kautsky's position represented that of the 'party centre' around Bebel and became the official viewpoint of the SPD. In October 1899, even before the appearance of Kautsky's 'anti-critique', the Hanover party congress had overwhelmingly passed a resolution proposed by Bebel rejecting any change in platform or tactics and specifically targeted at any endeavour 'attempting to conceal and shift its stance on the existing order of state and society and on the bourgeois parties'. The resolution did not oppose cooperation with bourgeois parties 'on a case by case basis', as long as the goal was 'to strengthen the party in elections, or to extend the political rights and liberties of the people, or to seriously improve the social position of the working class and promote cultural tasks, or to combat activities aimed against the workers and the people'. Even in such cases, however, the SPD insisted on maintaining 'its complete autonomy and independence' and on regarding every partial success merely as one step 'bringing it closer to its final goal'.

Neither the Hanover resolution nor Kautsky's book brought the revisionist conflict to an end. It occupied future party congresses and reached, with the sharp repudiation of revisionism at the Dresden congress in 1903, more of a climax than a denouement. Bernstein, who returned to Germany in 1901 and was elected to the Reichstag in a by-election the following year, along with his comrades-in-arms, among them Joseph Bloch, publisher of the *Sozialistische Monatshefte*, the agrarian revisionist Eduard David, and the Berlin attorney Wolfgang Heine, had no intention of renouncing arguments that had, in part, long been scientifically confirmed—like the thesis concerning the growth of the middle classes and the emergence of a new kind of small business, the repair shop.

More important than the small group of avowed 'revisionists', however, was the even greater number of influential 'reformists', pragmatic men like the leaders of the Free Trade Unions (*Freie Gewerkschaften*) under Carl Legien, head of the general commission, or the chairman of the Bavarian Social Democrats, Georg von Vollmar. It was Vollmar who, in his 'Eldorado' speeches in Munich in June 1891, was the first to exhort the party to move 'from the *theoretical to the practical*, from the general more to the particular' and not to forget 'present-day, immediate, urgent concerns' in a single-minded focus on the 'future'—that is, to engage in realpolitik. Conflicts over principle, like the one between Kautsky and Bernstein, held little interest for the 'reformists'. What they were interested in was exploiting the political options available to them without undue concern for the purity of tradition and dogma.

The majority of the party delegates, officials, and members stood with Bebel. Most Social Democrats approved of the parliamentary fraction's decision to renounce its right to a vice-presidential position, since part of the protocol of the Reichstag presidency was 'going to court', that is, official audiences visits with the emperor. At times, the party was even more doctrinaire than its head. At the 1895 party congress in Breslau, an agrarian programme advocated by Bebel, which would have opened the party to small farmers, was voted down by a large majority of delegates. The industrial workers feared an attenuation of the party's 'proletarian' identity. Unlike the Catholic milieu, social democracy was socially homogeneous. It had emerged from the era of anti-socialist legislation more firmly unified than Catholic Germany during or after the *Kulturkampf.* The social democratic workers had developed a proletarian class consciousness. And if class consciousness is a necessary part of social class, then the working class was the *only* one in Germany.

In shielding itself from the rest of society, the social democratic milieu was, to a certain extent, immune from the Wilhelmine zeitgeist. It was anti-militaristic, anti-nationalist, and—at least in principle—anti-colonialist. Anti-Semitism was uncommon, more so than in any other social stratum in Germany. Yet social democrats did not only reject and combat anti-Semitism, they also habitually underestimated it. The dictum that anti-Semitism was 'socialism for imbeciles' gave expression to a foolish optimism. A party pamphlet of the early 1890s put it in the following way:

> And the anti-Semites? . . . They are the avant-garde of social democracy, since they penetrate circles not yet accessible to the latter. In claiming the Jews to be the root of all social misery, they provoke their supporters into thinking about these issues, thus contributing to the emergence of class consciousness in backward social groups. The anti-Semites are an ephemeral party, such as tend to arise in times of social disintegration. In the long run, they will not be able to hide from the people the fact that the Christian capitalists behave just like the Jewish capitalists.[16]

The issue of anti-Semitism was connected with a crisis in French socialism that also rapidly affected the German Social Democrats, the uncontested leaders of the Second International founded in 1889. In May 1899 the Socialist Alexandre Millerand entered the radical-republican Waldeck-Rousseau cabinet, leading to the formation of a leftist government. The *cas Millerand*, the first instance of 'ministerialism' in the history of the European workers' movement, was a crisis ancillary to the Dreyfus affair, the scandal around the Jewish Captain Alfred Dreyfus, who was falsely accused of being a German spy, demoted, and exiled from France for life. The reform-minded forces within French socialism, led by Jean Jaurès, defended Millerand's decision, pointing to the danger from the right. For the supporters of the orthodox Marxist Jules Guesde, on the other hand, Socialist participation in a bourgeois government was absolutely irreconcilable with the doctrine of class struggle.

In September 1900 the congress of the International in Paris dealt with the French conflict. It passed a resolution drafted by Kautsky declaring the 'dangerous experiment' of Socialist participation in a bourgeois government acceptable only as a 'temporary and exceptional emergency measure'. But this formulation was not strict enough for Guesde and his friends. At the Amsterdam congress of the International in 1904, they presented another resolution (which had already been adopted by the Dresden congress of the SPD the year before), according to which the party, in the spirit of the 'Kautsky resolution', 'cannot aspire to share in the authority of the government within bourgeois society'. The congress adopted this resolution by 25 to 5 votes and 12 abstentions.

Unlike in the Third Republic, formal coalitions were not possible in the constitutional German Reich. Ever since the commercial treaties of the Caprivi era, it was considered acceptable for the Social Democrats to support individual government bills or proposals by the bourgeois parties, if such a decision could be justified in terms of the interests of the workers or the improvement of society. To approve budgetary measures, on the other hand, was treated by the party leadership as tantamount to a vote of confidence in the government, and was therefore rejected. In 1894, when Social Democrats in Bavaria, Baden, and Hesse nonetheless voted for a state budget for the first time, they were severely reprimanded by Bebel. The Dresden resolution of 1903, which was 'internationalized' a year later by the Amsterdam congress, went still further. By rejecting participation in any kind of coalition, it made the parliamentarization of the German Reich even less of a possibility than it already was.

The decision highlighted one of the main contradictions within the politics of German social democracy. The combination of a radical theory and a practice aimed at achieving small improvements had led the party to an impasse. With its militant refusal to participate in government, the SPD blocked precisely the kind of constitutional transformation it should have been its highest interest to promote. A revolutionary alternative to the parliamentarization of the Reich existed only in the imaginations of the party left around Rosa Luxembourg, Karl Liebknecht, Clara Zetkin, and Franz Mehring. It did not exist in reality. Social democracy was in the process furthering the isolation in which its adversaries sought to confine it.[17]

THE BÜLOW ERA

When, in October 1900, William II appointed the secretary of the foreign office, Count Bernhard von Bülow, to be Hohenlohe's successor as chancellor of the Reich and prime minister of Prussia, many observers believed the emperor was about to commence his 'personal regime'. Bülow, a suave career diplomat, was considered an intimate of the sovereign, who in turn considered Bülow much more 'his' chancellor than Caprivi and Hohenlohe had been. Yet it did not all depend on the emperor. The bureaucracy, the military, and the parliament each had their own interests and altogether too much influence to permit any plan for a 'personal regime' to be put into practice, even leaving aside William's own deficiencies as a statesman.

Bülow, who had been elevated to the title of prince in 1905, depended until 1906 on the support of the two conservative fractions, the National Liberals and the Centre. The latter, although slightly weakened after the 1903 federal elections, still remained the strongest fraction and was able to justify its support of the government above all with the social policy of Count Posadowsky-Wehner, the secretary of the federal interior ministry. Measures such as the extension of accident and health insurance, the prohibition of child labor in cottage industries, and state support in the construction of worker housing vindicated the policy of cooperation with the right among the Centre party's working-class constituency. The conservatives benefited from the parliamentary support of the chancellor not only through higher duties on grain (the 'Bülow tariff' of 1902); in 1905, after a bitter struggle, they also managed to block the construction of the decisive connecting section in the canal between the Elbe and Hanover. This was the greatest victory for the agrarian interests of the Reich to date. The majority of the parliament bowed to the pressure of the East Elbian Junkers, who opposed the canal for no other reason than to keep transportation costs for cheaper foreign grain as high as possible.

In December 1906 the governmental majority collapsed over a controversial issue of colonial policy. A native rebellion in German South-west Africa—first by the Herero, then by the Hottentots—prompted the government to petition the Reichstag for additional expenditures for the colonial troops. In the meantime, however, the behaviour of the colonial administration and military had come in for massive criticism at home. The battle against the Herero had turned into a campaign of annihilation. Since not only the Social Democrats, Guelfs, Alsace-Lorrainers, and Poles spoke out against the government's request, but also the Centre, under the influence of its left wing around the Württemberg delegate Matthias Erzberger, a narrow majority came together against the bill.

Bülow responded by dissolving the Reichstag. The ensuing election campaign was conducted by the government, German Conservatives, Free Conservatives, National Liberals, and the two liberal parties with nationalist slogans and a common front against the Social Democrats and Centre party. Since the 'national' forces supported each other in the run-off elections, they achieved a resounding victory in the second ballot of the 'Hottentot election' on 5 February 1905. The parties of the new liberal-conservative 'Bülow bloc' gained a total of 220 seats, the parties opposing the colonial policy only 177. The real loser was the SPD. Despite small increases in the number of votes they obtained, the Social Democrats lost nearly half of their power, falling from 81 to 44 seats.

The pact with the 'cartel parties' of 1887 allowed the left-liberals to achieve their primary tactical goal, the removal of the Centre party from the governmental camp. Liberalism and conservatism came together over a minimal 'national' consensus consciously excluding Social Democrats and Centre. Yet nationalism could not serve as the basis of a true reform policy. The most important legislative achievement of the 'Bülow bloc', the federal law of associations (*Reichsvereinsgesetz*) of April 1908, was a compromise. Liberals scored important successes: police authority in the dissolution of assemblies and associations was abolished, and most restrictions on political associations were removed. Women and young people over 18 years of age now finally had the right to become members of political associations and to participate in political assemblies. But the law also contained the controversial 'languages paragraph' (*Sprachenparagraph*), which mandated the use of German for all public occasions, with the exception of international conferences. In areas of mixed nationality (Posen, northern Schleswig, and parts of Alsace-Lorraine), an interim regulation applied, allowing the use of the native language for a period of twenty years.

On the international stage, the German Reich under Bülow drifted yet further into political isolation. The construction of the Baghdad railroad, a consortium of German and French banks and industrial concerns, provoked Great Britain and Russia. In 1904 London concluded an *entente cordiale* with Paris. On the face of it, the two powers did nothing more than agree that Morocco would be in the French, Egypt in the English sphere of influence. Germany, however, felt passed over and affronted. When, shortly afterwards, Russia suffered a serious defeat in its war with the Japanese, the leaders of Germany decided that the hour had come to teach France, the most important ally of the tzarist regime, a lesson. At the end of March 1905 William II, wishing to emphasize the German interest in Morocco, landed at Tangier. When two months later the French foreign minister, Delcassé, the architect of the anti-German policy of the Quai d'Orsay, was removed from office, many Germans saw the high-stakes *Weltpolitik* of their government confirmed.

But then Britain, the other ally of France, entered the scene. When Germany demanded an international conference on Morocco (held in April 1906 in Spanish Algeciras), British diplomacy saw to it that Berlin was completely isolated from the start. Germany reacted by stepping up naval production, which provoked Britain anew. London responded by concluding a treaty with St Petersburg in which the two powers came to an understanding about their respective spheres of interest in the Near and Middle East. What Germans felt to be 'encirclement' was the result of Bülow's 'free hand' policy—the Reich had done everything in its power to bring the other great powers (except for Austria-Hungary) closer together. The alliances of 1904 and 1907 were, first and foremost, the fruits of German foreign policy.

When Britain proposed to Germany a mutual limitation of naval expenditures in 1908, the emperor saw to it that the overture was brusquely rejected. At the same time, the situation in the Balkans was reaching a crisis point. In the autumn of 1908 Serbia responded to the annexation of Bosnia and Herzegovina by Austria-Hungary (which had occupied these still formally Ottoman territories since 1878, after a decision by the Congress of Berlin) with the mobilization of its armed forces. Vienna, with the firm support of Berlin, demanded good behaviour from Belgrade. Serbia and its ally Russia were forced to bow to the pressure of the central powers and recognize the annexations. Thus the Bosnia crisis seemed to end with a German success. In the long term, however, Germany's position deteriorated. Russia now increasingly sought the support of the western powers, and Wilhelmstrasse had committed itself to Austria-Hungary's Balkan interests in a way that was bound to compromise and endanger German diplomacy.

The most serious crisis of the Wilhelmine empire, the *Daily Telegraph* affair, also occurred during the era of the 'Bülow bloc'. On 28 October 1908, the London *Daily Telegraph* published an interview William II had granted to the English colonel Sir Edward James Stewart-Wortley during German military manoeuvres in Alsace. The emperor asserted in this conversation that the majority of Germans did not share his Anglophilia; that he had prevented a coalition of the Continental powers from forming against Britain during the Boer War of 1899 and had sent to his 'revered grandmother' Queen Victoria a war plan that the British had then obviously followed; and, finally, that the German fleet that so exercised the British was only a means of gaining worldwide respect for Germany, above all from Japan and China, as well as in the Pacific. 'It may even be that England herself will be glad that Germany has a fleet when they speak together on the same side in the great debates of the future.'

Following the strict constitutional and bureaucratic protocols to the letter, William II, in East Prussian Rominten at the time, had sent the text of the interview to the chancellor, who was taking the waters on the island of Norderney. Bülow, without reading the document, sent it to the foreign office, where a privy councillor by the name of Klehmet—the secretary and the chief of press were absent—dealt with it. Klehmet did not see fit to question the propriety of the emperor's words, making only a few minor corrections. From the undersecretary, who also did not think it necessary to read the text himself, the manuscript travelled back to the chancellor. According to his own testimony, Bülow once again refrained from reading the interview, returning it to the emperor along with Klehmet's emendations. William then sent it off for publication.

The British public was inclined to be amused at the German emperor's claims and boasts. The German public was shocked and outraged. In *Denkwürdigkeiten*, his posthumously published memoirs (1930), Bülow, one of the main responsible parties, accurately depicted the mood in the country:

> The Emperor's political observations and statements, published by the *Daily Telegraph*, were but the drop that brought the kettle of public exasperation to overflowing, filled to the rim as it was after all the careless remarks and gaffes His Majesty made time and time again. Like a punch in the ribs, the English conversations of William II violently reminded

the nation of all the political errors the Emperor had committed in the twenty years since the beginning of his rule, and of all the wrathful prophecies of the deposed Prince Bismarck. Something like a dark foreboding was felt in the widest circles, a premonition that such careless, brash, imprudent, indeed childish talk on the part of the head of the Reich could ultimately lead to catastrophe.

On 10 and 11 November speakers of all the party fractions, from the conservatives to the Social Democrats, sharply censured the emperor in the Reichstag. But the real sensation of the parliamentary reaction to the affair was that it prompted Bülow to issue William his first public warning. He was convinced, declared the chancellor, that the experiences of the previous few days would induce the emperor 'to observe even in private conversations that reserve which is equally indispensable to the interests of a consistent policy and to the authority of the crown. If this were not the case, neither I nor any of my successors could assume the responsibility.'

William II's reputation was so compromised by the affair that only a public gesture of humility and a promise of better behaviour could limit the damage. On 17 November 1908, after an interview with Bülow, he agreed to a statement to the effect that he had received the chancellor's comments and elucidations 'in great earnest' and saw 'his most noble imperial duty in securing the continuity of the Empire's policy in keeping with the constitution. Accordingly, H[is] M[ajesty] the Emperor commends the words of the Federal Chancellor in the Federal Parliament and assures Prince von Bülow of his continuing confidence.'

Regardless of how William really felt about his chancellor, in the autumn of 1908 he was unable to get rid of him. Bülow therefore had the opportunity to try his hand at the long-overdue 'great reform' of the imperial finances—and to fail. On 24 Juny 1909 the German Conservatives, Centre, and several smaller groups successfully blocked the centrepiece of the reform, the estate tax bill. There were, to be sure, good conservative as well as Catholic reasons to claim that the estate tax was hostile to property and family. But the rejection of the bill also had to do with factors that went far beyond the immediate legislative context. The Centre had not forgotten Bülow's role in the 'Hottentot election', and the Conservative vote was influenced by a strong ultra-royalist faction around the West Prussian landowner Elard von Oldenburg-Januschau that accused the chancellor of disloyalty to the emperor.

On 26 June, two days after the parliamentary failure of the Reich leadership, Bülow asked William II to allow him to resign from his post. The emperor, who had momentarily considered dissolving the Reichstag and even staging a *coup d'état*, gladly fulfilled his request, but wished Bülow to remain in office until the end of parliamentary debate over the other finance bills. An early dismissal would have made it seem as though the emperor were merely fulfilling the will of the Reichstag majority and tacitly assenting to parliamentary monarchy. In order to avoid this undesirable impression, Bülow was not dismissed until 14 July 1909, two days after the Reichstag had passed the remaining tax laws.[18]

THE PARTIES AND THE QUESTION OF PARLIAMENTARY RULE

Was Germany really 'poised on the threshold of parliamentary rule' in the summer of 1909, as one often reads? The two parties that had brought about Bülow's fall did *not* advocate such a change. The German conservatives emphatically rejected the parliamentarization of Germany, and the Centre party saw so many practical advantages in its policy of shifting alliances that it had no intention of committing itself to dependence on any kind of formal coalition. The Free Conservatives and National Liberals, too, sought only to preserve constitutional rule. Three parties endorsed parliamentary governance: the Liberal People's Party, the Liberal Union, and the German People's Party (active primarily in Württemberg). In March 1910 these parties joined together in the Progressive People's Party (*Fortschrittliche Volkspartei*). The position of the Social Democrats was not entirely clear. Parliamentary rule was in complete accordance with their desire for a total democratization of the state. Yet since they rejected cooperation with bourgeois parties, the possibility of their participation in a 'social-liberal' coalition did not exist for the time being.

Consequently, the German Reich of 1909 lacked one of the major prerequisites of parliamentary rule: a parliamentary majority aspiring to such a system and prepared to uphold it. And even if there had been such a majority in place, the Federal Council only needed a minority of fourteen votes to block any amendment to the constitution. Thus a veto from Prussia would have sufficed, and there was no doubt about where Prussia stood on the question of parliamentary rule. The Hohenzollern dynasty with the emperor and king on the throne, the army, the Junkers, and the high bureaucracy were all resolved to defend their power and interests. If the Reichstag had really forced the issue, the consequences would have been very serious indeed.

A conflict of similar proportions would have resulted if the opponents of Prussian three-class suffrage had banded together to fight for the introduction of the federal voting law in the largest German state. The injustice of the Prussian system was evident in the relationship between the number of votes and the number of parliamentary seats received by the Social Democrats. In 1903, the second time it ran for election to the Prussian House of Representatives, the SPD obtained 18.8% of the vote, but no seats. In 1908 the party, supported by 23.9% of the vote, entered the House for the first time, but received a mere 7 of 443 seats. It went without saying that the Social Democrats were the most vocal proponents of general direct suffrage in Prussia. They were joined only by the left-liberals. The Centre vacillated between the federal model and plural suffrage system friendly to propertied interests. Among the Prussian Free Conservatives and National Liberals there were probably supporters of plural suffrage, but no politicians who would have considered replacing the three-class with the federal system. The German Conservatives were uncompromising champions of the status quo and its main beneficiaries. With 14% of the vote in 1908, they obtained 143 seats, 34% of the total.

As progressive as federal suffrage was in comparison to the system in Prussia, it had one great deficiency: it only applied to men. Of all the political parties, only one fully endorsed equal political and social rights for women, the Social Democratic Party. Left-liberals were divided on the question. The followers of Friedrich Naumann were firm supporters of equal rights, but they were in the minority. In its March 1910 platform, the Progressive People's Party demanded the 'extension of the rights of women and their employment opportunities' as well as 'the right to vote and to stand for election to shop and commercial tribunals'. Significantly, however, nothing was said about parliamentary suffrage. The National Liberals had even greater reservations about women's rights, and the Centre Party and the Conservatives generally considered politics an area in which women had no business.

Things were not very much different within the women's movement itself. Women in the socialist movement, led by Clara Zetkin and Luise Zietz, fought for equal rights for women in all areas of social and political life, including the right to vote and to be candidates for election (active and passive suffrage). The bourgeois women's movement was divided. For the left wing around Minna Cauer, women's suffrage was an indispensable part of democracy. The moderates, led by Helene Lange, saw the vote not as part of their immediate political agenda, but as a goal to be achieved by women in the distant future and as a reward for especial merit. When, in 1907, the non-partisan League of German Women's Associations (*Bund Deutscher Frauenverbände*) demanded active and passive women's suffrage, it did not address the question of the legal framework (Reichstag system, three-class, or plural suffrage) in which the goal was to be realized. Of all the bourgeois women's movements, none was less radical than the German.[19]

By the first decade of the twentieth century, however, it could also no longer be said that the German workers' movement was especially radical. When revolution broke out in Russia in 1905 (first in St Petersburg, then in large parts of the country) in the wake of the Russo-Japanese war, leftist socialists in the west believed it to be the beginning of a new cycle of revolutions. It was true that Russia was considered the most backward country in Europe. For that very reason, however, Engels had predicted in the 1880s that 'the country is approaching its 1789' and that 'when the year 1789 has once begun there . . . the year 1793 will not be far off.' Engels predicted that the 'avant-garde of the revolution will go on the offensive' in Russia; indeed, he considered the tzarist empire to be one of the 'exceptional cases' 'in which a handful of people manage to *effect* a revolution'. If there was one place 'Blanquism' might conceivably work (the 'fantasy' of the French Communard Louis Auguste Blanqui, according to which a small group of conspirators could overturn a whole society), it would be, according to Engels, St Petersburg.

What the young Marx had expected from *Vormärz* Germany—that its backwardness would bring forth an especially radical revolution—the late Engels thus hoped for, at least momentarily, from Russia. Russia would make up for the lack of a revolutionary situation in the developed west, thereby driving forward the revolutionary agenda on the international stage. Once again, the revolutionary idea migrated from west to east. In 1843–4, Marx had proclaimed Germany the heir of the French revolutionary tradition. Four decades later, Engels continued the tradition of the '*translatio revolutionis*' in ascribing a special revolutionary mission to Russia.

After 1903 there really did exist a Marxist 'revolutionary avant-garde' in organized form in Russia, the group of 'Bolshevist' professional revolutionaries around Lenin. The party was formed when the Russian Social Democratic Workers' Party split into a majority (*Bolsheviki*) and a minority (*Mensheviki*) faction. However, Lenin and the Bolsheviks were not the ones who fascinated the German and west European left in 1905, but rather the Russian proletariat and its mass strikes. Rosa Luxemburg—who in 1904 had accused Lenin of seeking to eliminate the initiative of the masses for the sake of the tightly organized, centralized rule of a 'Blanquist' coterie—concluded from the revolution of 1905 (she was writing about a year later) that the mass strike was the '*form of movement of the proletarian masses, the manifestation of the proletarian battle in the revolution*', and thus that it was 'inseparable from the revolution'.

From her point of view, the backwardness of Russia was no reason *not* to learn from the Russian experience. On the contrary: 'Precisely because it has delayed its bourgeois revolution so unforgivably long, the most backward country can reveal to the proletariat of Germany and the most advanced capitalist countries ways and means of extending class struggle.' Unlike in Russia, the bourgeois order had had a long history in Germany; but since it had been completely exhausted in the meantime and since democracy and liberalism had had time 'to become extinct', then, 'in a period of open political warfare in Germany', it could 'only come down to the *dictatorship of the proletariat* as the ultimate, historically necessary outcome'.

Rosa Luxemburg's staunchest adversary within the party, Eduard Bernstein (whom she called an 'opportunist'), neither accepted her dialectics of backwardness nor had any interest in preparing the way for a 'dictatorship of the proletariat'. He, too, regarded the mass strike as a legitimate political weapon, *the* modern alternative to old revolutionary barricade-warfare, which he considered 'obsolete' (Engels wrote something very similar in 1895, shortly before his death, in the introduction to the new edition of Marx's *Klassenkämpfe in Frankreich*). Unlike the radical left around Luxemburg, however, Bernstein did not think of the political mass strike as an instrument to set the proletarian revolution in motion, but as a means of achieving democratic goals (such as the abolition of the Prussian House of Lords or the reform of Prussian suffrage) or defending against assaults on already existing democratic achievements (like the Reichstag suffrage law).

In an address to the party at the Bremen congress of the SPD in 1904, Bernstein said that although he had the reputation of being a 'moderate comrade' and considered the name a designation of honour, nonetheless moderation was not to be confused with weakness or lack of energy. If an attempt on the Reichstag voting law should be made, then the thought that the German workers 'may under no circumstances renounce this right must be so powerful that they use all forms of resistance at their disposal. And if they should be defeated, then it is better to go down with honour than to let the vote be taken away without any attempt to resist.'

With this statement, the revisionist Bernstein came very close to the Engels of 1895. Engels, too, regarded general, direct suffrage as an well-nigh revolutionary achievement allowing the workers' movement—at least in developed societies—to wage class struggle in new and more 'civil' forms and to proclaim an end to the 'era of surprise attacks, of revolutions made by a small, conscious minority at the head of unconscious masses'. The Free Trade Unions, however, who were as indispensable for political mass strikes as they were for industrial action, had no intention of letting politicians and theoreticians dictate what they should or should not do, no matter whether they were called Luxemburg or Bernstein, Engels or Bebel. With a membership of 1.6 million in 1906, nearly five times as large as the SPD (which had 384,000 members at the time), the social democratic trade unions were self-confident enough to give highest priority to preserving their own organization and avoid subordination to the party. At a trade union congress in Cologne in May 1905, an overwhelming majority of the delegates declared it 'reprehensible' 'to attempt to prescribe a particular tactic by agitating for political mass strikes'. A general strike, such as was endorsed by 'anarchists and people with no experience in the business of economic warfare', was 'out of the question'.

Since the Social Democratic left responded to the Cologne resolution with aggressive attacks against the Free Trade Unions, the SPD could also no longer avoid taking a position on the issue of mass strikes. In September 1905 a large majority of the Jena party congress passed a resolution drafted by Bebel declaring it the duty of the entire working class, 'in particular in the case of an attack on the general, equal, direct, and secret suffrage law or on the right to coalition . . . to employ any means that seems appropriate for their defence'. The congress designated the 'comprehensive mass walkout' as 'one of the most effective weapons to prevent such a political crime against the working class or to secure an important basic right for its liberation'. However, in order that this weapon might be made available and used to greatest effect, 'the greatest possible extension of the political and trade union organization of the working class is absolutely necessary, as well as vocal agitation.'

With the expression 'most effective weapon', the party leadership of the left sought to emphasize the defensive purpose of the political mass strike, thus accommodating moderates and the trade unions. But the Free Trade Unions, seeing the Jena resolution as a paternalistic attempt to co-opt their voice, resisted. After a series of confidential negotiations in February 1906, the leadership of the SPD agreed to a near-total self-correction: a general strike was not called for at the present time, and the party leadership would not call for one without the assent of the general commission of the Free Trade Unions.

That was not yet the end of the debate, however. Through an indiscretion, the confidential agreement was leaked to the public, causing a storm of outrage among the left wing of the party. The following party convention, which took place in September 1906 in Mannheim, passed, after heated exchanges, a resolution drafted by Bebel and Carl Legien, the head of the general commission of the Free Trade Unions. The so-called 'Mannheim agreement' confirmed the Jena resolution, but added that the latter did not contradict the Cologne resolution, and obliged the party leadership to consult the general commission 'as soon as it considered the necessity of a political mass strike to exist'. In sum, the result was a victory for the unions. The losers were not only the left-wing radicals, but also committed revisionists like Bernstein. After the 1906 SPD convention, political strikes for the democratization of Prussia were off the agenda for the time being.

The nature of the Mannheim 'compromise' corresponded to the distribution of power within the social democratic workers' movement. The party centre under Bebel, trying to reconcile the differences between 'left' and 'right', between the party and the unions, often could only do so with the help of a rhetoric that sounded more radical than was intended. The party's theoretical basis remained Marxist in the sense of the Erfurt platform of 1891. The day to day practice, however, was completely unrevolutionary, though in no way consistently reformist. The SPD fractions in the southern German state parliaments, repeatedly voting for state budgets against the party line, were regularly criticized, and when in 1909 the Baden Social Democrats formed a 'grand bloc' with the National Liberals and Liberals in order to push the Conservatives and Centre into the minority, their actions were regarded by most of the federal SPD as a betrayal of sacred principle.

In fact, under the prevailing conditions, the policy of the Baden Social Democrats was realistic and successful. It could not easily be transferred to the federal level, however, and to Prussia, so intimately linked to the Reich, not at all. A strategy with the goal of moving Germany and Prussia closer to democracy could not be discerned anywhere in the SPD. Everything undertaken by the party leadership was calculated to improve the material circumstances of the workers, to hold the party together, and to improve its performance in the next election. Consequently, the mixture of revolutionary doctrine and practical renunciation of revolution made a certain sense. Any real decision, whether for revolution or reform, would have split the party.[20]

The Centre found itself in a similar predicament at around this same time. After the turn of the century, differences of opinion with regard to the confessional character of the Christian Trade Unions, which had been supported by the Centre since their founding in the 1890s, led to a conflict (the so-called *Zentrumsstreit*) over the question of whether the Centre should consider itself a Catholic-clerical party or an interconfessional political party open to Protestants and independent of the clergy. The former position was represented by the Berlin 'integralists' around the Reichstag delegate Hermann Roeren, the latter view by the reformers of the 'Cologne school' around Julius Bachem, publicist and editor of the *Kölnischer Volkszeitung*. The integralists could count on the support of the pope, Pius X, the German episcopate, and the Berlin branch of the league of Catholic workers' associations. The reformers found allies in the Goerres Society for the Cultivation of Science in Catholic Germany (founded in 1876) under its leader, the Munich philosophy professor Georg Baron von Hertling, the Christian Trade Unions, and in the People's Association for Catholic Germany, which counted over 650,000 members in 1910, the tenth year of its existence.

The conflict escalated in spring 1906. Julius Bachem published in the *Historisch-politische Blätter für das katholische Deutschland* an essay entitled 'Wir müssen aus dem Turm heraus!'* calling for an end to the sequestration and confinement implicit in the popular image of the 'Centre tower'.

> We must not remain barricaded in our tower, we must plant ourselves in front of it and in an ever expanding circle with the means available to us in the present day. We must stand up for the platform of the political Centre party, a truly good platform. If the Centre is an authentic party in this state, then it ought to look upon and assert itself as such everywhere . . . The Centre must not slide into a *splendid isolation*† under the influence of the confessional antagonisms so many are working to sharpen. This would make the fulfilment of its duties to the Reich and to the people tremendously difficult. Let the above thoughts, those developed and those intimated, serve the effort to lessen these dangers.

The forceful integralist campaign launched by Roeren in response to Bachem's initiative missed its main target. The party leadership did not submit to the demand that it commit to the 'Catholic world view'. In the 'Berlin declaration' of 28 November 1909, it stressed that the Centre was 'basically a non-confessional political party'. But a clear assertion of its interconfessional character, such as the 'Cologne school' wished, was not contained in the declaration. Rather, the leading councils of the party referred explicitly to the 'fact that almost all of its voters and delegates belong to the Catholic Church'—a fact that was 'sufficient pledge that the Centre party will vigorously represent the just interests of German Catholics in all areas of public life'. This was a typical formal compromise; the Centre resolved neither to open nor to close itself, but confirmed the status quo.

The battle over the self-image of the Centre party died away after the autumn of 1909, but the trade union controversy continued. In the encyclical *Singulari quadam* of September 1912, Pope Pius X did not expressly forbid interconfessional Christian Unions, but he so clearly stressed Catholic unions as the rule that it was tantamount to an endorsement of the integralist position. The Christian Trade Unions, which counted 340,000 members by 1913, responded with massive protests, eventually forcing the German bishops to reinterpret the encyclical to accord with the prevailing conditions. The beneficiaries of the conflict between integralists and workers were the bourgeois politicians of the Centre, to whom Matthias Erzberger now also went over. The 'Catholic milieu' had become further

* Bachem, 'We Must Come Down from Our Tower'.

† [Translator's note: 'splendid isolation' is in English in the original.]

subdivided in the course of the conflict—so much so, in fact, that the curia and the episcopate could no longer compel acceptance of the integralist programme. The conservatives had lost influence. They were, however, not yet defeated.[21]

While Centre and Social Democrats were dealing with factional disputes, liberalism was enjoying a political renaissance of sorts. In June 1909 the liberal forces within German industry, weary of constant concessions to East Elbian agriculture, joined together to form the Hanse League for Commerce, Trade, and Industry (*Hansa-Bund für Handel, Gewerbe und Industrie*). Three-quarters of a year later, the three left-liberal parties united to form the Progressive People's Party. Among the National Liberals, too, there were signs of a reinvigorated bourgeois self-consciousness. Younger delegates like Gustav Stresemann (born in 1878 in Berlin, Ph.D. in economics, lawyer for the Association of Saxon Industrialists, and from 1911 member of the committee of the League of Industrialists) questioned the close relationship between their party and the Conservatives. Many National Liberal mayors became pioneers in cooperative economic policy, and such things as municipal transport offices, gas, electric, and water utilities were possible only because liberals of all political stripes had turned away from the 'Manchester' interpretation of laissez-faire economics and recognized the necessity of publicly funded social services. Liberalism thus became more reformist. Ironically, however, this transformation was not brought about by means of general, direct federal suffrage, but through local elections based on voting laws friendly to property. An 'opening towards the left', that is, to social democracy, was not part of the liberal renewal. Even in 1910, the vast majority of liberals and social democrats were still worlds apart.

Only a minority on the left-liberal fringe went so far as to categorically reject any kind of liberal–conservative joint policy and openly endorse cooperation with the Social Democrats. The old historian and Nobel Prize winner in literature, Theodor Mommsen, was still a lone voice in the wilderness when, at the end of 1902 (about a year before his death), he wrote an article in the liberal *Nation* calling for the collaboration of liberals and Social Democrats against the 'absolutism of a league of interest between the Junkers and the chaplainocracy' in order to prevent the 'overthrow of the federal constitution'. And that was not all. Mommsen proclaimed the Social Democrats the 'only large party at the present time that commands political respect' and wrote that everyone in Germany knew 'that equipped with a single mind like Bebel's between them, a dozen East Elbian Junkers would stand head and shoulders above their confreres.' It was no coincidence that the title of the piece, 'Was uns noch retten kann',* was the same as that of a pamphlet by Mommsen's friend Karl Twesten (died in 1870) from the year 1861, right before the beginning of the Prussian constitutional conflict.

Five and a half years later, in May 1908, the former editor of the *Nation*, Theodor Barth, together with two former members of the National Social Association, Hellmut von Gerlach and Rudolf Breitscheid, founded a party that put into practice Mommsen's appeal for a collusion between the liberal

* Mommsen, 'What Can Still Save Us'.

bourgeoisie and the social democratic workers: the Democratic Union (*Demokratische Vereinigung*). To be sure, with about 11,000 members in 1911 and about 30,000 votes in the federal elections of 1912, the new party never amounted to more than a splinter group. And it was only a minority of that minority that took the logical step of joining the Social Democratic Party. Rudolf Breitscheid was the first, in 1912. For this economics Ph.D. and former *Burschenschaft* member, this was the real beginning of his political career, which was to lead him to the leadership of the party in the Reichstag sixteen years later.

Within the Progressive People's Party, too, there were proponents of cooperation with the Social Democrats along the lines of the Baden 'grand bloc'. The advocates of an anti-feudal and anticlerical bloc 'from Bassermann to Bebel', among them Naumann, looked to the reformists and revisionists in the SPD and to the 'young liberals' in the National Liberal Party, who were led by the Baden jurist Ernst Bassermann after 1904. But the new left–liberal fusion party was by no means united in this matter, and, for the time being, only a few National Liberal and Social Democratic outsiders were prepared to take the idea of a 'social–liberal bloc' seriously. Thus, at the end of the Bülow era, there was no potentially majoritarian party constellation in sight that could have replaced the shattered 'Bülow bloc'.[22]

WORLD WAR AS A WAY OUT? THE SECOND MOROCCO CRISIS OF 1911

Bülow's successor as Reich chancellor, Prussian prime minister, and Prussian foreign minister, the administrative jurist Theobald von Bethmann Hollweg, who had led the federal ministry of the interior since 1907, was in many respects the opposite of his predecessor. He was not forceful of manner, but earnest and reflective; a vacillator, not a gambler. Close to the Free Conservatives, for whom he had been a delegate to the Reichstag for a few months in 1890, the new chancellor had to find his majorities where he could. He could not always depend on the support of the German Conservatives, who were drifting continually further to the right. On 29 January 1910, six months after Bethmann Hollweg came to power, the delegate Elard von Oldenburg-Januschau expressed the attitude of his party in a deliberately provocative manner by declaring before the Reichstag his allegiance to an 'old Prussian tradition': 'The king of Prussia and the German emperor must be ready at any moment to say to a lieutenant: Take ten men and shoot the parliament!'

Bethmann Hollweg suffered his first serious defeat in spring 1910 in the struggle for a modest reform of the Prussian three-class voting system. The centrepiece of the proposal was an education bonus for 'bearers of culture' (*Kulturträger*), including retired non-commissioned officers. The chancellor summarily withdrew the bill after the House of Representatives, with the votes of the Conservatives and the Centre, rejected an upper-house amendment to the draft.

He was more successful a year later in his attempt—vigorously contested by the Conservatives—to provide the province of Alsace-Lorraine with a constitution. The Alsace-Lorrainers now obtained a parliament with two chambers, the second of which they could elect. The fact that suffrage was general, equal, and direct was not the chancellor's doing, however (he had preferred a plural system), but that of the Reichstag. The province received three votes in the Federal Council, which, however, would not be counted if Prussia could find a majority only by means of them. The constitution of 1911 did not grant the Alsace-Lorrainers full equal rights with the other Germans, but it was an important step in this direction.

At the beginning of Bethmann Hollweg's chancellorship, the reins of foreign policy lay in the hands of Alfred von Kiderlen-Waechter (originally from Württemberg), the secretary of the foreign office. It was this man who, in the summer of 1911, brought Germany to the brink of a great war, though unintentionally. As in 1905, the catalyst of the international crisis was Morocco. Disturbances in the north African sultanate prompted France to occupy Fez and Rabat in spring 1911. Although the Wilhelmstrasse was prepared to leave Morocco to the French, it sought to make them pay for the concession by relinquishing extensive territories in the Congo to Germany. In order to underscore the German demands, Kiderlen sent the gunboat *Panther* to the port of Agadir, where it anchored on 1 July 1911.

The main instrument in the journalistic accompaniment to the '*Panther*'s leap to Agadir' was the Pan-German League. Its leader, the judicial official Heinrich Class, had been personally asked by Kiderlen for help with propaganda. The idea of war with France, which, given the state of international affairs, could rapidly expand into a world war, held no fear for Class and the Pan-Germans. Indeed a German West Morocco, such as the Pan-Germans demanded in one of their pamphlets, was not to be brought about without war. Numerous conservative, national-liberal, heavy-industrialist, and Evangelical newspapers expressly endorsed this idea. The chief of the general staff, Count Helmuth von Moltke, did the same. The 'younger Moltke' considered a great war unavoidable in any case and believed the present moment more favourable for it than later, when Germany's enemies would be stronger.

By 22 July it was clear that France would have the backing of Britain in the case of armed conflict with Germany. On this date Lloyd George, the chancellor of the exchequer, after a confidential agreement with the foreign minister, Sir Edward Grey, gave his support to Paris in a speech at the Mansion House. Neither William II nor Bethmann Hollweg wanted war, however, and even Kiderlen-Waechter sought a gain in prestige without violence. On 4 November 1911, after Russia, Austria-Hungary, and Italy had told their respective allies that they did not consider a war for Morocco to constitute a threat to their mutual defence agreements, Germany and France negotiated an end to the conflict. Germany renounced all forms of political influence in Morocco (which became a French protectorate in 1912) and contented itself with the assurance of most-favoured-nation treatment.

France ceded (not especially valuable) parts of its Congo territory to Germany, which granted France a strip of land in Togo in exchange.

The result of the Franco-German negotiations was the precise opposite of the hoped-for gain in prestige for the Reich. With his '*Panther*'s leap', Kiderlen-Waechter had demonstrated a classic example of unreflective Wilhelmine brinkmanship and, through the frivolous recourse to the Pan-German League, made himself hostage to extremist nationalism. Nonetheless, the Pan-Germans and the right-wing parties were not the only ones who stoked the fires of outrage over the 'cowardice' of the Reich leadership in the second Morocco crisis. Voices from the Centre were also heard lamenting the humiliation Germany received at the hands of Britain and France. Even left-liberal publications were not immune from invocations of 'Olmütz', Prussia's retreat in the face of Austria's threat of war in November 1850.

When, speaking before the Reichstag on 9 and 10 November 1911, Bethmann Hollweg defended the government's position and sharply rejected a pre-emptive war, the assembly responded with massive criticism. The leader of the Centre fraction, Count Georg von Hertling, concluded his speech with the remark that it would 'possibly' do no harm 'if at some point the authorities were to say that preservation of the peace is certainly a great good, but that it is too dearly bought if it can happen only at the price of our standing in the world'. The leader of the National Liberals, Ernst Bassermann, accused the chancellor of pursuing a 'politics of illusion', spoke of the 'defeat' Germany suffered in the Morocco crisis, and warned foreign nations to be 'cognizant of the fact that we shall not let our national honour be offended and that, if it should prove necessary to take up arms in defence of Germany, we shall be found a united nation'.

Even more extreme were the words of Ernst von Heydebrand und der Lasa, the leader of the German Conservative party, which up to that point had left 'world policy' mainly in the hands of the National Liberals and Free Conservatives. Yet the 'uncrowned king of Prussia', as Heydebrand liked to be called, had apparently come to the conclusion that old Prussiandom could successfully defend its endangered position only by placing itself at the forefront of the national movement demanding a better position in the world for Germany. 'What secures peace for us', said Heydebrand, 'is not this compliance, these agreements, these understandings. It is our good German sword. And it is also the feeling—one the French will have, with good reason—that we, too, hope to behold a government willing, when the time has come, to not let that sword go to rust.' At Britain the speaker aimed the comment that it had now been revealed to the whole German people 'where the enemy is. The German *Volk*, if it wishes to spread itself out in the world, if it wishes to find that place in the sun its right and destiny have appointed to it—then it now knows the location of the one who pretends to the right to pass judgment on whether it shall be permitted.'

The counterpoint to the belligerent language of the Conservatives and National Liberals was provided by the leader of the Social Democrats, the only party to call upon its supporters to protest over the war in the foregoing weeks. The end of Bebel's speech was prophetic. All sides will now arm themselves further

> until the moment when one or other of the parties says one day: better an end with horror than a horror without end . . . Then the catastrophe will come. Then, the general march will be struck up throughout Europe, at which point sixteen to eighteen million men, the flower of manhood of all the different nations, equipped with the latest instruments of murder, will confront each other as enemies on the field of battle. But in my view, hard on the heels of the great general march shall come the great crash-bang-wallop . . . It will not come through us, it will come through you yourselves. You are bringing things to a head. You are leading us into catastrophe . . . The twilight of the gods of the bourgeois world is upon us. Be assured: it is upon us! You are today in the process of undercutting your own political and societal order, sounding the death knell of your own political and societal order.

The minutes record outbursts of 'laughter' and 'great amusement' and the call from the right, 'It gets better after every war!'

During the second Morocco crisis, bourgeois Germany was in a state of agitation that can only be described as a kind of last-minute panic. This mood found its classic expression in a confidential letter Bassermann wrote to Kiderlen-Waechter on 24 July 1911. Referring to the increasing difficulty of 'concluding commercial treaties that even come close to meeting the interests of German industry', the National Liberal leader described it as

> unbearable for us that our competitors on the world market shut the doors of the last free areas before our noses. That must drive a nation like Germany, which must expand if she does not wish to suffocate on her own population surplus, to the point where only war remains as ultima ratio. This is the feeling of the thinking circles of the nation.[23]

The economic interests in Morocco to which Bassermann referred *did* exist in Germany. The Mannesmann brothers, in particular, to whom the sultan had assured the mining rights for many kinds of ore in the country, were eager to consolidate their position in Morocco and drive out French competition. They could count on the support of the Central Association of German Industrialists, the Pan-German League, and the National Liberals. However, the belligerent mood that seized the nation's 'thinking circles' in the summer of 1911 was not the product of the special interests of a steel company. The feeling that Germany always came up short in the international competition for power and markets had a long history in the German bourgeoisie. This feeling had grown stronger with the increasingly demonstrative solidarity between Britain and France after the *entente cordiale* of 1904. In 1911 British and French public opinion was hardly less nationalist, imperialist, and militarist than in Germany. When Italy, a 'belated nation' like Germany, turned imperialist words to deeds and initiated a war against Turkey for the conquest of Tripoli, there was a great deal of envy north of the Alps. Italy seemed to be pursuing the kind of self-confident power politics Germans were demanding in vain from their own government.

One of the reasons the Tripolitan war was popular in Italy was because it could be understood as an attempt to divert mass emigration away from South and North America towards a more proximate area on the north African coast, an area that considerably expanded Italian national territory and strengthened Italy's strategic position in the Mediterranean. Germany could claim no such interest in Morocco. As in other examples of Wilhelmine *Weltpolitik*, the second Morocco crisis was a case of prestige above interest. Germany was economically far stronger than France, not to mention Italy. Unlike its neighbour to the west, it did not need colonies and protectorates to compensate for the trauma of military defeat and the attendant territorial losses. The German economy was not far from overtaking that of Britain, the motherland of the Industrial Revolution and imperialism. The German share of world exports was continually rising, the British share just as continually sinking. The German Reich was among the world's great intellectual powerhouses, perhaps the greatest of them all. Yet all this was not enough for the political right. It was not enough that Germany should remain a mere 'great power'; it had to become the leading power of the world. This was the unequivocal message of the second Morocco crisis.

While the political events were still unfolding, Friedrich von Bernhardi, a former general and Pan-German writer on military affairs, was drawing his conclusions. *Deutschland und der nächste Krieg** was the title of his book, which drew great attention when it appeared at the beginning of 1912, was reprinted several times in rapid succession, and was immediately translated into the most important languages. Appealing to Darwin and his 'social Darwinist' disciples, the author declared the 'struggle for existence' to be the 'basis of all healthy development'. War was a means of selection, preventing inferior or decaying races from choking the growth of the healthy ones. But war was 'not merely a biological necessity, but also a moral requirement and, as such, an indispensable factor of culture'. The result was what Bernhardi termed the 'right to war' and the 'duty to war'.

'A deep rift has opened between the feeling of the nation and the diplomatic action of the government,' proclaimed the book's foreword. The only thing that could close this rift was a thoroughgoing re-education of the German *Volk* with the goal of preparing it for a hard decision—the decision 'whether we, too, wish to develop ourselves into a *World Power*, to assert ourselves as such, and to attain for the German Spirit and German Way of Life the worldwide respect they still lack to this day'. In consequence, movements such as social democracy and pacifism, which rejected this insight, were to be fought. Since it was a matter of 'World Power or downfall', 'existence or non-existence', it was imperative that the 'confusion of the political scene' and 'spiritual fragmentation' finally be overcome. Bernhardi thus resolutely opposed parliamentary government. 'No people is so little suited to the direction of its own fate as the German People, either in a purely

* Bernhardi, *Germany and the Next War.*

parliamentary or even republican government. For none does the commonplace liberal stencil fit so ill as for us.' Germany needed a strong government that would bring to an end the 'policy of peace and renunciation' pursued hitherto, putting in its place a 'propaganda of the deed'. It needed to strengthen the army and the fleet and to train the youth in military service from an early age.

These goals could only be reached in conjunction with a strong popular press dedicated to the task of maintaining the warlike disposition of the people. 'It must constantly draw attention to the importance and the necessity of war as an indispensable tool of politics and culture, as well as to the duty of sacrifice and personal dedication to state and Fatherland.' As their preceptors in these endeavours, Bernhardi held up to the Germans first and foremost Frederick the Great, then Bismarck, and, for their intellectual training for war, primarily Fichte, Arndt, and Treitschke. The book concluded with lines from a poem by Arndt from the year 1844:

Lass hell den Degen klirren
Von Deiner Sternenburg;
Hau von den wüsten Wirren
Den ganzen Jammer durch!*

Seventeen years before Bernhardi, Max Weber, in his 1895 Freiburg inaugural lecture, had lamented the 'hard lot of the political epigone', a fate history had imposed upon his generation. It was precisely this feeling of belonging to a lesser after-generation that the general wanted to overcome with violence. Through war, modern Germany would show itself equal to its forebears. Weber had considered *Weltpolitik* a tool to break the hegemony of the Prussian Junkers. Bernhardi wanted to preserve the spirit of the Prussian soldier-state so that Germany could advance to become a world power.

A resolute struggle against social democracy, such as Bernhardi preached, was a logical imperative for those who accepted the author's aims. Other contemporaries expressed themselves even more clearly on this point, hoping that war would have a salutary effect on the domestic political front. In the Reichstag debate on 9 November 1911, Bebel quoted two such voices. The *Deutsches Armeeblatt* had written during the second Morocco crisis: 'A generous passage at arms would also be a very good thing for the internal situation, even though it would bring tears and pain to individual families.' In the 26 August 1911 edition of the conservative *Post* one could read: 'In wide circles, the conviction is prevalent that a war can only be advantageous, since it would clarify our precarious political position and bring about the convalescence of many political and social conditions.' Bebel commented on these statements with the observation: 'Nobody

* Let bright the sword flash | From your stellar citadel; | Hack the whole miserable hash | asunder in one blow fell!

knows what to do about social democracy anymore. A foreign war would have been such an excellent distraction.'

There was no lack of groups pursuing the same goals as Bernhardi. The Colonial Association, the Eastern Marches Association, the Pan-German League, and the Navy League were joined in 1904 by the Imperial League against Social Democracy (*Reichsverband gegen die Sozialdemokratie*), endorsed by heavy industry and the parties of the right. By 1909 the organization counted over 200,000 members. Its pamphlets against the SPD were countless, but its success was modest. At best, its participation in the 'Hottentot election' of 1907 helped slow the increase in votes obtained by the Social Democrats.

In January 1912, in the wake of the second Morocco crisis, yet another nationalist organization was founded, whose primary aim was the strengthening of the German army: the German Army League (*Deutscher Wehrverein*), led by August Keim, another former general. The organization's top members came from the ranks of the Pan-German and Navy Leagues; it was no less *bürgerlich* in character than that of the other nationalist associations. Its idol was Bismarck. The Army League, which numbered 78,000 members in May 1912, was markedly anti-governmental, since the Bethmann Hollweg administration did not seem militaristic enough to its taste. It courted the masses and endeavoured to be populist. But it was too much of an assembly of notables to become the nucleus of mass movement transcending social class.

The Army League did not represent, any more than the Navy League or the Pan-German League, a new type of 'populist nationalism'. It also did not stand for a new kind of 'militarism from below'. Rather, it was a further expression of the nationalism of the 'right' that had existed from the first decade of the German Reich, spreading among bourgeois and petty-bourgeois Germany in several phases and becoming increasingly radical. The last phase, which began around 1911, was characterized by unprecedented militarism. Politicians, publicists, and propagandists heedlessly preached world war as a way out of foreign and domestic crisis.[24]

NATIONALISM AND ANTI-SEMITISM

At the beginning of 1912 the internal crisis of the German Reich came to a dramatic head. On 12 January the first round of the federal elections took place. The run-off elections followed on 20 and 25 January. The Social Democrats achieved a dramatic victory. Their tally of votes rose from 3.26 million in 1907 (29% of the total vote) to 4.25 million (34.8%). Their increase in parliamentary seats was even more dramatic. The SPD grew from 43 to 110 seats, primarily because of a run-off agreement with the Progressive People's Party. The Social Democrats had been the strongest party ever since 1890; now, for the first time, they represented the strongest fraction in the Reichstag.

A governmental majority without the Social Democrats was now possible only if the conservative parties, the National Liberals, the Progressives, and the Centre all voted together. A constellation of this kind was extraordinarily difficult to bring together. Yet the obstacles to a fixed alliance of parties including the Social Democrats were even greater. A centre-left bloc would have required the participation not only of the 42 delegates of the Progressive People's Party, but also of the 91 members of the Centre fraction. Considering the ideological antagonisms between the three parties, such a 'coalition' was, for the time being, pure fantasy.

The depth of the chasm still dividing the bourgeois parties from the Social Democrats was revealed in the struggle for the Reichstag presidency. On 9 February the Social Democrat Philipp Scheidemann was elected temporary first vice-president, provoking sharp public protest from the right and prompting the demonstrative resignations of the president, Peter Spahn from the Centre Party, and the National Liberal vice-president, Hermann Paasche. When Scheidemann, true to the Social Democratic 'code of conduct', refused to 'go to court' (i.e. participate in an audience of the presidency with the emperor), he lost the confidence of a majority and therewith his office. The final presidency was made up exclusively of members of the liberal fractions.

Shortly after the elections, a book appeared that seemed like the right's answer to the victory of the left. It bore the title *Wenn ich der Kaiser wär'*,* and was written by an author who named himself 'Daniel Frymann'. Behind the pseudonym stood Heinrich Class, after February 1908 the leader of the Pan-German League. The Mainz attorney embodied like no other the radical nationalism of the Wilhelmine era. Already in 1904, the year before the first Morocco crisis, Class was among the League officials calling for a war to conquer West Morocco. During the second Morocco crisis, he further demanded the cession of large parts of eastern France. Together with Alfred Hugenberg, the president of the directory of the Friedrich Krupp company in Essen, who had been the driving force behind the founding of the Pan-German League in 1890–1, Class helped the populist and anti-Semitic elements gain the ascendancy within the group. But the message of his 1912 book went far beyond what might have been called the organization's official opinion. There were good reasons for the pseudonym.

The *Kaiserbuch*,† as it came to be called, which had gone through five printings by 1914, had many points in common with Bernhardi's manifesto, which had appeared shortly before and won the praise of Class. 'Let war be holy to us like purifying fate', implored the Pan-German leader. 'Let it be welcome like the doctor of our souls, who shall heal us with the strongest of medicines.' Germany did not need to fear war either with Britain or with Russia. France was to be crushed, Belgium and the Netherlands annexed to the Reich under preservation of a

* Class, *If I Were the Emperor.*
† Class, *The Emperor Book.*

limited independence. 'The Gordian knot must be cut through; it cannot be undone amicably.'

In his domestic politics, Class was far more radical than Bernhardi. He demanded the abolition of general, equal suffrage and its replacement with a five-class system restricted to taxpayers, the exclusion of women from political life, inflexible resistance to the democratization of Prussia, a tenacious battle against the Poles, a readiness to a *coup d'état* against social democracy, this 'enemy of the Fatherland'—a step that was, to be sure, only to be expected under an 'emperor as leader'. Class directed his strongest attacks against the Jews, who, according to their inmost nature, were to the Germans as water to fire. The Jews were the 'agents and teachers of the materialism that rules the day', controlling theatres, the press, and the outcome of the recent 'Jew elections'. In order to avert the Jewish danger, the author called for a stop to Jewish immigration, the exclusion of the 'resident' (*landansässig*) Jews from public life, abolition of their active and passive suffrage, their placement under alien law, and the doubling of their tax burden. In addition, Jews were to be excluded from service in the army and navy, from leadership positions in the theatre and banks, and from the professions of attorney and teacher. Finally, newspapers with Jewish employees were to be designated as such.

Class sought to prove what he saw as the disproportionate societal influence of the Jews primarily with statistical data on the confessional background of university students. Measured according to their share of the population, five times as many Jews as Evangelicals studied at Prussian universities, and seven times as many as Catholics. Class's conclusion was 'that the life of our people, to the degree that it rests on, is connected with, or depends upon the activities of the learned professions, is falling victim at a rapidly increasing rate to a Jewish participation far beyond that which would normally be their right.' From his findings the author generalized: 'Never in history has a great, gifted, industrious people fallen so quickly and with so little resistance under the influence and intellectual sway of a foreign people so different in nature, as the Germans have with the Jews.' The battle cry Class hurled against the Jews was 'Germany to the Germans!' This challenge was to be turned into action by the 'leader'. The emperor was certainly the most desirable incarnation of the idea of the leader, but he was not necessarily the only conceivable one. 'If the leader were to arise this day, he will be amazed at how many faithful followers he has—and how valuable, selfless men rally round him.'

The *Kaiserbuch* amply demonstrated the demagogic qualities of its author. Nonetheless, it cannot easily be described as 'populist'. Class did not address the German *Volk* so much as the higher classes, especially the 'academically educated', who were to be the 'intellectual leaders of the people' and the 'backbone of political life'. The assertion that an 'aristocracy of merit' should take its place at the side of the 'aristocracy of birth' was quite as 'reactionary' as the wish to replace general direct suffrage with a class system. Class's anti-Semitism, too, was calculated to appeal primarily to the educated. The fact that the number of Jewish students, doctors, lawyers, and journalists was far greater than the proportion of Jews in the population was excellent fodder for an argument intended to stir the envy, inferiority complexes, and socio-economic anxieties of non-Jewish students and academics. Class used this method to gain support for goals that can best be epitomized in the term 'radical bourgeois conservatism'. This was a world-view that had long been on the ideological defensive. The outcome of the federal elections in January 1912 easily disposed it to panic.

German anti-Semitism seemed to have largely declined in political importance by the time Class's book came out. In the federal elections of 1907, only 5.5 per cent of the vote had gone to the fragmented anti-Semitic parties. Five years later, in January 1912, they managed only 2.5 per cent, their worst result since 1893. The public resonance to organized Jew-hatred had indeed decreased. Nonetheless, anti-Semitism was far from extinction. It lived on among the German Conservatives, in special interest associations like the Federation of Agriculturalists and the German League of Commercial Employees, in numerous student organizations, and in the Evangelical and Catholic churches. There were also a number of highly influential books by respected anti-Semitic authors, for example the *Deutsche Schriften** (1878 and 1881) by Paul de Lagarde, *Rembrandt als Erzieher*† by Julius Langbehn (first published 1890, but reworked and expanded a year later to include radically anti-Semitic arguments inspired by the fanatic Jew-hater Theodor Fritsch), and the 1899 two-volume work of Houston Stewart Chamberlain, an Englishman by birth but German by choice, entitled *Die Grundlagen des neunzehnten Jahrhunderts*,‡ which counted Emperor William II among its enthusiastic readership.[25]

Apart from the resolute liberals, the bourgeois culture of Germany had long been saturated with anti-Semitism. Only an external stimulus was required to bring it to the fore anew. The 1912 electoral victory of the left was one such stimulus, and Class's *Kaiserbuch* was only one of the first symptoms of the movement that now began. Shortly after the January elections, an 'Association against Jewish Arrogance' (*Verband gegen die Überhebung des Judentums*) was founded, including among its members not only well-known anti-Semitic publicists, but also the head of the German Gymnastics Association and the Association of German Gymnasts. In May 1912, at the instigation of Theodor Fritsch, the 'Hammer League' (*Reichshammerbund*) was formed, the inmost circle of which was a 'Germanic Order' (*Germanenorden*) organized as a system of lodges and using the swastika as its symbol. The Hammer League considered its most important task to be the coordination of all anti-Semitic activities and the infiltration of its agents into all sorts of different movements and associations.

* Lagarde, *German Writings.*
† Langbehn, *Rembrandt as Educator.*
‡ Chamberlain, *The Foundations of the Nineteenth Century.*

One of the organizations that drew Fritsch's special attention was the club that began the German youth movement, the *Wandervogel,** founded in Berlin-Steglitz in 1901. In 1912, a campaign began to exclude Jews from membership. Only a minority of the *Wandervögel* resisted. The controversy came to a provisional end in a compromise passed by the organization's federal congress in Frankfurt an der Oder during Easter 1914: it was left to the local groups to decide whether Jewish candidates would be accepted.

In 1913 came a new proposal for the 'solution to the Jewish question'. In a memorandum sent to two hundred prominent Germans, including Crown Prince William, Konstantin Baron von Gebsattel, a former Bavarian cavalry general (and at that time not yet a member of the Pan-German League), not only repeated the demands of the *Kaiserbuch*, but even outdid them. Any mixing of 'the Jewish and the German race' was to be punished, and all discriminatory measures were to be coordinated in such a manner as to leave the Jews only one course of action, emigration from Germany. Before they left the country, however, they were to be compelled to transfer the greater part of their property to the state.

It was true that William II and Bethmann Hollweg, to whom the crown prince (himself approached by Class in a letter) approvingly sent the memorandum, contradicted the general's scheme with economic and foreign policy arguments (and rejected his call for a *coup d'état* to abolish equal suffrage on 'practical' grounds, as too little likely to succeed). Off the record, however, both the emperor and the chancellor lamented the prominent role Jews played in the press. William also announced his firm intention 'to exclude Jewish influence from the army with all decisiveness and to limit it in all literary and artistic activities as much as possible'.

Only a minority of the German right went as far as Gebsattel and Class, and the membership in German racialist or '*völkisch*' organizations like the Hammer League remained small (nothing dependable is known of the numbers before 1914; the *Hammer*, the journal published by Fritsch, had an average circulation of 10,000). But the converse was also true. The resolute opponents of anti-Semitism enjoyed no wide support among the middle classes. The Association against Anti-Semitism (*Verein zur Abwehr des Antisemitismus*, founded in 1890), an initiative of liberal politicians, scholars, and publicists like Rudolf von Gneist, Heinrich Rickert, Theodor Barth, and Theodor Mommsen, numbered 18,000 members in 1897. There were probably not many more in 1912.

The organization's most active members were 'cultural Protestants' and left-liberals. In close alliance with the Central Association of German Citizens of Jewish Faith (*Centralverein deutscher Staatsbürger jüdischen Glaubens*, founded in 1893), it attempted to counteract the malignant effects of anti-Semitic horror stories of Jewish ritual murder (or later, after the First World War, forgeries like the *Protocols of the Elders of Zion*) by means of educational campaigns and appeals to reason.

* [Translator's note: the word means 'migratory bird.']

There was, on the other hand, no cooperation between the Association against Anti-Semitism and the Zionist Union for Germany (*Zionistische Vereinigung für Deutschland*), an organization established in 1897–8 by the German followers of Theodor Herzl, the Jewish publicist from Vienna. The Zionist response to anti-Semitism, the call for a Jewish national state in Palestine, was far more popular in eastern Europe than in Germany. Regardless of what the German Jew-haters said or did, the vast majority of German Jews considered Germany to be a country of the Enlightenment, of the rule of law, and of cultural progress—their *Vaterland.*

German Jews (i.e. those who were unbaptized) could find their political home only in parties firmly opposed to anti-Semitism, the liberal, especially left-liberal parties, and increasingly the Social Democrats. The workers' movement owed a great part of its ideological character to Jewish intellectuals, who had joined the Social Democratic Party in great numbers from the beginning. The organized left-liberalism of Wilhelmine Germany, for its part, is utterly inconceivable without the prosperous and educated Jewish bourgeoisie of the great cities like Berlin, Hamburg, Frankfurt am Main, or Breslau. The Jewish share in total tax revenues was many times the proportion of Jews in the population. In Berlin and environs, where the number of Jews in the population (5 per cent) was about five times greater than in the rest of the Reich, their contribution to the 1905 tax revenues amounted to 30 per cent of the total. The liberal press was financially just as dependent on the Jewish middle classes as it was intellectually dependent on the productivity of Jewish journalists. In contrast to the bureaucracy, judicial system, and armed forces, where massive discrimination against Jews continued, journalism was one of the fields in which Jews could freely engage, as they could in freelance academic and artistic professions, commerce, and banking. The great liberal newspapers in Germany—the *Frankfurter Zeitung*, *Berliner Tageblatt*, *Vossische Zeitung*, and so on—all showed the influence of Jewish spirit and wealth. The anti-Semitic activists knew full well why they attacked 'Jewish' liberalism and the 'Golden International' just as forcefully as 'Jewish' Marxism and the 'Red International'.

War against the 'Golden' and the 'Red International' was the rallying cry of a new interest group that presented itself to the public in Dresden in September 1911: the Imperial German Middle Class Association (*Reichsdeutscher Mittelstandsverband*), whose initiator was the indefatigable Theodor Fritsch, leader of the Middle Class Union for the Kingdom of Saxony (*Mittelstandsvereinigung für das Königreich Sachsen*). The new, militantly anti-social-democratic organization was established in order to draw craftsmen and small tradesmen out of the liberal Hanse League, bring them together under its own banner, and lead them into a firm alliance with the conservative forces in German society. To a certain extent, these efforts were successful. The *Mittelstand* organizations that joined the new federal association numbered over half a million members by 1913.

On 19 February 1912, four weeks after the Reichstag elections, the Association informed Chancellor Bethmann Hollweg that it was working 'in cooperation with a leading industrial association in order to create a community of interest among all independent productive estates'. One and a half years later, this task had largely been accomplished. At the third federal congress of the *Mittelstand* in Leipzig in August 1913, a 'Cartel of the Productive Estates' (*Kartell der schaffenden Stände*) was brought into existence (immediately branded 'cartel of the rapacious hands', *Kartell der raffenden Hände*, by its enemies), an alliance between the young federal *Mittelstand* association, the Federation of Agriculturalists, the Central Association of German Industrialists, and the Union of Christian Farmers' Associations (*Vereinigung der Christlichen Bauernvereine*). The Leipzig platform culminated in the call for the 'preservation of authority in all economic concerns', 'the protection of national labour, the guarantee of fair prices, and the protection of those willing to work' as well as the 'battle against Social Democracy and the false doctrines of socialism'.

The Cartel was a new attempt to reach an old goal, the reinforcement of the existing order through conservative *Sammlungspolitik*. Apart from declarations of common intention, however, the unequal partners achieved little. The textile industrialists of the Central Association protested against collusion with the agriculturalists. The heavy industrialists would also have refused to back the anti-Semitic position for which Fritsch campaigned. In the end, the August 1913 'gathering of all state-upholding forces' remained a mere demonstration, underscoring the desire of East Elbian agriculture, Rhenish-Westphalian industry, and the conservative wing of the old craft-industrial *Mittelstand* to fight anything and everything that amounted to a liberalization of society and a democratization of the body politic.[26]

Two months after the proclamation of the Cartel of the Productive Estates, Leipzig became the stage of a much more spectacular event. On 18 October 1913, the centennial of the victory over Napoleon, the monument to the Battle of the Nations was consecrated. Ernst Moritz Arndt had been the first to propose such a monument in 1814. In 1894 prominent members of the 'nationally' minded Leipzig bourgeoisie, led by the architect Clemens Thieme, took up the idea, and their organization, the German Patriots' League for the Erection of a Monument to the Battle of the Nations near Leipzig (*Deutscher Patriotenbund zur Errichtung eines Völkerschlachtsdenkmals bei Leipzig*) collected donations made by numerous groups, including associations of singers, marksmen, veterans, gymnasts, and cyclists, as well as by the emperor himself, the princes, and many cities and communities.

Proclaiming the Battle of the Nations at Leipzig the 'birthday of the German people' and the Battle of Sedan the 'birthday of the German Reich', the text of the 1913 dedication interpreted the 1871 founding of the Reich as the completion of the work undertaken by the German people in 1813. The nation was seen as a close-knit *Volksgemeinschaft* and, as such, was made into a standard the Germans of 1913 felt no less bound to live up to than their forebears a century before. The commemoration of 1813 had one overarching purpose: to convince the Germans that materialism and trivialization, cosmopolitanism and socialism, confessional and class antagonisms had to be overcome, and that they must elevate themselves again to the 'pure heights of German idealism' and to 'pure Germandom'. Seen in this way, the new monument was directed against internal no less than against external enemies. Like the Kyffhäuser monument of 1896, the monument to the Battle of the Nations was a monolithic bourgeois declaration of war on the 'the forces without Fatherland'.

In reference to the giant, sword-supported warrior figures on the peak of the dome and the archangel Michael on the main relief, Thomas Nipperdey has said that they are all 'characterized by a stern and ponderous seriousness, indeed of melancholy'. The pathos of sacrifice and suffering in the dedication literature is also present in the structure.

> The nation called upon to identify with itself in this monument is no longer a cultural and confessional community, but rather a community of war, fate, and sacrifice. It is no longer political in a concrete sense, that is, a monarchically and democratically ordered community. Rather, it is a nation bound together in the mythology of inwardness and solidarity—solidarity of an anti-socialist orientation.

The dedicatory speech, given by Thieme in the name of the Patriots' League in the presence of the German emperor, the king of Saxony, many German princes, the chancellor, ambassadors from the Russian, Swedish, and Austrian courts, military delegations, student corporations, and tens of thousands of onlookers, was in keeping with the dedication text. Thieme described the monument as a symbol of the 'spirit of sacrifice, courage, strength of faith, and the power of the German people'; it was the 'celebratory deed of the German people', commissioned to

> serve German meaning and spirit throughout centuries. What does all external glorification signify, if the commemoration of the deeds of the fathers fails to awaken new enthusiasm in the souls of the grandsons? The words of Ernst Moritz Arndt must remain true for all time: the monument to the Battle of Nations must be the Irminsul [the holy monument of the heathen Saxons, (H.A.W.)] of the German people, the place to which it directs its steps and its thoughts every 18 October, so that all may recall to mind that they are brothers of one tribe and one love and that, next to God, they must always respect and love German love and faithfulness.

The consecration of the Leipzig monument was the climax of the centenary celebrations of the wars of liberation. However, the year 1913 also saw the twenty-fifth anniversary of William II's accession to the throne. In countless speeches at countless celebrations, the ruler of the German Reich was hailed as the 'emperor of peace'. The will to peace and the readiness for war—both elements had their place in the invocations of German history old and recent. But the warlike tones were louder. Walther Rathenau, Jewish intellectual and member of the board of directors of the General Electricity Society, composed a cycle of poems entitled *1813. Ein Festgang zur Jahrhundertfeier.** One of them ran thus:

Frischauf! Wenn die zweite
Der Sonnen erwacht,
Sie leuchtet dem Streite,
Der Herrlichen Schlacht.

Und kauert in Gräben,
Und lauert der Tod,
Sprüht Freiheit und Leben
Aus funkelndem Rot.†

Hardly an hour of celebration passed in Germany of 1913 without the singing or quoting of songs from the era of the wars of liberation, especially those by Ernst Moritz Arndt and Theodor Körner, or Max Schneckenburger's 'Wacht am Rhein' from the year 1840. On 9 February 1913 the historian Dietrich Schäfer, student of Treitschke, avowed anti-Semite, leading member of the Pan-German League and founding member of the Navy and Army Leagues, gave a speech 'in remembrance of the uprising of the German Nation in 1813' at the University of Berlin. Turning to the emperor, who was in attendance, the speaker affirmed: 'If God should desire that Your Majesty should go into battle at the head of the German army in order to defend Germany's rights and Germany's honour, then the academic youth of today, too, would pray with Körner: "Bless me to life, to death! Father, I praise Thee!" '

There were voices in opposition to all this. In spring 1913 Social Democrats and progressive liberals drew attention to the obvious connections between the patriotic celebrations and the current policies of the government, namely its new military bill. At the first congress of the Free German Youth on the Hoher Meissner near Kassel in October 1913, the school reformer Gustav Wyneken warned against the 'mechanization of enthusiasm, which is now everywhere on the increase. Has it gone so far that they only need to shout certain words at you like "Germandom" and "national" in order to win your applause?'

Nonetheless, the prevalent opinion was certainly more like the one Ernst Müller-Meiningen, delegate from the Progressive People's Party, lamented before the Reichstag on 8 April 1913:

I spoke already last year of the 'national-psychological autosuggestive state' into which the peoples of Europe have allowed themselves to be cajoled. The development of this state has not yet been concluded. Its most dangerous phrase is now gradually beginning to get a

* Rathenau, *1813: A Contribution to the Centenary Celebrations.*

† Let's away! When the second | of the two suns awakes, | it will shine on the battle, | the fight of the glorious. || And if death crouches | and waits in trenches, | will flash freedom and life | out of fiery red.

serious hold on our middle class, perhaps the most worrying development of all: 'Better an end with horror than a horror without end!'[27]

BALKAN WARS AND THE ZABERN AFFAIR

The army bill that had caused such consternation among the left-liberal politicians in April 1913 was passed by the Reichstag with a large majority in June. The Progressive People's Party, too, agreed to the stepwise increase of the army by 136,000 men. Even the Social Democrats, though rejecting the bill in its final form, helped pass earlier legislation that made the army increase financially possible; the capital gains tax, passionately opposed by the Conservatives, was, according to the Social Democrats, a first step towards the federal income, wealth, and inheritance tax they had long desired.

About this same time, France introduced the three-year term of military service in response to the enlargement of the German army. The latter was, in its turn, a reaction to the peacetime strength of the Russian army as well as to the offensive strategy the French general staff had worked out with Russia after the German '*Panther*'s leap to Agadir'. The international arms race of 1912–13 took place against the background of two Balkan wars that once again brought Europe to the brink of a great war. The first began in summer 1912, when the Albanians revolted against Turkish rule and received the support of Bulgaria, Serbia, and Greece, which shortly before had formed a 'Balkan League' under Russian auspices. Within a few months, the allies had almost completely conquered Turkey's European territories. Russian and Austrio-Hungarian intervention was again held back—by Berlin's warnings to Vienna and London's warnings to St Petersburg.

The following year, the victors of the first Balkan war came into conflict over the partition of Macedonia. Bulgaria was on the one side, Serbia and Greece on the other, joined by Romania, which sought to take southern Dobrudja away from Bulgaria. Once again, Austria-Hungary threatened to intervene. Once again Germany, this time in cooperation with Rome, was able to convince its ally to back down. The Treaty of Bucharest of August 1913 led to the partition of Macedonia between Serbia and Greece; Albania gained its independence, though without the predominantly Albanian province of Kosovo, which fell to Serbia; Romania acquired southern Dobrudja. Austria-Hungary was the first great power to order the enlargement of its armed forces, which began while the crisis was still in progress. This was the start of the spiral that reached its—temporary—conclusion with the German army bill of 1912 and the French '*loi de trois ans*'.

Not until more than half a century later did the world learn how close Europe came to a great war in the Balkan crisis. The enlightenment came through the work of German historians evaluating documents detailing a conversation in

Berlin on 8 December 1912. Alarmed by the announcement of the British foreign secretary, Sir Edward Grey, that his country would not remain neutral if the Balkan crisis led to a German attack on France, William II had invited Moltke, chief of the general staff, Tirpitz, secretary of the imperial navy, Heeringen, chief of the admiralty, and Müller, chief of the navy cabinet, to a meeting. He did not invite the chancellor, the Prussian minister of war, or the secretary of the foreign office. The emperor was not the only one to urge an immediate war with France and Russia that day; Moltke agreed with him, saying: 'I consider war inevitable, and the sooner the better.' To Tirpitz's objection that the navy was not strong enough for a war with Britain and that the great battle should be postponed a year, Moltke responded that the navy would not be ready even at that point and that the army would be at a greater disadvantage, 'for our enemies are arming more than we, who are so restricted with respect to finances.'

The deliberations of 8 December had no immediate effects. Nor did William II's evaluation of the situation, such as he propounded a week later to his friend Albert Ballin, director of the joint-stock company Hamburg-American Paketfahrt ('Hapag') and most prominent of the 'emperor's Jews' (*Kaiserjuden*): if Germany were forced to resort to arms, then it would not be merely a matter of coming to the aid of Austria and fighting off Russia, 'but of fending off Slavdom in its entirety and remaining *German*. Id est, we were on the brink of a *racial war* of the Germanic peoples against the upstart Slavs. A *racial war* that we will not be spared, for the future of the Habsburg monarchy and the *existence* of our Fatherland are at stake.'

This was not Bethmann Hollweg's approach. For the present, the chancellor remained committed to avoiding a great war and to working out an understanding with Britain, and his policy proved decisive, at least temporarily. It was not at all certain that the chancellor and the foreign office would prevail against the emperor and the military in coming crises. There *was* a war party, both among the public and at the head of the Reich. Not only the pan-German, conservative, and national-liberal press, but also Catholic newspapers spoke, like the emperor, of an unavoidable war between the Germanic peoples and the Slavs. On 8 March 1913 *Germania*, the leading Centre paper, went so far as to reduce the whole of the 'oriental question' to a decision between 'the Teutonic world or the Slavic world' and to endorse the patriots of the 'Austrian war party' who had been ready in November 1912 'to strike against Serbia and Russia'. The German war party was a factor the civil leadership of the Reich could not ignore.[28]

The issue of 'race' also played a role in the domestic policies of Bethmann Hollweg's administration. On 25 June 1913 the Reichstag, by a large majority, passed a law on state and imperial citizenship against the votes of the Social Democrats and the Poles. According to the old law, which dated from the era of the North German Confederation (1 June 1870), imperial citizenship was attained through citizenship in one of the federal states. The new law added a 'direct imperial citizenship', the purpose of which was to bind expatriate Germans to the Reich. The precondition for citizenship in a German state remained, as a rule, descent from at least one German parent. At birth, the legitimate child of a German male assumed citizenship through the father; an illegitimate child acquired the citizenship of the mother. Under certain conditions, foreigners living in Germany could be naturalized, but there was no right to that status. When the Social Democrats (and, less emphatically, the progressive liberals) demanded one, the secretary of the federal ministry of the interior, Clemens von Delbrück, rejected the idea as an attempt 'to make it easier for alien elements to acquire citizenship'.

This comment was probably more anti-Polish than anti-Semitic in intent. But it was seriously meant. Delbrück explicitly endorsed the *jus sanguinis*, the law of descent through blood, and rejected the *jus soli*, which made place of birth decisive for citizenship. He thus defended an old German tradition, the nation defined as an objective community of fate, not a subjective community of will of the western type. During the deliberations, the Conservatives were the most eloquent advocates of this view of the nation. But the broad majority that voted the bill through made it clear that the traditional idea of 'Germanness' was still the predominant one.

After 1871 the Alsace-Lorrainers had never been asked if they *wanted* to be German. They were simply *considered* German, just as the law on state and imperial citizenship *considered* the imperial territory of Alsace-Lorraine a German state. Their initial rejection of the Reich had, over the years, given way to acceptance (as the federal elections demonstrate), and the constitution of 1911 seemed calculated to promote the organic integration of the province into the empire. On 6 November 1913 this development was suddenly interrupted. The *Zaberner Anzeiger* reported on hostile and coarsely derogatory statements a Prussian, Lieutenant von Forstner, had made to a group of recruits about the Alsace-Lorrainers (whom he referred to by the insulting name of *Wackes*).

The matter would probably have been quickly resolved if the commander, General von Deimling, had fulfilled the demand of Count Wedel, the governor, and not only punished Forstner with six days of house arrest, but sent him to another regiment. Since he failed to do so, the problem not only did not go away, it was exacerbated. Protests, clashes between soldiers and civilians, and military arrests increased in Zabern (Saverne).

The Reichstag turned its attention to the problem at the end of November and beginning of December. The Prussian minister of war, Falkenhayn, told the delegates that neither he himself nor the parliament had any authority in matters of disciplinary punishment, that this was the province of the military command, that is, of the monarch. Chancellor Bethmann Hollweg was so cautious in distancing himself from the behaviour of the military administration that the delegates took it as a provocation. When, on 4 December, he explicitly highlighted his agreement with the minister of war, it was the straw that broke the camel's back. An overwhelming majority of 193 to 34 votes with 3 abstentions agreed to a motion—lodged the day before by the Progressive People's Party—that the Reichstag officially declare itself in disagreement with chancellor's treatment of the Zabern affair. Only the two Conservative fractions voted against the first motion of disapproval in the history of the German Reichstag.

Political consequences there were none. The chancellor was not dependent upon the confidence of the delegates, a fact he stated openly after the vote. Behind the scenes, a few steps were taken toward restricting the high-handed behaviour of the military (including an expression of disapproval from the emperor, a punitive transfer of the two battalions stationed in Zabern, and a never-published decree from 19 March 1914 concerning the military's use of armed force). However, the military courts in Strasbourg decided, as a rule, in favour of the inculpated officers and against the soldiers who had informed the press. Lieutenant von Forstner, who, on 2 December, had struck a shoemaker's journeyman with the flat of his sabre when the latter was arrested for a public insult, was exonerated on 10 January 1914 after appeal to the military high tribunal, which recognized a situation of 'punitive self-defence'.

The real scandal of the 'Zabern affair' lay not in the events themselves, their public resonance, and their juridical consequences, but in the constitutional situation, upon which the crisis had shed a glaring light. The federal parliament, chancellor, and minister of war were all powerless in questions of royal military command. When necessary, the Prussian soldier-state could show the constitutional state its limits. In civil life, absolutism had been overcome. It lived on in the military.[29]

THE ROAD TO WAR

The shots that rang out in Bosnian Sarajevo on 28 June 1914 changed the world. The murder of Francis Ferdinand, heir to the Austrian throne, and his wife was the work of the 'Black Hand', a Serbian secret society. The key figure in this organization was Dragutin Dimitrijevic, a colonel in the Serbian general staff who stood in sharp opposition to the prime minister, Nikola Pasic. On the basis of its information, Vienna assumed that the Belgrade government was at least partly involved in the assassination. Austria-Hungary had to react, and Germany could not help but demonstrate solidarity with its ally.

German policy in the July crisis of 1914 was determined by the maxim 'now or never'. Instead of insisting that Vienna respond in moderation, Berlin allowed its partner a free hand, which was tantamount to supporting the Austrian war party. In the view of the German participants, the occasion seemed uniquely favourable for a radical solution to the Serbian question, and it could be expected that the 'national' public in Germany would support the call for 'satisfaction' in a manner in keeping with the duel mentality of the era. For like-minded Germans, an Austro-Hungarian war against Serbia was a just war. That it could hardly remain a local conflict, that it would almost certainly bring in Russia and France, and possibly Britain, on the one side, and Germany on the other, was a probability the moderate forces in the country, led by the chancellor, accepted. For the radicals within the military, political, and publicist war party, the prospect of a great war was the very reason to urge Vienna towards harsh treatment of Belgrade.

The proponents of a military solution were also swayed by other considerations, both foreign and domestic. For Moltke and the leading figures of the military, the arms race was the decisive factor: in a few years the adversaries would be even stronger, so the time to strike was now. The civilian war party, dominated by the Pan-German League, regarded war as an opportunity to resolve the internal situation: if the Social Democrats were to become any stronger, Germany would not be capable of waging any war at all; if Germany won the war, it would then be strong enough to bring the Social Democrats and pacifists to reason.

This was not the opinion of Bethmann Hollweg. He believed that if the Social Democrats supported the war, they would demand a high price in terms of domestic reforms. The cooperation of the SPD could only be secured if Russia could be made to appear as the real aggressor and warmonger. The more Russia sided with Serbia, the more plausible this scheme became.

In all other respects the chancellor was pessimistic. On 14 July he spoke to his adviser Kurt Riezler of a 'leap in the dark' that was nonetheless 'the most earnest of duties'. Since Italy, Germany's other partner in the Triple Alliance, could hardly be counted on any longer, everything would have to be done to keep at least Austria-Hungary, this multinational empire in a perpetual state of crisis, in firm partnership. By this time the chancellor, too, had come round to the military's view that within two or three years Germany would no longer be in a position to defend itself against an attack from France and Russia. For him, it would be a 'pre-emptive war', as he would tell Conrad Haussmann, delegate of the Progressive People's Party, in the summer of 1917.

Bethmann Hollweg was fully aware that Britain would not long remain neutral in a war that pitted Germany against France and Russia. After all, the 1905 'Schlieffen Plan' was still in effect, which called for an invasion through neutral Belgium in the case of a two-front war—a provocation that would amount to a declaration of war on Britain. But the military had made its decision, and a chancellor who had dared to confront the Prussian soldier-state after Sarajevo would probably soon have found himself out of office.

On 25 July Serbia responded with such accommodation to the remarkably far-reaching catalogue of demands Austria-Hungary had submitted to Belgrade on 23 July that even William II, who had supported a firm anti-Serbian line, decided on 28 July, upon his return from a 'trip to the north land', that there was no longer any reason for war. But it took a long time for Bethmann Hollweg to become active on behalf of the emperor's wishes, and he represented them less forcefully than they were intended. Consequently, William's change of opinion no longer had any effect in Vienna. At eleven o'clock in the morning of 28 July,

Austria-Hungary declared war on Serbia. Russia reacted the following day with a partial mobilization against Austria in several military districts. On 30 July Tzar Nicholas II, urged by his generals, ordered general mobilization.

When, on 30 July, the German chancellor (aware that Britain would join France and Russia in the event of war, but still ignorant of the general mobilization in Russia) pressured Vienna to accept an offer of mediation from Grey, the British foreign secretary, he was probably not motivated by a desire to rescue peace in Europe at the last minute; rather, he sought to make Russia appear as the aggressor. The next day Moltke encouraged his Austrian colleague, Conrad von Hötzendorf, to begin general mobilization immediately. This prompted the Austrian foreign minister, Count Berchtold, to ask sardonically: 'Who is in charge, Moltke or Bethmann?' The Habsburg monarchy followed the recommendation of the chief of the Prussian general staff. At noon on 31 July it declared general mobilization.

One hour later, Germany proclaimed a 'state of acute danger of war'. Since Russia failed to reply to a German ultimatum of that same day, Germany declared general mobilization and war against Russia on 1 July. Two days later, after Paris, responding to a German 'enquiry' of 31 August, said that it would act in keeping with its interests, Germany declared war on France. On 4 August Britain, which had mobilized its fleet three days before, demanded that Germany promise to respect Belgian neutrality by midnight. By this time, however, German troops had already crossed the border into Belgium, with the consequence that Britain declared war on the same day. Negatives came from two potential allies: Italy stated that Austria-Hungary was the aggressor, and that the situation did not therefore represent an attack against the Triple Alliance. Romania's position was similar. Only Turkey joined the central powers, and Bulgaria a year later. Thus began the First World War, which in 1979, after an interval of sixty-five years, the American historian and diplomat George F. Kennan would call '*the* great seminal catastrophe of this century'.

Although it is not correct to say that Germany was alone responsible for the war, Germany's was nonetheless the principal fault. Without German backing, Austria-Hungary could not have declared war on Serbia. The war parties in Berlin and Vienna added fuel to each other's fires, and both bolstered the war party in St Petersburg. The pan-Slavic movement demanded unflinching solidarity with Serbia, putting the Russian government under a pressure similar to that exerted by the rightist parties and associations of nationalist agitation on the leadership of the German Reich. But it was not initially successful: Russia did not encourage Serbia to remain inflexible to Vienna's demands of 23 July, but rather to fulfil them as much as possible.

In France, the ruling right did not want to endanger the alliance with the tzarist empire by urging St Petersburg to counsel moderation to Serbia. In addition Paris, much like Berlin, feared a further strengthening of the domestic left and, as a result, a majority against the three-year term of service. Whether the war would have been prevented if Britain had contradicted German speculations on its neutrality at an early date and with sufficient emphasis, is questionable. Such a policy might have had the opposite effect, making Russia and France even more willing to go to war.

And yet whatever the other participants could have done differently, one thing is certain: no great power worked for the escalation of the conflict more persistently than Germany. The fear that the military capabilities of the Reich would decline in the coming years does not alone justify the term 'pre-emptive war'. In summer 1914 no great power had any concrete plan to wage a war of aggression against Germany. The decisive actors in Germany, the leaders of the army and navy, were not concerned about preserving the status quo. They were after the hegemony of Europe. And their aspirations were shared by a strong current within the German bourgeoisie.

And yet, broad public support for the war—including the support of the Social Democrats—was only to be had if the government's aggressive intentions could be disguised as national defence. The Russian general mobilization permitted the Reich leadership to create this impression. On 1 August 1914 the head of the navy cabinet, Admiral von Müller, noted in his journal:

> The morning papers print the Emperor's and Chancellor's addresses to the enthusiastic people, gathered before the Emperor's residence and the Chancellor's palace. Atmosphere glorious. The government has had a lucky hand in making us out to seem like the ones who have been attacked.[30]

By this time the Reich leadership no longer needed to fear Social Democratic opposition to the war. In the years before, the largest political party in Germany had continually called for demonstrations and protests against the warmongering on the nationalist right—with especially strong resonance during the Balkan crisis in November 1912, when the Social Democrats, together with other parties of the Second International, gave expression to the common will for peace among the European proletariat at the cathedral in Basel. However, there were no clear indications of what the working class was actually to do in case of war. At the Stuttgart congress of the International in summer 1907, August Bebel (who died on 13 August 1913 at the age of 73) had impeded the passage of a motion explicitly designating 'mass strike' and 'uprising' as a means of averting and preventing war. His argument that 'mass strike amusements' made no sense after the outbreak of a war, since by then the masses would already have been called up, reflected the view of the majority of German Social Democrats.

At the end of July 1914, the SPD sponsored anti-war demonstrations in most of the large urban centres in Germany. The largest took place at Treptow Park in Berlin on 28 July. At the same time, however, the Reich leadership, attempting to secure the loyalty of the workers, was conducting negotiations with the leaders of the SPD, employing Albert Südekum, a 'revisionist', as intermediary. On 29 July Südekum was able to inform the chancellor that actions on the part of the SPD were neither planned nor to be feared in the event of war. Two days later a state of emergency was declared throughout the Reich. Not only the demonstrations against the war stopped suddenly, but all public criticism of the federal government—which, a few days before, the Social Democratic press (above all the *Vorwärts* and the *Leipziger Volkszeitung*) was accusing of being deeply complicit in the dramatic deterioration of the international situation.

The fear of government suppression and persecution of the party played a key role in the decision of the SPD leadership to ask the Social Democratic newspapers to 'exercise all due caution'. And in truth, had it called for resistance to the war, the party would have been subject to the harshest measures of the state, and it could not have been certain that the masses of its supporters would have obeyed such an appeal. The SPD and the labour unions had grown into mass organizations, upon whose preservation numberless lives depended. Even an August Bebel could not have afforded to jeopardize their existence.

On the other hand, the party leadership did not have to deal with any nationalist pressure from 'below' on the eve of the First World War. There was little 'hurrah patriotism' among the social democratic workers—but also little enthusiasm for the cause of the international proletariat. Neither the leaders nor the masses of the members were in any doubt about the fact that the looming war was going to be a war against *Russia*. To encourage the victory of the tzarist regime, considered, as in the time of Marx and Engels, the supreme reactionary power of Europe, was the last thing the SPD could wish. *This* fact, not a belief in the innocence of the Reich leadership, was decisive for the behaviour of the Social Democrats at the end of July and the beginning of August 1914.

The Russian general mobilization on 30 July made it easier for the party leadership to find support for its position and to move beyond its initial decision to abstain from the vote on war credits. On 3 August the Reichstag fraction of the SPD voted 78 to 14 for the approval of the government bill. On 4 August the head of the party, the Königsberg lawyer Hugo Haase, himself one of the defeated minority, read the fraction's statement before the plenum assembly of the Reichstag. It was a compromise between 'realists' and 'internationalists', attempting to do justice to both sides. Still, it was an honest statement, faithfully representing the motivations and the expectations of the party fraction.

Haase first attacked the imperialist policy of the arms race, which the SPD had 'fought with all its powers, but ultimately in vain'. He then spoke of the 'iron fact of war' confronting all, and of the 'looming horrors of enemy invasion'. He emphasized that the 'victory of Russian despotism' would place the German people and their future freedom in great danger, if not bring about their utter destruction; 'in harmony with the International', he invoked the right of every people to national independence and self-defence. He condemned all wars of conquest, demanding 'that, once the goal of security has been achieved and the adversary is prepared for peace, an end be made of war through a peace that permits of friendship with the neighbouring peoples.' The two most significant sentences of the speech were the following: 'We shall put into practice what we have always preached: in the hour of danger, we will not leave our own Fatherland in the lurch . . . Guided by these principles, we herewith approve the desired war credits.'

The minutes record 'spirited cheers' after the first sentence, 'spirited applause by the Social Democrats' after the second. When the Social Democrats stood up from their seats after the final vote on the war credits, there was 'repeated stormy applause and clapping in the house and in the stands'. At the salutation of the 'Emperor, People, and Fatherland', the Social Democrats, too, stood up. But only few of them joined in vocally. In doing so, they ignored the party resolution that Haase, incensed over the applause with which several of his party colleagues on the 'right' greeted the chancellor's speech, had brought about during a pause in the parliamentary session. Bethmann Hollweg had also made a demonstrative gesture towards the Social Democrats. Singling out the largest fraction, he proclaimed that the whole German people, 'united to the last man', stood behind the army and navy—a statement that set off 'joyous applause lasting several minutes'.

In November 1914, three months after the Social Democratic fraction had voted unanimously for the war credits, thus enabling their unanimous passage through the Reichstag, Lenin, living in exile in Switzerland, identified the 'transformation of the present imperialist war into a civil war' as 'the only authentic proletarian slogan'. In *this* sense, the SPD was no longer a 'proletarian' party, if indeed it had ever been one. It could not desire a civil war, which threatened to destroy everything it stood for. To prevent armed conflict was beyond its power, but it shared in the German war effort without making its support conditional upon far-reaching domestic reforms. And of course, there was absolutely no guarantee that the leadership of the Reich and the military would keep the promise made by the emperor in his speech on 4 August, a promise the Social Democrats referred to in order to justify their support for the war: 'We are not driven by a desire for conquest!'

When the war began, the social democratic movement had become far more integrated into German society than it and its adversaries had hitherto been willing to admit. In voting for the war credits and the 'truce' (*Burgfriede*), a kind of domestic-political ceasefire, the movement relinquished its commitment to class struggle, at least for the time being. This could have consequences for its relationship to the bourgeois centre, though such implications were not foreseeable on 4 August 1914. The consequences for the relationship between the SPD and the other socialist parties of western Europe, on the other hand, were already in evidence. The German Social Democrats had to accept the charge that they had opportunistically betrayed the international solidarity of the working class they themselves had invoked. In truth, the last phase of the July crisis witnessed the most radical transformation of the SPD in the party's history. Whether it would have survived the year 1914 politically intact without the new 'social patriotism' (so-called by leftist critics) is an open question.[31]

POLITICS AND SOCIETY UP TO NOVEMBER 1917

Before the Reichstag session on 4 August 1914, a church service was held in the Berlin cathedral in which, in addition to members of the imperial family and high officers, numerous Evangelical members of parliament from the bourgeois parties took part. Ernst von Dryander, the court chaplain, based his sermon on a passage from Paul's Letter to the Romans: 'If God is for us, who can be against us?' That God was indeed 'for Germany' was something the chaplain knew without a doubt: it was manifest in the events leading up to the war, such as he interpreted them.

> Like a sudden thunderstorm over the sunny countryside, the dark, ominous cloud of war has gathered over us and the lightning is already beginning to strike. With a wanton perverseness that beggars description war has been forced upon us, a war for whose justification the rational mind searches in vain. The Emperor, with untiring solicitude, has sought to spare the world nameless misery. It was in vain! The die has been cast. The mobilization has been proclaimed.

Dryander set the tone for war sermons throughout all of Evangelical Germany. As in 1813 and 1870–1, the war was seen as an atonement and a divine revelation at the same time, the sacrifice of the soldiers compared with Christian martyrdom or, indeed, with the crucifixion of the Saviour himself. Commemorations of the wars of liberation were omnipresent. The 1813 call 'With God for King and Fatherland' found its echo in the 1914 call 'With God for Emperor and Empire'. In 1914 the Holstein pastor Walter Lehmann published fourteen sermons under the title *Vom deutschen Gott*,* which he borrowed from Ernst Moritz Arndt. At the beginning of October 1918, shortly before the end of the war, Otto Dibelius, pastor in Berlin from 1915, was still proclaiming that whoever fought for his *Volkstum* and sacrificed everything for his *Volkstum* 'is fulfilling God's command . . . Whoever wants to be a Christian must place his *Volkstum* above all else in the world.' Even the liberal theologian Martin Rade, publisher of the *Christliche Welt*, warned in 1915 that the desire for peace becomes an 'injustice, when it seeks to wrest from God what the time is not yet ripe for'.

The Catholic bishops, theology professors, and priests felt and sermonized not one iota less nationalistically than their Evangelical colleagues. 'God can only protect the cause of justice,' wrote one of the military clergy, *Militäroberpfarrer* Balthasar Poertner, to his hometown in September 1914, 'and Germany's cause in this war, forced upon us with such wanton perversity, is the cause of justice, therefore of God'. In 1915 the Paderborn Old Testament scholar Norbert Peters called the war a 'holy war' and a battle 'for God against Satan', 'for the old commandments of Sinai against the hellish moral doctrine of modernity from beyond good and evil'. The bishop of Speyer, Michael von Faulhaber, declared that Jesus's

* Lehmann, *The German God.*

teaching 'Give to Caesar what is Caesar's' was to be considered the 'eternal precept of the civil conscience, even for the sacrificial journey to the fields of death . . . for the necessary holy war of the nations'.[32]

Sermons in the nations of the Entente were certainly no less patriotic than in the German Reich, and what was true of the pulpit was true of the lectern. However, the shrill tone of one particular early manifesto of German war nationalism provoked worldwide outrage. The October 1914 'Aufruf an die Kulturwelt',* signed by well-known artists and many of the most famous scholars, justified the attack on neutral Belgium without reservation, denied German crimes against the civil population of the country, and culminated in the statement: 'Without German militarism, German culture would long ago have been wiped from the face of the earth.'

German professors confronted the French-promoted 'ideas of 1789' with the 'ideas of 1914'. This term was coined in 1915 by the Münster economist Johann Plenge. Its most important popularizer was Rudolf Kjellén, a Swedish constitutional scholar whose advocacy of the German cause made him very popular in Germany. The 'ideas of 1914' represented a rejection of liberalism and individualism, democracy and universal human rights—in short, the values of the Western world. German values were duty, order, and justice, which could only be guaranteed by a strong state. 'Since 1789, there has been no revolution on earth like the German Revolution of 1914,' wrote Plenge.

> The twentieth-century revolution of the building up and unification of all state powers vs. the destructive liberation of the nineteenth century. For this reason, all the outcry over the new Napoleon contains a resonance of truth. For the second time, an Emperor is moving through the world as the leader of a people with the mighty, world-defining feeling of power of the highest unity. And we might claim that the 'ideas of 1914', the ideas of German organization, are destined for a triumphal march through the world, one as unremitting as that of the 'ideas of 1789'.

One of the 'ideas of 1914' was the concept of the *Volksgemeinschaft*, the 'community of the people', which had surmounted class divisions and with them Marxist internationalism. After the Social Democratic Party approved the war credits and made the 'truce' possible, the social democracy movement was treated in many bourgeois circles as the biblical prodigal son who had returned home. In a text published in 1916, Plenge wrote that the year 1914 had witnessed a radical transformation of socialism.

> For the first time in history, the vague philosophical goal of a movement pointing ahead to nowhere has given rise to the life-condition of a nation . . . Our war economy is, to be sure, to a great extent merely a temporary life-condition of our people . . . It is, nonetheless, the first authentic 'socialist' society and its spirit is the first authentically active emergence of a socialist spirit, as opposed to one made up exclusively of ill-defined demands. The pressure of war has driven the socialist idea into German economic life. Its organization grew together in a new spirit, and in this way the self-assertion of our nation gave birth to the

* 'Appeal to the Cultured World'.

new idea of 1914 for humanity, the idea of German organization, the people's cooperative of national socialism.

Such language found little resonance within the social democratic movement itself. Nonetheless, a few party intellectuals standing on the extreme left wing before the war (indeed, even as late as August 1914) actually did go over to the extreme right in the early autumn of 1914. Paul Lensch, Heinrich Cunow, and Konrad Haenisch, in intimate cooperation with Plenge, made the step from 'social patriotism' to 'social imperialism'. They portrayed Germany as a proletarian nation, Britain as a capitalist nation (a conceptual doublet first given currency around 1910 by Enrico Corradini and his *Associazione Nazionalista Italiana*). The war against Britain thus became a war for socialism, and internal class struggle was brought to an end—being transferred, in a sense, from the nation itself to the war between the nations, transforming the world war into the world revolution.

In the course of the war, Britain was drawn increasingly into the centre of Germany's ideological warfare. There were two primary reasons for this. In the first place, the world power of Great Britain was not, like France, Germany's 'hereditary enemy', but rather its model, as admired as it was envied. This led to a kind of love–hate relationship and made a dramatization of the German–English antagonism, which found popular expression in the salutation 'God punish England!', seem necessary. Secondly, Russia was 'used up' as Germany's most deadly enemy only one year after the beginning of the war, after the Eighth Army, under the nominal command of the reactivated General Paul von Hindenburg, confronted the numerically greatly superior Russian forces that had invaded East Prussia at the end of August 1914, defeating them first at Tannenberg, then, about two weeks later, on the Masurian Lakes. After the German military, in summer 1915, succeeded in conquering Lithuania, Courland, and Poland, the nation directed its undivided attention to the western theatre. There, after the indecisive outcome of the battle of the Marne in September 1914, the front stabilized and the war turned into a 'war of position' (*Stellungskrieg*).

The Catholic philosopher Max Scheler was one of the first to maintain that the war was 'first and last a German–English war'. His explanation, detailed in the book *Der Genius des Krieges und der deutsche Krieg*,* made it clear that the author was especially interested in convincing social democrats of the unavoidability of Britain's defeat. Every war against Britain, as the 'motherland of capitalism', Scheler wrote, was also a 'war against capitalism and its outgrowths as a whole'. The book appeared in 1915. This was the year Germany commemorated the centenary of the birth of Otto von Bismarck and the 500th anniversary of the Hohenzollern accession to power in Brandenburg.

That same year, the economist Werner Sombart characterized the war between Britain and Germany as a war between 'businessmen and heroes' (*Händler und*

* Max Scheler, *The Genius of War and the German War.*

Helden; this was the title of his *patriotische Besinnungen**). He contrasted British 'commercialism', which he described as execrable, with the positive example of German 'militarism'. 'Militarism is the heroic spirit elevated to the spirit of the warrior. It is the highest unity of Potsdam and Weimar. It is *Faust* and *Zarathustra* and Beethoven-score in the trenches. For the *Eroica* and the *Egmont*-overture, too, are purest militarism.'

For both scholars, however, justifying the war as such was more important than the emphasis on the German–British antagonism. Scheler quoted the statement, attributed to Treitschke, that war is an '*examen rigorosum* of states'. He himself called war the 'large-scale psychotherapeutics of peoples' and claimed that the 'genius of war' would become 'a religion of its own—a guide toward God'. Sombart believed that war could provide salvation from 'cultural pessimism', from 'the life of the vulgar, the life of an ant'. To raise 'German heroes', 'heroic men and heroic women', was to be the highest priority of all education, an education designed to

> harden the body and to develop all its powers in harmony, in order that we might see grow up a generation of courageous, broad-chested, bright-eyed young people. For the Fatherland needs them. Broad-hipped women to breed strong children, strong-boned, wiry, courageous men with endurance who will make good warriors.

Such warriors were necessary so that the Germans could prove themselves to be what Sombart knew they were: 'the chosen people of these centuries', the 'representative of divine thought on earth', 'the people of God'.

Less martial, but no less patriotic, was the 'intellectual service under arms' that Thomas Mann felt to be his duty. In the autumn of 1914, Mann compared the war to the battle Frederick the Great had to wage against a powerful alliance of enemies from 1756 to 1763. From 1916 to the end of 1917, the author of *Buddenbrooks* worked on his *Betrachtungen eines Unpolitischen*.† He was finishing this book when, in December 1917, the peace negotiations began between the German Reich and Bolshevik Russia in Brest-Litovsk. Thomas Mann was relieved that war now no longer had to be waged against the land of Dostoevsky, to whom he felt a kind of mystical connection, but only 'against the West alone, against the *trois pays libres* ['the three free countries' (H.A.W.)], against "civilization", "literature", politics, the rhetorical bourgeois'.

Against the West and its democracy, no matter whether in French, English, or American form, Mann sought to defend what he considered the profound essence of Germany: music, poetry, and philosophy. German *Kultur*, which he opposed to Western civilization, required the authoritarian state criticized in the West in order to protect it from the deleterious influence of politics. 'The politicization of the German concept of art would mean its democratization, an important feature

* Sombart, *Patriotic Meditations.*
† Mann, *Reflections of a Non-political Man.*

of the democratic levelling and realignment of Germany.' Since Mann saw the progress of democracy in Germany, too, and did not think it could be stopped, his protest was, at heart, without hope, an expression of the educated bourgeoisie's discontent with Western civilization and, at the same time, a farewell to that world 'of a resigned inwardness, sheltered by power' the poet was to commemorate many years later in his Munich speech on the 'Leiden und Grösse Richard Wagners'* of 10 February 1933.[33]

Initially, German intellectual war propaganda made no mention of concrete military goals. An open discussion of the goals the country pursued would have contradicted the notion of the war's purely defensive character; thus, such a discussion was forbidden until November 1916. Behind the scenes, however, plans of conquest were drawn up, both by the government and by political associations and business interests. In September 1914 the chancellor set down his ideas in a programme that amounted to a German-controlled central Europe and thus a German hegemony over Europe. His catalogue of demands included the annexation of the north Lorraine ore basin of Longwy-Briey, the city of Belfort, the transformation of Luxembourg into a German federal state, and the demotion of Belgium to a German 'vassal state'. The new Belgium was to cede Lüttich (Liège) and Verviers to Prussia and receive in return the French part of Flanders 'with Dunkirk, Calais, and Boulogne, mainly Flemish in population'. Concerning Russia, all that was said for the moment was that it had to be 'driven from the German border and its power over the non-Russian vassal nations broken'. The neighbour states, including Austria-Hungary, France, and possibly 'Poland' were to join a central European economic league, 'with its members in nominally equal partnership, but de facto under German leadership'.

It was no coincidence that Bethmann Hollweg's goals were in conspicuous agreement with those of Walther Rathenau, who in August 1914 had been given leadership of the war commodities department in the ministry of war. The demand for a central African colonial empire came from the imperial colonial office at about this same time. The government's war aims found the support of the most important branches of industry as well as the Deutsche Bank. The 'September programme' was thus a kind a lowest common denominator among the parties who thought clearly about Germany's war goals in the autumn of 1914.

The Pan-Germans and individual heavy industrialists went much further. Already at the end of August 1914 Heinrich Class, president of the Pan-German League, was demanding territorial concessions from France much more comprehensive than those of the chancellor shortly afterward. The face of Russia was to be 'powerfully redirected to the east' and 'basically thrown back into the borders of the time before Peter the Great'; the Baltic region, as well as parts of Russian Poland, White Russia, and northwest Russia, were to be settled by Germans, and the Russian Jews transferred to Palestine. In September 1915 the Centre delegate

* Mann, 'The Sufferings and Greatness of Richard Wagner'.

Matthias Erzberger, at that time a political confidant of the Thyssen concern, went so far as to demand the 'splitting up of the Russian colossus'. August Thyssen himself, in September 1914, had spoken out in support of the annexation of Belgium, certain *départements* of France, and, in the east, Russia's Baltic provinces. He also desired, if possible, German control of the territory around Odessa, the Crimea, the territory around Azov, and the Caucasus, in order to secure Germany's raw material needs for the future.

In May 1915, in separately published memoranda, the leading economic associations, among them the pillars of the 'Cartel of the Productive Estates' of 1913 (the Federation of Agriculturalists, the Central Association of German Industrialists, and the Imperial German Middle Class Association) and the export-oriented League of Industrialists, adopted the Pan-German programme. They were joined a month later by a large number of university teachers, civil servants, and artists. The 'professors' petition', inspired by the Berlin theologian and scholar Reinhold Seeberg, a native of the Baltic region, called for the expulsion of large segments of the native population from the territories to be ceded by Russia and, for the purposes of 'Germanization', their replacement with German farmers from other regions of the tzarist empire, or even with people from overpopulated Germany. Estonians, Latvians, and Lithuanians were to be employed as migrant labour in German agriculture. A more moderate group of German intellectuals, led by Theodor Wolff, publisher of the *Berliner Tageblatt*, as well as the historian Hans Delbrück, responded with another memorandum in July 1915. They rejected territorial gains in the west with the argument that 'the incorporation or annexation of politically independent peoples, who are long accustomed to independence, is reprehensible.' The path to expansion in the east, however, the moderate imperialists also left open.

Prominent signatures stood on both documents. Classical philologist Ulrich von Wilamowitz-Moellendorff, historians Eduard Meyer and Dietrich Schäfer, economist Adolf Wagner, and jurist Otto von Gierke signed the Seeberg petition; the Wolff–Delbrück text was endorsed by physicists Albert Einstein and Max Planck, theologians Adolf von Harnack and Ernst Troeltsch, sociologists Max and Alfred Weber, constititional scholar Gerhard Anschütz, historian Max Lehmann, and economist Gustav von Schmoller. There was, however, a conspicuous difference in the respective number of signatories. The moderate petition counted only 191 personalities from German intellectual life; the Pan-German document was signed by 1,347 people, including 352 professors.

The longer the war lasted, the more dissatisfied the Pan-Germans and with them the whole of the German right became with chancellor's policy, which Bethmann Hollweg himself later was to call a 'policy of the diagonal', meaning an attempt to square the circle. On the one hand, he had to make an effort to retain the support of the Social Democrats, who, at the end of June 1915, clearly reiterated their refusal to countenance German annexations. On the other hand, he had to make the expansionist military and the corresponding part of the German public believe that he was no less committed than the military leaders to enlarging and strengthening Germany through the war.

The chancellor's actual position was most closely represented by the advocates of a German-dominated *Mitteleuropa*. For this group, the hegemony of the Reich was to be primarily a material one secured by economic treaties, only secondarily through territorial expansions. Friedrich Naumann's 1915 book *Mitteleuropa*, which returned to Heinrich von Gagern's old idea of a 'wider federation' between Germany and Austria-Hungary (without referring explicitly to Gagern), rapidly became a kind of Bible for the moderate school of German war imperialism. In calling for the transformation of the federation into an 'existential partnership from top to bottom', the liberal parliamentarian and publicist not only took up the legacy of *grossdeutsch* foreign policy; he also forged domestic links to the forces that had resisted the *kleindeutsch* solution most tenaciously: Catholics, southern German democrats, and Social Democrats.

Naumann's appeal for a *Mitteleuropa* that was 'German at the core', organized around a federally structured German-Austrian-Hungarian economic area, had qualities that seemed to make it into a kind of 'Columbus's egg'. However, the author gave his plan a higher historical respectability by pointing out that a 'world-power of *Mitteleuropa*' had once existed in the past.

> The Germans filled the middle of Europe, but on all their borders they drew neighbouring peoples to themselves: the Holy Roman Empire of the German Nation. Now, during the war, this old Empire is shifting and pressing up again under the earth, for it wants to rise again after a long slumber.

Of course, in order to make the project of *Mitteleuropa* reality, the central powers first had to win the war. And the more extreme imperialists had to be put in their places.

Neither of these essentials was in sight, however. It was true that, in the east, the situation was developing favourably for Germany and Austria-Hungary, to the extent that Russia's military defeats plunged the country further and further into internal turmoil. In mid-March 1917 (the end of February, according to the Julian calendar), strikes and unrest changed suddenly into open revolution; a Provisional Government, dominated by the higher bourgeoisie, was set up, and Tzar Nicholas II abdicated. However, the new masters of Russia had no intention of renouncing Russian Poland, which the central powers had transformed into a formally independent 'Kingdom of Poland' in November 1916. And for their part, the German military and political right were less inclined than ever to agree to a 'separate peace' in the east without massive Russian territorial concessions.

In the west, the war of position continued after the failure of the Anglo-French Somme offensive and the bloody battles near Verdun in autumn 1916. The decision to conduct unrestricted submarine warfare, however, taken by the crown council on 9 July 1917 against the opposition of Bethmann Hollweg, proved fatal for the central powers. Torpedo attacks against British and French passenger liners by German submarines had already caused the death of a large number of American citizens since the start of the war. Now, the new resolution seemed like a calculated challenge to the United States, which responded by breaking off diplomatic relations and declaring war on Germany on 6 April 1917. The central powers had no realistic chance of winning the war after that.

By this time, the nationalist emotions and 'war enthusiasm' that had run high among the urban bourgeoisie and petty bourgeoisie at the war's start were gone. The disappointment of the hopes for a quick victory; widespread hunger in the course of the allied blockade of German ports, which cut off the import of foodstuffs; illicit trading and profiteering, which led to the sharpening of class antagonisms—all these things contributed to political discontent. This was not only true of the workers and farmers, who had rarely exhibited any surfeit of nationalist sentiment even at the beginning; it was also true of the broadest strata of the bourgeoisie, who identified themselves as thoroughgoingly *vaterländisch*. On the political right, Pan-Germans and anti-Semites tried to make the Jews into scapegoats. Rathenau's appointment to head the office of war commodities was seen as proof of their claim that Germany was falling increasingly under Jewish control. Already in 1915 Hans von Liebig, a chemistry professor in Giessen, was referring to Bethmann Hollweg as 'chancellor of German Jewry'.

On 19 October 1916 the Centre party delegate Matthias Erzberger called upon the chancellor to 'provide a detailed summary of the entire personnel of all war associations, divided according to sex, age of military service, salaries, confession'. A few days before, on 11 October, the Prussian ministry of war, reacting to a flood of complaints about supposed Jewish 'shirking of duty', had ordered 'statistics on the Jews' (*Judenstatistik*) to be compiled for the army. This survey represented nothing less than the official governmental recognition and legitimation of anti-Semitism. This was a profound historical caesura, and it shocked not only the Jews.

The results could only disappoint the initiators of the measure. The proportion of Jews among those who participated in the war, in both its achievements and its sacrifices, corresponded to the proportion of Jews in the population. To be sure, the statistics only became known after the war. Even if they had been published at the time, however, they would probably not have affected the views of the anti-Semites. When, in September 1914, the national economist Franz Oppenheimer paid tribute to the Jewish Social Democrat Ludwig Frank (originally from Baden), the first Reichstag delegate to fall in the war, the anti-Semitic press responded in a manner he summarized in one sentence: 'Don't get your hopes up; you are and remain the pariahs of Germany.'[34]

On the political left, protest against the policies of the Reich leadership and the Social Democrats supporting them began already in the autumn of 1914. On 2 December Karl Liebknecht, son of the party founder Wilhelm Liebknecht and a lawyer in Berlin, became the first Reichstag delegate to vote against new war credits. Nineteen other Social Democrats followed his example on 21 December 1915, among them Hugo Haase, the party head. In January 1916 Liebknecht was excluded from the parliamentary fraction. Following another 'breakdown of discipline', which the majority punished by excluding the offender from the fraction, eighteen opposition delegates united to form the Social Democratic Working Group (*Sozialdemokratische Arbeitsgemeinschaft*) in March 1916. Most of them belonged to the old pre-war left. Criticism of the official claim to a 'defensive war' was heard far beyond the left wing, however. The 'centrist' Kautsky, who held no parliamentary mandate, and the 'rightist' Bernstein also both rejected the majority line.

But the 'left' was by no means all of one mind. The delegates Haase and Wilhelm Dittmann, along with Rudolf Hilferding (originally from Vienna), a physician, Marxist theorist, editor of *Vorwärts*, and author of the popular 1910 book *Das Finanzkapital*, belonged to the moderate camp. Liebknecht, Rosa Luxemburg, party historian Franz Mehring, and Clara Zetkin, champion of the socialist women's movement, were among the radicals (though only Liebknecht was a parliamentary delegate). From the spring of 1915 the extreme left had its own organization, the *Gruppe Internationale*, which renamed itself the 'Spartacus League' (*Spartakusgruppe*) in the course of 1916. Other radical leftist groups included the 'Left Radicals' (*Linksradikalen*) in Hamburg and Bremen and the 'International Socialists of Germany' (*Internationale Sozialisten Deutschlands*) around the publisher of the journal *Lichtstrahlen*, Julian Borchardt.

The radicalization of the German left was closely connected to what happened among the left wing of the Second International. In September 1915 leftist socialists, some from countries at war (including Germany, France, Russia, and Italy), others from neutral states, convened in Swiss Zimmerwald. From there they issued a unanimous condemnation of socialist parties supporting the 'imperialist war', declaring them guilty of opportunistic treason against the principles of the International. The conference had been announced by Italian and Swiss socialists in mid-May 1915, one week before Italy joined the war on the side of the Entente. Moderate adversaries of the 'truce' policy, men like Bernstein, Kautsky, and Haase, whom Lenin disparagingly referred to as 'social pacifists', were not invited to Zimmerwald. But the extreme left around Lenin, which called for the 'truce' to be ended by a civil war, itself represented only a small minority of the participants. A unanimously passed resolution demanded a rapid end to the war, a peace without annexations and indemnities, and the right of national self-determination.

At the next conference, which took place in April 1916 in Kienthal outside Bern, Lenin and his supporters again remained in the minority. On two points, however, the Kienthal resolutions went beyond those of Zimmerwald. In the first place, the participants called for a 'rejection of all support for war policies by socialist parties' and a refusal to endorse war credits. Secondly, they accused the executive of the International of complete failure and of having 'collaborated in the policy of betraying its principles, the policy of the so-called "defence of the fatherland", and the policy of the "truce" '. The result fell short of Lenin's goal of splitting the Second International, and it was still very far away from laying the foundations for a new, revolutionary Third International. Nonetheless, it was a sign that the international workers' movement had polarized even more.

In Germany leftist opposition to the 'truce' policy of the Social Democrats increased measurably after the 'swede' or 'rutabaga winter' of 1916–17. Famine was not the only thing that radicalized the proletariat, however. Another factor was the increased exploitation of workers and the role the trade unions played in it. On 5 December 1916 the Reichstag, with the votes of the Social Democrats, passed the Patriotic Labour Service Act (*Vaterländisches Hilfsdienstgesetz*), which introduced national service for all men between the ages of 17 and 60 who had not already been called up for military service. It also required companies of more than fifty employees to institute workers' and employees' committees and created mediation commissions above the company level composed of representatives from labour and management in equal proportion.

The Labour Service Act was the Magna Carta of a programme that forced German industry to convert to the mass production of armaments. This was the so-called 'Hindenburg programme', which was designed by Erich Ludendorff, the quartermaster-general of the German army, and named after the 'victor of Tannenberg', Field Marshal Paul von Hindenburg, from the end of August 1916 chief of the Army High Command (*Oberste Heeresleitung* or OHL). While the act gave the unions more influence, they became so closely involved with the state and company management that, in the view of many workers, they ceased to represent the interests of the proletariat.

In April 1917 a wave of 'wildcat' mass strikes broke out in many large German cities, partly in response to the February revolution in Russia and the recent founding of the Independent German Social Democratic Party in Gotha (*Unabhängige Sozialdemokratische Partei Deutschlands* or USPD, formerly the *Sozialdemokratische Arbeitsgemeinschaft*). In Berlin, the 'Revolutionary Shop Stewards' (*Revolutionäre Obleute*) from the metal industry, who came from the left wing of the new USPD, first appeared on the scene. The prima facie goal of the uprising was an increase in the bread ration. In reality, however, it was the first large-scale workers' protest against the war, and it took place throughout the Reich. Within a few days, labour unions from all political camps—'free' social-democratic, Christian, and the liberal Hirsch–Dunker groups—managed to bring about the end of the demonstrations. But the antipathy to the 'truce' did not weaken. And the workers were not the only ones protesting against the war at this time; soldiers, too, became increasingly restless throughout 1917. In the German navy, hunger strikes and cases of absence without leave multiplied. The military courts responded with draconian—and legally untenable—punishments against the 'ringleaders'. Some ten sailors were condemned to death. Two, Max Reichpietsch and Albin Köbis, were executed on 5 September 1917. The outrage and bitterness of the sailors reached a new high.

The government's efforts to pacify the domestic scene in the spring of 1917 were insufficient. The 'Easter message' of 7 April, which Bethmann Hollweg had wrung from the emperor, promised constitutional reforms after the end of the war, including a restructuring of the Prussian House of Lords and House of Representatives. William also renounced the three-class voting system, but left the decision about whether it would be replaced by a plural system or general direct suffrage to the constitutional organs. This was not enough to satisfy the Social Democrats. It also did nothing to strengthen the chancellor's position on the 'right'.

Around this same time, Germany's most important ally showed increasing symptoms of crisis. Between January and April 1917 Emperor Charles, the successor of Francis Joseph, who had died in November 1916, had tried in vain to conclude a separate peace with France (and had brought a German renunciation of Alsace-Lorraine into the discussion). The failure of these peace feelers made the Habsburg monarchy even more dependent on Germany, but did not alter the wishes of the Vienna government to bring the war to an end as quickly as possible in order to preserve the multinational empire.

For this purpose Charles and his foreign minister, Count Czernin, attempted to act upon one of the most influential members of the German Reichstag, Matthias Erzberger, who, in agreement with Bethmann Hollweg, had gone to Vienna at the end of April. By this time the Centre delegate was acquainted with Czernin's extraordinarily bleak assessment of the military situation, which the latter had set down in a memorandum on 12 April (the foreign office in Berlin had permitted Erzberger to look at the document). The Vienna pessimism was partly responsible for Erzberger's transformation during those months from an annexationist to an advocate of a peace agreement and critic of unrestricted submarine warfare, the failure of which was obvious by that time. Erzberger's change of position influenced the attitude of his party, and the Centre moved somewhat to the left.

The Majority Social Democrats (the MSPD) did the same thing in June of 1917, but for other reasons. At an international conference in Stockholm, convened at the prompting of Dutch and Scandinavian socialists and attended by representatives from both German Social Democratic parties, the MSPD adopted the maxim of the Petrograd Workers' and Peasants' Soviet, 'peace without annexations and contributions'. Shortly thereafter, on 26 June 1917, the Social Democratic Party committee gave Bethmann Hollweg an ultimatum: the party would not take a final position on the new war credits bill until the administration had made a clear statement concerning both its war aims and its domestic plans. The Russian February revolution, the founding of the USPD, the April strikes—all these things came together to provoke the majority SPD into threatening an end to the 'truce'.[35]

Prisoner to his own 'policy of the diagonal', the chancellor could not satisfy the demands of the Social Democrats—neither in regard to a peace treaty nor with respect to the constitution—without provoking storms of protest from the right, where the Pan-Germans had long been waiting for an opportunity to call for a general mobilization against Bethmann Hollweg. On 2 July, having just returned to Berlin from the General Headquarters, the chancellor, in the presence of the most important ministerial secretaries, informed the leaders of the larger parliamentary fractions that he did not intend to comply with the wishes of the Social Democrats. In so doing, he stripped himself of the parliamentary majority that had supported him since 4 August 1914.

Ludendorff, too, went against Bethmann Hollweg, but for entirely different reasons than the Social Democrats. The strong man of the OHL wanted to replace Bethmann Hollweg with a head of government who would follow *his* instructions. Through Colonel Max Bauer, his most trusted confidant, the First Quartermaster-General informed Erzberger in June about the seriousness of the military situation. The politician could only interpret this communiqué as an exhortation to work for the chancellor's ouster. Erzberger also knew about Pope Benedict XV's intention to appeal to the warring countries for peace. When on 6 July, after consultation with the Majority Social Democrats and Progressives, the Centre delegate directed an impassioned attack against the policy of unrestricted submarine warfare and demanded a peace initiative from the parliament, he knew what he was doing. Erzberger's speech triggered the 'July crisis of 1917'.

That same day, National Liberals, Centre, Progressive People's Party, and Majority Social Democrats—who had been cooperating since April 1917 in the Reichstag's newly formed constitutional committee with the goal of reforming the federal constitution—founded a new body, the Interparty Committee (*Interfraktioneller Ausschuss*). But it was quickly evident that there were still sharp antagonisms between the fractions over the main questions. While the National Liberals had changed their mind about the appointment of parliamentarians to governmental office, they still had serious reservations against general direct suffrage for Prussia and rejected a peace resolution on the basis of the 'Peterograd formula'. Nonetheless, the chancellor's removal was a priority, especially for their delegate Gustav Stresemann, who had advanced to ever greater power and influence.

The three other parties considered the peace initiative more important. Out of consideration for its fraction in the Prussian House of Representatives, the Centre kept a low profile on the suffrage question. And despite certain remarks from Erzberger to the contrary, the majority of Centre delegates still found themselves unable to endorse the idea of parliamentary rule in the Reich. The Majority Social Democrats backed both the introduction of the Reichstag suffrage law in Prussia and, in principle, parliamentary rule. But with the exception of the party right wing, they did not desire to participate in a coalition government themselves, wishing to avoid conflict with the parliamentary and extraparliamentary left. The Progressive People's Party was unreservedly for both equal suffrage and parliamentarization and, in the unlikely event that Bethmann Hollweg did adopt these goals, for the chancellor's continuing in office. A part of the Centre around Erzberger and the National Liberals, on the other hand, was of one mind with the OHL on the chancellor issue: Bethmann Hollweg's predecessor, Prince Bernhard von Bülow, should also be his successor. Least concerned about the chancellor was the MSPD, although virtually nobody in the party trusted him any longer.

Then, for a short period, Bethmann Hollweg's position seemed to stabilize. William II was outraged over the machinations of the military and had no intention of appointing Bülow again. Prompted by Bethmann Hollweg, he even decreed (on 11 July) the introduction of equal suffrage in Prussia. After this, the anti-Bethmann Hollweg bloc began to crumble. But the next day, induced by Ludendorff, Crown Prince William intervened. The most important result of his conversations with selected opponents of the chancellor from almost all fractions was that Erzberger was able to commit the Centre to a statement against Bethmann Hollweg.

The dramatic climax of the crisis came on the afternoon of 12 July when Hindenburg and Ludendorff submitted their letters of resignation. The telegram in which Ludendorff announced his lack of confidence in Bethmann Hollweg was a historically unprecedented challenge to the monarch. But it had the desired effect. William II submitted to the will of the two generals, whom the great majority of the people still considered to be the guarantors of German victory.

On that same 12 July, the Majority Social Democrats, Centre, and Progressive People's Party agreed to the text of a peace resolution in the Interparty Committee. The Reichstag sought a peace through 'understanding and lasting reconciliation among the nations', the statement read. 'Forcible territorial expansion is incompatible with such a peace, as are other kinds of political, economic, and financial rape.' The language was chosen to allow an interpretative freedom sufficient to accommodate an expansion of the German sphere of influence. This was decidedly too little for the National Liberals, however, who not only did not endorse the resolution, but walked out on the committee. Nor did Bethmann Hollweg, who was still in office at this time, show any inclination to adopt the position of the three fractions (called 'majority parties' from this point forward). The OHL protested by telegram and demanded that the chancellor—in whom it had just officially declared its lack of confidence—prevent the adoption of the resolution. Bethmann Hollweg knew that he was no longer able to do this. On the evening of 12 July he personally asked the emperor to accept his resignation, submitting his request in writing the next day.

Hindenburg and Ludendorff, ordered to Berlin by William II, conducted interviews with the party leaders on the same day, 13 July. But there was no solution to the conflict over the peace resolution. The Social Democrats, Centre, and Progressives insisted on the text they had agreed to the day before. Shortly thereafter, William II accepted Bethmann Hollweg's resignation, appointing a successor on 14 July: Georg Michaelis, a government jurist, Prussian state commissioner for food procurement, and a complete novice to politics. Ludendorff had approved his appointment in advance. Michaelis himself reports in his memoirs that on the morning of 13 July, when he received the emperor's request, he had read in the 'Watchwords' of the Moravian Church (*Herrnhuter Brüdergemeinde*) the passage from Joshua 1: 9: 'Have not I commanded thee? Be strong and of a good courage; be not afraid, neither be thou dismayed'. He understood the passage as a sign that he ought not to refuse the entreaty of his highest superior.

The outcome of the July crisis of 1917 was *not* a success for the majority parties. They had allowed themselves—in part consciously, in part unconsciously—to be used as tools of the Army High Command, and now they had to suffer the consequences. After 14 July they were forced to deal with a chancellor far more remote from them than his luckless predecessor. In an article for the *Frankfurter Zeitung* at the beginning of September 1917, Max Weber described the crisis as a 'classic paradigm' of 'how the lack of normal parliamentary rule operates in crisis situations. There will never be any change unless the Reichstag parties are continually forced to express a clear position both on the questions of policy and with regard to the participants.' The 'German domestic question' was thus as follows: 'How may the parliament, condemned to a negative politics by dint of its current structure, be transformed into an agent of political responsibility?'

When Bethmann Hollweg's successor took office, the cause of parliamentary rule seemed, at first glance, to have advanced considerably. A significant number of politicians from the ranks of the majority parties and the National Liberals entered high positions in the federal administration and the Prussian ministries. The Centre politician Peter Spahn, for example, became Prussian minister of justice; Rudolf Schwander, the mayor of Strasbourg and close associate of the Progressive People's Party, became undersecretary, then, in October 1917, secretary of the newly formed Imperial Economic Office; the majority Social Democrat August Müller was appointed undersecretary of the War Nutrition Office. Nonetheless, these appointments did not make the majority parties and National Liberals into 'agents of political responsibility' in Weber's sense. It would be more accurate to speak of an attempt by the Reich leadership to discipline the parliamentary majority by drawing it into the bureaucracy. As far as the key question was concerned, Michaelis wasted no time in making it clear—though in somewhat qualified form—that he was no man of the majority. In the Reichstag debate on 19 July, which preceded the adoption of the peace resolution, he announced that the aims of the Reich leadership could be 'achieved within the framework of your resolution, as I interpret it'.

The majority parties seemed not to notice—or else they deliberately ignored—this reservation, which could be taken to turn the resolution into the very opposite of what it was intended to be. The parliamentary minutes record calls of ' "bravo!" and "very good"! from the Centre, Progressive People's Party, and Social Democrats'. The assembly passed the peace resolution by 212 to 126 votes with 17 abstentions. The MSPD delegates all voted positively; the Progressive People's Party did so with one exception, and the Centre with five. On the next day, the Majority Social Democrats assisted in the passage of the new war credits bill, approving 15 billion marks' worth of government expenditures.

The peace resolution was greeted with approval by the constituents of the majority parties. The right reacted with hostility. The nationalists responded by establishing the German Fatherland Party (*Deutsche Vaterlandspartei*) on 2 September 1917 in York Hall of the East Prussian *Landschaft* in Königsberg. The moving spirit behind the party's founding was the jurist Wolfgang Kapp, head of the *Landschaft*, a public credit office for agriculture. Despite its name, the new party did not look upon itself as a party among other parties, but as a supra-party association uniting all 'patriotic' forces. Its main catchment area was in Prussia east of the Elbe. The party activists came primarily from among the educated bourgeoisie employed in state offices, or from the manorial class, and they were mostly Evangelical in confession. The main constituents came from the ranks of the conservatives and National Liberals. Numerous nationalist associations joined the Fatherland Party as corporations, effectively doubling its direct and indirect membership. This fact must be taken into consideration when evaluating the party's own records; the claims of 450,000 members in March 1918 and 800,000 at the beginning of September 1918 both represent significant exaggerations.

It says much about the social character of the new association that its leadership was assumed by a member of the ruling house, Duke John Albert of Mecklenburg, co-founder of the Pan-German League and president of the German Colonial Society after 1895, and by the former secretary of the imperial naval office and creator of the German navy, Admiral of the Fleet von Tirpitz. The Fatherland Party was the culmination of *Sammlungspolitik* from above, called into life by servants of the state, represented by members of the old ruling elite, and supported by bourgeois and petty bourgeois devotees of the alliance of throne and altar, the two most important symbols of the authoritarian state. Despite the 'populism' of its platform and propaganda, however, it was not a mass organization of the new type. Among the lower classes of society, the 'party' that claimed it was not a party had virtually no support.

In its founding declaration, the Fatherland Party did emphasize that 'without strong backing from the people' the government would not be able 'to master the situation alone'. But the explanation that the government required 'a powerful tool for a powerful federal policy', a tool in the shape of 'a great people's party, supported by the broadest patriotic circles', quickly made clear that the party had no interest in the will of the people. Democracy was unequivocally rejected.

> Contrary to the lies of our enemies, we do not live under autocratic absolutism, but under the blessings of a constitutional state whose social engagement shames all the democracies of the world and has given the German people the power to defy the immense dominance of its enemies. German freedom stands sky-high above sham democracy with all its supposed blessings, which English hypocrisy and a Wilson seek to wheedle the Germans into accepting, so as to destroy Germany, which is invincible in arms.

The only thing that could save Germany was, according to the Fatherland Party, a 'Hindenburg peace', embracing 'enormous sacrifices and efforts as the price of victory'. While the founding declaration did not go into detail on this matter, countless speeches and petitions by the speakers of the national 'unity party' did. They wanted Germany to achieve a peace of conquests and aggrandizement at the expense of Belgium, France, Russia, and Britain. A 'Hindenburg peace' was the diametric opposite of the 'peace without annexations and contributions' endorsed by the Social Democrats—the 'Scheidemann peace' as the right called it, after its most eloquent proponent, the delegate Philipp Scheidemann.

If the founding of the German Fatherland Party was a response to the peace resolution of the moderate parliamentary majority, the founding of the People's Federation for Liberty and Fatherland (*Volksbund für Freiheit und Vaterland*) on 14 November 1917 was a response to the nationalist propaganda of the Fatherland Party. The new Federation sought to organize a movement for moderate war aims, redress of social conflicts and disparities, and inner reforms. Its participants included well-known professors like Friedrich Meinecke, Hans Delbrück, Max Weber, Hugo Preuss, Lujo Brentano, and Ernst Troeltsch; politicians and publicists from the ranks of the Progressive People's Party around Friedrich Naumann and Theodor Heuss; and eminent representatives of the trade unions, among them the Catholic labour leaders Johann Giesberts and Adam Stegerwald, and the Social Democrats Carl Liegen and Gustav Bauer.

The founding declaration of the People's Federation contained an appeal for the 'maximal concentration of our energies', necessary 'to break the destructive will of our enemies'. Domestic-political restructuring in the sense of a 'liberal consolidation of our state institutions' was to begin immediately, not wait until after the end of the war. It was essential 'to give a government willing to reform firm popular support, and to draw the necessary conclusions from the nature of the modern state, conclusions that today every nation must draw in the context of its development'. Finally, Germany needed a 'clear foreign policy, sustained by the people and the government, aspiring to a lasting peace, securing raw material imports and foreign markets, and placing the life, honour, and self-determination of the nations upon the basis of morality and law'.

The People's Federation did not explicitly endorse parliamentary rule for Germany, but it supported the call for more democracy. It did not demand annexations, but it also did not exclude them. The increase in German economic power was one of the common goals of all the signatories of the founding declaration. All in all, the proclamations of the Federation and its spokesmen gave the impression that the peace it sought was more the parliament's 'peace through understanding' than the Fatherland Party's 'peace through victory'.

The formation of a new socially inclusive, supra-confessional political centre met with a weaker public response than the shrill and arrogant tones of the Fatherland Party. The Federation's individual membership remained very modest, allegedly increasing from 1,000 in May to 2,800 by October 1918. If we count affiliate organizations, including all unions from diverse political camps, we arrive at the impressive but misleading figure of 4 million members. In reality the

Federation was far too heterogeneous ever to become a serious factor in domestic politics. Still, the cooperation between moderate representatives of the bourgeoisie and labour made it important. The People's Federation for Liberty and Fatherland (like the Association for Social Reform, which was involved in its founding) was an expression of the class compromise that had developed under the 'truce'. Without such a compromise, parliamentary democracy was inconceivable in Germany.

At the time of the Federation's founding, Michaelis was no longer the chancellor. The second chancellorship crisis of 1917 was provoked by extreme and untenable attacks by Eduard von Capelle, secretary of the naval office, against the leaders of the USPD, whom he accused on 9 October in the Reichstag of abetting a plan of revolt in the high seas fleet. The accusations enraged not only the party directly affected and the Majority Social Democrats, who, through their party and floor leader Friedrich Ebert, declared open war on the chancellor that same day. Among the Centre and the Progressive People's Party, too, Michaelis had lost all support by this time. The belief was widespread that he was proceeding against the Independent Social Democrats in the same way as the pre-war government had pursued the movement as a whole. Even for the National Liberals, who had been cooperating in the Interparty Committee again as of the end of August, it was clear by 9 October that Michaelis could no longer be supported as chancellor.

His successor, though a member of the Centre party, was not a man after the heart of the parliamentary majority from July. The Bavarian prime minister, Count Georg von Hertling, who assumed the offices of chancellor of the Reich and Prussian prime minister on 1 November 1917, rejected any further development towards parliamentary rule; as a resolute federalist, he feared that it would lead to a unified central government. He also gave no indication of being any more sympathetic to the July peace resolution than Michaelis. But his appointment also dissatisfied the political right. Militantly Evangelical circles among the military, the National Liberals, and the Fatherland Party felt the choice of a Catholic chancellor during the height of the 'Luther year' of 1917, the 400th anniversary of the Reformation, to be downright insulting.

Nonetheless, the change of chancellor was accompanied by signs that could be interpreted as a creeping parliamentarization of the state. For the second time in 1917, the Reichstag had brought about the collapse of the administration, this time without the help of the OHL, as in the case of Bethmann Hollweg. The vice-chancellorship was assumed not by the incumbent Karl Helfferich, favourite of the emperor and chancellor, but by the nominee of the Interparty Committee, Progressive delegate Friedrich von Payer from Stuttgart. The National Liberal parliamentarian Robert Friedberg from Berlin became vice-president of the Prussian state ministry. With these appointments, three of the Interparty Committee's four parties were represented in the executive of the Reich and Prussia.

But it was not yet clear in late 1917 whether the November reshuffle of the government would lead to an increase in the power of the July parliamentary majority to affect matters of 'grand policy'. It was no longer even certain that the July majority was still tenable. The Centre, for one, clearly distanced itself from the peace resolution in November. On the other hand, in the debate over Hertling's inaugural speech, the Majority Social Democrats expressly reserved the right to move against the new administration if it provoked them, the largest German party, through its actions or inaction. To begin the history of German parliamentary monarchy in November 1917 would thus be to exaggerate the significance of the caesura between Michaelis and Hertling.[36]

THE MILITARY DEFEAT AND THE 'REVOLUTION FROM ABOVE'

It is not because of the shake-up in the German chancellor's office that November 1917 represents a watershed in world history, but because of the revolution in Russia on 6 and 7 November. The second of the two Russian revolutions in 1917—called the October Revolution according to the Julian calendar—was, after the entrance of the United States of America into the war in April, the second event making 1917 into a year that marks a new epoch. When Lenin's Bolsheviks took power in Petrograd, former St Petersburg, most contemporaries did not yet perceive the events as a new kind of revolution, but as something that could influence the outcome of the world war.

This was the expectation that led the German foreign office and the Army High Command to grant Lenin and the other leading Bolsheviks, living in exile in Switzerland, passage through Germany and Sweden back to Russia from 9 to 12 April. With generous support from Germany, Lenin was to make his revolution and end the war in the east. As long as he did what the Reich leadership wanted, Lenin acted, 'objectively' speaking, as a German agent. Berlin was aware that he was pursuing radically different goals than those of the political and military leadership of Germany. It accepted this fact as the price for partial victory in the east and an end to the two-front war, which was more important to it than all else.

Bismarck had played a similar game with revolution before and after the outbreak of the war with Austria in 1866, when he took steps to mobilize the Hungarians, Czechs, and southern Slavic peoples against the Habsburg monarchy. After Prussia's military and diplomatic victories, he did not find it necessary to continue along this path. In 1917, faced with the prospect of an American landing in Europe, the political leaders of Germany saw themselves justified in acting according to a maxim Bethmann Hollweg had pronounced already on 4 August 1914 with regard to the invasion (which he himself considered 'unjust') of neutral Belgium: 'Necessity knows no law!'

At first, news of the Russian October Revolution was greeted in Germany with great relief. The 'decree on peace', resolved at Lenin's behest by the Second

All-Russian Congress of the Soviets on 8 November and calling all belligerent nations to cease fire and to start peace negotiations, impressed the war-weary working class in Germany and Austria-Hungary, since it seemed to promise a swift end to the war. The other appeal from Lenin's Russia—that the international working class lead the proletarian revolution to victory everywhere—showed, as yet, no tangible effect.

Even the Majority Social Democrats, whom Lenin castigated as 'social patriots', temporarily joined the chorus in praise of the peaceable Bolsheviks. Lenin and his followers had brought down without much bloodshed the government of Prime Minister Kerensky, which was obviously no longer politically tenable, but still not prepared to negotiate a peace. Now, for the first time, there was a chance for a separate agreement in the east. As early as the end of November, however, an increasing number of Social Democrats—both from the Majority party and among the moderate Independents—began to accuse the Bolsheviks of employing terrorist methods. After 19 January 1918 virtually no social democrat in Germany expressed sympathy with the Russian path. On this day, Lenin's revolutionary troops forcibly dissolved the Constituent Assembly (elected on 25 November), in which the Bolsheviks controlled only a quarter of the seats. With this act, Russia's path toward dictatorship was irreversible.

Not only the Majority Social Democrats, but also the moderate elements within the USPD were outraged at this violation of the democratic tradition within the European workers' movement. Karl Kautsky, an outspoken critic of the Bolsheviks even before 19 January 1918, wrote, condemning Lenin, that the dictatorship of one among several parties was not 'the dictatorship of the proletariat' according to Marx and Engels, 'but the dictatorship of one part of the proletariat over another'. The dictatorship of a minority, however, finds its strongest support in a loyal army, and the more the minority substitutes armed force for the majority, 'the more it compels all opposition to avail itself of the appeal to the bayonet and the fist instead of the appeal to the ballot, from which it is cut off. Then, *civil war* becomes the form in which political and social antagonisms are worked out.'

For Kautsky, civil war was the most brutal form of war, and therefore a catastrophe.

> In a civil war, every party fights for its existence, and the loser faces complete annihilation . . . Many people confuse civil war with social revolution, consider it the form social revolution takes, and are disposed to excuse the unavoidable violence of civil war by thinking that without such violence revolution is not possible . . . If, according to the example of the bourgeois revolution, we should say that the revolution is the same thing as civil war and dictatorship, then we must be consistent and say also that the revolution necessarily terminates in the rule of a Cromwell or Napoleon.

Even on the far left, in the 'Spartacus League', the opinions on the Bolsheviks' January *coup d'état* were divided. Clara Zetkin and Franz Mehring defended the dissolution of the Constituent Assembly without reservation. The champion of the socialist women's movement went so far as to claim that not taking this step 'would have been a crime, paired with foolishness.' Rosa Luxemburg, on the other hand, in 'preventive detention' since July 1916, considered it inexcusable that the Bolsheviks, after dissolving the Constituent Assembly (an act she, too, approved), did not immediately call for new elections. 'Freedom only for the supporters of the government, only for the members of one party—be it ever so numerous—is not freedom. Freedom is only ever the freedom of those who think differently.' These are the two most-quoted sentences of Luxemburg's posthumously published 'Die Russische Revolution'. They were not, however, intended as an argument for a liberal pluralism, but for a revolutionary, socialist pluralism. When she wrote about the 'freedom of those who think differently', the author was not thinking of 'class enemies' and 'class traitors'.[37]

By the time Lenin broke up the Constituent Assembly, Germany had come a good bit closer to a 'separate peace' in the east. The guns had been silent since 5 December 1917. On 22 January peace negotiations between Russia and the central powers commenced in Brest-Litovsk. The main point of contention was the right of national self-determination, which the Bolsheviks advocated, but which, in practice, they were resolved to subordinate to the exigencies of revolutionary class struggle, such as they interpreted it. The German side sought not only to permanently withdraw the entire Baltic region, Poland, and Finland from Russian rule, but also to secure German control over the Ukraine, its raw materials and grain fields, and these interests took precedence over the self-determination of the respective peoples. It took an interruption of the peace negotiations and a new German-Austrian offensive in February 1918 to force the Russian government to yield.

On 3 March 1918 the two sides signed the Treaty of Brest-Litovsk. The modern world had not yet known such a peace built on conquest and violence. Russia was compelled to give up not only Finland, Poland, Lithuania, and Courland,* but even the Ukraine. Shortly thereafter, the Transcaucasian states declared their independence. This cost Russia a third of its population and agricultural land, and more than half of its coal reserves. The formation of an independent Ukraine and the cession of Armenian territory to Turkey considerably weakened Russia's position on the Black Sea. It preserved only a narrow access to the Baltic. Further treaties at the end of August 1918 imposed 6 billion gold marks of reparations and cost Russia the north Baltic provinces of Livonia and Estonia. As before in the case of Courland, the greatest pressure for the cessions came from the German-Baltic upper class (as well as their representatives in Germany), who demanded that 'their' territories be separated from Russia. But even without this pressure, it would not have been difficult to persuade German public opinion in the spring

* [Translator's note: Courland part of present-day Latvia, was a separate province of the Russian empire from 1797 to 1918. It was bounded by the Baltic Sea to the west, Lithuania to the south, and the Drina River (now the Daugava) to the north.]

and summer of 1918 that it was necessary to create a buffer zone between Germany and the Bolsheviks out of the 'border states' of east central Europe.

The Treaty of Brest-Litovsk flagrantly violated the peace resolution of 19 July 1917. Nonetheless, the Reichstag accepted it on 22 March 1918 by a great majority. Among the votes in favour were those of the two bourgeois majority parties, the Centre and the Progressive People's Party. The MSPD, internally split into opponents, advocates, and 'neutrals', abstained from the vote. The USPD voted against the treaty. Before the vote the Majority Social Democrats, together with the two other majority parties, had passed a resolution expressing the expectation that the Reich would observe the right to national self-determination in the case of Poland, Lithuania, and Courland.

This resolution was also an attempt to overcome the tensions that had been building for months between the Majority Social Democrats and the bourgeois centre. The crisis between the majority parties came to a head in January 1918 in a great wave of strikes, provoked by the arrogant triumphalism that General Max Hoffmann, chief of the General Staff East, had demonstrated in his dealings with the Russian delegation in Brest-Litovsk under Leon Trotsky. The uprising began on 28 January in the greater Berlin area, where the Revolutionary Shop Stewards under Richard Müller succeeded in convincing at least 180,000 workers to down their tools. Most of the strikers worked in the metal industry, which was crucial for the production of armaments. Within a few days, workers from many German cities—Kiel, Hamburg, Leipzig, Brunswick, Cologne, Bochum, and others—joined the strike. On 30 January *Vorwärts*, the main Social Democratic Party organ, was banned. The next day saw the proclamation of a heightened state of siege and the arrest of Wilhelm Dittmann, Reichstag delegate of the USPD, as he spoke to striking workers in Treptow Park. A military tribunal condemned him to five years in prison on 4 February 1918.

The two leaders of the MSPD, Friedrich Ebert and Philipp Scheidemann, as well as the Prussian parliamentary delegate Otto Braun from Königsberg, had themselves elected to the strike committee on 28 January in order to bring the industrial action—in which the unions *did not* participate—to an end as quickly as possible. They achieved this goal on 4 February, when the strike was ended in Berlin (in most other parts of the Reich it was over earlier). Had it lasted any longer, the strike of the munitions workers would have threatened Germany's military power. For this reason, the counter-measures of the military, police, and judicial system were rigorous. Striking workers were arrested in large numbers or conscripted into the army.

In his 1928 book *Entstehung der Deutschen Republik, 1871–1918*,* the classical historian Arthur Rosenberg, a Communist party delegate in the Reichstag until his break with Stalin in 1927, described the January strike as a 'great mass uprising against the military dictatorship and General Ludendorff'. After the 1917 unrest

* Rosenberg, *The Birth of the German Republic, 1871–1918.*

in the navy, it represented the 'second act of direct mass action against the military dictatorship', followed by a third act, the revolution, in November 1918. The workers were rebelling against hunger, the 'state of siege', the militarization of industry, and the policy of a 'peace through victory'. The USPD joined in the strike, since, like the workers, it wanted to bring the war to an end as quickly as possible, without annexations and indemnities and on the basis of national self-determination. The MSPD joined the strike leadership in order to prevent the workers from falling entirely under the influence of the USPD, to avoid further deterioration in the domestic-political situation, and to counter the accusation that the social democratic proletariat was stabbing the armies on the battlefront in the back.

Such accusations were made during the Berlin strike of the munitions workers. In a sermon on 3 February Bruno Doehring, court chaplain and pastor of the Berlin cathedral, called the instigators of the strike 'worthless and cowardly creatures' who had 'treacherously defiled the altar of the Fatherland with fraternal blood' and 'poisoned the good blood of our people'. Then, foreshadowing the later myth of the 'stab in the back' (the so-called *Dolchstosslegende*), Doehring declared that the strike's initiators had rushed the misguided workers 'from the places of calm productive labour onto the streets, pressing the murder weapon into their hands' and ordering them to attack 'their brothers from the rear, even as they are lying before the enemy'.

The word 'treason' was also already part of Doehring's vocabulary. His sermon has the fallen crying from their graves, 'such that it screeches to high heaven, "Treason! Treason against our own people!"' It seemed like an echo of the chaplain's accusation when, on 26 February 1918, the Conservative Party leader Ernst von Heydebrand und der Lasa declared that the strike was 'nothing other than a simple matter of treason to country, instigated and influenced by foreign agents and, unfortunately, sustained partly by the influence of the German Social Democrats'.

It was this atmosphere, poisoned by accusations of treason, that made the Majority Social Democrats fear the worst, not only for themselves as a party and for the workers' movement, but for Germany as a whole. To end the war quickly was also *their* wish. But the peace at the end of all battles was, they hoped, not going to be only an external peace, but an internal one, too, as much as possible. That the 'truce' would survive the war was neither to be expected nor even desired. Without a certain amount of mutual understanding between the classes, however, Germany threatened to fall into civil war, such as was already happening in the Ukraine, Finland, and parts of Russia in the winter of 1917–18.

For this reason, the leaders of the Majority Social Democrats sought to build bridges between, on the one hand, the striking workers and, on the other, the bourgeois parties of the parliamentary majority and the leadership of the Reich. They did not entirely fail. Despite their disapproval of the Social Democratic strike tactics, the spokesmen of the bourgeois parties did not take up the accusations of treason. The Reichstag majority of July 1917 managed to hold together until 22 March 1918, when it was re-established after a fashion by means of a new resolution. In the end, the common front against the extreme nationalism of the Pan-Germans, the Conservatives, and the Fatherland Party proved stronger than what divided the bourgeois centre from the moderate left. The same was true with regard to another shared antagonism: the majority parties of July 1917 were united in rejecting the radicalism of the extreme left, regardless of whether it came from the Revolutionary Shop Stewards or from the German followers of the Bolsheviks in the Spartacus League. From this point of view, too, the centre parties could ill afford a rupture with the Majority Social Democrats.[38]

After the beginning of 1918, the inner development in Germany was far more affected by a power other than the Russia of Vladimir Ilyich Lenin—the America of Woodrow Wilson. The 'Fourteen Points' of 8 January and the 'Four Principles' of 11 February 1918, in which the president of the United States set down his ideas of a just international peace settlement, were not only an answer to the Bolsheviks, but also seemed to offer an alternative to the retributive peace proposed by the heads of government in Paris and London, Georges Clemenceau and David Lloyd George. Wilson's aspiration 'to make the world safe for democracy' appealed to many more Germans than did Lenin's call for a proletarian 'world revolution'. The idea of a 'League of Nations' was incomparably more attractive than the project of a 'Third International'. Even a victorious Entente might be made to accept the right to national self-determination for which the American president was campaigning. To be sure, Wilson's specific demands to Germany included several that seemed totally unacceptable to a majority of Germans, including the cession of Alsace-Lorraine to France and the formation of an independent Polish state to include the territories where the population was clearly Polish and with free access to the Baltic. The evacuation and restoration of Belgium, on the other hand, was far more difficult to baulk at—which did not prevent the political right from doing exactly that.

In terms of militarily power, too, the United States became increasingly important as the year 1918 progressed. American troops played a significant role in stopping the last German western offensive (begun at the end of March) in summer 1918. The decisive moment came on 8 August—the 'dark day of the German Army', as Ludendorff called it—when British tank battalions broke through at Amiens. Thereafter the much-lauded 'troop spirit' deteriorated with each successive day. Cases of refusal to obey orders, voluntary surrender to the enemy, absence without leave, and desertion increased rapidly. The recollections in Ludendorff's *Kriegserinnerungen** were not exaggerated and represented typical incidents: 'Retreating troops, passing by a fresh division that was fighting bravely, called out: "strike breakers!" and "war prolongers" . . . In many places the officers no longer had any influence, and allowed themselves to be swept along.'

'War morale' was in little better condition at home. Dissatisfaction had long become general, not confined only to the working class. Already in August 1917

* Ludendorff, *My War Memories.*

Ritter von Brettreich, a minister in the Bavarian government, declared that the *Mittelstand* was in 'a worse mood than all other circles at the moment'. A year later, in August 1918, Ernst Troeltsch had occasion to observe even among 'patriotic' and 'war-believing' farmers and cheese manufacturers of the Allgäu a 'veritably fanatical hatred breaking out against the whole of the officers' corps as the epitome of injustice and privilege'. On 23 September Oskar Geck, a Reichstag delegate from Baden, reported in a meeting between the SPD fraction and party committee that in southern Germany there was 'enormous bitterness against Prussia; not against the Prussian people, but against the Junkers and the military caste. The dominant feeling among us is that Prussia must bite the dust, and if Prussia does not bite the dust, Germany will bite the dust because of Prussia.'[39]

At that same meeting, SPD party chairman Friedrich Ebert discussed the practical implications of the traditional elite's loss of power. He placed before his party colleagues a clear choice:

> If we do not now seek an understanding with the bourgeois parties and the government, then we must let things take their course, adopt the revolutionary tactic, put ourselves on our own feet, and let the revolution decide the party's fate. Whoever has seen the situation in Russia cannot desire, in the interest of the proletariat, that things develop the same way here. On the contrary. We must hurl ourselves into the breach. We must see if we can gain enough influence to push our demands through. And if it is possible for us to link them with the rescue of the country, then it is our damned duty and responsibility to do it!

For Ebert, therefore, the question 'majority government or revolution?' answered itself. The outcome of the Bolshevik October Revolution was chaos and violence, terror and civil war. Given the circumstances, it was to be expected that a revolution in Germany might well take the same course. Thus the Social Democrats could not permit themselves to strive for revolution, but had to put their weight behind a peaceful reforms and back a class compromise with the moderate groups within the bourgeoisie.

Before the war, a majority of the party would have condemned such a policy as a betrayal of the fundamental Marxist principle of class struggle. The experience of class cooperation during the 'truce' and within the Interparty Committee had changed the situation. Nonetheless, the shift from parliamentary cooperation with the bourgeois centre to official participation in government was still going to require a political decision. This decision was made easier—indeed, made possible—by the fact that the dogmatic Marxists had left the party after the majority had voted to approve the war credits. This split *did* represent a burden on the social democratic movement and a handicap for the parliamentary democracy desired by a majority of Social Democrats. At the same time, however, it was something quite different. It was the very precondition of parliamentary governance, which was inconceivable without a coalition between the moderate elements within the bourgeoisie and the working class. It took the war, the splitting of the party, the Russian October Revolution, and the certainty of Germany's military defeat to convince the MSPD that it was necessary to take the decisive step towards a democratic Germany. The party committee and the parliamentary fraction took this step on 23 September by approving Ebert's course with a clear majority.

Ebert's speech to his party colleagues was based on consultations between Majority Social Democrats and Progressives in the Interparty Committee the day before. The Centre went along with most of the arrangements, including the agreement to general direct suffrage for all federal states and the evacuation of all occupied territories. But against the decisive point, the change to a parliamentary monarchy, the party of political Catholicism was still stubbornly resistant, even against the will of Erzberger. All too deep, for many delegates, was the fear that the rule of the parliamentary majority would cost the Catholic minority more political influence than under the constitutional system.

It also did not help that the Social Democrats wanted a change of chancellor. Hertling had shown himself to be as weak as Michaelis when dealing with the Army High Command and therefore not the right man to pursue the kind of peace agenda the MSPD wanted. Only on 28 September, when the National Liberals joined the call for full parliamentary rule, did the Centre yield, promising to accept parliamentarization and the appointment of a new chancellor endorsed by the majority.

Before the Reichstag majority could turn words into deeds, however, the Army High Command intervened and compelled both a change of chancellor and the shift to parliamentary government. On 14 September Austria-Hungary, acting on its own, had offered peace negotiations to the Allies. On 29 September Bulgaria, another German ally, accepted the Entente's ceasefire conditions. That same day, Hindenburg and Ludendorff convinced Emperor William II that Germany had definitively lost the war and should immediately approach Wilson with an offer of ceasefire and peace negotiations. The responsible party was not to be the OHL, however, but a new government endorsed by the parliamentary majority.

Ludendorff combined his initiative with a *Dolchstosslegende*. 'I have asked H.M. ['His Majesty' (H.A.W.)] to now bring those circles into the government whom we have to thank in great part for the present situation,' the First Quartermaster-General announced to a group of high officers on 1 October. 'Accordingly, we shall now see these gentlemen moving into the ministries. Let them conclude the peace that must now be made. Let them lie in the bed they made for us.'

William II accepted Ludendorff's solution. Since Hertling was not willing to introduce the parliamentary system himself, the emperor accepted his resignation on 30 September and, on 3 October, appointed as his successor Prince Max of Baden, who had already been approved by Ludendorff and the majority parties. The new chancellor, cousin and successor of the childless Duke Frederick II of Baden, had not distinguished himself as a supporter of parliamentary government or of the peace resolution of July 1917. Nonetheless the majority parties endorsed him, confident in their ability to influence his policymaking.

The Reichstag majority fractions were, in fact, much more strongly represented in the new Reich and Prussian governments than under Hertling. The Centre provided the new secretary of the federal ministry of the interior, Karl Trimborn; Friedrich von Payer from the Progressive People's Party continued as vice-chancellor; and the Social Democrats, too, now attained cabinet rank when Gustav Bauer, acting president of the general commission of the Free Trade Unions, took over leadership of newly created imperial labour office. Philipp Scheidemann became secretary without portfolio, a function also assumed by other leading parliamentarians such as Adolf Gröber and Matthias Erzberger from the Centre, as well as Conrad Haussmann, one of the 'discoverers' of Prince Max, from the Progressive People's Party. Otto Fischbeck, Haussmann's party colleague and president of the Interparty Committee, became Prussian minister of commerce. From the ranks of the National Liberals came the new secretary of the office of the judiciary, Paul von Krause, and Robert Friedberg, vice-president and president incumbent of the Prussian ministry, who regularly participated in the meetings of the federal cabinet.

In early autumn 1918, shortly before the change to the new government and governmental system, Paul von Hintze, secretary of the foreign office from the beginning of July to the beginning of August, spoke to Vice-Chancellor von Payer about a 'revolution from above'. According to Hintze, a 'revolution from above' was the only way to prevent a 'revolution from below'. For those involved at the time, the closest thing to a 'revolution from above' was what the OHL set in motion at the end of September. Parliamentarization, at least in a de facto sense, would no doubt have occurred in October 1918 even without the interference of the military, since the Reichstag majority was pursuing the same objective at the same time, albeit for different reasons. Nonetheless, the concept of a preventive 'revolution from above' can also be used to describe the actions of the party leaders, including those of the Majority Social Democrats.

The Russian example showed what a radical and determined revolutionary minority could do and the disastrous consequences of a *coup d'état* by such a group, an event well-schooled Marxists like Kautsky regarded as a relapse into 'Blanquism', which was generally thought of as historically superseded. Violent acts like the murder of the German ambassador Mirbach by anti-Bolshevist 'Leftist Social Revolutionaries' on 6 July 1918 and the murder of the tzar's family by the Bolsheviks ten days later cast a glaring light on the dynamics of terror and counter-terror. Lenin's statement 'Whoever resists is to be shot' on 21 February 1918, originally referring to men and women of the bourgeois class who refused to join special contingents digging trenches under the supervision of the Red Guard, had long become quotidian practice. Revolutionary rhetoric and action in Russia created fear of revolution in Germany, and they strengthened the resolve of the moderate forces within the working class and bourgeoisie to pre-empt a revolution from below through a peace settlement and a democracy.

The far right reacted to the formation of the first parliamentary government by declaring war against democracy—and against the Jews. On 3 October 1918 the president of the Pan-German League, Heinrich Class, called for the establishment of a 'great, courageous and dashing national party and the most ruthless war against Jewry, upon whom all of the only too justified anger of our good and misled people must be deflected.' In an article co-authored with Class for the League's official (since 1917) *Deutsche Zeitung* on 15 October, Baron von Gebsattel, Class's deputy, wrote that he and many like-minded people considered the new administration illegitimate and would do everything to bring it down. After the Jews had been so long active 'on behalf of the most extreme radicalization of Prussian suffrage', they had now once again been the real 'driving force' behind the 'bloodless coup' in Berlin. Democratic ideas were 'poison', and they were poison 'of Jewish origin'. The Jewish spirit of 'corrosion' (*Zersetzung*) was 'a real thing, not bound by good or evil will, a veritable law of nature that, as the legacy of a centuries-long development, is inseparably bound up with Jewry'.

The Pan-German diatribes against the Jews reached a climax at the congress of the group's leadership and executive committee on 19 and 20 October 1918 in Berlin. In the name of his friend Gebsattel, who was ill, Class called upon the audience 'to use the situation for fanfares against Jewry and the Jews themselves as lightning rods for all injustices'. Only when all available forces and means were exploited could 'fear and terror' be successfully stirred up among the Jews. Near the end of his speech, the president assured his listeners: 'I will not shrink from any means and direct myself in this respect according to the words of Heinrich von Kleist . . . : *Schlagt sie tot, das Weltgericht | fragt Euch nach den Gründen nicht!*'*

The formation of the cabinet of Prince Max of Baden represented a de facto parliamentarization, not yet the legal-constitutional introduction of parliamentary rule. The formal change from constitutional to parliamentary monarchy took place on 28 October 1918 through constitutional amendment. From this moment forward, the chancellor was dependent on the confidence of the Reichstag. If the Reichstag expressed its lack of confidence in him, he was compelled to resign. The chancellor became responsible for all acts of political significance performed by the emperor in the exercise of his constitutional powers. Thus the emperor's military command authority, to the extent it involved acts of 'political significance', was also placed under the control of parliament. Another constitutional amendment was hardly less important: no war could be declared nor peace concluded without the consent of the Reichstag.

While still preserving a monarchical form of government, the 'October reforms' transformed Germany into a democracy of the Western type, comparable to Great Britain, Belgium, the Netherlands, and the Scandinavian monarchies.

* 'Strike them dead! On Judgement Day | your reasons won't be questioned.'

The empire's fundamental contradiction, the antinomy between economic and cultural modernity on the one hand and the backwardness of its pre-parliamentary system of government on the other, was abolished on 28 October 1918. At least on paper.[40]

FROM REICH TO REPUBLIC

On 4 October 1918, immediately following its appointment, Max of Baden's administration, pressured by the OHL, submitted a request for an armistice to President Wilson. After messages had been sent back and forth several times, the final answer came on 23 October. Robert Lansing, the American secretary of state, demanded Germany's complete surrender and, in barely coded language, the abdication of William II. Thereupon the OHL called for an end to the negotiations with the USA and a continuation of the war 'with the utmost determination'. Given the military and political circumstances, this notion was an illusion and can only be interpreted as an attempt by Ludendorff to escape responsibility. When, on 24 October, the OHL sent a general telegram to the troop leaders ordering the continuation of hostilities, it was consciously provoking a showdown with the new parliamentary government. The latter petitioned the emperor to dismiss Ludendorff, which William II did on 26 October. The new First Quartermaster-General and de facto head of the OHL was General Groener, a native of Württemberg.

On 29 October, one day after he had signed the laws amending the constitution, William II, on the advice of Hindenburg, left Berlin for the General Headquarters in the Belgian town of Spa. Ernst Troeltsch, a keen observer of the events of the time, regarded this step as nothing more and nothing less than the final splitting of the government. 'The monarchic-military and the parliamentary-bureaucratic authorities were utterly divided and at war.' Indeed, there can be no doubt about the meaning of the emperor's departure. 'At the moment, it might well have been simply an instinctive reaction—the Hohenzollern monarchy, in the hour of danger, seeking to return to its military origins,' writes the historian Wolfgang Sauer. 'But, at the same time, this decision meant that the old powers severed their bond, formed so recently and with such difficulty, with the people's representatives and made the rash attempt to restore the old military monarchy.'

The most serious challenge to the new parliamentary government came not from the army, however, but from the navy. The leadership of the naval forces took the cessation of submarine warfare on 20 October as an opportunity to announce that the measure restored its 'operative freedom'. When the chancellor received news of this announcement from Admiral Scheer, he was unable to assess its implications. Nor was it intended that he do so. The plan was for the navy, which had not seen action since the battle of the Skaggerak (Jutland) at the end of May 1916, to write history once again and deal Britain a severe blow. It was a question of 'honour'. Heavy German losses, as well as conflict with the Reich leadership and the Reichstag majority sustaining it, were accepted as the necessary price. The navy command pursued its own foreign policy, and in a way that can be seen as a coup attempt.[41]

That the attempt failed was the result of resistance among the sailors. The revolt began on 29 October in a row of ships lying in the roads off Wilhelmshaven. The navy command took harsh counter-measures, but only succeeded in making things worse. On 1 November Kiel became the centre of the sailors' uprising. Dockyard workers joined the protests on 3 November. On the following day, at the request of Admiral Souchon, the commanding officer and governor of Kiel, the government intervened, sending Secretary Conrad Haussmann and the military expert of the Social Democratic Party fraction, Gustav Noske, to the city on the Baltic. Noske was able to pacify the rebellious sailors with a promise of amnesty, but he did not succeed in containing the unrest. On 4 November only Kiel was in the sailors' hands. Two days later Lübeck, Brunsbüttel, Hamburg, Bremen, and Cuxhaven were, too.

On 7 November the mutiny turned into revolution. The Wittelsbach throne was the first to fall. The Independent Social Democrat Kurt Eisner, a journalist from Berlin, seized power in Munich as the head of that city's workers' and soldiers' council, declaring Bavaria a 'free state' on the next day. Brunswick fell—also on 7 November—into the hands of sailors from Kiel and soldiers from the vicinity who had joined them. On 8 November Cologne, too, was taken over by a workers' and soldiers' council.* The mayor, Konrad Adenauer, was the first member of the city administration to 'accept the facts of the new situation without hesitation'. On the evening of the same day, the Prussian ministry of war listed the names of nine more cities that had gone 'red', among them Halle, Leipzig, Düsseldorf, Osnabrück, and Stuttgart.

While revolutionary unrest spread throughout the country, Berlin was the scene of a struggle over the emperor's abdication. The Majority Social Democrats, though republicans in principle, had long since become 'reasoned' or 'practical monarchists' (*Vernunftmonarchisten*). Distinguishing between the person of the monarch, who stood in the way of peace, and his office, they were willing to preserve the monarchical form of government for the time being. On 5 November *Vorwärts* declared its support for this social-democratic pragmatism: 'The prospect of having to mess around with royalist Don Quixotes for perhaps thirty years in a new republic, thereby setting back necessary developments, is not among the most pleasant of notions.'

William II's abdication was demanded not only—circuitously—by Wilson, but also—openly—by the sailors in Kiel. The first prominent Social Democrat to

* [Translator's note: the workers' and soldiers' councils are also frequently referred to as 'soviets'.]

declare on the matter was Philipp Scheidemann, who had written to the chancellor on 29 October requesting that the emperor voluntarily renounce the throne as a way of gaining more tolerable conditions for a ceasefire and peace. On 6 November party leader Friedrich Ebert, in an interview with Groener, urged William's abdication and the assignment of the regency to one of the imperial princes. To the chancellor he declared (if Prince Max quotes him correctly) on 7 November that, if the emperor did not step down, social revolution was unavoidable. 'But I don't want it; in fact, I hate it like sin.'

Ebert may have expressed himself somewhat differently in reality, but there was no doubt about his basic attitude. Once revolution broke out in Germany, there was no guarantee that it would not take a course similar to the revolution in Russia. As in Russia, moreover, radical social upheaval in Germany would prompt an allied intervention. Ebert saw things no differently than Groener, who, on the evening of 8 November, succeeded in persuading Hindenburg that the 'plan of a march on the home country', as contemplated by a minority of officers, was hopeless. 'In addition to certain civil war, there would also be the continuance of the bloody struggle with the Entente, which would be sure to press in from the west.'[42]

The 'emperor question' was not the only unresolved problem burdening the parliamentary majority and cabinet in the first week of November. On 24 October the Prussian House of Lords had adopted at first reading the bill introducing equal suffrage in Prussia, but it was uncertain that the House of Representatives would do the same. Under pressure from the majority parties, the mitigation of the war conditions proceeded apace. Karl Liebknecht, who had been condemned to four years in prison by the high military tribunal in July 1916 for attempted treason, was released on 23 October, and Rosa Luxemburg was released from preventive detention on 8 November. On the same day, the war cabinet followed the suggestion of Secretary Haussmann to release the sailors arrested during the 1917 navy mutiny. But the relaxation of the freedom of assembly, decreed on 2 November by the Prussian minister of war, Heinrich Scheüch, proved to be nothing more than a piece of paper. On 7 November General von Linsingen, regional commander of the Marks of Brandenburg, issued a ban on the formation of workers' and soldiers' councils as well as on gatherings of the USPD.

For the Social Democrats, this ban was the last straw. On the evening of 7 November the executive committees of the party and fraction placed before the war cabinet an ultimatum demanding the withdrawal of the ban, extreme forbearance on the part of the police and military, a reshuffle of the Prussian government to accord with the Reichstag majority, the strengthening of Social Democratic influence in the government of the Reich, and, finally, the abdication of the emperor and the renunciation of succession on the part of the crown prince.

On the evening of 8 November William II was still emperor of Germany and king of Prussia. Nonetheless, the Social Democrats announced publicly what Secretary Scheidemann had declared in the war cabinet the evening before: that the SPD did not wish to leave the government before the conclusion of a ceasefire agreement (the German negotiators, led by Matthias Erzberger, had left Berlin on 6 November but had not yet reached Allied headquarters; the armistice was not signed until 11 November in the forest of Compiègne). In extending its ultimatum, however, the MSPD could point to several successes in negotiations with the government and the majority parties. Equal suffrage on the basis of proportional representation was to be introduced per federal law in Prussia and the other states of the Reich; Prussia was to be immediately parliamentarized; and Social Democratic influence in the federal government was to be increased. In addition, the Majority Social Democrats were able to announce that the latest call-up of soldiers, which was stirring a great deal of public controversy, had been cancelled.

A further, last-minute concession came from the bourgeois majority parties on the evening of 8 November: the Centre and the Progressive People's Party agreed to the introduction of female suffrage. Both parties now also joined in the call for the emperor to step down, and even the National Liberals let it be understood that they would endorse an abdication. Thus the Social Democrats found themselves in a key strategic position, and they were able to take advantage of it. As an anonymous delegate from the Progressive People's Party frankly admitted to the midday edition of the *Berliner Zeitung*: 'In these times, Germany cannot be governed without the Social Democrats; otherwise the revolution would not proceed along an orderly and peaceful path, but along a Bolshevist path with all the horrors of civil war.'

The revolution reached the capital of the Reich on 9 November. Once again, developments were accelerated by the actions of General Linsingen, who arrested one of the leaders of the Revolutionary Shop Stewards, Ernst Däumig, and set up security posts in the large factories. Informed by party confidants in the plants that the Berlin workers were now also heading for the streets, Otto Wels, the district secretary, declared a general strike at 9 a.m. on 9 November in the name of the SPD and called the workers to a 'decisive battle under the old common banner'. One hour later Scheidemann resigned from his office as secretary. In a meeting of the Social Democratic parliamentary fraction, which commenced at the same time, Ebert could report that negotiations with the Independent Social Democrats and the workers had already been conducted. The SPD wished to cooperate with the workers and the soldiers in any necessary undertaking and then 'take over the government, completely and totally, like in Munich, but without bloodshed, if at all possible'.

The MSPD profited greatly from the fact that competing organizations among the workers had only limited power to act at this moment. The USPD was unwilling to make any agreement without its party leader Hugo Haase, who was in Kiel, and the Revolutionary Shop Stewards on the party left wing were not planning their move until 11 November. This temporary organizational and strategic vacuum to the left of the SPD was accompanied by a veritable vacuum in the military planning. There were almost no front-line troops in Berlin on 9 November, only three rifle battalions, and of these, it was none other than the Naumburg Rifle Battalion, considered especially loyal to the emperor, that took the initiative in seeking contact with the MSPD. Otto Wels seized the chance, and with resounding success. The soldiers responded enthusiastically to his call to join the people and the Social Democratic Party.

The news that the Naumburg Rifle Battalion had gone over to the revolution fell like a bomb on the chancellor's palace and the General Headquarters. Prince Max now knew that his government was no longer tenable. At about 11 a.m. he learned by telephone from distant Spa that the emperor had decided to abdicate. When, half an hour later, William's official declaration had still not been received, the chancellor took the initiative and announced the intention of the emperor and king over the Wolff Telegraph Agency. He himself, Prince Max, would remain in office until the question of the regency was resolved, would propose to the regent that Ebert be appointed to the chancellorship and that a law be passed for immediate elections to a Constituent National Assembly, which would then settle the German people's future form of government.

By 9 November, however, it was too late to rescue the monarchy, even through a regency. At 12.35, a delegation from the SPD led by Ebert appeared at the chancellor's palace, where Prince Max was meeting with the cabinet, and demanded the handover of power. This was necessary, the leader of the MSPD explained, in order to preserve the public order and avoid bloodshed. The Independent Social Democrats were united behind the majority in this question, he said, and it was possible that they would participate in the new government. Representatives of the bourgeoisie might also join, though the predominance of the Social Democrats would have to be assured. When the chancellor remarked that the question of the regency still had to be settled, Ebert replied that it was too late. Then Prince Max proposed that Ebert assume the chancellorship, whereupon the latter, after a short moment of hesitation, accepted.

At first, the Social Democrats also demanded the office of minister of war and the military command in the Marks of Brandenburg. But when Minister Scheüch, pointing out that the armistice negotiations were under way, proposed that he remain in office with a Social Democratic undersecretary at his side and a Social Democratic official at the side of the commander-in-chief of the Marks, the leaders of the delegation accepted. They also agreed that the secretary of the foreign office, Wilhelm Heinrich Solf, should remain in office. Then, after a short private consultation with the state secretaries, Prince Max of Baden took the revolutionary step of handing over the power of government, transferring to Ebert, as the latter put it in his first proclamation to the German people, 'the pursuance of the duties of imperial chancellor with the approval of all the ministerial secretaries'.

Thus, for the first time, a 'man of the people' stood at the head of the German Reich. Ebert was born in Heidelberg on 4 February 1871, the son of a master tailor. After a basic education at the primary school, he became a saddle-maker's apprentice, then travelled throughout Germany as a journeyman saddler, joining a trade union and the Social Democratic Party. In 1893 he became the editor of the party newspaper in Bremen, beginning a political career that would lead him, a gifted organizer, to the Reichstag by 1912 and to the head of the SPD (an office he shared with Hugo Haase) after Bebel's death the following year. Ebert was neither an ideologue nor a man of bold vision. He was a sober pragmatist, and one of the first within his party to realize that Germany was headed for a catastrophe unless the moderate forces within the labour movement and the bourgeoisie made an effort towards compromise and mutual understanding.

Philipp Scheidemann, born in Kassel in 1865, a printer by trade, from 1913 one of the three heads of the SPD Reichstag fraction and from October 1917 joint chairman of the SPD, did not fundamentally differ from Ebert in his view of the situation. On 2 October 1918, however, the gifted orator warned his party against 'entering into a bankrupt enterprise in this moment of greatest desperation'—that is, against joining Prince Max of Baden's cabinet. And on 9 November, too, he demonstrated greater sensitivity to the mood of the masses than Ebert. At about two in the afternoon, he proclaimed the German Republic from a balustrade of the Reichstag building, two hours before Karl Liebknecht, standing on the balcony over the portal of the royal palace in Berlin, proclaimed the 'free socialist republic of Germany'. Ebert was outraged at his colleague's announcement, wanting the freely elected constituent assembly to decide the question of Germany's form of government. But the jubilation of the crowd proved Scheidemann correct. The masses expected a demonstrative break with the old system of rule, which had led Germany to its current pass.

Ebert emphasized more the continuity than the break. Such signs were important above all to the government officials, judges, officers, and with them the German bourgeoisie. In an announcement on 9 November, the newly 'appointed' chancellor assured the government agencies and bureaucrats that the new government had 'taken over the leadership and duties in order to protect the German people from civil war and famine and to carry out its just demands for self-determination'. The government could fulfil these tasks only 'if all civil servants and agencies in the city and countryside lend a helping hand'. He, Ebert, was aware that many would find it difficult to work with the new men.

> But I appeal to their love for our people. A failure of organization in this difficult hour would deliver Germany over to anarchy and the worst kind of misery. Continue with me, therefore, to help the Fatherland by means of fearless and untiring labor, each at his post, until the hour of relief has come.[43]

The new government of which Ebert spoke did not yet exist at this time. Delegations from the MSPD and USPD were negotiating over its formation during the afternoon of 9 November while sporadic but intense fighting took place at the Marstall and the university. The starting point for the talks was Ebert's proposal that both parties be equally represented in the cabinet, to which members of the bourgeois parties could be admitted as special ministers. Among the Independents, however, scruples against cooperating with the 'government socialists' were still very strong. Liebknecht attempted to commit the fraction to the demand for 'all executive, all legislative, all judicial power to the workers' and soldiers' councils', which meant a system similar to that of the Russian soviets and a rejection of a constituent national assembly.

The USPD initially adopted this call, but the majority party rejected it out of hand: 'If this demand is aiming at a dictatorship of one part of one class, behind which the majority of the people does not stand, then we must reject it, since it does not accord with our democratic principles.' The USPD's wish to exclude the bourgeoisie was also denied, with the justification that such a step would considerably endanger the national food supply, if not lead to its complete interruption. The MSPD also declined the USPD's desire to participate in the government only until the armistice was concluded, insisting that cooperation between the socialist camps was necessary at least until the constituent assembly was in place. The USPD's catalogue of demands bore the mark of Liebknecht and the Revolutionary Shop Stewards. After Haase returned from Kiel on the evening of 9 November, more moderate voices prevailed. On the morning of the next day, the Independents agreed to accept bourgeois special ministers as technical assistants, on condition that one member from each of the Social Democratic parties monitor the activities of each special minister. The USPD gave up the idea of a provisional cabinet and declared that the question of the constituent assembly should only be addressed after the consolidation of the post-revolutionary situation. But the political power 'must lie in the hands of the workers' and soldiers' councils', which were 'to be straightway convened in a general assembly representing the whole Reich'.

The MSPD agreed to these conditions, since the leadership of the USPD no longer fundamentally rejected a constituent assembly and believed it would gain a majority in the planned assembly of workers' and soldiers' councils. The majority party also accepted the USPD's appointees to the government, the moderates Hugo Haase and Wilhelm Dittmann (who had been released from prison in October), as well as Emil Barth as representative of the Revolutionary Shop Stewards. The Majority Social Democrat members of the new 'Council of People's Commissars' (*Rat der Volksbeauftragten*) were Ebert, Scheidemann, and Otto Landsberg, a lawyer originally from Upper Silesia and delegate to the Reichstag since 1912.

Before entering upon its duties, the new Council had to be confirmed by an assembly of some 3,000 representatives of the workers' and soldiers' councils from the greater Berlin area. This gathering took place on the afternoon of 10 November in the Busch Circus. Even though the radicals, led by Karl Liebknecht, did not have a majority, the event was nearly cut short when Barth called for the government to submit to supervision by an action committee from the Revolutionary Shop Stewards and members of the Spartacus League threatened

Ebert. The latter considered the situation so serious that, after leaving the assembly, he secured the assent of the war minister, Scheüch, to protect the new government if it proved necessary.

It did not. The soldiers' representatives, whom Otto Wels had committed to the MSPD line, warned the Revolutionary Shop Stewards that they alone would form the government if the principle of parity were not also observed in the action committee. Thereupon the Revolutionary Shop Stewards submitted. By a great majority, the assembly elected a fourteen-member Action Committee of the Workers' Council (*Aktionskomitee des Arbeiterrates*), composed of seven representatives each from the MSPD and USPD. Most members of the Action Committee of the Soldiers (*Aktionskomitee der Soldaten*), also fourteen in number, had no party affiliation. The next day representatives from both committees formed the Executive Council of the Greater Berlin Workers' and Soldiers' Council (*Vollzugsrat des Arbeiter- und Soldatenrates Grossberlin*), which was to monitor the Council of People's Commissars until the convention of the general assembly of workers' and soldiers' councils. Finally, at Müller's motion, the assembly confirmed the Council of People's Commissars in the line-up agreed upon early that afternoon. Late in the evening on 10 November, the MSPD and USPD reaffirmed their coalition agreement in the imperial chancellery. Germany once again had a government.[44]

THE ORIGINS OF THE REVOLUTION FROM BELOW

On 10 November 1918 the left-liberal *Berliner Tageblatt* published a commentary on the recent events that did not stint on superlatives. 'Like a sudden typhoon,' wrote the editor-in-chief, Theodor Wolff,

> the greatest of all revolutions has brought down the regime of the Emperor with everything that belonged to it, above and below. We can call it the greatest of all revolutions, for never has such a firmly built bastille, ringed with such strong walls, been taken in one attack. Only one week ago there was a military and civil administrative apparatus so ramified, so enmeshed and deeply rooted, that its rule seemed secure for many ages. The grey automobiles of the officers raced through the streets of Berlin. The guards stood in the city squares like columns of power. A giant military organization seemed to embrace everything, and an only seemingly undefeated bureaucracy sat enthroned in the government offices and ministries. Yesterday morning that was all still there, at least in Berlin. Yesterday afternoon it was all gone.

Actually, some of it was still left. On the same 10 November, a Sunday, the inhabitants of Berlin took their usual stroll in Grunewald, as Ernst Troeltsch remarked.

> No elegant toilettes, just the citizenry, many dressed with intentional simplicity, no doubt. Everybody somewhat subdued, like people whose fate is being decided somewhere far away, but nonetheless calm and content that everything came off so well. The trams and subways ran as usual, the pledge that everything was in order for the immediate requirements of life. On all faces was written: 'Salaries are still being paid.'

In truth, 9 November 1918 was far from being a total collapse. Public offices continued to function as they had before. The fact that they had been taken over by local workers' and soldiers' councils, most of them firmly in the hands of the Social Democrats, hampered them less than it gave them a new legitimacy. The courts, gymnasia, and universities were hardly touched by the revolution. The OHL became the partner (albeit not yet a fully equal one) of the Council of People's Representatives already on the evening of 10 November. In a telephone conversation that became legendary, Groener claimed to have proposed an anti-Bolshevist 'alliance' to Ebert, who supposedly accepted. Everything seems to indicate that the First Quartermaster-General indeed made such an offer to the head of the Council of People's Commissars. Whatever Ebert's answer really was, he needed the help of the army leadership in bringing the troops home as rapidly and smoothly as possible, since demobilization was required for a smooth and rapid transition from a wartime to peacetime economy. For this, if for no other reason, the People's Commissars helped see to it that a collapse of the German military did not follow on the heels of the collapse of the German Reich.

What actually collapsed in November 1918 was the political system of the authoritarian state, which found its highest expression in the princes of the Reich and the individual German states. Only minorities were still backing the old order in the autumn of 1918, and the number of those prepared to defend the monarchy by force of arms was minuscule. But royalists did exist. There were more of them among the Protestants than among the Catholics, and nowhere were they as strong as in Prussia east of the Elbe. Although sovereigns had everywhere stood at the head of the church, an inner affinity to the unity of throne and altar and to the prince as the *summus episcopus* was above all a characteristic of German and especially northern and eastern German Lutheranism. It was not coincidentally Bruno Doehring, court chaplain and pastor of the cathedral in Berlin, who, in probably his last war sermon on 27 October 1918, called Wilson's demand for William II's abdication a 'satanic idea' and intoned: 'The monarchy in Prussia is a thousand times more than a political question for us Evangelicals. For us, it is a question of faith.'

Speaking of Germany after the First World War, Max Weber remarked that the 'history of the collapse of the authority legitimate until 1918' revealed 'how the war's destruction of traditional ways of life and the loss of prestige through defeat, in connection with the systematic habituation to illegal behaviour, contributed *equally* to undermining obedience to army and labour discipline and thus prepared the overthrow of the regime.' The sociological situation can be expressed in the argument that, by autumn 1918, the German Reich had largely lost the 'most common form of legitimacy today', namely 'belief in legality' (*Legalitätsglaube*), a resource of authority Weber defined as 'conformity to *formally* correct rules that have been imposed by accepted procedure'.

The war's erosion of traditional values, the looming military defeat of the central powers, and the spread of 'black markets' in the wake of economic and monetary policy failure—this was the triad of factors that caused, in Weber's astute analysis, the collapse of the Wilhelmine empire. The emperor was the embodiment of the old system. In the view of the broad masses, he was the one who bore ultimate responsibility for the length and the catastrophic outcome of the war as well as for the material deprivations of the people. And since he refused to take responsibility, he had to go. Wilson's 'Fourteen Points' nourished the hope that Germany could look forward to a just peace if it democratized its government. The longing for peace thus promoted the desire for democracy. By autumn 1918 these goals had the support of a broad majority. This majority formed the core of a societal consensus on the eve of 9 November 1918 and in the weeks following. It was not an all-inclusive consensus, to be sure, but nonetheless one that included all classes and confessions in Germany.

A good deal of democracy had, in fact, been achieved by this date. General direct male suffrage had been introduced in Germany at the founding of the Reich in 1871 (and even earlier in the North German Confederation, in 1867). On 8 November 1918 the majority parties agreed to extend this system to all states in the Reich, including Prussia, and to grant the right to vote and to stand for election to women. Furthermore, parliamentary government existed in a de facto sense after 3 October, and was made official on 28 October. However, the high-handed behaviour of the emperor, army, and navy command in the days after the constitutional reform made it clear that the new parliamentary system existed only on paper, and the inter-party agreements on 8 November came too late to alter the course of events.

The revolution from below broke out because the revolution from above, the October regime-change, had failed. This failure was the result of obstruction by the military. This obstruction, above all that of the navy command, made it impossible to preserve the institution of monarchy. Collapse, obstruction, and revolution led to the proclamation of the German Republic on 9 November 1918. This date did not mark the end of the German revolution, but only the beginning of a new period in its history.[45]

7

The Impaired Republic 1918–1933

FRAMING CONDITIONS AND THE LIMITS OF ACTION

When the First World War came to an end on 11 November 1918 with the signing of the armistice at Compiègne, it left both victors and vanquished in a state of deep trauma. It had been a different kind of war from those that unified Germany during the Bismarck era. It was the first in which modern technology—flame-throwers and poison gas, submarine torpedoes and bombs from aircraft—was employed in the anonymous slaughter of human masses. These devices and their effects inspired a horror that lived on among the war's survivors. But they also gave rise to a fascination, born of the discovery of what masses of men and technology could accomplish when they were permitted to cast off the trammels of civilization.

There was no single 'wartime experience', but many. Soldiers had experienced the war differently than civilians, soldiers on the front differently than those behind the lines, officers differently than the ranks, farmers differently than city-dwellers, academics differently than 'simple' folk, men differently than women, adults differently than young people and children. And of course, political alignment contributed decisively to how an individual perceived the war and evaluated it afterwards. Those who had refused already in 1914 to get caught up in the 'war enthusiasm', or who had turned against the war in the course of the conflict, could opt in 1918 for the most radical leftist position, calling for a civil war to end the capitalist order from which the 'imperialist' war had supposedly arisen. For those who affirmed the war as a necessity of nature and maintained to the end that a war for one's country could only be just, peace was little more than an interlude until the next armed conflict between the nations. At the end of 1918, both of these positions represented only small minorities, that of the extreme right no less than that of radical left. The vast majority in all countries, though not converted to principled pacifism, had had enough of war. How long the peace would last depended above all on how just or unjust it was perceived to be.[1]

In expectation of a just peace, Germany had separated itself from its monarchical system at the beginning of November 1918 and become a republic. What a just peace meant, however, was a matter of controversy. All Germans hoped that Germany would remain a unified state with its borders as intact as possible, and with no or only minor war reparations to pay. At the same time, most were aware that Alsace-Lorraine would be restored to France and the Polish-speaking parts of Prussia to the newly created Polish nation. Many looked to the *Anschluss* of Austria to provide a certain compensation for these losses. After the collapse of the Habsburg monarchy, Germany's closest ally in the war, a Provisional National Assembly in Vienna had proclaimed German-speaking Austria a republic and part of the German Republic. This was a solution according to Wilson's idea of the right to national self-determination. In both Germany and Austria the Social Democrats, who justly considered themselves the true heirs of the 1848 revolution, were the most eloquent proponents of a *grossdeutsch* national state. Realistically speaking, however, there could be no reason to expect the victors to permit such a large territorial increase on the part of their defeated foe.

It was more realistic to think that a common antipathy might bridge the gap between victors and vanquished—the antipathy to Bolshevist Russia. On 5 November, when Max of Baden's government was still in power, Germany had broken off diplomatic relations with Russia in protest over Russian payments to German revolutionaries. The armistice agreement of 11 November contained a point that fitted in with Berlin's calculations: with the consent of the Allies, German troops were to remain temporarily in the Baltic region in order to prevent further incursion by the Bolsheviks. The MSPD People's Commissars had more than one reason to emphasize the German–Allied consensus against Bolshevism. In the first place, only a moderate German government could expect a timely lifting of the blockade that still cut off food imports into Germany. Secondly, this very expectation necessarily strengthened the domestic political position of the moderate elements.

And in truth, there were good domestic as well as foreign policy reasons for Germany to disassociate itself from Bolshevism. When Karl Liebknecht—the leader of the Spartacus League, at that time still part of the USPD—attempted on 9 November to commit the Independent parliamentary fraction to the Russian agenda of 'all power to the councils', Eduard Bernstein, who was in attendance, 'was struck as if by lightning: "he will bring us counter-revolution." ' A counter-revolution would have provoked Allied intervention no less than a communist coup, and the war would have recommenced. For the moderates, therefore, democracy, and the Constituent Assembly that was to lay its foundations, represented both an earnest of peace abroad and the alternative to civil war.

Moreover, parliamentary government was a logical consequence of German history. Nobody worked this out as clearly as Bernstein, who, though still a member of the USPD, returned to the bosom of the majority party in December 1918 in order to set an example for the reunification of the Social Democrats. (He did not leave the Independents until March 1919, when the USPD banned such double memberships.) In his 1921 book *Die deutsche Revolution, ihr Ursprung, ihr Verlauf und ihr Werk*,* Bernstein, then 71 years old, sought to understand and explain to his contemporaries why the overthrow of the German government was so different from—that is, far less radical than —all great historical revolutions.

He saw two main reasons. The first was the high level of societal development. According to Bernstein's argument, the less developed societies are, the better they are able to cope with measures aimed at their radical restructuring.

> But the more intricate their inner subdivisions, the more elaborate the division of labour and the cooperation of their inner organs, the greater is the risk of great harm to their existential possibilities when the attempt is made to radically alter their form and content within a short time and with violent means. Regardless of how they account for it in theoretical terms, the authoritative leaders of the Social Democratic movement have comprehended this reality and modified their revolutionary praxis accordingly.

Bernstein saw the second reason for the moderate character of the German revolution in the degree of democracy that had already been achieved in the country.

> As backward as Germany was in important questions of its political life due to the continued existence of semi-feudal institutions and the power of the military, as an administrative state it had nonetheless achieved a stage of development at which simple democratization of the existing institutions meant a great step towards socialism. The first signs of this were already in evidence even before the revolution. Under the influence of the workers' representatives who had gained access to the legislative and administrative bodies of the Reich, the states, and the communities, the measure of democracy present at those levels has proved itself an effective lever to promote laws and policies endorsed by the socialist movement, so that even imperial Germany could rival politically progressive countries in these areas.

Germany, to summarize Bernstein's two-pronged argument, was already too industrialized and democratic to cope with a radical restructuring, either after the model of the French Revolution of 1789 or along the lines of the Russian Revolution of October 1917. The classic revolutions of the West, that of the Netherlands, the English Civil War, the American War of Indepedence, and the French Revolution of 1789, had all taken place in predominantly agricultural societies. The same is true of the Bolshevik revolution. The inhabitants of these societies were far less dependent on the services provided by the state and the

* Bernstein, *The German Revolution: Its Origins, Its Course, and Its Achievements.*

communities than were the inhabitants of industrialized nations with a complex division of labour. Consequently, the need for administrative continuity was far higher in developed than undeveloped societies.

The degree of democracy in Germany had a similarly inhibitive effect on revolutionary activity. Since Germany had already known general male suffrage for some fifty years, in 1918 it could only be a matter of extending the vote to women and all the separate states and introducing parliamentary rule in the government. The order of the day was more democracy, not less. The Social Democrats, the empire's staunchest advocates for democratization, would have sacrificed their political credibility if they had deviated from this course and fallen back on the orthodox Marxist 'dictatorship of the proletariat'.[2]

In contrast to Liebknecht, moderate Independents like the People's Commissars Haase and Dittmann did not fundamentally oppose the idea of a Constituent National Assembly. However, they did not want to hold elections until April or May 1919, three or four months later than what the Majority Social Democrats had in mind. They intended to use the intervening period to take precautionary measures securing democracy and socialism. The provisional government, as Rudolf Hilferding explained in the party organ *Freiheit* on 18 November 1918, must summon all its energies

> to perform the deeds that convince the proletariat that there is no way back, only a way forward. Democracy must be anchored in such a way as to make reaction impossible. The administration must not serve as a hotbed for counter-revolutionary activities. But above all, we must prove that we are not merely democrats, but also socialists. Pushing through a series of provisional measures is completely possible. They must be enacted so that here, too, positions can be set up that any capitalist counter-attack will be unable to take.

Hilferding's arguments for preventive intervention in the societal balance of power made a great deal of sense. A socialist majority in the Constituent Assembly was in no way certain, and it was likely that the enemies of democracy and socialism would emerge from their temporary retreat and grow stronger. Nonetheless, as Karl Kautsky, a close political friend of Hilferding, argued, such considerations did not automatically speak for the postponement of elections. A delay might, in fact, weaken the attraction of socialism. On one point the Majority Social Democrats around Ebert and Scheidemann were certainly correct: the longer the Council of People's Commissars, which had no democratic legitimacy, contrived to remain in power, the greater grew the danger of an attempted violent overthrow. This threat came not only from the far left, the direction the leaders of the MSPD tended to fix on, but also from the far right.

Could the Social Democrats have pursued a different, 'bolder' policy in the ten weeks between the fall of the monarchy and the election of the national assembly, a policy that would have placed the desired parliamentary democracy on a firmer societal foundation? Few questions in the history of the Weimar Republic are so controversial. One thing is certain: the People's Commissars were forced to work together with the old elites to a certain extent. In order to achieve rapid demobilization, they could not avoid cooperating with the Army High Command; in order to avoid administrative collapse, they had to leave the greater part of the bureaucratic system intact; and they were compelled to rely on the help of the business community in getting the economy going again.

Still, the cooperation was greater, and the changes fewer, than conditions demanded. It was certainly difficult to find workers for a republican people's militia whose task, in a crisis situation, it might have been to confront 'class brothers' from the ranks of the Spartacists. But virtually no effort was made to set up an armed force loyal to the republic. Even modest reform proposals by moderate workers' councils—the abolition of the compulsory salute when off-duty, the closing of officers' casinos, and the same provisions for officers and ranks, for example—were not undertaken. When Groener and Hindenburg's protested against these suggestions in December 1918, Ebert gave in almost immediately.

In the civil administration, too, nearly everything remained as it had been. Arch-conservative bureaucrats, making no secret of their contempt for the republic (they were especially common in agricultural East Elbia), remained in office despite the complaints of local workers' councils. Even when conservative provincial officials themselves wished to resign, Wolfgang Heine, Prussia's Majority Social Democratic interior minister, exhorted them to remain at their posts for the sake of public order. Eight months passed after the fall of the monarchy before the self-administrative bodies of the three-class suffrage system were replaced by new, democratically elected bodies.

Neither the Majority Social Democrats nor the Free Trade Unions had any intention of interfering with the existing system of private property. Workers' and employers' organizations, headed by Carl Liegen, president of the general commission of the Free Trade Unions, and Hugo Stinnes, a heavy industrialist, agreed on 15 November 1918 to form the Central Cooperative Union of the Industrial and Commercial Employers' and Employees' Federations of Germany (*Zentralarbeitsgemeinschaft der industriellen und gewerblichen Arbeitgeber- und Arbeitnehmerverbände Deutschlands*). The 'Stinnes–Liegen agreement' recognized the unions as wage-partners and introduced the eight-hour day (which, however, was to remain in place only if other civilized countries followed the German example). This agreement meant the de facto abandonment of nationalization, at least for the time being. This was true even in the coal-mining industry, where the socialization commission put in place by the People's Commissars called for nationalization in February 1919.

At no time in 1918–19 was the social dominance of the of East Elbian manorial lords seriously threatened—an elite that had resisted all efforts at democratic and parliamentary reform during the imperial era, perhaps even more tenaciously than the heavy industrialists. No movement arose among the agricultural workers and poor farmers to demand the expropriation of the Junkers. In fact, the Council of People's Commissars agreed to the formation of common councils for landowners, medium and small farmers, and agricultural labourers, which all but guaranteed the existing system of property relations. In January 1919 agricultural labourers were granted the right to engage in union activity and collective wage-bargaining. Nonetheless the manorial districts, one of the administrative foundations of Junker rule, remained in place until 1927. If the revolution cost the Junkers their access to state power, they preserved enough of their societal influence to work effectively towards the restoration of their political power.

The obstacles to land reform were very great in 1918–19, and probably insurmountable. The conversion of large estates into individual farms, as the agrarian reformers around Eduard David had long demanded, would have put the food supply at risk. For a 'state capitalist' solution, that is, the appropriation of the large estates by the governments of Prussia, Mecklenburg-Schwerin, and Mecklenburg-Strelitz and their cultivation by qualified tenant farmers, virtually no preliminary work had been done, and there was little awareness of the urgency of the problem. The proposal of the socialization commission under Karl Kautsky in the middle of February 1919 was no simple nationalization (which would immediately have raised the objection that the Allies, invoking the armistice agreement, could have used state property as a productive pledge to compel reparations). Rather, the experts proposed the creation of an independent economic body called the 'German Coal Community' (*Deutsche Kohlengemeinschaft*), in whose controlling board the management, workforces, federal government, and purchasers of coal were to have equal representation. However, the Social Democrats and Free Trade Unions believed that the time for a change in property relations had not yet come. Instead they followed the motto: 'Reconstruction, and then, where it makes sense, nationalization'. The result was that the coal mines, the bastion of those representing the 'lord in the manor' point of view, remained an anti-democratic bulwark after 1918.

The ruling Social Democrats justified their non-interference in the state bureaucracy by claiming they did not have personnel qualified to replace the current officials. This was true, but it is not sufficient to justify the 'hyper-continuity' that characterizes the German revolution of 1918–19. In taking it for granted that a state agency was to be headed by 'unpolitical' officials, not politicians, the Social Democrats showed that they had basically adopted the logic of the old imperial bureaucracy. And wherever expertise was really required (usually of a juristic nature), the new governments might have had recourse to a reservoir of competence among the liberal forces—a reservoir greater than the Social Democrats were willing to admit. To a certain extent the same was true of the military. Younger officers, prepared for reform, were certainly available, for example in the circles surrounding the *Republikanischer Führerbund*. But they were approached neither by the Council of People's Commissars nor by the coalition governments that succeeded it.

There is no need to speculate about the deeper reason why the Social Democratic People's Commissars concentrated on the most immediate tasks—preservation of the empire's unity, public order, restoration of the economy—and left everything else to the Constituent Assembly: they did not believe they had the democratic mandate to undertake drastic political and social change. 'We were literally the bankruptcy trustees of the old regime', as Friedrich Ebert put it in his report to the national assembly on 6 February 1919, to the lively applause of the Social Democrats.

All barns, all stockrooms were empty, all provisions were fast becoming exhausted, credit was shaken, morale had sunk low. Supported and aided by the Central Council of the Workers' and Soldiers' Councils, we devoted all our energies to fighting the dangers and afflictions of the interim period. We did not pre-empt the National Assembly. But where time was of the essence and the situation required it, we strove to accomplish the most pressing demands of the workers. We did everything we could to get the economy going again . . . If our success was not commensurate with our wishes, the circumstances that prevented it must be justly recognized.

What would have happened to the first German republic if the Social Democrats had thought of themselves less as the bankruptcy trustees of the old regime and more as the founding fathers of a democracy? We can only speculate. Ultimately, it seems very likely that the course of history would not have been radically different. The interim government was not capable of replacing whole classes of society with others. Had it made the attempt, the result would have been the civil war the Social Democrats so rightly abhorred as the worst of all evils. Civil war was certainly no way to bring about democracy, which required an understanding between the working classes and the bourgeoisie. Ebert and the Majority Social Democrats recognized this fact more clearly than most of the Independents, not to mention the far left, whose credo Rosa Luxemburg proclaimed on 20 November 1918 in the *Rote Fahne*, the mouthpiece of the Spartacus League: 'The "civil war", which some have anxiously tried to banish from the revolution, cannot be banished. For civil war is but another name for class struggle, and the notion of introducing socialism without class struggle, by decision of a parliamentary majority, is a ridiculous petty bourgeois illusion.'[3]

FROM THE COUNCIL CONGRESS TO THE NATIONAL ASSEMBLY

From 16 to 20 December, the First General Congress of the Workers' and Soldiers' Councils of Germany met in Berlin. It did so in compliance with a resolution of the Berlin Executive Council, which considered itself only the provisional head of the councils. Even before the congress, the Social Democrats could note with relief that they had a majority of the 514 delegates. Some 300 representatives of the local councils favoured the MSPD, about 100 the USPD; the rest were left-liberal or without party affiliation. Rosa Luxemburg and Karl

Liebknecht did not obtain mandates. A motion to include them as guests in an advisory capacity was rejected by a great majority at the very start of the congress.

Given the balance of power, the most important question the congress had to decide was already decided: elections to the Constituent German National Assembly would take place at an early date. Neither the advocates of a later date nor those of a pure 'council system'—that is, the transfer of all legislative, executive, and judicial authority to the workers' councils—had a chance. On 19 December the delegates took the step that Ernst Däumig, spokesman of the Revolutionary Shop Stewards, had beforehand called the 'death sentence' of the revolution: by 344 against 98 votes, they rejected the proposal to base the new republican constitution on the council system, endorsing instead—by about 400 against 50 votes—MSPD delegate Max Cohen-Reuss's motion to hold elections to the national assembly on 19 January 1919. This was an even earlier date than the one (16 February) the Council of People's Commissars had agreed to on 29 November.

In his arguments, which contributed strongly to the unambiguous outcome of the vote, Cohen-Reuss used the Russian revolution as an example of the domestic and international consequences of rule by council in Germany. In truth, the devotees of a 'pure council system' were labouring under an illusion. It was nothing but wishful thinking to imagine that the masses of a complex industrial society could be mobilized to keep permanent watch over their political representatives. Since only a privileged minority enjoyed the requisite free time, the transformation of council into dictatorial rule was foreordained. The great majority of German workers did not want a dictatorship, not even a 'dictatorship of the proletariat', which they foresaw would quickly become a dictatorship over the proletariat. They wanted to expand democracy, not abolish it. The decision of the council congress to set elections for 19 January 1919 made it clear that there was a broad, class-transcending consensus for a constituent assembly in Germany.

On two other questions, however, the 'leftist' tendencies of the congress emerged clearly. In the first place, a large majority of delegates called upon the Council of People's Commissars to immediately commence the nationalization of qualified branches of industry, especially mining. Secondly, they unanimously passed the so-called 'Hamburg points' on military policy. According to this resolution the Council of People's Commissars, under the auspices of a yet-to-be-elected Central Council (*Zentralrat*) of the workers' and soldiers' councils, was to function as commander-in-chief of the armed forces. All insignia of rank were eliminated 'as a symbol of the demolition of militarism and the abolition of blind obedience', and the wearing of arms while off-duty was banned. The soldiers elected their own leaders, and the enforcement of discipline became the responsibility of the soldiers' councils. Finally, the standing army was to be disbanded and a people's militia set up as expeditiously as possible.

The 'Hamburg points' were a reaction to negligence on the part of the government. If, in the weeks before, the People's Commissars had accommodated the moderate reform proposals of the soldiers' councils, the programme of the Hamburg soldiers' councils, parts of which were utopian, would hardly have been adopted. The delegates would probably also have responded to reasonable objections on Ebert's part if the latter had pushed for more realism. But the leader of the Council of People's Commissars took action only later, under the pressure of an ultimatum from the Army High Command. The 'executive resolutions' decreed by the People's Commissars on 19 January 1919 already showed the influence of the military, especially in matters of command authority. The law concerning the institution of a provisional army (*Reichswehr*), passed by the national assembly on 6 March 1919, no longer contained any trace of the 'Hamburg points'.

The last serious conflict fought out in the council congress was over the distribution of authority between the Council of People's Commissars and the Central Council. The MSPD proposed that, pending a final decision by the national assembly, legislative and executive authority be conferred on the Council of People's Commissars, the task of parliamentary supervision on the Central Council. Questioned by his party colleagues, Haase defined 'parliamentary supervision' to the effect that all laws were to be placed before the Central Council, the more important of them requiring consultation with that body. But the USPD delegates wanted more, namely the 'full right' of the Central Council to accept or reject bills before they became law. The MSPD, believing that such an arrangement would be fatal to the political effectiveness of the Council of People's Commissars, responded with an ultimatum: if the Independents' motion were accepted, the Majority People's Commissars, secretaries of state, and Prussian ministers would resign. After the congress had adopted Haase's concept of 'parliamentary supervision', the USPD's extreme left wing pushed through a boycott of the elections to the Central Council. As a result, only Majority Social Democrats were elected to the twenty-seven member Central Council of the German Socialist Republic.

Thus the People's Commissars of the USPD lost their voice in the government. The formal dissolution of the coalition of 10 November was ushered in by the 'Berlin Christmas battles', the dramatic climax to a two-week conflict over the payment of the 'people's naval division', which occupied the royal palace. On 23 December the rebellious sailors detained the government and 'arrested' Otto Wels, the commander of Berlin, in the Marstall. The ensuing bloody fighting in the vicinity of the palace and royal stables ended in a military defeat for the regular soldiers and a political defeat for the government. The USPD People's Commissars rightly complained that their MSPD colleagues, calling upon the Prussian minister of war for help, had given him carte blanche (and thus put the life of Otto Wels at risk). When the Central Council nonetheless approved the actions of Ebert and his colleagues on 28 December, Haase, Dittmann, and Barth decided to resign from the Council of People's Commissars.

Two days after the collapse of the coalition, the founding congress of the Communist Party of Germany (*Kommunistische Partei Deutschlands;* KPD) commenced in the Prussian House of Representatives in Berlin. The new party was a union of two political camps: the Spartacus League, hitherto the far left of the USPD, and the International Communists of Germany, formed by leftist radicals in Hamburg and Bremen. The mood in the chamber was radical in the extreme. Rosa Luxemburg sought in vain to convince the delegates that it was senseless and dangerous to endorse the motion of Otto Rühle from Pirna committing the party to a boycott of the elections to the national assembly. Endorse it they did, by 62 against 23 votes. The anti-parliamentary thrust of the measure was obvious. Arthur Rosenberg rightly called it 'an indirect call to coup-like ventures'.

On 4 January 1919, three days after the KPD's founding congress came to an end, Paul Hirsch, Prussia's Majority Social Democratic prime minister, dismissed the president of the Berlin police, Emil Eichhorn, who belonged to the left wing of the USPD. Since Eichhorn's security force had joined the rebellious 'people's naval division' during the Christmas battles, his removal was unavoidable. No government could entrust the capital's police force to a man who himself worked for that government's overthrow. The radical left saw things differently, and interpreted Eichhorn's dismissal as an intentional provocation. On the evening of the 4 January, leaders of the Berlin USPD and the Revolutionary Shop Stewards decided to hold demonstrations the next day in protest against the government's move. The manifesto was also signed by the KPD leadership.

The size and spirit of the masses that gathered on 5 January far exceeded the organizers' expectations. But events got out of control on the first day. While the Berlin USPD, the KPD, and the Revolutionary Shop Stewards were discussing strategy in police headquarters, armed demonstrators occupied the press centres of the Social Democratic *Vorwärts* and the left-liberal *Berliner Tageblatt* as well as the publishing houses of Mosse, Ullstein, and Scherl, the Büxenstein printing office, and the Wolff Telegraph Agency. At the same time, police headquarters received reports that all the Berlin troops and even garrisons from other parts of Germany like Frankfurt an der Oder stood behind the Revolutionary Shop Stewards and were prepared to overthrow the Ebert–Scheidemann government by force.

These reports—all false, as soon became evident—sent Karl Liebknecht into a revolutionary transport. He proclaimed that 'given this state of affairs, not only must the strike against Eichhorn be deflected, but the overthrow of the Ebert–Scheidemann government is also possible, and absolutely necessary.' Against the protests of Richard Müller and Ernst Däumig, a majority of the demonstrators called for the continued occupation of the newspaper buildings, a general strike of the Berlin workers, and battle against the government until it collapsed.

The January uprising—often called by the dubious name of 'Spartacus revolt'—was leaderless from the beginning. But it was not without goal. The cry to 'Overthrow the Ebert–Scheidemann government!' had no lesser aim than to block the elections to the Constituent National Assembly and set up the dictatorship of the proletariat. What the Russian Bolsheviks had accomplished in January 1918 by forcibly dissolving the Constituent Assembly, their German followers and sympathizers hoped to achieve before such a body was even elected. Consequently, the Council of People's Commissars had no choice but to accept the challenge of the radical minority of the Berlin proletariat and meet the attack on democracy with force.

This task fell to Gustav Noske, who had joined the Council of People's Commissars only on 29 December, one day after the Independents had abandoned the coalition. Noske, a woodworker by trade, later editor of a party newspaper and, as Reichstag delegate, the naval expert of the SPD, initially had at his disposal only a few Berlin reserve battalions, parts of the Republican Soldiers' Militia, and the Charlottenburg security forces, as well as the newly created 'auxiliary service' (*Helferdienst*) of the Social Democratic Party. These predominantly social democratic groups were joined by right-leaning 'free corps' (*Freikorps*), formed in response to an appeal from the government on 7 January ('Volunteers, come forward!'), and, after 8 January, by volunteer troops from the Army High Command.

At the beginning, armed conflict did not seem inevitable. On 6 January the government, urged by the USPD leadership, initiated talks with the insurgents. The MSPD demanded the immediate evacuation of the occupied newspaper buildings. Kautsky, representing the moderate forces within the USPD, proposed a compromise: the negotiations would be considered to have failed if they did not succeed in restoring full freedom of the press. It is not very probable that the rebels would have accepted this solution; their counter-proposal, the reinstatement of Eichhorn, was impossible. But the attempt was not even made, since the MSPD, and on 7 January the Central Council, spoke against it. The die was cast for violence.

There could be no doubt about the outcome of the struggle. On 11 January, after a bombardment lasting several hours, the occupiers of the *Vorwärts* building surrendered. Government troops stormed the other occupied buildings on the same day, and, on Noske's orders, the free corps organized by the OHL and commanded by General von Lüttwitz began to march on Berlin. With the uprising over by 12 January, there was no compelling military reason for them to enter the capital. But Noske and the OHL, thinking to prevent further coup attempts by setting a warning example, let them in.

Among their first victims were Karl Liebknecht and Rosa Luxemburg, murdered by officers on 15 January. The next day's newspapers claimed that Liebknecht was shot while trying to flee and that Luxemburg was killed by the crowd. In May 1919 a military tribunal acquitted several of the officers who had participated directly in the murders; two other accomplices were given light prison sentences. Those who had actually ordered the killings, the 'murderer central' of Waldemar Pabst at the Eden hotel, remained untouched.

The murdered Communist leaders were partly responsible for the blood spilled in the January fighting. This was especially true of Karl Liebknecht, whose call for the overthrow of the government flew in the face of all reason. Rosa Luxemburg praised the revolutionary masses, although their actions were diametrically opposed to the socialist theoretician's better insight. The January uprising in Berlin *was* an attempted *coup d'état* by a revolutionary minority. Had it not been defeated, civil war would have spread throughout Germany and provoked an Allied intervention.

However, there was no justification for the excesses of violence, which transformed the division between the moderate and radical forces in the workers' movement into a yawning abyss. The Majority Social Democrats availed themselves of the free corps—many of whom were no less ready than the Communists for civil war—more than was necessary. The young officers and students who dominated these volunteer forces had no interest in saving the republic. What drove them on was hatred of everything on the 'left'. It made sense to them to continue on the domestic front the war they had been waging against the external enemy. It was the Marxist left, after all, whom they considered responsible for Germany's defeat.[4]

By 12 January what the far left sought to prevent with their uprising could no longer be stopped: elections to the Constituent German National Assembly. For the bourgeoisie, there could be no more pressing goal than the prevention of a socialist majority. But this did not yet mean that the bourgeois parties had to work to overcome their fragmentation. The newly introduced proportional suffrage gave them the chance to be represented in the national assembly in a strength corresponding closely to their share of the vote. There was little motivation to pool their resources.

Of the two centre parties that had worked closely with the MSPD since 1917, one split immediately following the collapse of the imperial government. On 12 November 1918 the Bavarian Centre Party became the Bavarian People's Party (BVP; *Bayerische Volkspartei*). The founding of the BVP represented an attempt to thwart the shift to the centre that was to be feared from a coalition between Social Democrats, Centre, and left-liberals, and above all from Matthias Erzberger's agenda. For a few weeks after 9 November, the Centre Party itself considered becoming an interconfessional Christian popular party open to Protestants. But then Adolph Hoffmann, a sharply anti-clerical Independent Social Democrat and Prussian minister of education, came unwittingly to the aid of political Catholicism's conservative faction. Hoffmann's radically anti-ecclesiastical educational reforms had an effect opposite to the one intended, making for good propaganda for the traditional Centre.

In its appeal of 30 December 1918, the German Centre Party did emphasize that, as a Christian people's party, its membership was not confessionally restricted. Rather, it formed a common base for the political aspirations of all citizens of Christian faith. In terms of its personnel and platform, however, the party was the same as it had been under the imperial government. It addressed the question of the desirable form of government in language so reserved as to read like a veritable declaration of neutrality: 'Toppled in a violent overthrow, the old order of Germany has been destroyed. Some of the old authorities have been eradicated, others have been paralysed', reads the 30 December appeal. 'A new order is to be created on the basis of the present realities. After the collapse of the monarchy, this order must not take the form of a socialist republic, but must become a democratic republic.'

The Social Democrats' earlier liberal partner, the Progressive People's Party, was absorbed into the German Democratic Party (*Deutsche Demokratische Partei;* DDP). The call to found the new organization was published on 16 November 1918 by a circle around the editor-in-chief of the *Berliner Tageblatt*, Theodor Wolff, and the sociologist Alfred Weber, brother of the more famous Max. The architects of the DDP clearly proclaimed their commitment to the republican form of government and to the renewal of society. They even recommended 'taking up the idea of nationalization for monopolistically developed branches of the economy', and declared war on all forms of terror, 'Bolshevist' as well as 'reactionary'. Several National Liberals also joined the new party, among them Eugen Schiffer, but not including Gustav Stresemann, who had taken over leadership of the National Liberal Reichstag fraction after the death of Ernst Bassermann in 1917. Since Stresemann had advocated large-scale German annexations during the war, the Wolff circle regarded him as unacceptable. For his part, Stresemann mistrusted the 'leftist' proclivities of the intellectuals around Wolff and the *Berliner Tageblatt*.

On 15 December 1918 Stresemann, together with other National Liberals, founded the German People's Party (*Deutsche Volkspartei;* DVP). The DVP differed from the DDP in its stronger nationalist emphasis, the sharp delimitation of its platform vis-à-vis the Social Democrats, and its promotion of farmers' interests. With regard to nationalization, the party's 15 December election announcement stated that it was prepared 'to endorse . . . the transfer to the public authority of appropriate branches of industry, provided that a higher yield for society in general and better living conditions for the workers thereby be created'. On the question of form of government, the DVP kept all options open, but considered imperial monarchy, provided it could be re-established by popular will and through legal means, 'the most appropriate form of government for our people, according to our history and character'. At the same time, however, the party announced its willingness to participate 'in the current form of government, within the framework of its political principles'.

The two liberal parties had similar social agendas. They appealed primarily to the educated strata, independent businessmen, craftsmen, merchants, civil servants, and salaried employees. The right-liberal DVP gained strong and financially powerful backing from heavy industry, while the DDP enjoyed the support of leading entrepreneurs in the electrical industry and commerce, as well as of several banks. The Democratic Party was *the* party of the liberal Jewish bourgeoisie and had the support of several large Berlin and national newspapers like the *Berliner Tageblatt*, the *Vossische Zeitung*, and the *Frankfurter Zeitung*.

What liberalism failed to do at the end of 1918, conservatism accomplished right away: the unification of its forces. On 24 November 1918 the German National People's Party (*Deutschnationale Volkspartei;* DNVP) was founded, absorbing the German Conservative Party and the Free Conservative German Empire Party, as well as two anti-Semitic organizations, the Christian Social Party (*Christlich-soziale Partei*) and the German Ethnic Party (*Deutschvölkische Partei*). The DNVP avoided an open endorsement of monarchy at first; its inaugural platform demanded simply the 'return from the dictatorship of one class of the population to the parliamentary form of government, the only one possible after the recent events'.

Then, in its electoral announcement of 22 December, the German Nationalists proclaimed themselves convinced 'that even under the new democratic government, a monarchical head, standing above the parties as a factor of stability in political life', best accorded with the particular nature of the German people, such as it had developed historically. Nonetheless, the party was prepared to cooperate 'in any form of government created by the National Assembly'. The DNVP had its strongest backing in the Evangelical areas of old Prussia. It was the party of the large East Elbian landowners and the far right wing of heavy industry. It also found supporters among monarchist academics, above all pastors and higher government officials, farmers, small merchants, and 'nationalist' white-collar and blue-collar workers.[5]

In the elections to the Constituent National Assembly on 19 January 1919, the bourgeois parties achieved their most important common goal: the two socialist parties failed to gain a majority of votes and seats. With 37.9%, the MSPD received 3.1% more of the vote than the undivided party had attained in 1912 in the last elections under the imperial government. The USPD achieved 7.6%. The majority party owed its electoral gains not least to agricultural workers in rural east Elbia; its increase in seats was the result of the proportional suffrage system and a far more just division of electoral districts than under the Reich.

The most successful bourgeois party was the DDP, which received 18.5%. This was 6.2% more than its predecessor, the Progressive People's Party, had managed in 1912. The party of left-liberalism profited from the fact that bourgeois voters looked upon it as the future coalition partner of the Social Democrats, whom the DDP would, when necessary, put on the path of economic reason. The two parties of political Catholicism, the Centre and the Bavarian People's Party, also made electoral gains. Together they managed 19.7%, 3.3% more than the Centre had reached in 1912. According to widespread belief, the Centre's gains were primarily the result of Adolph Hoffmann's *Kulturkampf*.

The German Nationalists, the party of monarchic restoration, was among the losers. With 10.3% of the vote, it achieved considerably less than its predecessors, which together had attained 15.1%. The greatest losses, however, were suffered by the right-liberals. The DVP received 4.4%, compared with the National Liberals'

13.6% seven years before. To be sure, Stresemann's party was just getting organized in January 1919; it did not even contest the ballot in fifteen of the thirty-seven electoral districts.

Of the eligible population 83% voted in the elections, down somewhat from the 84.9% of 1912. At the same time, however, the introduction of female suffrage and the decrease in the minimum voting age from 25 to 20 greatly swelled the ranks of eligible voters, adding nearly 20 million, an increase of 136%. The Social Democrats, resolute champions of women's right to vote, did not benefit from their doing so. In the districts where men and women voted separately, many more men voted SPD than women. In Cologne, for example, the Social Democrats received 46% of the male vote, but only 32.2% of the female vote. The beneficiaries of women's suffrage were, along with the DDP, the explicitly church-friendly parties: the Centre and BVP among the Catholic constituency, the German Nationalists among Evangelicals.

There could be no doubt about the will of the majority. Most Germans wanted social reforms within the framework of parliamentary democracy, not political revolution and a radical restructuring of society. Revolution was to be guided as quickly as possible into the channel of peaceful evolution. It was not only bourgeois and farmers who thought so, but also most industrial workers.

The parallels to the last German revolution, that of 1848–9, were obvious. Both were to a certain extent 'unintentional'; the Social Democrats of 1918 were as much accidental revolutionaries as the liberals of 1848. When, at the end of February 1848, the liberals placed themselves at the head of the revolutionary movement, they did not suddenly become revolutionaries. They only wanted to make sure that they, and not the radicals, would be the ones to determine the course of events. Seven decades later, the Social Democrats were guided by the same thought, and, being democrats, they had to act accordingly. In both cases, a minority tried to prevent the election of a constituent national assembly, justifying its actions by claiming that the moderates had betrayed the revolution. Hecker's putsch of 1848 returned, after a fashion, in the 1919 January uprising in Berlin. Lenin's world-revolution was the latter-day echo of Marx's call to revolutionary world war.

The geographic directions of revolution and counter-revolution had, of course, changed. In 1848 the wave of revolution that spread across Europe began with the February Revolution in Paris. At the end of the First World War, it was the Russian October Revolution that provided the impetus. Just as a continuance of the 1848 revolution in Germany would have led to war with autocratic Russia, the Russian solution in post-1918 Germany would have provoked military intervention by the Western democracies. In neither case did things go so far. But the mere thought that they could was an important political factor in both revolutions, evoking fear and serving as a means to stir fear up—fear of the red revolution, of chaos and civil war.[6]

THE SECOND PHASE OF THE REVOLUTION

The election results of 19 January 1919 made only one outcome seem feasible: a coalition between the majority parties of the old Reichstag. While an alliance between the SPD and the DDP alone would have controlled a majority of the seats, the Democrats would have been subject to suffocating pressure from the numerically far superior Social Democrats. Accordingly, the DDP strongly desired the participation of the Centre Party, whose fraction had joined with that of the BVP. On 8 February the Centre opted to enter into a coalition with the SPD and DDP.

One particular solution, conceivable in theory, never came up for debate—a minority government of the two Social Democratic parties. Writing in 1921, Eduard Bernstein explained why there was no alternative to the coalition between the Social Democrats and the bourgeois centre. 'The Republic', he wrote in his book on the German revolution,

> could fight against *particular* bourgeois parties and classes, but not against all of them at once without putting itself in an untenable situation. It would not be able to bear the great burden that had fallen to its lot unless it managed to interest considerable portions of the bourgeoisie in its preservation and successful development. Even if the Social Democrats had gained a numerical majority in the elections to the National Assembly, their enlistment of the bourgeois-republican parties in government would have been imperative for the survival of the Republic. But it was also an existential necessity for Germany as a nation.

The decisions that led to the founding of the German Republic were taken between February and August 1919 in Weimar. The Thuringian 'temple of the muses' was chosen for two reasons. For one, the People's Commissars hoped it would provide the parliament and government with a measure of security and peace that Berlin, for the time being, was unable to guarantee. Secondly, the name of Weimar would tell the outside world that there existed another Germany apart from the Germany of militarism. As Friedrich Ebert told the Council of People's Commissars on 14 January: 'If we link the spirit of Weimar with the building of the new Germany, it will be received with pleasure the world over.' Philipp Scheidemann agreed with him: 'The city of Goethe is a good symbol for the young German Republic.'

On 10 February the National Assembly passed the provisional government law—that is, the provisional constitution—drafted by the secretary of the interior, Hugo Preuss, a liberal constitutional scholar from Berlin. The next day, the delegates elected Ebert as provisional president, who then assigned Scheidemann the task of forming the government. On 13 February the prime minister's coalition cabinet, consisting of ministers from the SPD, the Centre Party, and the DDP, commenced its work.

The new government's greatest domestic challenge was the wave of strikes that shook Germany in the first months of 1919. It began in the Ruhr area at the end of December 1918, spreading into the middle of the country by February. Its goal was the nationalization of the mining industry, although opinions were widely divided as to how this could best be accomplished. Syndicalist workers wanted to take the industry into their own hands; the socialist left wanted 'only' to set up works committees to deprive the management of power, at least for the time being. The strike movement in central Germany ended on 8 March after Scheidemann's government promised legislation introducing works committees and the nationalization of the coal and potash industry. In the Ruhr area, the miners' strike soon widened into a general strike, to which the government responded by sending troops. The most serious fighting took place in Berlin in March. On 9 March Noske, now minister of defence, issued an order without any legal backing: 'Any armed person met fighting against government troops is to be immediately shot.' Some thousand people died in the March uprising in Berlin.

The great strikes in spring 1919 formed the second wave of the German revolution. The radical part of the proletariat tried through industrial action to force the societal changes the revolution's first phase—between the fall of the monarchy and the national elections—had failed to bring. The immediate results of the workers' efforts were modest, compared to the expectations. The 'nationalization' that the government had promised their delegations, and that took shape in several laws in March and April 1919, made no changes in the property relations. In the coal and potash mining industry, syndicates with compulsory membership were set up whose supervisory boards, the Imperial Coal Council (*Reichskohlenrat*) and Imperial Potash Council (*Reichskalirat*), contained representatives from the Reich leadership, the states, mining entrepreneurs, processing industries, commerce, and workers. This kind of 'cooperative economy' did not entail a restriction of the entrepreneurs' power.

Of far greater importance to the workers were the works committees (*Betriebsräte*), introduced by a bitterly controversial law of 4 February 1920. Although the radical left was highly dissatisfied with the measure, it became the Magna Carta of employer–worker codetermination. The law on works committees made Germany into a pioneer of economic democracy.

The two Munich 'council republics' (*Räterepubliken*)* also belonged to the second phase of the revolution. The prehistory of the first began with the murder on 21 February 1919 of the Bavarian prime minister Kurt Eisner by Count Anton Arco-Valley, a law student and lieutenant on leave. Eisner, the head of the Bavarian USPD, was on his way to the Bavarian parliament, where he was intending to announce his resignation as head of the government, since his party had suffered a crushing defeat in the Bavarian elections on 12 January. On the day following the murder, a general Munich council assembly elected a Central Council of the Bavarian Republic, composed of delegates from the MSPD,

* [Translator note: *Räterepublik* is also frequently translated as 'soviet republic' (e.g. Munich Soviet Republic).]

USPD, KPD, and farmers' councils, and appointed Ernst Niekisch, a teacher from Augsburg and leftist Social Democrat, to lead it.

On 3 April the Augsburg councils, inspired by the proclamation of a Hungarian Council Republic by the Communist Béla Kun, came out in support of a Bavarian Council Republic. In the night of 6–7 April the central council in Munich decided to take up this demand. Its announcement, signed by Niekisch, declared the Bavarian parliament, 'this sterile assemblage from the outworn age of bourgeois capitalism', dissolved and the government of the Majority Social Democrat Johannes Hoffmann dismissed.

Within a very few days, the Munich Council Republic managed to make itself into an object of general derision. The breaking off of 'diplomatic relations' with the Reich, a telegraph message to Lenin reporting the unification of the upper Bavarian proletariat, and the announcement of 'free money' towards the abolition of capitalism—these were the highlights of the short-lived regime of the Schwabing literati. On 13 April, Palm Sunday, the Republican Soldiers' Militia, cooperating with the Hoffmann government in Bamberg, marched against Munich and engaged the leftist revolutionaries in heavy fighting. The victors were the 'Red Army' and the Communists, who had initially declined to join what they called the 'sham council republic'. On the evening of 13 April the Munich KPD, led by Eugen Leviné, who came from Russia, took over the leadership of what then became the Second Council Republic. Leviné was acting on his own, without orders from the Berlin party headquarters. After he commenced fighting, however, he received approval and support directly from Lenin. The latter even enquired on 27 April whether the Munich revolutionaries had assumed control of all the banks and taken hostages from among the bourgeoisie.

The attempt to impose on a predominantly agrarian, Catholic, and conservative country the dictatorship of a revolutionary clique—which had little backing even among the inhabitants of the capital—was foolish and doomed from the start. The red terror of the Communists was followed in the first days of May by the white terror of the Württemberg free corps, which came to the aid of the legitimate Bavarian government on Noske's orders and dealt out bloody punishment to the 'Spartacists', both real and imagined. By 3 May the Second Council Republic had been crushed, with a total of 606 killed in the fighting, including 38 government troops and 335 civilians. Eugen Leviné was accused of high treason, condemned to death, and executed on 5 June 1919. Ernst Niekisch got off with a two-year prison sentence.

The Munich council republics were one of the main reasons the Bavarian capital became a bulwark of the extreme right soon after the spring of 1919. Anti-Semitism, which was already strong, was made even stronger by the prominence of Jews in the Bavarian revolution: Kurt Eisner was a Prussian Jew; Eugen Leviné and Max Levien, another of the Communist council leaders, were eastern Jews; and numerous intellectual leaders of both council republics—including the writers Ernst Toller, Erich Mühsam, and Gustav Landauer, who was killed by free corps soldiers—came from Jewish families. For the most skilled of the anti-Semitic activists, Adolf Hitler, who began his political career in the summer of 1919 as an agent of the Reichswehr district command, the conditions in post-revolutionary Munich were highly opportune. Nowhere else would his propaganda have found such a strong echo.[7]

THE TREATY OF VERSAILLES

The defeat of the Second Munich Council Republic brought the second phase of the German revolution to an end. But there was little sign of a return to calm. On 7 May 1919, four days after the Bavarian capital had returned to 'normality', the German peace delegation was handed the 'peace terms of the Allied and associated governments' at Versailles. The Germans, who were still hoping for a 'Wilsonian' peace, a treaty on the basis of the right to national self-determination, reacted with a national outcry.

The terms of the peace included territorial cessions far in excess of the worst fears of the pessimists. It surprised nobody that Alsace-Lorraine would fall to France and the area around Posen to Poland. Beyond that, however, Poland was to receive all of Upper Silesia and the greater part of West Prussia, thereby cutting off East Prussia from the rest of the Reich. Danzig became a Free City under a commissioner to be appointed by the League of Nations when that assembly was established. The Memel district was to be administered by the Entente. In two further areas, East Prussian Masuria and the West Prussian territories east of the Vistula around Marienburg and Marienwerder, the population was to decide whether they wished to remain in Germany or join Poland. The right to self-determination was also accorded to North Schleswig with its part Danish-speaking, part German-speaking population.

In the west, the Eupen-Malmedy district fell to Belgium. The Saar district was not ceded to France, as Paris wished, but placed under the direction of the League of Nations for a period of fifteen years, after which the population was to be permitted to exercise its right to self-determination. In the Rhineland, too, French ambitions were downsized. The peace terms did not strip Germany of its territory left of the Rhine, but divided it into zones, which were to be occupied by the Allies for five, ten, and fifteen years, respectively. In addition, left-Rhenish Germany was to be permanently 'demilitarized'. Germany had to recognize Austria's independence as permanent, a status that could only be changed with the assent of the League of Nations. An article forbidding an *Anschluss* was written into the Peace Treaty of St Germain, which the Allies concluded with Austria on 10 September 1919. This treaty also forbade Austria to send representatives in an advisory capacity to the Reich Council (*Reichsrat*) until the future 'union with the German Reich', as Article 61 of the Weimar constitution had it. In a protocol of 22

September 1919, the Allies forced the Reich government to declare this passage invalid. The National Assembly agreed to this protocol on 18 December 1919.

The terms affecting the German military were also very strict. Conscription was abolished, the army reduced to 100,000 and the navy to 15,000 professional soldiers with extended periods of service. Germany was allowed no air force, submarines, tanks, or poison gas. The general staff was dissolved. With the exception of a few ships, the high seas fleet was to be turned over to the Allies (a condition the German navy skirted by scuttling the fleet at Scapa Flow on 21 June 1919).

The peace agreement cost Germany a seventh of its territory and a tenth of its population, as well as its colonies. If we take into consideration the partition of Upper Silesia in 1921, it lost a third of its coal reserves and three-quarters of its iron ore. The Allies had not yet agreed on a final figure for reparations. For the time being, Germany had to hand over its undersea telegraph cables, nine-tenths of its commercial fleet, and more than a tenth of its livestock. Moreover, it was to deliver some 40 million tons of coal yearly to France, Belgium, Luxembourg, and Italy for a period of ten years. The reparation demands were written into the Versailles Treaty in the fiercely controversial 'war guilt article', which compelled Germany to recognize, along with its allies, that it had been responsible for 'causing all the loss and damage to which the Allied and Associated Governments and their nationals have been subjected as a consequence of the war imposed on them by the aggression of Germany and her allies'.

At first, the governing parties were inclined to reject the terms of the peace treaty. At a demonstration held by the National Assembly at the University of Berlin on 12 May, Prime Minister Scheidemann asked a rhetorical question: 'What hand shall not wither that binds itself and us in these fetters?' The Prussian prime minister, Paul Hirsch, also a Majority Social Democrat, started the slogan 'Better dead than a slave!' The president of the National Assembly, the Centre delegate Konstantin Fehrenbach, called the treaty the 'eternalization of the war' and threatened the Allies with a second world war, first in Latin, then in German: '*Memores estote, inimici, ex ossibus ultor*. [The Latin phrase translates as: 'Remember, o enemies, from the bones [of the fallen] an avenger shall arise' (H.A.W.).] In the future, too, German women will give birth to children, and these children will smash the chains of bondage and cleanse the disgrace that is to be smeared on our German face.'

Nonetheless, only one party within the 'Weimar coalition' adopted an almost completely rejectionist position with regard to the Treaty of Versailles, the DDP. SPD and Centre were divided within themselves. The realists, among them Erzberger, David, and Noske, were alive to the fact that a German rejection would lead to an Allied occupation of Germany, which the nation's weakened military was in no position to prevent. This assessment was shared by Wilhelm Groener, who still held the office of quartermaster-general. The German peace delegation did manage to wring certain concessions from the Allies. On 16 June the victors agreed to a referendum in Upper Silesia to decide the nationality question. They also held out the prospect of an earlier end to the occupation of the Rhineland in the case of good behaviour on the part of Germany. With regard to the question of war guilt, however, the Allies were inflexible, sharply and comprehensively rejecting the German view on the matter.

Before an Allied ultimatum forced the National Assembly to decide whether it wanted to accept the treaty unconditionally, a new government came to power. Having committed himself to rejection, Scheidemann resigned on 21 June. He was replaced by a politically colourless party colleague, Gustav Bauer, the minister of labour, former second chairman of the general commission of the Free Trade Unions, and a personal confidant of Ebert. The DDP, solicitous of its newly acquired nationalist image, did not participate in Bauer's cabinet. The Centre, which did, vacillated between acceptance and rejection of the treaty. On 22 June the Allies refused to accept Germany's contention that it could neither accept sole culpability for the war nor the obligation of extraditing German war criminals and the politicians the Allies considered responsible for the outbreak of hostilities. Once again, the outcome of the decisive vote, which was to take place the next day, seemed completely open.

Two things tipped the scales. The first was a telegram from Groener emphasizing the hopelessness of the military situation. Secondly, the DNVP and DVP declared their willingness to accommodate the Centre by recognizing the 'patriotic motivations' of those—most of the Centre delegates—wishing to vote for the treaty. The National Assembly then voted by a show of hands to empower the government to sign. In addition to the Centre majority, the two Social Democratic parties and a minority of the DDP voted in favour. The German Nationalists, the DVP, a majority of the DDP, and a minority of the Centre opposed the signing. On 28 June Foreign Minister Hermann Müller, the newly elected head of the SPD, and the minister of transport, Johannes Bell of the Centre Party, affixed their signatures to the Treaty of Versailles in the Hall of Mirrors of the Versailles palace, the same place William I of Prussia had been proclaimed German emperor on 18 January 1871.

One of the main reasons German outrage over the 'diktat of Versailles' was so profound and lasting was that the Scheidemann government, against the entreaties of President Ebert, had consciously chosen not to inform the German public concerning the events leading up to the war. This it might well have done, given the availability of the German documents from the July crisis of 1914, which the Council of People's Commissars had entrusted to Karl Kautsky, at that time USPD representative in the foreign office, and Max Quark, MSPD representative in the ministry of the interior. The foreign office papers tell so heavily against the Reich leadership and the Austrian government that one can hardly avoid pronouncing Germany and its main ally primarily responsible for the outbreak of the war. This was precisely the reason a number of ministers, led by Scheidemann, refused to allow Kautsky's documents to be published. The fear was too great that Germany might give the Allies further justification for a hard peace.

In mid-June, shortly before the decisive ballot on the Treaty of Versailles, the Majority Social Democrats, gathering in Weimar for their first post-war party congress, closed ranks behind the prime minister. It was in vain that Eduard Bernstein urged his party colleagues to do justice to historical truth and free themselves from the prison of 4 August 1914. 'When I say the old system is guilty, I am not saying that we, the German people, are guilty. Rather, I am saying that the ones who lied to and deceived the German people at that time are guilty. From the German people I remove the blame.' The debate turned into a tribunal against those deviating from the party line. The sharpest attack came from Scheidemann. He called Bernstein 'an advocate of the devil' who, in his overdeveloped sense of justice, would defend even the imperialist enemies.

The majority of Germans not only repressed the German war guilt of 1914, but also the terms Germany dictated to Russia in spring 1918. The territorial and economic conditions of the Treaty of Versailles were milder than those of Brest-Litovsk. Neither treaty, of course, was just or sensible. The victors' representatives, while working on the preliminary agreements, were under pressure from their nations, who demanded punishment for the former central powers, Germany most of all, and compensation for the losses they had suffered. The victors violated the principle of national self-determination to the detriment of the vanquished. But had the Germans not done the same, when they were victorious? Had they not denied Poland the right to a state ever since the late eighteenth century? And was a viable Polish state even conceivable without access to the Baltic, and thus at the expense of German territory?

Versailles was harsh. But virtually nobody in Germany stopped to think that it might have been a great deal worse. The Reich remained in existence and the Rhineland in Germany. Germany was still the most populous country west of the Russian border and economically the most powerful nation in Europe. In a certain way, its international position had even improved over the period before 1914. The conflict between the western powers and communist Russia meant that Germany no longer had cause to feel 'encircled'. And even in Versailles, the first cracks in the western alliance—between France on the one hand, Britain and the United States on the other—had become visible. Membership in the League of Nations was not open to Germany, but it did not have to stay that way. Germany had good prospects of becoming a European great power again. Sober reflection on the new situation was all that was required to see 'Versailles' in realistic proportions.

But sober thinking was seldom to be found in Germany in the summer of 1919. Versailles provided grist for two historical legends that severely burdened the new republic from its very beginning and prevented a clean moral break with Wilhelmine Germany. The first was the myth of war innocence, which 'nationalist' Germany, with the backing of prominent historians, used to counter the putative 'war guilt lie' of the victors. In the view of the 'right', Germany was not to blame for the war, or at least no more to blame than any of the other nations that had taken part in it. The other myth was the so-called *Dolchstosslegende*, the legend of the 'stab in the back' that the German army, 'undefeated in the field', had received at the hands of the homeland. This story can be traced back to the last year of the war. It was given classic expression by Hindenburg, the last head of the Army High Command, who left office together with Groener on 25 June 1919. On 18 November 1919, speaking before a parliamentary committee investigating the causes of the German collapse, Hindenburg quoted an unknown British general as having said that the German army had been 'stabbed in the back'. The twin myths were already working their poison in the first days of 'Weimar'. There were many views on how Versailles could be revised. That it had to be revised was the unanimous opinion of all Germans from the day the treaty was signed.[8]

THE WEIMAR CONSTITUTION

Compared to the consensus for revision, the constitutional consensus in the German Republic was weak. This was already in evidence during the drafting of the text. The fact that the Social Democrats entrusted the overall control of constitutional matters to the left-liberal Hugo Preuss was both an expression of doubt about their own abilities in questions of national law and a sign of their willingness to reach an understanding with the bourgeois centre. But Preuss was unable to assert his will on significant questions. The 'father' of the Weimar constitution wanted to break up Prussia into smaller states, but ran into staunch and successful resistance from the Prussian Social Democrats, who regarded 'their' state as a bulwark against separatist aspirations in the west and a guarantor of the unity of the Reich. So Prussia remained intact. In two ways, however, the creators of the constitution sought to prevent the kind of hegemony the largest German state had exercised under the emperor. First, Prussia was allowed only two-fifths of the seats in the Reich Council, despite containing about three-fifths of the nation's population. Secondly, the rule whereby the German states were represented in the Council by members of their governments did not apply to Prussia. Half of the Prussian seats went to government officials, half to delegates from the provincial assemblies.

Preuss, who was secretary of the interior from 15 November until 13 February 1919, then minister of the interior until 20 June 1919, aspired to turn Germany into a decentralized unitary state. This provoked the federalists, from the Bavarian conservatives to the Social Democrats now in power in many of the German states. Ultimately, the Reich became more federal than the unitarians wished, and more unitarian than the federalists wished. The Weimar Republic was not a unitary state like the third French republic. The *Länder* were more than mere administrative units. Prussia's separation from the federal government had the effect of destroying the former's privileged status. On the other hand, the Reich Council had far less influence than the Federal Council under the monarchy. The southern German states lost the 'special rights' in matters of military, postal, and tax policy granted to them by Bismarck. Bavaria was the hardest hit by these losses, and there was little indication that the southern German Free State would long accept the diminution of its status.

In another area Preuss was much more successful. On the recommendation of Max Weber, he introduced the office of a Reich presidency. Democratically legitimated through direct election by the people, a strong president would prevent 'parliamentary absolutism' by providing a check on the Reichstag. As a non-partisan, integrating force, he would also both counterbalance the tendency of the party system towards fragmentation and represent the natural point of reference for the professional bureaucracy, itself obligated to be non-partisan, thus securing governmental continuity between the monarchy and the republic.

The conservative aspects of the institution initially provoked sharp criticism from the Social Democrats. In a meeting of the party fraction on 25 February 1919, the SPD veteran Hermann Molkenbuhr referred to the president as a 'replacement emperor' and spoke of the 'truly Napoleonic trick of the people electing the president'. On 28 February, at the first plenary reading of the draft of the constitution, the Social Democratic speaker, Richard Fischer, warned that the proposal gave the president greater and less restricted powers than those possessed by the presidents of the Republic of France or the United States of America. Furthermore, the new constitution should not be tailor-made to fit President Ebert, as the earlier constitution had been tailor-made to fit Bismarck. 'We must consider the fact that one day another man from another party—perhaps a reactionary, coup-plotting party—will stand in this place. We have to prepare against such chances, especially since the history of other republics provides very instructive examples of this kind of thing.'

Such reservations, articulated even more strongly by the USPD, found no resonance within the bourgeois parties. In response to the civil war-like conflicts in spring 1919, the desire for a powerful presidency grew strong, even within the MSPD. Contrary to their original intention, the Social Democrats eventually accepted a long, seven-year term of office, and they did not even resist when the bourgeois parties extended the presidency's extraordinary powers in emergency situations. The third reading on 30 July 1919 scrapped the drafting committee's decision to make measures pursuant to Emergency Article 48 dependent on the parliament's agreement. Instead, it was considered sufficient that the president immediately notify the Reichstag of his decisions. The right of that body to annul the president's measures was not affected by this modification, however.

The principle of parliamentary and representative democracy was not only restricted by the Reich president as a replacement legislative, but also by the possibility of direct popular legislation. The Social Democrats had demanded popular legislation in their 1869, 1875, and 1891 platforms. Consequently, they were now the driving force—despite second thoughts from some party members—behind the introduction of a referendum and a petition for a referendum. The DDP was less enthusiastic about such things than the MSPD and USPD, but nonetheless lent its support, along with some of the DNVP delegates. The DVP was strictly opposed.

Long debates ended in compromise. The Social Democrats' wish for popular ratification of the constitution and a petition for a referendum on the dissolution of the Reichstag were not adopted. But a majority did agree that a referendum should be held when a tenth of the electorate petitioned for one. A parliamentary bill was to be subject to referendum when a twentieth of the electorate so desired and a third of the Reichstag had opposed its passage. In order to annul a parliamentary decision, however, a majority of the electorate was required to participate in the referendum. The SPD, Centre, and DDP erected these hurdles in the third reading in order to make it more difficult for the president to oppose the Reichstag, since the constitutional committee—against the advice of SPD delegate Wilhelm Keil—had granted the president the right to call for a referendum against a parliamentary law.

For a time it looked as though the Reichstag would have yet another competitor in the legislative function, an 'economic parliament' (*Wirtschaftsparlament*). Such an organ was demanded by the Second Congress of the Workers', Farmers', and Soldiers' Councils of Germany in Berlin in April, as well as by the German Nationalists, who revived Bismarck's plan for a profession-based corporative chamber. But the majority of the National Assembly had no interest in such ideas, irrespective of their 'leftist' or 'rightist' provenance. Article 165 (the so-called *Räteartikel*) did provide for an federal economic council with a right to initiate and examine legislation. But lacking veto power, this body had no ability to limit the authority of the Reichstag.

The most important thing about Article 165 was not the economic council, but the codification of the principle of parity between capital and labour, and government recognition of *Tarifautonomie*, the right to free collective regulation of terms and conditions of employment. Generally, however, the National Assembly treated issues concerning the social order with great caution. The constitution made 'nationalization' optional, not obligatory. It allowed freedom of coalition, but not the right to strike, since then it would have had to define the limits of that right.

Several controversial matters of great symbolic importance could not be left open, however. One of these was the title of the constitution. The two Social Democratic parties favoured the 'Constitution of the German Republic', but were unable to prevail against the united front of the bourgeois parties, who insisted upon the 'Constitution of the German Reich'. On the question of the national flag, the USPD wanted red, the MSPD, invoking the legacy of 1848, black, red, and gold. The majority of the Centre and a minority of the DDP also favoured the colours of the German unification movement; the DNVP and DVP, along with the majority of the DDP and a minority of the Centre, desired to preserve the black, white, and red, the colours of the Bismarck empire. After heated debate a compromise was worked out here, too. The Reich colours would be black, red, and gold, but a separate flag was created for the commercial fleet (supposedly for reasons of 'better visibility') with the colours black, white, and red 'with a jack in black, red, and gold in the upper inner corner'. Clearly, not only the political right, but also elements within the 'Weimar' parties mourned the loss of the old Reich.

The most passionate battle was fought over the article dealing with schools. The Social Democrats sought to improve the social position of the lower classes through reform of the school system; the Centre desired to preserve confessional schools; the liberals wanted to curtail church influence in education. These antagonisms proved so tenacious that the SPD temporarily considered abandoning the whole section dealing with basic rights. This the Centre could not do, however, since the catalogue of basic rights included those dealing with matters of religion and religious organizations, rights of paramount importance to the Catholic Church. It was not until shortly before the third reading that the 'Weimar' parties agreed on the solution that made its way into the constitution: the interdenominational school (the so-called *Simultanschule*) was to be the ordinary school type, but it could be replaced by a confessional or non-religious school if the parent or guardian so desired.

This compromise saved the constitutional 'Basic Rights and Obligations of the German People' (which updated and expanded the 'Basic Rights of the German People' in the imperial constitution of 28 March 1849) and assured the Weimar constitution a broad majority in the final vote on 31 July 1919. Of the 420 members of the National Assembly 338 participated, 262 voting for adoption, 75 opposed, and one delegate abstaining. The votes in favour came from the SPD, Centre, and DDP (the 'Weimar' parties), the negatives from the USPD, DNVP, and DVP. President Friedrich Ebert signed the constitution on 11 August, and it took effect on 14 August through proclamation in the *Reichsgesetzblatt.* One week later, on 21 August, the president, National Assembly, and cabinet departed from Weimar. Henceforth Germany was governed from Berlin.

On 31 July Eduard David, the Social Democratic minister of the interior, hailed the adoption of the Weimar constitution: Germany was now the 'most democratic democracy in the world'; nowhere else had democracy been 'as thoroughly realized as in this constitution'. He was thinking primarily of its provisions for direct democracy. The attitude of the public was more one of passive acceptance than of active adoption. It was only in the course of the campaigns of hatred and violence waged by the far right that the constitution was to become a symbol of the republic. The document itself contained no guarantee against its own abolition, provided that the necessary majorities voted accordingly. To the fathers and mothers of the 1919 constitution, clauses limiting the will of the majority would have seemed like a relapse into the authoritarian state.

And yet the authoritarian state was by no means a thing of the past. It lived on not only apart from the new constitution, but also in it and through it. By granting the president legislative powers in vaguely defined emergency situations, the National Assembly provided ample scope for parliamentary opportunism. If the ruling parties were having difficulty reaching a compromise, the temptation was great to shift responsibility 'upstairs' to the head of state. An emergency measure on the basis of Article 48 then took the place of the regular legislative process, the parliamentary constitution giving way to a 'presidential reserve constitution' and the 'provisional dictatorship of the president'. While the Reichstag was authorized to dismiss the chancellor and any minister without naming a successor, the constitution made no provision for it to elect a new chancellor. All that was necessary was that the president's choice of a chancellor enjoy the confidence of the Reichstag. Since the president could dissolve the Reichstag, the parliamentary vote of no confidence was a weapon that would blunt rapidly. The president, not the parliament, had the whip hand.

The new constitution brought the Germans a great increase in personal liberty. But it did not guarantee the preservation of that liberty in difficult times. The 'most democratic democracy in the world' was not only endangered by the powers that rejected and fought it. It was also designed in such a way as to permit its own self-abolition.[9]

THE KAPP–LÜTTWITZ PUTSCH AND THE RUHR UPRISING

In summer 1919, after the signing of the Treaty of Versailles and the adoption of the Weimar constitution, a political calm set in. This was a welcome change for the Bauer government, especially for Matthias Erzberger, the minister of finance. When he entered office on 21 June, he found the government finances in a catastrophic condition. Under the emperor, Germany had financed the war mainly through domestic loans and pursued a credit policy that increasingly undermined the currency. The devaluation continued after the war, exacerbated by the high nominal wages the government, employers, and unions all saw as a kind of panacea against social unrest. As a staunch 'unitarian', Erzberger responded with the reform package that rightly bears his name. In order to assure federal sovereignty in all matters financial, he created a uniform tax administration for the Reich, 'nationalized' the rail system, imposed special taxes on the income and wealth of 'war profiteers', reformed the federal inheritance tax, and introduced a politically highly controversial one-off wealth tax, the so-called 'national emergency levy' (*Reichsnotopfer*) of December 1919. The final measure was a federal income tax, which the National Assembly passed in March 1920.

Apart from the war profiteers, the 'victims' of Erzberger's finance reform were the individual state and local governments. The *Länder* were now dependent on allocations from the Reich, and the municipalities, to a greater extent than before, on loans. This was one of the reasons the plan to control inflation by means of confiscatory taxes did not work. In fact, since businesses shifted the costs to consumers in the form of higher prices, the new revenues exacerbated the devaluation of the currency. Higher prices, in turn, stymied Erzberger's efforts towards social justice. All that survived of his finance reform was the unification of the tax system and finance administration, along with the political consequences that went along with it. The financial disempowerment of the *Länder* placed considerable strain on their relationship to the federal government, and the high indebtedness of the cities and communities, a result of the drastic curtailment of their sources of revenue, was to prove one of the main causes of Germany's financial weakness in the second half of the 1920s.

The political right had long hated Erzberger, author of the July 1917 peace resolution and signatory of the November 1918 armistice agreement. His levies on wealth made the hatred even more virulent. In January 1920, the finance minister found himself compelled to prefer charges against Karl Helfferich, former secretary of the interior, for accusing him of 'habitual untruthfulness' and the constant mingling of his business interests with his political duties. On 26 January Erzberger, leaving the courtroom in Moabit, was shot and badly wounded by a discharged cadet. At his trial on 21 February, the culprit was charged not with murder, but only with causing 'grievous bodily harm'. The next day, the campaign against Erzberger escalated even further with a newspaper article accusing him of tax evasion. Two days later, Erzberger requested to be temporarily relieved of his duties of office.

The trail against Helfferich was concluded on 12 March 1920, the former secretary of the interior condemned for defamation and libel. But the real loser, morally and politically, was Erzberger, whom the by no means impartial judges considered guilty of two instances of perjury and seven instances of corruption. Though he was later cleared of the charges of perjury and tax evasion, the public impact of the sentence was catastrophic. Later that day Erzberger resigned from his office as minister of finance.[10]

That same day, the Reich cabinet learned from Gustav Noske that a *coup d'état* was in the works. According to the defence minister, the wirepullers of the operation were Wolfgang Kapp, general director of the East Prussian *Landschaft*, and Captain Waldemar Pabst. In fact, considerable portions of the Reichswehr were behind the plan, which went down in history as the 'Kapp putsch'. Ever since the Treaty of Versailles went into effect on 10 January 1920, prominent officers, led by General Walter von Lüttwitz, commander of the District Command I in Berlin, had been steering towards a conflict with the government. That the Reich would fulfil the Allied demand to try German war criminals before German courts, if not extradite them, was an idea many officers found intolerable. The reduction of the army to 100,000 men, not yet complete, was an additional grievance. The free corps were most strongly affected, above all the so-called *Baltikumer*, who had fought against the Bolsheviks in Estonia and Latvia after the end of the war with the approbation of the Allies. Noske named one of the free corps by name: Marine Brigade Erhardt.

The civilian wing of the conspiracy consisted of politicians from the far right supported by Junkers and monarchist officials in the old Prussian provinces. Its planning centre was the National Alliance (*Nationale Vereinigung*) in Berlin, founded in October 1919 under Ludendorff's patronage. Its aim was an authoritarian—though not yet monarchical—regime that would actively pursue revisionist policies on the international stage.

Noske's defensive measures proved insufficient. On the morning of 13 March the Erhardt brigade entered Berlin. Kapp seized the chancellery towards seven o'clock. Since most of the generals, including the chief of the office of troops, Hans von Seeckt, considered military counter-measures hopeless, President Ebert, Chancellor Bauer, and most of the ministers had shortly before left for Dresden (whose commanding officer, General Maercker, Noske believed to be loyal). In the meantime, an appeal went out in Berlin proclaiming a 'general strike along the whole line' and calling for the unification of the proletariat. The author was the government chief of the press, the Social Democrat Ulrich Rauscher. The manifesto bore the name of Ebert and the Social Democratic ministers was well as that of Otto Wels, acting chairman of the SPD. At Maercker's reproach, the president and the Social Democratic ministers distanced themselves from the appeal. In fact, probably only Noske had read and approved the text in advance. We can also assume that Wels knew about and had agreed to it.

The danger of a general strike was that it could easily get out of control and turn into civil war. It was all but certain that Communists and syndicalists would not limit themselves merely to fighting for the restoration of the Bauer government. On the other hand, however, a general strike had a good chance of success in spring 1920. An inflation-induced economic boom had brought Germany to near-full employment. Striking workers did not have to worry that their jobs would be taken by the unemployed. A general strike against a military coup and for the constitutional authority of the state possessed an undeniable democratic legitimacy. And there was every reason to believe that a strong signal from workers and employees was necessary in order to convince the bureaucracy to unite against the putsch and to force its leaders to capitulate.

The leadership of the strike in March 1920 was assumed by the Free Trade Unions, in which Majority and Independent Social Democrats were still cooperating. The General German Trade Union Association (*Allgemeiner Deutscher Gewerkschaftsbund* or ADGB) and the Cooperative Union of Free Employees' Federations (*Arbeitsgemeinschaft freier Angestelltenverbände*) were able to organize the deeply divided workers' movement in common action. It was hoped that the Communists, if they could not be moved to cooperate, would at least be held in check. For its part, the KPD first announced on 13 March—the text was drafted by Ernst Reuter, the Berlin party leader—that the revolutionary proletariat would 'not lift a finger for the government of Karl Liebknecht's and Rosa Luxemburg's murderers, which has collapsed in shame and disgrace'. But since many Communists were already participating in the strike, the KPD made a new announcement the next day, now calling the strike the commencement of the battle against the military dictatorship and exhorting Communists 'to be bound and limited in their actions by the goals the majority of the workers provisionally sets for itself'. This was nothing less that an appeal to form the kind of unified proletarian front the party had rejected the day before.

The coup's supporters were limited from the beginning to the conservative forces in East Prussia. Since most of the ministerial bureaucracy refused to cooperate with the Kapp 'government', and since the protesting workers and employees had brought the whole economy to a standstill, the failure of the coup was already foreseeable on 14 March. Thus it is all the more astonishing that the German People's Party, despite all its reservations against a violent overthrow of the government, refused to actually condemn it. Instead, in a 14 March announcement drafted by its leader, Gustav Stresemann, the DVP blamed the 'recent government' for 'disrupting the path of organic development to which we are committed'. As a solution, the party limited itself to calling for the legalization of the 'current provisional government' and early elections. In the ensuing days Stresemann, who saw himself as a 'mediator' between the hostile camps, even spoke personally with Lüttwitz and Kapp.

The republican forces were even more exasperated by the fact that Vice Chancellor Schiffer, who had remained in Berlin (his party, the DDP, had joined the Bauer government again in October 1919), made far-reaching concessions to the coup leaders on 16 March in the presence and with the agreement of several Prussian ministers, including the Social Democrats Hirsch and Südekum: if 'Chancellor' Kapp and 'Commander-in-Chief' von Lüttwitz resigned, a new coalition government would be formed and new Reichstag elections held, including a direct election for president. This would have meant a partial success for the rebels.

The Bauer government, which had now retreated to Stuttgart, did well not to seek compromises. On 17 March, under pressure from the military, Kapp resigned, followed by Lüttwitz. Marching from the government district to the tune of the 'Deutschlandlied', the Erhardt brigade, clad in its usual gear ('*Hakenkreuz am Stahlhelm, schwarz-weiss-rotes Band | Die Brigade Erhardt werden wir genannt*'),* staged a parting massacre among the civilians gathered to protest. Twelve were killed, thirty wounded.

The end of the Kapp putsch was not the end of the general strike. The General German Trade Union Association, the Cooperative Union of Free Employees' Federations, and the German Civil Servants' Association (*Deutscher Beamtenbund*) decided to continue the action until a number of conditions were met. Noske, who was seen as responsible for alienating large portions of the Reichswehr, was not to return to Berlin as commander-in-chief of the troops. The undependable units were to be dissolved, disarmed, and the troops reorganized to make any future coup attempt impossible. In addition, the three groups demanded 'a key role in organizing the new situation'.

* 'Swastika on helmet, band of black-red-gold, | the Erhardt Brigade we are called.'

This announcement was followed on the same day by a nine-point programme by the workers' organization demanding, among other things, the punishment of all those involved in the coup; the fundamental democratization of the administration; the nationalization of the mining and energy industries; a security service organized and staffed by workers; and the resignation of two Prussian ministers, the Social Democratic minister of the interior, Wolfgang Heine, and the Democratic minister of transport, Rudolf Oeser. Heine, it was said, had been too tolerant of reactionary elements, and Oeser too soft on the rebels.

Negotiations between the unions, representatives of the majority parties, and the Reich and Prussian governments led to a partial agreement on 20 March. By this time, Noske and Heine had handed in their resignations. Units of the security police disloyal to the constitution were to be broken up and replaced by dependably republican groups. The socialization commission was to reconvene and prepare for the nationalization of selected industries. The Free Trade Unions then announced an end to the strike. The USPD did not do so until 23 March, after the Bauer administration had granted several further concessions.

The reorganization of the government was completed by 27 March. The colourless Gustav Bauer, whose reputation had sunk even further during the crisis, was replaced by Hermann Müller, one of the two chairmen of the SPD (the other being Otto Wels). Müller, who was born Mannheim in 1876, had learned several languages as a commercial employee, which helped his political career. Long before he assumed the office of German foreign minister in June 1919, he was the informal foreign minister of the SPD, speaking for the party in its negotiations with sister parties in western Europe. To replace the discredited minister of defence with another politician from their own ranks seemed to the Social Democrats neither important nor opportune. After Wels refused the post, it went to Otto Gessler, former mayor of Nuremberg and hitherto minister of reconstruction. A member of the DDP right wing, Gessler made no secret of his monarchist proclivities. General von Seeckt, who on 13 March had very forcefully refused to allow Reichswehr troops to fire on their own, took over leadership of the army.

The new government was not as leftist as the Free Trade Unions desired, and Müller's cabinet bore little resemblance to the kind of 'workers' government' Carl Legien, head of the ADGB, had called for. But such an administration was never more than a chimerical hope. The Weimar coalition could not support a 'trade union state', and it was wishful thinking to imagine that the social reforms left undone in the winter of 1918–19 could be made up in the spring of 1920.

Still, it was not too late to make the administration more democratic, as the new Prussian government under Otto Braun (hitherto minister of agriculture) proved. This agile Social Democrat from Königsberg, a printer by trade, appointed Carl Severing to the office of interior minister. Severing, a metalworker from Westphalia, was a long-time SPD delegate in the Reichstag and had shown great ability as federal and Prussian commissioner in the troubled Ruhr district. As minister of the interior, Severing initiated a large-scale reshuffle of offices in the provincial and police administrations. Officials who had collaborated with the putsch were replaced by men Severing trusted to stand firm in the republic's defence. This reorganization opened a new chapter in the history of Prussia. Within a few short years, the former Hohenzollern state would become a bulwark of the German Republic.

The opposite happened in Bavaria. On 14 March 1920 Munich experienced its own kind of coup. General Arnold Ritter von Möhl, commander of Group IV of the Reichswehr, after reaching an understanding with monarchist politicians like Georg Escherich, captain of the paramilitary civilian police forces (the so-called *Einwohnerwehren*), Gustav Ritter von Kahr, district president of Upper Bavaria, and the Munich police chief Ernst Pöhner, demanded that the Social Democratic prime minister, Johannes Hoffmann, transfer the executive authority to him, Möhl, in the interest of peace and the public order. The Bavarian coalition government—a minority cabinet made up of SPD, Bavarian Peasants' League (*Bayerischer Bauernbund*), and non-aligned politicians—tolerated by the BVP and DDP—submitted to the ultimatum. Hoffmann resigned, refusing to go along. Two days later, the Bavarian parliament elected Gustav von Kahr to the office of prime minister by a one-vote majority. His government was composed of members of the BVP, DDP, and the Bavarian Peasants' League. The Social Democrats went into the opposition, from which they did not emerge again during the life of the Weimar Republic. Bavaria became a rightist 'cell of order' (*Ordnungszelle*), a stronghold of all the forces seeking to redirect the Reich towards the right and replace parliamentary democracy with an authoritarian system of government.

It was not until the suppression of the Ruhr uprising that the Kapp–Lüttwitz putsch was finally over, however. The 'Red Ruhr Army', the paramilitary arm of a proletarian mass movement far larger than the KPD and its followers, had seized power in the industrial district of Rhineland-Westphalia after the rightist coup. Its leaders had no intention of relinquishing their position after the return to parliamentary government in Berlin. The most radical groups were the executive councils in the mining areas of the 'wild west', where syndicalists and leftist Communists were in command. In the eastern and southern parts of the district, where metalworking was the primary industry and the USPD was dominant, the federal and Prussian governments found a much greater willingness to cooperate.

Berlin took advantage of this political difference. The 'Bielefeld agreement' of 24 March (mainly a product of Severing's negotiation), which among other things provided for the workers to turn in their weapons under the common supervision of executive councils and local authorities, succeeded in convincing the moderate elements to stop fighting. But the more radical councils in Mülheim and Hamborn and the leaders of the Red Ruhr Army refused a ceasefire, and the Reichswehr and free corps were burning to settle accounts with the far left. The chaotic conditions among the anarchic leaders in Duisburg convinced the Reich government of the necessity for rapid action. The military repression of the rebellion took place between 30 March and 3 April. Among the forces deployed were units that shortly before had backed the Kapp–Lüttwitz putsch. The exact number of those killed in the Ruhr civil war has never been ascertained. The workers numbered well above 1,000 dead, the Reichswehr 208 dead and 123 missing, and the security police 41 dead.

The Ruhr uprising was the last of the great proletarian mass movements that had begun with the wildcat strikes of the year 1917. There is good reason to think of it as the third phase of the German revolution, which had entered a latent stage after the suppression of the Second Munich Council Republic in May 1919. The radical workers were protesting, on the one hand, against the political and social system they held responsible for the war and against those who wanted to restore this system after 1918, and, on the other hand, against the traditional workers' organizations, which they had come to regard as a part of the capitalist order. Of course, the unions and the Social Democrats still had far more and better qualified workers in their ranks than syndicalists, Communists, and independents. The political divide went right through the middle of the working class, and no one party and trade union could speak for it as a whole any longer.

The desire for a radical restructuring of the societal order survived the end of the revolutionary period in spring 1920. But the experiences of those weeks was sobering. The general strike had revealed itself to be a two-edged sword. To the extent that it helped bring the Kapp regime quickly to heel, it was certainly a success. Yet it developed a momentum of its own, one the unions and Social Democrats were powerless to stop. Against the will of the moderates, the radical left transformed the political strike into an armed conflict from which not the workers, but rather the military emerged victorious. Although the Ruhr uprising was followed by Communist rebellions like the 'March action' of 1921 in central Germany, the age of proletarian mass demonstrations was over, and there were no more general strikes in the Weimar Republic after 1920.

Those involved in the Ruhr uprising were punished far more severely than the participants in the recent putsch, most of whom were able to escape abroad, including Kapp and Lüttwitz. Pursued by the law, Lieutenant Commander Ehrhardt took refuge in the Bavarian *Ordnungszelle*, where, under bureaucratic cover, he set about preparing the next stage of the counter-revolution. The Reich government granted only a minimal part of the concessions it had made to the striking workers. The efforts of the new socialization commission remained as inconsequential as in 1919. Undependable police units were broken up only in places where the Social Democrats had sufficient power. Few workers joined the *Ortswehren*, the new local security forces. The Reichswehr, in order to avoid being implicated in anti-constitutional activities, was careful to display political restraint. At the same time, however, an amnesty in August 1920 allowed free corps officers who had supported the coup to be taken into the final-status army and navy. A staunch anti-republican attitude was no bar to professional advancement in the 'state within the state', which is what the German military in the Seeckt era in effect became.

The first Reichstag election after the revolution took place in Germany on 6 June 1920 (though 'Germany' must be qualified here; open border questions delayed the elections in Schleswig-Holstein, East Prussia, and Upper Silesia). They turned into a debacle for the republican forces. The parties of the Weimar coalition, who had possessed a two-thirds majority in the National Assembly, lost the majority of votes and seats. The MSPD sank from 37.9% to 21.6% of the vote, while the USPD was able to increase its share from 7.6% to 18.6%. The KPD, on the ballot for the first time, achieved only 1.7%. The DDP fell from 18.5% to 8.4%, while the DVP grew by almost the same amount, from 4.4% to 13.9%. The Centre Party's losses were comparatively minimal. In January 1919 it had gained 15.1% (without the BVP); now it managed 13.6%. The DNVP improved its share of the vote from 10.3% to 14.4%.

A shift to the right in the bourgeoisie, a shift to the left among the workers: this phrase sums up the election results. The elements that had refused to endorse the founding compromise of the German Republic were politically rewarded. The moderates were punished for what they had done—or neglected to do—after the beginning of 1919. The left blamed the republican governments for the resurgence of the 'reaction'. The right condemned the Weimar parties for everything that injured the national honour and harmed the interests of property. Versailles and the tax reform, the Kapp putsch and the ensuing battles: all this had an effect on the outcome of the election, which was, in effect, a vote of no confidence in the Weimar Republic.

Not that a new majority was anywhere in sight. A Grand Coalition from the Social Democrats to the German People's Party was not yet an imaginable way out of the crisis; the memories of the tactical opportunism of Stresemann and his party during the putsch were still too fresh among the SPD, and the 'anti-Marxist' sentiments of the DVP too strong. A bourgeois bloc including the German Nationalists was even less conceivable. The only solution was minority governments the opposition parties were willing to tolerate, either a Weimar coalition supported by the DVP and USPD or else a bourgeois cabinet shored up by the SPD. The SPD preferred the second variation, since the first seemed to offer even less scope for the party to display its distinctive image.

On 25 June 1920 Ebert appointed the Centre Party politician Konstantin Fehrenbach, president of the National Assembly, as chancellor. He formed a cabinet composed of members of the Centre, DDP, and DVP, along with two independent ministers. For the first time since October 1918, Germany had a government without the SPD. But the Reich could not be governed without the Social Democrats. This they knew, and the bourgeois minority cabinet adapted itself accordingly.[11]

RATHENAU, RAPALLO, REPARATIONS: GERMANY 1920–1922

The spring of 1921 saw two crises, both with a common root in questions left unresolved by the Treaty of Versailles. The first was in Upper Silesia. On 20 March, the plebiscite called for in the treaty took place. Those voting for Germany were 60% of the population, those for Poland 40%, the former predominantly in the industrial, the latter in agricultural areas. Thereupon the Reich government demanded all of Upper Silesia for Germany, while Poland and the Allies endorsed a partition. In order to underscore its demands, the Warsaw government secretly sponsored an uprising, in the course of which Polish insurgents occupied large parts of the plebiscite territory.

The Reich and Prussian governments responded by delivering arms to the Upper Silesian militia, a paramilitary formation established in 1920. Together with the *Oberland*, a Bavarian free corps, the militia stormed the Annaberg, the highest point in Upper Silesia, on 23 May. At the end of June an Allied commission brought about the withdrawal of the armed parties. On 20 October 1921 the Allied High Council decided the border dispute according to a League of Nations study: four-fifths of the industrial territory in Upper Silesia was to go to Poland, including the cities of Kattowitz and Königshütte, in which overwhelming majorities had voted for Germany. With no means to compel a more favourable resolution, Germany could do nothing but protest at this violation of the right to self-determination.

The second crisis in the spring of 1921 had to do with the war reparations. The payments were so high that they could not be raised in 'normal' fashion, by taxation, and thus made inflation worse. The fact that the peace treaty had not set the total amount Germany owed had fatal consequences. Perpetual uncertainty over the extent of the payments made it impossible for potential private creditors to realistically assess the creditworthiness of the country. Under such conditions, Germany could get no more long-term loans.

On 5 May 1921 the British prime minister, Lloyd George, handed the German ambassador in London an Allied ultimatum requiring reparations in the amount of 132 billion gold marks, to be paid in several stages at the current exchange value, that is, not including future interest, and with an additional 6 billion for Belgium, which had been attacked by Germany in 1914. A payment of 1 billion gold marks was required within twenty five days, by 30 May. Furthermore, the Allies demanded the payment of the 12 billion gold marks still outstanding from the total of 20 billion due, according to the Treaty of Versailles, on 1 May, disarmament in keeping with the Allied prescriptions, and the condemnation of German war criminals. In the case of non-fulfilment of Germany's obligations, the Allied threatened to begin occupation of the whole Ruhr area on 12 May (Düsseldorf, Duisburg, and Ruhrort had already been occupied on 8 March 1921 in punishment for non-compliance with the previous ultimatum).

The day before the London ultimatum was issued, Fehrenbach's cabinet, having failed to enlist the mediation of the United States, had announced its intention to resign. The reparations crisis thus coincided with a crisis of government, and both could only be solved in tandem. The DNVP, DVP, and KPD demanded that the ultimatum be rejected. SPD, Centre, and USPD wished to accept it, in view of the looming sanctions. The DDP was split.

A victory of the hard line would have meant the economic collapse of Germany. The rightist parties knew this, but they could assume, as with the vote over the Treaty of Versailles in June 1919, that there would be a majority for the lesser evil even without their support. Their calculations proved correct. SPD, Centre, and DDP assumed the responsibility of accepting the ultimatum and formed a new government, the first minority cabinet of the Weimar coalition. Its leader was Joseph Wirth of the Centre Party, appointed by Ebert on 10 May. Wirth, a former mathematics teacher from Baden, had succeeded Erzberger as finance minister in March 1920. He was a brilliant speaker and ardent nationalist, but also a committed republican and, as far as domestic issues were concerned, a 'leftist' within his party. Wirth's appointment to the chancellorship was the beginning of what came to be known as the 'policy of fulfilment' or *Erfüllungspolitik*.

Erfüllungspolitik meant that Germany would do its utmost to fulfil the requirements imposed upon it, thereby demonstrating the absurdity of the reparations policy. Since the reparations overburdened the country's economic capacities, catastrophic consequences could be expected. These would convince the Allies of the necessity of revising the London payment plan. Wirth was not the only one to adopt this logic; the Reichstag majority did, too. On 10 May 1921 it accepted the London ultimatum with 220 votes against 172. MSPD, USPD, and Centre voted unanimously in favour, along with a strong minority of the DDP and small minorities from the DVP and BVP. The Wirth government had passed its first test.

Among the London ultimatum's non-material requirements, one went all but unfulfilled—the condemnation of war criminals. Nine trials against twelve defendants did take place between May and July 1921 before the federal court in Leipzig, but only half of these led to convictions. The greatest stir was caused by the conviction of two lieutenants who had participated in the sinking of rescue boats from a torpedoed steamer. Both were condemned to four-year prison terms. This outraged the navy. In January 1922 the imprisonment came to an abrupt end when members of the right-wing radical 'Consul' organization, led by Lieutenant Commander Ehrhardt, freed the two officers from their prison cells. The Allied registered protest against the small number of convictions and the lenient sentences, but they undertook no action. Apart from the six 1921 convictions, German war crimes went unatoned.

The demand for disarmament was formally fulfilled by the early summer of 1921. It primarily affected the Bavarian *Einwohnerwehren*, which the Munich government had stubbornly refused to dissolve the year before. Under massive Allied pressure, Prime Minister Kahr finally had to order their disarmament in

June 1921. Three weeks later, on 24 June, the federal government declared the Bavarian *Einwohnerwehren*, the East Prussian local and border militias (*Ortswehren* and *Grenzwehren*), and Bavarian Forest Steward Georg Escherich's paramilitary 'Escherich Organization' (nicknamed *Orgesch*) disbanded throughout the whole Reich.

But that was not the end of the paramilitary influence on German politics. The *Ordnungszelle* Bavaria remained the El Dorado of numerous 'Patriotic Leagues' (*Vaterländische Verbände*) far more radical than the *Einwohnerwehren*. And in the rest of Germany, too, the Weimar state failed to secure the 'monopoly of legitimate use of physical force in enforcing its rules' that Max Weber identified as the main characteristic of the state as a compulsory political association with continuous organization (*politischer Anstaltsbetrieb*). This monopoly had already been undermined by the war. Widespread arms ownership, as Weber correctly noted, was one of the things that made the revolution of 1918–19 possible. To a certain extent, the transfer of arms from the Reichswehr to the free corps, local, and citizen's militias was understandable as a reaction to the forced, one-sided German disarmament and to attempted Communist takeovers. But it also contributed to the militarization of public life, and its consequences outlasted the civil war-like conflicts of the first five years after the war. Paramilitary organizations and party armies of the widest political description continued to block the development of a civil society, and a literature glorifying war did its part in keeping the spirit alive—a spirit that would construct its body, a militarily powerful Germany, capable of seeking vengeance for 1918.[12]

The hard core of the London ultimatum could not be softened. Already in 1921, Germany had to pay 3.3 billion gold marks in reparations, of which 1 billion was due on 30 May. The Reich was able to come up with only 150 million in cash for the first instalment. The remainder was financed through three-month treasury bills, which the government had the greatest difficulty redeeming by the due date. This operation clearly made inflation worse and induced the Social Democratic minister of trade and commerce, Robert Schmidt, to call on 19 May 1921 for fundamental financial reforms: the expropriation of 20 per cent of capital assets in agriculture, industry, commerce, banking, and housing.

Schmidt's call for the 'capture' of asset values spelled the end of the silent 'inflation consensus' that had characterized German economic, finance, and social policy since 1919. In the spring of 1921, the Social Democrats and Free Trade Unions began to realize that the devaluation of the currency steadily shifted the societal balance of power in favour of private property and against the workers. They also recognized that the reform of Germany's finances would not be possible without massive government intervention in existing property relations. Business interests and the bourgeois parties rejected this notion. Walther Rathenau, former president of the board of directors of the General Electricity Society, now minister of reconstruction and close to the DDP, said that Schmidt's proposals robbed Germany of economic freedom and that consumption could produce higher numbers than property. Joseph Wirth, who held both the chancellorship and the office of finance minister, agreed with his experts that 'the forces necessary to put these plans into action cannot be found.'

The political right morally condemned *Erfüllungspolitik* for the simple reason that 'Marxists'—that is, MSPD and USPD—had helped bring about the acceptance of the London ultimatum. The political centre, too, drew fire from the right, on account of its cooperation with the moderate left. In the *Miesbacher Anzeiger*, a provincial newspaper very popular in Bavaria, the writer Ludwig Thoma (who remained anonymous) called Chancellor Wirth the 'confidant of the shyster from Biberach', a reference to Erzberger. Thoma characterized Georg Gradnauer, the Social Democratic minister of the interior, in the following manner: 'Narrow, Saxon eyes; Hebrew nose and chin; the giant ears even more Hebrew.' When it was announced in the middle of June 1921 that Defence Minister Gessler would relocate the Reichswehr captain Franz Xaver Ritter von Epp, a former Bavarian free corps leader, to Prussia, Thoma commented: 'We will neither be ruled nor bullied by those Jewish swine on the Spree, and if Berlin has not yet been completely forsaken by God, they will throw Gessler out of the Reichswehr as quickly as possible.'

With their hate campaigns against the republic and its representatives, newspapers like the *Miesbacher Anzeiger* created an atmosphere that could discharge violently at any moment. On 9 June 1921 Carl Gareis, leader of the USPD fraction in the Bavarian parliament, was murdered in Munich by an unknown assailant, who shot him four times. The perpetrator of the next political murder was quickly identified by the police. On 26 August 1921, shortly after a judicial investigation had exonerated him of all charges of tax evasion and illegal flight of capital, Matthias Erzberger, the former minister of finance, was gunned down by two members of the 'Consul' organization and the Munich 'Germanic Order' while taking a walk in Griesbach in the northern Black Forest. The murderers, Heinrich Tillessen, a lieutenant, and Heinrich Schulz, a reserve lieutenant, escaped via Munich to Hungary. They were not sentenced until 1950, and even then served only two years of their prison terms (which were twelve and fifteen years, respectively). The leader of the 'Germanic Order,' Lieutenant Commander Manfred Killinger, who had ordered the murder, was acquitted by the Offenburg court of the charge of abetment to murder.

The commentary in the right-wing press amounted to a justification of the murder. The *Oletzkoer Zeitung*, a German Nationalist newspaper from East Prussia, wrote that the former minister had been overtaken by the fate that probably all national-minded Germans had wished upon him. 'A man who, like Erzberger, bore the main responsibility for the misfortune of our Fatherland, was a continual danger to Germany while he remained alive.' The like-minded *Berliner Lokalanzeiger* wrote that any other country would show 'limitless understanding' for conspirators like the officers who had shot Erzberger. The German Nationalist *Kreuz-Zeitung* compared the conspirators to Brutus, William Tell, and Charlotte

Corday, who had killed the Jacobin Marat in 1793, and accused 'Erzberger's present-day eulogists' of 'completely forgetting that the war waged against Erzberger was a war of defence'.

The trade unions and the Majority and Independent Social Democrats responded to Erzberger's murder and the right-wing glorification of violence with large demonstrations, which the KPD also joined. On 29 August the Reich government, at the behest of the president, passed an emergency measure on the basis of Article 48, Paragraph 2 of the Weimar constitution, which gave the interior minister the authority to ban all press, assemblies, and associations hostile to the republic. This provoked a new conflict with Bavaria, whose administration refused to enforce Gradnauer's ban against the *Miesbacher Anzeiger*, the *Münchner Beobachter*, and the *Völkischer Beobachter*, the central organ of the National Socialist German Workers' Party (*Nationalsozialistische Deutsche Arbeiterpartei;* NSDAP), founded in 1919.

On 28 September the president issued a second emergency measure in defence of the republic. This was the result of negotiations with the Bavarian government, now led by Count Lerchenfeld, a fairly moderate politician of the BVP who had replaced Kahr as prime minister the week before. The new ordinance promised to protect not only 'representatives of the republican-democratic form of government', but also, in accordance with the wishes of the Bavarian government, 'all persons in public life'. The authority to enforce prohibitions and confiscations in defence of the republic was transferred to the individual state agencies. In return, the Bavarian government committed itself to lifting the state of emergency, in effect in Bavaria since November 1919, by 6 October 1921 at the latest.

At the end of October 1921 another crisis, as superfluous as it was serious, struck the Wirth cabinet. The cause was the Allied High Council's decision regarding the partition of Upper Silesia. The DDP and—somewhat less forcefully—the Centre insisted that the Reich government resign immediately in order to demonstrate to the whole world Germany's protest against the violation of its right to national self-determination. The Social Democrats considered such a step both risky and useless, but they did not prevail. On 22 October Wirth informed the president of his cabinet's resignation.

There followed negotiations over the formation of a 'Grand Coalition', a crisis solution that even the Social Democrats now endorsed. This time, however, the DVP was unwilling, ostensibly because it doubted the SPD's commitment to a 'national defence front' on the Upper Silesia question. In reality, however, the business-friendly party was afraid of being outvoted by the other parties on controversial matters of tax policy. The DVP's rejection induced the DDP to withdraw from governmental responsibility. The only remaining solution was a 'black–red' minority cabinet under the current chancellor. The president had to threaten his resignation in order to overcome the Centre Party's resistance to a coalition with the SPD alone. The DDP, which no longer considered itself a coalition partner, nonetheless kept Gessler in the cabinet as a 'special minister'. This made the resignation of the government look like a farce. On 31 January 1922 Wirth transferred the office of foreign minister, which he himself had intermittently held, to the former reconstruction minister, Walther Rathenau. After a three-month interim, the DDP was once again a formal participant in the government.[13]

Two weeks before Rathenau assumed office, the Allied High Council invited Germany to attend an international conference in Genoa at which the victors and vanquished of the late war were to discuss the problems of economic reconstruction for the first time. Soviet Russia was also invited. It seemed logical for Berlin and Moscow, both 'have nots' in international affairs, to coordinate their policies in advance. While their diplomatic relations had not yet been restored, each country had a trade delegation in the other's capital after May 1921. Ideologically speaking, relations remained tense. In March 1921 the Communist International, founded two years previously in Moscow, had even tried to start a revolution in Germany, beginning in the industrial heartland—a plan Severing's Prussian police managed to stop in time. However, the Cominern's policy and the official policy of the Soviet government were not the same thing. While the 'internationalists' were preparing the way for world revolution, the 'realists' were seeking to strengthen Russia's position in cooperation with certain capitalist states, above all Germany.

This was especially the case in military affairs. In September 1921 the Red Army and the Reichswehr began top secret and increasingly systematic cooperation. The Russians were interested in superior German technology, and Germany sought Russia's support against the restrictions of the Treaty of Versailles, especially in the areas of air force and poison gas production. The common antipathy to Poland was also a factor. In 1920, Russia had suffered defeat in a war against Poland; the Treaty of Riga in March 1921 had forced it to recognize the Polish eastern border, which lay 200 to 300 kilometres east of the 'Curzon line' set by the Allies at the end of 1919.

Germany was as unwilling as Russia to accept its territorial losses to the new Polish national state. At the beginning of February 1920, on the eve of the Russo-Polish war, General von Seeckt, chief of the army command, had expressed the view that only in 'firm alliance with Great Russia' could Germany hope to recuperate its territories lost to Poland and its 'world power status'. Chancellor Wirth, an active promoter of secret military cooperation in his capacity as finance minister, shared Seeckt's opinion. Throughout 1922, he called for Poland to be crushed and for Germany and Russia to become neighbors once again.

Ago von Maltzan, the director of the eastern department of the foreign office, was not only a proponent of the 'eastern orientation' like Wirth and Seeckt, but the policy's actual architect. In the middle of January 1922 this diplomat from the school of Alfred von Kiderlen-Waechter negotiated with Karl Radek, the Soviet expert on Germany, working out the basis of a treaty that accommodated the Russian desire for closer economic cooperation with Germany. The plan did not include supervision by an international syndicate, as the Allies had suggested for the reconstruction of Russia.

However, the new foreign minister did not adopt this course. In contrast to Wirth, Seeckt, and Maltzan, Walther Rathenau was decidedly 'western' in orientation, wished to avoid German–Russian entanglements, and advocated an international economic consortium. Consequently, the German–Russian negotiations stalled, and were not revived until the Russian delegation under Foreign Minister Georgy Chicherin stopped in Berlin at the beginning of April on the way to Genoa. No treaty was concluded on this occasion, but there were so many points of convergence that one seemed possible in the near future.

On 5 April, before Wirth and the German delegation left for Genoa, President Ebert made his constitutional powers and political desires very clear to the cabinet. Since he was responsible for representing the Reich internationally, he insisted that no substantive agreements and commitments be made without his approval. It turned out differently. In Genoa the German representatives in the financial commission did succeed on one point: the Allied experts agreed that the reparations had contributed to the devaluation of the German currency and must not be permitted to overburden the country's economy. At the same time, however, a disconcerting rumour made the rounds that separate Allied–Russian negotiations might lead to an agreement at Germany's expense. Influenced by these reports, Rathenau finally submitted to pressure from Maltzan and authorized the latter to resume talks with the Russians.

As it turned out, there was no danger of a breakthrough in the Allied–Russian negotiations. Though Maltzan soon learned as much, he still did everything in his power to bring about a separate treaty with the Russians. An ambiguously worded telegram informing the president about the German–Russian talks was postponed by Maltzan for one day so that Ebert would have no opportunity to strengthen the already hesitant Rathenau in his resistance to a Russian treaty.

The decision was made in the night of 15–16 April at the legendary 'pyjama party' in Rathenau's hotel room. Maltzan informed those present, including the chancellor, about a phone conversation in which Chicherin had declared his willingness to conclude a treaty with the Germans immediately, and on their terms. Wirth and Maltzan managed to talk Rathenau out of informing the British prime minister, Lloyd George, of the latest developments. On the following day, Easter Sunday, the German delegation travelled to Rapallo, a seaside resort in northern Italy. That evening, Chicherin and Rathenau signed the treaty that bears this name, which very soon acquired quasi-mythical status. In the Treaty of Rapallo, Russia and Germany renounced all mutual claims to compensation for wartime damages, restored full diplomatic relations with each other, and committed themselves to a most-favoured-nation clause whereby any commercial advantages either country accorded to a third nation were automatically granted to the treaty partner.

The Berlin response to the treaty was mixed, but mostly positive. The president was—and remained—very upset that the chancellor and foreign minister had disregarded his instructions, but he supported the government in public. The Reichstag adopted the treaty at third reading on 4 July 1922 against a small number of votes from the DNVP. Among the warning voices was that of the USPD delegate Rudolf Breitscheid. At the end of April he called the Treaty of Rapallo the 'greatest possible disservice to German interests for the near future', since it stood to harm the emerging economic understanding with the West.

And so it happened. The manner in which Germany and Russia reached their agreement in April 1922 could not but cause the highest alarm among the Western powers, especially France. It is uncertain whether, absent Rapallo, the Genoa conference would have brought substantial progress on the reparations problem. After Rapallo there could be no hope for progress, at least for a long time.

And not only that. In a speech in Bar-le-Duc on 24 April, only one week after the signing of the treaty, Raymond Poincaré, the prime minister of France, hinted at the possibility of French military intervention. The commander-in-chief of the Allied forces in the Rhineland, General Degoutte, wrote in a letter to Defence Minister Maginot on 2 May that the German–Soviet agreement in Rapallo meant that France could not afford to lose any more time if it intended to occupy the Ruhr basin. The Treaty of Rapallo was a relapse into Wilhelmine brinkmanship, and it was guided by forces that thought in 'Wilhelmine' categories in more ways than one. When Wirth, speaking with Chicherin in Genoa, came out in support of a 'restoration of the 1914 borders', he knew he was also speaking for large portions of the German ruling class.[14]

The one reluctant German co-signatory of Rapallo did not live to see the treaty ratified by the parliament. In the late morning of 24 June 1922, Foreign Minister Walther Rathenau was shot to death by two men who overtook his automobile as he was driving to the foreign office from his villa in Grunewald. The murderers, quickly identified as Erwin Kern, a retired navy lieutenant, and Herman Fischer, a reserve lieutenant, were caught by the police on 17 July at Saaleck Castle near Kösen. Kern was shot while fleeing, whereupon Fischer committed suicide. Both were members of the 'German National Protective and Defensive League' (*Deutschvölkischer Schutz- und Trutzbund*), a 170,000-strong, militantly anti-Semitic group, and the 'Consul' organization, which had also planned Erzberger's assassination. The police were able to catch several other men involved in Rathenau plot, several of whom came from the same secret society.

The assassination of Rathenau was meant as an attack against the *Erfüllungspolitik* and the republic as a whole, and to a certain extent Rathenau really did stand for everything the murderers hated. He was a critic of the old Germany, who, as a Jew, could not have become foreign minister without the revolution. He represented the *Erfüllungspolitik* vis-à-vis the west without Joseph Wirth's ulterior motives with respect to the east. At the same time, however, he was a product of the Wilhelmine era and a German patriot, exhorting the Germans to a *levée en masse* in October 1918 and working to overcome the Versailles system from the summer of 1919. In a sense, Rathenau's own contradictions made him into a symbol of the young republic and into a target for the hatred of all who were out to bring Weimar down through a revolution on the right. According to the plans of the 'Consul' conspirators, the far left was to play the role of catalyst. In reaction to the assassination, the Communists would unleash the violence of the proletarian masses, which would be too great for the weak Weimar government to deal with. Only a national dictatorship would be able to restore order.

Rathenau's murder shook the republic like no other event since the Kapp–Lüttwitz putsch. But the 'Consul' conspirators waited in vain for the escalation of violence. The Communists joined Majority and Independent Social Democrats in the massive demonstrations sponsored by the General German Trade Union Association, and Chancellor Wirth, after paying tribute to the slain minister in the Reichstag on 25 June, hurled words at the political right the latter never forgave: 'There [on the right] the enemy is standing, dripping poison into the wounds of a nation. There he stands, and there can be no question about it—the enemy stands on the right.' The minutes record here 'tumultuous, incessant applause and clapping in the centre and left, in all the stands. Great, incessant commotion.'

As before, after Erzberger's assassination in 1921, the president and the government took legal action against the extreme right, and once again this led to a serious conflict with Bavaria. Two new ordinances pursuant to Article 48 were followed by a law 'in defence of the Republic' (*Republikschutzgesetz*), adopted by the Reichstag at third reading on 18 July 1922 with the two-thirds majority required for constitutional amendments. The support of the DVP made this possible. Actions hostile to the republic, from insulting the national flag to murdering the republic's official representatives, were sanctioned with severe punishments, and a special 'state court for the protection of the Republic' was established in Leipzig to try such crimes.

In response, Bavaria struck an unprecedented blow against the federal government. It abolished the new law on 24 July, one day after it took effect, and replaced it with an ordinance that, while adopting the material points of the *Republikschutzgesetz*, transferred the new court's jurisdiction to Bavarian courts. The Reich answered this violation of the constitution by proposing negotiations, which led to a compromise on 11 August ('Constitution Day'). To the new federal court was added a second senate with jurisdiction over crimes committed in southern Germany and staffed with southern German judges. The Bavarian government reciprocated on 25 August by abolishing its ordinance of 24 July. The rightist majority in the Bavarian parliament, considering this compromise an unacceptable retreat, forced Count Lerchenfeld to resign on 2 November. He was succeeded a week later by Eugen Ritter von Knilling, who was far more sympathetic to the 'Patriotic Leagues' and Adolf Hitler's National Socialists than Lerchenfeld had been.

The new federal law was a good deal less effective than its proponents had envisaged. The authoritarian-minded judiciary had no intention of strictly enforcing the new provisions. And when it did do so, then sooner against offenders from the left than from the right. For example, a Communist who used the expression 'republic of thieves' (*Räuberrepublik*) was sentenced to four weeks in prison, while a defendant from the *völkisch* scene got off with a fine of 70 marks for 'Jew republic' (*Judenrepublik*). In Bavarian courts, the term *Saurepublik* ('damned republic', literally 'sow republic') was not considered a term of opprobrium. Saying 'black-red-mustard' (*Schwarz-Rot-Mostrich*) or 'black-red-egg-yolk-yellow' (*Schwarz-Rot-Hühnereigelb*) for 'black-red-gold' was also not usually punished. One citizen who used the expression 'black-red-shit' (*Schwarz-Rot-Scheisse*) was first acquitted, then made to pay a fine of 30 marks after the case was appealed.

The religious community, too, continued to have strong feelings against the Weimar Republic. This was especially true of committed Protestants, many of whom had not come to terms with the fall of the monarchy. The official church attitude found expression in a popular rhyme: '*Die Kirche ist politisch neutral, aber sie wählt deutschnational*' ('The Church is politically neutral, but it votes German-National'). Like the DNVP, the German Evangelical Church Committee (*Deutscher Evangelischer Kirchenausschuss*) condemned the 1922 murder of Rathenau as a 'heinous crime', but it saw the Allied powers as the real perpetrators: 'We accuse our enemies, whose blindness has cast our people into disgrace and misery, out of which arise all of the demons of the abyss.'

The Catholic Church had not associated itself as intimately with the Hohenzollern state as the Evangelical church. Nonetheless, the German Catholic Congress in Munich at the end of 1922 showed how strong anti-republican attitudes still were among Catholics, too. Cardinal Faulhaber, the archbishop of Munich and Freising, condemned the November 1918 revolution as 'perjury and high treason', calling it an 'atrocity' that was not to be 'sanctified' simply because it had brought Catholics a few successes. When the president of the Catholic Congress, Cologne mayor Konrad Adenauer, distanced himself from Faulhaber in his closing address, the division within German Catholicism was plain to see.

The republican forces were well aware that anti-republican suspicions and antipathies could not be overcome by bans and punishments. For this reason, the president and government sought to promote and consolidate pro-republican attitudes through a 'positive' campaign. But success was modest here, too. 'Rightist' governments in the *Länder* torpedoed Interior Minister Adolf Köster's plan to make 11 August, the day the Weimar constitution was signed, into a national holiday. On another issue Köster had better success. It was his doing that the 'Deutschlandlied' was proclaimed the German national anthem by President Ebert on 11 August 1922. The words of Hoffmann von Fallersleben were not to serve as an expression of national arrogance, Ebert announced. 'But as once the poet did, so too do we today love "Germany above all". In fulfilment of his longing, let the song of unity and right and freedom under the banners of black, red, and gold be the festive expression of our patriotic feelings.'

Ebert's hope was not realized. The 'Deutschlandlied' did not make the national colours any more popular. To sing the first stanza was not sufficient to turn one into a republican. The republicans among the working class, for their part, found it difficult to join in singing a song that, despite its democratic, black-red-gold origins, was now more often sung on the black-white-red right than by the devotees of Weimar. '*Deutschland, Deutschland über alles*' had become the veritable signature tune of 'national Germany' ever since, on 10 November 1914, young volunteers—with this song on their lips, according to the official legend—had stormed enemy lines and fallen near Langemarck in Flanders. For the victors of the war, 11 November was the day of commemoration for the signing of the armistice in 1918. On the same day, to the strains of the 'Deutschlandlied', the German right cultivated the myth of Langemarck, a patriotic cult of sacrifice with a strong admixture of desire to wipe away the disgrace of 1918.[15]

Attempts to counter the kind of fanatical anti-Semitism that found expression in the campaign against and murder of the Jewish Walther Rathenau had virtually no chance of success. Three weeks after the murder, the Prussian government found it necessary to ban a general student congress in Marburg, since statements by the organizers seemed to indicate that public justifications for the assassination were in the offing. The *völkisch* camp of the German Students' Association (*Deutsche Studentenschaft*), with the *Deutscher Hochschulring* as its main organization, went to Bavarian Würzburg instead. The constitution drawn up there extended membership in the student body to German-Austrians and Germans from abroad 'of German heritage and mother tongue'. This was the first step along the way to an 'Aryan paragraph', which was already in effect in Austria.

The far right considered the Jews the authors of Germany's military defeat, believing they had systematically undermined the morale of the German workers with Marxist or Bolshevist ideas or had enriched themselves at the expense of the German people. The Jews were represented as instigators and beneficiaries of revolution, inflation, and the *Erfüllungspolitik*. They became, in effect, scapegoats for everything Germany suffered—or believed to be suffering—after November 1918. Rosa Luxemburg, Paul Levi, Kurt Eisner, Hugo Haase, Rudolf Hilferding, Eduard Bernstein, Otto Landsberg, Paul Hirsch, Ernst Heilmann, Hugo Preuss, Eugen Schiffer, Theodor Wolff, and Walther Rathenau—in the eyes of the fanatical anti-Semites, it made no difference whether these politicians and publicists were radical or moderate, Marxists or liberals, unbaptized or baptized. They were Jews, and thus enemies.

Anti-Semitism was especially virulent in higher education, since many academics and students perceived Jews mainly as competitors for prestigious positions in society. The fact that the 'Marxist' workers' movement had advanced to political power in 1918 was taken by many in the academy as a personal insult. They saw their claim to the leadership of the country called into question by people whom they believed to be lacking in the necessary intellectual and moral aptitude. The role of Jews in the politics of the left was enough to turn this feeling of downgraded status and prestige in an anti-Semitic direction. The *völkisch* students and young academics saw themselves in the tradition of the wars of liberation. In Fichte, especially, they found what they were looking for: the idea of the eternal German *Volk*, which they promptly put to use against the Jews as agents of a 'foreign' ethnic culture and against the Weimar state, which they saw as shaped by the Jews.

The favourite theme of anti-Semitic propaganda was the so-called *Ostjuden*, the 'Eastern Jews'. Names of Jews from Russia or Poland who had played a prominent role in the revolution of 1918–19 were as easy to learn as the names of eastern Jewish 'speculators' who profited from inflation. In contrast to the German Jews, who had long been settled and integrated in German society, the orthodox eastern Jews were of distinctly foreign appearance and formed, on account of their general destitution, a social problem group. What the anti-Semites studiously avoided mentioning was that the 'question of the Eastern Jews' was in good part the result of OHL policies in the occupied territories of Russian Poland in 1914. First largely stripping them of their material basis of existence, the Army High Command had then recruited Jews as labour for the German armaments industry. Some 35,000 came to Germany in this way, more or less under duress. About the same number were taken as prisoners of war or caught in Germany by the sudden outbreak of hostilities and interned. Added to the 80,000 eastern Jews living in Germany before 1914, the total figure at war's end was about 150,000.

Most of the eastern Jews working in the armaments industry lost their jobs after the war was over. But they could not easily return to their homes. The new states in eastern central Europe showed little initial willingness to take in large numbers of unemployed Jews. This was especially true of Poland, which had a strong tradition of anti-Semitism. In 1920–1 a considerable number—some 30,000—left for America, where eastern Jews had long found a new home. This emigration continued in the following years. In 1925, the year of the largest eastern Jewish immigration, there were about 108,000 living in Germany. That was 30,000 more than in 1910, but certainly no justification for the anti-Semitic claim that Germany was being flooded with eastern Jews.[16]

Even under the emperors, anti-Semitic parties and organizations had never held a monopoly on anti-Jewish sentiments. The German Conservative party had been unequivocally anti-Jewish from the moment of its inception and had made anti-Semitism an official part of its 'Tivoli platform' in 1892. The German Nationalists consciously adopted this tradition and offered a political home even to fanatical anti-Semites like the delegates Wilhelm Henning, Reinhold Wulle, and Albrecht Graefe. One of these, Henning, played a prominent role in the political and press campaign against Walther Rathenau. In the June 1922 edition of the *Konservative Monatsschrift*, the organ of the *völkisch* wing of the DNVP, Henning published an article claiming, among other things, that 'German honour' was 'no barter commodity for international Jew hands', and that Rathenau and his agents would be called to account.

After the murder of the foreign minister, the party leadership under former Prussian finance minister Oskar Hergt thought it advisable to make a clear distinction between the DNVP and the extremist *völkisch* elements on the right. Henning's removal from the party was calculated to demonstrate to the other bourgeois parties the DNVP's capacity to govern. The German Nationalist Reichstag fraction, which was given the final decision, decided it was enough to expel Henning from its own ranks; to exclude him from the party was not necessary. Shortly thereafter, Henning took this step himself, along with Wulle und Graefe. In September 1922 they founded the German Ethnic Cooperative Union (*Deutschvölkische Arbeitsgemeinschaft*), which gave rise to the German Ethnic Freedom Party (*Deutschvölkische Freiheitspartei*) in December.

One of the new party's strongest bastions was Munich, where the district chapter of the DNVP merged with it. The Bavarian capital provided a particularly favourable climate for the *völkisch* nationalists, though they also found a competitor there whose anti-Semitism was not to be outdone: the National Socialist German Workers' Party, led by Adolf Hitler. For the still very anti-Semitic DNVP, the departure of the radically *völkisch* elements had more advantages than disadvantages. Since the autumn of 1922, the German Nationalists had come a good distance towards their most important goal, participation in a bourgeois coalition that could govern without—and against—the Social Democrats.

On the left, too, Rathenau's assassination led to a realignment of political forces. In July 1922 the Reichstag fractions of the Majority and Independent Social Democrats formed a cooperative union. In September they reunited as one party. The USPD of 1922 was no longer the USPD of 1917. At the party congress in Halle in October 1920, a clear majority of the delegates had advocated joining the Communist International and merging with the KPD. To join the 'Third International' meant submitting to the 'twenty one conditions' the Comintern had set down at its Second World Congress in Moscow in summer 1920. According to these, all member parties were required to recognize the Bolshevist party type and method of obtaining political power. The moderate minority of the USPD, led by Wilhelm Dittmann and Artur Crispien along with the party intellectuals Rudolf Hilferding and Rudolf Breitscheid, refused to make such a radical break with the traditions of democratic socialism and remained independent.

This did not mean that a reunification with the Majority party would be automatic, however, especially since the MSPD took what many Independents considered a step to the right the following year. In its 1921 'Görlitz platform', co-authored by Eduard Bernstein, the MSPD defined itself as a 'party of the working people in the city and country' that aspired to fundamental societal reforms, was open to the middle classes, and no longer considered socialism the result of a natural and ineluctable economic development, but as a question of political will.

It took the rise of right-wing radicalism and, finally, Rathenau's murder to convince the two Social Democratic parties that they could no longer afford to be divided.

The 1922 reunification considerably strengthened the Social Democrats, especially in parliament. But it had its disadvantages. The MSPD's reformist Görlitz platform, designed for a leftist people's party, was invalid after only one year. The new 'Heidelberg platform' of September 1925, mainly the work of Hilferding, began with the old Marxist argument about the unavoidable and progressive destruction of small by big business. This effectively closed the party to the middle classes. The re-ideologization was accompanied by a more dogmatic party attitude towards participation in government. The union of the parliamentary fractions meant that 'rightist' notions of a Grand Coalition had to be abandoned, at least for the time being. Most of the USPD delegates, as well as the Majority left wing, would not have agreed to a coalition with the business-friendly DVP.

Nonetheless, Stresemann's party became a tacit participant in the Wirth administration. On 19 July 1922, five days after the union of the Social Democratic Reichstag fractions, the DVP, DDP, and Centre formed a 'cooperative union of the constitutional centre' (*Arbeitsgemeinschaft der verfassungstreuen Mitte*), which was intended to counter the new weight of the Social Democrats. With its endorsement of the *Republikschutzgesetz* the day before, the DVP had positioned itself in the political centre. On 24 October it facilitated the two-thirds majority necessary to amend the constitution and extend the term in office of (still only provisional) President Ebert until 30 June 1925. This step made the direct popular election set for December 1922 superfluous—an election the two liberal parties wished to avoid, fearing the consequences for public order.

There were good, indeed compelling reasons for a Grand Coalition in the autumn of 1922. Rathenau's murder destroyed in one blow all remaining confidence in the currency. Germans and non-Germans alike dumped their credits in marks on the market in a panic. The flight of capital took on gigantic proportions. At about the same time, the inflationary boom that had protected the Reich from the world economic crisis in the early 1920s came to an end. The interest in cheap German imports decreased in the same measure as German domestic industries regained strength. German exports lost the 'bonus' they had enjoyed when global production decreased after 1920. Inflation, which turned into hyperinflation in the autumn of 1922, lost its economic 'attraction'. Objectively speaking, this increased the chances for a currency reform. Politically, however, a reform was only possible through close cooperation between business and organized labour, between the moderate bourgeois parties and the Social Democrats.

This realization was far from widespread among the business community in autumn 1922. Hugo Stinnes, who had exploited inflation to erect a veritable industrial empire, wanted to strengthen the currency by making German workers work two hours longer per day without increased pay for ten to fifteen years. The proposals of the big industrialists, submitted to the federal economic council on 9

November, the fourth anniversary of the revolution, outraged the trade unions, Social Democrats, and Communists. Since Stinnes sat in the Reichstag for the DVP, his statements could also be taken as an indication that the heavy industrialist wing of the German People's Party would not be amenable to Wirth's and the bourgeois centre's efforts towards a Grand Coalition.

Yet Stinnes did not speak for all of German industry, nor even all of the DVP. The party head, Stresemann, was convinced of the necessity of reaching an understanding with the moderate forces in the workers' movement. This made it easier for Wirth, on 26 October, to talk the governing coalition and the DVP into forming a commission to look into a common platform for pressing economic questions, above all that of reparations. One of the architects of the Central Cooperative Union of November 1918, Hans von Raumer, an electrical industrialist, joined the commission for the DVP. The SPD was represented by Rudolf Hilferding. Internationally recognized as one of the leading Marxist theoreticians ever since the publication of his 1910 book *Das Finanzkapital*, Hilferding had been a member of the USPD before the reunification of the parties in September 1922.

The commission achieved what seemed like a 'miracle'. The experts agreed to a number of economic and fiscal measures, and the government was able to use these in its note on reparations to the Allies on 13 November 1922. Reductions in state expenditures and revenue increases were to help balance the budget. The real sensation, however, was one of the proposals for increasing productivity: a reform of the legislation governing working hours 'establishing the eight-hour day as normal working day and permitting legally restricted exceptions, which are to be worked out by contract or by the administration'. Without fundamentally abandoning one of the most important social achievements of November 1918, the commission was nonetheless suggesting, at least for certain branches of the economy, a temporary increase in working hours in order to make possible the reform of the currency, the economic reconstruction of the country, and the peaceful settling of differences with Germany's neighbors.

The Wirth government's note to the Allies was based primarily on the commission's suggestions. In response to an Allied demand, it also promised, for the first time, large-scale measures by the federal bank (*Reichsbank*) in support of the mark: if Germany were to receive an international loan of 500 gold marks, the federal bank would provide matching funds to stabilize the currency. The note was endorsed not only by the heads of the SPD, Centre, and DDP coalition fractions, but also by the representatives of the DVP. The foundations of a Grand Coalition thus seemed to be in place. But the appearance was deceptive. On the following day, 14 November, the fraction of the United Social Democratic Party of Germany (*Vereinigte Sozialdemokratische Partei Deutschlands*, the name of the party after its September unification congress in Nuremberg) voted against a Grand Coalition by three-quarters majority. Otto Braun, the prime minister of Prussia, would have supported such an alliance, but his was a lost cause. The party leadership did not want to risk another split with the former Independents, most of whom, in contrast to Hilferding, were still strictly opposed to joining the DVP, the 'business party'.

Joseph Wirth, in accordance with an agreement with the centre parties, resigned from the chancellorship on the same day. On 22 November the president named as his successor Wilhelm Cuno, the general director of the Hamburg-America Line. Cuno, a Catholic born in 1876 in Thuringian Suhl, stood clearly on the centre-right, though he did not belong to a political party. In appointing him, Ebert hoped that an experienced economics expert at the head of the cabinet would bring the German business community closer to the republic as well as make a good impression internationally. In addition to Cuno, four further non-aligned politicians joined the new administration, including the former mayor of Essen, Hans Luther, as minister of agriculture and the former quartermaster general, Wilhelm Groener, as minister of transport, which position he had already held under Fehrenbach and Wirth. The other ministers were members of the Centre, BVP, DDP, and DVP.

None of the republican governments hitherto had so resembled a cabinet of imperial bureaucrats. And never before had the selection of the chancellor been so exclusively the decision of the president. It would be only a slight exaggeration to say that the Cuno administration was a presidential cabinet in disguise. This relapse into the authoritarian state was not only Ebert's mistake. The main responsibility lay with the real governmental party of the Weimar Republic, the Social Democratic Party. Fearing for its internal unity, it turned away from a parliamentary solution to the crisis and thus made possible the presidential pathway.[17]

THE REPUBLIC ON THE BRINK: THE CRISIS YEAR OF 1923

Under the Cuno government, Germany began the year 1923, in the course of which the republic was to totter more than once on the brink of the abyss. On 11 January French and Belgian troops occupied the Ruhr district. The reason was mere pretence. According to the Allied Reparations Commission, Germany had failed to fulfil its obligations to deliver wood, telegraph poles, and coal. This neglect was the fault of the previous administration under Wirth, which after August 1922 had been following the popular maxim 'Bread first, then reparations'. This was foolish, for France had been waiting for an opportunity to occupy the Ruhr district ever since the Treaty of Rapallo. The purpose of the occupation was to obtain for France the kind of security vis-à-vis its eastern neighbor it had not been able to achieve in the Treaty of Versailles, owing to British and American resistance. Behind this security interest, however, lay more. The French wished to underscore their claim to hegemony over the European continent.

Germany responded to this act of aggression—for such the Ruhr invasion was—with a policy of 'passive resistance', that is, by refusing to follow the orders of the occupiers. The Cuno minority government, which hitherto had been able to rule only thanks to the acquiescence of the SPD, found a large Reichstag majority for this approach, as well as the active support of the unions. Only the extreme left and right refused to join the unified national front. On 22 January the Communists promulgated their solution: 'Strike Poincaré and Cuno on the Ruhr and on the Spree!' In the weeks following, however, out of consideration for the 'anti-imperialist', anti-French policy of the Union of Soviet Socialist Republics (officially founded in December 1922), the German Communists placed greater emphasis on the external enemy. The attitude of the National Socialists was more extreme. On 11 January Hitler declared to his followers in the Zirkus Krone in Munich that the proper response was not 'Down with France!' but 'Down with the November criminals!' He called the National Socialists the 'avenging army of the Fatherland'.[18]

The policy of passive resistance was generally successful until March 1923. Because of the German boycott, the French and Belgians were unable to force reparations payments. After that date, however, the occupiers began to confiscate coal mines and coking plants and to take over the rail system. The Reich not only had to keep paying the salaries of the rail employees, who were expelled from the occupied zone; it also gave millions in credit to the coal mining, iron, and steel industries for the continued payment of wages after the facilities were shut down. Financially speaking, the Ruhr occupation became a bottomless pit. Hyperinflation spiralled out of control. The mark's foreign value, which the federal bank had temporarily stabilized at about 21,000 to the dollar through the sale of gold reserves and foreign exchange from February through April 1923, fell in May to 48,000 and in June to 110,000 marks.

As the failure of passive resistance became clearer, the radical right went over to active resistance in the form of sabotage. In March and April 1923 a commando troop under Heinz Hauenstein, a former free corps leader, blew up several rail facilities in the occupied area. One of the commando's lower leaders, Albert Leo Schlageter, a National Socialist, was apprehended by the French criminal police in Essen on 2 April. On 9 May a French military tribunal in Düsseldorf convicted him of espionage and sabotage and condemned him to death. The sentence was carried out by firing squad on 26 May.

Schlageter's execution set off a storm of protest in Germany that echoed even in distant Moscow. In a speech before the expanded executive of the Communist International on 20 June 1923, Karl Radek, the organization's Germany expert, called the 'fascist' Schlageter a 'martyr of German nationalism' and 'courageous soldier of the counter-revolution', who deserved 'honest and manly recognition from us, soldiers of the revolution'.

If the circles of the German fascists who sincerely wish to serve the German people will not understand the meaning of Schlageter's fate, then Schlageter has fallen in vain, and they should write on his memorial: 'The Wanderer into the Void' . . . We desire to do everything so that men like Schlageter, who were prepared to die for a general cause, do not become wanderers into the void, but wanderers into a better future for all of humanity; so that they do not shed their hot, selfless blood for the profits of the coal and iron barons, but for the cause of the great working German people, who are a member of the family of nations fighting for their liberty.

Radek's 'Schlageter speech' was an attempt to separate the nationalist masses from their leaders and transform the national-revolutionary movement into a movement for social revolution. The term 'fascist' for the far right of the capitalist countries, including Germany, had become common currency on the communist and social democratic left ever since the fascist movement in Italy, led by the former socialist Benito Mussolini, had developed into the most powerful and successful of the radically anti-communist forces on the right, especially after it had come to power in the wake of the legendary 'March on Rome' at the end of October 1922. From the point of view of the Soviet Union and the Comintern, the Franco-German confrontation of 1923 offered a rare opportunity to bring down the entire post-war order of 1919. A war of national liberation waged by Germany against France might, with Russian help, quickly become the catalyst of world revolution—provided that the nationalist masses the fascists had seduced were prepared to fight with the Communists, and under Communist leadership. To turn this strategy into reality was the goal of the KPD's campaign of 'National-Bolshevist' agitation among the adherents of the nationalist right in summer 1923. Despite remarkable rhetorical concessions to anti-Semitism, however, the campaign generated few practical results.

Far greater was the KPD's success among the workers. Though not the actual initiators of the 'wildcat strikes' in the Ruhr district in mid-May, the Communists exploited them effectively, gaining strong support in the summer 1923 elections on all levels—works committees, trade unions, municipalities, and state parliaments. The membership of the KPD grew from 225,000 in September 1922 to 295,000 in September 1923. The number of local branches increased from some 2,500 to more than 3,300. By August 1923 a political explosion seemed to be in the offing. Deteriorating social conditions had created an atmosphere of desperation, which found expression in the so-called 'Cuno strikes'. The Free Trade Unions sought to protect the shops of the federal press, where money was printed, from the industrial action. But in vain. For one day, 10 August 1923, the press was shut down, and the resultant shortage of paper money was immediately felt.

The Social Democrats had been tolerating the Cuno administration up to this point. They did so, even though it stood further right than any other Weimar government, maintained contacts among the radical free corps, made no serious effort towards a diplomatic resolution of the Ruhr conflict, and undertook nothing to counter the growing destitution of the masses. In mid-April 1923 Theodor Leipart, president of the General German Trade Union Association, demanded the formation of a Grand Coalition, if necessary under Stresemann as chancellor.

But the Social Democrats refused. With left-wing resistance to cooperation with the DVP still so strong, the party leadership saw no alternative to continuing their toleration of the rightist cabinet. What is more, they feared that if the SPD were to assume governmental responsibility at the height of the crisis and break off the catastrophic passive resistance policy, 'nationalist' Germany would once again accuse the party of 'back-stabbing'.

It took the 'Cuno strikes' to convince the SPD party leaders that further toleration of the government was not a lesser, but a greater evil than a Grand Coalition. This remedy, long overdue, came together within a few short days, since not only the moderate bourgeois parties, the Centre and the DDP, but also powerful voices within the DVP and the business community had come to regard the policies of the minority cabinet as mistaken and dangerous. In its negotiations with the government parties, the SPD pushed through a number of measures, including the speedy containment of inflation, preparation of a gold currency, separation of the Reichswehr from all illegal organizations, 'foreign policy activity towards a solution of the reparations question while maintaining the complete unity of the nation and the sovereignty of the republic', and an application for German membership in the League of Nations. A Stresemann chancellorship, long in public discussion, was acceptable to the Social Democrats not least because they themselves, for domestic political reasons, were intent on avoiding the top position. Though they formed the strongest party, they contented themselves with the ministries of finance, economics, justice, and the interior. The remaining cabinet members came from the ranks of the DVP, Centre, and DDP, or were nonaligned, like the agriculture minister, Luther, who remained in office.

On 13 August, the day after Cuno's resignation, President Ebert appointed Gustav Stresemann chancellor and foreign minister. The following day, the new head of government won the vote of confidence from the Reichstag. A good third of the DVP and SPD delegates did not show up to vote, a clear sign that the Grand Coalition was still a highly controversial matter in the two wing parties. The political right, in Bavaria no less than in the occupied territories, was outraged by the SPD's return to government. Two cabinet members were targets of particular hostility: Rudolf Hilferding, the finance minister, since he was a Jew, and Gustav Radbruch, the minister of justice, who, holding the same office under Wirth, was seen as the embodiment of the hated *Republikschutzgesetz.* For the working class, on the other hand, the formation of the Grand Coalition had a calming effect. The 'Cuno strikes' subsided. There was no longer any immediate danger of a revolutionary situation in Germany.[19]

The leaders of the Third International were of a different opinion. In the middle of August, under the impact of the 'Cuno strikes', Grigory Zinoviev, the general secretary of the Comintern, called on the KPD to ready itself for the impending revolutionary crisis. On 23 August the politburo of the Russian Communist Party held a secret meeting. Against a hesitant party secretary Stalin, Zinoviev, Radek, and the people's commissar for defence, Leon Trotsky, pushed through a resolution to set up a special committee with the task of systematically preparing for a communist revolution in Germany.

In September came the final decision for the 'German October', which Trotsky wished to set for 9 November 1923, the fifth anniversary of the German revolution. On 1 October Zinoviev directed the KPD leadership to involve the party as much as possible in the minority government of Saxony under the leftist Social Democrat Erich Zeigner, which the Communists had been tolerating since March. The next step was to be the arming of the Saxon proletariat. Saxony would be the starting point of the German revolution, a civil war that would end with the triumph of the Communists over the fascists and the bourgeois republic.

While the Communists were planning the revolution, the political crisis in Germany came to a head. On 26 September, after long hesitation, the president and government announced the end of the policy of passive resistance. The Bavarian government responded that same day by declaring a state of emergency and transferring executive power to the president of Upper Bavaria, Gustav Ritter von Kahr. To this the Reich reacted on 26 September with its own decree declaring a state of emergency in all of Germany and transferring the executive authority to the minister of defence, who could delegate it in turn to the military commanders. Legally speaking, the Bavarian government was obligated to annul its measures at the behest of the Reich president or parliament. But Stresemann and the bourgeois ministers in his cabinet, believing that Bavaria would not obey such a request, thought it better to avoid a trip to Munich in the first place.

Shortly thereafter, the weakness of the federal government became even more clearly manifest. On 27 September the *Völkischer Beobachter*, the mouthpiece of the NSDAP, directed sharp anti-Semitic attacks against 'dictators Stresemann and Seeckt', since the latter was married to a 'half-Jewess', the former to a 'Jewess'. Defence Minister Gessler ordered Kahr to ban the newspaper. Kahr refused, and he was backed up by the commander of the federal troops in Bavaria, General von Lossow. This was a clear case of refusal to obey orders. Nonetheless Seeckt, the head of the Reichswehr, was as little inclined as he had been in the spring of 1921 to order federal troops to fire on their own. Instead, he prepared himself for a role on the federal level similar to Kahr's in Bavaria, and there were many who supported him. A 'national dictatorship' under a 'directory' led by Seeckt—this was the demand of prominent heavy industrialists like Hugo Stinnes and all those whose political home was the German National People's Party.

Even Ebert and Stresemann, in their conversation on 22 September (Defence Minister Gessler and Sollmann, the Social Democratic interior minister, were also present), discussed the possibility of a temporary Seeckt dictatorship as a last resort to protect the unity of the Reich against Bavarian particularism and the separatist aspirations in the Rhineland. Another kind of dictatorship was proposed at the cabinet meeting on 30 September by Labour Minister Brauns, a Centre politician, and Finance Minister Hilferding: an 'enabling act' (*Ermächtigungsgesetz*) allowing the government to take whatever financial and political steps were necessary. One such necessary step, in the view of both, was the extension of the working day, a measure supported by business but opposed by the Free Trade Unions.

The SPD, however, was not prepared to countenance the kind of executive authority over working hours Hilferding and Brauns desired. Hermann Müller, the party head, made this clear in a meeting of the coalition party leaders on 2 October. The governmental right wing was far less ceremonious in its rejection of the Stresemann cabinet's policies. At that same meeting Ernst Scholz, head of the DVP fraction, demanded the complete elimination of the eight-hour day, a 'break with France', and the inclusion of the German Nationalists in the Grand Coalition. He was acting as the mouthpiece of Stinnes, who sought nothing less than to bring down Stresemann and erect a 'national dictatorship'. The next day saw the failure of final attempts to arrive at a compromise on working hours, since the Social Democratic Reichstag fraction refused to do battle with the Free Trade Unions. With no options left, Stresemann handed in his resignation.

By 6 October, however, the chancellor was once again Gustav Stresemann, and once again he presided over a Grand Coalition cabinet. The rapid end to the government crisis was the work of President Ebert, who charged Stresemann with the task of forming a new government immediately after the old cabinet's resignation. In addition, the majority of the DVP refused to uphold the hard-line policy of its industry-dominated right wing. The decisive breakthrough came in the night of 5–6 October. The party leaders agreed to the compromise formula on working hours their experts had worked out eleven months previously, on 13 November 1922: the eight-hour day was to be fundamentally preserved, but could be extended by contractual agreement or legislation.

At this juncture the SPD, too, was ready to endorse an enabling act that did not affect working hours and that would remain in force only for the duration of the current coalition. On 13 October the Reichstag passed this law with the necessary constitutional two-thirds majority, and it formed the basis of ordinances dealing with unemployment assistance, staff cuts in public services, and introducing compulsory government mediation in wage disagreements. The latter measure, which made the state the final arbiter of industrial action, brought about what Hilferding summarized in 1927 in the concept of the 'political wage' and celebrated as the expression of a higher, 'organized capitalism', indeed as a step towards socialism: the veritable abolition of wage autonomy and market forces. The parallels to Article 48 were obvious. Just as the parties could shift responsibility 'upstairs' to the president in difficult situations, the wage partners could now relegate their conflicts to the minister of labour. This was the first time changes of such magnitude had been initiated in Germany by government ordinance.

While the fate of the Grand Coalition was being decided in Berlin, rightist-authoritarian forces and Communists were working for regime change. In Bavaria, Hitler had himself elected on 25 September as the leader of the 'German Combat League' (*Deutscher Kampfbund*), a new umbrella organization of the 'Patriotic Leagues'. Four days later, Kahr abolished the enforcement of the

Republikschutzgesetz. Another measure by the general state commissar was even more clearly intended to attract the support of the National Socialists: considerable numbers of eastern Jews were deported from Bavaria after the middle of October. However, Kahr's heaviest blow against the Reich came on 20 October, when Defence Minister Gessler ordered the long-overdue dismissal of von Lossow, the Munich district commander. Kahr promptly appointed him commander-in-chief of the Bavarian forces and declared the Seventh Division of the Reichswehr under the authority of the Free State.

Neither Kahr, nor Lossow, nor their ally, Colonel von Seisser, commander of the Bavarian police, had any intention of seceding from the Reich. Rather, the Bavarian triumvirate wished to model the Reich after Bavaria. What they had in mind was a 'march on Berlin' culminating in the establishment of a 'national dictatorship'. The National Socialists were permitted to participate in the march. The role of the German Mussolini was not intended for Hitler, however, but reserved for Kahr and, later, on the federal level, for a man of comparable outlook. Seeckt was considered a candidate, even after the events of 20 October. Yet despite his sympathies for Kahr's political vision, the chief of the army command was a legalist. It was improbable that he would launch an attack against the expressed will of the Reich president.

The main theatre of Communist activities was central Germany. On 10 October the KPD was able to report that it had carried out the orders of the general secretary of the Comintern issued nine days before: the Communists had entered Erich Zeigner's Saxon government, where they assumed the posts of the minister of finance, minister of economics, and, in the person of party head Heinrich Brandler, director of the state chancellery. In Thuringia, too, an SPD–KPD coalition government under the Social Democrat August Frölich was formed on 16 October, the Communists acquiring the economics and justice ministries.

The Dresden and Weimar governments of the unified leftist front were formed legally, and both were endorsed by parliamentary majorities. The Zeigner and Frölich cabinets undertook no steps that could be considered hostile to the Reich. But nobody in Berlin, including the ruling Social Democrats, had any doubt about the intention of the Communists to use Saxony and Thuringia to launch the struggle for power in Germany. The Reich reacted accordingly. On 13 October the Saxon district commander, General Müller, who from 27 September held the executive power, banned the paramilitary 'Proletarian Hundreds' (*Proletarische Hundertschaften*) of the KPD. On 16 October, after consultation with Defence Minister Gessler, Müller announced that the Saxon police was to be immediately placed under the command of the Reichswehr. This move stripped the Dresden government of its only instrument of power.

Until 21 October, the danger of a communist uprising in Saxony was quite real. The KPD had planned for this day a workers' conference in Chemnitz that was supposed to call a general strike and give the signal for the uprising. But when

Brandler, speaking at this conference, demanded the immediate commencement of the general strike in response to the dictatorship of the Reichswehr, he met with no agreement. The Social Democratic minister of labour, Graupe, threatened to desert the meeting with his party colleagues if the Communists persisted in this direction. He met with no resistance. The timetable for the 'German October' was thus frustrated, and with it the attempt to repeat in Germany the example set in Russia by the Bolsheviks in October (and November) 1917. Only Hamburg witnessed a putsch-like communist rebellion. After three days of bloodshed, the police were once again in control of the Hanse city by 25 October.

At about this same time, between 21 and 27 October, the Reichswehr took control throughout Saxony. Armed clashes cost lives in several cities. On 27 October Stresemann sent Zeigner an ultimatum. Pointing to the revolutionary propaganda of Communist members of the administration, including Brandler, he demanded that the Saxon prime minister form a government without Communists. If Zeigner refused, Stresemann would appoint a commissar with the task of governing Saxony until a constitutional government was put in place. Zeigner refused.

The process of federal executive action began the next day. Invoking Article 48 of the Weimar constitution, the Reich president empowered the chancellor to remove the members of the Saxon government from office and to entrust other persons with the business of state. Stresemann then appointed the DVP Reichstag delegate Karl Rudolf Heinze, former federal minister of justice, as the commissar for Saxony. On the afternoon of 29 October, the Reichswehr expelled the Saxon ministers from the government buildings. Zeigner resigned the next day. In the presence of Otto Wels, head of the Social Democratic Party, and Wilhelm Dittmann, a member of the party executive, the SPD fraction of the Saxon parliament nominated Alfred Fellisch, former economics minister, to lead a Social Democratic minority cabinet. The DDP promised to tolerate the new government. On 31 October, the Saxon parliament elected Fellisch as Zeigner's successor, whereupon President Ebert, at Stresemann's request, withdrew Heinze as federal commissar.

The federal executive action against Saxony proceeded differently from what the Reichswehr had had in mind. Stresemann's solution was a state of emergency in its most civil form, preserving the primacy of politics. Nonetheless the Social Democrats, though they had fundamentally endorsed the chancellor's 27 October ultimatum, raised serious objections after the fact. Although they were critical of their Saxon and Thuringian comrades, what really upset both the leadership and the rank and file of the SPD was the discrepancy between the treatment of Saxony and the treatment of Bavaria. In a meeting of the Reichstag fraction on 31 October, Stresemann's critics prevailed. They now issued an ultimatum in their own right, demanding that the Reich government lift the military state of emergency, declare the behaviour of the Bavarian leaders unconstitutional, and immediately undertake the necessary steps against the Free State. The bourgeois ministers, convinced of the political and military impossibility of a civil war over

Bavaria, rejected these demands. On 2 November the SPD withdrew from the government. Stresemann's second cabinet was now a bourgeois minority government.

In leaving the Grand Coalition, the Social Democrats were acting out of the fear that many of their supporters would turn to the Communists if they continued to countenance what were felt to be 'rightist' policies. But the retreat from government was a risk; it left a power vacuum that could be exploited by the plotters of dictatorship. In a fraction meeting on 31 October the Prussian interior minister, Carl Severing, who represented Münster in the Reichstag, warned against the danger that the French could conspire with German separatists to establish a 'Rhenish Republic' and the forces of the extreme right start a war with France. 'Back to pure class struggle!', the solution of Reichstag president Paul Löbe, was not a realistic alternative for the Social Democrats. Even if they were not part of the government, Germany's largest party was obligated to see to it that the country remained governable. Anything else would have been a politics of catastrophe, an option not open to the party that had founded the Weimar state.

Four days after the end of the Grand Coalition the Reichswehr, with Ebert's authorization, moved into central and eastern Thuringia, forcibly dissolving the Proletarian Hundreds over the ensuing days. On 12 November the Thuringian SPD, submitting to the pressure from Berlin, terminated the coalition with the KPD. Prime Minister Frölich stayed on as head of a minority cabinet until early *Landtag* elections on 24 February 1924. These elections took the SPD out of power; for the next three years, Thuringia was governed by a bourgeois minority cabinet tolerated by the DVP. In Saxony, the interim of the SPD minority government lasted until January 1924, when it was succeeded by a SPD–DDP–DVP cabinet bitterly opposed by the Social Democratic left wing. Two years later the Saxon SPD split, and the Social Democratic Party thereafter stood in opposition to a government headed by a prime minister from the rightist 'Old Social Democrats' until 1929.

At the beginning of November 1923 very few people imagined that Stresemann's rump cabinet would last very long. Ebert was not one of them. In a letter of 4 November, the president authorized General von Seeckt to find out if Otto Wiedfeldt, the German ambassador in Washington, would be prepared to assume the chancellorship at the head of a 'small, directory-type cabinet with emergency powers'. Wiedfeldt's letter of refusal had not yet arrived in Berlin by the time the Bavarian crisis reached its spectacular peak. On the evening of 8 November, Adolf Hitler took advantage of an assembly of Kahr supporters in the Bürgerbräukeller, one of Munich's large beer halls, to call for a 'national revolution'. Wielding a pistol, the National Socialist leader forced Kahr, Lossow, and Seisser to participate. Erich Ludendorff, however, whom Hitler appointed on the spot as commander-in-chief of the national army, soon restored the triumvirate's freedom of action, and Hitler's coup was rapidly countered. At noon on 9 November the bullets of the Bavarian police brought the putsch to an end at the

Munich Feldherrnhalle. Hitler himself managed to make his escape, but was arrested two days later. Sixteen of his followers paid for the 'national revolution' with their lives.

The Munich events led to dramatic changes in Berlin, too. In the night of 8 November, Ebert transferred to the chief of the army leadership the command over the Reichswehr and, in modification of the ordinance of 26 September 1923, the executive authority. The president and parliament were seemingly convinced that Seeckt's empowerment was the only way to get the Bavarian Reichswehr to oppose the rebels. There was, of course, no guarantee that Seeckt himself would not try to take over. Ebert probably thought that the army chief would be less dangerous to the republic as his, the president's, direct subordinate than in his previous position, which was virtually free from control.

The Hitler putsch was a watershed, not only for Bavaria, but for the Reich as a whole. The events of 8 November thoroughly discredited the 'serious' dictatorial plans of Kahr and his associates and deeply compromised the authority of the general state commissar. But without the firm backing of the Bavarian political leadership, a 'national' revolution was virtually inconceivable in Germany. As a result, Hitler's putsch achieved the exact opposite of what the National Socialist leader had sought, contributing greatly to the consolidation of the endangered republic.[20]

On 15 November, one week after the Munich putsch, Stresemann's rump cabinet succeeded in performing the '*Rentenmark* miracle'. The new currency, introduced on this day, was conceived as a provisional measure. According to the proposal of Hans Luther, who had succeeded Rudolf Hilferding as finance minister on 6 October, debenture bonds and mortgages on agricultural and industrial land would guarantee the market value of the *Rentenmark* until a permanent, gold-supported currency could be introduced. On 20 November the mark's exchange rate, which had been 1.26 trillion to the dollar on 14 November, was stabilized at 4.2 trillion. At that point, the federal bank set an analogous rate of 1 trillion paper marks to 1 *Rentenmark*, thereby achieving once again the pre-war exchange rate between mark and dollar.

The victim of the currency reform was the Rhineland. Until the introduction of the gold-backed *Reichsmark* on 30 August 1924, the occupied territory was all but abandoned by the Reich and forced to get along with municipal emergency money as a means of payment. On 13 November the mayor of Cologne, Konrad Adenauer, protested that 'the Rhineland must be worth more than one or two or even three new currencies', but in vain. From the perspective of Berlin, the danger that the Rhineland would temporarily become politically independent, in whatever form, seemed like the lesser of two evils compared with the economic collapse threatening all of Germany if the new currency were to be ruined by the continued complete subsidization of the occupied territories.

Another kind of 'miracle' became manifest after 25 October. On this day Poincaré, the French prime minister, informed the British government that he was prepared, under certain conditions, to agree to a re-examination of the reparations question. He was responding to a suggestion the American secretary of state, Charles Hughes, had originally made at the end of December 1922, and which the British government had adopted on 12 October, that the economic aspects of the reparations question be discussed at an international conference. The French conditions were the following: the panel of experts was to be appointed by the Allied Reparations Commission; the amount of Germany's reparation debt, imposed on the Reich by the May 1921 London ultimatum, was to be independent of the examination's findings; and a second commission was to determine the amount and the whereabouts of German foreign currency assets. After America also agreed to this proposal, Paris officially petitioned the Reparations Commission on 13 November to set both commissions to work. This set the course for the Dawes Plan, the 1924 reparations treaty to which the economic upswing of the middle Weimar years was inextricably linked.

There were many reasons for Poincaré's about-face. The occupation of the Rhine had become too much of a burden and was endangering the French currency; the domestic opposition of the left had grown stronger, and France had increasingly isolated itself on the international stage. But more important was another reason. On 23 October Hughes, the American secretary of state, informed the French prime minister that the United States would accept France's participation in the inter-Allied expert commission and link the discussion of the reparations question with the problem of debts between the Allies. By accommodating Germany to a certain extent, France could thus expect to improve its position as America's debtor.

Paris's new policy on reparations did not yet mean that France had renounced its aim of separating the Rhineland from Germany. On 25 October, the same day he informed the British of his change of course, Poincaré also decided to adopt a policy of active and official support for the autonomy of the occupied territories. After 21 October there were movements afoot in a number of cities—including Aachen, Trier, Koblenz, Bonn, and Wiesbaden—to proclaim a 'Rhenish Republic.' These separatist aspirations were supported by the French and Belgian occupying authorities, but not by larger circles of the population. By November 1923 it was clear both in the Prussian Rhineland and in the Bavarian Palatinate that a voluntary secession from the Reich would not occur.

Thus the chances of a gradual de-escalation of tensions were looking favourable, both internally and externally, when a new governmental crisis broke out in Berlin. On 22 November, against all of Ebert's warnings, the SPD brought a motion of no confidence in Stresemann's minority cabinet. The justification was that the government had proceeded with utmost harshness against Saxony and Thuringia but had done nothing decisive about the anti-constitutional situation in Bavaria. The motion was consciously formulated such that the German National People's Party, on whose vote everything depended, would not be able to endorse it. The Social Democrats did not want to bring down Stresemann's government, but to make a statement and thus to calm emotions on the party's left wing. Stresemann, however, was not about to allow his position to be further undermined, and countered the SPD initiative by calling for a vote of confidence. On 23 November, by 231 against 156 votes and 7 abstentions, the Reichstag rejected the motion of the governmental parties. For the first time in the history of the German Republic, as the deposed chancellor afterwards told foreign correspondents, a government had fallen 'on the open field of battle'.

The settling of the crisis was mostly the work of Ebert. On 30 November 1923 Stresemann was succeeded by the head of the Centre Party and parliamentary fraction, Wilhelm Marx, a judge from Cologne and a somewhat colourless personality. He led a bourgeois cabinet composed of members from the Centre, DVP, DDP, and BVP, including the former chancellor as foreign minister. The new administration was subject to the toleration of the SPD, which, again under massive pressure from the president, even assisted in the passage of another enabling act. This law, in effect until 14 February 1924, empowered the government to 'take the measures it considers necessary and urgent with regard to the distress of the people and the state'. One of the things now subject to government control was the length of the working day. A new policy was a matter of pressing concern, since the demobilization ordinances from the revolutionary period, which had been extended several times, had expired on 17 November. Thereafter, according to law, the pre-war working day was in effect wherever hours were not regulated by contract.

By the time the enabling law expired a quarter of a year later, many things had changed in Germany. Although the eight-hour day continued to be considered the norm, the ten-hour day was legally permitted in large portions of the economy. The Free Trade Unions answered this defeat in January 1924 by terminating the Central Cooperative Union of November 1918. But this was little more than a symbolic protest. In December 1923 the salaries of civil servants were set at a level far below that of pre-war Germany. On 14 February 1924 an emergency tax measure initiated the dismantling of state control in the housing market. This was an important step towards ending the 'war socialism' that had outlasted the war by more than half a decade.

The same ordinance regulated the fiercely controversial revaluation of outstanding debts from certain kinds of capital investments destroyed by inflation, such as mortgages, bonds, debentures, savings accounts, and life insurance policies. The flat revaluation rate of 15 per cent of the value in gold marks contained the tacit admission that Finance Minister Luther's principle of 'mark for mark' simply could not be reconciled with an elementary sense of justice, since it would have meant complete dispossession. However, repayment of revaluation debts was extended until 1932, the repayment of the principal and interest on public loans, including the war loans, until the final amortization of the reparations—that is, for an indefinite period of time.

The embittered protest of the millions who were affected had no effect on the measure. The Marx government could do nothing else, at the risk of jeopardizing the new currency. The real victims of the inflation were people with savings and the underwriters of war loans. 'A concentration of property in a few but powerful hands has taken place,' wrote the economist Franz Eulenburg in 1924.

The capital assets of the middle classes were destroyed, and with them the claim to a part of the other properties. The appropriation has occurred above all in industry. The smaller and medium-sized companies have not been expropriated, but are now more strongly dependent on the concerns. Accordingly, the distribution of wealth is significantly less equitable than before.

The devaluation, though it did not bankrupt the middle class as a whole, nonetheless ruined or permanently weakened considerable portions of it. Those who had lived from their savings or derived their income from securities were left, at the end of the inflationary period, with literally nothing. Academic families, who traditionally paid for their children's studies out of savings, were also hard hit. On the other hand, many in the middle class benefited from the devaluation. House and property owners were now debt-free and profited from the general valorization of material assets.

The real winners were the large landowners, most of whom had been deeply in debt, and the owners of large industrial properties. In a material sense the state, too, profited from inflation. The repayment of its debts in worthless paper money, especially the gigantic sums of the war credits, was tantamount to a general debt-release. In a non-material sense, of course, the state was among the losers. Its credibility had been fundamentally shaken, and it was against the republic that the inflation's victims directed their resentment. Five years after the end of the war, the monarchy, which had initiated the inflation in 1914, appeared to many Germans in a rosy light once more.

The inflation had had a levelling effect. The income difference between the higher and lower government officials had shrunk, and the same was true of the gap between the bureaucracy as a whole and the working classes. But the workers by no means benefited. According to the calculations of the federal statistics bureau, real weekly wages in December 1923 amounted to 70 per cent of the pre-war level. Unemployment was also high. In December 1923, 28 per cent of union members were without work. The membership of the ADGB fell from 7.7 million in September 1923 to 4.8 million in March 1924. The role the unions had played in the Ruhr conflict, where they had shored up the state, was disregarded by large numbers of workers. In fact, at the beginning of 1924 everything seemed to indicate that the potential for mass proletarian protest was much higher than a year before.

Nonetheless, there were also unmistakable signs of an easing of tensions on the domestic front. In the Ruhr district, normal work resumed at the end of November after an agreement between the Mining Association (*Bergbaulicher Verein*) and the MICUM (*Mission interalliée de contrôle des usines et des mines*) on 23 November 1923. The stabilization of the economy in the Rhineland and Ruhr district increasingly undermined the project of a Rhenish federal state loosely connected with the

Reich, such as Adenauer had been pursuing with the support of Stinnes in autumn 1923. The plan was sharply rejected by Foreign Minister Stresemann in January 1924, whereupon the mayor of Cologne put it aside.

On 28 February the military state of emergency was ended at Seeckt's initiative. On the one hand, the general wanted to avoid eroding the authority of the Reichswehr in a running battle with civil agencies, above all in Saxony and Thuringia, but also in Prussia. On the other hand, Seeckt feared an infiltration by right-wing radical organizations. Internal consolidation of the army was more important to him than an exercise of power with no political payoff.

There was some initial controversy about whether the bans against the KPD, NSDAP, and the German Ethnic Freedom Party, which the army chief had pronounced on 23 November 1923 as head of the executive, should remain in effect. Seeckt wanted to maintain them; Severing demanded they be lifted. The Prussian interior minister was able to prevail, for the most part. The party bans came to an end at the same time as the state of emergency. Public demonstrations in the open air were still forbidden for the time being, though the central agencies of the *Länder* were permitted to authorize exceptions. This 'civil' state of emergency lasted eight months, ended by presidential decree on 25 October 1924.

The conflict between Bavaria and the Reich was officially brought to an end in February 1924. As per a settlement of 14 February, the Reichswehr commander in Bavaria could only be recalled in agreement with the Bavarian government and in accord with its legitimate wishes. Furthermore, the wording of the oaths for the army and navy were modified to include a pledge of loyalty to the constitution of the recruit's home state. This settled the right of the Munich government to use the troops of the Reichswehr stationed in Bavaria. Four days later, Kahr resigned as general state commissar and Lossow as commander-in-chief in Bavaria. Their anti-Reich and anti-constitutional activities in the autumn of 1923 had no legal consequences of any kind.[21]

On 1 April 1924 the Munich court handed down the judgments in the cases against the rebels of 8–9 November 1923. General Ludendorff was acquitted of the charge of high treason. Five other participants in the putsch, among them Ernst Röhm, organizer of the National Socialist 'Storm Troopers' (*Sturmabteilungen* or SA), were sentenced to three months in prison and a fine of 100 marks. Hitler himself, along with three other conspirators, was condemned to five years in prison and a fine of 200 marks. For this latter group, too, probation was possible, once six months of the sentence had been served. (In the event, Hitler was released at Christmas 1924 from his imprisonment at Landsberg, which he had used to write his book *Mein Kampf.**) All of the accused were recognized by the court as having 'acted in a purely patriotic spirit and according to the noblest and most selfless will' and in the sincere belief 'that they were compelled to act in order to save the Fatherland and that they did exactly what the intentions of

* Hitler, *My Struggle.*

the leading Bavarian men had been shortly before.' Morally speaking, this amounted to an acquittal, and it was understood as such throughout all of Germany.

The controversy of the Munich decision had not yet passed when an event that was to decisively affect the further development of the republic made headlines. On 9 April 1924 the commission of experts under the American banker Charles Dawes, which had gone to work in Paris in January, published its report on the reparations question. While no total amount owed by Germany was named, the study evidently assumed that the 132 million gold marks demanded by the London ultimatum of May 1921 was beyond the capacity of the German economy. In order not to endanger the currency, it was recommended that the creditor nations appoint a reparations agent to arrange for 'transfer protection', a payment method that sought to safeguard the stability of the mark. The yearly instalments, or annuities, began with a billion gold marks, to be increased to 2.5 billion over the course of five years. In order to accommodate the French desire for guarantees, the rail system of the Reich was changed into a corporation with specific obligations to fulfil and with a board of directors including representatives from the creditor nations (an internationally composed general council was also installed in the Reichsbank). Several other sources of federal revenue and a 5 billion mark, interest-bearing mortgage of German industrial corporations were to provide further securities.

These restrictions on German sovereignty were far-reaching, and yet considerably easier to bear than the territorial guarantees France and Belgium had seized in January 1923 in the Ruhr occupation. The Dawes Plan also contained an element of good news for the German economy: a 800 million mark foreign loan, which was to provide the foundation for a new bank of issue and secure the stability of the currency. The proceeds were to be directed exclusively towards the payment of domestic obligations to the Allies like materials shipments and occupation costs. But the provision contained the prospect of future American loans and investments, and this prospect had a stimulating effect. Germany, which had been one of the most important markets for American goods before 1914, could well assume that the United States had recognized the opportunity that lay in engagement with its productive, albeit capital-hungry economy.

The Dawes Plan was America's contribution towards the stabilization of Germany. The Union of Soviet Socialist Republics made its own contribution at about the same time. After Lenin's death in January 1924, Moscow's drive towards world revolution abated. As Stalin's position grew stronger, the 'development of socialism in one country'—that is, in the Soviet Union—became the priority. The improvised revolutions attempted in Germany by the Comintern in March 1921 and again in the autumn of 1923 did not accord with the new policy, proclaimed by Stalin in 1925 but already in practice earlier.

The world-political change of scene in 1923–4 also included new developments in London and Paris. In Great Britain, the Labour Party and the Liberals triumphed over the Conservatives in the elections for the House of Commons on

6 December 1923. In January 1924 Ramsay MacDonald became the first British head of government from the Labour Party. In France, Poincaré's *Bloc national* lost the majority to the *Cartel des gauches*, an electoral alliance between the Socialists and the bourgeois Radical Socialists, on 11 May 1924. The Radical Socialist Édouard Herriot, an admirer of German Idealist philosophy, became prime minister without opposition from the Socialists. Germany could expect a friendlier attitude from the new British and French governments than from the previous rightist cabinets.

It was evident by the spring of 1924 that France's attempt to forcibly revise the post-war order in its favour had failed. Germany emerged from the Ruhr conflict economically weakened but, thanks to the intervention of the United States, politically stronger. The post-war period had come to an end between November 1923 and April 1924. A relative stabilization in Germany and in the relations between the most important states was unmistakable.[22]

FROM MARX TO LUTHER

The second Reichstag elections on 4 May 1924 revealed the limits of this political calm. The radicals on both sides of the political spectrum made strong gains at the expense of most of the moderate parties. The German Nationalists, whose electoral campaign had targeted the portions of the middle classes harmed by inflation, increased their share of the vote from 15.1 to 19.5%. (Both here and subsequently, I include in the 1920 figures the results of the 1921 elections in Schleswig-Holstein and East Prussia and the 1922 elections in Upper Silesia.) This made the DNVP the strongest force in the bourgeois camp and the second largest party in the country. The German Ethnic Freedom Party, in alliance with the leaderless National Socialists, achieved 6.5 per cent straight off. All in all, over a quarter of the German electorate voted for the anti-republican right.

Two changes were conspicuous left of centre: a strong shift from the Social Democrats to the Communists, and a considerable weakening of 'Marxist' voices across the board. In the 1920 elections the workers' parties had together achieved 41.7% of the vote. In May 1924 they managed only 34%. The SPD fell from 21.7% to 20.5%. This seems like only a small loss at first glance. In reality, however, it was a disaster: the reunited SPD gained fewer votes in May 1924 than the Majority party alone had obtained in 1920. Clearly, a considerable number of the 17.9% of Germans who had voted USPD in 1920 had migrated to the KPD, which, with 12.6% of the 1924 vote, became a proletarian mass party in the Reich for the first time.

Some of the parties of the bourgeois centre and the moderate right took considerable losses—losses which became the gains of the German Nationalists and the German Ethnic Freedom Party. The DVP fell from 13.9% to 9.2%, the DDP from 8.3% to 5.7%. The Catholic parties suffered comparatively little: the Centre

Party sank from 13.6% to 13.4%, the BVP from 4.2% to 3.2%. Bourgeois splinter groups garnered a total of 8.5% of the vote, a 5.3% gain from the previous elections.

After the elections, the DNVP demanded the office of chancellor and presented the former Admiral of the Fleet von Tirpitz as its candidate. The centre parties rejected the Father of the German Navy with the same resolution the German Nationalists showed with regard to the centre's exhortation that they embrace the Dawes Plan, the rejection of which had been one of the main themes of their electoral campaign. The upshot was that, on 3 June, Wilhelm Marx formed another bourgeois minority cabinet, which, however, the BVP refused to join on account of acute tensions.

After the defeat of the SPD, a Grand Coalition was no longer seen as a serious option. At the Social Democratic Party congress in Berlin from 11 to 14 June 1924, the left wing denounced the leadership's coalition policy to date. The president of the Metalworkers' Association, the former Independent Robert Dissmann, confronted the 'solicitude for the state and bourgeois coalition parties' with a 'policy of uncompromising class struggle', which Dissmann saw as the only way to win back the proletarian voters who had gone over to the Communists. Müller, the party head, expressed the mitigating view that if the coalitions of the recent years were examined, it would be seen that 'we have only been in the government when we *had* to be in the government. The reasons that compelled us were almost always reasons of foreign policy.' In a proposal submitted by Müller and adopted by the delegates with a large majority, the congress characterized the coalition policy as a matter of tactics and not of principle. Participation in government was to be undertaken only 'after an examination of all advantages and disadvantages for the interests of the less well-off, so that we can be sure that the working class will not alone be called upon to make sacrifices'. The message was clear: non-participation in the government of the Reich was to be considered the norm for the Social Democratic Party.

Non-participation did not mean unconditional opposition, of course. In matters of foreign policy, Chancellor Marx and Foreign Minister Stresemann could regularly count on the votes of the SPD. This was also true with regard to the Dawes Plan and the supplementary agreements worked out at a conference in London in August 1924. The German negotiators were able to achieve a notable success there: the French and Belgians promised to withdraw from the areas they had occupied in 1921 and 1923—not immediately, as the Germans had demanded, but within a year's time. The Dortmund-Hörde zone, however, as well as all territories on the right bank of the Rhine occupied in January 1923, would be restored to Germany the day after the final signing of the agreement. This made it officially clear that the Rhineland would remain part of Germany and would be economically and financially fully reintegrated into the Reich.

The votes of the SPD were not sufficient to pass all the laws of the Dawes Plan. The railway bill, which restricted German sovereignty and thus entailed modifying the constitution, required a two-thirds majority. This could only be achieved with the support of a considerable number of German Nationalist votes. In order to soften DNVP opposition, the government made a clearly 'national' statement about the question of war guilt on 29 August, one day before the signing of the London agreement. But even this gesture failed to achieve the hoped-for effect. Several influential interest groups pressed the German Nationalists to accept the bill. These included the National Association of German Industry (*Reichsverband der Deutschen Industrie*, which united in 1919 the Central Association of German Industrialists, the Federation of Industrialists, and the Association for the Protection of the Interests of the Chemical Industry), the Christian-national Labour unions, and, for a time, though in a qualified manner, even the National Land League (*Reichslandbund*), the powerful successor of the Federation of Agriculturalists. In the case of the bill's rejection, the president and the chancellor threatened to dissolve the Reichstag. The DVP held out the prospect of a share in the government if the DNVP helped it pass. In the decisive ballot on 29 August, 52 German Nationalist delegates voted against, 48 in favour. That was sufficient to pass the railroad law with a two-thirds majority and the London agreement as a whole.

The next day, the 'good behaviour' of the DNVP was to be rewarded. On the parliamentary agenda stood the first reading of a bill proposed by the government to reintroduce the agricultural customs of the 1902 'Bülow tariff', which had expired in 1914. The law was to take effect on 25 January 1925, the day Germany's Versailles Treaty obligation to grant the victorious powers most-favoured-nation privileges expired, restoring the Reich's commercial freedom. But the plan foundered on the opposition of the left: the SPD and KPD walked out of the plenum assembly, leaving the Reichstag without a quorum. It adjourned until 15 October. Three days before it reconvened, the government withdrew the bill. The attempt to restore the privileges of the large landowners at the expense of the consumers had failed, at least for the moment.

The impossibility of finding a dependable parliamentary majority for the business of government was so obvious that the Marx cabinet decided, on 20 October, to petition the president for the dissolution of the Reichstag. Ebert agreed that same day, setting new elections for 7 December. The second parliamentary electoral campaign was influenced by the economic recovery the country was experiencing. On 30 August, the provisional *Rentenmark* gave way to the new *Reichsmark*, which was covered to 40% of its value by gold or foreign currencies. Once the London agreement had been concluded, foreign credit poured into Germany. The unemployment rate fell from 12.4% of union labour in July to 7.3% in November. Contract wages climbed from an average of 57 pfennigs per hour in January 1924 to 72.5 in January 1925 (according to information from twelve selected branches of industry). At the same time, the percentage of workers who had to work more than 48 hours per week fell from 54.7% in May to 45.5% in November.

The economic upswing led to a political de-radicalization. The extremists on the outer party wings—the German Ethnic Freedom Party, which now called itself the National Socialist Freedom Party (*Nationalsozialistische Freiheitspartei*), and the Communists—emerged from the 7 December elections weaker than before. The winners were the Social Democrats and, to a lesser extent, the German Nationalists. The SPD climbed from 20.5% to 26% of the vote, the DNVP from 19.5% to 20.5%. The Communists fell from 12.6% to 9%, the union of the National Socialists and the German Ethnic Freedom Party from 6.5% to 3%. The changes in the centre and moderate right were fairly minor. Of the small parties, the Economic Party (*Wirtschaftspartei*), representing the small and medium-sized business community, was the most successful with 3.3%. The revaluation parties achieved a mere 0.4%, mainly because the German Nationalists had once again campaigned strongly as the party of those harmed by the inflation.

The election results allowed only two possibilities for a majority government: either a Grand Coalition or a bourgeois centre-right cabinet. The DVP declared its unwillingness to work with the Social Democrats, and the DDP refused to join with the German Nationalists—which did not make a bourgeois bloc impossible, however, since the latter already had a majority without the left-liberal party. On 15 January 1925, after arduous negotiations, the first Reich government with DNVP participation came together under the non-aligned chancellor Hans Luther. Stresemann remained foreign minister, the Centre politician Heinrich Brauns minister of labour. Despite the fact that his party, the DDP, was not in the government, Otto Gessler remained the director of the defence department as a 'special minister'. The German Nationalists assumed the leadership of the interior, finance, and economics ministries. Right at the beginning of his term, the new minister of economics, Karl Neuhaus, found himself compelled to bitterly disappoint a large portion of the DNVP constituency. Supported by the unanimous vote of the leading organizations in agriculture, industry, commerce, and banking, he announced in a memorandum at the end of January that a revaluation of more than 15 per cent (that is, the rate set by the emergency tax measure of 14 February 1924 and vehemently attacked by the DNVP) would be intolerable for the owners of material assets and thus unworkable.[23]

EBERT'S DEATH AND THE ELECTION OF HINDENBURG

On 28 February 1925 the party conflict set off by the German Nationalists with their about-face on the revaluation question paused for a moment. On this day, President Ebert died at the age of 54. The immediate cause of death was appendicitis and peritonitis. But his physical powers of resistance had been crippled by emotional injuries. The worst was the accusation of treason levelled at him by—among others—a *völkisch* journalist by the name of Erwin Rothardt, editor of the *Mitteldeutsche Presse*, for Ebert's role during the strike of the Berlin munitions workers in January 1918. On 23 December 1924 an enlarged jury of the Magdeburg district court handed down its judgment in the libel action Ebert had undertaken against the journalist. Although the court sentenced the accused to three months in prison for libel against the president, the opinion noted that Rothardt's claim that Ebert's participation in the strike represented treason was, in a legal sense, valid. Accordingly, defamation of character had not taken place.

Powerful voices were immediately raised against this character assassination on the part of the Magdeburg judges, a typical case of judiciary anti-republicanism. The lawyers for the prosecution appealed the case. The Reich government, the Marx cabinet, issued a statement in defence of the president's honour. Famous scholars, including the historians Friedrich Meinecke and Hans Delbrück as well as the jurists Gerhard Anschütz and Wilhelm Kahl, made an official statement on his behalf. In an open letter to Ebert printed in the *Berliner Tageblatt*, the Evangelical theologian Adolf von Harnack (who was also president of the Kaiser Wilhelm Society for the Advancement of Science, the later Max Planck Society, and had written one of the drafts for the emperor's appeal to the German people in August 1914) spoke of a 'miscarriage of justice' that filled him with outrage:

A disgraceful thing has taken place here, and we are saddened and alarmed. All the more do I, along with all good Germans, feel the gratitude the Fatherland owes you, most honoured Herr President of the Reich, for all of your patriotic work and efforts, especially during the years 1918 and 1919. And since this gratitude lives on today in thousands of hearts, the judgement of history shall confirm it for all future. Nonetheless, such voices were the exception and became, in their turn, the target of hateful commentaries from the right. The Magdeburg decision had a powerful effect, and it was directed against Ebert and the republic for which he stood.

Many of the obituaries for the first president of the Reich seemed like attempts at a posthumous redress. The cabinet, including its German Nationalist members, declared that Ebert had 'administered the office of a President of the German Reich with exemplary conscientiousness and statesmanlike intelligence . . . in the most difficult of times'. In the Social Democratic press, too, there was no lack of effort to smooth over past conflicts. After the federal executive action against Saxony, there had been sharp criticism of Ebert in the SPD and even petitions to expel him from the party. His own union, the Saddlers' Association, did in fact throw him out. *Vorwärts* alluded to such conflicts with the observation that the non-partisan nature of Ebert's office had distanced him from the life of the SPD and brought him into contact with the masses only on official occasions. But this did not subtract from an overall positive assessment. 'After the great theoreticians and the great agitators, Ebert was the first great *statesman* of the German labour movement . . . In honouring Friedrich Ebert, it does itself honour.'

Those who had hated and despised Ebert while he was alive continued to do so after his death. This was equally true of the National Socialist, German Nationalist, and *völkisch* right as of the Communists, for whom the delegate

Hermann Remmele spoke when he told the Reichstag on 1 March 1925 that the deceased president had 'gone to the grave with the curse of the German proletariat'. In retrospect, this reproach shows precisely where Ebert's greatest historical achievement lay: in his untiring efforts towards rapprochement and cooperation between the moderate forces in the labour movement and the bourgeoisie. Ebert had recognized earlier than many of his party colleagues that this compromise formed the existential core of the republic, and no one matched him in his persistent devotion to the goal of achieving it.

At the same time, however, Ebert's limitations were clear. He depended all too often on the judgement of military and bureaucratic advisers, whom he had every reason to mistrust. Much to the consternation of his friend Otto Braun, he had no instinct for the dangers inherent in frequent recourse to Article 48 (in 1923 alone Ebert signed forty two emergency measures, most of them aimed at economic crises). By the time of his death, the law concerning the formal execution of this article, required by the constitution, still had not been passed. It never was.

We would thus probably not be justified in calling Friedrich Ebert a great German statesman. He was a staunch democrat, a German patriot, and an exponent of balance and conciliation both at home and abroad. His knowledge of politics and humanity made him, who had no more than a basic school education, far superior to the many academics who condescended to him. Only after he was gone did many of his political friends realize what it meant to have a republican at the head of the republic. His death, a few short months before the end of his term and the election of his successor, marks a deep caesura in the history of the first German Republic.[24]

The first ballot in the first popular election for a Reich president took place on 29 March 1925. The candidate for the governmental right was Karl Jarres, former interior minister and at that time mayor of Duisburg, endorsed by the DVP (his own party), the German Nationalists, and the Economic Party. The SPD put forward Otto Braun, who had just resigned from the office of Prussian prime minister in the wake of a governmental crisis. The Centre was represented by the former chancellor, Wilhelm Marx, the DDP by Willy Hellpach, president of Baden, and the BVP by Heinrich Held, prime minister of the Free State of Bavaria since April 1924. The Communists ran their party head, Ernst Thälmann, a former shipyard worker who had cut his political teeth during the uprising in his home town of Hamburg at the end of October 1923. The National Socialist candidate was Erich Ludendorff.

Nobody achieved the absolute majority necessary in the first ballot. Jarres did best with 38.8% of the vote, followed by Braun with 29% and Marx with 14.5%. The rest of the field was far behind: Thälmann managed 7%, Hellpach 5.8%, Held 3.9%, and Ludendorff 1.1%.

The 'Weimar' parties realized they could not defeat the right unless they agreed to a common candidate. They chose Marx, among other reasons because the SPD knew from its experience with runoff agreements during the monarchy that its adherents followed party recommendations in a far more disciplined manner than bourgeois voters. The Centre, in turn, agreed to elect Braun as Prussian prime minister (which occurred on 3 April 1925).

Since Jarres would have no chance against Marx backed by a unified republican *Volksblock*, the right looked around for a more attractive option. The law on the election of the Reich president (of 4 April 1920) permitted a candidate who had not taken part in the first ballot. This gave 'nationalist' circles around the former Admiral of the Fleet von Tirpitz the chance to court a popular non-politician who was already a living legend: Field Marshal Paul von Beneckendorff und von Hindenburg. At 77 years of age (he was born in Posen on 2 October 1847), Hindenburg had been living in retirement in Hanover since his departure from the Army High Command in the summer of 1919.

The 'victor of Tannenberg' had become a kind of 'substitute emperor' already during the First World War. The nationalist right had first identified him as a possible future Reich president in spring 1920, at the time of the Kapp–Lüttwitz putsch. Once again, German Nationalists from the old Prussian provinces, big landowners from the high councils of the National Land League, and former senior officers were the most active on behalf of his candidacy. There was, to be sure, strong initial resistance in the committee of the conservative *Reichsbürgerrat* around the former Prussian interior minister Friedrich Wilhelm von Loebell, which had backed Jarres in the first ballot. Big industry saw Hindenburg as the spokesman for agrarian interests. Stresemann feared that a President Hindenburg would provoke a negative reaction from abroad. After Jarres withdrew his candidacy, however, such reservations lost force. As a loyal monarchist, Hindenburg first sought the blessing of the former emperor, living in exile in Holland, before announcing on 7 April his willingness to run as the candidate of the *Reichsblock*.

Hindenburg's electoral prospects were good. He could depend not only on the votes of staunch monarchists and most churchgoing Protestants; the Bavarian People's Party, too, backed him, a Prussian Lutheran, mainly because Marx, though a Bavarian Catholic, was supported by the despised Social Democrats. It also helped Hindenburg that the KPD leadership decided on 11 April to keep Thälmann in the running—a decision the Communists justified by saying that it was not the duty of the proletariat 'to seek out the cleverest representative of bourgeois interests or choose the lesser of two evils between the civilian dictatorship of Marx and the military dictatorship of Hindenburg'. Accordingly, Marx could not count on making up on the 'left', among the Communist voters, what he would lose on the 'right' in conservative Bavaria.

The *Volksblock* kept warning until the end about the dangers Hindenburg's election would represent for the interests of the republic and of peace. But it was of no use. On 26 April 1925 the *Reichsblock* candidate emerged from the second ballot with a margin of 900,000 votes over Marx. With electoral participation at 77.6%, 8.7% higher than in the first ballot, Hindenburg achieved 48.3% of votes cast, followed by Marx with 45.3% and Thälmann at 6.4%. The field marshal missed an absolute majority by only a small margin—but an absolute majority was not necessary this time.

The Communists could have prevented Hindenburg's election. The *Vorwärts* headline 'Hindenburg, President by the Grace of Thälmann' accurately described the effect of the KPD leader's candidacy. But the BVP was at least equally responsible. Other 'fathers' and 'mothers' of Hindenburg's success were anti-Catholic liberals in Württemberg and anticlerical Social Democrats in Saxony; the former had voted for Hindenburg, the latter for Thälmann as a 'lesser evil' than Marx, a 'vassal of Rome'. The shift from one of the 'black, red, and gold' candidates to Hindenburg was especially marked in East Prussia. Nowhere was the myth of the 'victor of Tannenberg' as strong as in the province where the battle had taken place.

Hindenburg's triumph was not a plebiscite for the restoration of the monarchy, but it did represent a referendum against parliamentary democracy, such as the Germans had become acquainted with it in the time since 1919. Disillusionment with the grey republican daily routine went hand-in-hand with a nostalgic transfiguration of the past. The liberal *Frankfurter Zeitung* wrote that it was mainly unpolitical Germans who were responsible for the outcome of the election:

> Indeed, we all know what brought the large masses of habitual non-voters to the polls this time. It is the romantic nimbus that the fevered fantasies of the impoverished strata of the people, hard hit in their national self-consciousness, have woven about the head of the commander, without their becoming aware that they owe their personal and national misery entirely to that very system of old imperial governance and warfare, as whose representative they honour that commander. The romantic longing for the glory and greatness of the past—that is what brought these unpolitical strata to the polls and Hindenburg the victory.

The *Berliner Tageblatt*, also a liberal paper, felt 'shame over the political immaturity of so many millions'; the Social Democratic *Vorwärts* spoke of a 'shock victory of the reaction, won by Communist treason to the republic'. Both newspapers—along with the writer Heinrich Mann at about the same time—compared Hindenburg's election to an event early in the history of the third French republic, the victory of the clerical monarchist Marshal MacMahon in the presidential election of 1873. *Vorwärts* saw a modicum of comfort in the historical analogy:

> As fifty years ago in France, so now in Germany a marshal and monarchist appears, after a lost war, as president of the republic. The French republic passed through the danger zone successfully. It will be the duty of German republicans, especially the German Social Democrats, to see to it that Germany emerges no less successfully.

Several staunch republicans soon began to console themselves with the thought that Hindenburg's presidency could reconcile portions of the right to republican governance. As the writer Count Harry Kessler, who had fought on the side of the DDP for a Marx victory, wrote on 12 May (one day after Hindenburg took the oath upon the constitution and was sworn into office by the Social Democratic Reichstag president Paul Löbe before the black, red, and gold standard of the Reich president), 'Hindenburg will now make the republic acceptable, including the Black, Red, and Gold, which will now appear everywhere together with Hindenburg as his personal colours. Some of the admiration directed at him must necessarily rub off on it.'

Such hopes were not completely without foundation. The fact that Hindenburg promised to respect the constitution made it difficult for many of the republic's enemies to persist in their inveterate hatred of the new state. The 'realist' shift in the Evangelical church was a characteristic example; only in 1925 did it finally accept the republic as a fact, albeit an unpleasant one. If it had been legally possible to elect a replacement emperor, the German people might one day have accepted or even sought outright a return to the monarchy. For the time being, however, the main goal of the black, white, and red camp seemed to be within reach—the development of a strong state, as capable and effective as imperial Germany had been in putting the parliament and the parties in their place.

The milieu with the greatest cause for satisfaction after the second presidential ballot was the one from which Hindenburg himself came and with which he continued to be on intimate terms, the world of the military and the Prussian nobility. It was of singular importance to the army and the great manorial lords to have, once again, direct contact to the head of state, one who held supreme executive authority in times of crisis. The relations of power in society and politics did not suddenly change after 26 April 1925. But, as of that day, the old Prussian power elite of pre-republican Germany had the whip hand again, which it could use anytime the parliament was unwilling to recognize the demand of the hour. From the perspective of the 'right', this was a great step forward. It was certainly a step away from the Weimar of 1919. The events of spring 1925 represented nothing less than a silent constitutional metamorphosis, a conservative re-founding of the German Republic.[25]

CULTURAL CRITICISM AND CLASS STRUGGLE: 'WEIMAR' INTELLECTUALS

In 1928 Kurt Tucholsky, one of the leading intellectuals of the left, enquired in *Die Weltbühne* about the progress of the 'republican idea' in Germany. Hindenburg had been in office three years, and had celebrated his eightieth birthday in October 1927. The writer came to the conclusion that 'out in the country', that is, outside the capital, 'there is only sporadic evidence of it. East of the Elbe things look bad, on the right side of the Oder, mega-bad.' Berlin massively overestimated itself in believing itself to be the heart and core of the nation.

The Berlin editorialist would do well to go incognito to a large Silesian estate, or a Prussian one, or to a Pomeranian town. There he will experience something. The farcical characters that crawled out of the woodwork and into Berlin on Hindenburg Day [Hindenburg's eightieth birthday (H.A.W.)], the commemorative Kaiser Wilhelm toppers, the ancient frock coats, the chief forester beards—all this was only a small catalogue sample. The well-sorted warehouse stocks are to be found in the small cities, where they can be inspected at any time, though not without risk. Not without risk if, for example, the 'Berliner' tried energetically to turn off the terror, dictatorship, and insolence of the local bourgeoisie. No court supports him there, no administrative agency, no newspaper. He is forsaken and must quit the field.

Tucholsky's thoughts in 'Berlin und die Provinz' (published in 1928) shed retrospective light on the presidential election in spring 1925. Hindenburg's victory was, in part, an expression of cultural protest—protest against everything that now makes Weimar seem modern. As the historian Peter Gay has noted, the 'Weimar style' actually appeared *before* Weimar. This was true of the expressionist revolution in painting, literature, and drama in the first decade of the twentieth century, as well as of the no less revolutionary breakthrough to atonality in music. It was equally true of the great revolutions in the natural sciences, Sigmund Freud's psychoanalysis, Albert Einstein's theory of relativity, and Max Weber's sociology. Even the 'new objectivity' (*neue Sachlichkeit*), which after 1923 replaced expressionism in all artistic media, could be traced back to the pre-war period. Walter Gropius, whose 1926 Bauhaus building in Dessau created a new functional aesthetics that was both admired and hated, had developed his style before the First World War. Weimar culture thus preceded the founding of the republic. Still, the political regime change had a liberating effect. The innovators now had opportunities they had not enjoyed under the old system, and their impact was wide enough to justify calling Weimar a large-scale experiment in classical modernism.

Weimar modernism provoked a cultural-political reaction, which had no lack of symbolic targets. The incessant campaign against the Bauhaus, the bastion of modern architecture, was one example (Tucholsky also referred to it). In 1925 the Bauhaus was forced to leave its original home in Weimar after the Thuringian parliament cut its funds by half in the autumn of 1924, making it de facto impossible for the institution to keep running. But even the new location in Dessau, the capital of Anhalt, where a Social Democratic prime minister was in office almost continually from 1918 to May 1932, the Bauhaus was a blot on the landscape for the forces of the right. In 1929, at the dedication of a colony Gropius had designed for the workers and employees of the Junker's factory in Dessau-Törten, National Socialists and German Nationalists protested against the 'Moroccan huts' of the 'nigger colony'. The main cause for alarm was the fact that the houses did not have the characteristic German pointed roofs, but were flat-roofed in the style of the 'new objectivity'.

The war against the Weimar spirit also expressed itself in more elevated forms. The intellectual critics on the right regarded the republic as a product of collectivist levelling, in which the masses triumphed over the individual personality. One of these critics was the philosopher Martin Heidegger. In *Sein und Zeit*,* his 1927 magnum opus, Heidegger spoke of a dictatorship of 'the they' (*das Man*):

The they is always present, but in such a manner that it has always stolen away whenever existence presses for a decision. Since the they presents every judgement and decision as its own, however, it strips the individual existence of responsibility. The they can afford, so to speak, to have 'them' constantly appealing to its authority. It can most easily take responsibility for everything, because it is not someone who needs to take a stand for anything. It 'was' always the they who did it, and yet it can be said that it was 'no one'. In the daily routine of existence, most things come about in such a way that we must say, 'it was no one.'

As common as the cliché of oppressive collectivism was the idea of a corrosive pluralism deforming the parliamentary system and ultimately leading to the disintegration of the state. In the foreword to the second, 1926, edition of his book *Die geistesgeschichtliche Lage des heutigen Parlamentarismus*† (first published in 1923), the legal scholar Carl Schmitt wrote that the parliament was no longer a forum where arguments were exchanged freely and publicly, but was now only a place where organized interests collided. Rational argument had been supplanted by ideological polarization, and consequently the present parliamentary system lacked the ability to bring forth political unity.

In some states, parliamentary governance has gone so far as to transform all public affairs into spoils and objects of compromise for parties and followings, with the result that politics is no longer the business of an elite, but has become the fairly contemptible occupation of a fairly contemptible class of men.

After Hindenburg's election, rightist intellectuals like Carl Schmitt no longer entertained any doubt about the cure for the disease that was parliamentary government: plebiscitary democracy, which had ordained the Reich president as the agent of the general will. The directly elected head of state as the incarnation of the Rousseauist *volonté générale* had to be made stronger in confrontation with a parliament articulating the *volonté de tous*, the sum of the many individual wills. According to the Weimar constitution, as Schmitt wrote in his 1928 book *Verfassungslehre*,‡ there were two political leaders, the chancellor and the president.

The former determines the guidelines of policy, but only because he is supported by the confidence of the parliament, that is, of a shifting and unreliable coalition. The president, by contrast, enjoys the confidence of the entire people, communicated not through the medium of a factious and partisan parliament, but unified directly in his person.

The president was set against the chancellor, democracy against the parliament, and the people were called as witness against their representatives: it was the fundamental contradiction of the Weimar constitution that allowed Schmitt to 'democratically' rationalize his appeal for authoritarian leadership and acclamation.

* Heidegger, *Being and Time.*
† Schmitt, *The Crisis of Parliamentary Democracy.*
‡ Schmitt, *Constitutional Doctrine.*

Carl Schmitt represented a school of thought that has come to be known as the 'conservative revolution'. This term distinguishes its exponents from traditional Weimar conservatives, the great majority of whom favoured some manner of restoration of the fallen monarchic system, as well as from the Leninist revolutionaries, who strove to realize their goal of a classless communist society through international class struggle, the proletarian revolution, and the dictatorship of the proletariat. For most intellectuals of the 'conservative revolution', the term 'revolution' was more a metaphor than a concrete programme. It stood for a radical break with bourgeois liberalism and Western democracy. The 'revolution from the right'—the title of a 1931 book by the sociologist Hans Freyer—set the *Volk* against society, the order of the whole against the pluralism of competing interests, the political decision binding for all against uncontrolled parliamentary debate, the leader against the masses.

Their opposition to the capitalist and democratic west brought a number of 'conservative revolutionaries' into a certain proximity with the communist and dictatorial east. Cooperation between Germany and the Soviet Union, both strongly revisionist powers, had its supporters among communists and nationalists alike. Moreover, among the so-called 'national Bolshevists' (a questionable name) around Ernst Niekisch, former leader of the Augsburg and Munich councils of 1919, this foreign policy orientation found its counterpart in a sharply anticapitalist rhetoric, albeit of a more 'Prussian' than 'Russian' colouring.

Even staunchly anti-Marxist intellectuals like Oswald Spengler, author of *Der Untergang des Abendlandes*,* advocated for a 'German' or 'Prussian socialism'. The great question for the world, as Spengler wrote in his 1920 book *Preussentum und Sozialismus*,† was the choice between the Prussian and the English idea, socialism and capitalism, state and parliament.

> Prussiandom and socialism stand *together against the inner England*, against the world-view that infuses our entire life as a people, crippling it and stealing its soul . . . The working class must liberate itself from the illusions of Marxism. Marx is dead. As a form of existence, socialism is just beginning, but the socialism of the German proletariat is at an end. *For the worker, there is only Prussian socialism or nothing* . . . For conservatives, there is only conscious socialism or destruction. But we need liberation from the forms of Anglo-French democracy. We have our own.

Spengler's socialism had nothing to do with a change in property relations. It was less a question of economic order than of economic attitude or philosophy. 'The meaning of socialism is that life is controlled not by the opposition between rich and poor, but by the rank that achievement and talent bestow. That is *our* freedom, freedom from the economic despotism of the individual.' The points of contact between the socialism of 'conservative revolutionaries' like Spengler and the socialism of the National Socialists were obvious. Nonetheless, the proximity remained

* Spengler, *The Decline of the West.*
† Spengler, *Prussianism and Socialism.*

primarily one of language. Prior to 1933, the new conservative intellectuals tended to sympathize more with the Italian Fascists than the German National Socialists, whom they considered vulgar. But simply to call them 'fascists' would also be inaccurate. Both the Italian Fascists and the German National Socialists mobilized masses and deployed organized violence. The authors of the 'conservative revolution' remained, in everything they wrote and thought, within the pale of the educated public, whence they came and for whom they wrote.

Both 'conservative revolutionaries' and National Socialists represented a radical nationalism initially directed primarily at domestic politics and affairs. Fragmented and divided German society was to be replaced by the unified nation. In this way, integral nationalism was a response to Marxism and liberalism. The latter was seen as the precondition for the former, and both were enemies. Nobody understood the domestic-political serviceability of nationalism as a weapon against all forms of the Marxist left as well as Hitler. At the beginning of 1924 the leader of the National Socialists wrote in an essay in defence of the putsch of 8–9 November 1923:

> *Marxist internationalism can only be broken by means of a fanatically extreme nationalism of the highest social ethics and morality.* We cannot take the false gods of Marxism away from the people without giving them a better god . . . It is the world-important achievement of Benito Mussolini to have recognized this most clearly and put it into practice with the greatest consistency by replacing international Marxism, the enemy to be eradicated, with fanatical national Fascism, with the result that almost all of the Marxists organizations of Italy have been dissolved.[26]

Nonetheless, the 'conservative revolutionaries' and the National Socialists were only in partial agreement about German nationalism. The nationalism of the new conservative intellectuals lacked the 'totalitarian' comprehensiveness of the Fascists and National Socialists. Its anti-liberalism was stronger than its anti-Marxism. Though they were, as a rule, anti-Semites, the 'conservative revolutionaries' were less emphatic than the National Socialists about the importance of anti-Jewish hatred. Their anti-Semitism generally remained within the limits of what can be called German 'consensus anti-Semitism'. It was not at the centre of a quasi-religion, as for the National Socialists.

In general, anti-Semitism was not as widespread and intense during the relatively 'good' Weimar years between 1924 and 1929 as it had been during the republic's first half-decade. But it was still strong in Germany society, especially with respect to the putative cultural hegemony of the Jews, that is, in journalism, the publishing industry, theatre, and film. Those who saw the Jewish spirit at work in corrosive, subversive intellectualism and the decadent civilization of the metropolis could count on an audience not only on the right, but even in the environs of the political centre. Otto Dibelius, Evangelical superintendent of the Kurmark, delegate for the DNVP, and confessed anti-Semite, wrote in a 'confidential' letter to the pastors of his parish in 1928 that it was undeniable that the Jews had always 'played a leading role . . . in all the subversive phenomena of modern civilization'. *Der grosse Herder*, a Catholic reference work, observed in a 1926 article under the correspondng rubric that anti-Semitism was 'an antipathy felt by the majority against what it considers to be a foreign minority, one that closes itself off to a certain extent but is nonetheless unusually influential, demonstrating high spiritual values and, at the same time, an exaggerated self-importance.' That same year, an advertising brochure for the Vitte seaside resort on the island of Hiddensee, distributed by island management, stated: 'It must be said that the Jews make a point of avoiding Vitte.' Anti-Semitism was a quotidian affair in Germany of the Weimar Republic, and among conservatives it was socially acceptable, provided it did not go beyond the limits imposed by traditional notions of 'decency'.

Jews played a very prominent role in the circles normally associated with the spirit of Weimar. They were not present on the political right simply because the right was anti-Semitic. To oppose the discrimination of minorities was, by definition, to be a leftist or a liberal. One of the main reasons Jews were strongly involved in the labour movement was because nowhere else did there exist a mass movement fighting for a society of equal rights. But since Weimar society was very far from being egalitarian, it could not satisfy the left. Criticism of the prevalent order thus became one of the primary characteristics of the leftists intellectuals of the Weimar Republic, Jews and non-Jews alike.

A considerable number of these thinkers went so far in their critique as to condemn the new Weimar state in its entirety. For the Communists and their adherents, the 'bourgeois' republic was not worth defending. The intellectuals acting under the aegis of Willy Münzenberg, the press and propaganda chief of the KPD, aspired to what the party proclaimed: the revolutionary destruction of the existing system and the creation of 'Soviet Germany'. Even the most prominent among them, people like Bertolt Brecht, Arnold Zweig, Anna Seghers, Johannes R. Becher, and Kurt Weill, were 'Weimar' intellectuals only in the period sense, not because they had any inner attachment to the republic of 1919.

One such leftist Jewish intellectual was Kurt Tucholsky. Though he was certainly no KPD propagandist, Tucholsky's view of Weimar was nonetheless radically critical. The main target of his mockery and contempt was the SPD. When the Social Democrats adopted a reformist platform at their party congress in Görlitz in 1921, Tucholsky wrote a poem referring to them as 'Skat brothers . . . who have read Marx'. Five years later he compared 'the completely pigheaded dear good SPD' with 'modest radishes: red on the outside, white on the inside'. For the *Weltbühne* author, the necessity of compromise, which the SPD could not avoid even when they were out of power, was nothing more than 'parliament rote' (*Parlamentsroutinendreh*). In terms of its effects, the battle Tucholsky and his colleagues waged against the Social Democrats was a battle against parliamentary democracy. In this respect, the intellectuals of the *Weltbühne* circle were much closer to the anti-parliamentarians of the 'conservative revolution' than both sides were aware.

Most of the intellectuals who supported Weimar were conscious of its inner weakness. Thomas Mann, who had still been defending the authoritarian German state at the end of the war, made a very famous speech in defence of the German Republic to an auditorium of partially hostile Berlin students in October 1922, on the occasion of Gerhart Hauptmann's sixtieth birthday. At the end of November, at an event sponsored by the DDP in Munich, Mann, who strongly identified with the Bavarian capital, expressed his anger and sadness over the alienation that had been growing between Munich and Berlin since the pre-war years. Before the war, Munich had been democratic and Berlin feudal-military, but now it was practically the reverse.

> We have felt shame at the refractory pessimism those in Munich set against the political insight of Berlin and the political longing of a whole world. With concern we have seen its healthy and cheerful blood poisoned with anti-Semitic nationalism and God knows what kinds of sinister foolishness. We were forced to look on as Munich was decried in Germany and beyond Germany as the refuge of reaction, as the headquarters of all obstinacy and contumacy against the will of the age. We were forced to listen to it being referred to as a stupid city, as *the* stupid city.

Thomas Mann hoped to bring about a change by calling things by their proper names. But the fundamental defensiveness of his attitude was as unmistakable as that of Friedrich Meinecke. At a congress of German university teachers in Weimar in April 1926, a meeting of republican professors and lecturers, the Berlin historian tried to build bridges to the moderate faction of the German Nationalist party. He, a 'republican by virtue of reason' (*Vernunftrepublikaner*), lamented that there had been no compromise between the black-white-red and black-white-gold camps in 1919, but instead a 'complete change of colour'. He admitted that parliamentary government was not necessarily implicit in a democratic republic, and showed, one year after Hindenburg's election, a willingness to consider the question of 'whether the Weimar constitution might be further developed by strengthening the Reich presidency'.

The indecision manifest in such statements was typical of intellectual *Vernunftrepublikanismus*. Nonetheless, Meinecke was far ahead of the rest of academic Germany in calling attention to the existential law of the Weimar Republic. 'The republic is the great vent for the class struggle between the workers and the bourgeoisie. It is the social peace between them in state form,' the historian declared in a lecture to the Democratic Students Association in Berlin in January 1925. 'Social discord no longer exists between the working class and the bourgeoisie in general. The rift has shifted to the right and now goes right through the middle of the bourgeoisie itself.'

Meinecke could also have said that the rift had shifted to the left as well as the right, going through both the middle of the working class and the middle of the bourgeoisie. Indeed, the political lines of division reflected those in society less than ever before. Between the bourgeois *Vernunftrepublikaner* and the far right yawned a veritable abyss. But the same was true of the relationship between Social Democrats and Communists. Both workers' parties still employed some of the same Marxist concepts, but understood completely different things by them. 'Class struggle', for example, meant for the Communists the sharpening of social conflict towards the ultimate goal of proletarian revolution, whereas for the Social Democrats and the Free Trade Unions it meant a pluralist politics in the interest of the workers.

The republic still rested on the shoulders of the moderate forces within the bourgeoisie and the working class. In the middle of the 1920s there were both signs pointing toward a renewal of the 'class compromise' of 1918–19 and developments that seemed to indicate political polarization. Only one thing was certain: the stabilization of Weimar after 1923 was only relative, measured according to the instability of the previous years. The internal threat to democracy had not ceased to exist, but only ebbed somewhat.[27]

THE CONSERVATIVE REPUBLIC

The year 1925 has gone down in history not only because of Hindenburg's election to the Reich presidency. A second event also ranks high in historical importance: the conclusion of the Locarno accords on 26 October, which sealed Germany's readmission into the circle of European great powers. This treaty system was designed to consolidate the post-war order, but it did so, in accordance with German wishes, in an asymmetric manner. Only the German western borders were secured by international law. Germany, France, and Belgium renounced all use of force to alter the existing borders, and their inviolability was further guaranteed by Britain and Italy. With its eastern neighbors Poland and Czechoslovakia, on the other hand, Germany only concluded arbitration treaties. However, France promised military support for both countries in the event of a German attack.

Locarno in no way closed off the possibility of a peaceful revision of the German eastern border. Foreign Minister Stresemann left no doubt that he was working towards this goal, in full agreement with German public opinion. As he informed the German embassy in London on 19 April, a peaceful solution to the Polish border question would not be achievable

> without the precarious economic and financial situation in Poland having reached the most extreme point, placing the whole Polish state in a condition of powerlessness . . . Thus, overall, it will have to be our goal to delay Poland's final and permanent rehabilitation until such time as the country is ready for a border agreement corresponding to our wishes and until our own position of power is strong enough . . . Only the unrestricted return of sovereignty over the territories in question can satisfy us.

Two further international events were closely connected with Locarno: the Treaty of Berlin with the Soviet Union and Germany's admission into the League of Nations. The German–Soviet agreement, which the Reichstag passed almost unanimously on 10 June 1926, was designed, on the one hand, to dispel Moscow's suspicions concerning Germany's Locarno policies. Its other purpose was to increase the pressure on Warsaw. The treaty signatories promised mutual neutrality in case of an unprovoked attack by one or more third parties and non-participation in any coalition using an economic boycott against either power. Germany promised Russia what it had itself required from the western nations the year before in Locarno: de facto non-involvement in any League of Nations sanctions against Moscow. In all other areas, the Rapallo Treaty of 1922 was to remain the foundation of German–Soviet relations.

The second great international event of 1926, Germany's accession to the League of Nations, took place in Geneva on 10 September. As its governments had so persistently demanded, the Reich immediately became a permanent member of the League council, the organization's most important organ. Poland, Germany's main competitor for this prestigious position, had to make do with a non-permanent council seat and the assurance it would be re-elected to it. For the Social Democrats, who had canvassed for League membership earlier and more consistently than any other German political party, the achievement was a cause for great celebration. 'Germany and Europe are progressing from the crisis of international anarchy to a condition of international order, in which the liberty of all peoples will be realized in due course,' wrote *Vorwärts*, which called the event a veritable 'world-historical leap'.[28]

German's entrance into the League of Nations represented the zenith of the 'Stresemann era'. Ardent annexationist of the war years, opportunistic tactician during the Kapp–Lüttwitz putsch, Gustav Stresemann had since matured into a *Vernunftrepublikaner* and a statesman. As chancellor during the autumn 1923 crisis, he had done more than anyone else to preserve the unity of the Reich and the democratic government of the republic. As foreign minister, he was the champion of peaceful understanding with the west—though to Germany's eastern neighbor Poland he was, it is true, no less 'nationalist' than most German politicians on the right and the left. The foreign minister of the years 1923–9 was an enlightened representative of German great power politics and an advocate of a narrower union among the states of Europe. He could be both, since in his perspective there was no contradiction between the two. No German politician of the post-war period was so highly respected abroad. On 10 December 1926 he was awarded the Nobel peace prize along with his French colleague, Aristide Briand.

The firmest pillar in Stresemann's foreign policy was the Social Democratic Party. When the German Nationalists, dissatisfied with the western concessions in Locarno, abandoned the Luther government in October 1925, the SPD stepped into the breach and helped pass the treaties in the Reichstag on 27 November. It would have been natural to make this support contingent upon participation in the administration, but the SPD made no such demand.

In June 1926 it let another chance for a Grand Coalition slip by. On 12 May 1926, Luther's minority bourgeois cabinet was compelled to step down after a conflict over flags. (The cause was a cabinet decision on 1 May allowing the embassy and consular agencies to fly the black, white, and red commercial flag along with the black, red, and gold of the Reich.) The successor, a bourgeois minority cabinet under Marx, was open to SPD participation. But now the Social Democrats paid the price for their active support during the previous months of a KPD-sponsored plebiscite—the first on the federal level—involving a petition and referendum on the expropriation without compensation of the former German princes. The referendum, which took place on 20 June 1926, fell short of its goal, since only 36.4 per cent of eligible Germans voted for the bill, well below the necessary majority. After this episode of common extra-parliamentary action with the Communists, the SPD did not find it within its power to return immediately to a politics of 'class compromise' with the bourgeois centre. The Grand Coalition, which Stresemann had also supported, did not come off.

In mid-December 1926 arose yet a third opportunity to replace bourgeois minority governance with a majority government in the shape of a centre–left alliance. At Stresemann's behest, the Marx administration offered the Social Democrats a Grand Coalition as a way of avoiding a debate over the armed forces, which the SPD was pushing for. The latter refused. On 16 December 1926 Philipp Scheidemann gave a speech before the Reichstag that went down in the annals of German parliamentary history. To the outrage of all the bourgeois parties, the former prime minister of the Reich spoke of the secret weapons production going on in the country and described how its financing was being covered up. He detailed the interplay between the Reichswehr and extremist right-wing organizations, and mentioned the so-called 'black Reichswehr', the numerous small-calibre shooting clubs the army used to circumvent the limit of 100,000 troops. And he shocked the Communists by disclosing that their cell at the port of Stettin had been fully informed about the arms and munitions shipments Soviet ships had unloaded there in September and October.

On 17 December, the day after this spectacular speech, the parliament brought down the Marx government by 249 against 171 votes. The DVP, DNVP, and KPD joined the SPD vote of no confidence. The question of the Grand Coalition was now definitively put to rest; after Scheidemann's speech, no bourgeois politician would have supported or even seriously considered one.[29]

The outcome of the governmental crisis in the winter of 1926–7 was a centre-right administration under Wilhelm Marx, which took office on 29 January 1927. In this fourth Marx cabinet, which included the Centre Party, BVP, DVP, and DNVP, the German Nationalists provided the ministers of the interior, justice, agriculture, and transport. Interior Minister von Keudell, who, as *Landrat* of Königsberg in the Neumark (East Brandenburg), had cooperated with the Kapp–Lüttwitz government in March 1920, was the main target of criticism from the left, a target he offered on numerous occasions.

On 27 November 1927, for example, the DNVP interior minister sent a telegram to the German Students' Association assuring them of his 'inner solidarity'. This was a demonstration of sympathy in the conflict between the umbrella organization of the German Students' Associations and the Prussian government. The German Student Association also included the Austrian organizations that had expressly excluded Jews from membership. In September 1927 the non-aligned Prussian minister of education and ecclesiastic affairs, Carl Heinrich Becker, one of the great university reformers of the Weimar Republic, had prevailed upon the Braun administration to strip Prussian student associations of their government recognition, since they persistently refused to leave the German Students' Association. In a letter to Chancellor Marx on 27 November, Braun threatened to break off all contact between the Prussian government and the federal interior minister if incidents like the latter's supportive letter to the German Students' Association were repeated. Motions of no confidence, brought forward by the SPD and KPD on account of the 'Keudell case', failed on 6 December 1927 against a majority of the government coalition.

The new government's agricultural policy also bore the German Nationalist trademark. The DNVP had already effected a return to the grain tariffs of 1902 in August 1925, under Luther's chancellorship. Amendments in July 1927 extended and, in some cases, increased the existing tariffs for a number of agricultural products, including potatoes, sugar, and pork. On the whole, however, the government of the bourgeois bloc was in no way unambiguously 'reactionary'. In May 1927 the *Republikschutzgesetz* was extended for two years—though in somewhat milder form—with the votes of the German Nationalist Party. In July of the same year the Reichstag passed, by an overwhelming majority, the most important social policy reform measure of the Weimar Republic, unemployment insurance. As the unions had demanded, the law changed the previous welfare programme into an insurance fund, into which employers and employees paid equal contributions, 3 per cent of the wage. This insurance programme, along with an employment agency, was administered by an independent federal office, the *Reichsanstalt für Arbeitsvermittlung und Arbeitslosenversicherung*, with district and local branches. There were also standardized administrative boards on all levels, composed of representatives of the insured, the employers, and the public corporations, all with an equal number of votes.

The unemployment insurance programme represented the greatest increase in social security achieved by workers and employees during the Weimar Republic. The 1927 law took up one of the central ideas of Bismarck's social policy, social responsibility as the joint obligation of business and government. For the costs of the unemployment insurance were not borne by employers and workers alone, but by the state, too. In emergency situations, the Reich would have to provide a loan to the federal unemployment agency if the latter's 'emergency funds' proved insufficient. There was no provision for direct state allocations, however. The government, parliament, and organizations apparently did not consider mass unemployment on a gigantic scale to be a threat. If such a situation occurred, the 1927 system was doomed.

Indeed, there would hardly have been such broad support for the reform if unemployment had been high in 1927. The numbers were especially low in July, with 630,000 unemployed workers drawing state support. The year 1927 was also the high water mark for German industrial profits during the Weimar Republic. Not only workers and employees benefited, but also civil servants. The December 1927 salary reform raised state pay by an average of 16–17 per cent, with the greatest increases on the lower levels. With this reform, Finance Minister Köhler, a Centre politician, sought to address the fact that state salaries had increased much less than workers' wages since 1924. Nonetheless, it caused serious problems for public budgets, and Heinrich Brüning, the Centre Party's budget expert, abstained from the final vote on 15 December 1927. His concerns about the financial consequences of the law were shared by the employers' associations and the reparations agent, the American Parker Gilbert, who had written a memo in October accusing municipalities of irresponsible financial behaviour. But 1928 was an election year, and to insist on financial solidity was to swim against the current.

By the time the salary reform law was passed, the disintegration of the bourgeois bloc was already in sight. Ever since July 1927, the coalition partners had been fighting over an education measure introduced by Interior Minister von Keudell. The bill proposed placing Christian interdenominational schools (the *Simultanschule*) and confessional schools on the same legal footing. It was endorsed by the Centre, BVP, and DNVP. The DVP, the heirs of the National Liberals of the *Kulturkampf*, rejected it, pointing out that the Weimar constitution had codified the priority of the interdenominational school. On 15 February 1928 Count Westarp, head of the DNVP parliamentary fraction and leader of the coalition council meetings, found himself forced to announce that no agreement on the controversial question was possible and that the coalition was thus dissolved.

It seemed as though every kind of parliamentary majority in Weimar contained the seeds of its own destruction. For a Grand Coalition, the crisis zone was social policy. For a coalition of the right, it was foreign policy and cultural issues. The parties, which the era of constitutional monarchy had not habituated to the necessity of compromise, tended continually to regard their individual goals as non-negotiable. Even 'state' parties behaved this way again and again, as if the decisive line of division still ran between the government and the parliament, as in the time before October 1918, instead of between the parliamentary majority and the opposition, as the logic of the parliamentary system dictated. The government was often considered the 'adversary' even by parties playing an important role in it. This legacy from the Wilhelmine era goes far towards explaining the weakness that characterized German parliamentary rule even during the relatively peaceful years of the first republic.

On 31 March 1928 President Hindenburg dissolved the Reichstag and set new elections for 20 May. But 31 March was important for another reason, too. On this day, the Reich Council decided concerning a project that would plunge the next government into its first crisis: 'battleship A'. The navy planned this ship as the beginning of a series of replacement vessels and wanted to commit the legislature to a long-term programme lasting several legislative periods. In December 1927 the Reich Council, led by Prussia, had come out against the spending for the project. In the Reichstag, however, the bourgeois bloc put together a majority that approved the first budgetary instalment at the end of March. On 31 March the Reich Council responded by requesting that the acting cabinet not authorize work on the battleship until further examination of the finances and in any case until after 1 September 1928. Since the government had to rely on the cooperation of the Reich Council more than usual in the ensuing weeks, Groener, the non-aligned minister of defence (who had replaced the worn-out Gessler on 19 January 1928), saw himself forced to agree to this stipulation.

'Battleship A' provided the leftists parties with a rousing campaign theme. The KPD, which, under Ernst Thälmanns leadership, had become more and more the obedient tool of Stalin, opposed the battleship with the popular demand for free meals for school children. (The bourgeois parliamentary majority had rejected the 5 million marks intended for this programme.) The slogan 'Food for kids, not battleships!' was also used by the Social Democrats, who thus made themselves seem more radical than they actually were. At its party congress in Kiel in May 1927, the SPD had left no doubt about its resolve to prevent a new rightist cabinet and, election results permitting, to assume governmental power.

On the far right margin of the political spectrum, a consolidated NSDAP entered the campaign in the spring of 1928. Adolf Hitler was the uncontested *Führer* of the National Socialists. Ever since the 'Führer congress' in February 1926, the left wing around the brothers Otto and Gregor Strasser, which was strong in northern Germany, no longer provided a counterweight to the party headquarters in Munich. Though the NSDAP still represented itself as a 'socialist' party friendly to the worker, it was clear already before the election that its greatest resonance was not in the large cities, but in hard-hit rural areas, especially after the collapse of pork prices in 1927, the prelude to a worldwide agricultural crisis. It was the rural population Hitler had in mind with his new, binding interpretation of point 17 of the 1920 party platform: the demand for uncompensated expropriation of land for community purposes referred, in the new reading, only to unlawfully acquired property, above all that of 'Jewish land speculation companies'.

In society as a whole, however, there was little sense of an impending crisis on the eve of the election. The economic data were positive, and the unemployment figures were below those of the previous year. The democratic forces of Germany had never entered a Weimar parliamentary election with such reason for optimism as they did the election of 20 May 1928.[30]

THE GRAND COALITION UP TO THE DEATH OF STRESEMANN

The radiant victors of the fourth Reichstag election were the Social Democrats with 29.8% of the vote, a 3.8% increase over the previous election in December 1924. The greatest losers were the German National People's Party, which fell from 20.5% to 14.3%. Of the moderate bourgeois parties, the Centre's loss of 1.5% was the worst, the two liberal parties each falling by 1.4%. If there had been a 5 per cent hurdle in the Weimar Republic, the DDP would have been out of the parliament; it managed only 4.9%. Pure interest-group parties, on the other hand, did comparatively well. The national party of small and medium-sized businesses, called the Economic Party for short, grew from 3.3% of the vote to 4.6%. The newly founded Christian National Farmers' and Rural People's Party (*Christlich-Nationale Bauern- und Landvolkpartei*) achieved 2.9% in its first election. On the far left, the KPD increased its share of the vote from 9% to 10.6%, while on the extreme right, the NSDAP had to accept a national average of only 2.6%. In several zones of agricultural crisis on the west coast of Schleswig-Holstein, however, the popularity of the National Socialists was truly sensational. In North Dithmarschen they gained 28.9%, in South Dithmarschen no less than 36.8%.

The election outcome allowed practically only one kind of parliamentary majority: a Grand Coalition, which finally came together on 28 June 1928 after arduous negotiations. This was not yet a formal coalition government, but at first only a 'cabinet of personalities'. The political independence of the ministers suggested by this term was an illusion. In fact, the objections of the DVP to the coalition—led by the head of the SPD, Hermann Müller—were so strong that it required an ultimatum from Stresemann before his party would temporarily agree to two DVP cabinet members (himself as foreign minister and Julius Curtius as minister of the economy).

The government had only been in power a few weeks when it was plunged into a serious crisis. On 10 August 1928, the cabinet approved the construction of 'battleship A', against which the SPD had actively campaigned before the election. The Social Democratic finance minister, Hilferding, was unable to raise fiscal objections, since the project's costs were covered by cuts in other areas of the military budget. Thus the confirmation of the previous parliament's decision was correct. What is more, a negative vote from the Social Democratic ministers would have meant the immediate end of the Müller administration. But many members and supporters of Germany's largest party saw things differently, and they had a powerful ally: Otto Wels, the de facto leader of the SPD as long as party co-chair Müller was chancellor. On 31 October, after the end of the parliament's summer break, Wels brought forward a motion by the SPD fraction to halt construction on the ship and use the savings for school lunch programmes.

If this motion was a slap in the face for Hermann Müller, even more so was the notion that the chancellor and SPD ministers should vote with the fraction and against the cabinet decision of 10 August. But this is exactly what happened on 16 November 1928 in the Reichstag plenum. By endorsing the motion, Chancellor Müller, Interior Minister Carl Severing, Finance Minister Rudolf Hilferding, and Labour Minister Rudolf Wissell all but registered a vote of no confidence in their own administration.

The effect on the public was disastrous. Though the government was spared an actual defeat, since all the bourgeois parties and the National Socialists voted against the SPD motion and were able to bring it down, the strongest party in the government had nonetheless caused great harm to the image of parliamentary governance in Germany. The *Vossische Zeitung* rightly accused the Social Democrats of lacking credibility. Wels had given 'an opposition speech of the heaviest calibre', the liberal Berlin paper wrote.

A sensational result, if it had been seriously intended. Its logical conclusion would have been the announcement that the Social Democratic Party was pulling its ministers out of the government. It has no such intention. It wishes to continue in power, simply to save face . . . Shall we be content to allow the Social Democrats to pound the table in the house while hoping that others prevent anything from breaking?

Then, in April 1929, the government parties finally achieved what many had come to believe a lost cause, a formal Grand Coalition. It was preceded by an agreement on the federal budget for 1929 after Finance Minister Hilferding and, following him, the finance experts of the fractions had adjusted upwards the estimations of the expected tax revenues. But the decisive reason for the surprising rapprochement had to do with foreign policy. At the beginning of February, negotiations over reparations had commenced in Paris. The Dawes Plan of 1924, we recall, was only a provisional agreement, leaving the question of the total amount of reparations Germany owed undecided. And in 1928–9 the country's annual payments under the treaty reached their full amount—2.5 billion marks—for the first time.

Confronted with a worsening economic situation, all the governing parties were interested in reducing this burden as quickly as possible. But the reparations agent himself wanted to revise the Dawes Plan. As long as Parker Gilbert was authorized to determine whether Germany's balance of payments and currency situation justified a transfer of the reparations, the Germans could hide behind him, as it were. Gilbert considered this state of affairs harmful and wanted to use a new treaty to force Germany to become economically independent.

The Paris negotiations resulted in the Young Plan, named after Owen D. Young, the American director of the conference of experts that ended on 7 June 1929. According to this plan, Germany was to pay reparations for nearly six decades, until 1988. During the first ten years, the annuities would be below their average amount of 2 billion marks. Thereafter they would rise, and not decrease again for thirty-seven years. No further foreign monitoring of German finances was planned, nor mortgages on industry and federal revenue. The German government was to take over responsibility for the transfer from the reparations agent. It was granted the right to distinguish between the 'protected' and 'unprotected' portions of the reparations, the latter to be paid unconditionally and on time, the former subject, upon application, to deferment of up to two years. The payments would be received by a new agency, the Bank of International Settlements in Basel. If Germany had difficulty making the payments, it could have recourse to an international board of experts. This body would have to make suggestions for the revision of the Young Plan in the event that the German economy was unable to fulfil its obligations. Another eventuality was also covered: if the United States granted its Allied debtors a debt reduction, two-thirds of that amount was to be subtracted from the German reparations.

Compared to the Dawes Plan, the Young Plan had one great advantage for Germany: it restored the country's economic sovereignty. The termination of transfer protection was a disadvantage, however, since it meant that the Reich would now have to keep paying reparations during an economic depression. And the prospect of having to pay them for fifty-eight years was bleak. Still, there was a kind of political recompense for this harshness. The German government's acceptance of the Young Plan made France willing to accommodate Germany on the Rhineland question. On 30 August 1929 a conference in The Hague between Great Britain, France, Italy, Belgium, Japan, and Germany came to an end with the signing of an agreement for early withdrawal from the Rhineland. The Allied troops were to pull out of the second zone by 30 November 1929 (the occupation of the first zone had been ended in the winter of 1925–6); the third and last zone would be vacated on 30 June 1930, five years before the date fixed in the Treaty of Versailles.

The staunch right did not wait for the outcome of the negotiations before mobilizing its followers against the Young Plan. On 6 July the National Committee of German Agriculture (*Reichsausschuss der deutschen Landwirtschaft*) declared the results of the negotiations economically unacceptable. Two days later the heavy-industrial Langnam association, whose actual name was the Association for the Protection of the Common Economic Interests in Rhineland and Westphalia (*Verein zur Wahrung der gemeinsamen wirtschaftlichen Interessen in Rheinland und Westfalen*), declared that the experts' report would overburden the German economy. On 9 July a National Committee for the German Referendum (*Reichsausschuss für das Deutsche Volksbegehren*) convened in Berlin. The Pan-German League was represented by Heinrich Class, the Steel Helmet (*Stahlhelm*), a paramilitary League of Front Soldiers (*Bund der Frontsoldaten*) founded at the end of 1918, by its national leader Franz Seldte, the DNVP by the film and press magnate Alfred Hugenberg, who had assumed the party leadership in October 1928, and the NSDAP by Adolf Hitler. This meeting produced a manifesto calling on the German people to fight against the Young Plan and the 'war guilt lie' and launching the drive for a plebiscite.

While the right was gathering its forces, the gulf between the moderate and the radical left was growing deeper. In the summer of 1928 the Sixth World Congress of the Communist International in Moscow had set a course sharply to the left, defining the new general party line in terms of a theory of the 'third period'. According to this doctrine, the relative stability of capitalism, which had superseded the acute revolutionary post-war crisis in the autumn of 1923, was now at an end throughout the world. The hallmarks of the 'third period' of post-war development were the increasing contradictions within the capitalist order and the preparation of an imperialist war against the Soviet Union. The outcome of the new crisis was historically inevitable. Led by the Communist parties, the labouring masses in the capitalist countries and their colonies would rise up against the capitalist systems of exploitation and bring about a proletarian victory through revolutionary war. The most pressing task for the Communist International was to fulfil the precondition for the final battle: to destroy the 'bourgeoisified' Social Democratic movement, whose ideology of class cooperation now demonstrated many points of contact with fascism.

The reasons for the Comintern's 'ultra-leftist' turn were to be found both within the Soviet Union itself and within Germany. In the Soviet Union, a power struggle was raging between Stalin, the general secretary of the Communist Party, and a group around Nikolai Bukharin. The latter group, stamped as 'rightist' by its enemies, spoke against Stalin's programme of forced collectivization of agriculture and accelerated industrialization. If the other parties of the Third International could be committed to an offensive against rightist tendencies, this would help Stalin in his battle against Bukharin. The German cause of the leftward shift lay in the fact that a Grand Coalition under a Social Democratic chancellor was in power after June 1928. The SPD was regarded as the party that had done more than any other to promote rapprochement with the western powers, especially with France. This alone made it, in Stalin's view, a dangerous political enemy of the Soviet Union.

Were it not for Bloody May Day in Berlin, the Sixth World Congress's declaration that the Social Democratic parties were growing closer to the fascists and would therefore have to be more strongly fought might have remained mere abstract theory. But in the spring of 1929 the Social Democratic president of the Berlin police, Karl Friedrich Zörgiebel, unintentionally came to Stalin's aid. Zörgiebel upheld a ban on open-air assemblies and demonstrations, decreed by him the previous December, for 1 May, the workers' traditional 'day of struggle'. When the Communists ignored the ban and erected several barricades, the police promptly moved against them with armoured vehicles and firearms. The outcome of the battle was 32 dead, all civilians, almost 200 wounded, and far more than 1,000 arrests.

The police action was followed by an administrative measure, a country-wide ban of the League of Red Front Fighters (*Roter Frontkämpferbund*), a paramilitary group founded in 1924. The KPD responded in June in Wedding, the part of the capital that had seen the heaviest fighting at the beginning of May. A party congress originally planned for Dresden was convened there. Bloody May Day and the ban of the Red Front Fighters were proof to the party leadership that the Social Democrats were becoming 'social fascists'. Ernst Thälmann went so far as to call the 'social fascism' of the SPD an especially dangerous form of fascist development. The delegates hailed the party head in a manner that can only be described as a 'cult of the leader'. According to the minutes of the meeting, he was received with calls of 'bravo!' and prolonged applause even before commencing his two-hour speech. 'The Party Congress welcomes Comrade Thälmann with tumultuous applause. The delegates rise to their feet and sing the "International". The youth delegation greets the First Chairman of the Party with a threefold "Hail Moscow!" '

The political radicalization on the left was closely connected with increasing unemployment. In February 1929 economic recession brought the unemployment rate above 3 million for the first time, and the usual spring recovery was weak; there were still 2.7 million people out of work in March. The federal unemployment agency was only able to cover 800,000 workers with 'primary support' from its contribution fund and was forced to take out a loan from the government. Since the government lacked the money, the finance minister had to seek help from a bank consortium. Only this unorthodox solution prevented the collapse of the federal unemployment agency.

At this point it was clear to all that the federal finances could not be straightened out without a reform of the unemployment insurance programme. Unfortunately, on no issue were the two wing parties of the Grand Coalition so divided as on social insurance policy. The SPD, in conjunction with the Free Trade Unions, supported increased contributions from employers and workers. The DVP, with a view to the business community, rejected this solution, demanding that contributions be reduced.

At the end of September, despite countless conferences of experts, still no agreement was in sight. On 1 October Chancellor Müller indicated for the first time that he might resign if the government could not resolve the problem. But the DVP yielded that same day: if the SPD and Centre were willing to postpone their proposed half per cent increase in the contributions until December 1929, the People's Party would enable (by abstaining from the ballot) the passage of a bill lowering the rates of unemployment support and correcting defects in the insurance programme. The Social Democrats and Centre agreed, and the bill passed on 3 October. The Grand Coalition had passed its most difficult test to date.

By the time the president of the Reichstag announced the results of the ballot, the man who had done the most to save the Müller government was no longer alive. In the early morning of 3 October 1929 Gustav Stresemann died of a stroke. Long in a declining state of health, the foreign minister had spent his last reserves attempting to prevent any change of government that threatened to undermine his rapprochement policy in the parliament. In order to secure his foreign policy on the 'right', Stresemann had occasionally behaved more nationalistically than he actually was. But he firmly held to his belief that the desired revision of

Versailles did not justify starting a new war. The prerequisite for a foreign policy based on this belief was a cooperation between the moderate forces within the bourgeoisie and the working class. Since Stresemann knew this, he was the staunchest advocate of the Grand Coalition within his party, and his death considerably weakened this alliance. The only statesman the Weimar Republic produced was soon to prove—both domestically and in terms of foreign policy—irreplaceable.[31]

THE END OF PARLIAMENTARY DEMOCRACY

The primary beneficiary of a collapse of the Grand Coalition in the autumn of 1929 would have been the 'national opposition' that had formed at the beginning of July for the German plebiscite. On 29 September the group submitted to the interior minister its application—in the required form of a legislative bill—for a referendum against the Young Plan and the 'war guilt lie'. The bill's most spectacular provision was in § 4, which read: 'The Chancellor and Ministers of the Reich, as well as their authorized representatives, who, contrary to § 3, sign treaties with foreign powers, are subject to the punishments as per § 92, no. 3 of the Criminal Code.' This paragraph sanctioned treason with a prison term of no less than two years. In its first draft, § 4 had read somewhat differently, threatening imprisonment to 'Chancellor, Ministers, and authorized representatives of the Reich'—that is, including the Reich president. Since Hindenburg was an honorary member of the Stahlhelm (as of 1924), Franz Seldte, the organization's national leader, pushed through an amendment with the help of the German Nationalists excepting the head of state from the threat of punishment.

The 'liberty law' cleared the first hurdle, though barely: 10.02% of the voting population participated in the referendum, just 0.02% more than required by the constitution. The Reichstag was thus forced to deal with the bill, and did so between 27 and 30 November 1929. That it would fail was clear from the start, given the overall distribution of votes. How the DNVP would act—that is, to what extent Hugenberg would be able to impose his will on the fraction—was very much an open question, however. The vote on the imprisonment paragraph revealed that he by no means enjoyed the full support of his party; only 53 out of the 72 DNVP delegates voted in favour. Hugenberg's sharp counter-measures split the fraction. At the beginning of December twelve delegates, including former interior minister von Keudell, landowner Hans Schlange-Schöningen, Walter Lambach, director of the German Nationalist Commercial Employees' Federation, and the retired lieutenant commander Gottfried Treviranus, left the DNVP and joined together to form the German Nationalist Cooperative Union (*Deutschnationale Arbeitsgemeinschaft*). The DNVP floor leader, Count Westarp, resigned from his post in protest against Hugenberg.

The referendum on the 'law against the enslavement of the German people' took place on 22 December 1929, when 5.8 million Germans, or 13.8% of eligible voters, came out in support of the bill. Since 21 million were necessary to pass it, the failure of the National Committee was obvious. But it was significant that more than a fifth of the electorate voted in favour of the bill in nine of the thirty-five electoral districts and that Hitler was well on his way to being recognized by 'decent society' as a political partner. With the participation of the NSDAP in the National Committee, the leader of the 1923 putsch had achieved an important intermediate goal: the established right reckoned with him and granted him access to financial means that benefited the further advancement of the NSDAP.

By the autumn of 1929 there was no more mistaking that the National Socialists were on the rise. They achieved great gains in all elections they entered in November and December: for the parliaments of Baden and Thuringia, for the city parliament of Lübeck and the provincial assemblies of Prussia, for the municipalities in Hesse and Berlin. The latter election, which was held on 17 November, saw the Social Democrats fall from 73 to 64 seats and the DDP from 21 to 14, whereas the NSDAP, which had not yet been represented in the city council assembly, obtained 13 seats right away. The National Socialist conquest of German universities began at about the same time. The National Socialist German Students' League (*Nationalsozialistischer Deutscher Studentenbund*) was the big winner in the General Student Committee (*Allgemeiner Studentenausschuss*; AStA) elections of the 1929–30 winter semester. In Würzburg it achieved 30%, at the Technical University in Berlin 38%, and in Greifswald no less than 53%.

The shift to the right among the students was an expression of social protest. A young generation of academics was rebelling against its 'proletarization' and declaring war against the 'system', which it held responsible for its financial difficulties and uncertain career prospects. Hatred of the Weimar state and animosity towards the Jews went hand in hand. While the Jews represented only 1 per cent of the population, they formed 4–5 per cent of the student body. The percentages were even higher in certain fields, like medicine and law, and at a number of universities, such as Frankfurt am Main and Berlin. For many of their non-Jewish fellow students, this meant that the Jews were taking advantage of unfair privileges. The advance of the National Socialist student organizations was based in part on the mass mobilization of social envy.

We need not search long for the economic causes of the far right's popularity in the autumn of 1929. The agricultural crisis had grown even more serious and radicalized the rural population in northern Germany. Bomb attacks on finance agencies and district administration offices had been making headlines repeatedly since the spring, above all in Schleswig-Holstein. The number of those looking for work in Germany rose from 1.5 million in September to 2.9 million in December, 350,000 more than the same month the previous year. Share prices had reached their highest point in the boom year of 1927. If we equate their level between

1924 and 1926 to 100 points, 1927 would represent 158. They fell to 148 points in 1928 and to 134 in 1929. But the most alarming news came from America. On 24 October 1929, the infamous Black Friday, the prices on the New York stock exchange suffered a massive drop. They continued to fall in the ensuing days, and within a short time the gains of an entire year had been wiped out.

The cause of the stock market crash was a sustained period of over-speculation. Trusting in the longevity of the boom, small shareholders and large investment corporations had invested ever more money in industry, thus raising production. In October 1929 it became clear that supply had far outpaced demand. The decrease in stock prices suffered by companies such as General Electric and investment firms like the Goldman Sachs Trading Company caused a panic among the shareholders.

The consequences were immediately felt on the other side of the Atlantic. In order to remain liquid, American banks began to demand the return of funds they had placed in short-term European investments. Hardest hit was Germany, where the sum total of short-term foreign—and that meant primarily American—credit amounted to 15.7 billion marks in 1929. However, some three-quarters of short-term and medium-term loans, a considerable portion of which came directly or indirectly from abroad, were regularly used for long-term investments. The municipalities, in particular, tended to be involved in this kind of activity, which had long drawn the criticism of Parker Gilbert, the reparations agent. Thus diverted, the funds were practically frozen. They could not be made liquid on demand, but repaid only through new loans.

The Reich, too, found it increasingly difficult to obtain foreign credit. For the president of the federal bank, Hjalmar Schacht (a founding member of the DDP at the end of 1918, but now leaning more to the right), this was a welcome predicament. He used the looming December deficit as a means of pressuring the government into committing itself to a long-term reform of national finances. The cabinet and coalition considered this goal achieved on 14 December 1929, when the Reichstag agreed—despite uncertainty with regard to its final legislative form—to a fiscal programme containing an increase in unemployment contributions from 3 to 3.5 per cent, an increase in the tobacco tax, a decrease in direct taxes for the purpose of shoring up capital formation, and the announcement of a law dealing with the national debt.

Two days later, however, Schacht declared the cabinet's short-term measures to be inadequate. Backed by the reparations agent, he demanded a sum of 500 million marks for debt repayment in the 1930 budget (an amount he reduced by 50 million marks in the negotiations during the ensuing days). On 22 December the Reichstag passed the necessary legislation, and the government received a bridging loan from a domestic banking consortium headed by the federal bank, allowing the Reich to remain solvent.

By this time, Rudolf Hilferding was no longer finance minister. The Social Democrat had handed in his resignation on 20 December, declaring that 'outside intervention' had prevented him from pursuing his policies. Schacht was indeed the victor in his duel with Hilferding. But the coalition, government, and finance minister had only themselves to blame. Their attempt to manipulate the revenue estimates in the spring of 1929 had only been a trick to avoid real finance reform—not to mention the questionable finance policies of the previous governments, especially the fourth Marx cabinet.[32]

By the end of 1929 and the beginning of 1930, there could no longer be any doubt about the fact that parliamentary democracy was in deep crisis in Germany. The power struggle between the government and the president of the federal bank was not the only indication. There were also signs that large portions of the 'power elite' were beginning to turn away from the government, if not entirely from parliamentary rule. The large-scale agricultural interests, represented by the National Land League, had been against the Grand Coalition from the start. In December 1929 the National Association of German Industry sent the Müller cabinet a memorandum entitled *Aufstieg oder Niedergang?*,* which demanded—in language tantamount to an ultimatum—that social expenditures be adjusted to the productivity of the economy and that the government have the right to veto spending increases authorized by the parliament. By the end of 1929 at the latest, Defence Minister Groener and his closest adviser, General Kurt von Schleicher, head of the new Ministerial Office (*Ministeramt*), were working together with Otto Meissner, the secretary in the office of the Reich president, for a government without Social Democrats. Given the state of affairs at the time, this could only have been a presidential cabinet. Hindenburg himself had come out in favour of such a reform in spring 1929. Count Westarp, at that time still floor leader of the DNVP, was one of the first to learn of his intentions.

Hindenburg made himself clearer at the beginning of 1930. On 6 January he enquired of Hugenberg, and on 15 January of Westarp, whether the German Nationalists would support, either directly or indirectly, a cabinet put together by the president if the financial reform in February or March should lead to a governmental crisis. 'There is a great concern', wrote Westarp, paraphrasing the head of state, 'that the opportunity to form an anti-parliamentary and anti-Marxist administration would then fail because of the DNVP and that *Hindenburg* would not be able to free himself from governing with the Social Democrats.' The president received two different answers from his German Nationalist interlocutors: the party head responded negatively, the former floor leader favorably. At the beginning of 1930 it was clear that the path from parliamentary to presidential rule still contained many obstacles.

What held the government together during this period was the interest all the coalition parties shared in passing the Young laws. On 20 January, after the details had been discussed for months in subcommittees of the expert commission, the Young Plan was passed in The Hague. The most important thing for Germany was that the payment schedule and total amount remained what the experts had proposed in June 1929. Eight days later began the last chapter in the history of the

* *Rise or Decline?*

Grand Coalition. On 28 January, at the suggestion of Heinrich Brüning, who had been elected floor leader in December, the Centre decided to make its support of the Young Plan conditional upon an agreement on financial reform. Brüning's proposal was neither a repudiation of the Grand Coalition nor of the new reparations agreement. It was an attempt to use the coalition's foreign policy goals as a means of leveraging a reform of the national finances.

Though a small number of SPD delegates wanted to put forward the counter-proposal of a financial reform in the spirit of the Social Democrats, they were unable to prevail. The great majority of the fraction staunchly rejected linking domestic and foreign policy measures in this way. But this attitude had the unintended effect of weakening the SPD's negotiating position. On the right wing of the coalition, the DVP refused any further concessions on unemployment insurance, increases in direct taxes, and an emergency levy from civil servants and others with fixed salaries. At the end of February, it looked like an agreement was no longer possible.

The president shared this assessment. In a personal interview on 1 March, Hindenburg asked Brüning if the Centre would be willing to support a different government. Brüning rejected the idea. It was the shared opinion of the fraction leadership, he said, that the present coalition was to be maintained as long as possible, in order to pass the Young Plan and a series of important domestic reforms. An attempt to carry through these plans without the Social Democrats would lead to great turmoil, and, in any case, without the SPD a majority was very uncertain. Towards the end of the conversation, Brüning summarized the position of the Centre by telling Hindenburg 'that we at least demand a commitment of the party leaders to the finance laws and have all of us the wish that the current coalition be preserved for a while'.

On 5 March, against the expectations of nearly all observers, the cabinet of the Grand Coalition came to an agreement on the proposals to cover the 1930 federal budget. One of the most significant points was the increase in the 'industry burden'—which was actually slated to be abolished after the passage of the Young Plan—from 300 to 350 million marks in January 1930. This fulfilled the SPD's demand for a direct property tax, albeit only for a year. Equally important was another concession by Rudolf Hilferding's successor as finance minister, Paul Moldenhauer of the DVP: the board of directors of the unemployment office was authorized to raise the contributions from 3.5 to 4 per cent. In exchange, the Social Democratic ministers agreed that there would be no refund of the payroll tax in 1931.

The cabinet's agreement was a triumph of the moderate forces in all camps, but it was built on sand. On 6 March the DVP fraction, supported by the Association of German Employers' Associations (*Vereinigung der deutschen Arbeitgeberverbände*) and the National Association of German Industry, rejected key provisions of the compromise. The BVP, which occupied the postal ministry in the Müller cabinet, refused to go along with an increase in the beer tax. On 11 March the president intervened again. In conversations with Brüning and Müller,

Hindenburg declared his willingness to grant the government the plenary powers of Article 48. This seemed to accomplish Brüning's purpose of linking the finance reform to the reparations agreement. On 12 March the Young laws were passed at the third reading by 265 against 192 votes and 3 abstentions. Almost all Centre delegates voted in favour.

Whatever Hindenburg's intentions were on 11 March, however, his 'camarilla' was determined to exploit the new situation presenting itself *after* the passage of the Young laws for a decisive shift to the right, away from a parliamentary and towards a presidential system. Already on 18 March, heavy-industry circles in the German People's Party learned that the president, 'apparently at the instigation of Groener and Schleicher', had decided not to permit the Müller cabinet to use Emergency Article 48 after all. On 19 March Hindenburg, in an imperious tone, demanded that the government pass measures to help east German agriculture. His state secretary, Otto Meissner, remarked on this step to General von Schleicher in the following words: 'This is the first stage of *your* solution! It also lays the foundation for the best thing we can have, "for the Hindenburg leadership".'[33]

Knowing the president's plans, the DVP could afford to adopt a relatively moderate stance vis-à-vis the Social Democrats at its party congress in Mannheim on 21 and 22 March. On 26 and 27 March Brüning again tried to work out a compromise, the main effect of which would have been to postpone the battle over unemployment insurance reform. The unemployment office was to introduce austerity measures, and the government was to decide at a later date whether it wished to raise the level of the contributions, lower the level of payments, or increase indirect taxes for the purpose of financing federal loans. This proposal, which weakened the cabinet decision of 5 March to the detriment of the unemployed, obtained a majority of People's Party votes on 27 March. At the meeting of the SPD fraction, however, union representatives and Labour Minister Wissell were especially vocal in their rejection of the 'Brüning compromise'. Chancellor Müller and the other Social Democratic members of the cabinet were among the small minority endorsing the Centre's proposal. The cabinet had no choice but to record its failure and tender its resignation to the president.

The decisions made on 27 March 1930 mark one of the deepest ruptures in the history of the Weimar Republic. In retrospect, it is clear that the period of relative stability came to an end on this day and that the first phase in the dissolution of the first German democracy began. But many contemporaries, too, were conscious of the significance of the day's events. On 28 March the *Frankfurter Zeitung* spoke of a 'black day . . . doubly ominous, because the trivial cause of the battle stands in such a grotesque disproportion to the disastrous consequences that may arise from it'. Criticism was also soon heard in the ranks of the SPD, whose decision had sealed the fate of the Müller government. In the May issue of *Die Gesellschaft*, the theory-oriented journal he edited, Rudolf Hilferding explained why he could not follow the argument of the party majority that a reduction in unemployment compensation would have been unavoidable in the autumn if Brüning's proposal had been accepted:

In terms of the very goal of securing the unemployment insurance, the resignation from the government seems to be, at best, no improvement. The fear that things would have got worse in the autumn does not seem sufficient for such a momentous step. The fear of death is no good justification for committing suicide.

By 27 March 1930 it was foreseeable that the breakdown of the Grand Coalition would lead to a shift in power from the parliament to the president. The parliamentary and extra-parliamentary right had wanted this outcome, mainly because there seemed to be no other way to vanquish the Weimar social welfare state. *This* was the immediate objective of the pioneers of the presidential solution, not merely the defeat of a minor increase in the unemployment contributions. It was therefore the right that bore the main responsibility for what occurred after the collapse of the Müller government.

The moderate left cheerily accepted the departure from parliamentary democracy and thus shared the blame for the shift to a presidential system. The Social Democrats could have prevented the disintegration of the Grand Coalition at the end of March—though only at the price of a party crisis and probably only for a short time, since the coalition would hardly have outlasted the passage of the Young laws, its most important goal, in the autumn of 1930. Nonetheless, it would have been the right thing for the SPD to have stepped onto the bridge Brüning had thrown, for the self-reproach the Social Democrats now had to suffer was bitter. At the decisive moment, they had not done everything within their power to preserve parliamentary democracy and to prevent a relapse into the authoritarian state.[34]

THE SHIFT TO A PRESIDENTIAL SYSTEM AND THE RISE OF THE NSDAP

Hindenburg's circle had been considering Heinrich Brüning as a possible successor to Hermann Müller for some time. This ascetic bachelor from Westphalian Münster, 44 years old at the time of his appointment to the chancellorship of the Reich on 30 March 1930, had been an officer at the front in 1915 after a broad course of study in history and political science, which he completed with a doctoral thesis in national economy. He had been wounded and decorated in the war. The fact that he had been the director of the Christian-national trade unions after 1920 preserved him from party-internal accusations of being a 'rightist'. On the other hand, he had also gained high regard in Conservative circles as a finance expert in the Reichstag, to which he had belonged since 1924. While his Catholicism was a liability in the view of *Kulturkampf* liberals, for the architects of the presidential state it was, if anything, an asset. Through Brüning's mediation, political Catholicism became one of the buttresses of the silent constitutional revolution Hindenburg and his circle sought to effect.

Initially, the Brüning government was not an openly presidential cabinet, but a covert one. In addition to Groener, the non-aligned minister of defence, it included representatives from the bourgeois parties that had participated in the previous administration—the Centre Party, DVP, DDP, and BVP—as well as one minister each from the DNVP, the Economic Party, and the People's National Reich Association (*Volksnationale Reichsvereinigung*), formed by former members of the DNVP and the Farmers' and Rural People's Party. But since Martin Schiele, the German Nationalist minister of agriculture, resigned his seat in the Reichstag upon entering office, it was not clear at first how his party would react to the Brüning cabinet. And in fact the DNVP voted inconsistently several times in April 1930, delivering narrow parliamentary minorities to the government—very much against the will of Hugenberg.

Then, about a quarter of a year after Brüning's appointment, there arose the kind of situation Hindenburg had had in mind when he made him chancellor: a government bill to cover the budget was rejected in the parliament's tax committee. Thereafter, on 16 July, the president made it officially known that he had authorized the chancellor to put the budgetary programme into effect on the basis of Article 48 in case it should fail to pass the Reichstag, and to dissolve the latter if it should call for the annulment of the emergency measures or pronounce a vote of no confidence in the chancellor.

Speaking for his party, Rudolf Breitscheid, the SPD floor leader, immediately protested that the purpose of Article 48 was 'to help the state and to protect the state when need arises, not to help a particular government out of its predicament when it cannot find the majority it is looking for'. But government by emergency decree could now no longer be averted. On 16 July, after the rejection of the budget bill in the plenum assembly of the Reichstag, Brüning announced that the government had no interest in further debate. The first two emergency measures went into effect that same day, though they lasted only two days. On 18 July the Reichstag accepted the SPD's motion to lift the measures, whereupon it was immediately dissolved by the president. New elections were set for 14 September. On 26 July Hindenburg decreed a new 'emergency measure to remedy financial, economic, and social crises'. Among other things, it introduced a 'civic tax' (*Bürgersteuer*) that, unlike in the previous emergency measures, was graduated to a certain extent. Moreover, it formed the legal basis for a programme of federal assistance for people on fixed incomes, an income tax supplement, a tax on unmarried people (*Ledigensteuer*), and—unavoidable in view of increased unemployment—an increase in unemployment contributions from 3.5% to 4.5%.

The transition from covertly to openly presidential rule in July 1930 was characterized by a certain ineluctability. Four months before, the president had rejected rule by parliamentary majority; now, the July crisis represented the fulfilment of the law that had guided the new chancellor into office on 30 March. Brüning was unable to accommodate the Social Democrats without alienating the right wing of the governing coalition, which would have been at cross-purposes with the logic of his appointment. The Social Democrats, for their part, could not accept the non-graduated civic tax the government had insisted upon up to the dissolution of parliament without causing massive harm to their supporters' sense of justice and handing the Communists a cheap victory. The main protagonists of the July crisis had so little room to manoeuvre that a parliamentary solution was all but impossible.

The parliamentary elections were preceded by attempts to concentrate the forces of the bourgeois parties. The success was not great. The DDP allied itself with the People's National Reich Association, the political arm of the conservative and—for the period, relatively moderately—anti-Semitic Young German Order (*Jungdeutscher Orden*), to form the German State Party (*Deutscher Staatspartei*). This deeply upset many of the DDP's Jewish supporters, and not only them. The industrial interests promoted the Conservative People's Party (*Konservative Volkspartei*), formed at the end of July by the *volkskonservativ* forces around Treviranus and the anti-Hugenberg faction around Count Westarp. On the left, everything remained as it had been, organizationally speaking. The only innovation was the vehement nationalism put on display by the KPD. In its 24 August 'programatic declaration on the national and social liberation of the German people', the Communist party said that the leaders of the SPD were

> not only assistants to the hangmen of the bourgeoisie, but, at the same time, the willing agents of French and Polish imperialism. All the actions of the traitorous, corrupt Social Democrats represent one continuous act of high treason against the existential interests of the labouring masses of Germany.[35]

Of the voting population of the country 82% participated in the Reichstag elections on 14 September 1930, more than in any other parliamentary election since 1920. But the real sensation was the performance of the National Socialists, who grew from somewhat more than 800,000 votes in May 1928 to 6.4 million. This represented an increase from 2.6% to 18.3% of the vote and from 12 to 107 seats in parliament. Communist gains were also considerable, though less dramatic. The KPD grew from 10.6% to 13.1% of the vote and gained 77 seats, up from 54.

All other parties took losses. The German Nationalists were reduced by half, falling from 14.3% to 7%. The downfall of the liberal parties continued, the DVP sinking from 8.7% to 4.5%, and the German State party, the former DDP, from 4.9% to 3.8%. The Catholic parties' losses were comparatively minor. The Centre, which had obtained 12.1% in 1928, now came off with 11.8%. The BVP's 3% was down from 3.1% two years previously. Much greater were the losses of the SPD, which still remained Germany's largest party. It fell from 29.6% to 24.5%. The newly founded Conservative People's Party, together with the 'Guelf' German-Hanover Party (*Deutsch-Hannoversche Partei*), achieved all of 1.3% of the vote.

The National Socialists were the main beneficiaries of the increased electoral participation. Yet the non-voters in previous elections were not the main source of 'brown' success. Most of the NSDAP constituency had previously voted for other parties. A methodical calculation has revealed that probably one in three DNVP voters, one in four DVP or DDP voters, one in seven non-voters, and one in ten SPD voters chose Hitler's party in the 1930 elections. The conservative and liberal 'camps' thus contributed far more to the rise of National Socialism than the Social Democrats. Several other facts can also be considered certain. Protestants were twice as susceptible to the NSDAP as Catholics. Farmers, government officials, the self-employed, retirees, and pensioners were, proportionally speaking, more strongly represented in the NSDAP constituency than in the general working population. The opposite was true of workers and employees. The unemployed (whose official number was somewhat more than 3 million in September 1930) contributed little to National Socialist success; they were far more likely to vote for the party of Ernst Thälmann than that of Adolf Hitler.

National Socialism's appeal to the middle classes was so obvious that the Social Democratic sociologist Theodor Geiger, writing in the autumn of the same year, interpreted the NSDAP success as the expression of a 'panic in the *Mittelstand*'. Though accurate, this diagnosis was not the whole story. The National Socialists won over not only bourgeois and rural voters who were dissatisfied with their previous parties or who had not voted before; they also succeeded in penetrating the working class. It was to their advantage that a significant number of German workers had never developed the kind of proletarian class consciousness that led others to vote for one of the 'Marxist' parties.

Thus the NSDAP of 1930 was, in a purely sociological sense, a 'people's party', far more so than all other parties, which drew their main support from a particular social or confessional 'milieu'. It was true that, by 1930, these social and confessional 'milieus' were not nearly as segregated from each other as during the imperial era. Gramophone, film, and radio had begun to prepare the way for a new mass culture that would ride roughshod over the boundaries between social groups. But the 'old' parties barely recognized the challenge that lay in these developments. The National Socialists, on the other hand, exploited the new media of mass communication to great effect, responding to a widespread need for a sense of community beyond the confines of estate, class, and confession—a need that was especially vigorous in the younger generation, but which had lain politically dormant until this moment. As backwards-looking as were many of its promises to its voters, the NSDAP owed its success mainly to its ability to adapt to the conditions of the era of mass culture and, in this sense, to demonstrate its 'modernity'.

The National Socialist answer to the need for community was no different in 1930 than it had been in the years before: extreme nationalism. Nationalism would envelop in one giant embrace everything that divided Germans from each other. The rhetorics of anti-Semitism and nationalism often went hand-in-hand. If the former was less prominent in 1930 than in previous electoral campaigns, the main reason was because the National Socialists were out for the votes of the working classes, who were generally unresponsive to anti-Jewish agitation. The concept of 'socialism', which tended to irritate many bourgeois voters, especially the older among them, was assiduously reinterpreted by the National Socialists. Hitler's version of socialism did not entail the abolition of private property, but rather an equality of opportunity in society and an economic philosophy derived from a principle anchored in the 1920 party platform: *Gemeinnutz vor Eigennutz*, 'the common good before the good of the individual' or 'service before self'.

The republican parties, as nationalist as they believed themselves to be, could not attempt to outdo the nationalism of the National Socialists. But the pledge of allegiance to the democratic republic, the answer of Weimar's staunch defenders to the challenge from the radical right, was only able to mobilize a minority. Even within the Weimar coalition, which still held together in Prussia, republican pathos could achieve but little. Opinions were too divided on what, precisely, was worth saving about Weimar. In any case, the most obvious thing to do in light of the political polarization reflected in the electoral results of 14 September was for each party to return to the sources of its own strength. For the Social Democrats, this meant binding their supporters more firmly to socialism as a cultural movement and a lifestyle. For the Centre, it meant a return to the Catholic part of political Catholicism.

Bourgeois liberalism was a far less clearly delineated and less tightly 'networked' milieu than the social democratic movement or political Catholicism. Its political convictions were less firmly entrenched. Both liberal parties, the DVP no less than the DDP, responded to the rightward migration of their voters by re-orienting themselves in that direction. Indeed, within a few short months of Stresemann's death, there was very little left of the DVP that could be called 'liberal'. In January 1930 it joined a rightist government in Thuringia in which the National Socialists, with Wilhelm Frick, occupied the ministry of the interior and public education (until April 1931). For the German Democratic party, the alliance with the anti-Semitic People's National Reich Association in the 14 September elections had not paid off. Middle-class tradesmen continued to abandon the party, and, presumably, no small number of disillusioned Jews went over to the Social Democrats. A few short weeks after the elections, the newly founded German State Party split. On 7 October, led by their High Master, Artur Mahraun, the Young Germans announced their departure from the party, citing 'insurmountable philosophic differences'. Henceforth, the only reminder of the July 1930 fusion was the new party name, which no longer contained the word 'democratic'.[36]

The downfall of German liberalism prompted not only many Jewish voters to look for a new political home, but also one of the most famous German writers. In October 1930 Thomas Mann delivered his 'German Address' in Beethoven Hall in Berlin. Continually interrupted by hostile calls from the audience, Mann exhorted the German bourgeois to take their political place at the side of the Social Democrats. This party, he said, stood for the peaceful rebuilding of Europe and had provided the most dependable support for the policies of Gustav Stresemann.

Marxism or no Marxism, it is the intellectual and spiritual traditions of the German bourgeoisie themselves that point it to this seat. For a foreign policy dedicated to Franco-German understanding is the only one to which corresponds a domestic atmosphere offering the bourgeois claims to happiness—liberty, spirituality, culture—any chance of survival. Any other involves a nationalist asceticism and uptightness that would mean the most fearsome conflict between Fatherland and Culture, bringing misfortune to us all.

Thomas Mann intended his speech to be an 'appeal to reason'. That sounded like a response to the much-discussed entreaty made by Otto Braun in an interview with the American news agency United Press on the day after the election. For the Prussian prime minister, the outcome of the vote meant that a 'Grand Coalition of all rational people' must join together 'in order to concentrate energetically, with a no doubt sufficient governmental majority, first of all on fighting unemployment and improving the economic conditions of existence for the broad masses'.

But Otto Braun's appeal to all rational people had, in the autumn of 1930, hardly a better chance of being heard than Thomas Mann's appeal to the reason of the bourgeoisie. Hindenburg had not detached himself from the Social Democrats in the spring only to allow them a share in the power of the Reich half a year later, and the governmental right wing thought the same. Conversely, there was massive resistance within the SPD to any kind of cooperation with Brüning and the forces backing him. Max Seydewitz, a Reichstag delegate from Saxony, spoke for the party left wing when he wrote in the 15 September issue of the journal *Klassenkampf* that the intentions of the Centre Party chancellor were no less fascist than the methods proposed by the National Socialists, and it thus made no sense 'for the Social Democratic movement to differentiate between Brüning's and Hitler's fascism in its struggle for democracy and against fascism'.

For the governmental camp, a widening to the right was just as impossible as a widening to the left. A coalition with the NSDAP was unthinkable for the bourgeois centre parties, and the army and industrial interests also did not consider the National Socialists fit for government in autumn 1930. Even Hitler's spectacular performance in the trial for high treason of the Reichswehr officers from Ulm, Scheringer, Ludin, and Wendt, was as yet unable to change this fact. Summonsed by the defence of the three young National Socialists before the federal court in Leipzig on 25 September 1930, Hitler maintained under oath that the NSDAP would take power only by legal means. However, after the presiding judge enquired about his comment that heads would roll in the sand after a National Socialist victory, Hitler then added that a national court would be created through the normal legislative process with the task of condemning the criminals of November 1918. Their execution would be accomplished by legal means, that is.

Since neither the National Socialists nor the Social Democrats were acceptable, the bourgeois minority cabinet under Brüning was forced into toleration agreements. Political reasons militated against seeking NSDAP support, which Hitler strictly rejected in any case. Consequently, there was no realistic alternative to an arrangement with the Social Democrats.

The SPD leaders shared this assessment. From their post-election point of view, there were three main reasons to work with the Brüning administration. First, it was the only way to avoid a government even further to the right, dependent on the National Socialists. Secondly, the Weimar coalition in Prussia under Otto Braun would be in great danger if the Social Democrats brought down the national government under the Centre Party chancellor. The loss of government power in Germany's largest state would also have meant giving up control of the Prussian police, the state's most powerful force in dealing with National Socialists and Communists. Thirdly, there was a wide field of substantive agreement between the Social Democrats and the government camp, based on the shared realization that the consequences of the questionable 'debt economy' after 1924 could be overcome only by means of a rigorous cost-cutting policy. The reform consensus did not preclude dissent over the distribution of the social costs of austerity, but it was not undone by this continuing antagonism.

The foundation of the cooperation policy was laid at the end of September in confidential interviews between Brüning and the Social Democratic Party leadership, with Rudolf Hilferding and Hermann Pünder, the state secretary of the federal chancellery, playing active roles. On 3 October the SPD fraction passed a resolution justifying its support of the government. In view of the election outcome, the party considered its foremost task to be the preservation of democracy, the safeguarding of the constitution, and the defence of parliamentary governance. Furthermore, the SPD was fighting for democracy in order to defend the social welfare programmes and raise the living standards of the working class. 'While safeguarding the existential interests of the laboring masses, the Social Democratic fraction will stand up for the defence of the parliamentary foundation and for a resolution of the most pressing fiscal concerns.'

The Weimar Republic had experienced many fiery debates in the Reichstag, but none were as tumultuous as those of 17 and 18 October 1930. In protest against a ban on uniforms in Prussia, the 107 National Socialists entered the main hall of the parliament dressed in the brown shirts of the SA. Gregor Strasser, the leader of the party's national organization (*Reichsorganisationsleiter*), announced that the National Socialists, 'anti-parliamentarians on principle', were practically compelled to become 'the defenders of the Weimar constitution' against the current dictatorial plans of the bourgeoisie. 'We are now for the democracy of Weimar, we are for the law in defence of the republic, as long as it suits us. And we will demand and maintain every position of power on the basis of this constitution for as long as we wish.'

The Communist speaker, the delegate Wilhelm Pieck, did not trouble himself with drawing a cloak of legality over the subversive plans of his party. There was, he declared, only one way to bring down the accursed system of capitalist exploitation and slavery:

Revolution and thus the destruction of capitalism and the removal of all those who support this system. That is the task the Communist party has set itself, and the day will come when the labouring masses, when the unemployed, under the leadership of the Communist Party, will drive out this parliament of businessmen and fascists. Then the German Soviets will come together in its stead and erect the Dictatorship of the Proletariat, setting up a free socialist Soviet Germany in place of this rotten bourgeois society and this republic of starvation.

Nonetheless, after the Social Democrats had committed themselves to working with the Brüning administration, there was little doubt about the outcome of the ballots. On 18 October the parliament, with the votes of the SPD, passed the government's bill on the repayment of the debt, then a measure transferring the petitions to lift the emergency measures of 26 July to the budgetary committee, then finally a motion by the coalition parties to bypass all votes of no confidence and resume the regular business of government. With this accomplished, the Reichstag adjourned until 3 December, to the outrage of the National Socialists and the Communists. The government had won not only a battle, but also—equally important—time.

With the assistance of the SPD, Brüning's cabinet also survived the similarly turbulent December session. But it had to pay the price in a number of social welfare concessions. The civic tax was graduated more sharply and the unemployed were granted health insurance free of charge. In exchange, the SPD assumed part responsibility for an increase in unemployment contributions from 4.5 to 6.5 per cent, a 6 per cent cut in the salaries of government employees, and new measures for the protection of agriculture, including higher customs duties for wheat and barley. On 7 December the Reichstag adjourned until 3 February 1931.

Vorwärts welcomed its departure. Three months after the new elections, as the 13 December issue of the SPD party organ announced, everybody was probably of one mind that 'this Reichstag is a failure and that we can be glad if we hear and see nothing of it.' The party's floor leader in the Prussian parliament, Ernst Heilmann, who was also a delegate in the Reichstag, wrote that, in reality, a Reichstag with 107 National Socialists and 77 Communists could not function effectively. 'A people that elects such a parliament is effectively renouncing self-governance. And its legislative privilege is automatically replaced by Art. 48.' In a broadcast speech on 17 December, Otto Braun argued that if the Reichstag, partly owing to its infiltration by anti-parliamentary groups, was unwilling and unable to accomplish the tasks conferred upon it by the constitution, 'then, but only then, the political SOS-signal must be given, and the safety valve of the constitution must be opened long enough to deal with the acute crisis the parliament was unable, or unwilling, to master.' *Vorwärts* published Braun's speech under the title 'An Education in Democracy'.[37]

When the Social Democrats convened in Leipzig on 31 May 1931 for their first party congress after their departure from power, the policy of cooperation drew a great deal of criticism. Nonetheless, the negative views were outweighed by the support for the main argument of the policy's defenders: 'National Socialism has been held back from governmental power by us,' declared Wilhelm Sollmann, deputy floor leader of the fraction,

> and if, in October 1930, the National Socialists were prevented from taking over the presidency of the parliament, from taking over the army and the police force, then, I believe, no criticism in point of detail ought to stop us from saying that that is not only a great success, it is a European success for German Social Democracy.

There was, in fact, no responsible alternative to the toleration policy for the SPD, in view of the distribution of political power after the September 1930 elections. But toleration had drawbacks, and these were obvious to all observers by spring 1931. The fact that the parliament now met infrequently (on 26 March it had adjourned until 13 October) was grist for the mills of the anti-parliamentary forces of the extreme left and right, and nobody knew how to exploit this opportunity as effectively as Hitler. He could now appeal to both the widespread resentment against the western-style—and thus 'un-German'—parliamentary democracy of 1919, which had become a mere façade after the autumn of 1930, *and* to the people's right to political participation in the form of general equal suffrage, first codified under Bismarck, but largely vitiated under Brüning's presidential cabinet. And what is more, the Social Democratic toleration of Brüning's unpopular austerity policy enabled the leader of the National Socialists to present his party as the only popular opposition movement to the right of the Communists and, at the same time, as an alternative to 'Marxism' in both its Bolshevist and its reformed versions.

On 5 June 1931, the day the SPD congress in Leipzig came to an end, President Hindenburg decreed a new emergency measure, one that had been anticipated for some time. The harshness of its social impact was worse than all expectations. Unemployment payments were reduced by an average of 10–12 per cent. The salaries of state officials and company employees were cut by between 4 and 8 per cent. Invalids and disabled veterans received lower pensions. The Social Democrats joined in the general cry of outrage. Their demand that the Reichstag—or at least the budgetary committee—be convoked met with unqualified rejection by Brüning, who believed the country to be on the brink of insolvency, if not of civil war. The only prospect he held out to the Social Democrats was that some of the harsher social consequences might be mitigated in the provisions for the measure's enforcement. In order to force the SPD to back down, he threatened to terminate the Prussian coalition. This worked. On 16 June the Social Democratic fraction withdrew its motion to convoke the budgetary committee.

The party left wing revolted. On 1 July it published an 'admonition' against the continuation of the cooperation policy. This was to become the seed of a new organization, the Socialist Workers' Party of Germany (*Sozialistische Arbeiterpartei Deutschlands*), founded at the beginning of October. But the majority of the SPD was not prepared to break with Brüning and to give up power in Prussia. In the July issue of *Die Gesellschaft*, Rudolf Hilferding spoke of the 'tragic predicament' of his party, resulting from the collision between the economic crisis and the situation of political emergency created by the elections on 14 September 1930:

> The Reichstag is a parliament against parliamentary rule, its existence a threat to democracy, to the working classes, to foreign policy . . . Defending democracy against a majority that rejects it, and doing so with the political tools of a democratic constitution that presupposes a functional parliament—it is almost like squaring the circle, the problem presented to the Social Democrats to solve. It is truly a situation that has never occurred before.

It was not until well into 1931 that most Germans began to realize that the nadir of the economic crisis was still to come and that the world was in the middle of a Great Depression. On 20 June there was still what appeared to be a ray of hope. The American president, Herbert Hoover, proposed a year-long international 'debt holiday' from the payment of compulsory state debts, including the German reparations, and on 6 July, after the USA had overcome French resistance, the Hoover Moratorium really did take effect. Shortly afterward, however, Germany was shaken by a bank crisis that further undermined confidence in capitalism and the market economy. The buying and selling of foreign exchange was rigorously cut back. The drastic increase of the minimum lending rate and the rate for loans on security had a fatal effect on the prostrate economy. Tax revenues were used to rehabilitate the banks, amounting to a partial nationalization of the banking system.

In September 1931 the Brüning government was faced with a serious foreign policy crisis when the project of an Austro-German customs union ended in a debacle. Julius Curtius, Stresemann's successor in the foreign ministry, was the main responsible party, but in a larger sense Brüning too was at fault. The customs union, which Vienna had also been pushing since 1930, was designed to strengthen German influence in central and south-eastern Europe, prepare the way for eventual political union between the two German-speaking countries, and, above all, demonstrate renewed German self-confidence both domestically and internationally—an agenda in full agreement with Brüning's emphatically nationalist foreign policy.

When, on 18 March 1931, the cabinet committed itself to the customs union, the Wilhelmstrasse foresaw an unfriendly reaction from France. But it was not prepared for the intensity and the sharpness with which Paris responded to the initiative. Austria, which was in dire need of international and especially French assistance, was so impressed that it began to withdraw from the project in May. On 3 September Curtius, along with his colleague in Vienna, Johannes Schober, announced to the European committee of the Council of the League of Nations in Geneva that the two countries would no longer pursue the project. Two days later, in response to a Council request motivated by Great Britain, the International Court of Justice in The Hague decided by eight votes against seven that the customs union violated the 1922 Geneva Protocol on the economic and financial reconstruction of Austria.

After the humiliating failure of his Austria policy, Curtius's position as foreign minister became untenable. On 3 October he asked the chancellor to apply to the president for his resignation. By this point, however, it was no longer simply a matter of a change of leadership in the foreign office. In September Schleicher, followed by Hindenburg, had exhorted the chancellor to perform a decisive turn to the right. Brüning sought to accommodate these demands by reshuffling his cabinet on 9 October. He himself took over the foreign office. Defence Minister Groener also temporarily assumed the interior ministry, succeeding the 'leftist' Centre politician and former chancellor, Joseph Wirth. Curt Joël, the arch-conservative state secretary, advanced to minister of justice.

The DVP, Curtius's party, was no longer represented in the Brüning cabinet. Its heavy-industry wing had demanded on 3 October that it go over to the opposition and bring forward a parliamentary motion of no confidence in the government. This the party leadership and Reichstag fraction agreed to do one week later. Thus, one year after the beginning of the cooperation policy, the chancellor was presented the bill for his occasional concessions to the Social Democrats, on whom he depended in parliament. The right wing of the business camp broke with Brüning because his policies were not right enough for the industrial right.[38]

On 11 October the conservative portion of the Ruhr industrial interests had the chance to go one step further and publicly join ranks with the 'nationalist opposition'. On that day, the parties and associations of the staunch right held a military parade in Bad Harzburg. But apart from Ernst Brandi, one of the coal mine directors of the United Steel Works Corporation, no prominent heavy industrialist took part in this meeting, which had been initiated by Hugenberg. Even Brüning's harshest critics in the business world evidently still had reservations about openly joining the radical right.

The 'Harzburg front' was made up of the NSDAP, DNVP, Stahlhelm, National Land League, and Pan-German League, along with numerous members of former ruling houses, the former chief of the Army High Command, General von Seeckt (from 1930 a DVP delegate in the Reichstag), and Hjalmar Schacht, former president of the Reichsbank, who had resigned his office in March 1930 in protest against the Young Plan. Schacht's attacks on the bank succeeded in starting a hectic debate that lasted several days. Hitler, who had been officially received by Hindenburg for the first time on the previous day, caused a stir by leaving the parade before the Stahlhelm formations could follow his SA—a consciously provocative gesture intended to demonstrate his independence from the 'old' right.

The events in Harzburg made it easier for the Social Democrats to come to terms with the more rightist second cabinet under Brüning. The massive attacks against it by the 'fascist reaction' were by themselves almost sufficient to make the government seem tolerable to the SPD. Schacht's elucidations on monetary policy inspired the headline 'The Harzburg Inflation Front' in the 12 October issue of *Vorwärts*. On this point there was full agreement with Brüning, who was equally opposed to any experimentation with the currency. In the short parliamentary session that began two days after the Harzburg assembly, the chancellor could once again count on the support of the SPD. On 16 October the votes of the Social Democrats were decisive in rejecting all motions of no confidence.

HINDENBURG'S RE-ELECTION AND THE FALL OF BRÜNING

Brüning used the renewed strength of his position to promulgate a new emergency decree on 9 December linking wage and price reductions together in such a way so as not to significantly damage the purchasing power of the masses and to increase the attractiveness of German exports. However, the chancellor still categorically rejected the kind of loan-financed job creation programmes some portions of business and even experts of the General German Trade Union Association had been demanding, the former since the summer, the latter since December. Such ideas contradicted not only his fundamental belief in the absolute necessity of a balanced budget, but also his foreign policy priorities. If Germany created the impression that it still possessed financial resources, the argument that the reparations burden was strangling the German economy would have lost its force. The end of the reparations was the immediate goal Germany had to achieve in order to cast off all the other shackles of Versailles—the military ones not least—and regain its traditional great-power status.

This was the reason Brüning also did not jump at the chance for a reparations compromise when one presented itself at the end of 1931. On 23 December the Special Advisory Committee of the Bank of International Settlements in Basel presented the report that the German government, in accordance with the procedure set out in the Young Plan, had requested in November. The committee came to the conclusion that, in order to avoid a new catastrophe, all debts between states, including the German reparations, would have to be immediately adjusted to the shattered conditions of the world economy.

That meant nothing more nor less than a total revision of the Young Plan. But the reparations conference planned in Lausanne at the beginning of 1932 in response to the report did not interest Brüning in the slightest, since, in his view, it would lead only to a new moratorium and a reduction in the amount Germany owed, that is, to a provisional half-measure, not to the desired complete and final end to the reparations payments. Consequently, the German government sought to postpone the conference, and was successful. Set to begin on 25 January 1932, the meeting was called off on 20 January. The domestic price for this foreign policy decision was momentous. The drastic deflationary course continued unabated, and social destitution and political radicalization spread.

At the beginning of 1932 all of German domestic political life was focused on the presidential election planned for the spring of the year. Brüning would have preferred a quick parliamentary solution to the problem: Hindenburg's re-election by the Reichstag with the two-thirds majority necessary to revise the constitution. But the German Nationalists and National Socialists refused to go along. For his part the incumbent, who had celebrated his eighty-fourth birthday in October 1931, did not want to run in a popular election unless he had sufficient backing from his friends on the right, those who had urged him to run in 1925.

That he would have this backing was not at all certain at the beginning of 1932. Among those involved in the 'Hindenburg committee', whose 1 February declaration called for the re-election of the aged field marshal, were the poet Gerhart Hauptmann, the painter Max Liebermann, the director of the National Association of German Industry, Carl Duisberg, the High Master of the Young German Order, Artur Mahraun, and two former defence ministers, Otto Gessler and Gustav Noske. But none of the leaders of the 'nationalist associations' or big agriculture had signed the document. Since the Stahlhelm, which counted Hindenburg as an honorary member, did not want to vote for him, the Kyffhäuser Union, of which he was honorary president, also hesitated to endorse him openly. Only on 14 February did the organization's central executive come out in support of the president, and one day later Hindenburg finally announced that, in recognition of his 'responsibility for the fate of our Fatherland', he would be available for possible re-election.

Hindenburg's announcement prompted the parties of the moderate right and centre to publicly side with him. The Harzburg front disintegrated. The Stahlhelm and the German Nationalists resisted the National Socialists' pretensions to leadership and, on 22 February, nominated their own candidate, the Stahlhelm deputy national leader, Theodor Duesterberg. That same day Joseph Goebbels, district leader (*Gauleiter*) of the NSDAP in Berlin, declared in the Sportpalast that 'Hitler will become our president.' Four days later, the leader of the National Socialists had himself appointed to an official post, that of *Regierungsrat*, in the Brunswick legation in Berlin. With this step Adolf Hitler, born in Austria, stateless since 1925, obtained the last thing that stood in the way of his candidacy for the Reich presidency, German citizenship.

The far left had had a candidate ever since 12 January: Ernst Thälmann, nominated by the central committee of the KPD as the 'red workers' candidate' for the succession to Hindenburg. The Comintern and the Communist party leadership expected Thälmann to draw a large number of votes from the Social Democratic workers if the SPD opted to endorse the incumbent. This calculation was not entirely chimerical. It was true that, since the beginning of the cooperation policy in October 1930, the members and supporters of the SPD had put up with a great deal that ran diametrically counter to the traditional ideas of the party. Nonetheless, an election recommendation for the staunch monarchist Hindenburg would have been beyond the pale for many Social Democrats.

The National Socialists also sharply attacked the SPD for its expected endorsement of Hindenburg. On 23 February, the first day of a short parliamentary session characterized by constant tumult, Goebbels caused a great stir by remarking that Hindenburg was 'praised by the Berlin asphalt press, praised by the party of the deserters'. He meant the Social Democrats, on whose behalf the delegate Kurt Schumacher, a seriously wounded volunteer of 1914, then hurled back the wildly applauded rejoinder that the whole National Socialist agitation was 'a continual appeal to the inner bastard in people', and that if anything about National Socialism deserved recognition, it was the fact 'that, for the first time in German politics, it has successfully accomplished the total mobilization of human stupidity'.

On 26 February, the last day of the session, the SPD made its decision for Hindenburg officially known. The election statement by the party leadership declared that on 13 March, the day of the first presidential ballot, the German people would stand before the question of whether Hindenburg should remain or be replaced by Hitler.

> Hitler instead of Hindenburg—that means chaos and panic in Germany and all of Europe, radical exacerbation of the economic crisis and the unemployment emergency, the most extreme threat of bloody conflicts among our own people and with other nations. Hitler instead of Hindenburg—that means victory of the most reactionary over the most progressive elements of the bourgeoisie and over the working class, destruction of all civil liberties, the press, political, trade union, and cultural organizations, increased exploitation and wage slavery . . . Defeat Hitler! Vote for Hindenburg!

Hindenburg's most passionate champion within the governmental camp was the chancellor. On 11 March, at his last great election rally in the Berlin Sportpalast, Brüning drew a picture of the president that was painfully at odds with reality. He would, he said, like to see the man who was Hindenburg's equal 'in assessing a situation sharply and quickly and summing it up in a few short, pithy sentences'. Brüning counted Hindenburg among the 'real leaders' and the 'men sent by God', called him the 'symbol of German power and unity in the whole world', and concluded with the call: 'Hindenburg must prevail, for Germany must live.'[39]

By late evening on 13 March 1932, it was clear that there would be a second ballot. With 49.6% of the vote, Hindenburg was just shy of the necessary absolute majority. Hitler was second with 30.1%, followed at a great distance by Thälmann with 13.2% and Duesterberg, who managed 6.8%.

To assure the victory of the incumbent, 173,000 more votes would have been enough. Unlike in 1925, Hindenburg did especially well in all those areas where Social Democrats had their strongholds and where the Catholic proportion of the population was greater than the average. In Evangelical-rural areas, in contrast, where he had won decisively seven years before, his results were far below the national average. Outside of Bavaria, Hindenburg lost among his erstwhile loyal voters and won among his former adversaries.

Although Hitler won 5 million more votes than his party achieved during the last parliamentary election in September 1930, his chances of defeating Hindenburg in the now mandatory second ballot were small. The Communists decided to run Thälmann again, despite the fact that it was now even more clear than before that it was a choice between Hitler and Hindenburg. Faithful to Stalin's maxim of November 1931 that the 'main blow in the working class' was to be aimed at the Social Democrats, the KPD emphasized the main purpose of the 'battle candidacy of Comrade Thälmann': it was a matter of 'clearly exposing the character of the SPD as the moderate wing of fascism and the twin brother of Hitler-fascism'. Duesterberg did not run in the second ballot. The Stahlhelm recommended abstention, and the German Nationalists opted against 'active participation' in the vote.

The second ballot was held on 10 April 1932. By evening it was obvious that the incumbent had a clear mandate for a second term in office. Hindenburg obtained 53%, Hitler 36.8%, and Thälmann 10.2% of the vote.

Hindenburg's triumph was, in great part, the result of the SPD's policy of cooperation. If the Social Democrats and their supporters had not had the chance to get used to a 'policy of the lesser of two evils' since the autumn of 1930, it would have been virtually impossible to convince them in spring 1932 that they had to vote for a dyed-in-the-wool monarchist in order to prevent a National Socialist dictatorship. But precisely this was the choice. Nobody but the field marshal could count on the backing of a portion of the traditional right in addition to what support remained for the Weimar coalition, thus relegating Hitler to second place. The Social Democrats knew as well as anybody that Hindenburg was no democrat. So far, however, the second president of the Reich had shown himself to be a man of law and justice, one who respected even the constitution he did not love. As things stood, nothing more could be redeemed in the presidential elections of 1932. But compared to what was yet again avoided on 10 April, the proclamation of the 'Third Reich', it was a great deal.

For the victor, however, the election outcome was tainted. Hindenburg was deeply upset that he owed his victory not to the right, but primarily to the Social Democrats and Catholics. He took his resentment out on the man who had been his most active campaigner, Heinrich Brüning, finding a convenient excuse to upbraid the chancellor in the 'emergency measure to secure the authority of the state' of April 13, which banned Hitler's private armies, the SA (*Sturmabteilungen* or Storm Troopers) and the SS (*Schutzstaffeln* or Security Force). The ban had been pushed by the interior ministers of the most important states—Prussia, Bavaria, Württemberg, Baden, Hesse, and Saxony—and was based on information the Prussian police had secured in house searches in mid-March concerning the secret military policy of the National Socialists.

This information had prompted even General von Schleicher, head of the ministerial office in the defence ministry, to support the ban of the SA and SS at first. Even before the second ballot of the presidential election, however, he had reversed his position. Using his former regiment comrade Oskar von Hindenburg, son of the field marshal, as a go-between, Schleicher succeeded in persuading the president that the ban was not politically opportune, since it would necessarily lead to a new conflict with the right. Hindenburg did reluctantly sign the measure, but two days later he went behind Groener's, the defence minister's, back to obtain information from General von Hammerstein, head of the army command, concerning the activities of the *Reichsbanner Schwarz-Rot-Gold*, a republican paramilitary organization founded in 1924 and dominated by

Social Democrats. In Hindenburg's view, this information was incriminating and thus justified banning the organization.

That did not happen. Groener, who was also temporary interior minister, determined the information provided by the defence ministry to be of no importance and came to an agreement with the leader of the Reichsbanner, Karl Höltermann, on a tactical measure: the elite units of the Reichsbanner, the so-called *Schufos* (short for *Schutzformationen*), were sent on leave. The emergency measure of 13 April remained in effect, but Groener had gained three influential adversaries in the course of the conflict: Kurt von Schleicher, who had been his *Kardinal in politicis* up to that point, and both Hindenburgs, the father and the son.

Two weeks after the second presidential ballot, most Germans were called to the ballot box yet again. On 24 April elections to state parliaments took place in Prussia, Bavaria, Württemberg, Anhalt, and in the Free and Hanse City of Hamburg. The NSDAP achieved massive gains in all five *Länder*, and in all of them but Bavaria—where the BVP was able to maintain an advantage of two seats—it was now the strongest party. In Prussia, the Weimar coalition lost the majority, but without the rightist parties, NSDAP, DNVP, and DVP, being able to put one together on their own account. On 12 April, in its last session before the election, the previous parliament—that is, the governing majority—had provided for this eventuality, voting to change election procedure. Hitherto, a second ballot for the prime minister was to be conducted as a run-off between the two most viable candidates; a relative majority was sufficient. After the change, an absolute majority of votes was needed for the second and all subsequent ballots.

The effect was the same as a constructive vote of no confidence. The parliament could only replace the incumbent head of government by voting for a successor with a majority. The *Vorwärts* made surprisingly clear what the Social Democratic initiators of the amendment were aiming to accomplish: if, after 24 April, the 'national opposition' and the Communists should constitute a negative majority, it would be up to the KPD to decide whether it would bring the right to power by restoring the old procedure.

There had been cooperation between the extreme right and the extreme left in Prussia in the summer of 1931 when the Communists, on instructions from Stalin, joined the parties and the organizations of the 'national opposition' in their campaign for a referendum to dissolve the Prussian parliament. The negative majority that did not yet exist on 9 August 1931, the day of the referendum, was a reality by 24 April 1932. Still, it was unlikely that the Communists would assume the responsibility for the election of a prime minister from or close to the National Socialist Party.

On 25 April the executive committee of the Comintern, together with representatives of the KPD and the 'Revolutionary Trade Union Opposition', published a manifesto that adopted a new tone with regard to the Social Democrats. The manifesto 'To the German Workers' announced the Communists' willingness 'to fight together with any organization in which workers are organized and that really wishes to do battle against the reduction of wages and supports'. While this proclamation, too, contained the typical sharp attacks against the leaders of the SPD and the Free Trade Unions, the 'unitary battle front' against the 'capitalist thieves and the increasingly shameless fascist bands', an alliance it considered long overdue, was no longer expressly limited to a 'unitary front from below', that is, directed against the leaders of the reformist organizations. The May manifesto of the KPD central committee expressed the new message in one short sentence: 'National Socialist participation in government would be a dangerous step along the way to open, bloody dictatorship.'

The crisis in the Prussian parliament could only have been solved in the form of a 'black–brown coalition'. The NSDAP and Centre held talks about such an alliance, as they had done before in Hesse after parliamentary elections on 15 November 1931. But since Brüning was unwilling to give Hitler's party the key positions of prime minister and interior minister, the chances for an agreement were small. On 24 May the newly elected parliament convened for its first session. The Braun government announced its resignation on the same day, but remained in office in a caretaker capacity, since there was no majority for a restoration of the old procedure.[40]

On 9 May 1932 began a four-day Reichstag session. It would form the immediate prelude to Brüning's dismissal. Events were set in motion by Groener, who, on 10 May, delivered a speech that was drowned out by a flood of scornful heckling from the National Socialist delegates and that, as Goebbels recorded in his journal, proved to be the minister's 'funeral dirge'. Brüning tried to limit the damage. His speech the next day emphasized the approaching reparations conference in Lausanne and urged parliament and public not to lose composure 'in the last hundred metres before the finish line'.

On 12 May the government, with the help of the SPD, once again won all votes. By this point, however, the Reichswehr leadership, headed by Schleicher, had decided not only to break with Groener, but also to bring down Brüning. Groener himself declared on 12 May that he intended to step down as defence minister and to concentrate solely on the interior ministry (which he had been directing in a temporary capacity). This would have required Hindenburg's assent. But the president, at the instigation of Schleicher, insisted that Groener leave the government entirely. Before leaving to spend his Whitsun holidays at Neudeck, his estate in East Prussia, Hindenburg ordered Brüning to make no changes in personnel while he was away.

The ban on the SA was one but not the only reason for Schleicher's break with Brüning. By April 1932 at the latest, the politically active general had become convinced that the crisis of the German state could only be solved in cooperation with National Socialists. On 28 April and 7 May he conducted secret talks with Hitler. The second of these (if not also the first) dealt with the conditions under which the NSDAP would be willing to tolerate a cabinet reformed or reshuffled towards the 'right'. By 7 May Schleicher knew Hitler's price: the dissolution of the

Reichstag, new elections, and the lifting of the ban on the SA and SS. Hindenburg knew about these interviews. What further weakened Brüning's position in the eyes of both Schleicher and Hindenburg was the fact that the chancellor and the foreign minister had returned on 30 April from the disarmament conference in Geneva with almost completely empty hands. The press had good reason to think that the chancellor would not be able to maintain himself in office for very long after Groener had announced his resignation as defence minister.

While Hindenburg was vacationing in Neudeck, another power elite long desirous of Brüning's fall got involved in the action—the Junkers. The National Land League, firmly in the hands of the 'national opposition' by the autumn of 1930, was the only significant economic interest group that had come out in support of Hitler before the second presidential ballot. It was the government itself that, on 21 May, provided the most important agrarian umbrella organization with the watchword it needed to launch a large-scale campaign against Brüning. The national commissioner for 'eastern assistance' (*Osthilfe*), Hans Schlange-Schöningen, presented the parliament-approved draft of a settlement decree that held out the possibility of obtaining excessively indebted estates for the state by 'private contract' (*freihändig*) or via compulsory auction, and using them for farming settlements.

Immediately after the draft was made public, Count Kalckreuth, president of the National Land League, and Ernst Brandes, president of the German Agricultural Conference (*Deutscher Landwirtschaftstag*), along with several of the Land League's administrative offices, lodged complaints with Hindenburg. The message was uniform: the right to compulsory auction, as Baron von Gayl, director of the East Prussian *Landgesellschaft*, put it, represented a further 'descent into state socialism' and weakened the 'power of resistance of those circles that have traditionally upheld the national animosity towards the Poles'. Men like Elard von Oldenburg-Januschau, who owned estates in the vicinity of the president's, attempted to persuade him in the same direction in personal conversations.

The pressure soon had the desired effect. On 25 May Hindenburg informed Schlange-Schöningen through State Secretary Meissner that he could not approve the measure in its current form. A resolution of the German Nationalist fraction two days later called the settlement measure 'unqualified Bolshevism'. By 27 May at the latest, Hindenburg was unable to retreat from his position; the German Nationalists were standing in the way of the rightward shift he sought to effect.

After his return to Berlin, on 29 May, the president received Brüning in order to tell him that he awaited the resignation of the government. In the late morning of 30 May, the chancellor informed the cabinet of his conversation with Hindenburg. Shortly before noon, Brüning submitted his resignation to the head of state. The interview lasted only a few minutes. At noon, Hindenburg received a parade of the Skagerrak Guard, an honorary naval unit, before the entrance to the presidential palace.[41]

Of all the chancellors of the Weimar Republic, Heinrich Brüning is historically the most contested. Partisan favour and hatred have distorted the evaluation of his character, making it difficult to assess. In the view of some, he systematically undermined the foundations of German democracy and thereby inadvertently prepared the way for Hitler. Others see him as the representative of a conservative alternative both to failed parliamentary governance and to National Socialist dictatorship. According to the second interpretation, Brüning's policies were historically necessary to a great extent; the path to catastrophe did not begin until his fall from power.

The truth is that the parliamentary system had already failed by the time Brüning became chancellor on 30 March 1930. After the collapse of the Grand Coalition, the shift to an openly presidential system was only a matter of time. Brüning became the executor of policies, the guidelines of which were largely determined by the president and his circle. Economically he represented the broad-based, supra-party reform consensus, which basically amounted to a deflationary policy, until well into the second half of 1931. There was, moreover, an 'objective' obstacle standing in the way of an alternative, anti-cyclical economic policy until the end of 1931 and the beginning of 1932, the unsolved reparations problem. Brüning could only have changed his economic course after it became clear that a return to the Young Plan was impossible. But he did not wish to do so, believing that a reparations compromise would have had a deleterious effect on national prestige, and because of his far-reaching foreign policy objectives. And it is quite likely that he even had little choice about the latter, since a more elastic foreign policy would certainly have met with Hindenburg's veto.

The president's position was so strong that the question of Brüning's own long-range goals is only of limited interest. In exile and in his memoirs (published in 1970, shortly after his death), the chancellor of the years 1930–2 maintained that he worked assiduously for the restoration of the monarchy, seeking in this way to erect a barrier against a dictatorship of the National Socialists. There can be no doubt about Brüning's feelings for the pre-war imperial order. In a cabinet meeting on 24 February 1932, he made it clear that he had had nothing to do with the events of 9 November 1918, having been on that day among the troops 'who formed the head of the Winterfeldt group to put down the revolution'. But there is no evidence from his term in office that Brüning was actually working for the restoration of the monarchy. His retrospective explanation is obviously a self-stylization, an attempt to monumentalize himself as a conservative statesman of far-reaching vision.

In reality, Brüning was the half-willing, half-unwilling executor of a politics that cannot be adequately described as 'conservative'. The real centre of power in the late republic was Hindenburg and his camarilla. These men aspired to set up an authoritarian state in which the will of the people would find only very limited expression. Brüning, in contrast, was content to restrict the rights of the Reichstag, especially with regard to state expenditures (a practical reform policy he successfully implemented in February 1931). He believed the National Socialists could be domesticated, but made their participation in government subject to conditions they could not accept without radically changing their political identity. Like the head of the Centre Party, the prelate Ludwig Kaas, Brüning endorsed a shift to the right in German politics, but wanted to adhere strictly to the constitution. When, in spring 1932, Hindenburg and his circle decided to abandon all consideration for the toleration policy of the Social Democrats and to accommodate the National Socialists to a greater extent than Brüning considered acceptable, the chancellor was forced to go.

The fall of Brüning was of profound historical significance. On 30 May 1932 the first, moderate, parliamentarily tolerated phase of the presidential system came to an end, and a second, authoritarian, openly anti-parliamentary phase began. The leaders of the Reichswehr and the great east Elbian landowners who had brought about the change in government wanted to enlist the National Socialists as junior partners, so to speak—not in order to let them rule, but to transform them into supporters of their own regime. The fulfilment of Hitler's conditions for accepting the rightist cabinet necessitated the dissolution of the Reichstag, whose legislative period was not scheduled to come to an end until September 1934. If new elections had taken place at that time, Germany would have looked very different than it did in the summer of 1932. The popularity of the extremist parties would have receded in the course of the expected economic recovery. The new, anti-parliamentary presidential system of Hindenburg and the Prussian power elite destroyed this opportunity. They brought the crisis of state to a dramatic head and Germany into a situation virtually impossible to master by constitutional means.[42]

THE DEEPENING OF THE CRISIS

Franz von Papen (born in 1879), whom Kurt von Schleicher chose as Brüning's successor, was a former officer of the general staff, a landowner in Westphalia, an enthusiastic equestrian, the principal shareholder of the Centre Party newspaper *Germania*, and a member of the board of directors in several agricultural interest groups. Until the elections on 24 April 1932 he was a delegate in the Prussian parliament, one of the Centre Party's backbenchers furthest to the right. In Schleicher's calculation, Papen would bind the Centre Party to the new government just as Brüning had done before him. On 31 May, however, immediately after the new chancellor was authorized by Hindenburg to form his cabinet, the Centre leader, Monsignor Kaas, made it clear to Papen that the party would look upon any attempt on his part to take up Brüning's succession as treason. But when Hindenburg appealed to his sense of patriotic duty, Papen decided for the chancellorship and left the Centre Party.

The 'strong man' of the new cabinet was General Kurt von Schleicher, who was 50 years of age at the time. A native of Brandenburg, Schleicher took over the defence ministry, entering the full limelight of public life for the first time. The new minister of the interior was Baron Wilhelm von Gayl, who had been the director of the East Prussian *Landgesellschaft*. The minister of agriculture, Baron Magnus von Braun, was also from East Prussia. Like Gayl, he had belonged to the DNVP before entering the cabinet. The foreign ministry fell to the man who had been the ambassador in London up to this time, Baron Konstantin von Neurath, who was close to the German National People's Party and was a native of Württemberg. The new finance minister was a staunch monarchist, Count Lutz Schwerin von Krosigk, who from 1929 had been the assistant head of the department he now led. Among the ministers were one count, three barons, two further members of the nobility, and only three bourgeois—a state of affairs that prompted *Vorwärts* to the famous headline of 1 June, 'The Cabinet of Barons'.

On 4 June the president dissolved the Reichstag, thus fulfiling one of the conditions Hitler had placed on his toleration of the new government. New elections were set for 31 July. On 14 June Hindenburg signed the Papen cabinet's first emergency measure. Based on preliminary work of the Brüning government, it decreased unemployment payments by an average of 23 per cent and shortened the period of coverage from twenty to six months. Thereafter, practically all social welfare claims and obligations were ended, replaced by a system on a level far below what was generally considered the 'subsistence level'. Two days later, the government fulfilled a promise Schleicher had made to Hitler on 4 June: the ban on the SA and the SS was lifted and the wearing of uniforms once again generally permitted.

On the same day, 16 June, the reparations conference (originally planned for January, but postponed at Brüning's entreaty) began in Lausanne. Papen could now reap the rewards of his predecessor's firmness. According to the agreement, which the new chancellor signed on 9 July, Germany's final payment would be no more than 3 billion marks, which was to be paid only after the expiration of a three-year period and over a longer period of time in the form of national debenture bonds—provided the economic equilibrium had been fully restored in the interim. Though the treaty's ratification by the parliaments in Paris and London still depended on whether the United States was prepared to accept an inter-Allied debt settlement, it was highly unlikely that Germany would ever have to pay reparations again, apart from the final sum, which was little more than symbolic.

This foreign policy coup, which only the Social Democrats and the liberal press recognized as such, did nothing to calm the domestic political scene. The electoral campaign in the summer of 1932 was the bloodiest in German history. The Communists and National Socialists were responsible for most of the violence. Immediately following the lifting of the SA ban, many areas of the Reich experienced murderous clashes between political opponents. They were especially frequent in the industrial districts of the Rhine and Ruhr. In Prussia, 3 men died in political riots in the first half of June, 2 National Socialists and 1 Communist. In the second half of the month, after the SA and uniform ban was lifted, the number of politically motivated deaths rose to 17, 12 National Socialists and 5 Communists. Among the 86 deaths in July, 38 were National Socialists, 30 Communists. Sundays were particularly sanguinary. On 10 July, for example, 17 people died in Germany, 10 were fatally wounded, and 181 seriously wounded.

Although the escalation of violence and terror on the streets was clearly connected to the lifting of the SA ban, the 'cabinet of barons', in holding the Prussian police responsible, laid the blame on the shoulders of the custodial government of Germany's largest state. In a ministers' conference on 11 July, Interior Minister von Gayl accused Carl Severing—after 1930 once again interior minister of Prussia—of giving his police force orders to combat the National Socialist movement, despite the fact that it continued to grow stronger. Gayl came to the conclusion that a commissioner from the Reich should be sent to Prussia, and that it would be best if the chancellor assumed this task and appointed sub-commissioners. The next day, the government set the deadline for 20 July. But Severing wasted no time in thwarting its plans. A decree on the same day, 12 July, making it easier to ban outdoor assemblies and requiring the police to proceed with utmost rigour against illegal bearing of arms, temporarily undermined the cabinet's manoeuvre against Prussia.

What saved the government's original timetable was the Bloody Sunday of Altona on 17 July 1932. An unusual combination of bad political, administrative, and police decisions was partly responsible for nineteen civilian deaths in the course of a demonstrative march by the SA through strongly 'red' districts of the—at that time still Prussian—town. Most of the victims were killed by bullets from the police. Perhaps Severing could have prevented a federal strike against Prussia by immediately declaring a state of emergency in Altona. But the Prussian interior minister refrained from a demonstration of strength. The Reich government acted instead. On 18 July, without consulting the *Länder*, it promulgated a general ban on outdoor assemblies and ordered three members of the Prussian cabinet—Welfare Minister Hirtsiefer of the Centre Party representing Otto Braun, who had been relieved of his duties, Interior Minister Severing, and Otto Klepper, the independent finance minister—to appear at the Reich chancellery on 20 July at ten o'clock in the morning.

The content of Papen's interview with the three ministers became known as the *Preussenschlag*, the 'strike against Prussia'. Using Article 48, the president appointed the chancellor federal commissioner of Prussia, empowering him to dismiss the members of the Prussian state ministry, take personal charge of the prime minister's affairs, and assign the leadership of the Prussian ministries to other persons as commissioners of the Reich. Thereupon Papen announced that, by virtue of his new authority, he was dismissing Braun and Severing from their offices and appointing Franz Bracht, the mayor of Essen, to be interior minister.

Since the actions of the Reich violated both the national and the Prussian constitutions, the custodial Prussian government responded with a suit in the federal court. However, the people, or the masses of workers, did not call upon the Prussian government, the SPD, the Free Trade Unions, and the Reichsbanner Schwarz-Rot-Gold to fight against the attack from the Reich government. Instead, the Social Democrats responded by saying that the 'cabinet of barons' would have to answer for their acts in the parliamentary elections on 31 July. Young Reichsbanner activists were particularly outraged at the lack of resistance, interpreting it as a surrender in the face of violence, a judgement that has been echoed in German historiography.

But there were good, indeed compelling reasons for the Social Democrats to behave as they did. The 'people' had declared on 24 April that they no longer supported the Prussian government. The outcome of the Prussian parliamentary elections had dealt a heavy blow to the SPD's belief in its democratic legitimacy. With unemployment as high as it was—officially 5.5 million in June 1932, but in reality somewhat higher—a general strike was out of the question. The situation was very different than in the spring of 1920, during the Kapp–Lüttwitz putsch. At that time, Germany was experiencing near-full employment. Moreover, the strikers knew themselves to be in agreement with the legitimate authority of the state. The *Preussenschlag*, on the other hand, was ordered by the newly elected president of the Reich. It would not have been realistic to expect a large number of officials and policemen to rise up against him.

Another important difference was that, in the summer of 1932, the working class was more divided than ever. On 14 July, in response to signs of creeping 'social democratization' within its own ranks, the KPD had ended the more flexible tactic of the unitary front initiated in April, warning against 'any neglect of our battle against the social-fascist leaders, any obscuring of the principal antagonism between ourselves and the SPD'. Common cause with the Communists for the restoration of the Braun government was simply inconceivable. When, therefore, the Communists asked the Social Democrats and Free Trade Unions on 20 July whether they were prepared for a general strike, it was nothing more than a rhetorical question. In any case, the Reichsbanner was neither militarily nor psychologically equipped to take up armed resistance against the army. In this respect, the paramilitary organization of the republicans was also inferior to those of the right, the SA, SS, and Stahlhelm, which would certainly have taken active part in a battle against the 'Marxists'. A civil war would have been the democratic left's to lose in the summer of 1932, probably with enormous casualties.

The reasons went back far beyond the year 1932. The SPD's passivity in the face of the *Preussenschlag* was not least a consequence of its twenty-month policy of cooperation and long-standing leadership in the Prussian government. It was objectively impossible to be a governmental party—formally in Prussia, informally on the national level—while preparing for civil war. On 20 July 1932 the Social Democrats lost what little power they had left, power they had managed to maintain for so long *because* they had staked everything on one card in the autumn of 1930: the fight against National Socialism on the basis of the constitution and in alliance with the moderate forces within the bourgeoisie.

A sharp observer in the ranks of the Social Democratic left, Arkadij Gurland, wrote in June 1932—that is, before the *Preussenschlag*—that the toleration policy had been based on the assumption 'that the main threat to democracy lies in the danger of civil war. Accordingly, its practical goal was less the preservation of democracy than the preservation of *legality*, less the prevention of unparliamentary rule than the prevention of *civil war*.' The SPD adhered to this postulate on 20 July 1932, too. In doing so, it stuck to the principle it had followed on its path to power in November 1918, during the founding of the first German republic.

It was in keeping with this priority of the 'prevention of civil war' that the Social Democratic interior minister of Prussia saw the Papen government's takeover of the Prussian police as the 'lesser evil', compared to a National Socialist ascendancy in Prussia. Even before 20 July, Severing had made comments to the arch-conservative interior minister of the Reich that the latter could interpret as encouragement to appoint a federal commissioner for the Prussian police. And Gayl, too, was no stranger to thoughts of a preventive strike against the extreme right. While it was not the main cause, the 'nationalization' (*Verreichlichung*) of the Prussian police as a precaution against a National Socialist grab for the executive power of Germany's largest state was certainly a recognizable secondary reason for the Reich's strike against Prussia.

The dismissal of the Braun government brought an unusual chapter in the history of Prussia to an end. After 1918 the Hohenzollern state had turned into the most dependable buttress of the republic among all the German *Länder*. Though old Prussia had not disappeared, the political scene was controlled by the three Weimar coalition parties until spring 1932. Immediately after the *Preussenschlag* the great purification began. State secretaries and department heads, provincial, district government, and police presidents, as well as other officials belonging to the coalition parties were sent into temporary retirement and replaced by conservatives, often from the German National People's Party. Only one of the four Social Democratic *Oberpräsidenten* remained, Gustav Noske in Hanover. In the opinion of the Reich government, the former defence minister stood so far to the right of his party that he could hold onto his post, which he had occupied since July 1920.[43]

The Social Democrats' desire to make the Papen government pay for the *Preussenschlag* in the Reichstag election on 31 July 1932 did not come to fruition. The outcome at the polls was a triumph for Hitler, at least at first glance. With electoral participation at 84.1%, the highest since 1920, 37.4% of the vote went to the NSDAP. This represented an increase of 19.1% over the previous election on 14 September 1930. The number of National Socialist seats in the Reichstag grew from 107 to 230. The Communists' gains were much less significant; they climbed from 13.1% to 14.5%. The two Catholic parties also grew, the Centre from 11.8% to 12.5%, the BVP from 3% to 3.2%. All other parties were losers. The SPD fell from 24.5% to 21.6%, the DNVP from 7% to 5.9%, the DVP from 4.5% to 1.2%, and the German State Party from 3.8% to 1%. The remaining parties together totalled 2.5% of the vote.

The National Socialists had succeeded in making themselves the heirs to the parties of the liberal centre and the moderate right, as well as of the splinter parties. They also mobilized many first-time and traditional non-voters. The north and the east of Germany were much more strongly 'brown' than the south and the west. But also in Hesse, Franconia, the Palatinate, and the north of Württemberg, the NSDAP overtook all other parties. With 51% of its vote falling to the party of Hitler, Schleswig-Holstein was the National Socialist 'frontrunner' among the thirty-five electoral districts in the country.

As in 1930, the Catholic milieu and, to a lesser extent, the fragmented 'Marxist' constituency proved relatively immune to National Socialist rhetoric. Among the bourgeois-Protestant groups, only the conservatives managed to preserve a modicum of independence from the NSDAP. The 5.9% of the vote that went to the DNVP, whose power was still concentrated in east Elbia, was the nucleus of the monarchist camp, formerly much larger. Political liberalism had been nearly wiped away. The National Socialists had become *the* great protest movement against the 'system', and whoever did not have strong ideological or political reservations against it was susceptible to its call. The fact that Hitler's party made very contradictory promises was little noticed by its voters. What counted was the hope that a 'national revolution' would bring about positive changes for Germany and the Germans.

There were, however, no signs of a parliamentary majority after the election. Although the National Socialists were by far the strongest party in the Reichstag, they had actually improved very little on their performance in the second ballot of the presidential race on 10 April and in the state parliamentary elections on 24 April. Even with the help of the DNVP and the smaller rightist parties, they were far from a majority. A black–brown coalition was theoretically possible, but the experiences in Hesse and Prussia made it very doubtful that such an alliance would take shape.

The National Socialists were bitterly disappointed that political ascendancy was not yet in sight even after their great electoral success. They gave vent to their disappointment in a wave of bloody attacks against political enemies at the beginning of August. The SA struck primarily where they were especially strong, in the east. On 9 August the Reich government found it necessary to proclaim a new emergency measure against political terror extending the death penalty to cases of politically motivated homicide and setting up special tribunals in the most affected districts.

The decree went into effect at midnight on 10 August. One and a half hours later, a crime of unusual brutality, even for the increasingly brutal times, was committed in the town of Potempa in the district of Gleiwitz. Inebriated members of the SA attacked an unemployed supporter of the Communist party, shot at him and kicked him to death before the eyes of his mother. The police succeeded in apprehending most of the suspects within two days. Given the new legal situation, it was probable that the special court in Beuthen would pronounce death sentences—unless the National Socialists came to power in the interim.

For several days in the first part of August, Hitler seemed very close to doing just that. On 6 August he met with the defence minister for a long confidential interview in the vicinity of Berlin. The National Socialist leader succeeded in convincing Schleicher that he, Hitler, should take over the leadership of the national government, his party assuming the offices of Prussian prime minister; the departments of the interior, education, and agriculture in Prussia and on the national level, each in personal union; the ministry of justice, and a new ministry of aviation. With his fundamental assent to Hitler's demands, the 'strong man' of the cabinet performed a dramatic about-face. Apparently, at the beginning of August 1932, Schleicher considered the Reichswehr a sufficient counterweight to a National Socialist monopoly of political power.

Hindenburg, who was vacationing in Neudeck at this time, saw things very differently. He brusquely rejected Schleicher's proposal. His reaction was no different after his return to Berlin, when, on 10 August, Papen suggested appointing Hitler chancellor at the head of a majority government inclusive of the Centre Party. This was the occasion of Hindenburg's much quoted comment that it was a bit much to expect him to make the 'Bohemian private' into the chancellor of the German Reich.

The cabinet, too, was very divided over the question of putting governmental power in Hitler's hands, as became clear in the late afternoon of 10 August 1932. In favour were—indirectly—Justice Minister Gürtner and—much more openly—Finance Minister Schwerin von Krosigk. The latter made the crude comment that civil war could best be avoided by 'turning the poacher into the forest warden'. The staunchest resistance came from the interior minister, Gayl, who was even prepared to wage a 'battle to the death' with the NSDAP, referred to a 'revolution from above', and openly advocated a solution at odds with the constitution: the dissolution of the Reichstag, postponement of new elections beyond the constitutionally mandated deadline of sixty days, and the imposition of a new voting law.

On the next day, 11 August, the government's traditional celebration of the constitution took place, with the president in attendance. For the first time in the history of the Weimar Republic, the main speaker held an oration *against* the constitution of 1919. Interior Minister von Gayl commenced with the observation that the Weimar constitution did not unite the German people, but divided them. He called for constitutional reform in an authoritarian sense, the main aspects of which were an elevation of the voting age, extra votes for breadwinners and mothers, detachment of governmental power from the parliament, and the creation of a profession-based, corporative first chamber as a counterweight to the Reichstag.

During the next two days, Hitler was scheduled to negotiate first with the chancellor, then with the president. In order to emphasize his claim to power, the National Socialist leader had marshalled strong forces of SA all around Berlin. The interview with the chancellor, set for 12 August, he postponed at short notice until the next day. In the late morning of 13 August Hitler, accompanied by SA chief of staff Ernst Röhm, called on Schleicher, then, together with Wilhelm Frick, the NSDAP floor leader, on Papen. From the defence minister and chancellor Hitler learned that Hindenburg had thus far proved unwilling to grant him the chancellorship. Without the president's express authorization, Papen offered Hitler the post of vice chancellor in his administration and even gave him his word that he would resign in Hitler's favour after a period of cooperation, during which Hindenburg could become better acquainted with him. But Hitler rejected the offer and continued to insist on the chancellorship.

The interview with the president of the Reich took place in the afternoon of 13 August 1932. Papen and Meissner were also present, as well as Röhm and Frick on the side of the National Socialists. This meeting was Hitler's greatest political defeat since the failed Munich putsch on 8 and 9 November 1923. According to Meissner's protocol, Hindenburg answered Hitler's demand for the chancellorship with a 'clear, definite no'.

> He could not, as he said, answer to God, his conscience, and his Fatherland for granting the entire authority of government to one party, especially to a party that was one-sidedly against those who thought differently. There were also, he added, a number of other reasons he did not wish to list in detail, such as fear of greater unrest, the reaction abroad, etc.

The official announcement about the meeting was terse and sharply worded. The key sentence stated that Hindenburg had rejected Hitler's demand because he 'could not answer to his conscience and to his duties to his Fatherland for granting the entire power of government exclusively to the National Socialist movement, which is determined to exercise it in a one-sided manner.'

Hitler was humiliated. Immediately after the interview with Hindenburg, he reproached the chancellor for not making it clear ahead of time that the president had already made up his mind, and he went so far as to warn Papen and Meissner that 'further developments would lead inevitably to the solution proposed by him or to the fall of the President. The government would find itself in a difficult situation. The opposition would become very sharp, and he would not be answerable for the consequences.' That was undisguised blackmail. Hitler was threatening to renounce legality and resort to revolutionary violence and civil war in the event that his claims were not met.

An opportunity soon arose to declare open war on the government. On 22 August the special court at Beuthen handed down its judgments in the Potempa case. On the basis of the emergency measure of 9 August, five National Socialist defendants were condemned to death, four for joint politically motivated homicide, one for incitement to politically motivated homicide. Hitler immediately assured the perpetrators via telegram that the battle for their liberty was, 'from this moment on, a matter of our honour, and the battle against a government under which this was possible, a matter of our duty'. Two days later, Hitler announced in the *Völkischer Beobachter* that Herr von Papen had 'written his name into German history in the blood of national warriors'. Goebbels tried to outdo his leader. In the *Angriff*, of which he was the editor, he identified the Jews as those responsible for the Beuthen sentences. 'Never forget, comrades! Say it a hundred times a day to yourselves, so that it pursues you even into your dreams—the Jews are responsible! And they will not escape the judgement they deserve.'

The cabinet knew full well that the execution of the sentences could lead to open civil war. On the other hand, there was the danger that a pardon for the perpetrators would be interpreted as a capitulation to the National Socialists. But this seemed the lesser risk. Hindenburg stated on 30 August that he personally supported a pardon not for political, but for legal reasons. The deed was committed only one and a half hours after the emergency measure against political terror had gone into effect, and it could not be assumed that the offenders had known about the increase in the severity of the penalties. This was the rationalization (which could be found even in liberal newspapers like the *Frankfurter Zeitung*) used by the acting Prussian government under Papen on 2 September when it commuted the sentences of the Potempa murderers to life in prison.[44]

Hindenburg gave his vote in the Potempa case on 30 August at Neudeck, where Papen, Gayl, and Schleicher had joined him for a meeting. The main subject of discussion was the internal political situation after 13 August. Papen assumed that the parliament would soon have to be dissolved again, since it had produced no majority willing to cooperate with the president and since a conceivable black–brown coalition could only lead to an 'illusory' or 'negative' majority. After the Reichstag was dissolved again, there was the question of whether new elections were to be held within the constitutionally mandated deadline of sixty days. It was true that a delay was a formal violation of Article 25.

> However, we have a situation of national emergency that clearly authorizes the Herr President to postpone the vote. The Herr President has also, in his oath, taken it upon himself to defend the German people from harm. In these politically agitated times, with all the acts of terror and murder, new elections would indeed cause great harm to the German people.

Gayl, who had been the first to propose postponing elections (in the cabinet meeting on 10 August), seconded the chancellor. At the end of the meeting, Hindenburg made the announcement the three visitors had been waiting for:

> The Herr *President* made a statement to the effect that he, in order to avert detriment to the German people, could, in the state of national emergency following the dissolution of the parliament, answer to his conscience for interpreting the provisions of Article 25 to the effect that new elections be postponed to a later date, given the extraordinary situation in the country.

For Papen, Gayl, and Schleicher, this go-ahead was just as important as full authorization to dissolve the Reichstag, which Hindenburg granted without reservation and immediately signed. In the view of the president and the three highest members of the government, it was a valid argument to claim that the state of national emergency left them no alternative to the breach of the constitution. There was legal opinion to justify such a step as *ultima ratio*. In his book *Legalität and Legitimität** (completed on 10 July, ten days before the *Preussenschlag*), Carl Schmitt, the most notable such voice, developed the thesis of the two constitutions into which the Weimar constitution broke down—a first, organizational main part, formal and value-neutral, and a second part, dealing with basic rights, which Schmitt characterized as substantive and value-based. The two parts could only have remained together under favourable circumstances. Now, however, the main part had been suspended by the organs of state themselves, while the second remained in effect. According to Schmitt, this second, core part of the constitution could only be preserved by abandoning the first part. By virtue of his higher, plebiscitary 'legitimacy', the Reich president, the true 'guardian of the constitution', was thus justified in declaring war on and superseding the merely formal 'legality' of the pluralist party state.

It also lay in the logic of Schmitt's construction to extend the aura of legitimacy to a constitutional revision from 'above', provided that the president succeed in establishing the new constitution by virtue of his authority. The arguments of Johannes Heckel, a colleague of Schmitt, were far more sophisticated in this respect. In an essay published in the *Archiv des öffentlichen Rechts* in October 1932, Heckel explained that Germany had entered a state of constitutional paralysis after the parliamentary elections. Since two openly anti-constitutional parties, the NSDAP and KPD, held an absolute majority of seats, the Reichstag was no longer capable of exercising its function as an organ of constitutional government. It was not to be expected that new elections would alter this situation. In such a state of acute constitutional crisis, Heckel argued, the president could invoke his duty 'to carry out the overarching political purpose of the constitution despite the abnormal situation, and adapting to it'. To be sure, he was not permitted to use the postponement of new elections to the purpose that Gayl, for one, had in mind: the setting up of a new, authoritarian constitution. In exercising provisional dictatorial power, the president could only be a '*dictator ad tuendam constitutionem*', not a '*dictator ad constituendam constitutionem*'—that is, a dictator for the preservation of the existing constitution, not for the promulgation of a new one.[45]

The day of the emergency meeting at Neudeck, 30 August 1932, was also the day of the constituent session of the newly elected Reichstag. In the conclusion to her address, the president by seniority, the Communist Clara Zetkin (born on 5 July 1857), expressed her hope that she would live long enough to give the opening address as *Alterspräsidentin* of the first council congress of Soviet Germany. Then a strong majority elected the National Socialist Herman Goering as

* Schmitt, *Legality and Legitimacy.*

Reichstag president. The Centre Party also voted for him, pointing to the parliamentary tradition that the presidency fell to the strongest fraction.

The second Reichstag session was held on 12 September. The only item on the agenda was the chancellor's inaugural speech. Right at the beginning, however, the Communist delegate Ernst Torgler made a motion to change the agenda, proposing that his party's motions to revoke two new emergency measures (one for the stimulation of the economy of 4 September and a related decree for the increase and preservation of job opportunities of 5 September) and the motions for a vote of no confidence in the government be dealt with first. It would have taken only one delegate to prevent this change of procedure, but—to the surprise of all—no one objected, not even the German Nationalists. The NSDAP, in order to consult with Hitler, requested a half-hour pause, during which the Centre urged the National Socialists to reject the KPD's motions. But Hitler opted to vote for them. This brought negotiations between the two parties—in which Hitler was personally involved, having met with Brüning on 29 August—to an end for the time being.

Papen was taken completely by surprise by this turn of events. Anticipating neither the initiative of the KPD nor the absence of resistance, he had appeared in the Reichstag without the dissolution order Hindenburg had signed in Neudeck on 30 August (the document was not dated). He did not get hold of the 'red file' until the pause, brandishing it upon his returned to the main hall. Goering, the president of the parliament, ignored Papen's two requests to speak, as well as the file the chancellor finally placed on his desk. Instead, he called for a vote on the two KPD motions, the results of which he announced long after the cabinet had left the hall. Of 560 ballot papers, one was invalid, 512 delegates voted in favour, 42 against, and 5 abstained. The negative votes came from the DNVP and DVP. The members of several smaller groups, the German State Party, the Christian-Social People's Service (*Christlich-Sozialer Volksdienst*), the German Farmers' Party (*Deutsche Bauernpartei*), and the Economic Party, were absent from the vote. All other parties voted for the Communist motions.

The vote was invalid; from the moment the chancellor lay the order on the desk of the Reichstag president, the assembly was dissolved. But the political effect could no longer be undone. More than four-fifths of the delegates had voted no confidence in the Papen government, and the chancellor had only his own neglect to blame for the debacle.

When the cabinet met two days later to discuss what was to be done, Papen no longer had the confidence to undertake the trial of strength for which he had gained the support of Hindenburg on 30 August. Only Gayl and Schleicher argued for the indefinite postponement of new elections, the latter pointing out that the legal scholars Carl Schmitt, Erwin Jacobi, and Carl Bilfinger, all defenders of the national government in the case of 'Prussia vs. the Reich', had agreed that a 'true state of emergency' existed in this case. Papen and the other ministers believed that the moment had not yet come to depart from the constitution. On 17 September the cabinet decided to propose to the president 6 November, the last possible date, for new parliamentary elections. Hindenburg signed off on the proposal three days later.

The chancellor did not abandon the idea of constitutional reform. In his inaugural speech, which he gave by radio on the evening of 12 September, Papen addressed the subject in a manner similar to Gayl at the constitution ceremony. The system of formal democracy, which in the judgement of history and in the view of the German nation had come to ruin, had to be replaced by a new order, a 'truly non-partisan national leadership' supported by the power and authority of the popularly elected president of the Reich. The voting age was to be raised and the organ of popular representation organically linked with the self-governing bodies, evidently in the form of a first chamber based on professional corporations. The Prussian and national governments were to be 'organically' joined, bringing independent and antagonistic courses to an end—here Papen retrospectively presented the *Preussenschlag* as a breakthrough to the long-discussed 'reform of the Reich'. The German people had the chancellor's assurance that they themselves would be able to decide concerning the new constitution, which the government would present to them after thorough scrutiny. Papen concluded his address with the call: 'With Hindenburg and for Germany!'

The last part of this speech was an outline of the 'new state' the cabinet had been aspiring to establish since the summer of 1932. In a pamphlet with an introduction by the chancellor, and which therefore acquired official status, the publicist Walther Schotte described in greater detail how the 'new state' would differ from the parliamentary democracy of Weimar. The 'new state' was an authoritarian presidential state with professional-corporative elements. The will of the people found expression primarily through a one-time elective act, the plebiscitary legitimation of the head of state. The president, not the parliament, embodied the general will and was the centre of power. The Reichstag, de-radicalized through a new voting law taking age, marital status, and number of children into consideration, was to share the legislative function with an upper house. In this first chamber, appointed by the president, the professional corporations would cooperate harmoniously. At least, this was how the architects of the 'new state' saw things. Had a majority of Germans voted for a constitutional plan oriented on this scheme, they would have been electing to divest themselves of the greater part of their political power.

Papen, Gayl, and their publicist friends could depend on the fact that by 1932, parliamentary democracy had very few committed supporters left in Germany. In a much-read book from 1927, the *jungkonservativ* writer Edgar Jung—who would become Papen's speech-writer in the spring of 1933—denounced the parliamentary system of the west as the 'rule of the inferior'. The idea of an authoritarian, ostensibly non-partisan presidential state—indeed, a state that would render political parties obsolete—was the common denominator of the reform plans that rightist groups like the 'Ring movement' around Heinrich von Gleichen-Russwurm, founder of the *Herrenklub*, and the circle around the newspaper *Die Tat* and its publisher, Hans

Zehrer, had been developing for some time. In other respects, however, the 'conservative revolution' was not a monolithic bloc. The '*Tat* circle', which was closely connected to Schleicher, emphasized the role of the masses far more than did the intellectuals of the *Herrenklub* around Papen. It was true that the role played by the defence minister in the discussions about new links between 'right' and 'left' often had more to do with the changing projects of his advisers than with any concrete plans of his own. Still, by September 1932 it was clear that Schleicher was increasingly sceptical about the distance the chancellor—who had been selected by Schleicher himself—was putting between himself and the *Volk*.

At no other time during his term in office was the fundamentally backward-looking nature of Papen's politics so in evidence than on 12 October 1932. Prompted, it seems, by Edgar Jung, a Protestant who admired Catholicism, the chancellor, speaking at a meeting of the Bavarian Industrialists' Association in Munich, invoked the 'invisible current of power of the *sacrum imperium*, the indestructible idea of the holy German Empire'. During the crisis of the German state, the myth of the Reich gained in charisma what the republic lost. But the imperial idea also served to justify the German claim to be something different and more than a nation state in the western sense, shaped by the ideas of 1789. 'Only a Europe led by Germany can be a Europe at peace,' declared Wilhelm Stapel in 1932, publisher of the *jungkonservativ* journal *Deutsches Volkstum*. 'The Reich is becoming a watchword, in both domestic and foreign policy,' observed the Catholic publicist Waldemar Gurian, a critic of the new political romanticism, also in 1932. 'For the Reich, and against Versailles and parliamentary democracy . . . We can call the Reich the German image of humanity, placed over against western humanitarianism and yet differing from eastern apocalypticism by virtue of its intimate connection with European history.'

The idea of the empire, the *Reichsidee*, experienced a supra-confessional renaissance in the early 1930s. It was usually accompanied by an assertion of the *grossdeutsch* idea and also, frequently, by a trans-national view of the German *Volk*. Both Protestant and Catholic imperial ideologues considered the opposition between *kleindeutsch* and *grossdeutsch* obsolete anyway, now that the Habsburg empire no longer existed, and they saw themselves in agreement with current German historiography on this point. One could, in order to give a 'positive' answer to the west and the Weimar Republic, invoke the idea of a supra-national German empire as a force for order in central Europe, or the Prussia of Frederick the Great, or even both myths together. Most authors of the 'conservative revolution', as well as well-known German historians, did just that. The mystical grand narrative of the *sacrum imperium*, on the other hand, belonged primarily to the Catholic right of which Papen was a member. It was a credo that gave many people—and not just his political enemies—cause to doubt the chancellor's grasp on reality.[46]

That reality caught up with Papen on 25 October at the latest, when the federal court in Leipzig handed down its judgment in the matter of the *Preussenschlag*. The presidential decree of 20 July 1932 was declared constitutional, to the extent that it appointed the chancellor federal commissioner of Prussia, authorizing him to temporarily divest Prussian ministers of their powers of office and to exercise them himself. But this empowerment was, as the text continued, 'not to be extended such as to strip the Prussian state ministry and its members of the power to represent Prussia in the Reich Council or vis-à-vis the Prussian Parliament, the State Council, or other countries'.

The Leipzig decision did *not* abolish the 'dualism' between Prussian and the Reich. It declared both sides, the accuser and the plaintiff, partially in the right. In consequence, the authority of the Prussia state was divided between the custodial Braun administration and the provisional government installed by the Reich. The latter retained the actual executive authority, whereas the former's most important right was to represent Prussia in the Reich Council. Though the Braun cabinet regained no real power, it could count as a success the fact that no dereliction of duty could be proven. The Reich government, while continuing to exercise the administrative authority of Germany's largest state, including its police, had to accept the judgment that it had acted unconstitutionally on 20 July in dismissing the Prussian government. This verdict also pertained to the president, in whose name the measure had been pronounced.

However one looked at it, the Leipzig decision was a defeat for the Reich government—which was not the same thing as a victory for the former Prussian cabinet. In *Vorwärts* appeared a commentary from 'a special source' (possibly Hermann Heller, the counsel for the prosecution) hitting the nail on the head. The Leipzig decision was not a legal, but rather a political decision, wrote the author of the article.

> The court avoided the serious conflict with the Reich government that would have resulted if it had recognized the claim of the Prussian government to the *full* extent . . . Its judgment is the opposite of a Solomonic decision; it has sliced the contested child neatly in two and given each of the two mothers a half . . . How that is intended to work in practice, and how it will work, the gods know.

The decision had virtually no effect on the year's second electoral campaign for the Reichstag. The opposite was true of an event that made headlines in the whole country only a few days before the vote: the public transport strike in Berlin, which began on 3 November. The sensation was less the strike itself than the fact that the Communists and National Socialists fought together against the state and the labour unions. Four people were killed and eight seriously wounded by the police on 4 November. Goebbels observed with satisfaction that his party's reputation among the workers 'has risen splendidly within very few days'. The Communist–National Socialist cooperation gave the chancellor occasion to make a radio broadcast over all stations in the country denouncing wildcat strikes as a 'crime against the whole of the nation' and citing Berlin as an example of how the state would deal very harshly with all disturbers of the peace. Not until 7 November, the day after the election, did regular traffic begin to flow again in the capital of the Reich.[47]

The most striking result of the elections on 6 November was the poor performance of the National Socialists, not only in Berlin, but in the whole country. Compared to the previous elections on 31 July, the NSDAP lost over 2 million voters. Its share of the returns fell from 37.3% to 33.1%, its seats from 230 to 196. The SPD was also among the losers, receiving more than 700,000 fewer votes than in July and sinking from 21.6% to 20.4%. The winners were the German Nationalists and the Communists. Hugenberg's party gained over 900,000 more votes, an increase from 5.9% to 8.9%. The KPD, with some 600,000 more votes, climbed from 14.5% to 16.9% and from 89 to the magic number of 100 seats. The other parties experienced only small changes. But the decrease in electoral participation was conspicuous. From 84.1% in July, it fell to 80.6%

The outcome of the vote was primarily a manifestation of political frustration. For most Germans, the 6 November elections represented the fifth trip to the polls in 1932, including the two presidential ballots and the five provincial elections on 24 April. The NSDAP, whom the politicization of the traditionally non-voting population had earlier benefited the most, now suffered the worst from the decrease in participation, for 'non-political' voters were the soonest to feel that their vote had had little effect on practical politics.

Also in evidence was a modicum of greater confidence in the Papen cabinet, reflected in the comparatively good performances of the DNVP and DVP. The government and the parties supporting it benefited from the first signs of economic recovery, which could be interpreted as the result of the active economic policy Papen had initiated in September. In addition, the political and social radicalism of the National Socialists had had a sobering effect on many in Germany. The cooperation with the Communists during the Berlin transport strike shocked not only the affluent circles of the capital, but scared away many bourgeois voters throughout the country. Nonetheless, the government had no cause for triumph. Nearly nine-tenths of the population had voted for parties in opposition to the 'cabinet of barons.'

The National Socialists' losses filled their political adversaries with satisfaction, the Social Democrats most of all. As Otto Wels, the party chair, put it in an executive meeting on 10 November, the SPD had fought five battles under the watchword 'Defeat Hitler!' in the course of 1932, 'and after the fifth he was defeated'. However, the election outcome also had a very disturbing side for the Social Democrats, their own losses and the Communists' gains. The gap between the two workers' parties had shrunk by half, from 7.1% in July to 3.5%. If this trend continued into new elections at the beginning of 1933, at the height of mass unemployment, a dramatic crisis was almost certain to result. 'We are at the final spurt with the Communists,' observed Karl Böchel, a Chemnitz district chairman and 'leftist', at the same meeting.

We only have to lose a dozen seats, then the Communists are stronger than us . . . That would be the famous psychological moment for the Communist agitation . . . Then comrades who have remained faithful to the party will say, 'the voice of the people has decided', and they will try to get out quickly.

The Communists came to similar conclusions. The central committee of the KPD spoke of an acceleration in the advance of the revolution and called the Communists the victors of the election. This was also the view of *Pravda*, the central organ of the Communist Party of the Soviet Union. The KPD was the 'unitary party of the proletarian revolution in Germany', and as such had won the electoral victory.

Ever larger masses of workers are going over to the camp of the revolution. Great revolutionary struggles are imminent. The present wave of economic struggles will lead to ever greater strike movements in whole branches and districts of industry, to the political mass strike and political general strike under the leadership of the Communist Party, to the battle for the proletarian dictatorship.

It did not escape astute observers in Germany that the combination of Communist gains and National Socialist losses held greater possibilities for Hitler than for Thälmann. In the *Vossische Zeitung* of 8 November, Julius Elbau commented:

A hundred Communists in the Reichstag! Transports of joy on the fifteenth anniversary of the October revolution in Moscow! Eighty-nine made no difference, neither in the Reichstag nor in the country. But one hundred! That's something, at the very least a nice round number. And for Hitler a true gift from God.

For now, in the view of the liberal editorialist, it could be foreseen 'that the citizens, frightened out of their wits, will rush into the arms of the only true patent saviour.' The National Socialists were counting on exactly that happening. 'Rationally thinking journalists seem to be slowly realizing that the situation is not as rosy for the reaction as they imagined it to be during the election campaign,' Goebbels wrote in his journal on 10 November. 'Now the great test of nerves begins, probably the last. If we pass it, then we will come to power'.[48]

On 8 November, speaking before the foreign press club, Chancellor von Papen made his first official announcement concerning the election outcome. He spoke of a 'welcome increase in understanding for the work of the government', then expressed his hope that a true national concentration would be possible, now that the election was over. 'Questions of personnel, as I have always emphasized, will play no role in this matter.' In a cabinet meeting on the next day, Gayl sharply criticized the chancellor's statement, calling it a 'sign of weakness'. The interior minister recommended negotiations with the parties in order to sound out the potential for a toleration agreement. 'If this aim cannot be achieved, then the consequences are clear. The possibility of another dissolution of the parliament arises, and with it a state of constitutional emergency. Then, for a certain time, dictatorship will be unavoidable.'

The debate then returned to the government's emergency plan of 30 August. But none of the ministers supported Gayl. Schleicher managed to find agreement for his suggestion to postpone constitutional reform and take up negotiations with the parties, so as to put them in the wrong. He himself, he said, was prepared to speak with Hitler, although he, the defence minister, was 'absolutely convinced that the National Socialists will not participate in the government'. Hindenburg, for his part, wanted to maintain the presidential cabinet and not switch chancellors, as he explained to Papen the following day.

The president's position was much more lucid than that of the chancellor. On the one hand, Papen was willing to follow Hindenburg loyally. On the other hand, his own desire was to reach an understanding with the National Socialists, and he did not personally wish to exclude the possibility of giving the chancellorship to Hitler. His comments to the foreign press were meant in this way and no other, and if the information sent on 13 November by Wilhelm Keppler, the leader of a circle of pro-National Socialist industrialists, to the Cologne banker Kurt von Schröder was true, the chancellor had twice expressed his support for a Hitler government to Ewald Hecker, chairman of the board of the Ilseder Steelworks, in the days before the press conference. For his part, Papen learned from Hecker that a large circle of leading personalities in industry, banking, and agriculture was preparing to send a message to Hindenburg demanding that Hitler be made chancellor.

This letter reached the president on 19 November. The key sentence was the following:

> The conferral of the authoritative leadership of a presidential cabinet equipped with the best material and personal resources onto the leader of the largest national group will eradicate the weaknesses and errors that necessarily accompany every mass movement and make an affirmative force out of millions who today stand on the sidelines.

The text contained twenty signatures, among them eight from the circle around Keppler, which included Schacht, Hecker, and Kurt von Schröder. Most of the signatories were *Mittelstand* businessmen, bankers, and landowners. The letter was also signed by Count Eberhard von Kalckreuth, acting president of the National Land League, and Fritz Thyssen, who had long been a National Socialist supporter. Along with August Rosterg, an owner of potash mines, Thyssen was the only major industrialist actively engaged on Hitler's behalf in this way. Albert Vögler, general director of the United Steel Works, who did not himself sign the letter, told Schröder on 21 November that two other heavy industrialists, Paul Reusch, chairman of the board of Good Hope Steel and Iron Works, and Fritz Springorum, general director of Hoesch, 'basically share the view expressed in the letter and consider it a real solution to the present crisis'. They did not wish to sign, however, since they both feared that such a political statement would make the antagonisms within the industry of the Ruhr district all too clear.

Clearly, then, the letter to Hindenburg did not represent the position of big industry as a whole. But it was also evident that, after 6 November, the Papen government could no longer count on the same, virtually unified support of the 'business community' as in September and October. The election outcome was disappointing for industry, which had given the greater part of its 'political' funds to the two parties friendly to the government, the DVP and DNVP. Particularly alarming were the KPD's gains, for which Hitler held the Papen cabinet responsible, and not entirely without cause. Finance Minister von Krosigk expressed a broadly held opinion when, in a cabinet meeting on 9 November, he justified his support of NSDAP participation in government by saying that otherwise a large number of National Socialists, 'including the nationalist youth', would migrate into the Communist camp. Similar fears led industrialists to change their opinion in Hitler's favour in the wake of the Reichstag elections. An observer at a meeting of the heavy industrialist Langnam association in Düsseldorf at the end of November gained the—certainly exaggerated—impression 'that nearly all of industry wants Hitler to be appointed, regardless of the circumstances'.[49]

On 17 November the cabinet took stock of the chancellor's efforts to negotiate with the parties. The results were negative. Two parties, the SPD and NSDAP, had refused to agree to an interview. The Centre and BVP, on the other hand, demanded the resignation of the cabinet and the inclusion of the National Socialists in the government (which, given the distribution of seats in the new Reichstag, was no longer possible in the shape of a 'purely' black–brown coalition). The head of the BVP, Fritz Schäffer, even approved of giving the chancellorship to Hitler. Papen himself came to the conclusion that a 'national concentration' was not possible under his own chancellorship, and recommended proffering the resignation of the entire cabinet. The ministers agreed. Hindenburg accepted the government's resignation later that same day, but asked them to remain in office for the time being.

The next day, Hindenburg himself took up negotiations with selected party leaders. The most important exchanges were those with Hitler on 19 and 21 November. They led to no workable result. Since Hugenberg rejected a Hitler chancellorship out of hand, an NSDAP majority was not possible, and Hindenburg, too, was unwilling to entrust Hitler with the leadership of a presidential cabinet. He seemed unimpressed with the latter's warning that there would be '18 million Marxists, including perhaps 14 to 15 million Communists' in Germany if his movement fell apart, and equally unavailing was Hitler's prophecy that a continuation of the authoritarian government threatened to unleash a new revolution and Bolshevist chaos in the coming months.

On 24 November Hindenburg, through the agency of State Secretary Meissner, sent Hitler a letter—communicated to the press at the same time—containing essentially the same message as his decision on 13 August: the president believed

> he could not answer to the German people for granting plenary presidential authority to the leader of a party emphasizing again and again its sole claims to power and negatively disposed towards himself personally as well as towards the political and economic measures he has considered necessary. Under such conditions, the Herr Reich President would have to fear that a presidential cabinet under your direction must needs lead to a party dictatorship, with all attendant consequences for an extraordinary sharpening of antagonisms

among the German people, consequences he could not answer to his oath and his conscience for having brought about.

After his talks with Hitler, Hindenburg was convinced that there was no longer any alternative to proclaiming a state of national emergency. The chancellor and cabinet, however, were not nearly so ready for battle. When, in a private conversation with Papen on 26 November, Krosigk spoke of the bloody battles that would occur between the army and the 'national' youth if the chancellor declared a state of emergency, the latter was impressed. In an interview with Hindenburg on the same day (with the defence minister also attending), the chancellor requested that the formation of the new government not be entrusted to him. When Hindenburg insisted Papen remain chancellor, the defence minister, according to his own account, advised that 'the atmosphere be tested beforehand', 'given the general opposition to Papen, which is making itself felt even in the industry of the Ruhr'. The president had no objection, set no date for Schleicher, and gave him a completely free hand in his choice of interlocutors.

The most important talks the defence minister held in the following days were those with the heads of the ADGB and the Social Democratic party fraction on 28 November. Schleicher gained union leader Theodor Leipart's support for a 'ceasefire into the next year' by promising to abolish the measure of 5 September allowing employers to undercut contract wages. The interview with Rudolf Breitscheid went very differently. The critical point was reached when the minister asked what the SPD would do if new elections were postponed until the spring of 1933. Schleicher's question, 'whether the Social Democrats would then immediately go onto the barricades', elicited the following answer from Breitscheid:

> I replied to him that I would not commit myself to the 'barricades', but that I was compelled to inform him that the Social Democrats would resist such a violation of the constitution with all their strength. Under these conditions, said Schleicher, the future does indeed look very grim.[50]

Perceptive observers were not surprised by the difference between the ADGB and the SPD. The Social Democrats were worried that the mere appearance of a new 'cooperation' policy would both lay the party open to unparalleled attacks from the Communists and split it from within. The Free Trade Unions, on the other hand, had for some time been underscoring their independence from the SPD and emphasizing their nationalist attitude. Leipart's speech on the 'cultural tasks of the unions' at the national school of his organization in Bernau on 14 October was programatic in this regard. According to one of its key sentences, 'No social stratum can escape the national development.' The unions had organized the workers in order to 'awaken the feeling of community within them and to cultivate the community spirit'. They performed 'service for the people' and waged their 'social struggle in the interest of the nation'. Though socialists, they were not lacking in 'religious feeling, and what is more, they knew the soldierly spirit of falling into line and of sacrifice for the good of the whole'.

Ernst Jünger's book *Der Arbeiter. Herrschaft und Gestalt** had come out a short time before this speech. Leipart did not quote it directly, but it was obvious that his speech-writer—Lothar Erdmann, editor of the union monthly *Die Arbeit*—borrowed central ideas from the right's most notable writer. The worker as soldier of labour, who, in contrast to the liberal civilian, served the nation as a whole, had little to do with the class-conscious proletarian, but much in common with Jünger's *Gestalt*.

It was no accident that, of all newspapers, the *Tägliche Rundschau* printed Leipart's speech. Taken over (with financial assistance from the defence ministry) by the '*Tat* circle' around Hans Zehrer in 1932, the *Tägliche Rundschau* was thereafter regarded—though not always justly—as Schleicher's mouthpiece. Even more spectacular was the applause the Social Democrat Leipart received from Gregor Strasser, a National Socialist. On 20 October the leader of the NSDAP national party organization declared in the Sportpalast in Berlin that Leipart's speech included sentences 'that, if sincerely intended, open up wide prospects for the future'. After the report in the *Tägliche Rundschau* Strasser, 'in unqualified recognition of the *sine qua non* of their professional existence', exhorted the unions 'to draw the necessary conclusions from the declaration of their director and openly demonstrate their political neutrality by separating themselves from the party of "Heilmann and Hilferding", from the SPD, directed as it is by a caste of internationally inclined intellectuals'.

The Bernau speech and the resonance it found seemed to prove that the 'cross-front' from Leipart to Strasser, propagated by the '*Tat* circle' and promoted by Schleicher, was more than just an expression of political wishful thinking. Nonetheless, events at the end of November 1932 revealed that the obstacles to such an axis were greater than Schleicher and Zehrer had expected. The inflexible attitude of the SPD reduced the value of Leipart's willingness to work with Schleicher. And on the right side of the political spectrum, Strasser failed to win Hitler over to an arrangement with the defence minister. The NSDAP leader rejected the offer of vice-chancellorship in the new cabinet on 30 November. To be sure, even if he had accepted, the left flank would not have held together. National Socialists in ministerial positions would have been confronted with resolute Social Democratic opposition—and also, all differences between the ADGB and SPD notwithstanding, with the hostility of the Free Trade Unions. The polarization Schleicher sought to contain would have been even stronger than before.

The alternative to an arrangement with the NSDAP as a whole—even if only a 'ceasefire'—was, for Schleicher, a pact with the forces he imagined to be backing Strasser. If Strasser acted on his own and brought a large number of National Socialists into the government camp, it would open up entirely new prospects. Indeed, it would have a veritably revolutionary effect on the internal political situation of the country. For the time being, however, this too was pure speculation.

* Jünger, *The Worker: Mastery and Form.*

It was true that the NSDAP national leader knew the party's dismal financial situation better than anyone else, and if any National Socialist apart from Hitler had a broad following among the 'old guard', it was he. But Strasser had always avoided any trial of strength with Hitler, and this made a split in the NSDAP improbable.

In sum, Schleicher's investigations did not lead to any kind of breakthrough. There was no sign of a parliamentary majority for a cabinet under his leadership. Nonetheless, he knew that large portions of the working class considered him a lesser evil than Papen. 'Papen means war! The President does not have the power to declare war on his own people!' Thus declared *Vorwärts* on 29 November, as rumours about a Papen 'battle cabinet' were circulating in Berlin and causing '*a tremendous stir among the workers*', according to the Social Democratic party organ. Schleicher was *not* facing a declaration of war by the Social Democrats, but only their opposition; *Vorwärts* hastened to assure readers that opposition was a '*normal function* of political life'. The relationship between the defence minister and the Reichsbanner could almost be called one of mutual trust. He had even better relations with the Christian-national and liberal unions than with the Free Trade Unions. Among the Centre and other moderate parties, Schleicher had never inspired the same aversion as Papen, and from the leading industrial associations he had no opposition to fear.

In a word, Schleicher enjoyed considerably greater backing in society and political life than Papen. If Germany was facing a long period of non-parliamentary rule under a state of emergency, this fact could be crucially important. Schleicher's attitude towards the necessity of declaring a state of emergency did not, at the end of November 1932, differ from that of the incumbent chancellor. But he did see the risks of military dictatorship—however veiled—more realistically than Papen, and this was the reason he wanted to do everything possible to preclude a civil war.[51]

For his part, Papen was not out to put himself at the head of a dictatorship. Only when there was no other choice was he willing to do what Hindenburg asked of him. The latter, however, after hearing on 1 December what Schleicher had to report concerning the talks of the previous few days (Oskar von Hindenburg, Papen, and Meissner were also present), was in no way persuaded that a Schleicher chancellorship would improve the situation, and insisted Papen form the new government. Papen gave in, but requested that the president 'place all presidential rights at his disposal for the conflict with the Reichstag, certain to come'. After detailed legal-constitutional elucidations from Meissner, Hindenburg agreed 'to take, in the event of conflict with the Reichstag, all necessary measures to protect Germany from any harm that might arise from a violation of the duties of the Reichstag'.

Weary of the back-and-forth in the cabinet, the president was determined to cut the Gordian knot. It was in keeping with his military way of thinking to not postpone a battle that, sooner or later, was inevitable, but to fight it out quickly. Schleicher, the 'desk general', saw things more clearly. The kind of dictatorship Hindenburg had chosen was the most dangerous, since there was no popular support for it. To command the army to march against the overwhelming majority of the people would undermine its morale and risk its very existence. Finding himself unable to countenance such a course, the defence minister rebelled against the president.

Schleicher's opportunity lay in the fact that he knew the majority of the cabinet to be on his side—as well as in the outcome of a military 'war game', known as *Planspiel Ott*, which he had conducted at the end of November. In an improvised ministerial meeting on the morning of 2 December, Lieutenant Colonel Eugen Ott, at Schleicher's behest, presented the lessons of the exercise. The Reichswehr, it was concluded, could not win a two-front war against Communists and National Socialists, and certainly not if it had to ward off a Polish attack (part of the war-game scenario) on the eastern border of Germany at the same time. The cabinet was deeply impressed. When Papen reported on the meeting to the president, the latter gave up his resistance to a Schleicher chancellorship. 'I am grown too old to assume responsibility for a civil war at the end of my life.' Such, according to Papen's records, were the words Hindenburg used to justify the reversal of a position he had held the day before.

Schleicher took a great risk with *Planspiel Ott*. If, as chancellor, he opted to declare a state of national emergency, the president could use the results of the exercise against him. Schleicher might hope that he, unlike Papen, would be able to keep the unions from calling a general strike, thus eliminating one of the scenario's central assumptions. But he also faced the prospect that the belief would become firmly ensconced that the Reichswehr, police, and Technical Emergency Corps would not be able to defend the country in the event that the elections were postponed.

Whether or not the defence minister was thinking of these risks on 2 December, his main focus was the immediate effect of the demonstration, and in this he was successful. On 3 December 1932 Hindenburg appointed Schleicher chancellor. His predecessor, however, still enjoying the president's special confidence, remained in his official residence in the Wilhelmstrasse, to which Schleicher assented. Thus Papen preserved what was perhaps even more important than a government office, the privilege of immediate access to the president of the Reich.[52]

THE HANDING OVER OF THE STATE

The news of Schleicher's appointment was greeted with relief by a large portion of the population. His chancellorship, it was thought, would at least not make the internal situation any worse, since the general promised to not to engage in experiments with the constitution and committed himself to easing social tensions. It was true that as defence minister (a post he kept as chancellor), Schleicher had been something of an enigma to observers from all parts of the political spectrum.

His attitude toward the National Socialists was nothing less than contradictory and volatile. And yet, in the political centre and on the moderate left, he was credited with far more tactical skill than Papen, the 'gentleman rider', who notoriously underestimated currents of political resistance—one of the reasons for his failure. From industry-friendly newspapers like the *Deutsche Allgemeine Zeitung* and the *Rheinisch-Westfälische Zeitung*, the new chancellor heard primarily one message: that he would have no choice but to seek out the active support of the National Socialists.

Schleicher cleared his first hurdle without much effort: no petitions for a vote of no confidence in the government were brought forward during the short parliamentary session that began on 6 December. With his assent, the Reichstag lifted the part of the emergency decree of 4 September empowering the government to institute the wage measure from 5 September. The cabinet also agreed to the passage of an amnesty law. Furthermore, in response to an NSDAP petition, the parliament amended Article 51 of the constitution, which provided that the chancellor would represent the president if the latter was unable to exercise the functions of his office or in the event of an early termination of his presidency. Hindenburg had celebrated his eighty-fifth birthday on 2 October 1932. If he died or took seriously ill during Schleicher's chancellorship, the powers of the president, chancellor, and defence minister of the Reich would be unified in the hands of the general. In order to preclude this, the National Socialists proposed that the Reichstag president assume the representation of the Reich presidency. They found the agreement of most of the bourgeois parties and the Social Democrats, for whom the prospect of a further increase in Schleicher's power was equally threatening. The proposal passed with the necessary two-thirds majority on 9 December. This was the last day of the session, the Reichstag adjourning for an indefinite period of time.

That same day, the *Tägliche Rundschau* published a sensational announcement: Gregor Strasser had resigned from all party offices. The leader of the NSDAP national organization, whom Schleicher had offered the vice chancellorship five days previously, was reacting to Hitler's refusal to tolerate the Schleicher government. The newspaper, which was considered the chancellor's mouthpiece, interpreted Strasser's decision as a declaration of war against Hitler. But Strasser had no such intention, despite the fact that he was, up to that point, the second most powerful man in the party. On 9 December he departed for Munich, where his family resided, then spent two weeks vacationing in the southern Tyrol. Hitler very quickly succeeded in securing the allegiance of the party's district leaders, inspectors, and parliamentary delegates. The differences of opinion between the *Führer* and the former *Reichsorganisationsleiter* were swept under the rug as well as possible. 'Palace revolution failed,' Goebbels noted in his journal. 'Strasser is isolated. Dead man!'

Schleicher saw things differently. He continued to place his bets on Strasser. In a meeting of group and district commanders, which took place from 13 to 15 December, the chancellor announced that it was still his policy to work towards 'a cooperation of the Nazis under Strasser under the messianic blessing of Hitler'. By January, he said, the question of a firm parliamentary majority would be answered. As soon as the Reichstag was convened, the National Socialists would be asked if they wished to cooperate. If they said no, it would mean a fierce battle, including the dissolution of the Reichstag and the Prussian parliament. In order to win such a battle, the right would have to be on the side of the government. Therefore, nobody was to be surprised if repeated attempts were made to bring the National Socialists on board and confront them with responsibility. A destruction of the NSDAP was not in the interest of the state.

Thus, even in the middle of December, Schleicher still believed he could reach an understanding with both Strasser and Hitler. He would fight only after one last attempt to involve the National Socialists in the government had been made and rejected. In both cases, it was necessary to avoid as much as possible any confrontation with the unionized working class. In this regard, the chancellor had cause for optimism. On 8 December Heinrich Imbusch, head of the Association of Christian Trade Unions, had spoken extremely positively to Hindenburg about the new chancellor and his cabinet. Similar comments from Leipart had appeared in the Parisian *Excelsior* three days before. While this was a far cry from the 'cross-front', it was clear that by mid-December the government was no longer politically isolated.

When the chancellor announced his governing platform in a radio address on 15 December, he did so with great self-confidence. His views concerning a military dictatorship were generally well known, he said, but he would state them again: 'It is uncomfortable to sit on the point of the bayonet. In the long run, that is, no government can rule without broad popular backing.' He greeted the Reichstag with 'a strong dose of healthy mistrust', but it was imperative that his government be accorded the opportunity to carry out its programme, and this consisted in a single point: 'Job creation!' He, Schleicher, was neither a devotee of capitalism nor of socialism and had nothing against being seen as a 'social general'.

The chancellor stressed the close relationship between job creation, farm settlement, and border security in the east, and he endorsed the idea of general conscription for a militia. In his conclusion, Schleicher distanced himself clearly from Papen, whom he had called his 'friend' and a 'fearless and irreproachable knight' at the beginning of his address. To those who thought that an authoritarian government could get along without popular support, Schleicher replied

> that will and courage do not alone suffice for those who would govern; it is also necessary to understand the sentiments of the people and recognize the psychological moment. For that reason, my government will take the best Moltke-proverb for the guiding principle of its endeavours: 'Look before you leap.'[53]

The 'fearless and irreproachable knight' did not agree that the general was the better chancellor. He wanted to return to the centre of power, and to that end he got together with another of Schleicher's adversaries. On 4 January 1933 Papen and Hitler met at the house of the banker Kurt von Schröder in Cologne. What was intended as a secret interview soon made headlines in both the German and the international press. The purpose of the talks was to find common ground between the National Socialist leader and the Reich president and to bring about the end of the Schleicher government. Before Papen could mediate between Hitler and Hindenburg, however, he first had to clear up his personal relationship with Hitler, which had been very tense since 13 August. After this was accomplished, the two men agreed to a sort of 'duumvirate', whereby the question of the real leader of the government was to remain unanswered for the time being.

It is certain that Hitler reiterated his demand for the chancellorship at this meeting. Papen, according to what we know about his position in August and November 1932, probably did not insist on the leadership role in a future 'cabinet of national concentration'. But he would not have failed to mention Hindenburg's continuing reservations against a Hitler chancellorship. In the further course of the interview, then, Hitler apparently no longer absolutely rejected the possibility of a temporary alternative to his chancellorship. On 10 January, after a conversation with his *Führer* the day before, Goebbels wrote in his journal:

> Hitler gives me the report. Papen sharply against Schleicher, wants to bring him down and get him completely out of the way. Still has the old man's ear. Lives with him, too. Arrangement prepared with us. Either the Chancellorship or ministries of power. Defence and Interior. That sounds pretty good.

The assumption that Hitler did not categorically reject a nominal Papen chancellorship as a temporary solution is also supported by comments the former head of government made privately in the days following the meeting. When, on 7 January, Papen met with the leading industrialists Krupp, Reusch, Springorum, and Vögler in Dortmund in order to report on the talks, he communicated the impression that Hitler would probably be content to play the role of 'junior partner' in a cabinet controlled by conservative forces. This kind of arrangement would have suited the heavy industrial right wing perfectly, and by pushing for it, Papen could be sure of the support of *some* of the most important industrialists. Krupp, however, was not one of them, nor was the National Association of German Industry he directed. Despite its criticism of Schleicher, this organization saw no reason to trade the current government for a cabinet that, it was feared, would stir up even more political unrest among the people.

On 9 January Papen held talks first with Schleicher, who put on a brave front, and then with Hindenburg. The president gained from Papen the impression that Hitler was no longer insisting on the entire authority of the government and was prepared to participate in a coalition. He therefore asked the former chancellor to keep up the dialogue with Hitler on this basis, and under the strictest confidence. Hindenburg now set his sights on the reconstitution of a Papen cabinet, a goal he justified to Meissner by telling him that Hitler would not support or tolerate the current government under Schleicher.[54]

Two days later the National Land League—which had actively participated in Brüning's ouster eight months before—mobilized against the Schleicher administration. After a meeting with the chancellor, Agricultural Minister von Braun, and Economics Minister Warmbold, at which the president presided, the cabinet learned of a decision the League had communicated to the press a few hours before. It was tantamount to a declaration of war. 'The current administration has suffered the immiseration of German agriculture, especially the peasant economy of breed improvement, to take on dimensions that would not have seemed possible even under a Marxist government,' the League's statement declared. 'The pillaging of agriculture for the sake of the almighty pocketbook interests of the internationally-minded export industry and its servants continues apace . . . For this reason the actions of the government hitherto also do not satisfy the instructions the president has also repeatedly issued.'

On 13 January the leader of the NSDAP Agrarian-Political Apparatus, Richard Walther Darré, launched another attack. In an open letter to Schleicher, he demanded from the government a 'decisive change of course towards the domestic market', though he recognized that such a move was not to be expected from the current administration. As Count Kalckreuth, president of the National Land League, had done at his meeting with the Reich president and chancellor on 11 January, Darré invoked the 'disturbing spread of Bolshevism among the German people'. His letter concluded with an allusion to the export-friendly policy of Bismarck's successor: 'German agriculture's tale of woe began with "*General*" von Caprivi. Let us hope to God that "*General*" von Schleicher will be the last representative of this unhappy and anti-agricultural era.'

Schleicher could afford to ignore Darré's letter, but not the broadside from the National Land League. In the evening of 11 January the chancellor had an official announcement made accusing the organization of demagogic and factually incorrect attacks against the government. This reproach was followed by sanctions: the cabinet broke off all relations with the League. But the president did not join the boycott. On 17 January he addressed a letter to the leadership of Germany's largest agricultural interest group expressing his hope that the measure he had just signed for more effective stays of execution would help ease tensions in the agricultural community.

By 11 January, when he settled accounts with the National Land League, Schleicher had also been wanting for over a week to clarify things between his government and the Reichstag. On 4 January he let State Secretary Planck of the parliamentary advisory committee know that the cabinet was ready at any time to appear before the delegates and elucidate its platform. Thereafter he expected the situation to be straightened out, and was not prepared to accept that petitions for votes of no confidence be deferred. But the advisory committee decided (with the NSDAP abstaining) not to convene the Reichstag until 24 January, instead of 10 January, as the SPD and KPD wanted. Rudolf Breitscheid observed that the behaviour of the National Socialists was 'practically tantamount to a toleration of the Schleicher government'.

The National Socialists, unlike Schleicher, were playing for time. Their first aim was to patch things up in the wake of the 6 November parliamentary elections and after the local elections in Thuringia on 4 December, which had also been very disappointing for the NSDAP. The parliamentary elections in Lippe-Detmold, the second smallest German state, on 15 January offered an opportunity. In the first part of the month, the party flooded the northern German state with a wave of demonstrations and rallies. Hitler himself spoke at sixteen large events. The effort paid off. The NSDAP gained some 6,000 votes more than on 6 November, climbing from 34.7% to 39.6% of the vote. Party propaganda interpreted this outcome as proof the National Socialists were once again on the rise. In reality, the success was comparatively modest. In comparison with the Reichstag elections on 31 July 1932, the NSDAP had lost 3,500 votes, and on the national level it could never have organized an electoral campaign as intensive as in a small state with 160,000 inhabitants.

Nonetheless, the psychological effect was what counted at the moment. The party of Hitler seemed to be on the advance again, and this strengthened Hitler's hand vis-à-vis the bourgeois right, especially the German Nationalists, from whom he had taken the most votes. From now on, it was once again out of the question that he would give up the post of chancellor in a 'national' government. Against Strasser, too, he could now take the decisive step. On 16 January, at a meeting of district leaders in Weimar, Hitler went on the offensive against the former head of the national party organization. The result was unambiguous: Strasser found no more defenders, and Hitler's position within the party was stronger than ever.[55]

On the day after the Lippe elections, the cabinet met for the first time in the new year in order to discuss the political situation. Schleicher showed himself determined to force a rapid decision about the future of his cabinet and, with it, the future of German politics. Though he still talked about the possibility of getting the National Socialists to cooperate in some way, he concentrated entirely on the consequences of their refusal. If the Reichstag set the petitions for a vote of no confidence at the top of its agenda for the coming session, Schleicher would send them the written order of dissolution. There were, he said, strong reasons against holding new elections within the constitutionally mandated period of sixty days. The business community rejected them, and this attitude was widespread among workers, too. 'With things as they are, he believes the idea of postponing the new elections until the autumn very worthy of consideration.'

Unlike on the last day of Franz von Papen's chancellorship, there was virtually no objection to the promulgation of a state of emergency on 16 January 1933. Interior Minister Bracht, who had succeeded Gayl on 3 December, emphasized that 'one thing, at least, has been achieved: a united front against the government no longer exists.' He proposed to set the new Reichstag elections for 22 October or 12 November 1933. Finance Minister Count Schwerin von Krosigk, too, who in November and at the beginning of December 1932 had been one of the staunchest opponents of violating the constitution, now supported the delay of elections without qualification.

The possible legal and political consequences of the delay were never discussed. Nor was an alternative plan of action that had originated in the Wehrmacht department of the defence ministry and been inserted into the protocol of the cabinet session: the 'non-recognition of a vote of no confidence and the confirmation of the government by the president'. According to its author, ignoring a vote of no confidence from a 'negative' majority represented, 'relatively speaking, a lesser conflict with the constitution' than postponing new elections or forcing the Reichstag to adjourn. Article 54, which made the chancellor and ministers subject to the confidence of the parliament, did not prevent a government that had been voted out from remaining in office in a custodial capacity. It also did not establish a time limit for the life of an administration after its parliamentary 'death'.

In his 1928 book *Verfassungslehre* Carl Schmitt, one of Germany's most prominent constitutional scholars, had called a vote of no confidence from a parliamentary majority itself incapable of forming a government an 'act of pure obstruction'. In such a case there was no obligation to resign, 'at least not when the dissolution of the Reichstag is ordered at the same time'. In the December 1932 edition of *Die Gesellschaft*, the Social Democratic jurist Ernst Fraenkel came to the conclusion—as Carl Schmitt and Johannes Heckel, whom he cited, had already done—that the Reichstag, as the central organ of the Weimar constitution, would be unable to fulfil its obligations as long as Communists and National Socialists had a majority. Fraenkel suggested a referendum to amend the constitution as a means of preventing the 'delinquent parliament' from bringing the machinery of state to a halt and giving the enemies of the constitution the longed-for pretext for a *coup d'état*. According to his proposal, a parliamentary vote of no confidence in the chancellor or a minister would legally compel resignation only 'if the representative body combines the vote of no confidence with a positive suggestion to the President naming the person who is to be appointed minister in place of the fallen governmental official'.

Around the end of 1932 and beginning of 1933, political pragmatists were advising the chancellor to the effect that a constructive vote of no confidence be introduced in a de facto sense, without explicit emendation of the constitution (on 1 December 1932 Franz Sperr, the Bavarian envoy to the Reich, and on 19 and 26 January 1933 Wilhelm Simpfendörfer, Reichstag delegate and head of the Christian Social People's Service, a party originating in the Pietist movement in Württemberg). But Schleicher did not respond to any of these suggestions, which sought to resolve the crisis below the threshold of an openly declared state of emergency. He believed that delaying new elections would cause a smaller loss of governmental authority than a vote of no confidence. He could hold out to the president the fact that his government was less isolated than that of his predecessor and that the conditions of *Planspiel Ott* did not therefore obtain. But it was very unclear whether Hindenburg would accord Schleicher what he had promised Papen—the dissolution of the Reichstag and the non-constitutional delay of new elections. Since both those things were uncertain, the 16 January plan for a national state of emergency rested on very shaky foundations.[56]

A few short days after the cabinet meeting, the press was full of speculations about the imminent proclamation of a state of emergency. At a meeting of SPD party officials in Berlin-Friedrichshain, Rudolf Breitscheid revealed what Schleicher had told him on 28 November concerning a possible delay of new elections. The Social Democratic floor leader also quoted the response he had given to the defence minister at the time: 'Such a provocation will doubtless cause the greatest convulsions.'

Another revelation on the same day drew even greater attention. Joseph Ersing, Centre delegate and secretary of the Christian Trade Unions, reported to the parliamentary budget committee on what became known as the '*Osthilfe* scandal', the misuse of public funds for the rehabilitation of deeply indebted manorial estates, especially in East Prussia. If the groups behind the National Land League, which had continually received immense sums from the entire German people, adopted the kind of language they had recently used to the Reichstag, then, Ersing said, the Reichstag would have to look into the matter. And if the federal funds were not used to cover debt, but for the purchase of luxury automobiles and racehorses and trips to the Riviera, the government would have to demand the repayment of the funds. The circles of the great landowners, Ersing said, were seeking to prevent further parliamentary deliberation over the issues of eastern assistance. This was the reason such intense efforts were being made behind the scenes to dissolve the Reichstag.

One of the reasons Ersing's disclosures caused such a stir was because, shortly before, the name of a personal friend of the president had appeared in press reports on the issue of eastern assistance. Elard von Oldenburg-Januschau had allegedly done extremely well in the distribution of public funds. The public was also informed in detail about how Hindenburg came into the possession of Neudeck. The ownership of this estate, which he had received from the German business community in 1927 on the occasion of his eightieth birthday, had been registered in the name of his son Oskar (a son 'not provided for in the constitution', as people sneered at the time) in order to spare the latter the payment of the inheritance tax. Although this manipulation was not actually illegal, it damaged the reputation of the head of state.

One day after Ersing's sensational speech, the advisory committee decided to postpone the convocation of the plenum from 24 to 31 January. The cause of the delay was the National Socialists, who had every reason to avoid a plenary session at the moment. There were to be no disturbances in the political negotiations Hitler had resumed shortly after the Lippe elections. On 17 January he had an interview with Hugenberg. It failed to produce concrete results, however, since the DNVP leader refused to hand over to the National Socialists control of the Prussian interior ministry and, with it, the police. The next day, Hitler met Papen in the Dahlem villa of Joachim von Ribbentrop, a politically active champagne salesman who had recently joined the NSDAP. Pointing to his electoral successes, the National Socialist leader pressed his demand for the chancellorship much more firmly than on 4 January in Cologne. Nonetheless, whatever the former chancellor thought of the idea, Hindenburg still rejected a Hitler chancellorship.

In the meantime, the political pressure on Schleicher continued to grow. On 21 January the German Nationalist parliamentary fraction declared open opposition to the cabinet. In a statement immediately communicated to the chancellor, but not published until 24 January, the DNVP stated that the policy of deferment and hesitation cast doubts upon all attempts to improve the situation. The main target of criticism was the government's economic policy, which was 'straying ever further into socialist-internationalist ideas'. 'It is a particular danger when antagonisms between big and small are permitted to arise, especially in agriculture, and with them the threat of Bolshevism in the countryside.' The claim that Schleicher was pursuing such a policy was as demagogic and nonsensical as the accusation the German Nationalists had levelled against Brüning in the Reichstag in May 1932, describing his settlement measure as 'pure Bolshevism'. Nevertheless, their language once again seemed calculated to impress Hindenburg and to repeat the rhetorical success of the previous spring.

On 22 January, one day after the DNVP went on the attack against Schleicher, Hitler and Papen met again at Ribbentrop's house. The presence of Meissner and Oskar von Hindenburg, as well as Goering and Frick for the National Socialists, lent particular weight to the occasion. Hitler assured Papen that bourgeois ministers could be well represented in a presidential government under his leadership, as long as they were not beholden to their parties. Goering told Meissner something similar. Papen's words indicate that he was prepared to be satisfied with the office of vice chancellor in a Hitler cabinet. The most important part of the meeting was a lengthy conversation Hitler held privately with the son of the president of the Reich. On their drive back to the Wilhelmstrasse, Oskar von Hindenburg told Meissner that he thought Hitler's views made a good deal of sense.

Hindenburg had already been informed about the Dahlem meeting by the time he received the chancellor for an interview the next day, on 23 January. Schleicher reported on the cabinet's emergency plans and was rebuffed. He would still have to consider the dissolution of the parliament, said Hindenburg, but he could not at the present time justify delaying new elections:

> Such a step would be interpreted by all sides as a violation of the constitution. Before deciding on such a step, the party leaders would have to be consulted in order to ascertain that they would recognize the state of national emergency and refrain from raising the accusation that it represents a violation of the constitution.

Earlier, between the end of August and the beginning of December 1932, Hindenburg and Meissner had expressed no such constitutional reservations against a postponement of new elections. The legal situation was still the same. But the political situation had changed. Hindenburg may have been influenced by Schleicher's own efforts to demonstrate, with *Planspiel Ott*, how the declaration of a state of emergency could provoke a civil war. But there were also other reasons for the discrepancy, including personal ones. The revelations of corruption in the eastern assistance programme continued in the budgetary committee without any attempt by the chancellor to protect the president. This was the main reason Hindenburg's fellow landed aristocrats, men like 'old Januschau', pressed for Schleicher's dismissal and Hitler's appointment to the chancellorship, and the army district commander in East Prussian, General von Blomberg, sought to urge the president in the same direction.

Whatever doubts Hindenburg still entertained about the parties' reaction to a delay in new elections were dispelled in the days that followed. On 25 January the SPD executive and the leadership of the parliamentary fraction registered 'the strongest possible protest against the planned proclamation of a so-called national state of emergency'. The realization of this plan would be tantamount to a *coup d'état*, and that would create an extra-legal situation 'against which every resistance is permitted and required'. The next day, Monsignor Kaas wrote a letter to the chancellor warning him in the name of the Centre Party against an 'emergency delay of the date of new elections' and reminding him of their last conversation on 16 January, in which Kaas had vehemently criticized 'the fundamental tendency of Carl Schmitt and his followers, which is to relativize the whole legal framework of the state'. 'The postponement of elections would be an undeniable violation of the constitution, with all the legal and political consequences that would necessarily arise from it . . . The illegality from above will give an incalculable impetus to the illegality from below.' At Brüning's suggestion, a copy of the letter was sent to the president of the Reich.

At the end of January 1933 the Centre and Social Democratic parties were behaving as if Schleicher represented a greater threat to the Weimar Republic than Hitler. For these, the two largest democratic parties in the country, the violation of a single article of the Weimar constitution represented the greatest possible danger, not the abolition of the constitution itself. The Centre had been saying publicly for a long time that it considered a Hitler chancellorship—provided it was backed by a parliamentary majority and swore fealty to the constitution—to be a democratically correct solution to the crisis, if not the only legitimate one. The SPD had not, as yet, endorsed this point of view. On 25 January, however, the delegate Siegfried Aufhäuser, head of the a group of employees' associations (the *Arbeitsgemeinschaft freier Angestelltenverbände*) linked with the Free Trade Unions, demanded that the parliament 'convene and take action to express the lack of confidence of the entire population in the current governmental authority'. This could only be understood as an attempt to gain National Socialist support for the fight against Schleicher. The campaign against the delay of new elections does seem to indicate that the Social Democrats also believed that a Hitler government, coming to power by legal means, was a lesser evil than a provisional Schleicher dictatorship.[57]

On 27 January Berlin was full of rumors about another kind of dictatorship, a Papen-led 'battle cabinet'. It was true that Hindenburg still wanted to appoint

Papen as Schleicher's successor, not Hitler. But he was counting on the cooperation of the National Socialists and sufficient backing for this move in the Reichstag. The German Nationalists, on the other hand, were propagating the idea of an anti-parliamentary battle cabinet. Their party leader, Hugenberg, got into such a row with Hitler on 27 January over the vexed question of which party would obtain the Prussian interior ministry that Hitler cancelled a meeting with Papen planned for that day. When the NSDAP declared publicly that it would fight with all possible intensity against a dictatorial government headed by the former chancellor, Papen was impressed. Speaking to Ribbentrop that evening, he declared himself in favour of a Hitler chancellorship in stronger language than he had used previously. Ribbentrop considered it 'the turning point of the whole issue'.

One of those who believed a presidential government led by Papen or Hugenberg to be the greatest evil was the incumbent chancellor himself. Such a cabinet, Schleicher announced in a ministers' conference on the morning of 28 January, could 'soon provoke a national and presidential crisis, since the sentiments of the broad masses would oppose it in the strongest possible way'. The difficulties would perhaps not be so great if the president decided to appoint Hitler chancellor. According to his knowledge, however, Hindenburg was not prepared to do that. Schleicher did not believe his own government had any further chance of survival. He was right. When, shortly after noon, he repeated his request for an order to dissolve the Reichstag (there was no further mention of delaying elections), the president tersely turned him down. Thereupon Schleicher announced the resignation of his cabinet.

An even greater public stir than Schleicher's dismissal was caused by the official announcement that the Reich president had authorized former chancellor Franz von Papen 'to clarify the political situation through negotiations with the parties and to determine the available recourses'. Greatly alarmed, the acting leaders of the National Association of German Industry and the German Industry and Trade Association, Ludwig Kastl and Eduard Hamm, warned State Secretary Meissner about the harm the political crisis threatened to cause to the German economy. Labour unions of all political stripes sent a telegram to the president informing him that the whole of the German working class would look upon the 'appointment of a socially reactionary and labour-hostile government' as a provocation. The Centre Party and the Bavarian prime minister, Heinrich Held, expressed themselves similarly.

For a short time it seemed as though the SPD, too, believed a rightist 'battle cabinet' without a majority to be a greater threat than a Hitler government backed by a parliamentary majority. Along the road that began with Schleicher's fall, wrote the *Vorwärts* on the evening of 28 January,

> constitutional rule will only be preserved if a parliamentary majority can be created for Hitler and if it is guaranteed that Hitler will vanish as soon as he loses this majority. In other words, a Hitler–Hugenberg government is constitutionally only viable if the Centre gives it its blessing . . . A Harzburg government *without* a parliamentary majority means coup d'état and civil war.

The next morning, the mouthpiece of the Social Democratic party corrected itself: 'A *Hitler cabinet*, even if the Centre wished to afford it a parliamentary basis through toleration, would be a *cabinet of provocation more than ever*! . . . A Hitler cabinet—that means Hitler's will—would serve as a *springboard for fascist dictatorship*.' Even before Schleicher's dismissal, the SPD had called its followers to a mass demonstration in the Lustgarten on the afternoon of 29 January. According to the party newspaper 100,000 people heeded the call. The watchword for the event was 'Berlin remains red!'

Papen succeeded in winning over members of the former Schleicher government—including Foreign Minister von Neurath and Finance Minister Count Schwerin von Krosigk—to a cabinet with Hitler as chancellor and himself as vice chancellor. When, on the evening of 28 January, he was able to inform Hindenburg that reliable conservative politicians would determine the character of Hitler's cabinet, the president was impressed. For the first time, he was prepared to give up his reservations against a Hitler chancellorship.

The German Nationalists caused Papen the greatest difficulties. Hugenberg was under pressure from politicians like Ewald von Kleist-Schmenzin and Otto Schmidt-Hannover, who advocated an authoritarian government and demanded that Hitler be fought energetically. The party head himself had strong objections to the National Socialists' demand for new elections. In his view, what made participation in a Hitler–Papen cabinet a possibility was the fact that Hindenburg agreed to one of Hugenberg's major demands, his appointment as minister of economics and agriculture, both in the Reich government and in Prussia.

Hitler, for his part, had to accept that Papen would be the federal commissioner for Prussia, not Hitler. In exchange, Goering was given the office of deputy commissioner, responsible for the Prussian interior ministry and therefore in control of the police forces of the largest German state. Goering also received the posts of federal minister without portfolio and federal commissioner for air transport. The federal ministry of the interior was granted to Wilhelm Frick. Thus only three members of the NSDAP sat in the cabinet. In numerical terms the conservatives—including Labour Minister Franz Seldte, the leader of the Stahlhelm—were clearly dominant.

One minister was appointed by Hindenburg himself. The district commander for East Prussia, General von Blomberg (who on 29 January was in Geneva as technical adviser to the German delegation at the disarmament conference) became Schleicher's successor as defence minister. Rumours that the Potsdam garrison was planning a coup (false, as it turned out) caused Hindenburg to swear Blomberg into office on the morning of 30 January, immediately after his arrival in Berlin. This was a violation of the constitution. The president could only appoint ministers when asked to do so by the chancellor, and the chancellor was not yet in office.

It long remained unclear whether the president would grant the National Socialist demand for the dissolution of the Reichstag and new elections, a demand Hitler justified by claiming that there was no majority in the current parliament for the enabling law he considered absolutely necessary. On 29 January Papen seems to have convinced Hindenburg to agree to the move if the Centre and the Bavarian People's Party proved unwilling to support the new government in any way. Hitler did not find it difficult to announce negotiations with the two Catholic parties. Finally, after Hugenberg, too, had given in on the question of new elections, Hitler and the members of his cabinet took their oaths of office on the Weimar constitution in the late afternoon of 30 January 1933. Hindenburg concluded the brief ceremony with the words: 'And now, gentlemen, forward with God!'[58]

While in the Wilhelmstrasse the die was being cast for Germany's fate, the executive of the SPD was meeting with representatives of the party fraction and the ADGB in the nearby Reichstag building. When they received the news of the appointment of Hitler's cabinet, the leaders of the party and fraction reacted by issuing an appeal cautioning against 'undisciplined behaviour by individual organizations and groups acting on their own' and calling 'cool-headedness, resolve' the demands of the hour. In a meeting of the party executive on the next day, Rudolf Breitscheid, representing Otto Wels, who was ill, emphatically rejected extra-parliamentary action:

> If at first Hitler remains within the constitution, and be it hypocrisy a hundred times over, it would be wrong to give him an excuse to violate the constitution . . . If Hitler takes the path of the constitution, then he stands at the head of a government we can and must fight, even more than the previous ones. But it is still a government by constitutional right.

Breitscheid's words were met with strong agreement by those present, including members of the parliamentary fraction and the 'iron front', the alliance of the SPD, Free Trade Unions, Reichsbanner Schwarz-Rot-Gold, and workers' sporting clubs.

The central committee of the KPD, on the other hand, believed the time for more direct action had come. On 30 January it spoke directly to the leaders of the SPD and Labour unions for the first time since the *Preussenschlag* on 20 July 1932. The SPD, the General German Trade Union Association, the Cooperative Union of Free Employees' Federations, and the Christian Trade Unions were exhorted to 'join the Communists in executing the general strike against the fascist dictatorship of Hitler, Hugenberg, Papen, against the destruction of the workers' associations, for the liberty of the working class.'

But a unitary proletarian front had even less chance of success on 30 January 1933 than on 20 July 1932. With over 6 million Germans officially registered as unemployed, a longer general strike was out of the question, and a limited general strike would have been interpreted by the new government more as a sign of weakness than as a demonstration of strength. Moreover, it was extremely improbable that the Communists would have heeded any call to bring the strike to an end. The Communist rhetoric of a common defensive action lacked the key ingredient: credibility. For years, the KPD had been waging war against the Social

Democrats as the 'main social buttress of the bourgeoisie' and as 'social fascists'. As late as 26 January, the *Rote Fahne* had rejected the *Vorwärts* proposal that the SPD and KPD should conclude a 'non-aggression pact' as an 'infamous disparagement of anti-fascist Berlin'. The Social Democrats and the Free Trade Unions could not but expect that the Communists would immediately go over to the kind of revolutionary violence the National Socialists were waiting for in order to lend their terror a semblance of legitimacy. A civil war could end only with the bloody defeat of the workers' organizations. A divided left had no chance against the forces that rightist groups, the police, and the army could call in.

On the evening of 30 January 1933 the streets belonged to Hitler's 'brown battalions', not only in Berlin, but in many places in Germany. On the next day, in accordance with his promise to Papen, the new chancellor began his negotiations with the Centre. But they were mere pretence. Hitler's true aim was to show that no governance was possible with the parliament elected on 6 November 1932. For its part, the Centre was still interested in a bona fide coalition with the NSDAP and much less indignant about Hitler's chancellorship than about the 'reactionary' character of his cabinet. Nonetheless, Kaas had to reject Hitler's demand that the Reichstag be adjourned for one year, and in doing so, he gave the chancellor the excuse he needed to declare the negotiations a failure and to bring about the first major decision of his cabinet, the request to Hindenburg for the dissolution of the Reichstag. The order was given by the president on 1 February, as well as another setting new elections for 5 March 1933. Until that date, the Hitler cabinet would be able—indeed compelled—to govern by means of the emergency powers of Article 48.[59]

THE TRANSFER OF POWER TO HITLER: ORIGINS AND ALTERNATIVES

Hitler's appointment as chancellor of the Reich was *not* the ineluctable outcome of the German political crisis that had begun with the breakdown of the Grand Coalition on 27 March 1930 and had come to a dramatic head after Brüning's dismissal on 30 March 1932. Hindenburg was not forced to break with Schleicher, any more than he had been forced to replace Brüning with Papen. In the event of a parliamentary vote of no confidence, he could have kept Schleicher in office at the head of a custodial government or replaced him with a less polarizing, 'non-partisan' figure. He was not barred from dissolving the Reichstag again within the constitutional limit of sixty days; a delay of new elections until the autumn of 1933, however, was no less risky than it had been the year before, considering the declarations from the political centre and the Social Democrats. Nothing compelled the president to make Hitler chancellor. It was true that, despite the NSDAP losses in the 6 November elections, Hitler was still the leader of the strongest party. But he did not have a majority in the Reichstag.

Hindenburg had opposed a Hitler chancellorship until January 1933, seeking to prevent a National Socialist Party dictatorship. He changed his position after his closest political advisers put pressure on him, and also because he believed that the predominance of conservative ministers in Hitler's cabinet would reduce, if not eliminate, the risk of dictatorship. The pressure came—directly—from the large-scale agricultural interests in the east and—indirectly, via Papen—from the right wing of heavy industry. It came, as well, from nearly everybody who had access to Hindenburg. To withstand this pressure was now beyond the capacity of the old man. In January 1933 the power centre around Hindenburg decided to take its chances with Hitler, and Hindenburg the person was only one part of this centre of power.

Thus 30 January 1933 was neither the inevitable result of prior political developments nor the product of chance. Hitler's mass support made his appointment possible, but it was the will of Hindenburg and of the political milieu he embodied that made him chancellor. The power of the 'old elite' demanding a 'government of national concentration' under Hitler was, no less than the popularity of his party, a social fact with a long history. The erosion of confidence in the democratic state was a part of this history. If the 'belief in legitimacy' (*Legitimitätsglaube*), which Max Weber considered the most important non-material resource of rulership, was weak in Weimar from the very beginning, the reasons lay both in the nature of this beginning—the republic's birth out of Germany's defeat in the First World War—as well as in events, personalities, and phenomena that lay far back in German history. If the collapse of the first German Republic can be traced back to a single root cause, it lies in the long historical deferment of the question of liberty in the nineteenth century—or, to put it another way, in the non-simultaneity of Germany's political modernization: the early democratization of suffrage and the late democratization of the system of government. Hitler was, after 1930, the main beneficiary of this contradiction and built the foundations of his success upon it.

In his plan to destroy Weimar democracy, Hitler availed himself of all the possibilities the Weimar constitution had to offer. The tactics of legality he imposed on his party were far more successful than the revolutionary violence he had professed ten years previously—a credo to which the KPD, the other totalitarian party, continued to subscribe. In openly advocating civil war, the Communists gave the National Socialists—who had the largest civil war army of all—the opportunity to present themselves as guardians of the constitution, as a factor of order, standing ready with the police and, if necessary, the army to strike down a coup attempt from the left. At the same time, Hitler could himself threaten the rulers of the country with revolutionary violence and civil war if they broke the law or changed it to the detriment of the National Socialists, as in the case of the emergency measure against political terror of 9 August 1932.

Hitler's conditional promise of legality, which contained an implicit threat, fulfilled its purpose. The traditional right's fear of the revolutionary character of

National Socialism ultimately gave way to the belief that the leader of the 'national' masses would provide the urgently needed popular basis for an authoritarian politics. The illusions of the authoritarians were flanked by the illusions of the democrats. In order to preserve the state under the rule of law, its defenders would have had to violate—even if only by accepting a 'negative' vote of no confidence—the letter of a constitution that was, ultimately, neutral with regard to its own validity. What stopped them was the predominance of a 'functionalist' view of legality, an attitude Carl Schmitt had lambasted in the summer of 1932, saying that 'it will remain neutral to the point of suicide.' Ernst Fraenkel had the same thing in mind when, at the end of 1932, he castigated the widespread 'constitutional fetishism' of the period. Weimar had fallen into the legality trap, which the fathers and mothers of the constitution themselves had set.[60]

Looking ahead

During the night of 17–18 December 1941, nearly nine years after he had come to power, Hitler, sitting in his main headquarters in the 'Wolf's Den' near Rastenburg, attempted to put the events of the day in historical perspective. 'At the time of the accession to power,' he said,

it was a decisive moment for me: do we want to stick with the traditional calendar? Or should we interpret the new world order as a sign of the beginning of a new calendar? I told myself that the year 1933 was nothing other than the renewal of a millennial condition. The concept of the Reich had, at that time, been nearly extirpated, but today it has victoriously asserted itself with us and in the world. Germany is referred to everywhere simply as 'the Reich'.[1]

Hitler overestimated his 'achievement'. Among educated Germans, the concept of the Reich had already attained new—albeit only abstract—greatness in the years *before* 1933. It was the response of rightist intellectuals to Weimar and Versailles, both the Versailles of 1919 and the Versailles of 1871. In their view, the Reich was something higher than the republic. It was also something more than the Bismarck empire of 1871, which had been humiliated and decimated by the forces of the Entente in 1919. It was more than one state among other states. As the political right of the early 1930s saw it, the Reich was a 'Greater Germany' by its very nature. Bismarck's 'Little Germany', according to the dominant opinion of the time, may have been the only viable answer to the German question of *those days*; ever since the downfall of the Habsburg monarchy, however, the nation state of 1871 was thought to be unperfected and no longer the last word of history. The end of the multinational Austrian empire had removed the strongest argument against the Greater Germany solution and in favour of a Little Germany. After 1918, there were two republics that considered themselves German, whose unification was prevented not by the right to national self-determination, but by the will of the victorious powers.

In 1920, shortly before the fiftieth anniversary of the founding of the Reich, the historian Hermann Oncken pronounced the following judgement:

Now that Austria-Hungary has completely broken apart and the bloodless body of the German Reich has been rendered incapable of pursuing an active foreign policy for a long time, we have only one last line of retreat: the *return to the idea of Greater Germany*. This is, for us, the result of the world crisis . . . Greater Germany has now become possible, since the Austrian dynastic state no longer exists, and it has become necessary, since German Austria cannot survive by itself. Thus not only has the theoretical *raison d'être* of the Little Germany idea of 1848/1866 been invalidated; the Little German Reich itself, as it existed between 1871 and 1918, has lost the realpolitical justification of its existence. The Little Germany idea, along with its supplement in the narrower and wider federation, must automatically be absorbed into the idea of Greater Germany.

The Bismarck empire as a 'preliminary step to something higher, to the entire Greater German national state, which absolutely must become our ideal today'—the National-Liberal *Vernunftrepublikaner* Oncken spoke here for the great majority of German historians of the Weimar period. Like Oncken, the Prussian-influenced educated bourgeoisie, both conservatives and liberals, had come round to the *grossdeutsch* idea rather late in the day. Southern German Catholics, on the other hand, for whom Königgrätz was still a painful memory, had always been *grosseutsch* in attitude, along with the Social Democrats, who saw themselves as the guardians of the legacy of 1848. Paul Löbe, long-time Social Democratic president of the Reichstag, was the leader of the *grossdeutsch*-minded Austro-German People's Union (*Österreichisch-deutscher Volksbund*), and no paramilitary organization was so resolute in its support for a German–Austrian unification as the Social Democratic Reichsbanner Schwarz-Rot-Gold. In the words of Hermann Schützinger, one of the 'military' leaders of the Reichsbanner, in the year 1925: 'The German republic . . . will be a Greater Germany, or it will not be.'[2]

Thus the ruling classes of the late Weimar Republic could count on broad support within German society when they added another demand to their pursuit of a revision of the Treaty of Versailles: the revision of the founding of the Reich. The failure of the Austro-German customs union in 1931 was seen as a setback along the road to the realization of a Greater Germany, not as its refutation. The complete and not merely commercial *Anschluss* of Austria was itself considered only an intermediate stop along the road to a German hegemony in central Europe—a vision that had before inspired the liberals in the Frankfurt Paulskirche and liberal imperialists like Friedrich Naumann during the time of the Austro-German alliance in the First World War.

A part of this project was the economic-political attachment to Germany of *Zwischeneuropa* ('Europe-in-Between'), a term appearing in the title of a 1932 book by the *jungkonservativ* publicist Giselher Wirsing, who would later become a *Sturmbann* leader in the SS and, later still, editor-in-chief of the Evangelical weekly *Christ und Welt*. During the economic crisis, voices calling for a great central European economic area controlled by Germany became louder. For intellectuals of the 'conservative revolution', the myth of the old, supra-national Reich served to lend an aura of historical legitimacy to the German claims to ascendancy.[3]

An active German ethnic politics was narrowly linked to the cultivation of Reich ideology. Ethnic Germans outside the borders of the Reich—in Poland, Czechoslovakia, and in the rest of eastern central and southeastern Europe—were actively supported by organizations like the League for Germans Abroad (*Verein für das Deutschtum im Ausland*) and by official agencies, led by the foreign office. This support was both defensive and offensive. The defensive side was the opposition to efforts aimed at the assimilation—that is, denationalization—of the German minorities in the new national states. The offensive side was the attempt to exploit Germans abroad for the purposes of German hegemonial politics. This second aspect was a great deal more pronounced in the period of presidential cabinets beginning with Brüning than during the Stresemann era. The material furtherance of Germans living abroad was accompanied by the scholarly investigation of ethnic German communities outside of Germany. After 1931 these studies were coordinated by research instututes like the *Volksdeutschen Forschungsgemeinschaften*. The idea of the *Volk* became, along with the idea of the Reich, a central part of the *jungkonservativ* drive to intellectually supersede the Weimar state.[4]

In many ways, therefore, the ground was prepared for Hitler's rise to power. The National Socialist leader pursued incomparably more radical goals than the academics in the circles of the 'conservative revolution'. But since there was a wide field of agreement between them and the National Socialists, they could become a kind of intellectual reserve army for Hitler's intellectually challenged movement.

The mythology of the Reich was the most important bridge between Hitler and large numbers of educated Germans. Hitler's intuitive grasp of the opportunities implicit in this concept was one of the conditions for his success. The *Reichsidee* was the memory of the greatness of the German Middle Ages and of the burden Germany had taken upon itself in those days, the defence of the whole of the Christian west against the threat from the heathen east. In the heads and hearts of its devotees, the idea of the Reich had survived the humiliations to which Germany had been subjected from the west, by France, for centuries: the Peace of Westphalia, the conquests of Louis XIV and Napoleon, the Treaty of Versailles. 'The Reich' stood for a European order determined by Germany, and as such was the German answer to the revolutions and ideas of 1789 and 1917. 'The Reich' was the earthly reflection of the Eternal, and as such formed the ultimate ground of a particular German mission. They, the Germans, must lead Europe, for only they had a universal calling, one elevating them far above the other nations and their nation states.

Like the *Volksgemeinschaft*, the 'community of the *Volk*', the 'Reich' was a vision well suited to counter and transcend the fragmentation of Germany into parties, classes, and confessions. In Hitler's opinion the Weimar Republic, unable to bring forth a unitary political will, had failed in this task. He, the *Führer*, claimed to embody the will of the nation. He knew the deep longing for a saviour of Germany, who would extinguish the disgrace of Versailles and all other humiliations and overcome the internal divisions. He saw himself as this saviour. He was convinced that the rescue of Germany demanded the suppression of the Jews, and he allowed no doubts on this point among his faithful. At no time did he distance himself from the anti-Jewish excesses of his SA, which were especially frequent after the Reichstag elections of September 1930 and July 1932. For Hitler himself, however, anti-Semitism was not the most important aspect of National Socialist agitation in the final years of the Weimar Republic. He had long before won over the radical anti-Jewish minority. A 'moderate' anti-Semite was not offensive to the majority of Germans, but raw violence was. Hitler took this into account in his campaign speeches.

In the last years before 1933, Hitler no longer referred to the great war he was always resolved to wage. He spoke of 'work and bread', of the reconciliation between the bourgeois citizen and the worker, between nationalism and socialism, of the end of class struggle and civil war, of the community of the German people. He promised to drive the 'thirty parties' from the country, and invoked the 'new German Reich of greatness, of might and strength, of power and of glory and of social justice'.

What Hitler did not say was that his German Reich would no longer be what it had been during the time of the monarchy and the republic—a constitutional state under the rule of law. But nobody who had read *Mein Kampf* or listened to his speeches could doubt his resolve to break radically with everything even remotely connected with liberalism and enlightenment. When, on 30 January 1933, Hindenburg appointed him chancellor, Hitler had the chance to suit his actions to his words and to shape Germany in his own image.[5]

Notes

CHAPTER 1. LEGACY OF A MILLENNIUM

1. Geoffrey Barraclough, *Tatsachen der deutschen Geschichte* (Berlin: Weidmannsche Verlag, 1947), orig. *Factors in German History* (Oxford: Blackwell, 1946).
2. Werner Goez, *Translatio Imperii. Ein Beitrag zur Geschichte des Geschichtsdenkens und der politischen Theorien im Mittelalter und in der frühen Neuzeit* (Tübingen: Mohr, 1958), esp. 74 ff.; P. A. van den Baar, *Die kirchliche Lehre der Translatio Imperii Romani bis zur Mitte des 13. Jahrhunderts* (Rome: Gregorian University, 1956), 27 ff.; Horst Dieter Rauh, *Das Bild des Antichrist im Mittelalter: Von Tyconius zum Deutschen Symbolismus*, 2nd edn (Münster: Aschendorff, 1979), 55 ff.; Bernhard Töpfer, *Das kommende Reich des Friedens. Zur Entwicklung chiliastischer Zukunftshoffnungen im Hochmittelalter* (Berlin: Akademie Verlag, 1964); Herfried Münkler, 'Das Reich als politische Macht und politischer Mythos', in *Reich—Nation—Europa. Modelle politischer Ordnung* (Weinheim: Beltz Athenaeum, 1996), 11–59; Willy Marxsen, *Einleitung in das Neue Testament*, 2nd edn (Gütersloh: G. Mohn, 1964), 64, tr. as *Introduction to the New Testament* (Oxford: Blackwell, 1968).
3. Otto Bischof von Freising, *Chronik oder die Geschichte der zwei Staaten*, trans Adolf Schmidt (Latin–German), ed. Walter Lammers, 5th edn (Darmstadt: Wissenschaftliche Buchgesellschaft, 1990), 464–5, tr. as *The Two Cities: A Chronicle of Universal History to the Year 1146 AD*, tr. Charles Christopher Mierow, ed. Austin P. Evans and Charles Knapp (New York: Columbia University Press, 1928).
4. Karl Ferdinand Werner, 'Les nations et le sentiment national dans l'Europe médiévale', *Revue Historique*, 244 (1970), 285–304; id., 'Mittelalter' in the article 'Volk, Nation, Nationalismus', in *Geschichtliche Grundbegriffe. Historisches Lexikon zur politisch-sozialen Sprache in Deutschland*, ed. Otto Brunner, Werner Conze, Reinhart Koselleck, vii (Stuttgart: E. Klett, 1992), 171–281 (esp. 199 ff.); the article 'Reich', ibid., v. 423–508; Joachim Ehlers, 'Schriftkultur, Ethnogenese und Nationsbildung in ottonischer Zeit', *Frühmittelalterliche Studien*, 23 (1989), 302–17; Johannes Fried, *Der Weg in die Geschichte. Die Ursprünge Deutschlands bis 1024* (Berlin: Propyläen Verlag, 1994), esp. 9 ff., 853 ff.; Peter Moraw, 'Vom deutschen Zusammenhalt in älterer Zeit', in *Identität und Geschichte*, ed. Matthias Werner (Weimar: Böhlau, 1997), 27–59; Percy Ernst Schramm, *Kaiser, Rom und Renovatio. Studien und Texte zur Geschichte des römischen Erneuerungsgedankens vom Ende des karolingischen Reiches bis zum Investiturstreit*, 2 vols. (Berlin: B. G. Teubner, 1929), i. 12 ff.; Gerd Tellenbach, *Libertas. Kirche und Weltordnung im Zeitalter des Investiturstreites* (Stuttgart: W. Kohlkammer, 1936), 16 ff., tr. as *Church, State, and Christian Society at the Time of the Investiture Contest* (Oxford: Blackwell, 1940).
5. Karl Ferdinand Werner, 'Das hochmittelalterliche Imperium im politischen Bewusstsein Frankreichs (10.–12. Jahrhundert)', *HZ* 200 (1965), 2–60 (esp. 50 ff.); Heinz Löwe, 'Kaisertum und Abendland in ottonischer und frühsalischer Zeit', *HZ* 196 (1963), 529–62.

6. *The Letters of John of Salisbury*, ed. W. J. Millor and H. E. Butler (Latin-English), i (London, 1955), 206 (letter 124, to Master Ralph of Sarre, June/July 1160); a German translation can be found in *Das Reich des Mittelalters*, 3rd edn, ed. Joachim Leuschner (Stuttgart 1972), 20–1; Horst Fuhrmann, ' "Wer hat die Deutschen zu Richtern über die Völker bestellt?" Die Deutschen als Ärgernis im Mittelalter', *GWU* 46 (1995), 625–41.
7. Rauh, *Bild* (note 2), 365 ff.; Friedrich Heer, *Die Tragödie des Heiligen Reiches* (Stuttgart: W. Kohlhammer, 1952), 118 ff., 141 ff., 240 ff.; Gottfried Koch, *Auf dem Weg zum Sacrum Imperium. Studien zur ideologischen Herrschaftsbegründung der deutschen Zentralgewalt im 11. u. 12. Jahrhundert* (Berlin: Akademie Verlag, 1972), 149 ff.; Timothy Reuter, 'The Medieval German "Sonderweg"? The Empire and its Rulers in the High Middle Ages', in *King and Kingship in Medieval Europe*, ed. Anne Duggan (London: 1993), 179–211; Karl Langosch, *Geistliche Spiele. Lateinische Dramen mit deutschen Versen* (Darmstadt: Wissenschaftliche Buchgesellschaft, 1957), 179–239 (*Das Spiel vom deutschen Kaiser und vom Antichrist* [*Ludus de Antichristo*]).
8. Karl Jordan, 'Investiturstreit und frühe Stauferzeit (1056–1197)', *Frühzeit und Mittelalter*, 9th edn, ed. Herbert Grundmann (= Bruno Gebhardt, *Handbuch der deutschen Geschichte*, i) (Stuttgart: Union Verlag, 1970), 223–425 (391 ff).
9. Hartmut Boockmann, *Stauferzeit und spätes Mittelalter. Deutschland 1125–1517* (Berlin: Siedler, 1987), 165 ff.
10. Geoffrey Barraclough, *Die mittelalterlichen Grundlagen des modernen Deutschland* (Weimar: Herman Böhlaus Nachfolger, 1955), 195 ff., orig. *The Origins of Modern Germany* (Oxford: Blackwell, 1946).
11. Alexander von Roes, *Schriften*, ed. Herbert Grundmann and Hermann Heimpel (Monumenta Germaniae Historica [MGH]. *Staatsschriften des späteren Mittelalters*, i. *Die Schriften des Alexander von Roes und des Engelbert von Admont, 1. Stück: Alexander von Roes*) (Stuttgart: A. Hiersemann, 1958), 91–148 (*Memoriale de prerogativa Romani Imperii*, 126–7). A German translation can be found in Alexander von Roes, *Schriften*, ed. Herbert Grundmann and Hermann Heimpel, Deutsches Mittelalter. Kritische Studientexte der MGH, 4 (Weimar, 1949), 18–67 (49); Hermann Heimpel, 'Alexander von Roes und das deutsche Selbstbewusstsein des 13. Jahrhunderts', *Deutsches Mittelalter* (Leipzig, 1941), 79–110.
12. Leuschner, *Reich* (note 6), 38–9.
13. Eugen Rosenstock-Huessy, *Die europäischen Revolutionen und der Charakter der Nationen*, 1st edn (1931), 3rd edn (Stuttgart: W. Kohlhammer, 1961), 131 ff.
14. Ibid. 239.
15. Marsilius von Padua, *Der Verteidiger des Friedens (Defensor Pacis)*, ed. Horst Kusch, based on the trans by Walter Kunzmann (Latin–German) (Berlin: Rütten & Loening, 1958), part 2, 1078–85, tr. as *The Defender of Peace*, tr. and introd. Alan Gewirth (New York, Harper & Row, 1967); Wilhelm von Ockham, *Texte zur politischen Theorie. Exzerpte aus dem Dialogus*, selected, trans., and ed. Jürgen Miethke (Latin–German) (Stuttgart, 1995), 226–309; William of Ockham, *On the Power of Emperors and Popes*, ed. and trans. Annabel S. Brett (Durham: University of Durham; Sterling, VA: Thoemmes Press, 1998).
16. Alois Dempf, *Sacrum Imperium. Geschichts- und Staatsphilosophie des Mittelalters und der politischen Renaissance* (Munich: Oldenbourg, 1929), 544; Ernst Troeltsch, *Die Soziallehren der christlichen Kirchen und Gruppen*, in *Gesammelte Schriften*, i (Tübingen:

J. C. B. Mohr, 1912), 420, 432 ff., 794 ff., 858 ff., tr. as *The Social Teaching of the Christian Churches* (Chicago: University of Chicago Press, 1931, repr. 1981).

17. Eberhard Isenmann, 'Kaiser, Reich und deutsche Nation am Ausgang des 15. Jahrhunderts', *Ansätze und Diskontinuität deutscher Nationsbildung im Mittelalter*, ed. Joachim Ehlers (Sigmaringen: Thorbecke, 1989), 145–246 (esp. 155 ff.); Alfred Schröcker, *Die Deutsche Nation. Beobachtungen zur politischen Propaganda des ausgehenden 15. Jahrhunderts* (Lübeck: Matthiesen Verlag, 1974), esp. 116 ff.; Ulrich Nonn, 'Heiliges Römisches Reich Deutscher Nation. Zum Nationen-Begriff im 15. Jahrhundert', *Zeitschrift für Historische Forschung*, 9 (1982), 129–42.
18. Heinz Angermeier, *Die Reichsreform 1410–1555. Die Staatsproblematik in Deutschland zwischen Mittelalter und Gegenwart* (Munich: C. H. Beck, 1984); Georg Schmidt, *Geschichte des Alten Reiches. Staat und Nation in der Frühen Neuzeit 1495–1806* (Munich: C. H. Beck, 1999), 33 ff. (the ideas of the '*komplementärer Reichs-Staat*', the '*Verstaatung des Alten Reiches*' around 1500 and of the Old Reich as state of the German nation); Wolfgang Reinhard, *Geschichte der Staatsgewalt. Eine vergleichende Verfassungsgeschichte Europas von den Anfängen bis zur Gegenwart* (Munich: C. H. Beck, 1999), 52 ff.
19. Max Wehrli, 'Der Nationalgedanke im deutschen und schweizerischen Humanismus', *Nationalismus in Germanistik und Dichtung. Dokumentation des Germanistentages in München vom 17.–22. Oktober 1966*, ed. Benno von Wiese and Rudolf Henss (Berlin: E. Schmidt, 1967), 126–43 (quote: 131); Goez, *Translatio* (note 2), 248–57; Bernd Schönemann, 'Frühe Neuzeit und 19. Jahrhundert', in the article 'Volk, Nation, Nationalismus' (note 4), 281–431 (esp. 288 ff.); Herfried Münkler et al., *Nationenbildung. Die Nationalisierung Europas im Diskurs humanistischer Intellektueller. Italien und Deutschland* (Berlin: Akademie Verlag, 1998); id., 'Nation als politische Idee im frühneuzeitlichen Europa', *Nation und Literatur im Europa der Frühen Neuzeit*, ed. Klaus Garber (Tübingen: Niemeyer, 1989), 56–86; Wolfgang Hardtwig, 'Ulrich von Hutten. Zum Verhältnis von Individuum, Stand und Nation in der Reformationszeit', in *Nationalismus und Bürgerkultur in Deutschland 1500–1914* (Göttingen: Vandenhoeck & Ruprecht, 1994), 15–33; Frank L. Borchardt, *German Antiquity in Renaissance Myth* (Baltimore: Johns Hopkins University Press, 1971); Ludwig Krapf, *Germanenmythos und Reichsideologie. Frühhumanistische Rezeptionsweisen der taciteischen 'Germania'* (Tübingen: Niemeyer, 1979).
20. Martin Luther, *An den christlichen Adel deutscher Nation von des christlichen Standes Besserung* (1520), in *D. Martin Luthers Werke*, complete critical edition, vi (Weimar, 1888), 381–469 (462–5), tr. as *To the Christian Nobility of the German Nation concerning the Reform of the Christian Estate* (1520), in *Luther's Works* (St Louis and Philadephia: Concordia Publishing House and Fortress Press, 1958–), xliv. 123–217 (207–10). For a modern German translation, see Martin Luther, *An den christlichen Adel deutscher Nation und andere Schriften*, 2nd edn (Stuttgart, 1964), 98–103.
21. Georg Wilhelm Friedrich Hegel, *Vorlesungen über die Philosophie der Geschichte*, in *Sämtliche Werke*, xi, 3rd edn (Stuttgart: Fromman, 1949), 519, 521 ff., 524, tr. as *The Philosophy of History*, trans. J. Sibree (New York: Wiley, 1944), 414–17.
22. Karl Marx, 'Zur Kritik der Hegelschen Rechtsphilosophie. Einleitung', Karl Marx and Friedrich Engels, *Werke* (= MEW; Berlin, 1956–), i. 385–6, tr. as 'Contribution to the Critique of Hegel's Philosphy of Law', Karl Marx/Friedrich Engels, *Collected Works* (= MECW; International Publishers: New York, 1975–2004), iii. 175–87 (182).

23. Friedrich Nietzsche, *Der Antichrist*, in *Werke* (complete critical edition, ed. Giorgio Colli and Mazzino Montinari), pt 6 (Berlin, 1969), iii. 248–9, tr. in *Complete Works*, ed. Oscar Levy and Robert Guppy (New York: Russell & Russell, 1964), xvi. 228–9.
24. Marx, 'Kritik' (note 22), 391; Friedrich Engels, *Zum 'Bauernkrieg'* (1884), MEW, xxi. 402, tr. as; 'On *The Peasants' War*', MECW, xxvi. 554–5; Marx, 'Critique' (note 22), 187.
25. Peter Blickle, *Die Revolution von 1525*, 2nd edn (Munich: Oldenbourg, 1981), tr. as *The Revolution of 1525: The German Peasants' War from a New Perspective* (Baltimore: Johns Hopkins University Press, 1981), id., *Gemeindereformation. Die Menschen des 16. Jahrhunderts auf dem Weg zum Heil* (Munich: Oldenbourg, 1985), tr. as *Communal Reformation: The Quest for Salvation in Sixteenth-Century Germany* (Atlantic Highlands, NJ: Humanities Press, 1992); Richard von Dülmen, *Reformation als Revolution. Soziale Bewegung und religiöser Radikalismus in der deutschen Reformation* (Munich: Deutscher Taschenbuch Verlag, 1977).
26. Rosenstock-Huessy, *Revolutionen* (note 13), 234–5.
27. Heinz Schilling, *Aufbruch und Krise. Deutschland 1517–1648*, 2nd edn (Berlin: Siedler, 1994), 184 ff.
28. Troeltsch, *Soziallehren* (note 16), 518.
29. Ibid. 519, 684.
30. Franz Borkenau, 'Luther: Ost oder West', in *Zwei Abhandlungen zur deutschen Geschichte* (Frankfurt: V. Klostermann, 1947), 45–75 (59).
31. Ibid. 74; Helmuth Plessner, *Die verspätete Nation. Über die politische Verführbarkeit bürgerlichen Geistes* (1st edn under the title *Das Schicksal deutschen Geistes im Ausgang seiner bürgerlichen Epoche* (Zurich, 1935)) (Stuttgart: W. Kohlhammer, 1959), 58 ff.
32. Martin Luther, *Von den Juden und ihren Lügen* (1543), in *Werke* (note 20), liii (Weimar, 1920), 413–552 (esp. 522 ff.; quote: 479), tr. as *On the Jews and their Lies* (1543), in *Works* (note 20), xlvii. 121–306 (esp. 267 ff.; quote: 213–14). Klaus Deppermann, 'Judenhass und Judenfreundschaft im frühen Protestantismus', *Die Juden als Minderheit in der Geschichte*, ed. Bernd Martin and Ernst Schulin (Munich: Deutscher Taschenbuch Verlag, 1981), 110–30; Heiko A. Oberman, *Wurzeln des Antisemitismus. Christenangst und Judenplage im Zeitalter von Humanismus und Reformation*, 2nd edn (Berlin: Severin und Siedler, 1983), 56 ff., 125 ff., tr. as *The Roots of anti-Semitism in the Age of Renaissance and Reformation* (Philadelphia: Fortress Press, 1984); Joshua Trachtenberg, *The Devil and the Jews: The Medieval Conception of the Jew and its Relation to Modern Antisemitism* (New Haven: Yale University Press, 1943).
33. Leopold von Ranke, *Deutsche Geschichte im Zeitalter der Reformation*, in *Leopold von Ranke's Werke* (complete edition of the Deutsche Akademie) (Munich: Duncker & Humblot, 1925), i. 4, tr. as *History of the Reformation in Germany* (New York: F. Unger, 1905, repr. of 1966); Rosenstock-Huessy, *Revolutionen* (note 13), 224; Paul Joachimsen, *Vom deutschen Volk zum deutschen Staat. Eine Geschichte des deutschen Nationalbewusstseins* (1916), 3rd edn, ed. and updated Joachim Leuschner (Göttingen: Vandenhoeck & Ruprecht, 1956), 25 ff.; Heinrich Lutz, 'Die deutsche Nation zu Beginn der Neuzeit. Fragen nach dem Gelingen und Scheitern deutscher Einheit im 16. Jahrhundert', *HZ* 234 (1982), 529–59.
34. Schilling, *Aufbruch* (note 27), 243.
35. Max Weber, 'Die protestantische Ethik und der Geist des Kapitalismus', *Archiv für Sozialwissenschaft und Sozialpolitik*, 20 (1905), 1–54; 21 (1905), 1–110, tr. as *The Protestant Ethic and the Spirit of Capitalism* (New York: Scribner, 1958); Alfred

Müller-Armack, *Genealogie der Wirtschaftsstile. Die geistesgeschichtlichen Ursprünge der Staats- und Wirtschaftsformen bis zum Ausgang des 18. Jahrhunderts* (Stuttgart: W. Kohlhammer, 1941); Herbert Lüthy, 'Nochmals: "Calvinismus und Kapitalismus". Über die Irrwege einer sozialhistorischen Diskussion' (1961), repr. in *Gesellschaft in der industriellen Revolution*, ed. Rudolf Braun et al. (Cologne: Kiepenheuer & Witsch, 1973), 18–36; Hartmut Lehmann, 'Asketischer Protestantismus und ökonomischer Rationalismus: Die Weber-These nach zwei Generationen', in *Max Webers Sicht des okzidentalen Christentums*, ed. Wolfgang Schluchter (Frankfurt: Suhrkamp, 1988), 529–53.

36. Schilling, *Aufbruch* (note 27), 282 ff., 412 ff.; id., 'Nationale Identität und Konfession in der europäischen Neuzeit', in *Nationale und kulturelle Identität. Studien zur Entwicklung des kollektiven Bewusstseins in der Neuzeit*, i, ed. Bernhard Giesen (Frankfurt: Suhrkamp, 1991), 192–252.
37. Johannes Burkhardt, *Der Dreissigjährige Krieg* (Frankfurt: Suhrkamp, 1992), 30 ff.; Georg Schmidt, *Der Dreissigjährige Krieg* (Munich: C. H. Beck, 1995); Günter Barudio, *Der Teutsche Krieg 1618–1648* (Frankfurt: Fischer, 1988); Adam Wandruszka, *Reichspatriotismus und Reichspolitik zur Zeit des Prager Friedens von 1635. Eine Studie zur Geschichte des deutschen Nationalbewusstseins* (Cologne: H. Böhlaus Nachfolger, 1955).
38. Christoph Dipper, *Deutsche Geschichte 1648–1784* (Frankfurt: Suhrkamp, 1991), 263 ff.; Schilling, *Aufbruch* (note 27), 396, 436 ff.
39. Burkhardt, *Dreissigjähriger Krieg* (note 37), 90 ff.
40. Samuel von Pufendorf, *Die Verfassung des Deutschen Reiches* (Latin–German), ed. and trans. Horst Denzer (Frankfurt: Insel, 1994), 198–9; Norbert Elias, *Über den Prozess der Zivilisation. Soziogenetische und psychogenetische Untersuchungen*, 2 vols., 1st edn (1939), 18th edn (Frankfurt: Suhrkamp, 1993), ii. 129 ff., tr. as *The Civilizing Process* (Oxford: Blackwell, 1994); Rudolf Vierhaus, *Staaten und Stände. Vom Westfälischen zum Hubertusburger Frieden 1648–1763* (Berlin: Propyläen Verlag, 1984), 22 ff.
41. Johann Gustav Droysen, *Geschichte der preussischen Politik*, ii, pt 2 (Leipzig: Veit, 1870), 436.
42. Otto Hintze, 'Kalvinismus und Staatsräson in Brandenburg zu Beginn des 17. Jahrhunderts', in id., *Geist und Epochen der preussischen Geschichte. Gesammelte Abhandlungen*, ed. Fritz Hartung (Leipzig: Koehler & Amelang, 1943), 289–346 (in the order of the quotes: 289, 324–5, 345, 315–16, 302–3).
43. Müller-Armack, *Genealogie* (note 35), 147.
44. Hintze, *Kalvinismus* (note 42), 300, 315.
45. Troeltsch, *Soziallehren* (note 16), 599–600.
46. Otto Hintze, 'Die Hohenzollern und der Adel', in *Geist* (note 42), 38–63; Hans Rosenberg, *Bureaucracy, Aristocracy, and Autocracy: The Prussian Experience* (Cambridge, MA: Harvard University Press, 1958).
47. Otto Büsch, *Militärsystem und Sozialleben im alten Preussen 1713–1807. Die Anfänge der sozialen Militarisierung der preussisch-deutschen Gesellschaft* (Berlin: De Gruyter, 1952), 164–5, tr. as *Military System and Social Life in Old Regime Prussia, 1713–1807: The Beginning of the Social Militarization of Prusso-German Society* (Atlantic Highlands, NJ: Humanities Press, 1997).
48. Heinz Schilling, *Höfe und Allianzen. Deutschland 1648–1763*, 2nd edn (Berlin: Siedler, 1994), 392 ff.; Carl Hinrichs, *Preussentum und Pietismus. Der Pietismus in Brandenburg-Preussen als religiös-soziale Reformbewegung* (Göttingen: Vandenhoeck & Ruprecht, 1971); Richard L. Gawthrop, *Pietism and the Making of Eighteenth-Century Prussia* (Cambridge: Cambridge University Press, 1993); Gerhard Kaiser, *Pietismus und*

Patriotismus im literarischen Deutschland. Ein Beitrag zum Problem der Säkularisation (Wiesbaden: F. Steiner, 1961), 39 ff.; Koppel S. Pinson, *Pietism as a Factor in the Rise of German Nationalism* (New York: Octagon, 1934); Hartmut Lehmann, 'Pietism and Nationalism: The Relationship between Protestant Revivalism and National Renewal in Nineteenth-Century Germany', *Church History*, 51 (1982), 39–53; *Geschichte des Pietismus*, ed. Martin Brecht et al. (Göttingen: Vandenhoeck & Ruprecht, 1993–).

49. Sibylle Badstübner-Gröger et al., *Hugenotten in Berlin* (Berlin: Nicolai, 1988), 14 ff.
50. Schilling, *Aufbruch* (note 27), 415 ff.
51. Ibid. 303 ff.
52. Theodor Schieder, *Friedrich der Grosse. Ein Königtum der Widersprüche* (Berlin: Propyläen Verlag, 1983), tr. as *Frederick the Great* (London, New York: Longman, 2000); Ingrid Mittenzwei, *Friedrich II. von Preussen* (Berlin: Deutscher Verlag, 1979); Rudolf Augstein, *Preussens Friedrich und die Deutschen* (Frankfurt: S. Fischer, 1968).
53. Rudolf von Thadden, *Fragen an Preussen. Zur Geschichte eines aufgehobenen Staates* (Munich: C. H. Beck, 1981), 58–9, 167; Hans Joachim Schoeps, *Preussen. Geschichte eines Staates* (Berlin: Propyläen Verlag, 1966), 98; Schilling, *Höfe* (note 48), 431.
54. Reinhart Koselleck, *Preussen zwischen Reform und Revolution. Allgemeines Landrecht, Verwaltung und soziale Bewegung von 1791 bis 1848* (Stuttgart: Klett, 1967), 24–5.
55. Alexis de Tocqueville, *L'Ancien Régime et la Révolution*, in *Œuvres complètes* (Paris: Gallimard, 1952), ii, pt 1. 269, tr. as *The Old Régime and the Revolution* (Chicago: University of Chicago Press, 1955), i. 262.
56. Schilling, *Höfe* (note 48), 320 ff.; Horst Möller, *Fürstenstaat oder Bürgernation. Deutschland 1763–1815* (Berlin: Siedler, 1989), 308 ff.
57. Johann Wolfgang von Goethe, *Aus meinem Leben. Dichtung und Wahrheit*, pt 1, bk II, in *Werke*, Weimar edition (Munich: Deutscher Taschenbuch Verlag, 1987), xxvi. 71, tr. as *From My Life* (New York: Suhrkamp Publishers, 1987); Theodor Schieder, 'Friedrich der Grosse—eine Integrationsfigur des deutschen Nationalbewusstseins im 18. Jahrhundert?', in *Nationalismus in vorindustrieller Zeit*, ed. Otto Dann (Munich: Oldenbourg, 1986), 113–27.
58. Thomas Abbt, *Vom Tode für das Vaterland*, in *Vermischte Werke* (repr. Hildesheim: G. Olms, 1978), i. 17; Christoph Prignitz, *Vaterlandsliebe und Freiheit. Deutscher Patriotismus von 1750 bis 1850* (Wiesbaden: Steiner, 1981), 17; Benjamin W. Redekop, 'Thomas Abbt and the Formation of an Enlightened German "Public" ', *Journal of the History of Ideas*, 58 (1997), 81–103.
59. Harm Klueting, ' "Bürokratischer Patriotismus". Aspekte des Patriotismus im theresianisch-josephinischen Österreich', *Patriotismus*, ed. Günter Birtsch, *Aufklärung* 4/2 (1991), 37–52.
60. Christoph Martin Wieland, 'National-Poesie' (1773), in *Sämmtliche Werke* (Leipzig: G. J. Göschen, 1839–40), xxxv. 327–35 (327); Prignitz, *Vaterlandsliebe* (note 58), 7 (Wieland); Rudolf Vierhaus, ' "Patriotismus"-Begriff und Realität einer moralisch-politischen Haltung', in *Deutsche patriotische und gemeinnützige Gesellschaften*, ed. id. (Munich: Kraus International Publ., 1980), 9–29 (14: Goethe, Möser, Nicolai); Horst Möller, *Aufklärung in Preussen. Der Verleger, Publizist und Geschichtsschreiber Friedrich Nicolai* (Berlin: Colloquium Verlag, 1974), 565 ff.
61. Pufendorf, *Verfassung* (note 40), 46–7; Hermann Conrad, *Deutsche Rechtsgeschichte*, ii (Karlsruhe: C. F. Müller, 1966), 113 ff.; Jürgen Luh, *Unheiliges Römisches Reich. Der konfessionelle Gegensatz 1648 bis 1806* (Potsdam: Verlag für Berlin-Brandenburg,

1995); Reinhard Stauber, 'Nationalismus vor dem Nationalismus? Eine Bestandsaufnahme der Forschung zu "Nation" und "Nationalismus" in der Frühen Neuzeit', *GWU* 47 (1996), 139–65; Manfred Jacobs, 'Die Entwicklung des deutschen Nationalgedankens von der Reformation bis zum deutschen Idealismus', in *Volk—Nation—Vaterland. Der deutsche Protestantismus und der Nationalismus*, ed. Horst Zillessen (Gütersloh: G. Mohn, 1970), 51–110.

62. Pufendorf, *Verfassung* (note 40), 46 ff.; Christoph Martin Wieland, 'Über Deutschen Patriotismus. Betrachtungen, Fragen und Zweifel' (May 1793), in *Werke* (note 60), 245–59 (252); Prignitz, *Vaterlandsliebe* (note 58), 7 ff.; Gertrude Lübbe-Wolff, 'Die Bedeutung der Lehre von den vier Weltreichen für das Staatsrecht des römisch-deutschen Reichs', *Der Staat*, 23 (1984), 387–91; Notker Hammerstein, ' "Imperium Romanum cum omnibus suis qualitatibus ad Germanos est translatum". Das vierte Weltreich in der Lehre der Reichsjuristen', *Zeitschrift für historische Forschung*, suppl. 3 (1987), 187–202.

63. Reinhard Rürup, *Johann Jacob Moser. Pietismus und Reform* (Wiesbaden: Steiner, 1965), esp. 151–2; Notker Hammerstein, 'Das politische Denken Friedrich Carl von Mosers', *HZ* 212 (1971), 316–38; Michael Stolleis, 'Reichspublizistik und Reichspatriotismus vom 16. zum 18. Jahrhundert', *Aufklärung*, 4 (1989), 7–23; Karl Otmar Freiherr von Aretin, 'Reichspatriotismus', in *Patriotismus*, ed. Birtsch (note 59), 25–36; id., *Das Alte Reich 1648–1806*, 3 vols. (Stuttgart: Klett Cotta, 1993–); John G. Gagliardo, *Reich and Nation: The Holy Roman Empire as Idea and Reality, 1763–1806* (Bloomington: Indiana University Press, 1980), esp. 49 ff. The quotes: Friedrich Carl von Moser, *Von dem Deutschen Nationalgeist* (1766; repr. Selb: Notos, 1976), 19, 21, 40 (emphases in the original).

64. Wolfgang Hardtwig, 'Vom Elitebewusstsein zur Massenbewegung. Frühformen des Nationalismus in Deutschland 1500–1840', in *Nationalismus* (note 19), 34–54 (quote from Gottsched: 44; from Hardtwig: 46); Hagen Schulze, *Staat und Nation in der europäischen Geschichte* (Munich: C. H. Beck, 1994), 108 ff., 142 ff.; Otto Dann, *Nation und Nationalismus in Deutschland 1770–1990* (Munich: C. H. Beck, 1990), 28 ff.; Bernhard Giesen and Kay Junge, 'Vom Patriotismus zum Nationalismus. Zur Evolution der "Deutschen Kulturnation" ', in *Identität*, ed. Giesen (note 36), 255–303; Helga Schultz, 'Mythos und Aufklärung. Frühformen des Nationalismus in Deutschland', *HZ* 261 (1996), 31–67; *Dichter und ihre Nation*, ed. Helmut Scheuer (Frankfurt: Suhrkamp, 1993); Winfried Woesler, 'Die Idee der deutschen Nationalliteratur in der zweiten Hälfte des 18. Jahrhunderts', *Nation*, ed. Garber (note 19), 716–33; Hans Peter Herrmann et al., *Machtphantasie Deutschland. Nationalismus, Männlichkeit und Fremdenhass im Vaterlandsdiskurs deutscher Schriftsteller des 18. Jahrhunderts* (Frankfurt: Suhrkamp, 1996); Jörg Echternkamp, *Aufstieg des deutschen Nationalismus (1770–1840)* (Frankfurt: Campus, 1998), 41 ff.

65. Conrad Wiedemann, 'Deutsche Klassik und nationale Identität. Eine Revision der Sonderwegs-Frage', *Klassik im Vergleich. Normativität und Historizität europäischer Klassiken*, ed. Wilhelm Vosskamp (Stuttgart: Metzler, 1993), 541–69 (547–8); Franz Josef Worstbrock, 'Translatio artium. Über Herkunft und Entwicklung einer kulturhistorischen Theorie', *Archiv für Kulturgeschichte*, 47 (1965), 1–22; Manfred Landfester, 'Griechen und Deutsche: Der Mythos einer "Wahlverwandtschaft" ', in *Mythos und Nation. Studien zur Entwicklung des kollektiven Bewusstseins in der Neuzeit*, iii. ed. Helmut Berding (Frankfurt: Suhrkamp, 1996), 198–219.

66. Gotthold Ephraim Lessing, *Hamburgische Dramaturgie*, parts 101–4, in *Werke*, iv (Munich: C. Hanser, 1973), 698; Goethe, *Werke* (note 57), v. 218.
67. Johann Gottfried Herder, *Briefe zur Beförderung der Humanität*, in *Werke in zehn Bänden*, vii (Frankfurt: Deutscher Klassiker Verlag, 1991), 687 (letter 115 [1797]); id., *Ideen zur Philosophie der Geschichte der Menschheit*, ibid. vi (Frankfurt: Deutscher Klassiker Verlag, 1989), 630, 639 (pt III, 15, I, II); id., *Philosophical Writings* (Cambridge: Cambridge University Press, 2002); id., *Reflections on the Philosophy of the History of Mankind* (Chicago: University of Chicago Press, 1968).
68. Immanuel Kant, *Reflexionen zur Anthropologie*, in *Gesammelte Schriften* (Akademie edn), xv (Berlin: G. Reimer, 1913), 590–1; Schönemann, *Frühe Neuzeit* (note 19), 320.
69. Johann Wolfgang von Goethe, *Faust. Der Tragödie erster und zweiter Teil*, pt 1 (Auerbach's Keller in Leipzig), in *Werke* (note 57), xiv. 99, tr. as *Faust*, pt 1, trans. Randall Jarrell (New York: Farrar, Straus & Giroux, 1976); Rudolf Schlögl, 'Die patriotisch-gemeinnützigen Gesellschaften. Organisation, Sozialstruktur, Tätigkeitsfelder', in *Aufklärungsgesellschaften*, ed. Helmut Reinalter (Frankfurt: P. Lang, 1993), 61–81.
70. Herder, *Briefe* (note 67), 305 letter 57 [1795]; supplement: 'Haben wir noch das Publikum und Vaterland der Alten?'); Otto Dann, 'Herder und die Deutsche Bewegung', in Gerhard Sauder, *Johann Gottfried Herder 1744–1803* (Hamburg: F. Meiner, 1987), 308–40; Harro Segeberg, 'Germany', in *Nationalism in the Age of the French Revolution*, ed. Otto Dann and John Dinwiddy (London: Hambledon Press, 1988), 137–56.
71. Wilhelm Dilthey, 'Die dichterische und philosophische Bewegung in Deutschland 1770–1800', in *Die geistige Welt. Einleitung in die Philosophie des Lebens. Gesammelte Schriften*, v, 6th edn (Stuttgart: Teubner, 1974), 12–27 (13).
72. Dann, 'Herder' (note 70), 324 ff.; Wilhelm Abel, *Massenarmut und Hungerkrisen im vorindustriellen Deutschland* (Göttingen: Vandenhoeck & Ruprecht, 1972), esp. 191 ff., 252 ff.; R. R. Palmer, *The Age of Democratic Revolution: A Political History of Europe and America, 1760–1800*, 2 vols. (Princeton: Princeton University Press, 1964); Eric J. Hobsbawm, *The Age of Revolution: Europe 1789–1848* (London: Weidenfeld and Nicolson, 1962), tr. as *Europäische Revolutionen 1789–1848* (Zurich: Kindler, 1973); Reinhart Koselleck, *Kritik und Krise. Eine Studie zur Pathogenese der bürgerlichen Welt* (Freiburg: K. Alber, 1959); id., 'Introduction', *Geschichtliche Grundbegriffe* (note 4), i. pp. xii–xxvii (for 'Sattelzeit', see from about 1750); Jürgen Habermas, *Strukturwandel der Öffentlichkeit. Untersuchungen zu einer Kategorie der bürgerlichen Gesellschaft* (Neuwied: Luchterhand, 1961), esp. 104 ff., tr. as *The Structural Transformation of the Public Sphere: An Inquiry into a Category of Bourgeois Society* (Cambridge, MA: MIT Press, 1989).

CHAPTER 2. HAMPERED BY PROGRESS 1789–1830

1. Georg Wilhelm Friedrich Hegel, *Vorlesungen über die Philosophie der Geschichte*, in *Sämtliche Werke*, 3rd edn, xi (repr. Stuttgart: Fromman, 1949), 557–8, tr. as *The Philosophy of History*, trans J. Sibree (New York: Wiley, 1944), 447; Joachim Ritter, *Hegel und die französische Revolution* (Cologne: Westdeutscher Verlag, 1957), tr. as *Hegel and the French Revolution: Essays on the Philosophy of Right* (Cambridge, MA: MIT Press, 1982).
2. Rudolf Vierhaus, 'Montesquieu in Deutschland. Zur Geschichte seiner Wirkung als politischer Schriftsteller im 18. Jahrhundert', in *Deutschland im 18. Jahrhundert.*

Politische Verfassung, soziales Gefüge, geistige Bewegungen (Göttingen: Vandenhoeck & Ruprecht, 1987), 9–32; id., 'Politisches Bewusstsein in Deutschland vor 1789', ibid. 183–201; id., ' "Sie und nicht wir." Deutsche Urteile über den Ausbruch der Französischen Revolution', ibid. 202–15.

3. Christoph Martin Wieland, 'Kosmopolitische Adresse an die Französische Nationalversammlung, von Eleutherius Philoceltes' (Oct. 1789), in *Sämtliche Werke*, xxxi (Leipzig: G. J. Göschen, 1857), 30–58 (58); id., 'Unparteiische Betrachtungen über die Staatsrevolution in Frankreich' (May 1790), ibid. 69–101 (73); id., 'Zufällige Gedanken über die Abschaffung des Erbadels in Frankreich' (July 1790), ibid. 102–25 (123–4); id., 'Worte zur rechten Zeit und an die politischen und moralischen Gewalthaber. Nachträge' (Jan. 1793), ibid. 319–25 (320); Irmtraut Sahmland, *Christoph Martin Wieland und die deutsche Nation. Zwischen Patriotismus, Kosmopolitismus und Griechentum* (Tübingen: M. Niemeyer, 1990).
4. Johann Gottfried Herder, *Briefe die Fortschritte der Humanität betreffend* (1792), in *Werke in zehn Bänden*, vii (Frankfurt: Deutscher Klassiker Verlag, 1991), 774 (letter 13), 779 (letter 16), 780 (letter 17; emphases in original), tr. in *Philosophical Writings* (Cambridge: Cambridge University Press, 2002); Hans-Wolf Jäger, 'Herder und die Französische Revolution', in *Johann Gottfried Herder 1744–1803*, ed. Gerhard Sauder (Hamburg: F. Meiner, 1987), 299–307.
5. Georg Forster, 'Darstellung der Revolution in Mainz' (1793), in *Werke. Sämtliche Schriften, Tagebücher, Briefe*, x. *Revolutionsschriften 1792/93* (Berlin: Akademie Verlag, 1990), 505–91 (556); Volker Mehnert, *Protestantismus und radikale Spätaufklärung. Die Beurteilung Luthers und der Reformation durch aufgeklärte deutsche Schriftsteller zur Zeit der Französischen Revolution* (Munich: Minerva, 1982), 52–3 (Forster), 55, 117 (Rebmann); Walter Grab, *Norddeutsche Jakobiner. Demokratische Bestrebungen zur Zeit der ersten französischen Republik* (Hamburg: Europäische Verlagsanstalt, 1967); Heinrich Scheel, *Süddeutsche Jakobiner. Klassenkämpfe und republikanische Bestrebungen zur Zeit der Französischen Revolution* (Berlin: Akademie Verlag, 1962); Franz Dumont, *Die Mainzer Republik 1792/93. Studien zur Revolutionierung in Rheinhessen und der Pfalz* (Alzey: Verlag der Rheinhessischen Druckwerkstätte, 1993); Wolfang Reinbold, *Mythenbildungen und Nationalismus. 'Deutsche Jakobiner' zwischen Revolution und Reaktion (1789–1800)* (Bern: Lang, 1999); Jacques Droz, *L'Allemagne et la Révolution Française* (Paris: Presses Universitaries de France, 1949); Volker Press, 'Warum gab es keine deutsche Revolution? Deutschland und das revolutionäre Frankreich', in *Revolution und Krieg. Zur Dynamik historischen Wandels seit dem 18. Jahrhundert*, ed. Dieter Langewiesche (Paderborn: Schöningh, 1989), 67–85; Ernst Wolfgang Becker, *Zeit der Revolution!—Revolution der Zeit? Zeiterfahrungen in Deutschland in der Ära der Revolutionen 1789–1848/49* (Göttingen: Vandenhoeck & Ruprecht, 1999), 37 ff.
6. Friedrich Meinecke, *Das Zeitalter der deutschen Erhebung (1795–1815)* (1906), new (6th) edn (Göttingen: Vandenhoeck & Ruprecht, 1957), 46 (Struensee), tr. as *The Age of German Liberation, 1795–1815* (Berkeley: University of California Press, 1977); Max Braubach, 'Von der Französischen Revolution bis zum Wiener Kongress', in *Von der Französischen Revolution bis zum Ersten Weltkrieg* (= Bruno Gebhardt, *Handbuch der deutschen Geschichte*, iii), 9th edn (Stuttgart: Union Deutsche Verlagsgesellschaft, 1970), 2–96 (35); Reinhart Koselleck, *Preussen zwischen Reform und Revolution. Allgemeines Landrecht, Verwaltung und soziale Bewegung von 1791 bis 1848* (Stuttgart: Klett,

1967); Hanna Schissler, *Preussische Agrargesellschaft im Wandel. Wirtschaftliche, gesellschaftliche und politische Transformationsprozesse von 1763 bis 1847* (Göttingen: Vandenhoeck & Ruprecht, 1978).

7. Immanuel Kant, *Zum ewigen Frieden*, in *Gesammelte Schriften* (Akademie edn; Berlin: G. Reimer, 1900–), viii. 351 ff., 378; id., *Der Streit der Fakultäten*, ibid., vii. 88; id., *Die Metaphysik der Sitten/Rechtslehre*, ibid., vi. 338–42 (§§ 51 and 52; emphases in original); tr. as *Perpetual Peace*, ed. and introd. Lewis White Beck (New York: Liberal Arts Press, 1957); id., *The Conflict of the Faculties*, trans. and introd. Mary J. Gregor (New York: Abaris Books, 1979); id., *The Philosophy of Law: An Exposition of the Fundamental Principles of Jurisprudence as the Science of Right*, trans. W. Hastie (Clifton, NJ: A. M. Kelley, 1974); Karl Vorländer, 'Kants Stellung zur französischen Revolution', *Philosophische Abhandlungen. Festschrift für Hermann Cohen* (Berlin: B. Cassirer, 1912), 247–69; Peter Burg, *Kant und die Französische Revolution* (Berlin: Duncker und Humblot, 1974); Zwi Batscha, 'Bürgerliche Republik und bürgerliche Revolution bei Immanuel Kant', in *Studien zur politischen Theorie des deutschen Frühliberalismus* (Frankfurt: Suhrkamp, 1981), 43–65; Volker Gerhardt, *Immanuel Kants Entwurf 'Zum ewigen Frieden'. Eine Theorie der Politik* (Darmstadt: Wissenschaftliche Buchgesellschaft, 1995), esp. 88–9; Leonard Krieger, *The German Idea of Freedom: History of a Political Tradition* (Boston: Beacon Press, 1957), 86 ff.; Vierhaus, 'Montesquieu' (note 2), 9 ff.; the article 'Demokratie', in *Geschichtliche Grundbegriffe. Historisches Lexikon zur politisch-sozialen Sprache in Deutschland*, ed. Otto Brunner, Reinhart Koselleck, Werner Conze, i (Stuttgart: Klett, 1972), 820–99 (esp. 822 ff.); Hajo Holborn, 'Der deutsche Idealismus in sozialgeschichtlicher Beleuchtung', *Moderne deutsche Sozialgeschichte*, ed. Hans-Ulrich Wehler (Cologne: Kiepenheur und Witsch, 1966), 85–108.

8. Rudolf Stadelmann, 'Deutschland und die westeuropäischen Revolutionen', in *Deutschland und Westeuropa* (Laupheim: Schloss Laupheim-Württemberg, U. Steiner, 1948), 11–33 (28).

9. Edmund Burke/Friedrich Gentz, *Über die Französische Revolution. Betrachtungen und Abhandlungen*, ed. and with an appendix by Hermann Klenner (Berlin: Akademie Verlag, 1990); Friedrich Meinecke, *Weltbürgertum und Nationalstaat. Studien zur Genesis des deutschen Nationalstaates* (1907), in *Sämtliche Werke* (Munich: Oldenbourg, 1957–68), v. 113 ff., tr. as *Cosmopolitanism and the National State* (Princeton: Princeton University Press, 1970); Fritz Valjavec, *Die Entstehung der politischen Strömungen in Deutschland 1770–1815* (Munich: Oldenbourg, 1951), esp. 244 ff.; Frieda Braune, *Edmund Burke in Deutschland. Ein Beitrag zur Geschichte des historisch-politischen Denkens* (Heidelberg: C. Winter, 1917); Golo Mann, *Friedrich von Gentz. Geschichte eines europäischen Staatsmannes* (Zurich: Europa Verlag, 1947), 36 ff.

10. Christoph Martin Wieland, 'Patriotischer Beitrag zu Deutschlands höchstem Flor, veranlasst durch einen im Jahr 1780 gedruckten Beitrag dieses Namens', in *Werke* (note 3), xxxi. 349–68 (364, 365, 367); id., 'Betrachtungen über die gegenwärtige Lage des Vaterlandes', 208–59 (237–8); Vierhaus, 'Montesquieu' (note 2), 9 ff.

11. Heinrich August Winkler, 'Der Nationalismus und seine Funktionen', in *Nationalismus*, ed. id., (Königstein: Verlagsgruppe Athenäum, Hain, Scriptor, Hanstein, 1978), 5–46; Herfried Münkler, 'Nation als politische Idee im frühneuzeitlichen Europa', in *Nation und Literatur im Europa der Frühen Neuzeit*, ed. Klaus Garber (Tübingen: M. Niemeyer, 1989), 56–86; *Nationalismus in vorindustrieller Zeit*, ed. Otto Dann (Munich: Oldenbourg, 1986).

12. Thomas Abbt, *Vom Tode für das Vaterland*, in *Vermischte Werke*, i (repr. Hildesheim: G. Olms, 1978), 51, 62, 70, 72. In the last sentence I (H.A.W.) have corrected the word *Stimme* ('voice'), which is obviously an error, to *Summe* ('sum').
13. Karl Otmar Freiherr v. Aretin, *Heiliges Römisches Reich 1776–1806. Reichsverfassung und Staatssouveränität*, 2 vols. (Wiesbaden: F. Steiner, 1967), i. 318 ff.; John S. Gagliardo, *Reich and Nation: The Holy Roman Empire as Idea and Reality, 1763–1806* (Bloomington: Indiana University Press, 1980), 165 ff.; Horst Möller, *Fürstenstaat oder Bürgernation. Deutschland 1763–1815* (Berlin: Siedler, 1989), 532 ff.; Georg Schmidt, *Geschichte des Alten Reiches* (Munich: C. H. Beck, 1999).
14. Friedrich Schiller, 'Deutsche Grösse', in *Schillers Werke. Nationalausgabe*, ii, pt I (Weimar: Hermann Böhlaus Nachfolger, 1983), 431–7; on the question of date see ibid., ii, pt II B (Weimar: Hermann Böhlaus Nachfolger, 1993), 257–9; Meinecke, *Weltbürgertum* (note 9), 54 ff.; Jörg Echternkamp, *Der Aufstieg des deutschen Nationalismus (1770–1840)* (Frankfurt: Campus, 1998), 163 ff.
15. Georg Wilhelm Friedrich Hegel, *Die Verfassung Deutschlands* (1802), in *Politische Schriften* (Frankfurt: Suhrkamp, 1966), 23–138 (23, 62, 106, 122, 132, 136); Hermann Heller, *Hegel und der nationale Machtstaatsgedanke in Deutschland* (Berlin: B. G. Teubner, 1921), 12 ff.
16. Arnold Berney, 'Reichstradition und Nationalstaatsgedanke (1789–1815)', *HZ* 140 (1929), 57–86; Gerhard Schuck, *Rheinbundpatriotismus und politische Öffentlichkeit zwischen Aufklärung und Frühliberalismus. Kontinuitätsdenken und Diskontinuitätserfahrung in den Staatsrechts- und Verfassungsdebatten der Rheinbundpublizistik* (Stuttgart: F. Steiner, 1994); Georg Schmidt, 'Der Rheinbund und die deutsche Nationalbewegung', in *Die Entstehung der Nationalbewegung in Europa 1750–1849*, ed. Heiner Timmermann (Berlin: Duncker & Humblot, 1993), 29–44.
17. Elisabeth Fehrenbach, *Traditionelle Gesellschaft und revolutionäres Recht. Die Einführung des Code Napoléon in den Rheinbundstaaten* (Göttingen: Vandenhoeck & Ruprecht, 1974) (quote: 12); Eberhard Weis, 'Ergebnisse eines Vergleichs der grundherrschaftlichen Strukturen Deutschlands und Frankreichs vom Hochmittelalter bis zum Ausgang des 18. Jahrhunderts', in *Deutschland und Frankreich um 1800. Aufklärung—Revolution—Reform* (Munich: C. H. Beck, 1990), 67–81; Ernst Rudolf Huber, *Deutsche Verfassungsgeschichte seit 1789*, i. *Reform und Restauration 1789 bis 1830*, 3rd edn (Stuttgart: Kohlhammer, 1990), 314 ff.
18. Helmut Berding, *Napoleonische Herrschafts- und Gesellschaftspolitik im Königreich Westfalen 1807–1813* (Göttingen: Vandenhoeck & Ruprecht, 1973), esp. 15; *Napoleonische Herrschaft und Modernisierung*, ed. id., *GG* 6/4 (1989).
19. Lorenz von Stein, *Geschichte der sozialen Bewegung in Frankreich*, 3 vols., i. *Der Begriff der Gesellschaft und die soziale Geschichte der Französischen Revolution bis zum Jahre 1850* (1850; repr. Darmstadt: Wissenschaftliche Buchgesellschaft, 1959), 426 (427, 429–30; emphases in original); Heinrich August Winkler, 'Gesellschaftsform und Aussenpolitik. Eine Theorie Lorenz von Steins in zeitgeschichtlicher Perspektive', in *Liberalismus und Antiliberalismus. Studien zur politischen Sozialgeschichte des 19. und 20. Jahrhunderts* (Göttingen: Vandenhoeck & Ruprecht, 1979), 235–51.
20. Thomas Nipperdey, *Deutsche Geschichte 1800–1866. Bürgerwelt und starker Staat* (Munich: C. H. Beck, 1983), 25; Braubach, 'Von der Französischen Revolution' (note 6), 45.

21. Friedrich Gentz, *Fragmente aus der neuesten Geschichte* (1806), in *Ausgewählte Schriften*, iv (Stuttgart: L. F. Rieger, 1837), 33–4 ('Teutschland' and 'teutsch' in the original); Mann, *Gentz* (note 9), 167 ff.; 'Hinrich C. Seeba, Zeitgeist und deutscher Geist. Zur Nationalisierung der Epochentendenz um 1800', *Deutsche Vierteljahrschrift für Literaturwissenschaft und Geistesgeschichte*, 61 (1987), Sonderheft, 185–215.
22. Georg Wilhelm Friedrich Hegel, *Grundlinien der Philosophie des Rechts oder Naturrecht und Staatswissenschaft im Grundrisse*, in *Sämtliche Werke* (note 1), vii (Stuttgart: Fromman, 1952), 241 ff. (§ 257 ff.; quote: 241); Hans-Ulrich Wehler, *Deutsche Gesellschaftsgeschichte*, i. *Vom Feudalismus des Alten Reiches bis zur Defensiven Modernisierung der Reformära 1700–1815* (Munich: C. H. Beck, 1987), 397 ff. (quote: 446); Nipperdey, *Geschichte* (note 20), 331 ff.; Koselleck, *Preussen* (note 6), 163 ff.; Schissler, *Agrargesellschaft* (note 6), 105 ff.
23. Johann Gottlieb Fichte, *Beitrag zur Berichtigung der Urtheile des Publicums über die Französische Revolution* (1793), in *Fichtes Werke*, 8 vols. (Berlin: De Gruyter, 1845–6, repr. Berlin, 1971), vi. 39–256 (esp. 152 ff.); id., *Reden an die deutsche Nation* (1808), ibid. 259–499 (quotes in order: 278, 355, 346, 380–1, 384–5, 456, 470–1, 496), tr. as *Addresses to the German Nation* (New York: Harper & Row, 1968).
24. Fichte, *Reden*, 467–8, 386–7, 353–4, 387–8, 385–6; id., *Aus dem Entwurfe zu einer politischen Schrift im Frühlinge 1813*, ibid. in *Fichtes Werke*, vi. 554, 565 (emphases in original); Meinecke, *Weltbürgertum* (note 9), 84 ff.; Eugene Newton Anderson, *Nationalism and the Cultural Crisis in Prussia 1806–1815* (New York: Octagon, 1939), 16–63; Becker, *Zeit* (note 5), 108 ff.; Huber, *Verfassungsgeschichte* (note 17), i. 478–9 (Kalisch).
25. Stein, *Geschichte* (note 19), i. 481, 428 (emphases in original).
26. Georg Wilhelm Friedrich Hegel, *Phänomenologie des Geistes* (1807), in *Werke* (note 1), ii. 132, tr. as *Phenomenology of Spirit* (Oxford: Clarendon Press, 1977).
27. O. C. C. Höpffner [Friedrich Ludwig Jahn], 'Über die Beförderung des Patriotismus im Preussischen Reiche' (1800), in *Friedrich Ludwig Jahns Werke* (Hof: G. A. Grau, 1884–7), i. 3–22; Friedrich Ludwig Jahn, *Deutsches Volkstum* (1810), ibid. 143–380 (146 ff., 159–63, 203; emphases in original); Rainer Wiegels and Winfried Woesler, *Arminius und die Varusschlacht. Geschichte—Mythos—Literatur* (Paderborn: Schöningh, 1995); Andreas Dörner, *Politischer Mythos und symbolische Politik. Sinnstiftung durch symbolische Formen am Beispiel des Hermannmythos* (Opladen: Westdeutscher Verlag, 1995).
28. Jahn, *Volkstum* (note 27), 285, 307 ff., 235–45 (emphases in original); Hans Kohn, *Wege und Irrwege. Vom Geist des deutschen Bürgertums* (Düsseldorf: Droste, 1962), 73 ff., orig. *The Mind of Germany: The Education of a Nation* (New York: Scribner, 1960).
29. Ernst Moritz Arndt, *Geist der Zeit* (1806–17) (Leipzig: Max Hesse, n.d. [1908]), pt 2 (1809), 85; id., 'Gebet', in *Arndts Werke* (Berlin: Deutsches Verlagshaus Bong, n.d. [1912]), pt 1, 74; id., 'Katechismus für den deutschen Kriegs- und Wehrmann' (1813), pt 10, 131–62 (142–3, 147); id., 'An die Preussen' (1813), ibid. 163–70 (169); id., 'Was bedeutet Landsturm und Landwehr?' (1813), ibid. 171–86 (176); id., 'Über Volkshass und den Gebrauch einer fremden Sprache' (1813), in *Ernst Moritz Arndt's Schriften für und an seine lieben Deutschen. Zum ersten Mal gesammelt und durch Neues vermehrt* (Leipzig: Weidmann, 1845), 353–73 (358, 361, 367–8; all emphases

in the original), tr. as *Arndt's Spirit of the Times* (London: Printed by and for W. M. Thiselton and the author, 1808).

30. *Arndt's Schriften*, 372; id., 'Der Rhein, Teutschlands Strom, aber nicht Teutschlands Graenze' (1813), in *Werke* (note 29), pt 11, 37–82 (42); id., 'Das preussische Volk und Heer im Jahre 1813' (1814), ibid. 7–36 (29, 32); id., 'Bemerkungen über Teutschlands Lage im November 1814', id., *Blick aus der Zeit auf die Zeit* (Germanien, n.d. [1814]), 1–79; id., 'Noch eine Vermahnung an die politischen teutschen Philister', ibid. 257–81; id., 'Über Preussens Rheinische Mark und über Bundesfestungen' (1815), in *Werke* (note 29), pt 11, 143–99 (164, 187, 190); Günther Ott, *Ernst Moritz Arndt. Religion, Christentum und Kirche in der Entwicklung des deutschen Publizisten und Patrioten* (Bonn: Presseverband der Evangelischen Kirche im Rheinland, 1966), 197 ff.; Alexander Scharff, *Der Gedanke der preussischen Vorherrschaft in den Anfängen der deutschen Einheitsbewegung* (Bonn: K. Schroeder, 1929), 39–40 (on Arndt's position in 1814); Klaus Vondung, *Die Apokalypse in Deutschland* (Munich: Deutscher Taschenbuch Verlag, 1988), 152 ff., tr. as *The Apocalypse in Germany* (Columbia, MO: University of Missouri Press, 2000).
31. Arndt, *Geist der Zeit* (note 29), pt 2 (1809), 134–5; pt 3 (1813), 156; id., 'Über künftige ständische Verfassungen in Teutschland' (1814), in *Werke* (note 29), pt 11, 83–130 (106, 121); Anderson, *Nationalism* (note 24), 64–103; Michael Jeismann, *Das Vaterland der Feinde. Studien zum nationalen Feindbegriff und Selbstverständnis in Deutschland und Frankreich 1792–1918* (Stuttgart: Klett-Cotta, 1992), 27 ff.
32. Fichte, *Reden* (note 23), 464–5; Arndt, 'Preussens Rheinische Mark' (note 30), 191; Otto Kallscheuer and Claus Leggewie, 'Deutsche Kulturnation versus französische Staatsnation? Eine ideengeschichtliche Stichprobe', *Nationales Bewusstsein und kollektive Identität. Studien zur Entwicklung des kollektiven Bewusstseins in der Neuzeit*, ii ed. Helmut Berding (Frankfurt: Suhrkamp, 1994), 112–62; Bernhard Giesen, *Die Intellektuellen und die Nation. Eine deutsche Achsenzeit* (Frankfurt: Suhrkamp, 1993), 27 ff.; Conrad Wiedemann, 'Zwischen Nationalgeist und Kosmopolitismus. Über die Schwierigkeiten der deutschen Klassiker, einen Nationalhelden zu finden', in *Patriotismus*, ed. Günter Birtsch, *Aufklärung*, 4/2 (1991), 75–101.
33. Ernst Moritz Arndt, 'Bemerkungen' (note 30), 59 ff.; id., 'Die Schweitzer, Holländer und Elsässer', in *Blick* (note 30), 80–112; id., 'Noch etwas über die Juden', ibid. 180–201 (181, 199, 188); Fichte, *Beitrag* (note 23), 150–1; Jacob Katz, *Vom Vorurteil zur Vernichtung. Der Antisemitismus 1700–1933* (Munich: C. H. Beck 1989), 61, orig. *From Prejudice to Destruction: Anti-Semitism, 1700–1933* (Cambridge, MA: Harvard University Press, 1980), Hans Rothfels, 'Grundsätzliches zum Problem der Nationalität', in *Zeitgeschichtliche Betrachtungen. Vorträge und Aufsätze* (Göttingen: Vandenhoeck & Ruprecht, 1959), 89–111.
34. Otto W. Johnston, *Der deutsche Nationalmythos. Ursprung und politisches Programm* (Stuttgart: Metzler, 1990), orig. *The Myth of a Nation: Literature and Politics in Prussia under Napoleon* (New York: Camden House, 1989); Eric J. Hobsbawm, *Nationen und Nationalismus. Mythos und Realität seit 1780* (Frankfurt: Campus, 1991), orig. *Nations and Nationalism since 1780: Programme, Myth, Reality* (Cambridge: Cambridge University Press, 1990); *The Invention of Tradition*, ed. id. and Terence Ranger (Cambridge: Cambridge University Press, 1983); Benedict Anderson, *Die Erfindung der Nation* (Frankfurt: Campus, 1988), orig. *Imagined Communities: Reflections on the Origin and Spread of Nationalism* (London: Verso, 1983); Anthony D. Smith, 'The

Nation: Invented, Imagined, Reconstructed?', *Millennium: Journal of International Studies*, 20 (1991), 353–68.

35. Meinecke, *Weltbürgertum* (note 9), 58 ff., 113 ff.; Kohn, *Wege* (note 28), 53 ff.; Carl Schmitt, *Politische Romantik* (1919), 3rd edn (Berlin: Duncker & Humblot, 1968), tr. as *Political Romanticism* (Cambridge, MA: MIT Press, 1986); Hermann Kurzke, *Romantik und Konservatismus. Das 'politische' Werk Friedrich von Hardenbergs (Novalis)* (Munich: W. Fink, 1983).
36. Ernst Moritz Arndt, *Was ist des Deutschen Vaterland?* (1813), in *Werke* (note 29), pt 1, 126–7; id., *Geist der Zeit* (note 29), pt III, 177; Heinz Angermeier, 'Deutschland zwischen Reichstradition und Nationalstaat. Verfassungspolitische Konzeptionen und nationales Denken zwischen 1801 und 1815', in *Das alte Reich in der deutschen Geschichte. Studien über Kontinuitäten und Zäsuren* (Munich: Oldenbourg, 1991), 449–521; Meinecke, *Weltbürgertum* (note 9), 142 ff.; Scharff, *Gedanke* (note 30), 8 ff.; the article 'Ideologie', *Geschichtliche Grundbegriffe* (note 7), iii (Stuttgart: Klett, 1982), 131–69; 'Humboldts "Denkschrift über die deutsche Verfassung" vom Dezember 1813', in *Wilhelm von Humboldt. Eine Auswahl aus seinen Schriften*, ed. Siegfried A. Kaehler (Berlin: R. Hobbing, 1922), 88–103 (quote: 92–3).
37. Leopold Zscharnack, 'Die Pflege des religiösen Patriotismus durch die evangelische Geistlichkeit 1806–1815', in *Harnack-Ehrung. Beiträge zur Kirchengeschichte. Festschrift für Adolf von Harnack* (Leipzig: J. C. Hinrichs, 1921), 394–423 (on the appearance of the concept of 'religious patriotism', see 400); Gerhard Graf, *Gottesbild und Politik. Eine Studie zur Frömmigkeit in Preussen während der Befreiungskriege 1813–1815* (Göttingen: Vandenhoeck & Ruprecht, 1993); Artie J. Hoover, *The Gospel of Nationalism: German Patriotic Preaching from Napoleon to Versailles* (Stuttgart: F. Steiner, 1986), 6 ff.; Georg Schmidt, 'Von der Nationaleinheit zum Nationalstaat. Der gedankliche Kontinuitätsbruch in Deutschland zu Beginn des 19. Jahrhunderts', *Die evangelische Diaspora. Jahrbuch des Gustav-Adolf-Werks*, 63 (1994), 59–75; Jerry Dawson, *Friedrich Schleiermacher: The Evolution of a Nationalist* (Austin: University of Texas Press, 1966); Otto Dann, 'Schleiermacher und die nationale Bewegung', in *Internationaler Schleiermacher-Kongress Berlin 1984*, 2 vols. (Berlin: De Gruyter, 1985), ii. 1107–20; Rudolf von Thadden, 'Schleiermacher und Preussen', ibid. 1099–1106; Kurt Nowak, *Schleiermacher und die Frühromantik. Eine literaturgeschichtliche Schule zum romantischen Religionsverständnis und Menschenbild am Ende des 18. Jahrhunderts in Deutschland* (Weimar: Hermann Böhlaus Nachfolger, 1986), 92 ff.; Karin Hagemann, 'Nation, Krieg und Geschlechterordnung. Zum kulturellen und politischen Diskurs in der Zeit der antinapoleonischen Erhebung Preussens 1806–1815', *GG* 22 (1996), 562–91; Hasko A. Zimmer, *Auf dem Altar des Vaterlands. Religion und Patriotismus in der deutschen Kriegslyrik des 19. Jahrhunderts* (Frankfurt: Thesen Verlag, 1971); Reinhard Wittram, 'Kirche und Nationalismus in der Geschichte des deutschen Protestantismus im 19. Jahrhundert', in *Das Nationale als europäisches Problem. Beiträge zur Geschichte des Nationalitätsprinzips vornehmlich im 19. Jahrhundert* (Göttingen: Vandenhoeck & Ruprecht, 1954), 109–48; Lothar Gall, 'Die Germania als Symbol nationaler Einheit im 19. und 20. Jahrhundert', in *Nachrichten der Akademie der Wissenschaften in Göttingen. I. Philologisch-Historische Klasse, Jg. 1993*, 2 (Göttingen: Vandenhoeck & Ruprecht, 1993); Gerhard Brunn, 'Germania und die Entstehung des deutschen Nationalstaates. Zum Zusammenhang

von Symbolen u. Wir-Gefühl', in *Politik der Symbole, Symbole der Politik*, ed. Rüdiger Voigt (Opladen: Leske + Budrich, 1989), 101–22.

38. Anthony D. Smith, *Theories of Nationalism*, 3rd edn (London: Duckworth, 1983); Hagen Schulze, *Staat und Nation in der europäischen Geschichte* (Munich: C. H. Beck, 1994), 150 ff. tr. as *States, Nations, and Nationalism: From the Middle Ages to the Present* (Oxford: Blackwell, 1996); Miroslav Hroch, 'Das Erwachen kleiner Nationen als Problem der komparativen Forschung', in *Nationalismus* (note 11), ed. Winkler, 155–72; Jürgen Wilke, 'Der nationale Aufbruch der Befreiungskriege als Kommunikationsereignis' *Volk—Nation—Vaterland*, ed. Ulrich Herrmann (Hamburg: F. Meiner, 1996), 353–66.
39. Dieter Grimm, *Deutsche Verfassungsgeschichte 1776–1866* (Frankfurt: Suhrkamp, 1988), 68 ff., 113 ff.; Karsten Ruppert, *Bürgertum und staatliche Macht in Deutschland zwischen Französischer und deutscher Revolution* (Berlin: Duncker & Humblot, 1998); Huber, *Verfassungsgeschichte* (note 17), i. 314 ff., 475 ff., 583 ff.
40. Huber, *Verfassungsgeschichte*, 704 ff.; Wehler, *Gesellschaftsgeschichte* (note 22), ii. *Von der Reformära bis zur industriellen und politischen 'Deutschen Doppelrevolution' 1815–1848/49* (Munich: C. H. Beck, 1987), 333 ff.; Franz Schnabel, *Deutsche Geschichte im neunzehnten Jahrhundert*, ii. *Monarchie und Volkssouveränität*, 2nd edn (Freiburg: Herder, 1949), 218 ff.; *175 Jahre Wartburgfest. 18. Oktober 1817–18. Oktober 1992. Studien zur politischen Bedeutung und zum Zeithintergrund der Wartburgfeier*, ed. Karl Malettke (Heidelberg: Winter, 1992); Wolfgang Hardtwig, 'Studentische Mentalität—Politische Jugendbewegung—Nationalismus. Die Anfänge der deutschen Burschenschaft', in *Nationalismus und Bürgerkultur in Deutschland 1500–1914* (Göttingen: Vandenhoeck & Ruprecht, 1994), 108–48; Peter Brandt, 'Das studentische Wartburgfest vom 18./19. Oktober 1817', in *Öffentliche Festkultur. Politische Feste in Deutschland von der Aufklärung bis zum Ersten Weltkrieg*, ed. Dieter Düding et al. (Hamburg: Rowohlt, 1988), 89–112. Quote from Görres in 'Wiedererneuerung des Vertrags von Chaumont', *Rheinischer Merkur*, 225, 19 Apr. 1815. Facsimile edition in Joseph von Görres, *Gesammelte Schriften*, ix, 11 (Cologne: Gilde-Verlag, 1928).
41. Dieter Düding, *Organisierter gesellschaftlicher Nationalismus in Deutschland (1808–1847). Bedeutung und Funktion der Turner- und Sängervereine für die deutsche Nationalbewegung* (Munich: Oldenbourg, 1984); Karin Luys, *Die Anfänge der deutschen Nationalbewegung von 1815 bis 1819* (Münster: Nodus Publikationen, 1992); Wolfgang v. Groote, *Die Entstehung des Nationalbewusstseins in Nordwestdeutschland 1790–1830* (Göttingen: Musterschmidt-Verlag, 1955); Otto Dann, 'Nationalismus und sozialer Wandel in Deutschland 1806–1850', in *Nationalismus und sozialer Wandel*, ed. id. (Hamburg: Hoffmann und Campe, 1978), 77–128; Wehler, *Gesellschaftsgeschichte*, ii (note 40), 394 ff.; Koselleck, *Preussen* (note 6), 284 ff.; Friedrich Meinecke, *1848. Eine Säkularbetrachtung* (Berlin: L. Blanvalet, 1948), 9; Theodor Schieder, 'Partikularismus und Nationalbewusstsein im Denken des deutschen Vormärz', *Staat und Gesellschaft im deutschen Vormärz 1815–1848*, ed. Werner Conze (Stuttgart: Klett, 1962), 9–38; Werner Conze, 'Das Spannungsfeld von Staat und Gesellschaft im Vormärz', ibid. 207–69; Volker Sellin, 'Nationalbewusstsein und Partikularismus in Deutschland im 19. Jahrhundert', in *Kultur und Gedächtnis*, ed. Jan Assmann and Tonio Hölscher (Frankfurt: Suhrkamp, 1988), 241–64; Dieter Langewiesche, 'Reich, Nation und Staat in der jüngeren deutschen Geschichte', *HZ* 254 (1992), 341–81.

42. Lothar Gall, *Benjamin Constant. Seine politische Ideenwelt und der deutsche Vormärz* (Wiesbaden: F. Steiner, 1963); *Liberalismus im 19. Jahrhundert*, ed. Dieter Langewiesche (Göttingen: Vandenhoeck & Ruprecht, 1988); Wolfram Siemann, *Vom Staatenbund zum Nationalstaat. Deutschland 1806–1871* (Munich: C. H. Beck, 1995), esp. 29 ff.; Christoph Hauser, *Anfänge bürgerlicher Organisation. Philhellenismus und Frühliberalismus in Südwestdeutschland* (Göttingen: Vandenhoeck & Ruprecht, 1990).
43. Katz, *Vorurteil* (note 33), 95 ff.; Helmut Berding, *Moderner Antisemitismus in Deutschland* (Frankfurt: Suhrkamp, 1988), 42 ff. (Marwitz: 46); Reinhard Rürup, *Emanzipation und Antisemitismus. Studien zur 'Judenfrage' der bürgerlichen Gesellschaft* (Göttingen: Vandenhoeck & Ruprecht, 1975), esp. 37 ff. (Rotteck: 61); Wolfgang Altgeld, *Katholizismus, Protestantismus, Judentum. Über religiös begründete Gegensätze und nationalreligiöse Ideen in der Geschichte des deutschen Nationalismus* (Mainz: Matthias-Grünewald-Verlag, 1992), 47 ff.; Eleonore Sterling, *Judenhass. Die Anfänge des politischen Antisemitismus in Deutschland (1815–1850)*, 2nd edn (Frankfurt: Europäische Verlagsanstalt, 1969), 77 ff.; Rainer Erb and Werner Bergmann, *Die Nachtseite der Judenemanzipation. Der Widerstand gegen die Integration der Juden in Deutschland 1780–1860* (Berlin: Metropol, 1989), 15 ff., 217 ff.; Stefan Rohrbacher, *Gewalt im Biedermeier. Antijüdische Ausschreitungen in Vormärz und Revolution (1815–1848/49)* (Frankfurt: Campus, 1993), 94 ff.; Rüdiger von Treskow, *Erlauchter Vertheidiger der Menschenrechte! Die Korrespondenz Karl von Rottecks*, 2 vols. (Freiburg: Ploetz, 1990), i. 160 ff.
44. Ludwig Börne, 'Der ewige Jude', in *Ludwig Börnes gesammelte Schriften. Vollständige Ausgabe in sechs Bänden* (Leipzig: M. Hesse, n.d.), iii. 139–71 (141, 171).
45. Katz, *Vorurteil* (note 33), 107 ff.; Ernst Schulin, 'Weltbürgertum und deutscher Volksgeist. Die romantische Nationalisierung im frühen neunzehnten Jahrhundert', in *Deutschland in Europa. Ein historischer Rückblick*, ed. Bernd Martin (Munich: Deutscher Taschenbuch Verlag, 1992), 105–21; Thomas Nipperdey, 'Auf der Suche nach Identität. Romantischer Nationalismus', in *Nachdenken über die deutsche Geschichte* (Munich: C. H. Beck, 1986), 110–25.

CHAPTER 3. LIBERALISM IN CRISIS 1830–1850

1. Lorenz von Stein, *Geschichte der sozialen Bewegung in Frankreich von 1789 bis auf unsere Tage*, 3 vols., ii. *Die industrielle Gesellschaft, der Sozialismus und Kommunismus Frankreichs von 1830 bis 1844* (1850, repr. Darmstadt: Wissenschaftliche Buchgesellschaft, 1959), 1, 6, 10–11.
2. Eberhard Kolb, 'Polenbild und Polenfreundschaft der deutschen Frühliberalen. Zu Motivation und Funktion aussenpolitischer Parteinahme im Vormärz', *Saeculum*, 26 (1975), 111–27; Hans-Henning Hahn, 'Die Organisation der polnischen "Grossen Emigration" 1831–1847', in *Nationale Bewegung und soziale Organisation*, i. *Vergleichende Studien zur nationalen Vereinsbewegung des 19. Jahrhunderts in Europa*, ed. Theodor Schieder and Otto Dann (Munich: Oldenbourg, 1978), 131–279; *Der polnische Freiheitskampf 1830/31 und die liberale deutsche Polenfreundschaft*, ed. Peter Ehlen (Munich: J. Berchmanns, 1982).
3. Hans-Ulrich Wehler, *Deutsche Gesellschaftsgeschichte*, ii. *Von der Reformära bis zur industriellen und politischen 'Deutschen Doppelrevolution' 1815–1845/49* (Munich: C. H. Beck, 1987), 345 ff.; Wolfram Siemann, *Vom Staatenbund zum Nationalstaat*

1806–1871 (Munich: C. H. Beck, 1995), 343 ff.; Elisabeth Fehrenbach, *Verfassungsstaat und Nationsbildung 1815–1871* (Munich: Oldenbourg, 1992), 9 ff.; Dieter Langewiesche, *Europa zwischen Restauration und Revolution 1815–1849* (Munich: Oldenbourg, 1985), 65 ff.; Hartwig Brandt, 'Die Julirevolution (1830) und die Rezeption der "principes de 1789" in Deutschland', in *Revolution und Gegenrevolution 1789–1830. Zur geistigen Auseinandersetzung in Frankreich und Deutschland*, ed. Roger Dufraisse (Munich: Oldenbourg, 1991), 225–35; Hans-Gerhard Husung, *Protest und Repression im Vormärz. Norddeutschland zwischen Restauration und Revolution* (Göttingen: Vandenhoeck & Ruprecht, 1983), 43 ff.; *Die Französische Julirevolution von 1830 und Europa*, ed. Manfred Kossok and Werner Loch (Berlin: Akademie-Verlag, 1985), esp. 177 ff.; Kurt Holzapfel, 'Der Einfluss der Julirevolution von 1830/31 auf Deutschland', in *Demokratische und soziale Protestbewegungen in Mitteleuropa 1815–1848/49*, ed. Helmut Reinalter (Frankfurt: Suhrkamp, 1986), 105–40; Ernst Wolfgang Becker, *Zeit der Revolution!—Revolution der Zeit? Zeiterfahrungen in Deutschland in der Ära der Revolutionen 1789–1848/49* (Göttingen: Vandenhoeck & Ruprecht, 1999), 147 ff.

4. Lothar Gall, 'Gründung und politische Entwicklung des Grossherzogtums bis 1848', in *Badische Geschichte. Vom Grossherzogtum bis zur Gegenwart*, ed. Josef Becker et al. (Stuttgart: Theiss, 1979), 11–36 (Welcker motion: 32); Manfred Meyer, *Freiheit und Macht. Studien zum Nationalismus süddeutscher, insbesondere badischer Liberaler 1830–1848* (Frankfurt: P. Land, 1994), 102 ff., 170 ff.; Reiner Schöttle, *Politische Theorien des süddeutschen Liberalismus im Vormärz. Studien zu Rotteck, Welcker, Pfizer, Murhard* (Baden-Baden: Nomos, 1994), 147 ff., 183 ff.; Friedrich Meinecke, *Weltbürgertum und Nationalstaat* (1907), in *Werke*, v (Munich: Oldenbourg, 1962), 281 ff., tr. as *Cosmopolitanism and the National State* (Princeton: Princeton University Press, 1970).
5. Ernst Rudolf Huber, *Deutsche Verfassungsgeschichte seit 1789*, ii. *Der Kampf um Einheit und Freiheit 1830 bis 1850*, 3rd edn (Stuttgart: W. Kohlhammer, 1988), 133 ff.; Heinrich von Treitschke, *Deutsche Geschichte im Neunzehnten Jahrhundert*, pt 4, *Bis zum Tode König Friedrich Wilhelms IV.*, 5th edn (Leipzig: S. Hirzel, 1907), 261 ff., tr. as *History of Germany in the Nineteenth Century* (London, Jarrold & Sons, 1915–19), vii; Hans Kohn, *Wege und Irrwege. Vom Geist des deutschen Bürgertums* (Düsseldorf: Droste, 1962), 125–6, orig. *The Mind of Germany: The Education of a Nation* (New York: Scribner, 1960); Cornelia Foerster, *Der Press- und Vaterlandsverein von 1832/33. Sozialstruktur und Organisationsformen der bürgerlichen Bewegung in der Zeit des Hambacher Festes* (Trier: Verlag Trierer Historischer Forschungen, 1982); Wolfgang Schieder, 'Der rheinpfälzische Liberalismus von 1832 als politische Protestbewegung', in *Vom Staat des Ancien Régime zum modernen Parteienstaat. Festschrift für Theodor Schieder*, ed. Helmut Berding et al. (Munich: Oldenbourg, 1978), 169–95; *Liberalismus in der Gesellschaft des deutschen Vormärz*, ed. id., GG, Sonderheft 9 (Göttingen: Vandenhoeck & Ruprecht, 1983); Hans Fenske, 'Politischer und sozialer Protest in Süddeutschland nach 1830', in *Protestbewegungen* (note 3), ed. Reinalter, 143–201; Jörg Echternkamp, *Der Aufstieg des deutschen Nationalismus (1770–1840)* (Frankfurt: Campus, 1998), 420 ff. Quotes von Siebenpfeiffer and Wirth in J. G. A. Wirth, *Das Nationalfest der Deutschen zu Hambach*, 1 (Neustadt: In Commission bei Philipp Christmann, 1832, repr. Vaduz: Topos, 1977), 38–9, 46 (emphases in original). Quote from Rotteck in: Meyer, *Freiheit* (note 4), 149.

6. Huber, *Verfassungsgeschichte* (note 5), ii. 92 ff., 125 ff., 151 ff.; Wehler, *Gesellschaftsgeschichte* (note 3), ii. 366 ff. (quote from Metternich: 367); Treitschke, *Geschichte* (note 5), pt 4, 657 (quote: 666).
7. Huber, *Verfassungsgeschichte* (note 5), ii. 177 ff.; Lothar Gall, 'Liberalismus und "bürgerliche Gesellschaft". Zu Charakter und Entwicklung der liberalen Bewegung in Deutschland', in *Liberalismus*, ed. tr., 3rd edn (Königstein: Verlagsgruppe Athenäum, Hain, Scriptor, Hanstein, 1985), 162–86; Wolfram Fischer, 'Das Verhältnis von Staat und Wirtschaft in Deutschland am Beginn der Industrialisierung', in *Industrielle Revolution. Wirtschaftliche Aspekte*, ed. Rudolf Braun et al. (Cologne: Kiepenheuer & Witsch, 1972), 287–304; *Staat und Gesellschaft im deutschen Vormärz 1815–1848*, ed. Werner Conze (Stuttgart: Klett, 1962); James J. Sheehan, *Der Ausklang des alten Reiches. Deutschland seit dem Ende des Siebenjährigen Krieges bis zur gescheiterten Revolution 1763 bis 1850* (Berlin: Propyläen, 1994), 546 ff.; id., *Der deutsche Liberalismus. Von den Anfängen im 18. Jahrhundert bis zum Ersten Weltkrieg 1770–1914* (Munich: C. H. Beck, 1983), 26 ff., orig. *German Liberalism in the Nineteenth Century* (Chicago: University of Chicago Press, 1978).
8. Wolfram Fischer, 'Der Deutsche Zollverein. Fallstudie einer Zollunion', in *Wirtschaft und Gesellschaft im Zeitalter der Industrialisierung*, ed. id. (Göttingen: Vandenhoeck & Ruprecht, 1972), 110–28; Hans-Werner Hahn, *Geschichte des Deutschen Zollvereins* (Göttingen: Vandenhoeck & Ruprecht, 1984); Thomas Nipperdey, *Deutsche Geschichte 1800–1866. Bürgerwelt und starker Staat* (Munich: C. H. Beck, 1983), 358 ff.; Wehler, *Gesellschaftsgeschichte* (note 3), ii. 125 ff.
9. Treitschke, *Geschichte* (note 5), pt 5, *Bis zur Märzrevolution*, 4th edn (Leipzig 1899), 3 ff. (quote: 57–8), tr. as *History of Germany* (note 5), vii; Nipperdey, *Geschichte* (note 8), 396 ff.; David E. Barclay, *Anarchie und guter Wille. Friedrich Wilhelm IV. und die preussische Monarchie* (Berlin: Siedler, 1995), 85 ff.; orig. *Frederick William IV and the Prussian Monarchy, 1840–1861* (Oxford: Oxford University Press, 1995); Walter Bussmann, *Zwischen Preussen und Deutschland. Friedrich Wilhelm IV. Eine Biographie* (Berlin: Siedler, 1990), 101 ff.; Frank-Lothar Kroll, *Friedrich Wilhelm IV. und das Staatsdenken der deutschen Romantik* (Berlin: Colloquium-Verlag, 1990); Dirk Blasius, 'Friedrich Wilhelm IV. Persönlichkeit und Amt', HZ 263 (1996), 589–607.
10. Irmline Veit-Brause, 'Die deutsch-französische Krise von 1840. Studien zur deutschen Einheitsbewegung', Ph.D. thesis, Cologne, 1967 (Rheinlieder: 125 ff.); Ute Schneider, *Politische Festkultur im 19. Jahrhundert. Die Rheinprovinz von der französischen Zeit bis zum Ende des Ersten Weltkrieges (1806–1918)* (Essen: Klartext, 1995), 79 ff.; Dietmar Klenke, *Der singende 'deutsche Mann'. Gesangvereine und deutsches Nationalbewusstsein von Napoleon bis Hitler* (Munich: Waxmann, 1998), 82 ff.; Meyer, *Freiheit* (note 4), 205 ff.; Echternkamp, *Aufstieg* (note 5), 464 ff.; *Deutscher Liberalismus im Vormärz. Heinrich von Gagern, Briefe und Reden 1815–1848*, ed. Paul Wentzcke and Wolfgang Klötzer (Göttingen: Musterschmidt, 1959), 99–101 (letter to Hans Christoph von Gagern, 13 July 1832), 261–3 (letter to Friedrich von Gagern, 4 Jan. 1843; quote: 263).
11. Karl Biedermann, 'Die Fortschritte des nationalen Prinzips in Deutschland (1842)', in *Vormärz und Revolution 1840–1849*, ed. Hans Fenske, 2nd edn (Darmstadt: Wissenschaftliche Buchgesellschaft, 1991), 54–64 (58, 60); Veit-Brause, *Krise* (note 10), 219 (Pfizer), 244 (Steinacker), 251–2; Meyer, *Freiheit* (note 4), 193 ff.; Hans Fenske,

'Ungeduldige Zuschauer. Die Deutschen und die europäische Expansion 1815–1880', in *Imperialistische Kontinuität und nationale Ungeduld im 19. Jahrhundert*, ed. Wolfgang Reinhard (Frankfurt: Fischer Taschenbuch Verlag, 1991), 87–123. For a summary of Paul Pfizer's national-political ideas from the early 1840s see id., *Das Vaterland. Aus der Schrift: Gedanken über Recht, Staat und Kirche* (1842) (Stuttgart: Hallberger'sche Verlagshandlung, 1845) (on the connection between Austria and Germany see esp. 197). Quote from Friedrich List in id., 'Die politisch-ökonomische Nationaleinheit der Deutschen', in *Schriften, Reden, Briefe*, vii (Berlin: R. Hobbing, 1931), 441–502 (444). The quasi-biblical passage is taken from Matthew 16: 26 ('For what is a man profited, if he shall gain the whole world, and lose his own soul?')

12. Friedrich Julius Stahl, *Der christliche Staat. Vortrag über Kirchenzucht* (1847), 2nd edn (Berlin: L Oehmigke, 1858); Bussmann, *Zwischen Preussen* (note 9), 172 ff.; Barclay, *Anarchie* (note 9), 85 ff.; Wehler, *Gesellschaftsgeschichte* (note 3), ii. 407, 571; Huber *Verfassungsgeschichte* (note 5), ii. 185 ff.; Heinrich Lutz, *Zwischen Habsburg und Preussen. Deutschland 1815–1866* (Berlin: Siedler, 1985), 211 ff.; Meyer, *Freiheit* (note 4), 197; Richard Hinton Thomas, *Liberalism, Nationalism, and the German Intellectuals 1822–1847* (Cambridge, MA: W. Heffner, 1951), 81 ff., 114–15; Georg Bollenbeck, *Bildung und Kultur. Glanz und Elend eines deutschen Deutungsmusters* (Frankfurt: Insel, 1994), 186 ff.; Thomas Nipperdey, 'Der Kölner Dom als Nationaldenkmal', in *Nachdenken über die deutsche Geschichte*, ed. id. (Munich: C. H. Beck, 1986), 156–71; id., 'Nationalidee und Nationaldenkmal im 19. Jahrhundert', *Gesellschaft, Kultur, Theorie*, ed. id. (Göttingen: Vandenhoeck & Ruprecht, 1976), 133–73.

13. Gustav Mayer, 'Die Anfänge des politischen Radikalismus im vormärzlichen Preussen' (1913), in *Radikalismus, Sozialismus und bürgerliche Demokratie* (Frankfurt: Suhrkamp, 1969), 7–107; Hans Rosenberg, 'Theologischer Rationalismus und vormärzlicher Vulgärliberalismus' (1930), in *Politische Denkströmungen im deutschen Vormärz* (Göttingen: Vandenhoeck & Ruprecht, 1972), 18–50; Jörg Echternkamp, 'Religiosität und Nationskonzeption. Zum Verhältnis von Theologischem Rationalismus und Liberalnationalismus im deutschen Vormärz', *Jahrbuch zur Liberalismusforschung*, 6 (1994), 137–51; Jörn Brederlow, *'Lichtfreunde' und 'Freie Gemeinden'. Religiöser Protest und Freiheitsbewegung im Vormärz und in der Revolution von 1848/49* (Munich: Oldenbourg, 1976); Friedrich Wilhelm Graf, *Die Politisierung des religiösen Bewusstseins. Die bürgerlichen Religionsparteien im deutschen Vormärz: Das Beispiel des Deutschkatholizismus* (Stuttgart: Frommann-Holzboog, 1978); Stephan Walter, *Demokratisches Denken zwischen Hegel und Marx. Die politische Philosophie Arnold Ruges* (Düsseldorf: Droste, 1995), 101 ff.; Karl Löwith, *Von Hegel zu Nietzsche. Der revolutionäre Bruch im Denken des neunzehnten Jahrhunderts. Marx und Kierkegaard*, 3rd edn (Stuttgart: W. Kohlhammer, 1953), 78 ff., tr. as *From Hegel to Nietzsche: The Revolution in Nineteenth-Century Thought* (New York: Holt, Rinehart and Winston, 1964); Wolfgang Schieder, 'Kirche und Revolution. Sozialgeschichtliche Aspekte der Trierer Wallfahrt von 1844', *Archiv für Sozialgeschichte*, 14 (1974), 419–54; Kurt Nowak, *Geschichte des Christentums in Deutschland. Religion, Politik und Gesellschaft vom Ende der Aufklärung bis zur Mitte des 20. Jahrhunderts* (Munich: C. H. Beck, 1995), 64 ff.; Manfred Botzenhart, *Reform, Restauration, Krise. Deutschland 1789–1847* (Frankfurt: Suhrkamp, 1985), 120 ff.; Wehler, *Gesellschaftsgeschichte* (note 3), ii. 413 ff.

14. Johann Jacoby, *Vier Fragen, beantwortet von einem Ostpreussen* (1841; Munich, 1910); Arnold Ruge, *Preussen und die Reaction. Zur Geschichte unserer Zeit* (Leipzig: Otto Wigand, 1838), 69 ff.; id., 'Selbstkritik des Liberalismus' (1841), in *Gesammelte Schriften*, pt 13 (Mannheim, 1846), 76–116 (116); Mayer, 'Anfänge' (note 13), 9; Friedrich Zunkel, *Der rheinisch-westfälische Unternehmer 1834–1879. Ein Beitrag zur Geschichte des deutschen Bürgertums im 19. Jahrhundert* (Cologne: Westdeutscher Verlag, 1962); Elisabeth Fehrenbach, 'Rheinischer Liberalismus und gesellschaftliche Verfassung', in *Liberalismus* (note 5), ed. Schieder, 272–94; Paul Nolte, *Gemeindebürgertum und Liberalismus in Baden 1800–1850. Tradition—Radikalismus—Republik* (Göttingen: Vandenhoeck & Ruprecht, 1994); Walter, *Denken* (note 13), 112 ff., 145 ff., 269 ff.
15. Karl Marx, 'Zur Kritik der Hegelschen Rechtsphilosophie Einleitung', MEW i. 378–91 (quotes: 379, 385, 391; emphases in original); Karl Marx/Friedrich Engels, *Manifest der Kommunistischen Partei*, ibid., iv. 459–93 (493); Karl Marx, 'Contribution to the Critique of Hegel's Philosphy of Law', MECW iii. 175–87 (quotes: 176, 182, 187), tr. as *Manifesto of the Communist Party*, MECW, vi. 477–519 (519); Heinrich August Winkler, 'Zum Verhältnis von bürgerlicher und proletarischer Revolution bei Marx und Engels', in *Revolution, Staat, Faschismus. Zur Revision des Historischen Materialismus* (Göttingen: Vandenhoeck & Ruprecht, 1978), 8–34.
16. Wehler, *Gesellschaftsgeschichte* (note 3), ii. 241 ff., 585 ff.; Wolfgang Hardtwig, *Vormärz. Der monarchische Staat und das Bürgertum* (Munich: Deutscher Taschenbuch Verlag, 1985), 88 ff.; Jürgen Kocka, *Weder Stand noch Klasse. Unterschichten um 1800* (Bonn: J. H. W. Dietz, 1990); id., *Arbeitsverhältnisse und Arbeiterexistenzen. Grundlagen der Klassenbildung im 19. Jahrhundert* (Bonn: J. H. W. Dietz, 1990), esp. 373 ff.; Wolfgang Schieder, *Anfänge der deutschen Arbeiterbewegung. Die Auslandsvereine im Jahrzehnt nach der Juli-Revolution von 1830* (Stuttgart: Klett, 1963); Werner Conze, 'Vom "Pöbel" zum "Proletariat", Sozialgeschichtliche Voraussetzungen für den Sozialismus in Deutschland', in *Moderne deutsche Sozialgeschichte*, ed. Hans-Ulrich Wehler (Cologne: Kiepenheuer und Witsch, 1966), 111–36; Frolinde Balser, *Sozial-Demokratie 1848/1863. Die erste deutsche Arbeiterorganisation 'Allgemeine Deutsche Arbeiterverbrüderung' nach der Revolution*, 2 vols., 2nd edn (Stuttgart: Klett, 1966).
17. Heinrich von Sybel, *Die politischen Parteien der Rheinprovinz, in ihrem Verhältniss zur preussischen Verfassung* (Düsseldorf: Verlag von Julius Buddeus, 1847), 63, 81–2; Huber, *Verfassungsgeschichte* (note 5), ii. 492 ff. (Frederick William IV quote: 495); Nipperdey, *Geschichte* (note 8), 399 ff.; Wehler, *Gesellschaftsgeschichte* (note 3), ii., 677 ff.; Michael Neumüller, *Liberalismus und Revolution. Das Problem der Revolution in der deutschen liberalen Geschichtsschreibung des 19. Jahrhunderts* (Düsseldorf: Pädagogischer Verlag Schwann, 1963); *1848/49 in Europa und der Mythos der Französischen Revolution*, ed. Irmtraud Götz von Olenhusen (Göttingen: Vandenhoeck & Ruprecht, 1998).
18. Peter J. Katzenstein, *Disjoined Partners: Austria and Germany since 1815* (Berkeley: University of California Press, 1976), 35 ff.; Nipperdey, *Deutsche Geschichte* (note 8), 337 ff.; Lutz, *Zwischen Habsburg* (note 12), 169 ff.; Langewiesche, *Europa* (note 3), 116 ff.; Huber, *Verfassungsgeschichte* (note 5), ii. 451 ff.
19. Huber *Verfassungsgeschichte*, ii. 448–51 (here also quotes from the Offenburg and Heppenheim demands), 502 ff., 663 ff.; Ulrike von Hirschhausen, *Liberalismus und Nation. Die Deutsche Zeitung 1847–1850* (Düsseldorf: Droste, 1998); Veit Valentin,

Geschichte der deutschen Revolution 1848–1849, 2 vols., i. *Bis zum Zusammentritt des Frankfurter Parlaments* (1931; Cologne: Kiepenheuer & Witsch, 1970), 161 ff.; Treitschke, *Geschichte*, pt 5, (note 9), 564 ff.; Reimer Hansen, 'Was bedeutet *up ewig ungedeelt*? Das Ripener Privileg von 1460 im deutsch–dänischen Nationalkonflikt des 19. Jahrhunderts', *Grenzfriedenshefte* 1996/4, 215–32. Quote from Engels: id., 'Die Bewegungen von 1847', MEW, iv. 494–503 (502–3), tr. as 'The Movements of 1847', MECW, vi. 520–9 (529).

20. Marx, 'Kritik' (note 15), 391 (emphases in original), tr. 'Critique' (note 15), 182 (emphases in original); Roger Price, *The Second French Republic: A Social History* (London: Batsford, 1972); Gilbert Ziebura, *Frankreich 1789–1870. Entstehung einer bürgerlichen Gesellschaftsformation* (Frankfurt: Campus, 1979), 142 ff.
21. Valentin, *Geschichte* (note 19), i. 338 ff., 410 ff. (quotes: 426, 451); ii. *Bis zum Ende der Volksbewegung* (1932; Cologne: Kiepenheuer & Witsch, 1970), 75 ff.; Rudolf Stadelmann, *Soziale und politische Geschichte der Revolution von 1848*, (1948), 2nd edn, Darmstadt: Wissenschaftliche Buchgesellschaft, 1962), 22 ff., tr. as *Social and Political History of the German 1848 Revolution* (Athens, OH: Ohio University Press, 1975); Wehler, *Gesellschaftsgeschichte* (note 3), ii. 642 ff., 703 ff.; Huber, *Verfassungsgeschichte* (note 5), ii. 502 ff., 547 ff., 571 ff.; *Die Revolutionen von 1848/49. Erfahrung—Verarbeitung—Deutung*, ed. Christian Jansen/Thomas Mergel (Göttingen: Vandenhoeck & Ruprecht, 1998); *Revolution in Deutschland und Europa 1848/49*, ed. Wolfgang Hardtwig (Göttingen: Vandenhoeck & Ruprecht, 1998); Wolfgang J. Mommsen, *1848. Die ungewollte Revolution* (Frankfurt: Fischer, 1998); *Europa 1848. Revolution und Reform*, ed. Dieter Dowe et al. (Bonn 1998); Dieter Hein, *Die Revolution von 1848/49* (Munich: C. H. Beck, 1998); *1848. Revolution in Europa. Verlauf, politische Programme, Folgen und Wirkungen*, ed. Heiner Timmermann (Berlin: Duncker & Humblot, 1999); *1848. Revolution in Deutschland*, ed. Christof Dipper and Ulrich Speck (Frankfurt: Insel, 1998); Helmut Berding, *Moderner Antisemitismus in Deutschland* (Frankfurt: Suhrkamp, 1988), 74 ff.; Stefan Rohrbacher, *Gewalt im Biedermeier. Antijüdische Ausschreitungen in Vormärz und Revolution (1815–1848/49)* (Frankfurt: Campus, 1993), 181 ff.
22. *Verhandlungen des deutschen Parlaments. Officielle Ausgabe. Mit einer geschichtlichen Einleitung über die Entstehung der Vertretung des ganzen deutschen Volkes, 2 Lieferungen*, ed. F. S. Jucho (Frankfurt: J. D. Sauerländer, 1848), i. 172 (Poland resolution); *Dokumente zur deutschen Verfassungsgeschichte, i. Deutsche Verfassungsdokumente 1803–1850*, 3rd edn, ed. Ernst Rudolf Huber (Stuttgart: Kohlhammer, 1978), 448–9 (Frederick William IV's proclamation on 21 Mar. 1848); Huber, *Verfassungsgeschichte* (note 5), ii. 571 ff.; Valentin, *Geschichte* (note 19), i. 466 ff., 520 ff.; Meinecke, *Weltbürgertum* (note 4), 301 ff.; Franz X. Vollmer, 'Die 48er Revolution in Baden', in Becker et al., *Badische Geschichte* (note 4), 37–64; Rüdiger Hachtmann, *Berlin 1848. Eine Politik- und Gesellschaftsgeschichte der Revolution* (Bonn: J. H. W. Dietz, 1997), 157 ff.; Hans Christof Kraus, *Ernst Ludwig Gerlach. Politisches Denken und Handeln eines preussischen Altkonservativen*, 2 vols. (Göttingen: Vandenhoeck & Ruprecht, 1994), i. 395 ff.; Wolfram Siemann, *Die deutsche Revolution von 1848/49* (Frankfurt: Suhrkamp, 1985), 146 ff., tr. as *The German Revolution of 1848–49* (New York: St Martin's Press, 1998); Reinhard Wittram, *Die Nationalitätenfrage in Europa und die Erschütterung des europäischen Staatensystems (1848–1917)* (Stuttgart: Klett, 1954),

2–3 (Palacký); Hans Rothfels, 'Das erste Scheitern des Nationalstaates in Ost-Mittel-Europa 1848/49', in *Zeitgeschichtliche Betrachtungen* (Göttingen: Vandenhoeck & Ruprecht, 1959), 40–53; *1848/49. Revolutionen in Ostmitteleuropa*, ed. Rudolf Jaworski/Robert Luft (Munich: Oldenbourg, 1996).

23. *Stenographischer Bericht über die Verhandlungen der deutschen constituierenden Nationalversammlung zu Frankfurt am Main. Hg. auf Beschluss der Nationalversammlung durch die Redactions-Commission und in deren Auftrag von Prof. Franz Wigard*, 9 vols. (Leipzig: Breitkopf & Härtel, 1848–9), iii. 1182 (Dahlmann, 5 Sept. 1848; emphases in original), 2048 (Venedey, 14 Sept. 1848); Gustav Rümelin, *Aus der Paulskirche. Berichte aus dem Schwäbischen Merkur aus den Jahren 1848 und 1849* (Stuttgart: G. J. Göschen, 1892), 85 ff.; Valentin, *Geschichte*, ii. (note 21), 1 ff., 95 ff., 149 ff.; Huber, *Verfassungsgeschichte* (note 5), ii. 587 ff., 682 ff.; Wehler, *Gesellschaftsgeschichte* (note 3), ii. 706 ff.; Nipperdey, *Geschichte* (note 8), 617 ff.; Manfred Botzenhardt, *Deutscher Parlamentarismus in der Revolutionszeit 1848–1850* (Düsseldorf: Droste, 1977), 184 ff.; Werner Boldt, *Die Anfänge des deutschen Parteiwesens. Fraktionen, politische Vereine und Parteien in der Revolution 1848* (Paderborn: Schöningh, 1971), 18 ff.; Frank Eyck, *Deutschlands grosse Hoffnung. Die Frankfurter Nationalversammlung* (Munich: P. List, 1973), 77 ff., orig. *The Frankfurt Parliament 1848–1849* (London: St Martin's Press, 1968); Vollmer, 'Revolution' (note 22), 53 ff.; Franz Mehring, *Geschichte der deutschen Sozialdemokratie* (1897–8), 2 vols., pt 1, *Von der Julirevolution bis zum preussischen Verfassungsstreite 1830 bis 1863* (Berlin: Dietz, 1960), 429 ff.; Balser, *Sozial-Demokratie* (note 16); Jürgen Bergmann, *Wirtschaftskrise und Revolution, Handwerker und Arbeiter 1848/49* (Stuttgart: Klett-Cotta, 1986); Thomas Mergel, *Zwischen Klasse und Konfession. Katholisches Bürgertum im Rheinland 1794–1914* (Göttingen: Vandenhoeck & Ruprecht, 1994), 117 ff. The battles named by Venedey: Fehrbellin, 1675, Prussian victory under the Great Elector over Sweden; Rossbach, 1757, Prussian victory under Frederick the Great in the Seven Years War over the French and the army of the Reich; Katzbach, 1813, Prussian victory under Blücher over the French.

24. *Verhandlungen der Versammlung zur Vereinbarung der Preussischen Staats-Verfassung*, 3 vols. (Berlin: Verlag der Deckerschen Geheimen Ober-Hofbuchdruckerei, 1848), i. 417 (Waldeck), iii. 154–5 (Temme); Manfred Botzenhardt, 'Das preussische Parlament und die deutsche Nationalversammlung im Jahre 1848', in *Regierung, Bürokratie und Parlament in Preussen und Deutschland von 1848 bis zur Gegenwart*, ed. Gerhard A. Ritter (Düsseldorf: Droste, 1983), 14–40; Peter Borowsky, 'Was ist Deutschland? Wer ist deutsch? Die Debatte zur nationalen Identität 1848 in der deutschen Nationalversammlung zu Frankfurt und der preussischen Nationalversammlung zu Berlin', in *Vom schwierigen Zusammenwachsen der Deutschen. Nationale Identität und Nationalismus im 19. und 20. Jahrhundert*, ed. Bernd Jürgen Wendt (Frankfurt: P. Lang, 1992), 81–95; Meinecke, *Weltbürgertum* (note 4), 327 ff.

25. Karl Marx, 'Die revolutionäre Bewegung', MEW, vi. 148–50 (150; emphasis in original); Friedrich Engels, 'Der magyarische Kampf', ibid. 165–76 (172, 176); id., 'Der demokratische Panslawismus', ibid., 271–86 (286); Karl Marx, 'The Revolutionary Movement', MECW, viii. 213–15 (215; emphases in original); Friedrich Engels, 'The Magyar Struggle', ibid. 227–38 (234, 238); id., 'Democratic Pan-Slavism', ibid., 362–78 (377–8); Valentin, *Geschichte* (note 21), ii. 183 ff.; Huber, *Verfassungsgeschichte* (note 5), ii. 710 ff.; Lutz, *Zwischen Habsburg* (note 12), 292 ff.

26. Joseph Hansen, *Gustav von Mevissen. Ein rheinisches Lebensbild 1815–1899*, ii. (Berlin: G. Reimer, 1906), 448 (letter to Georg Mallinckrodt); *Stenographischer Bericht* (note 23), vi. 4096–7 (Dahlmann, 15 Dec. 1848); Hachtmann, *Berlin* (note 22), 688 ff.; Wehler, *Gesellschaftsgeschichte* (note 3), ii. 753 ff.; Nipperdey, *Geschichte* (note 8), 647 ff.; Valentin, *Geschichte* (note 21), ii. 227 ff.; Huber, *Verfassungsgeschichte* (note 5), ii. 737 ff.; Meinecke, *Weltbürgertum* (note 4), 349 ff.; Kraus, *Gerlach* (note 22), i. 430 ff.; Konrad Canis, 'Ideologie und politische Taktik der junkerlich-militaristischen Reaktion bei der Vorbereitung und Durchführung des Staatstreiches in Preussen im Herbst 1848', *Jahrbuch für Geschichte*, 7 (1972), 461–503; Blasius, 'Friedrich Wilhelm IV' (note 9), 600 ff. Quote from Jacoby: *Verhandlungen* (note 24), iii. 325; Waldecks speech on 31 Oct. 1848: ibid., 292–3.
27. *Stenographischer Bericht* (note 23), i. 183 (declaration in defense of the nationalities from of 31 May 1848), 214–15. (Arndt, 5 June 1848); ii. 1145 (Jordan, 24 July 1848), 1156 (Vogt, 12 Aug. 1848); iv. 2779–80. (Arneth, 20 Oct. 1848), 2855 (Mühlfeld, 24 Oct. 1848), 2859 (Vincke, 24 Oct. 1848), 2869 (Reichensperger, 24 Oct. 1848), 2876 (Uhland, 26 Oct. 1848), 2881 (Deym, 26 Oct. 1848), 2898 ff. (Gagern 26 Oct. 1848); Dokumente (note 22), i. ed. Huber, 395 (Art. XIII, § 188 of the imperial constitution in defense of the nationalities); id., *Verfassungsgeschichte* (note 5), ii. 792 ff.; Valentin, *Geschichte* (note 21), ii. 215 ff.; Günter Wollstein, *Das 'Grossdeutschland' der Paulskirche. Nationale Ziele in der bürgerlichen Revolution 1848/49* (Düsseldorf: Droste, 1977), 266 ff.; Rudolf Lill, 'Grossdeutsch und kleindeutsch im Spannungsfeld der Konfessionen', in *Probleme des Konfessionalismus in Deutschland seit 1800*, ed. Anton Rauscher (Paderborn: Schöningh, 1984), 29–47.
28. *Stenographischer Bericht* (note 23), vi. 4626 ff. (Beseler, 13 Jan. 1849), 5807 ff. (Radowitz, 17 Mar. 1849), 5823 (Vogt, 17 Mar. 1849), 5839 ff. (Mohl, 17 Mar. 1849); Huber, *Verfassungsgeschichte* (note 5), ii. 814 ff.; Siemann, *Revolution* (note 22), 192 ff.; Valentin, *Geschichte* (note 22), ii. 305 ff.; Jörg-Detlef Kühne, *Die Reichsverfassung der Paulskirche. Vorbild und Verwirklichung im späteren deutschen Rechtsleben*, 2nd edn (Neuwied: Luchterhand, 1998).
29. Valentin, *Geschichte* (note 21), ii. 381 ff., 448 ff.; Huber, *Verfassungsgeschichte* (note 5), ii. 854 ff.; Hachtmann, *Berlin* (note 22), 798 ff.; Barclay, *Anarchie* (note 9), 272 ff.; Bussmann, *Zwischen Preussen* (note 9), 284 ff.; Christoph Klessmann, 'Zur Sozialgeschichte der Reichsverfassungskampagne von 1849', *HZ* 218 (1974), 283–337; Friedrich Engels, *Die deutsche Reichsverfassungskampagne* (1850), MEW, vii. 109–97 (196), tr. as *The Campaign for the German Imperial Constitution*, MECW, x. 147–239 (237); Fürst Otto von Bismarck, *Die gesammelten Werke* (Friedrichsruh edition, Berlin: O. Stollberg, 1924–); x. 103 ff. The 'mud and clay' quote is from a letter of Frederick William IV to the Prussian envoy in London, Christian Karl Josias von Bunsen, on 13 Dec. 1848; see Leopold von Ranke, *Aus dem Briefwechsel Friedrich Wilhelms IV. mit Bunsen* (Leipzig: Duncker & Humblot, 1873), 233–4.
30. Rümelin, *Paulskirche* (note 23), 14, 240–1; *Stenographischer Bericht* (note 23), ii. 1101 (Ruge), vi. 4596 (Beckerath); Nipperdey, *Geschichte* (note 8), 663 ff.; Wehler, *Gesellschaftsgeschichte* (note 3), ii. 759 ff.; Siemann, *Revolution* (note 22), 223 ff.; Becker, *Zeit* (note 3), 294 ff.; *Die deutsche Revolution von 1848*, ed. Dieter Langewiesche (Darmstadt: Wissenschaftliche Buchgesellschaft, 1983); Hans Rothfels, *1848. Betrachtungen im Abstand von hundert Jahren* (Darmstadt: Wissenschaftliche Buchgesellschaft, 1972, orig. '1848: One Hundred Years after', *Journal of Modern*

History, 20 (1948); Wolfgang Schieder, '1848/49: Die ungewollte Revolution', in *Wendepunkte deutscher Geschichte 1948–1990*, ed. Carola Stern and Heinrich August Winkler (Frankfurt: Fischer Taschenbuch, 1994), 17–42; Lothar Gall, 'Die Germania als Symbol nationaler Einheit im 19. und 20. Jahrhundert', in *Nachrichten der Akademie der Wissenschaften in Göttingen. I. Philologisch-Historische Klasse, Jg. 1993*, 2 (Göttingen: Vandenhoeck & Ruprecht, 1993), 10–11.

CHAPTER 4. UNITY BEFORE LIBERTY 1850–1871

1. Hans-Ulrich Wehler, *Deutsche Gesellschaftsgeschichte*, iii. *Von der 'Deutschen Doppelrevolution' bis zum Beginn des Ersten Weltkrieges 1849–1914* (Munich: C. H. Beck, 1995), 7 ff.; Reinhard Rürup, *Deutschland im 19. Jahrhundert. 1815–1871* (Göttingen: Vandenhoeck & Ruprecht, 1984), 197 ff.; Wolfgang J. Mommsen, *Das Ringen um den nationalen Staat. Die Gründung und der innere Ausbau des Deutschen Reiches unter Otto von Bismarck 1850 bis 1890* (Berlin: Propyläen, 1993), 33 ff.; Johannes Willms, *Nationalismus ohne Nation. Deutsche Geschichte von 1789 bis 1914* (Düsseldorf: Claassen, 1983), 301 ff.; Hans Rosenberg, *Die Weltwirtschaftskrise von 1857–1859* (1934, 2nd edn Göttingen: Vandenhoeck & Ruprecht, 1974). Quote from the *National-Zeitung* in Oscar Stillich, *Die politischen Parteien in Deutschland*, ii. *Der Liberalismus* (Leipzig: W. Klinkhardt, 1911), 36.
2. Harm-Hinrich Brandt, *Der österreichische Neoabsolutismus. Staatsfinanzen und Politik 1848–1860*, 2 vols. (Göttingen: Vandenhoeck & Ruprecht, 1978); Ernst Rudolf Huber, *Deutsche Verfassungsgeschichte seit 1789*, iii. *Bismarck und das Reich*, 3rd edn (Stuttgart: W. Kohlhammer, 1988), 35 ff.; Dieter Grimm, *Deutsche Verfassungsgeschichte 1776–1866* (Frankfurt: Suhrkamp, 1988), 214 ff.; Hans Boldt, 'Die preussische Verfassung vom 31. Januar 1850. Probleme ihrer Interpretation', in *Preussen im Rückblick*, ed. Hans-Jürgen Puhle and Hans-Ulrich Wehler, GG, Sonderheft 6 (Göttingen: Vandenhoeck & Ruprecht, 1980), 224–46; Günther Grünthal, *Parlamentarismus in Preussen 1848/49–1857/58. Preussischer Konstitutionalismus, Parlament und Regierung in der Reaktionsära* (Düsseldorf: Droste, 1982); Hartwin Spenkuch, *Das Preussische Herrenhaus. Adel und Bürgertum in der Ersten Kammer des Landtags 1854–1918* (Düsseldorf: Droste, 1998), 47 ff.; Wilhelm Füssl, *Professor in der Politik: Friedrich Julius Stahl (1802–1861). Das monarchische Prinzip und seine Umsetzung in die parlamentarische Praxis* (Göttingen: Vandenhoeck & Ruprecht, 1988), 44 ff., 108 ff. (quotes from Stahls 'Entwurf für eine conservative Partei' of Feb./Mar. 1849: 183 ff.); Gerhard Masur, *Friedrich Julius Stahl. Geschichte seines Lebens. Aufstieg und Entfaltung, 1802–1840* (Berlin: E. S. Mittler, 1930), 200 ff.; Horst Zillessen, *Protestantismus und politische Form. Eine Untersuchung zum protestantischen Verfassungsverständnis* (Gütersloh: G. Mohn, 1971), 67 ff.; Hans-Christof Kraus, *Ernst Ludwig von Gerlach. Politisches Denken und Handeln eines preussischen Altkonservativen*, 2 vols. (Göttingen: Vandenhoeck & Ruprecht, 1994), ii. 586 ff.; David E. Barclay, *Anarchie und guter Wille. Friedrich Wilhelm IV. und die preussische Monarchie* (Berlin: Siedler, 1995), 308 ff., orig. *Frederick William IV and the Prussian Monarchy, 1840–1861* (Oxford: Oxford University Press, 1995).
3. Helmut Böhme, *Deutschlands Weg zur Grossmacht. Studien zum Verhältnis von Wirtschaft und Staat während der Reichsgründungszeit 1848–1881* (Cologne: Kiepenheuer & Witsch, 1966), 19 ff.; Richard Löwenthal, 'Internationale Konstellation und innerstaatlicher

Systemwandel', HZ 212 (1971), 41–58; Anselm Doering-Manteuffel, *Vom Wiener Kongress zur Pariser Konferenz. England, die deutsche Frage und das Mächtesystem 1815–1856* (Göttingen: Vandenhoeck & Ruprecht, 1991), 187 ff.; Winfried Baumgart, *Der Friede von Paris 1856. Studien zum Verhältnis von Kriegführung, Politik und Friedensbewahrung* (Munich: R. Oldenbourg, 1972), tr. as *The Peace of Paris, 1856: Studies in War, Diplomacy, and Peacemaking* (Santa Barbara, CA: ABC-Clio, 1981); Werner E. Mosse, *The Rise and Fall of the Crimean System 1855–1871: The Story of a Peace Settlement* (London: Macmillan, 1963); Hans Joachim Schoeps, *Das andere Preussen. Konservative Gestalten und Probleme im Zeitalter Friedrich Wilhelms IV.*, 2nd edn (Honnef: Peters, 1957), 124 ff.; Ernst Engelberg, *Bismarck. Urpreusse und Reichsgründer* (Berlin: Siedler, 1985), 417 ff.; Lothar Gall, *Bismarck. Der weisse Revolutionär* (Berlin: Propyläen, 1980), 167 ff., tr. as *Bismarck, the White Revolutionary* (London: Allen & Unwin, 1986). For the quotes from Bismarck's letters to Leopold von Gerlach, see Fürst Otto von Bismarck, *Die gesammelten Werke*, Friedrichsruh edition (Berlin: O. Stollberg, 1924–), xiv/i: 464 ff. (2 May 1857), 470 ff. (30 May 1857; emphasis in original).

4. Ludwig August von Rochau, *Grundsätze der Realpolitik. Angewendet auf die staatlichen Zustände Deutschlands* (1853), ed. and introd. Hans-Ulrich Wehler (Frankfurt: Ullstein, 1972), 25–6, 67, 169, 173; Siegfried A. Kaehler, 'Realpolitik zur Zeit des Krimkrieges. Eine Säkularbetrachtung', *HZ* 174 (1952), 417–78; Hans Rothfels, 'Zeitgeschichtliche Betrachtungen zum Problem der Realpolitik', in *Zeitgeschichtliche Betrachtungen* (Göttingen: Vandenhoeck & Ruprecht, 1959), 179–98; Karl-Georg Faber, 'Realpolitik als Ideologie. Die Bedeutung des Jahres 1866 für das politische Denken in Deutschland', *HZ* 203 (1966), 1–45.
5. Rochau, *Grundsätze* (note 4), 126 ff., 146 ff., 150–1.
6. Lorenz von Stein, *Geschichte der sozialen Bewegung in Frankreich von 1789 bis auf unsere Tage*, 3 vols., iii. *Das Königtum, die Republik und die Souveränität der französischen Gesellschaft seit der Februarrevolution 1848* (1850; new edn Darmstadt: Wissenschaftliche Buchgesellschaft, 1959), 406, 408.
7. Ibid. 7, 37–41; id., *Zur preussischen Verfassungsfrage* (1852; 2nd edn Darmstadt: Wissenschaftliche Buchgesellschaft, 1961) 4, 6, 12, 34 ff. (emphases in original); Dirk Blasius, 'Lorenz von Stein', in *Deutsche Historiker*, i., ed. Hans-Ulrich Wehler (Göttingen: Vandenhoeck & Ruprecht, 1971), 25–38; Hermann Beck, *The Origins of the Authoritarian Welfare State in Prussia: Conservatives, Bureaucracy, and the Social Question, 1815–1870* (Ann Arbor: University of Michigan Press, 1995), esp. 71 ff.
8. Karl Marx, *Die Klassenkämpfe in Frankreich* (1850), MEW, vii. 9–107 (89–90); id., 'Die moralisierende Kritik und die kritisierende Moral' (1847), MEW, iv. 331–59 (339); id., 'Sieg der Kontrerevolution in Wien' (7 Nov. 1848), MEW, v. 455–7 (457; all emphases in the original); id., letter to Joseph Weydemeyer of 5 Mar. 1852, MEW, xxviii. 503–9 (508); Marx, *The Class Struggles in France*, MECW, x. 45–146 (127); id., 'Moralising Criticism and Critical Morality', MECW, vi. 312–40 (319); id., 'Victory of the Counter-Revolution in Vienna', MECW, vii. 503–6 (505–6); letter to Joseph Weydemeyer of 5 Mar. 1852, MECW, xxxix. 60–6 (62–5).
9. Rochau, *Grundsätze* (note 4), 184; Karl Marx, *Der achtzehnte Brumaire des Louis Bonaparte*, MEW (note 8), viii. 111–207 (in the order of the quotes: 118, 204, 154); Karl Marx/Friedrich Engels, *Manifest der Kommunistischen Partei*, MEW, iv. 459–93 (464); 'Die politischen Parteien in England—Die Lage in Europa' (24 June 1858), MEW, xii. 503–6 (505; emphases in original); id., 'Die französische Abrüstung' (12 Aug. 1859), ibid. 447–9 (448); Engels's letter to Marx of 15 Nov. 1857, ibid. xxix. 208–12 (211–12);

Karl Marx, 'Das neue Ministerium' (9 Nov. 1858), xii. 636–9; Friedrich Engels, 'Europa im Jahre 1858' (23 Dec. 1858), ibid., 654–8 (658); Karl Marx, *The Eighteenth Brumaire of Louis Bonaparte*, MECW, xi. 99–197 (in the order of the quotes: 106–7, 194, 143); Karl Marx/Friedrich Engels, *Communist* Party *Manifesto* MECW, vi. 477–519 (486); Marx, 'Political Parties in England—Situation in Europe', MECW, xv. 566–9 (568); id., 'The French Disarmament' MECW, xvi. 442–4 (443); Engels's letter to Marx of 15 Nov. 1857; MECW, xl. 200–4 (203); Marx, 'The New Ministry', MECW, xvi. 101–5; Engels, 'Europe in 1858', ibid. 120–4 (124); Heinrich August Winkler, 'Zum Verhältnis von bürgerlicher und proletarischer Revolution bei Marx und Engels', in *Revolution, Staat, Faschismus. Zur Revision des Historischen Materialismus* (Göttingen: Vandenhoeck & Ruprecht, 1978), 8–34; id., 'Primat der Ökonomie? Zur Rolle der Staatsgewalt bei Marx und Engels', ibid. 35–64. Marx's 'translation' of 'Hic Rhodus, hic salta!' is from Georg Wilhelm Friedrich Hegel, *Grundlinien der Philosophie des Rechts oder Naturrecht und Staatswissenschaft im Grundrisse (Vorrede)*, in *Sämtliche Werke*, 3rd edn, vii (Stuttgart: Fromman, 1952), p. xxii.

10. Felix Salomon, *Die deutschen Parteiprogramme* (Leipzig: B. G. Teubner, 1907), i. 41–2; Ludolf Parisius, *Deutschlands politische Parteien und das Ministerium Bismarck* (Berlin: J. Guttentag, 1878), 15 ff.; Huber, *Verfassungsgeschichte*, iii. (note 2), 269 ff.; Heinrich August Winkler, *Preussischer Liberalismus und deutscher Nationalstaat. Studien zur Geschichte der Deutschen Fortschrittspartei 1861–1866* (Tübingen: Mohr, 1964), 3 ff.
11. *Bismarck und der Staat. Ausgewählte Dokumente*, introd. Hans Rothfels (Stuttgart: Kohlhammer, n.d. [1953]), 111–15 (113–14; Bismarck's letter to Alvensleben of 5 May 1859); Ferdinand Lassalle, *Der italienische Krieg und die italienische Aufgabe Preussens. Eine Stimme aus der Demokratie* (1859), in *Gesamtwerke*, ed. Erich Blum (Leipzig: Pfau, n.d. [1899–1909]), ii. 369–442 (391–2, 435–8); Friedrich Engels, *Po und Rhein* (April 1859), MEW, xiii. 225–68 (227, 268), tr. as *Po and Rhine*, MECW, xvi. 213–55 (215, 255). Hans Rosenberg, *Die nationalpolitische Publizistik Deutschlands vom Eintritt der Neuen Ära in Preussen bis zum Ausbruch des deutschen Krieges. Eine kritische Bibliographie*, 2 vols. (Munich: R. Oldenbourg, 1935), i. 20–158; Hermann Oncken, *Lassalle. Zwischen Marx und Bismarck* (1904: 5th edn (Stuttgart: Kohlhammer, 1966), 131 ff.; Arnold Oskar Meyer, *Bismarck. Der Mensch und der Staatsmann* (Stuttgart: K. F. Koehler, 1949), 123 ff.; Erich Portner, *Die Einigung Italiens im Urteil liberaler deutscher Zeitgenossen* (Bonn: L. Röhrscheid, 1959); Huber, *Verfassungsgeschichte*, iii (note 2), 254 ff.; Wehler, *Gesellschaftsgeschichte*, iii. (note 1), 228 ff. On Rochau see Ludwig August von Rochau, 'Die Frage von Krieg und Frieden', introd. to the 2nd edn of id., *Grundsätze* (note 4), 192–203.
12. Peter Katzenstein, *Disjoined Partners: Austria and Germany since 1815* (Berkeley: University of California Press, 1976), 66 ff.; Heinrich Lutz, *Zwischen Habsburg und Preussen, Deutschland 1815–1866* (Berlin: Siedler, 1985), 403 ff.; Thomas Nipperdey, *Deutsche Geschichte 1800–1866. Bürgerwelt und starker Staat* (Munich: C. H. Beck, 1983), 704 ff.; Huber, *Verfassungsgeschichte*, iii (note 2), 138 ff., 378 ff., 384 ff.; Georg Franz, *Liberalismus. Die deutsch-liberale Bewegung in der habsburgischen Monarchie* (Munich: G. D. W. Callwey, 1955), 264 ff.; Andreas Biefang, *Politisches Bürgertum in Deutschland 1857–1868. Nationale Organisationen und Eliten* (Düsseldorf: Droste, 1994), 17 ff., 185 ff., 301 ff.; Shlomo Na'aman, *Der Deutsche Nationalverein. Die politische Konstituierung des deutschen Bürgertums 1859–1867* (Düsseldorf: Droste, 1987), 41 ff.; Rainer Noltenius, 'Schiller als Führer und Heiland. Das Schillerfest 1859 als

nationaler Traum von der Geburt des zweiten deutschen Kaiserreiches', *Öffentliche Festkultur. Politische Feste in Deutschland von der Aufklärung bis zum Ersten Weltkrieg*, ed. Dieter Düding et al. (Hamburg: Rowohlt, 1988), 237–58; Dieter Düding, 'Nationale Oppositionsfeste der Turner, Sänger und Schützen im 19. Jahrhundert', ibid. 166–90; id., 'Die deutsche Nationalbewegung des 19. Jahrhunderts als Vereinsbewegung. Anmerkungen zu ihrer Struktur und Phänomenologie zwischen Befreiungskriegszeitalter und Reichsgründung', *GWU* 42 (1991), 601–24; Hans-Thorwald Michaelis, *Unter schwarz-rot-goldenem Banner und dem Signum des Doppeladlers. Gescheiterte Volksbewaffnungs- und Vereinigungsbestrebungen in der Deutschen Nationalbewegung und im Deutschen Schützenbund 1859–1869* (Frankfurt: P. Lang, 1993), 229 ff.; Dietmar Klenke, 'Nationalkriegerisches Gemeinschaftsideal als politische Religion. Zum Vereinsnationalismus der Sänger, Schützen und Turner am Vorabend der Einigungskriege', *HZ* 260 (1995), 395–448; id., *Der singende 'deutsche Mann', Gesangvereine und deutsches Nationalbewusstsein von Napoleon bis Hitler* (Münster: Waxmann, 1998); Svenja Goltermann, *Körper der Nation. Habitusforschung und die Politik des Turnens 1860–1890* (Göttingen: Vandenhoeck & Ruprecht, 1998); Stefan Illig, *Zwischen Körperertüchtigung und nationaler Bewegung. Turnvereine in Bayern 1860–1890* (Cologne: SH-Verlag, 1998); Dieter Langewiesche, 'Nation, Nationalismus und Nationalstaat: Forschungsstand und Forschungsperspektiven', *NPL* 40 (1995), 190–236.

13. *Deutsche Parteiprogramme*, ed. Wilhelm Mommsen (Munich: Isar, 1960), 132–5 (platform of the German Progressive Party); Bismarck, *Werke* (note 3), x. 139–40 (budget commission, 30 Sept. 1862), xv. 179–80, 194 ff. (*Erinnerung und Gedanke*); Heinrich von Sybel, *Die Begründung des Deutschen Reiches durch Wilhelm I.*, 3 vols. (new edn Meersburg: F. M. Hendel, 1930), i. 508 ff., tr. as *The Founding of the German Empire by William I* (New York: Greenwood Press, 1968); Thomas Nipperdey, *Die Organisation der deutschen Parteien vor 1918* (Düsseldorf: Droste, 1961), 196 ff.; Fritz Löwenthal, *Der preussische Verfassungsstreit 1862–1866* (Munich: Duncker & Humblot, 1914), 120 ff.; Rolf Helfert, *Der preussische Liberalismus und die Heeresreform von 1860* (Bonn: Holos, 1989), 67 ff.; Winkler, *Liberalismus* (note 10), 10 ff.; Huber, *Verfassungsgeschichte*, iii (note 2), 275 ff.
14. *National-Zeitung* [*NZ*], 2 Oct. 1862, Morgenblatt [*Mbl*], on Bismarck's 'napoleonic ideas'; (Löwenstein); *NZ*, 23 Oct. 1862, *Abendblatt* [*Abl*]; 'Politische Correspondenz', *Preussische Jahrbücher*, 10 (1862), 402–18 (412); [Karl Twesten], 'Lehre und Schriften Auguste Comtes', ibid. 4 (1859), 279–307 (306); *Stenographischer Bericht über die Verhandlungen des preussischen Abgeordnetenhauses* [*Sten. Ber., LT*], 1866 (1st session), I, 79 ff. (Twesten, 22 Feb. 1866); Otto Westphal, *Welt- und Staatsauffassung des deutschen Liberalismus. Eine Untersuchung über die Preussischen Jahrbücher und den konstitutionellen Liberalismus in Deutschland, 1858 bis 1863* (Munich: Oldenbourg, 1919), 297 ff.; Winkler, *Liberalismus* (note 10), 16 ff.
15. Ludolf Parisius, *Leopold Freiherr von Hoverbeck*, 2 vols. (Berlin: J. Guttentag, 1897–), ii. 53–5 (letters to Karl Witt of 27 June and 30 July 1865); Ferdinand Lassalle, *Über Verfassungswesen* (speech on 16 Apr. 1862) (repr. Darmstadt: Wissenschaftliche Buchgesellschaft, 1958), 56–7; Oncken, *Lassalle* (note 11), 178 ff., 296 ff.; Shlomo Na'aman, *Demokratische und soziale Impulse in der Frühgeschichte der deutschen Arbeiterbewegung der Jahre 1862/63* (Wiesbaden: F. Steiner, 1969); id., *Lassalle* (Hanover, 1970), 527 ff.; Gustav Mayer, 'Lassalle und Bismarck', in id., *Arbeiterbewegung und Obrigkeitsstaat*, ed. Hans-Ulrich Wehler (Bonn: Verlag Neue

Gesellschaft, 1972), 93–118; Wolfgang Schieder, 'Das Scheitern des bürgerlichen in Radikalismus und die sozialistische Parteibildung in Deutschland', in *Sozialdemokratie zwischen Klassenbewegung und Volkspartei*, ed. Hans Mommsen (Frankfurt: Athenäum-Fischer Taschenbuch-Verlag, 1974), 17–34; Rita Aldenhoff, *Schulze-Delitzsch. Ein Beitrag zur Geschichte des Liberalismus zwischen Revolution und Reichsgründung* (Baden-Baden: Nomos, 1984), 161 ff.

16. Heinrich Bernhard Oppenheim, 'Ein Wort über politische und staatsbürgerliche Pflichterfüllung', *Deutsche Jahrbücher*, 13 (1864), 112–28 (118–19, 122; emphasis in original); Wilhelm Löwe (von Calbe), 'Preussens Beruf in der deutschen Sache', ibid. 2 (1861), 169–90 (179); *NZ*, 17 Apr. 1862, *Mbl.*; Parisius, *Hoverbeck* (note 15), i. 164–5. (Forckenbeck's letter of 21 Aug. 1859); Winkler, *Liberalismus* (note 10), 26 ff.; Ernst Rudolf Huber, *Deutsche Verfassungsgeschichte seit 1789*, i. *Reform und Restauration 1789–1830*, 3rd edn (Stuttgart: Kohlhammer, 1990), 610 ff.; *Dokumente zur deutschen Verfassungsgeschichte*, i. *Deutsche Verfassungsdokumente 1803–1850*, ed. id., 3rd edn (Stuttgart: Kohlhammer,1978), 119–20 (*Bundeskriegsverfassung* of 9 Apr. 1821).
17. *Der Deutsche Nationalverein 1859–1867. Vorstands- und Ausschussprotokolle*, ed. Andreas Biefang (Düsseldorf: Droste, 1995), 246–8 (resolution of the committee of 25 May 1863); Sybel, *Begründung* (note 13), i. 581 ff.; Huber, *Verfassungsgeschichte*, iii (note 2), 393 ff., 421 ff.; Biefang, *Bürgertum* (note 12), 221 ff.; Willy Real, *Der deutsche Reformverein. Grossdeutsche Stimmen und Kräfte zwischen Villafranca und Königgrätz* (Lübeck: Matthiesen, 1966); Hans Rosenberg, 'Honoratiorenpolitiker und grossdeutsche Sammlungsbestrebungen im Reichsgründungszeitalter', in *Machteliten und Wirtschaftskonjunkturen. Studien zur neueren deutschen Sozial- und Wirtschaftsgeschichte* (Göttingen: Vandenhoeck & Ruprecht, 1978), 198–254. On the controversy between Sybel und Ficker see *Universalstaat oder Nationalstaat. Macht und Ende des Ersten Deutschen Reiches. Die Streitschriften von Heinrich von Sybel und Julius Ficker zur deutschen Kaiserpolitik des Mittelalters*, 2nd edn, ed. Friedrich Schneider (Innsbruck: Universitätsverlag Wagner, 1943).
18. *Sten. Ber.*, *LT*, 1862 (2nd session), VI, enclosure 78 (report of the unified commissions for finances and customs and trade and industry in the commercial treaty with France); Victor Böhmert, 'Deutschlands wirtschaftliche Neugestaltung', *Preussische Jahrbücher*, 18 (1866), 269–304 (270); Böhme, *Weg* (note 3), 91 ff.; Huber, *Verfassungsgeschichte*, iii (note 2), 615 ff.; Winkler, *Liberalismus* (note 10), 71 ff.; Eugen Franz, *Der Entscheidungskampf um die wirtschaftspolitische Führung Deutschlands (1856 bis 1867)* (Munich: Verlag der Kommission, 1933); Volker Hentschel, *Die deutschen Freihändler und der volkswirtschaftliche Kongress 1858–1885* (Stuttgart: Klett, 1975), 61 ff.
19. Lawrence D. Steefel, *The Schleswig-Holstein Question* (Cambridge, MA: Harvard University Press, 1932), 3 ff.; Otto Brandt, *Geschichte Schleswig-Holsteins. Ein Grundriss*, 4th edn (Kiel: Mühlau, 1949), 168 ff.; Joachim Daebel, 'Die Schleswig-Holstein-Bewegung in Deutschland 1863/64', Ph.D. thesis, Cologne, 1969, 45 ff.; Theodor Schieder, 'Vom Deutschen Bund zum Deutschen Reich', *Von der Französischen Revolution bis zum Ersten Weltkrieg* (= Bruno Gebhardt, *Handbuch der Deutschen Geschichte*, iii), 9th edn, ed. Karl Erich Born et al. (Stuttgart: Union-Verlag, 1970), 99–220 (183 ff.); Ernst Rudolf Huber, *Deutsche Verfassungsgeschichte seit 1789*, ii. *Der Kampf um Einheit und Freiheit 1830 bis 1850*, 3rd edn (Stuttgart: Kohlhammer,

1988), 933 ff.; id., *Verfassungsgeschichte*, iii (note 2), 449 ff. Quote from Lerchenfeld in Real, *Reformverein* (note 17), 185.

20. *Sten. Ber., LT*, 1863/64, I, 274 (Twesten, 2 Dec. 1863), 497–8 (Waldeck, 18 Dec. 1863); *NZ*, 29 May 1864, *Mbl.*; 11 Aug. 1864, *Mbl.*; 12 Aug. 1864, *Mbl.*; *Volkszeitung* [*VZ*], 8. 16. 1864; Winkler, *Liberalismus* (note 10), 50 ff.; Real, *Reformverein* (note 17), 170 ff.; Gall, *Bismarck* (note 3), 312 ff.; Huber, *Verfassungsgeschichte*, iii (note 2), 482 ff.; Schieder, 'Vom Deutschen Bund' (note 19), 188 ff.; Rudolf Stadelmann, *Das Jahr 1865 und das Problem von Bismarcks deutscher Politik* (Munich: Oldenbourg, 1933); Andreas Kaernbach, *Bismarcks Konzepte zur Reform des Deutschen Bundes. Zur Kontinuität der Politik Bismarcks und Preussens in der deutschen Frage* (Göttingen: Vandenhoeck & Ruprecht, 1991), 98 ff.; Eberhard Kolb, 'Grosspreussen oder Kleindeutschland? Zu Bismarcks deutscher Politik im Reichsgründungszeitalter', in *Umbrüche deutscher Geschichte 1866/71, 1918/19, 1929/33* (Munich: Oldenbourg, 1993), 11–33.

21. Theodor Mommsen, *Die Annexion Schleswig-Holsteins. Ein Sendschreiben an die Wahlmänner der Stadt Halle und des Saalkreises* (Berlin: Weidmannsche, 1865), 17, 23; *Sten. Ber., LT*, 1865, III, 2117 (Michaelis, 13 June 1865); *NZ*, 1 June 1865, *Mbl.*; 2 Aug. 1865, Mbl.; 3 Aug. 1865, *Mbl.*; *VZ*, 6 Aug. 1865; 16 Aug. 1865; 25 Aug. 1865, *Mbl.*; *VZ*, 12 Oct. 1865 (Harkorts declaration); *Schulthess' Europäischer Geschichtskalender*, 6 (1865) (Nördlingen: C. H. Beck, 1866), 120–1 (declaration of the Delegate Congress of 1 Oct. 1865); *Nationalverein* (note 17), 366–7 (resolution of the general assembly of 29 Oct. 1865); *Die Sturmjahre der preussisch-deutschen Einigung 1859–1870. Politische Briefe aus dem Nachlass liberaler Parteiführer*, sel. and ed. Julius Heyderhoff (= *Deutscher Liberalismus im Zeitalter Bismarcks. Eine politische Briefsammlung*, i) (1925; repr. Osnabrück: Biblio-Verlag, 1967), 253–5 (Mommsen's letter of 28 Sept. 1865), 255–7 (Twesten's letter of 28 Sept. 1865); Huber, *Verfassungsgeschichte*, iii (note 2), 506 ff.; Winkler, *Liberalismus* (note 10), 60 ff.; Andreas Biefang, 'National-preussisch oder deutsch-national? Die Deutsche Fortschrittspartei in Preussen 1861–1867', GG 23 (1997), 360–83; Alfred Heuss, *Theodor Mommsen und das 19. Jahrhundert* (Kiel: F. Hirt, 1956), 177 ff.

22. *Nationalverein* (note 17), 212–13 (Miquel, Oct. 1865); Na'aman, *Nationalverein* (note 12), 186 ff.; Adolf Rapp, *Die Württemberger und die nationale Frage 1863–1871* (Stuttgart: Kohlhammer, 1910), 98 (*Beobachter*, 17 Apr. 1864), 84 (*Beobachter*, 10 Feb. 1864), 99–100 (*Beobachter*, 23–9 Apr. 1864); Dieter Langewiesche, *Liberalismus und Demokratie in Württemberg zwischen Revolution und Reichsgründung* (Düsseldorf: Droste, 1974), 309 ff.; Gerlinde Runge, *Die Volkspartei in Württemberg von 1864 bis 1871. Die Erben der 48er Revolution im Kampf gegen die preussisch-kleindeutsche Lösung der nationalen Frage* (Stuttgart: Kohlhammer, 1970), 25 ff.

23. Gustav Mayer, 'Die Trennung der proletarischen von der bürgerlichen Demokratie in Deutschland, 1863–1870', in *Radikalismus, Sozialismus und bürgerliche Demokratie*, ed. Hans-Ulrich Wehler (Frankfurt: Suhrkamp, 1969), 108–78; Rolf Weber, *Kleinbürgerliche Demokraten in der deutschen Einheitsbewegung 1863–1866* (Berlin: Rütten & Loening, 1962), 81 ff.; Schieder, 'Scheitern' (note 15), 17 ff.

24. Lothar Gall, *Der Liberalismus als regierende Partei. Das Grossherzogtum Baden zwischen Restauration und Reichsgründung* (Wiesbaden: F. Steiner, 1968), 169 ff.; id., 'Die partei- und sozialgeschichtliche Problematik des badischen Kulturkampfes', *Zeitschrift für die Geschichte des Oberrheins*, 113 (1965), 151–96; Josef Becker, *Liberaler Staat und Kirche*

in der Ära von Reichsgründung und Kulturkampf. Geschichte und Strukturen ihres Verhältnisses in Baden 1860–1876 (Mainz: Matthias-Grünewald-Verlag, 1973), 35 ff.; Böhme, *Weg* (note 3), 197 ff.; Kaernbach, *Konzepte* (note 20), 204 ff.

25. Bismarck, *Werke* (note 3), v. 421 (edict to the Prussian envoy in Munich, Heinrich VII Prince Reuss, of 24 Mar. 1866); *NZ* 5 Apr. 1866, *Mbl.*; 12 Apr. 1866, *Abl.*; 18 Apr. 1866, *Abl.* (Twesten); Kaernbach, *Konzepte* (note 20), 211 ff.; Huber, *Verfassungsgeschichte*, iii (note 2), 510 ff.; Lutz, *Zwischen Habsburg* (note 12), 552 ff.; Sybel, *Begründung* (note 13), ii. 390 ff.; Heinrich Ritter von Srbik, *Deutsche Einheit. Idee und Wirklichkeit vom Heiligen Reich bis Königgrätz*, 4 vols. (Munich: F. Bruckmann, 1935), iv. 320 ff.; Theodor Schieder, *Die kleindeutsche Partei in Bayern in den Kämpfen um die nationale Einheit 1863–1871* (Munich: C. H. Beck, 1936), 93 ff.; Rapp, *Württemberger* (note 22), 162 ff.; Gall, *Liberalismus* (note 24), 345 ff.; Winkler, *Liberalismus* (note 10), 83 ff.
26. Franz, *Liberalismus* (note 12), 261–2 (*Neue Freie Presse*, 19 June 1866); *NZ* 30 June 1866, *Mbl.*; 1 July 1866, *Mbl.* (Duncker); Rapp, *Württemberger* (note 22), 134 (manifesto of the People's Party of 2 Apr. 1866), 157 (Upper Swabia), 159 (*Beobachter*, 24 June 1866); Winkler, *Liberalismus* (note 10), 88 ff.; Gall, *Liberalismus* (note 24), 352 ff.; Huber, *Verfassungsgeschichte*, iii (note 2), 555 ff.; Sybel, *Begründung* (note 13), ii. 591 ff.; *Die nationalpolitische Publizistik von 1866 bis 1871. Eine kritische Bibliographie*, 2 vols., ed. Karl-Georg Faber (Düsseldorf: Droste, 1963), i. 13 ff.
27. *Denkwürdigkeiten des Fürsten Chlodwig zu Hohenlohe-Schillingsfürst*, 2 vols. (Stuttgart: Deutsche Verlagsanstalt, 1907), i. 168–9 (13 July 1866), tr. as *Memoirs of Prince Chlodwig of Hohenlohe-Schillingsfuerst*, 2 vols., ed. George W. Chrystal (New York: AMS Press Edition, 1970); Christa Stache, *Bürgerlicher Liberalismus und katholischer Konservatismus in Bayern 1867–1871. Kulturkämpferische Auseinandersetzungen vor dem Hintergrund von nationaler Einigung und wirtschaftlich-sozialem Wandel* (Frankfurt: Lang,1981), 42–3 (declaration of the Progressive party of 28 Aug. 1866); Schieder, *Partei* (note 25), 129 ff.; Gall, *Liberalismus* (note 24), 376 ff.; Langewiesche, *Liberalismus* (note 22), 324 ff.; Rapp, *Württemberger* (note 22), 184 ff.; Wehler, *Gesellschaftsgeschichte*, iii (note 1), 283 ff. (civil war argument).
28. *NZ* 31 July 1866, *Mbl.*; 25 July 1866, *Mbl.* (emphases in original); [Edmund Jörg], 'Das deutsche Volk zwischen heute und morgen', *Historisch-politische Blätter für das katholische Deutschland* [*HPB*], 58 (1866/II), 313–28 (324, 328); Adolf M. Birke, *Bischof Ketteler und der deutsche Liberalismus. Eine Untersuchung über das Verhältnis des liberalen Katholizismus zum bürgerlichen Liberalismus in der Reichsgründungszeit* (Mainz: Matthias-Grünewald-Verlag, 1971), 74 (Ketteler's to Emperor Franz Joseph of 28 Aug. 1866); Wilhelm Emmanuel von Ketteler, *Deutschland nach dem Kriege von 1866* (Mainz: F. Kirchheim, 1867), 82–4; Faber, 'Realpolitik' (note 4), 1 ff.
29. [Ernst Ludwig v. Gerlach], 'Krieg und Bundesreform', *Neue Preussische Zeitung* (*Kreuz-Zeitung*), 8 May 1866; Kraus, *Gerlach* (note 2), ii. 804 (quote from the pamphlet 'Die Annexionen und der Norddeutsche Bund'; emphases in original); Winkler, *Liberalismus* (note 10), 99 ff.; Rapp, *Württemberger* (note 22), 190 (Österlen); August Bebel, *Aus meinem Leben*, (1911; repr. Bonn: J. H. W. Dietz, 1997), 127–8 (platform of the Saxon People's party), tr. as *My Life* (New York: H. Fertig, 1973); Weber, *Demokraten* (note 23), 237 ff.; Mayer, 'Trennung' (note 23), 129 ff.; Werner Conze and Dieter Groh, *Die Arbeiterbewegung in der nationalen Bewegung. Die deutsche Sozialdemokratie vor, während und nach der Reichsgründung* (Stuttgart, 1966); Michael Stürmer, *Das ruhelose Reich.*

Deutschland 1866–1918 (Berlin: Klett, 1983), 143 ff. Quote from Jacoby in *Sten. Ber., LT*, 1866/67, I, 72; on Klopp see Lorenz Matzinger, *Onno Klopp 1822–1903. Leben und Werk* (Aurich: Ostfriesische Landschaft, 1993), 78 ff.

30. MEW, xxxi. 240–1 (Engels to Marx, 25 July 1866); xxxvi. 238–9 (Engels to Bebel, 18 Nov. 1884; all emphases in the original); MECW, xl. 297–8 (Engels to Marx, 25 July 1866); xlvii. 220–3 (Engels to Bebel, 18 Nov. 1884; all emphases in the original); Bismarck, *Werke* (note 3), vi. 120 (Bismarck to Manteuffel, 11 Aug. 1866), viii. 459 (conversation with the writer Paul Lindau and the bank director Löwenfeld on 8 Dec. 1882; here the quote from the conversation with Napoleon III, probably Oct. 1864 or 1865); Hans Joachim Schoeps, *Der Weg ins Deutsche Kaiserreich* (Berlin: Propyläen, 1970), 147–8 (Bluntschli, Hess); *Sten. Ber., LT*, 1866/67, III, 1299–300 (Twesten), II, 833 (Unruh); Jacob Burckhardt, *Über das Studium der Geschichte. Der Text der 'Weltgeschichtlichen Betrachtungen'*, ed. Peter Ganz (Munich: C. H. Beck, 1982), 373 (emphases in original); Winkler, *Liberalismus* (note 10), 106 ff.; id., 'Primat' (note 9), 52–3; Henry A. Kissinger, 'Der weisse Revolutionär: Reflexionen über Bismarck', in *Das Bismarck-Problem in der Geschichtsschreibung nach 1945*, ed. Lothar Gall (Cologne: Kiepenheuer & Witsch, 1971), 392–428; Gustav Adolf Rein, *Die Revolution in der Politik Bismarcks* (Göttingen: Musterschmidt, 1957), 325 ff.; Meyer, *Bismarck* (note 11), 328 ff.; Ernst Engelberg, 'Über die Revolution von oben', *Zeitschrift für Geschichtswissenschaft*, 22 (1974), 1183–1212; Dieter Langewiesche, ' "Revolution von oben"? Kriege und Nationalstaatsgründung in Deutschland', in *Revolution und Krieg. Zur Dynamik historischen Wandels seit dem 18. Jahrhundert*, ed. id. (Paderborn: Schöningh, 1989), 117–34.

31. Parisius, *Parteien* (note 10), 77; Huber, *Verfassungsgeschichte*, iii (note 2), 352–3; Winkler, *Liberalismus* (note 10), 91 ff.; id., 'Bürgerliche Emanzipation und nationale Einigung. Zur Entstehung des Nationalliberalismus in Preussen', in *Liberalismus und Antiliberalismus. Studien zur politischen Sozialgeschichte des 19. und 20. Jahrhunderts* (Göttingen: Vandenhoeck & Ruprecht, 1979), 24–35.

32. Huber, *Verfassungsgeschichte*, iii (note 2), 305 ff. (argument about the legitimacy of Bismarck's policies, 1862–6); Hans Boldt, 'Verfassungskonflikt und Verfassungshistorie. Eine Auseinandersetzung mit Ernst Rudolf Huber', in *Der Staat*, suppl. 1, *Probleme des Konstitutionalismus im 19. Jahrhundert* (Berlin: Duncker & Humblot, 1975), 75–102; Ernst Wolfgang Böckenförde, 'Der Verfassungstyp der deutschen konstitutionellen Monarchie im 19. Jahrhundert', in *Moderne deutsche Verfassungsgeschichte (1815–1914)*, ed. id. (Cologne: Kiepenheuer & Witsch, 1972), 146–70; Rainer Wahl, 'Der preussische Verfassungskonflikt und das konstitutionelle System des Kaiserreichs', ibid. 171–94. For Bismarck's conversation with Twesten on 1 Oct. 1862 see Bismarck, *Werke* (note 3), vii. 59–60.

33. *Sten. Ber., LT*, 1866/67, I, 151 (Waldeck, 1 Sept. 1866), 182 ff. (Lasker, 3 Sept. 1866), 161 (Michaelis, 1 Sept. 1866), 198–9 (Twesten, 3 Sept. 1866), 72 (Virchow), 23 Aug. 1866), 252–3 (Harkort, 7 Sept. 1866); *NZ* 19 Aug. 1866, *Mbl.*; 7 Nov. 1866, *Mbl.* (Twesten); 4 Dec. 1866, *Mbl.* (Bamberger); Hermann Baumgarten, 'Der deutsche Liberalismus. Eine Selbstkritik', *Preussische Jahrbücher*, 18 (1866), 455–515 (470–1), 575–628 (596–7, 624–5, 627; emphases in original); repr. ed. Adolf M. Birke (Berlin: Ullstein, 1974); Parisius, *Parteien* (note 10), 78 ff. (announcement of 24 Oct. 1866); Burckhardt, *Studium* (note 30), 378; Carl Schmitt, *Verfassungslehre* (Berlin 1928), 31–2; id., *Staatsgefüge und Zusammenbruch des zweiten Reiches. Der Sieg*

des Bürgers über den Soldaten (Hamburg: Hanseatische Verlagsanstalt, 1934), 7 ff.; Winkler, *Liberalismus* (note 10), 113 ff.; Biefang, 'National-preussisch' (note 21), 360 ff.

34. Heinrich von Treitschke, 'Bundesstaat und Einheitsstaat' (1864), in *Historische und politische Aufsätze*, 6th edn (Leipzig: Hirzel, 1903), 77–241; Gerhard Ritter, *Die preussischen Konservativen und Bismarcks deutsche Politik 1858 bis 1876* (Heidelberg: C. Winter, 1913), 147 ff.; Klaus-Erich Pollmann, *Parlamentarismus im Norddeutschen Bund, 1867–1870* (Düsseldorf: Droste, 1985), 93 ff. (fraction strength: 171); Andreas Biefang, 'Modernität wider Willen. Bemerkungen zur Entstehung des demokratischen Wahlrechts des Kaiserreichs', in *Gestaltungskraft des Politischen. Festschrift f. Eberhard Kolb*, ed. Wolfram Pyta and Ludwig Richter (Berlin: Duncker & Humblot, 1998), 239–59; Otto Becker, *Bismarcks Ringen um Deutschlands Gestaltung* (Heidelberg: Quelle & Meyer, 1958), 211 ff.; Wolfgang J. Mommsen, 'Das deutsche Kaiserreich als System umgangener Entscheidungen', in *Der autoritäre Nationalstaat. Verfassung, Gesellschaft und Kultur im deutschen Kaiserreich* (Frankfurt: Fischer Taschenbuch, 1990), 11–38, tr. as *Imperial Germany 1867–1918: Politics, Culture, and Society in an Authoritarian State* (London: Edward Arnold; New York: St Martin's Press, 1995); id., 'Die Verfassung des Deutschen Reiches von 1871 als dilatorischer Herrschaftskompromiss', ibid. 39–65; Huber, *Verfassungsgeschichte*, iii (note 2), 629 ff., 643 ff. (659); Böhme, *Weg* (note 3), 236 ff.; Schieder, 'Vom Deutschen Bund' (note 19), 198 ff.

35. Hans Georg Aschoff, *Welfische Bewegung und politischer Katholizismus 1866 bis 1918. Die Deutsch-Hannoversche Partei und das Zentrum in der Provinz Hannover während des Kaiserreiches* (Düsseldorf: Droste, 1987), 19 ff.; Schieder, 'Scheitern' (note 15), 31 ff.; Mayer, 'Trennung' (note 23), 138 ff.; Conze and Groh, *Arbeiterbewegung* (note 29), 78 ff.; Runge, *Volkspartei* (note 22), 115 ff.; Rapp, *Württemberger* (note 22), 289 ff.; Gall, *Liberalismus* (note 24), 376 ff.; Becker, *Staat* (note 24), 201 ff.; Stache, *Liberalismus* (note 27), 45 ff.; Schieder, *Partei* (note 25), 193 ff.; Friedrich Hartmannsgruber, *Die Bayerische Patriotenpartei 1868–1887* (Munich: C. H. Beck, 1986), 33 ff.; Rolf Wilhelm, *Das Verhältnis der süddeutschen Staaten zum Norddeutschen Bund (1867–1870)* (Husum: Matthiesen, 1978), 97 ff.; Lothar Gall, 'Bismarcks Süddeutschlandpolitik 1866–1870', in *Europa vor dem Krieg von 1870. Mächtekonstellation—Konfliktfelder—Kriegsausbruch*, ed. Eberhard Kolb (Munich: Oldenbourg, 1987), 23–32.

36. Pollmann, *Parlamentarismus* (note 34), 259 ff., 433 ff.; Wilhelm, *Verhältnis* (note 35), 103 ff. (quote from the *NZ* of 22 Feb. 1870: 103–4), 183–4 (Bismarck's conversation with Spitzemberg of 27 Mar. 1870); Meyer, *Bismarck* (note 11), 379–80; Gall, *Bismarck* (note 3), 466 ff.

37. 'Die confessionelle Leidenschaft im Ruine Deutschlands', *HPB* 58 (1866/II), 781–96 (783–4: quote from the*Protestantischen Kirchenzeitung*); *Sten. Ber., LT*, 1873, I, 631 (Virchow, 17 Jan. 1873); Georg Franz, *Kulturkampf. Staat und katholische Kirche in Mitteleuropa von der Säkularisation bis zum Abschluss des preussischen Kulturkampfes* (Munich: D. W. Callwey, 1954), 61 ff. (89: Antonelli quote); Adam Wandruszka, *Schicksalsjahr 1866* (Graz: Verlag Styria, 1966), 13 ff.; Karl Heinrich Höfele, 'Königgrätz und die Deutschen von 1866', *GWU* 17 (1966), 393–416; Rudolf Lill, 'Italien im Zeitalter des Risorgimento (1815–1870)', in *Europa von der Französischen Revolution zu den nationalstaatlichen Bewegungen des 19. Jahrhunderts* (= *Handbuch der*

europäischen Geschichte, ed. Theodor Schieder, v) (Stuttgart: Klett-Cotta, 1981), 827–85 (879 ff.); id., 'Katholizismus und Nation bis zur Reichsgründung', in *Katholizismus, nationaler Gedanke und Europa seit 1800*, ed. Albrecht Langner (Paderborn: Schöningh, 1985), 51–64; Thomas Mergel, *Zwischen Klasse und Konfession. Katholisches Bürgertum im Rheinland 1794–1848* (Göttingen: Vandenhoeck & Ruprecht, 1994), 263 ff.; Ernst Rudolf Huber, *Deutsche Verfassungsgeschichte seit 1789*, iv. *Struktur und Krisen des Kaiserreichs*, 2nd edn (Stuttgart: Kohlhammer, 1969), 645 ff.; Becker, *Staat* (note 24), 201 ff.; Stache, *Liberalismus* (note 27), 162 ff. On the German Protestant Association, founded in 1863, see Claudia Lepp, *Protestantisch-liberaler Aufbruch in die Moderne. Der Deutsche Protestantenverein in der Zeit der Reichsgründung* (Gütersloh: Chr. Kaiser, 1996), esp. 298 ff.

38. Bismarck, *Werke* (note 3), xiii 468 (address to the delegation from the University of Jenaon, 30 July 1892); Gall, *Bismarck* (note 3), 417 ff. (431: Gramont); Otto Pflanze, *Bismarck. Der Reichsgründer* (Munich: C. H. Beck, 1997), 449 ff., orig. *Bismarck and the Development of Germany: The Period of Unification, 1815–1871* (Princeton: Princeton University Press, 1963); Huber, *Verfassungsgeschichte*, iii (note 2), 702 ff.; Jochen Dittrich, 'Ursache und Ausbruch des deutsch-französischen Krieges', in *Reichsgründung 1870/71. Tatsachen, Kontroversen, Interpretationen*, ed. Theodor Schieder and Ernst Deuerlein (Stuttgart: Seewald, 1970), 64–94; Eberhard Kolb, *Der Kriegsausbruch 1870* (Göttingen: Vandenhoeck & Ruprecht, 1970), 143 ff. (argument about France's sole responsibility for the outbreak of the war); *Europa* (note 35), ed. id.; Josef Becker, 'Zum Problem der Bismarckschen Politik in der spanischen Thronfrage 1870', *HZ* 212 (1971), 529–607; id., 'Von Bismarcks "spanischer Diversion" zur "Emser Legende" des Reichsgründers', in Johannes Burkhardt et al., *Lange und kurze Wege in den Ersten Weltkrieg. Vier Augsburger Beiträge zur Kriegsursachenforschung* (Munich: Ernst Vögel, 1996), 87–113 (argument about Bismarck's war plans from the beginning of the Spanish succession question)
39. MEW, xvii. 3–7 (5: 'Erste Adresse des Generalrats'); Conze and Groh, *Arbeiterbewegung* (note 29), 86 ff.; Rapp, *Württemberger* (note 22), 364 (*Reutlinger Neue Bürgerzeitung*), 383 (Mayer), 396 (flags); Runge, *Volkspartei* (note 22), 161 ff.; Hans Fenske, *Der Weg zur Reichsgründung 1850–1870* (= *Quellen zum politischen Denken der Deutschen im 19. u. 20. Jahrhundert. Freiherr vom Stein-Gedächtnisausgabe*, v) (Darmstadt: Wissenschaftliche Buchgesellschaft, 1977), 419–21 (Jörg, 19 July 1870), 421–4 (Sepp, 19 July 1870); Huber, *Verfassungsgeschichte*, iii (note 2), 724 (vote in Bavarian parliament); Hartmannsgruber, *Patriotenpartei* (note 35), 362 ff.; Lothar Gall, 'Zur Frage der Annexion von Elsass und Lothringen 1870', *HZ* 206 (1968), 265–326; id., 'Das Problem Elsass-Lothringen', in *Reichsgründung* (note 38), ed. Schieder and Deuerlein, 366–85; Rudolf Buchner, 'Die deutsche patriotische Dichtung vom Kriegsbeginn 1870 über Frankreich und die elsässische Frage', ibid. 327–36; Heinrich von Treitschke, 'Was fordern wir von Frankreich?' (manuscript completed on 30 Aug. 1870), *Preussische Jahrbücher*, 26 (1870), 367–409 (371, 380, 406); Eberhard Kolb, *Der Weg aus dem Krieg. Bismarcks Politik im Krieg und die Friedensanbahnung 1870/71* (Munich: Oldenbourg, 1989), 113 ff.
40. Paul Piechowski, *Die Kriegspredigt von 1870/71* (Leipzig: Scholl, 1917), esp. 78 ff.; Hasko Zimmer, *Auf dem Altar des Vaterlandes. Religion und Patriotismus in der deutschen Kriegslyrik des 19. Jahrhunderts* (Frankfurt: Thesen Verlag, 1971), 71 ff.; Michael Jeismann, *Das Vaterland der Feinde. Studien zum nationalen Feindbegriff und*

Selbstverständnis in Deutschland und Frankreich 1792–1918 (Stuttgart: Klett-Cotta, 1992), 161 ff., 246 (Rittershaus), 267 (Leipzig theatre prologue), 276 (*Vossische Zeitung*, 24 July 1870); *Marianne und Germania 1789–1889. Frankreich und Deutschland. Zwei Welten—Eine Revue*, ed. Marie-Louise von Plessen (Berlin: Argon, 1996), 405–48; Kolb, *Weg* (note 39), 1 ff., 195 ff.; Klaus Hildebrand, *No intervention. Die Pax Britannica und Preussen 1865/66–1869/70. Eine Untersuchung zur englischen Weltpolitik im 19. Jahrhundert* (Munich: Oldenbourg, 1997); Ernst Moritz Arndt, 'Ein Wort über die Feier der Leipziger Schlacht' (1814), in *Werke* (Berlin: Deutsches Verlagshaus Bong, n.d.), 131–42 (133); Theodor Schieder, *Das deutsche Kaiserreich von 1871 als Nationalstaat* (Cologne: Westdeutscher Verlag, 1961), 72 ff., 125–53 (Bodelschwingh's speech on 27 June 1871: 135–45); Hartmut Lehmann, 'Friedrich von Bodelschwingh und das Sedanfest', *HZ* 202 (1966), 542–73; Claudia Lepp, 'Protestanten feiern ihre Nation—Die kulturprotestantischen Ursprünge des Sedantages', *Historisches Jahrbuch*, 118 (1998), 201–22; MEW xvii. 268–70 (269: Marx and Engel's letter to the committee of the Social Democratic Workers' party, written between 22 and 30 Aug. 1870), 271–9 (275: 'Zweite Adresse des Generalrats', 9 Sept. 1870; all emphases in the original), tr. MECW, xxii. 260–2 (Marx and Engels's letter to the committee of the Social Democratic Workers' party), 263–70 (267: 'Second Address of the General Council', 9 Sept. 1870); *Stenographischer Bericht über die Verhandlungen des Reichstags des Norddeutschen Bundes*, 1870, *II. ausserordentliche Session*, 187–8 (Lasker's motion); *Neue Preussische Zeitung* (*Kreuz-Zeitung*), 10 Feb. 1870; Ritter, *Konservative* (note 34), 355; Hartmannsgruber, *Patriotenpartei* (note 35), 368 (*Bayerisches Vaterland*, 13 Jan. 1871); *Sturmjahre* (note 21), 494 (Sybel to Baumgarten, 27 Jan. 1871); Elisabeth Fehrenbach, *Wandlungen des deutschen Kaisergedankens 1871–1918* (Munich: Oldenbourg, 1969), 14 ff.; Schoeps, *Weg* (note 30), 189 ff.; Huber, *Verfassungsgeschichte*, iii (note 2), 724 ff.

CHAPTER 5. THE TRANSFORMATION OF NATIONALISM 1871–1890

1. *Bismarck im Urteil der Zeitgenossen und der Nachwelt*, 2nd edn, ed. Walter Bussmann (Stuttgart: Klett, 1956), 28 (Disraeli); *Hansard's Parliamentary Debates*, Third Series, cciv (London: Cornelius Buck, 1871), 81–2; Ludwig Dehio, 'Deutschland und die Epoche der Weltkriege' (1951), in *Deutschland und die Weltpolitik im 20. Jahrhundert* (Munich: Oldenbourg, 1955), 9–36 (15); Eberhard Kolb, 'Der Pariser Commune-Aufstand und die Beendigung des deutsch-französischen Krieges', in *Umbrüche deutscher Geschichte. 1866/71. 1918/19. 1929/33. Ausgewählte Aufsätze* (Munich: Oldenbourg, 1993), 163–88; id., 'Kriegsniederlage und Revolution: Pariser Commune 1871', ibid. 189–206.
2. Günter Brakelmann, 'Der Krieg von 1870/71 und die Reichsgründung im Urteil des Protestantismus', in *Kirche zwischen Krieg und Frieden. Studien zur Geschichte des deutschen Protestantismus*, ed. Wolfgang Huber and Johannes Schwerdtfeger (Stuttgart: Klett, 1976), 293–320 (303: *Neue Evangelische Kirchenzeitung* [*NEKZ*], 7 Jan. 1871; 304: *NEKZ* 18 Mar. 1871; 306: quotes on the French as 'satanic' people and 'Antichrist'; 307–8: quotes from the *Evangelischen Kirchenzeitung*, 1871); Walter Frank, *Hofprediger Adolf Stoecker und die christlichsoziale Bewegung* (Berlin: R. Hobbing, 1928), 32–3 (Stoecker, 27 Jan. 1871); Fürst Otto von Bismarck,

Die gesammelten Werke (Friedrichsruh edition) (Berlin: O. Stollberg, 1924–), xi. 256–7 (speech on 6 Mar. 1872), xiii. 475 (speech on 31 July 1892 in Jena); Theodor Schieder, *Das deutsche Kaiserreich von 1871 als Nationalstaat* (Cologne: Westdeutscher Verlag, 1961), 175 (Bennigsen, 26 Jan. 1881); Elisabeth Fehrenbach, *Wandlungen des deutschen Kaisergedankens 1871–1918* (Munich: Oldenbourg, 1969), 14 ff.; Helmuth Walser Smith, *German Nationalism and Religious Conflict: Culture, Ideology, Politics, 1870–1914* (Princeton: Princeton University Press, 1995); Horst Dippel, '1871 versus 1789: German Historians and the Ideological Foundations of the Deutsche Reich', *History of European Ideas*, 16 (1993), 829–37; Dieter Langewiesche, 'Deutschland und Österreich: Nationswerdung und Staatsbildung in Mitteleuropa im 19. Jahrhundert', *GWU* 42 (1991), 754–66; Adam Wandruszka, 'Grossdeutsche und kleindeutsche Ideologie 1840–1871', in *Deutschland und Österreich. Ein bilaterales Geschichtsbuch*, ed. Robert A. Kann and Friedrich Prinz (Vienna: Jugend und Volk, 1980), 110–42; Karl Heinrich Höfele, 'Sendungsglaube und Epochenbewusstsein in Deutschland 1870/71', *Zeitschrift für Religions- und Geistesgeschichte*, 15 (1963), 265–76.

3. Bismarck, *Werke* (note 2), xv. *Erinnerung und Gedanke*, 199; Manfred Hanisch, 'Nationalisierung der Dynastien oder Monarchisierung der Nation? Zum Verhältnis von Monarchie und Nation in Deutschland im 19. Jahrhundert', in *Bürgertum, Adel und Monarchie. Wandel der Lebensformen im Zeitalter des bürgerlichen Nationalismus*, ed. Adolf M. Birke and Lothar Kettenacker (Munich: K. G. Saur, 1989), 71–91; id., *Für Fürst und Vaterland. Legitimitätsstiftung in Bayern zwischen Revolution 1848 und deutscher Einheit* (Munich: Oldenbourg, 1991), 20 ff.; Siegfried Weichlein, 'Sachsen zwischen Landesbewusstsein und Nationsbildung 1866–1871', in *Sachsen im Kaiserreich—Politik, Wirtschaft und Gesellschaft im Umbruch*, ed. Simone Lässig and Karl Heinrich Pohl (Dresden: Böhlau, 1997), 241–70; Gerhard Ritter, *Die preussischen Konservativen und Bismarcks deutsche Politik 1858–1876* (Heidelberg: C. Winter, 1913), 359 (Kleist-Retzow); Hans Booms, *Die Deutschkonservative Partei. Preussischer Charakter, Reichsauffassung, Nationalbegriff* (Düsseldorf: Droste, 1954), 5 ff.; James N. Retallack, *Notables of the Right. The Conservative Party and Political Mobilization in Germany, 1876–1918* (London: Unwin Hyman, 1988), 13 ff.; Oliver Janz, *Bürger besonderer Art. Evangelische Pfarrer in Preussen 1850–1914* (Berlin: Walter de Gruyter, 1994), esp. 58 ff.
4. Christoph Weber, *'Eine starke, enggeschlossene Phalanx'. Der politische Katholizismus und die erste deutsche Reichstagswahl 1871* (Essen: Klartext, 1992), 54 ff.; (Edmund Jörg,) 'Das grosse Neujahr', *HPB* 67 (1871), 1–15 (6); Wilhelm Emmanuel von Ketteler, *Die Katholiken im Deutschen Reiche. Entwurf zu einem politischen Programm* (Mainz: F, Kirchheim, 1873), 5; Adolf M. Birke, *Bischof Ketteler und der deutsche Liberalismus. Eine Untersuchung über das Verhältnis des liberalen Katholizismus zum bürgerlichen Liberalismus in der Reichsgründungszeit* (Mainz: Matthias-Grünewald-Verlag, 1971), 78 ff.; Rudolf Lill, 'Die deutschen Katholiken und Bismarcks Reichsgründung', in *Reichsgründung 1870/71. Tatsachen, Kontroversen, Interpretationen*, ed. Theodor Schieder and Ernst Deuerlein (Stuttgart: Seewald, 1970), 345–65; Schieder, *Kaiserreich* (note 2), 125 ff. (152: Ketteler, 19 Aug. 1874); Fehrenbach, *Wandlungen* (note 2), 20 ff.
5. Brakelmann, 'Krieg' (note 2), 318 (Wichern); *Stenographischer Bericht über die Verhandlungen des Deutschen Reichstags* [*Sten. Ber.*], xx. 920–1 (Bebel, 25 May 1871);

August Bebel, *Aus meinem Leben* (1910–14; Bonn: J. H. W. Dietz, 1997), 299 ff., tr. as *My Life* (New York: H. Fertig, 1973); Karl Marx, 'Der Bürgerkrieg in Frankreich' (1871), MEW, xvii. 313–65; Friedrich Engels, 'Einleitung zu Karl Marx *Bürgerkrieg in Frankreich*' (1891), MEW, xx. 188–99 (199), tr. as Marx, 'The Civil War in France', MECW, xx. 307–57; Engels, 'Introduction to Karl Marx's *The Civil War in France*', MECW, xxvii. 179–91 (190–1); Dieter Groh and Peter Brandt, *'Vaterlandslose Gesellen'. Sozialdemokratie und Nation 1860–1990* (Munich: C. H. Beck, 1992), 26 ff. On the 'inner Düppel' see Lothar Gall, *Bismarck. Der weisse Revolutionär* (Berlin: Propyläen, 1980), 331.

6. Franz Mehring, *Geschichte der deutschen Sozialdemokratie*, 1st edn (1897–8), 2 vols., ii. *Von Lassalles 'Offenem Antwortschreiben' bis zum Erfurter Programm 1863 bis 1891* (Berlin: J. H. W. Dietz, 1960), 378, 434–5 (Jacoby); Ernest Renan, *Was ist eine Nation? Und andere politische Schriften*, ed. Walter Euchner (Vienna: 1995), 57 (Paris address 'What is a nation?', 11 Mar. 1882), 59 (the Franco-German war [Sept. 1870]), 118 (Strauss to Renan, 29 Sept. 1870), 131–2 (Renan to Strauss, 15 Sept. 1871); id., *Qu'est-ce qu'une nation?/What is a Nation?* (Toronto: Tapir Press, 1996); Jörg, 'Neujahr' (note 4), 9 (the German Reich as 'pure' but 'incomplete nation-state'); Helmuth Plessner, *Die verspätete Nation. Über die politische Verführbarkeit bürgerlichen Geistes* (1st edn under the title *Das Schicksal deutschen Geistes im Ausgang seiner bürgerlichen Epoche* (Zurich, 1935)) (Stuttgart: Kohlhammer, 1959), 39.
7. *Sten. Ber.*, xxiv. 356 (Bismarck, 14 May 1872); *Sten. Ber., LT*, 1873, I, 631 (Virchow, 17 Jan. 1873); Bismarck, *Werke* (note 2), xv. 333 (*Erinnerung und Gedanke*); *Der Kulturkampf in Italien und in den deutschsprachigen Ländern*, ed. Rudolf Lill and Francesco Traniello (Berlin: Duncker & Humblot, 1993); Winfried Becker, 'Der Kulturkampf als europäisches und deutsches Phänomen', *Historisches Jahrbuch*, 101 (1981), 422–46; id., 'Liberale Kulturkampf-Positionen und politischer Katholizismus', in *Innenpolitische Probleme des Bismarck-Reiches*, ed. Otto Pflanze (Munich: Oldenbourg, 1983), 47–72; Winfried Grohs, *Die Liberale Reichspartei. 1871–1874. Liberale Katholiken und föderalistische Protestanten im ersten Deutschen Reichstag* (Frankfurt: Peter Lang, 1990), 26 ff.; Weber, *Phalanx* (note 4), 42 ff.; Ritter, *Konservative* (note 3), 361 ff.; Claudia Lepp, *Protestantisch-liberaler Aufbruch in die Moderne. Der Deutsche Protestantenverein in der Zeit der Reichsgründung und des Kulturkampfes* (Gütersloh: Chr. Kaiser, 1996), 319 ff.; Ernst Rudolf Huber, *Deutsche Verfassungsgeschichte seit 1789*, iv. *Strukturen und Krisen des Kaiserreichs*, 2nd edn (Stuttgart: Kohlhammer, 1969), 672 ff.
8. *NZ* 21 Oct. 1876, *Mbl.*; *NZ* 2 Sept. 1877, *Mbl.*; Thomas Mergel, *Zwischen Klasse und Konfession. Katholisches Bürgertum im Rheinland 1794–1914* (Göttingen: Vandenhoeck & Ruprecht, 1994), 235 ff.; Gottfried Korff, 'Kulturkampf und Volksfrömmigkeit', in *Volksreligiosität in der modernen Sozialgeschichte*, ed. Wolfgang Schieder, *GG*, Sonderheft 11 (Göttingen: Vandenhoeck & Ruprecht, 1986), 137–51; Margaret L. Anderson and Kenneth Barkin, 'The Myth of the Puttkamer Purge and the Reality of the Kulturkampf', *Journal of Modern History*, 54 (1982), 647–86; Margaret L. Anderson, 'The Kulturkampf and the Course of German History', *Central European History*, 19 (1986), 82–115; ead., *Windthorst. Zentrumspolitiker und Gegenspieler Bismarcks* (Düsseldorf: Droste, 1988), 130 ff., orig. *Windthorst: A Political Biography* (Oxford: Clarendon Press, 1981); 130 ff.; Jonathan Sperber, *Popular Catholicism in Nineteenth-Century Germany* (Princeton: Princeton University Press, 1984), 207 ff.;

David Blackbourn, 'Progress and Piety: Liberalism, Catholicism, and the State in Imperial Germany', *History Workshops Journal*, 26 (1988), 57–78; id., *Wenn ihr sie wieder seht, fragt, wer sie sei. Marienerscheinungen in Marpingen—Aufstieg und Niedergang des deutschen Lourdes* (Reinbek: Rowohlt, 1997), orig. *Marpingen: Apparitions of the Virgin Mary in Bismarckian Germany* (Oxford: Clarendon Press, 1993); Gustav Schmidt, 'Die Nationalliberalen—eine regierungsfähige Partei? Zur Problematik der inneren Reichsgründung 1870–1878', in *Die deutschen Parteien vor 1918*, ed. Gerhard A. Ritter (Cologne: Kiepenheuer & Witsch, 1973), 208–23; Hans-Ulrich Wehler, *Deutsche Gesellschaftsgeschichte*, iii. *Von der 'Deutschen Doppelrevolution' bis zum Beginn des Ersten Weltkrieges 1849–1914* (Munich: C. H. Beck, 1995), 892 ff.

9. Heinrich Heine, 'Gedanken und Einfälle', in *Sämtliche Werke in zwölf Bänden* (Leipzig: Hesse & Becker, n.d.), xii. *Vermischte Schriften*, 3–50 (9); Richard Wagner, 'Das Judentum in der Musik' (1850), in *Gesammelte Schriften und Dichtungen*, v, 2nd edn (Leipzig: E. W. Fritsch, 1888), 66–85 (68–9); tr. as *Judaism in Music* (London: W. Reeves, 1910); id., 'Was ist deutsch?' (1865 and 1878), ibid. 9 (Berlin 1913), 36–53 (50–1); *Sten. Ber., LT*, 1873, I, 937–51 (Lasker, 7 Feb. 1873); (Franz Perrot), 'Die Ära Bleichröder-Delbrück-Camphausen und die neudeutsche Wirtschaftspolitik', *Neue Preussische Zeitung* (*Kreuz-Zeitung*), 29 June 1873; Otto Glagau, *Deutsches Handwerk und historisches Bürgertum* (Osnabrück: B. Wehberg, 1879), 80; id., *Der Börsen- und Gründungs-Schwindel in Berlin*, 2 vols. (Leipzig: P. Frohberg, 1876–7); 'Milliarden-Noth und Krach-Segen', *HPB* 74 (1874), 963–76 (976: cosmopolitan powers of finance); [Edmund Jörg], 'Vor fünfundzwanzig Jahren', *HPB*, 79 (1877), 1–17 (10: The Kulturkampf as a tool of the stock market); id., 'Das "Gründer"-Unwesen mit Staatshülfe', ibid. 237–52 (239: 'Jewified liberalism'); Mergel, Klasse (note 8), 258–9 (Catholic Press); Birke, Ketteler (note 4), 92 (Ketteler, 1873); Gordon A. Craig, *Deutsche Geschichte 1866–1945. Vom Norddeutschen Bund bis zum Ende des Dritten Reiches* (Munich: C. H. Beck, 1980), 85 (Freytag, Raabe, Dahn), orig. *Germany, 1866–1945* (Oxford: Oxford University Press, 1978), George L. Mosse, 'The Image of the Jew in German Political Culture: Felix Dahn and Gustav Freytag', Publications of the Leo Baeck Institute of Jews from Germany. Year Book 2 (1957), 218–27; id., *Germans and Jews: The Right, the Left and the Search for a 'Third Force' in Pre-Nazi Germany* (London: Orbach & Chambers, 1971), 34 ff.; Hans Rosenberg, *Grosse Depression und Bismarckzeit. Wirtschaftsablauf, Gesellschaft und Politik in Mitteleuropa* (Berlin: de Gruyter, 1967), 22 ff. (29); James F. Harris, *The People Speak! Anti-Semitism and Emancipation in Nineteenth-Century Bavaria* (Ann Arbor: University of Michigan Press, 1994), esp. 209 ff.; Olaf Blaschke, *Katholizismus und Antisemitismus im deutschen Kaiserreich* (Göttingen: Vandenhoeck & Ruprecht, 1997), 42 ff.; Fritz Stern, *Gold und Eisen. Bismarck und sein Bankier Bleichröder* (Reinbek: Rowohlt, 1988), 680 ff. (Germania article: 682 ff.) orig. *Gold and Iron: Bismarck, Bleichröder, and the Building of the German Empire*, 2nd edn (New York: Vintage Books, 1979); Erik Lindner, *Patriotismus deutscher Juden von der napoleonischen Ära bis zum Kaiserreich. Zwischen korporativem Loyalismus und individueller deutsch-jüdischer Identität* (Frankfurt: Lang, 1997), 267 ff.; A. Sartorius von Waltershausen, *Deutsche Wirtschaftsgeschichte 1815–1914*, 2nd edn (Jena: G. Fischer, 1923), 275 ff. (statistics of the economic crisis).

10. Carl Wilmanns, *Die 'goldene' Internationale und die Nothwendigkeit einer socialen Reformpartei* (Berlin: Niendorf, 1876); Constantin Frantz, *Der National-Liberalismus*

und die Judenherrschaft (Munich: Literarische Institut von M. Huttler, 1874), 49 (Fichte), 64 (quote); id., *Literarisch-politische Aufsätze* (Munich: Literarische Institut von M. Huttler, 1876), p. xvii (foreword; all emphases in the original); Wilhelm Marr, *Der Sieg des Judenthums über das Germanenthum. Vom nicht confessionellen Standpunkt aus betrachtet* (Bern: Rudolph Costenoble, 1879), 3, 46; Helmut Berding, *Moderner Antisemitismus in Deutschland* (Frankfurt: Suhrkamp, 1988), 86 ff.; Reinhard Rürup, *Emanzipation und Antisemitismus. Studien zur 'Judenfrage' der bürgerlichen Gesellschaft* (Göttingen: Vandenhoeck & Ruprecht, 1975), 74 ff., 101 ff. (Marr, Frantz, Dühring); Jacob Katz, *Vom Vorurteil bis zur Vernichtung. Der Antisemitismus 1700–1933* (Munich: C. H. Beck, 1989), 253 ff. (also on the reception of Rohling), orig. *From Prejudice to Destruction: Anti-Semitism, 1700–1933* (Cambridge, MA: Harvard University Press, 1980); Paul W. Massing, *Vorgeschichte des politischen Antisemitismus* (Frankfurt: Europäische Verlagsanstalt, 1959), 5 ff., orig. *Rehearsal for Destruction: A Study of Political Anti-Semitism in Imperial Germany* (New York: Harper, 1949); Peter G. J. Pulzer, *Die Entstehung des politischen Antisemitismus in Deutschland und Österreich 1867–1914* (Gütersloh: S. Mohn, 1966), orig. *The Rise of Political Anti-Semitism in Germany and Austria* (New York: Wiley, 1964); John Weiss, *Der lange Weg zum Holocaust. Die Geschichte der Judenfeindschaft in Deutschland und Österreich* (Hamburg, Hoffmann & Campe, 1997), 118 ff., orig. *Ideology of Death: Why the Holocaust Happened in Germany* (Chicago: I. R. Dee, 1996); Rainer Erb and Werner Bergmann, *Die Nachtseite der Judenemanzipation. Der Widerstand gegen die Integration der Juden in Deutschland 1780–1860* (Berlin: Metropol, 1989), 97 ff.; Shulamit Volkov, *The Rise of Popular Antimodernism in Germany: The Urban Master Artisans 1873–1896* (Princeton: Princeton University Press, 1978), 215 ff.; ead., 'Antisemitismus als kultureller Code', in, *Jüdisches Leben und Antisemitismus im 19. u. 20. Jahrhundert* (Munich: C. H. Beck, 1990), 13–36; Blaschke, *Katholizismus* (note 9), 48 ff., 74 ff. (on Rohling); Thomas Nipperdey, *Deutsche Geschichte 1866–1918*, i. *Arbeitswelt und Bürgergeist* (Munich: C. H. Beck, 1990), 396 ff.; ii. *Machtstaat vor der Demokratie* (Munich: C. H. Beck, 1992), 289 ff.; Wehler, *Gesellschaftsgeschichte*, iii (note 8), 924 ff. For Fichte's views on the Jews, see above p. 60.

11. Adolf Stoecker, 'Unsere Forderungen an das moderne Judentum' (19 Sept. 1879), in *Christlich-Sozial. Reden und Aufsätze*, 2nd edn (Berlin: Buchhandlung der Berliner Stadtmission, 1890), 359–69 (359–60, 367 ff.); id., 'Notwehr gegen das moderne Judentum' (26 Sept. 1879), ibid., 369–82 (381); id., 'Die Selbstverteidigung des modernen Judentums in dem Geisteskampf der Gegenwart' (5 Jan. 1880), ibid. 382–89 (385: on Treitschke); Frank, *Stoecker* (note 2), 88 ff.; Heinrich von Treitschke, 'Unsere Aussichten' (Nov. 1879), in *Der Berliner Antisemitismusstreit*, ed. Walter Boehlich (Frankfurt: Insel, 1965), 5–12 (6 ff., 11); Manuel Joël, 'Offener Brief an Heinrich von Treitschke' (1879), 13–25 (23: on Lasker's defeat); Hermann Cohen, 'Ein Bekenntnis in der Judenfrage' (Jan. 1880), ibid. 124–49; Ludwig Bamberger, 'Deutschthum und Judenthum' (1880), ibid. 149–79 (165 ff.); 'Erklärung' (by Forckenbeck et al., 12 Nov. 1880), ibid. 202–4; Theodor Mommsen, 'Ein Brief an die Nationalzeitung' (19 Nov. 1880), ibid. 208–9; id., 'Auch ein Wort über unser Judenthum' (1880), ibid. 210–25 (208, 220, 224); Hans-Michael Bernhardt, ' "Die Juden sind unser Unglück!" Strukturen eines Feindbildes im deutschen Kaiserreich', in *Feindbilder in der deutschen Geschichte. Studien zur Vorurteilsgeschichte im 19. u. 20. Jahrhundert*, ed. Christoph Jahr et al. (Berlin: Metropol, 1994), 25–54; John C. G. Röhl, *Wilhelm II. Die Jugend*

des Kaisers 1859–1888 (Munich: C. H. Beck, 1993), 414–15 (Crown Prince Frederick on anti-Semitism); Katz, *Vorurteil* (note 10), 217 ff.; Günter Brakelmann, *Protestantismus und Politik. Werk und Wirken Adolf Stoeckers* (Hamburg: Christians, 1982); Grit Koch, *Adolf Stoecker 1835–1909. Ein Leben zwischen Politik und Kirche* (Erlangen: Palm & Enke, 1993).

12. Heinrich Heine, *Zur Geschichte der Religion und Philosophie in Deutschland* (1834), in *Werke* (note 9), viii. *Über Deutschland*, I, 3–122 (120–1); Eugen Dühring, *Die Judenfrage als Frage der Racenschädlichkeit für Existenz, Sitte und Cultur der Völker* (1st edn under the title *Die Judenfrage als Racen-, Sitten- und Culturfrage* (1880)), 3rd edn (Karlsruhe: H. Reuther, 1886), 159; Paul de Lagarde, 'Juden und Indogermanen' (1887), in *Ausgewählte Schriften* (Munich: Lehmann, 1924), 195–216 (209); Bamberger, 'Deutschthum' (note 11), 176–7; Frank, *Stoecker* (note 2), 118 (anti-Semite petition); Katz, *Vorurteil* (note 10), 275 ff.; Berding, *Antisemitismus* (note 10), 99 ff.; Gerd-Klaus Kaltenbrunner, 'Vom Konkurrenten des Karl Marx zum Vorläufer Hitlers', in *Propheten des Nationalismus*, ed. Karl Schwedhelm (Munich: List, 1969), 36–55; Fritz Stern, *Kulturpessimismus als politische Gefahr. Eine Analyse nationaler Ideologie in Deutschland* (Bern: Scherz, 1963), orig. *The Politics of Cultural Despair: A Study in the Rise of the Germanic Ideology* (Berkeley: University of California Press, 1961); Kurt Wawrzinek, *Die Entstehung der deutschen Antisemitenparteien (1873–1890)* (Berlin: E. Ebering, 1927); Stefan Scheil, *Die Entwicklung des politischen Antisemitismus in Deutschland zwischen 1881 und 1912. Eine wahlgeschichtliche Untersuchung* (Berlin: Duncker & Humblot, 1999); Norbert Kampe, *Studenten und 'Judenfrage' im Deutschen Kaiserreich. Die Entstehung einer akademischen Trägerschicht des Antisemitismus* (Göttingen: Vandenhoeck & Ruprecht, 1988), 23 ff.; Plessner, *Nation* (note 6). For the quote from the *Antisemitische Correspondenz*, see the article 'Antisemitische Parteien 1879–1914', in *Lexikon zur Parteiengeschichte. Die bürgerlichen und kleinbürgerlichen Parteien und Verbände in Deutschland (1789–1945)*, ed. Dieter Fricke et al., 4 vols. (Leipzig: VEB Bibliographisches Institut Leipzig, 1983–), i. 77–88.

13. *NZ* 4 Dec. 1866, *Mbl.* (Bamberger); Hermann Oncken, *Rudolf von Bennigsen. Ein deutscher liberaler Politiker*, 2 vols., ii. *Von 1867 bis 1902* (Stuttgart: Deutsche Verlags-Anstalt, 1910), 297 ff.; Huber, *Verfassungsgeschichte*, iv (note 7), 129 ff., 351 ff.; Karl Erich Born, 'Von der Reichsgründung bis zum 1. Weltkrieg', in *Von der Französischen Revolution bis zum Ersten Weltkrieg* (= Bruno Gebhardt, *Handbuch der deutschen Geschichte*, ed. Herbert Grundmann, iii), 9th edn (Stuttgart: Union-Verlag, 1970), 261 ff., 296 ff.; Hans Gerhard Benzig, *Bismarcks Kampf um die Kreisordnung von 1871* (Hamburg: Kovac, 1996), 173 ff.; Hartwin Spenkuch, *Das Preussische Herrenhaus. Adel und Bürgertum in der Ersten Kammer des Landtags 1854–1918* (Düsseldorf: Droste, 1998), 93 ff.; Schmidt, 'Nationalliberale' (note 8), 208 ff.; Booms, *Deutschkonservative Partei* (note 3), 17 ff.; Ritter, *Konservative* (note 3), 361 ff.; Gall, *Bismarck* (note 5), 359 (Grand Duke Frederick I's letter to Heinrich Gelzer, 3 Apr. 1878); *Lexikon* (note 12), iv, ed. Fricke et al., 358–67 (the article 'Vereinigung der Steuer- und Wirtschaftsreformer 1876–1928'), 509–43 (the article 'Zentralverband Deutscher Industrieller 1876–1919').

14. *Norddeutsche Allgemeine Zeitung*, 31 July 1878; 'Auf den Grund', *Neue Preussische Zeitung* (*Kreuz-Zeitung*), 30 July 1878; 'Unsere Hauptanklagen gegen den Liberalismus', part III, ibid. 15 Aug. 1878, part VI, 21 Aug. 1878 (emphases in original); Otto Pflanze, *Bismarck. Der Reichskanzler* (Munich: C. H. Beck, 1998), 118 ff.,

orig. *Bismarck and the Development of Germany: The Period of Unification, 1815–1871* (Princeton: Princeton University Press, 1990); Wolfgang Pack, *Das parlamentarische Ringen um das Sozialistengesetz 1878/90* (Düsseldorf: Droste, 1961); Vernon L. Lidtke, *The Outlawed Party: Social Democracy in Germany, 1878–1890* (Princeton: Princeton University Press, 1966); Lucian Hölscher, *Weltgericht oder Revolution. Protestantische und sozialistische Zukunftsvorstellungen im deutschen Kaiserreich* (Stuttgart: Klett-Cotta, 1989), 221 ff.; Gerhard A. Ritter and Klaus Tenfelde, *Arbeiter im Deutschen Kaiserreich 1871 bis 1914* (Bonn: J. H. W. Dietz, 1992), esp. 679 ff.; Mehring, *Geschichte*, ii (note 6), 492 ff. (673–4: statistics on the effects of the anti-socialist law); Wehler, *Gesellschaftsgeschichte*, iii (note 8), 902 ff.

15. *Bismarck und der Staat. Ausgewählte Dokumente*, introd. Hans Rothfels (Stuttgart: Kohlhammer, n.d. [1953]), 329 ff. (329: Bismarck's letter to Itzenplitz, 17 Nov. 1871); Wolfgang Saile, *Hermann Wagener und sein Verhältnis zu Bismarck. Ein Beitrag zur Geschichte des konservativen Sozialismus* (Tübingen: Mohr, 1958), 49 ff. (on L. v. Stein's influence on the Prussian conservatives); Helmut Böhme, *Deutschlands Weg zur Grossmacht. Studien zum Verhältnis von Wirtschaft und Staat während der Reichsgründungszeit 1848–1881* (Cologne: Kiepenheuer & Witsch, 1966), 530 ff.; Karl W. Hardach, *Die Bedeutung wirtschaftlicher Faktoren bei der Wiedereinführung der Eisen- und Getreidezölle in Deutschland 1879* (Berlin: Duncker & Humblot, 1967); Anderson, *Windthorst* (note 8), 226 ff.; Hans Rosenberg, 'Die Pseudodemokratisierung der Rittergutsbesitzerklasse', in *Machteliten und Wirtschaftskonjunkturen. Studien zur neueren deutschen Sozial- und Wirtschaftsgeschichte* (Göttingen: Vandenhoeck & Ruprecht, 1978), 83–101; id., 'Zur sozialen Funktion der Agrarpolitik im Zweiten Reich', ibid. 102–17; id., *Depression* (note 9), 169 ff.; Wehler, *Gesellschaftsgeschichte*, iii (note 8), 934 ff.
16. Ludwig Bamberger, 'National' (September 1888), in *Politische Schriften* (Berlin 1897), v. 203–37 (217); *NZ* 14 Nov. 1878, *Abl.* (quote from the *Volkswirtschaftliche Correspondenz*); *NZ* 13 Nov. 1878, *Mbl.* (on the 'Jewification' of Posen); E. v. d. Brüggen, 'Die Kolonisation in unserem Osten und die Herstellung des Erbzinses', *Preussische Jahrbücher*, 44 (1879), 32–51 (35); 'Sozialismus und Deportation', *Grenzboten*, 37/2 (1878), 41–50 (46); 'Die Julitage des deutschen Liberalismus', ibid. 38/3 (1879), 124–6 (124); 'Die natürliche Gruppierung deutscher Parteien', ibid. 200–4 (203–4); *Im Neuen Reich 1871–1890. Politische Briefe aus dem Nachlass liberaler Parteiführer*, sel. and ed. Paul Wentzcke (= *Deutscher Liberalismus im Zeitalter Bismarcks. Eine politische Briefsammlung*, ii) (1925; repr. Osnabrück: Biblio-Verlag, 1967), 307–11 (Lasker's letter to his constituents, March 1880; quotes: 309), 356 (statement upon leaving the party, 30 Aug. 1880); Heinrich August Winkler, 'Vom linken zum rechten Nationalismus. Der deutsche Liberalismus in der Krise von 1878/79', in *Liberalismus und Antiliberalismus. Studien zur politischen Sozialgeschichte des 19. u. 20. Jahrhunderts* (Göttingen: Vandenhoeck & Ruprecht, 1979), 36–51; id., 'Der Nationalismus und seine Funktionen', ibid. 52–80.
17. Huber, *Verfassungsgeschichte*, iv (note 7), 767 ff.; Nipperdey, *Geschichte*, ii (note 10), 428 ff.; Wehler, *Gesellschaftsgeschichte*, iii (note 8), 897 ff.; Winfried Becker, 'Die Deutsche Zentrumspartei im Bismarckreich', in *Die Minderheit als Mitte. Die Deutsche Zentrumspartei in der Innenpolitik des Reiches 1871–1933*, ed. id. (Paderborn: Schöningh, 1986), 9–46; David Blackbourn, 'Die Zentrumspartei und die deutschen

Katholiken während des Kulturkampfes und danach', in *Probleme* (note 7), ed. Pflanze, 73–94; Anderson, *Windthorst* (note 8), 278 ff.

18. *Deutsche Parteiprogramme*, ed. Wilhelm Mommsen (Munich: Isar, 1960), 157 (platform of the German Liberal Party from 5 Mar. 1884), 158–160 (Heidelberg declaration of the National Liberals from 23 Mar. 1884); *Bismarck* (note 15), ed. Rothfels, 359 (Bismarck's statement to Busch, 26 June 1881); id., *Theodor Lohmann und die Kampfjahre der staatlichen Sozialpolitik (1871–1905)* (Berlin: C. S. Mittler und Sohn, 1927), 48 ff.; Gerhard A. Ritter, *Der Sozialstaat. Entstehung und Entwicklung im internationalen Vergleich* (Munich: Oldenbourg, 1989), 60 ff.; Wehler, *Gesellschaftsgeschichte*, iii (note 8), 936 ff.; Wolther von Kieseritzky, *Liberalismus und Sozialstaat. Liberale Politik zwischen Machtstaat und Arbeiterbewegung in Deutschland (1878–1893)* (Cologne: Böhlau, 2001); Dan S. White, *The Splintered Party. National Liberalism in Hessen and the Reich, 1867–1918* (Cambridge, MA: Harvard University Press, 1976), 84 ff.
19. Hans-Ulrich Wehler, *Bismarck und der Imperialismus*, 1st edn (Cologne: Kiepenheuer & Witsch, 1969), 112 ff. (164: Miquel, 166: Hohenlohe-Langenburg); id., 'Von den "Reichsfeinden" zur "Reichskristallnacht": Polenpolitik im Deutschen Kaiserreich 1871–1918', id., *Krisenherde des Kaiserreichs 1871–1918* (Göttingen: Vandenhoeck & Ruprecht, 1970), 181–199 (193 f.); id., 'Unfähig zur Verfassungsreform: Das "Reichsland" Elsass-Lothringen von 1870 bis 1918', ibid. 17–63; id., *Gesellschaftsgeschichte*, iii (note 8), 961 ff.; Schieder, *Kaiserreich* (note 2), 95 ff.; Christoph Klessmann, *Polnische Bergarbeiter im Ruhrgebiet 1870–1945. Soziale Integration und nationale Subkultur einer Minderheit in der deutschen Industriegesellschaft* (Göttingen: Vandenhoeck & Ruprecht, 1978), 23 ff.; Hermann Hiery, *Reichstagswahlen im Reichsland. Ein Beitrag zur Landesgeschichte von Elsass-Lothringen und zur Wahlgeschichte des Deutschen Reiches 1871–1918* (Düsseldorf: Droste, 1986), 60 ff.; *Nationale Minderheiten und staatliche Minderheitenpolitik in Deutschland im 19. Jahrhundert*, ed. Hans Henning Hahn and Peter Kunze (Berlin: Akademie Verlag, 1999).
20. *Die Grosse Politik der Europäischen Mächte 1871–1914. Sammlung der Diplomatischen Akten des Auswärtigen Amtes*, ii. *Der Berliner Kongress und seine Vorgeschichte* (Berlin: Deutsche Verlagsgesellschaft für Politik und Geschichte, 1922), 153 f. (Kissinger Diktat, 15 June 1877, also on the '*cauchemar des coalitions*'); Klaus Hildebrand, *Das vergangene Reich. Deutsche Aussenpolitik von Bismarck zu Hitler* (Stuttgart: Deutsche Verlags-Anstalt, 1995), 34 ff.; Andreas Hillgruber, *Bismarcks Aussenpolitik* (Freiburg: Rombach, 1972), 175 ff.; George W. F. Hallgarten, *Imperialismus vor 1914. Die soziologischen Grundlagen der Aussenpolitik europäischer Grossmächte vor dem Ersten Weltkrieg*, 2 vols. (Munich: C. H. Beck, 1963), i. 160 ff.; Hans-Ulrich Wehler, 'Bismarcks späte Russlandpolitik 1879–1890', in *Krisenherde* (note 19), 163–81; id., *Gesellschaftsgeschichte*, iii (note 8), 970 ff.; Gall, *Bismarck* (note 5), 634 (Herbert von Bismarck to Bill von Bismarck, 19 June 1887), 636 (Bismarck to Bronsart von Schellendorf, 30 Dec. 1887), 642 ff. ('system of expedients'); Horst Müller-Link, *Industrialisierung und Aussenpolitik. Preussen–Deutschland und das Zarenreich von 1860* (Göttingen: Vandenhoeck & Ruprecht, 1977), 191 ff.
21. Theodor Fontane, *Der Stechlin, Roman*, id., *Werke, Schriften, Briefe*, ed. Walter Keitel and Helmuth Nürnberger, v, pt 1 (Munich: Hanser, 1980), 307; Röhl, *Wilhelm II.* (note 11), 711 ff.; id., 'Staatsstreichspläne oder Staatsstreichbereitschaft? Bismarcks

Politik in der Entlassungskrise', *HZ* 203 (1966), 610–24; Huber, *Verfassungsgeschichte*, iii (note 7), 202 ff. (theory on the coup plan as a means of 'concealing the intention to resolve the crisis in a manner in keeping with the constitution'); Anderson, *Windthorst* (note 8), 401 ff.; Wehler, *Gesellschaftsgeschichte*, iii (note 5), 684 ff.; Gall, *Bismarck* (note 5), 684 ff.; Erich Eyck, *Bismarck. Leben und Werk*, 3 vols., iii (Erlenbach: E. Rentsch, 1944), 500 ff.

22. *Sten. Ber.*, cii. 725, 733 (Bismarck, 6 Feb. 1888); liiv. 28–31, 33–4 (Bismarck on Lasker, 13 Mar. 1884); liv/2. 2249 (Hänel, 10 July 1879); Fontane, *Werke* (note 21), iii, pt 4, 674 (letter to Georg Friedlaender, 7 Jan. 1889); Lothar Wickert, *Theodor Mommsen*, 4 vols., iv (Frankfurt: Klostermann, 1980), 93 (Mommsen to Brentano, 3 Jan. 1902); Friedrich Nietzsche, *Unzeitgemässe Betrachtungen. David Strauss. Der Bekenner und der Schriftsteller*, in *Werke* (critical edition, ed. Giorgio Colli and Mazzino Montinari), i, pt 3 (Berlin: de Gruyter, 1972), 153–238 (155–6; emphasis in original), tr. as *Thoughts out of Season*, in *Complete Works*, ed. Oscar Levy and Robert Guppy (New York: Russell & Russell, 1964), iv, pt 1/4 Jacob Burckhardt, *Briefe*, v, ed. Max Burckhardt (Basel: B. Schwabe, 1949–86), 184 (letter to Friedrich von Preen, 31 Dec. 1872); Emil Du Bois-Reymond, 'Der deutsche Krieg' (3 Aug. 1870), id., *Reden*, i. *Literatur, Philosophie, Zeitgeschichte* (Leipzig: Veit, 1886), 65–92 (92); *NZ* 5 Dec. 1878, *Mbl.*; Louis L. Snyder, 'Bismarck and the Lasker Resolution 1884', *Review of Politics*, 79 (1967), 41–64; Craig, *Geschichte* (note 9), 156 ff.; Eyck, *Bismarck*, iii (note 21), 543 ff.; Hans Kohn, *Wege und Irrwege. Vom Geist des deutschen Bürgertums* (Düsseldorf: Droste, 1962, 179 ff., orig. *The Mind of Germany: The Education of a Nation* (New York: Scribner, 1960); Wehler, *Gesellschaftsgeschichte*, iii (note 8), 327 ff.; Huber, *Verfassungsgeschichte*, iv (note 7), 190 ff. (Geffcken affair); Hiery, *Reichstagswahlen* (note 19), 200 ff.; Peter Steinbach, 'Politisierung und Nationalisierung der Region im 19. Jahrhundert. Regionalspezifische Politikrezeption im Spiegel historischer Wahlforschung', in *Probleme politischer Partizipation im Modernisierungsprozess*, ed. id. (Stuttgart: Klett-Cotta, 1982), 321–49, 241 ff.; *Bismarck und der deutsche Nationalmythos*, ed. Lothar Machtan (Bremen: Temmen, 1994); Arno Borst, 'Barbarossas Erwachen—Zur Geschichte der deutschen Identität', in *Identität, Poetik und Hermeneutik, VIII*, 2nd edn, ed. Odo Marquard and Karlheinz Stierle (Munich: W. Fink, 1996), 17–60. On the crisis provoked by 'Is War in Sight? see Otto Pflanze, *Bismarck. Der Reichsgründer* (note 14), 775 ff.

CHAPTER 6. WORLD POLICY AND WORLD WAR 1890–1918

1. Max Weber, 'Der Nationalstaat und die Volkswirtschaftspolitik', in *Gesamtausgabe*, pt I: *Reden und Schriften*, iv, pt 2 (Tübingen: J. C. B. Mohr, 1993), 545–74 (571; emphasis in original); id., 'Diskussionsbeiträge zum Vortrag von Karl Oldenberg' (8th Evangelical-Social Congress in Leipzig, 10–11 June 1897), 623–40 (633–4: 'feudalization of bourgeois capital'); Werner Sombart, *Die deutsche Volkswirtschaft im neunzehnten Jahrhundert und im Anfang des 20. Jahrhunderts* (1912), 7th edn (Berlin: G. Bondi, 1927), 469 ff.; Hugo Preuss, 'Die Junkerfrage', *Die Nation*, 14 (1896–7), 507–8, 522–5, 537–41, 541–52, 552–7, 570–3, 586–9, 603–6, 616–19, 632–5; Oscar Stillich, *Die politischen Parteien in Deutschland*, ii. *Der Liberalismus* (Leipzig: W. Klinkhardt, 1911), 2, 105 ff.; Wolfgang J. Mommsen, *Max Weber und die deutsche*

Politik 1890–1920, 2nd edn (Tübingen: Mohr, 1974), 97 ff., tr. as *Max Weber and German Politics, 1890–1920* (Chicago: University of Chicago Press, 1984); Gregor Schöllgen, *Max Weber* (Munich: C. H. Beck, 1998); Cornelius Torp, *Max Weber und die preussischen Junker* (Tübingen: Mohr Siebeck, 1998); Hartmut Berghoff, 'Aristokratisierung des Bürgertums? Zur Sozialgeschichte der Nobilitierung von Unternehmern in Preussen und Grossbritannien', *VSWG* 81 (1994), 178–204; Hans-Ulrich Wehler, *Deutsche Gesellschaftsgeschichte*, iii. *Von der 'Deutschen Doppelrevolution' bis zum Beginn des Ersten Weltkrieges 1849–1914* (Munich: C. H. Beck, 1995), 718 ff.; Thomas Nipperdey, *Deutsche Geschichte 1866–1918*, ii. *Machtstaat vor der Demokratie* (Munich: C. H. Beck, 1992), 595 ff. On Michaelis see above, p. 151.

2. The article 'Bund der Landwirte 1893–1920', in *Lexikon zur Parteiengeschichte. Die bürgerlichen und kleinbürgerlichen Parteien und Verbände in Deutschland (1789–1945)*, 4 vols., iv, ed. Dieter Fricke et al. (Leipzig: VEB Bibliographisches Institut Leipzig, 1983), 241–70 (Dec. 1892 manifesto: 243; membership: 242); Hans-Jürgen Puhle, *Agrarische Interessenpolitik und preussischer Konservatismus im Wilhelminischen Reich 1893–1914. Ein Beitrag zur Analyse des Nationalismus in Deutschland am Beispiel des Bundes der Landwirte und der Deutsch-Konservativen Partei*, 2nd edn (Bonn: Verlag Neue Gesellschaft, 1975), 28 ff.; id., *Von der Agrarkrise zum Präfaschismus. Thesen zum Stellenwert der agrarischen Interessenverbände in der deutschen Politik am Ende des 19. Jahrhunderts* (Wiesbaden: F. Steiner, 1972). Quote from Caprivi in *Sten. Ber.*, cxviii. 3307 (10 Dec. 1891).
3. John C. G. Röhl, *Deutschland ohne Bismarck. Die Regierungskrise im Zweiten Kaiserreich 1890–1900* (Tübingen: Rainer Wunderlich Verlag, 1969), 57 ff., orig. *Germany without Bismarck: The Crisis of Government in the Second Reich, 1890–1900* (London: Batsford, 1967); Hans-Jörg v. Berlepsch, *'Neuer Kurs' im Kaiserreich? Die Arbeiterpolitik des Freiherrn von Berlepsch 1890–96* (Bonn: Verlag Neue Gesellschaft, 1987); Karl Erich Born, *Staat und Sozialpolitik seit Bismarcks Sturz 1890–1914* (Wiesbaden: F. Steiner, 1957); Gerhard A. Ritter, *Die Arbeiterbewegung im Wilhelminischen Reich. Die Sozialdemokratische Partei und die Freien Gewerkschaften 1890–1900*, 2nd edn (Berlin: Colloquium Verlag, 1963), 15 ff.; Ludwig Elm, *Zwischen Fortschritt und Reaktion. Geschichte der liberalen Bourgeoisie 1893–1918* (Berlin: Akademie-Verlag 1968); Ernst Rudolf Huber, *Deutsche Verfassungsgeschichte seit 1789*, iv. *Struktur und Krisen des Kaiserreichs*, 2nd edn (Stuttgart: Kohlhammer, 1969), 247 ff., 554 ff., 950 ff., 1075 ff., 1220 ff.; Wehler, *Gesellschaftsgeschichte*, iii (note 1), 1000 ff.
4. Hans Herzfeld, *Johannes von Miquel. Sein Anteil am Ausbau des Deutschen Reiches bis zur Jahrhundertwende*, 2 vols. (Detmold: Meyersche Hofbuchhandlung, Verlag Dr. Catharina Staercke, 1938), i. 394 (Miquel, 26 Jan. 1879); Heinrich August Winkler, 'Der rückversicherte Mittelstand: Die Interessenverbände von Handwerk und Kleinhandel im deutschen Kaiserreich', in *Liberalismus und Antiliberalismus. Studien zur politischen Sozialgeschichte des 19. und 20. Jahrhunderts* (Göttingen: Vandenhoeck & Ruprecht, 1979), 83–98; Dirk Stegmann, *Die Erben Bismarcks. Parteien und Verbände in der Spätphase des Wilhelminischen Deutschland. Sammlungspolitik 1897–1918* (Cologne: Kiepenheuer & Witsch, 1970), 59 ff. (66: William II, 18 June 1897; manifesto of the free traders of 1898); Hartmut Kaelble, *Industrielle Interessenpolitik in der Wilhelminischen Gesellschaft. Centralverband Deutscher Industrieller 1895–1914* (Berlin: de Gruyter, 1967), 51 ff.; Hans-Peter Ullmann, *Der Bund der Industriellen. Organisation, Einfluss und Politik klein- und mittelbetrieblicher*

Industrieller im Deutschen Kaiserreich 1895–1914 (Göttingen: Vandenhoeck & Ruprecht, 1976), 165 ff.; Röhl, *Deutschland* (note 3), 224 ff.

5. *Sten. Ber.*, cxlix. 5149 (Marschall, 18 Mar. 1897); Eckart Kehr, 'Englandhass und Weltpolitik' (1928), in *Der Primat der Innenpolitik. Gesammelte Aufsätze zur preussisch-deutschen Sozialgeschichte im 19. u. 20. Jahrhundert*, ed. and introd. Hans-Ulrich Wehler (Berlin: de Gruyter, 1965), 149–75 (quotes from Kehr: 164, Tirpitz, 21 Dec. 1895: 165); id., *Economic Interest, Militarism, and Foreign Policy: Essays on German History* (Berkeley: University of California Press, 1977); id., *Schlachtflottenbau und Parteipolitik 1894–1901* (Berlin: E. Ebering, 1930; repr. Vaduz: Klaus Reprint, 1965), esp. 276 ff.; Volker Berghahn, *Der Tirpitz-Plan. Genesis und Verfall einer innenpolitischen Krisenstrategie unter Wilhelm II.* (Düsseldorf: Droste, 1971); Kenneth D. Barkin, *The Controversy over German Industrialization 1890–1902* (Chicago: University of Chigaco Press, 1970), 211 ff.; Konrad Schilling, *Beiträge zu einer Geschichte des radikalen Nationalismus in der Wilhelminischen Ära 1890–1909* (Cologne: Gouder & Hansen, 1968); Geoff Eley, *Reshaping the German Right: Radical Nationalism and Political Change after Bismarck* (New Haven: Yale University Press, 1980), 68 ff.; id., 'Die Umformierung der Rechten: Der radikale Nationalismus und der Deutsche Flottenverein 1898–1908', in *Wilhelminismus, Nationalismus, Faschismus. Zur historischen Kontinuität in Deutschland* (Münster: Westfälisches Dampfboot, 1991), 144–73; Huber, *Verfassungsgeschichte*, iv (note 3), 565 ff.; Wehler, *Gesellschaftsgeschichte*, iii (note 1), 1129 ff.; the article 'Deutscher Flottenverein 1898–1934', in *Lexikon* (note 2), ii, ed. Fricke et al., 67–89 (membership: 68).
6. *Sten. Ber.*, clix. 60 (Bülow, 6 Dec. 1897); Konrad Canis, *Von Bismarck zur Weltpolitik. Deutsche Aussenpolitik 1890 bis 1902* (Berlin: Akademie-Verlag, 1997), 223 ff.; Gustav Schmidt, *Der europäische Imperialismus* (Munich: Oldenbourg, 1985), 90 ff.; Klaus Hildebrand, *Das vergangene Reich. Deutsche Aussenpolitik von Bismarck bis Hitler* (Stuttgart: Deutsche Verlags-Anstalt, 1995), 149 ff.
7. The article 'Alldeutscher Verband 1891–1939', in *Lexikon* (note 2), i, ed. Fricke et al., 13–47 (membership: 13, quotes from the statutes: 16, of the year 1894: 19); the article 'Deutscher Ostmarkenverein 1894–1934', ibid., ii. 225–50 (membership: 225–6, quote from the statutes: 228); Roger Chickering, *We Men Who Feel Most German: A Cultural Study of the Pan-German League 1886–1914* (London: Allen & Unwin, 1984), 44 ff.; Mildred S. Wertheimer, *The Pan-German League 1890–1914* (New York: Octagon, 1924); Hans-Ulrich Wehler, 'Von den "Reichsfeinden" zur "Reichskristallnacht": Polenpolitik im Deutschen Kaiserreich 1871–1918', in *Krisenherde des Kaiserreichs 1871–1918. Studien zur deutschen Sozial- und Verfassungsgeschichte* (Göttingen: Vandenhoeck & Ruprecht, 1970), 181–200; id., 'Deutsch-polnische Beziehungen im 19. und 20. Jahrhundert', ibid. 201–18; Martin Broszat, *200 Jahre deutsche Polenpolitik* (Munich: Ehrenwirth, 1963), 25 ff.
8. Thomas Rohkrämer, *Der Militarismus der «kleinen Leute». Die Kriegervereine im Deutschen Kaiserreich 1871–1914* (Munich: Oldenbourg, 1990), esp. 34 ff.; Jakob Vogel, *Nationen im Gleichschritt. Der Kult der 'Nation in Waffen' in Deutschland und Frankreich, 1871–1914* (Göttingen: Vendenhoek & Ruprecht, 1997); Robert von Friedeburg, 'Klassen-, Geschlechter- oder Nationalidentität? Handwerker und Tagelöhner in den Kriegervereinen der neupreussischen Provinz Hessen-Nassau 1890–1914', *Militär und Gesellschaft im 19. und 20. Jahrhundert*, ed. Ute Frevert (Stuttgart: Klett-Cotta, 1997), 229–44; the article 'Kyffhäuser-Bund der Deutschen

Landeskriegerverbände 1899/1900–1943', in *Lexikon* (note 2), iii, ed. Fricke et al., 325–44 (membership: 326–7).

9. Thomas Nipperdey, 'Nationalidee und Nationaldenkmal in Deutschland im 19. Jahrhundert', in *Gesellschaft, Kultur, Theorie. Gesammelte Aufsätze zur neueren Geschichte* (Göttingen: Vandenhoeck & Ruprecht, 1976), 133–73 (143–4); *Das Kyffhäuser-Denkmal 1896–1996. Ein nationales Monument im europäischen Kontext*, ed. Gunther Mai (Cologne: Böhlau, 1997); Wolfgang Hardtwig, 'Bürgertum, Staatssymbolik und Staatsbewusstsein im Deutschen Kaiserreich 1871–1914', in *Nationalismus und Bürgerkultur in Deutschland 1500–1914. Ausgewählte Aufsätze* (Göttingen: Vandenhoeck & Ruprecht, 1994), 191–218 (208); Charlotte Tacke, *Denkmal im sozialen Raum. Nationale Symbole in Deutschland und Frankreich im 19. Jahrhundert* (Göttingen: Vandenhoeck & Ruprecht, 1995), 80 ff.; ead., 'Die 1900-Jahrfeier der Schlacht im Teutoburger Wald 1909. Von der "klassenlosen Bürgergesellschaft" zur "klassenlosen Volksgemeinschaft"?', in *Bürgerliche Feste. Symbolische Formen politischen Handelns im 19. Jahrhundert*, ed. Manfred Hettling and Paul Nolte (Göttingen: Vandenhoeck & Ruprecht, 1993), 192–230; Reinhard Alings, *Monument und Nation. Das Bild vom Nationalstaat im Medium Denkmal—zum Verhältnis von Nation und Staat im deutschen Kaiserreich 1871–1918* (Berlin: de Gruyter, 1996); Michael S. Cullen, *Der Reichstag. Die Geschichte eines Monumentes*, 2nd edn (Stuttgart: Parkland Verlag, 1990), 219 (William II, 25 Apr. 1893 in Rome), 242 (*Vossische Zeitung*, 6 Dec. 1894), 246 (William II to Eulenburg, 8 Dec. 1894); Fritz Schellack, 'Sedan- und Kaisergeburtstagsfeste', in *Öffentliche Festkultur. Politische Feste in Deutschland von der Aufklärung bis zum Ersten Weltkrieg*, ed. Dieter Düding et al. (Hamburg: Rowohlt, 1988), 278–97; Beatrix Bouvier, 'Die Märzfeiern der sozialdemokratischen Arbeiter: Gedenktage des Proletariats—Gedenktage der Revolution. Zur Geschichte des 18. März', ibid. 334–51; Georg L. Mosse, *Die Nationalisierung der Massen. Politische Symbolik und Massenbewegungen in Deutschland von den Napoleonischen Kriegen bis zum Dritten Reich* (Frankfurt: Ullstein, 1976), 62 ff., orig. *The Nationalization of the Masses: Political Symbolism and Mass Movements in Germany from the Napoleonic Wars through the Third Reich* (New York: H. Fertig, 1975).

10. Kurt Wawrzinek, *Die Entstehung der deutschen Antisemitenparteien, 1873–1890* (Berlin: E. Ebering, 1927); Richard S. Levy, *The Downfall of the Anti-Semitic Parties in Imperial Gemany* (New Haven: Yale University Press, 1975); Stefan Scheil, *Die Entwicklung des politischen Antisemitismus in Deutschland zwischen 1881 und 1912: eine wahlgeschichtliche Untersuchung* (Berlin: Duncker & Humblot, 1999), 72 ff.; *Handbuch zur 'Völkischen Bewegung' 1871–1918*, ed. Uwe Puschner et al. (Munich: K. G. Saur, 1996); the article 'Antisemitische Parteien 1879–1894', *Lexikon* (note 2), i, ed. Fricke et al., 77–88; 'Deutschsoziale Partei 1900–1914', ibid. ii. 534–7; 'Deutschsoziale Reformpartei 1894–1900', ibid. 540–9; Hans Booms, *Die Deutschkonservative Partei. Preussischer Charakter, Reichsauffassung, Nationalbegriff* (Düsseldorf: Droste, 1954), esp. 97 ff.; James N. Retallack, *Notables of the Right: The Conservative Party and Political Mobilization in Germany, 1876–1918* (London: Unwin Hyman, 1988), 91 ff.; *Deutsche Parteiprogramme*, ed. Wilhelm Mommsen (Munich: Isar Verlag, 1960), 78–80 ('Tivoli platform'); *Handbuch der Deutsch-Konservativen Partei*, 4th edn (Berlin: Reimar Hobbing, 1911), 4–9 (the article 'Antisemitismus'); Uwe Mai, ' "Wie es der Jude treibt". Das Feindbild der antisemitischen Bewegung am Beispiel der Agitation Hermann

Ahlwardts', *Feindbilder in der deutschen Geschichte. Studien zur Vorurteilsgeschichte im 19. u. 20. Jahrhundert*, ed. Christoph Jahr et al. (Berlin: Metropol, 1994), 55–80; Puhle, *Interessenpolitik* (note 2), 130 (quote from 1895); Iris Hamel, *Völkischer Verband und nationale Gewerkschaft. Der Deutschnationale Handlungsgehilfen-Verband 1893–1933* (Frankfurt: Europäische Verlagsanstalt, 1967), 14 ff. (quote from the statutes: 53); Jürgen Kocka, *Unternehmensverwaltung und Angestelltenschaft am Beispiel Siemens 1847–1914. Zum Verhältnis von Kapitalismus und Bürokratie in der deutschen Industrialisierung* (Stuttgart: Klett, 1969), 148 ff., 536 ff.; Gerhard A. Ritter with Merith Niehuss, *Wahlgeschichtliches Arbeitsbuch. Materialien zur Statistik des Kaiserreiches 1871–1918* (Munich: C. H. Beck, 1980), 38 ff.; Nipperdey, *Geschichte* (note 1), 289 ff.

11. *Parteiprogramme* (note 10), ed. Mommsen, 166–8 (*Grundlinien des Nationalsozialen Kreises*, 25 Nov. 1896); Friedrich Naumann, 'Demokratie und Kaisertum', in *Werke. Politische Schriften*, ii. *Schriften zur Verfassungspolitik* (Cologne: Westdeutscher Verlag, 1964), 266–7; Werner Conze, 'Friedrich Naumann. Grundlagen und Ansatz seiner Politik in der national-sozialen Zeit', in *Schicksalswege deutscher Vergangenheit. Festschrift für Siegfried A. Kaehler*, ed. Walther Hubatsch (Düsseldorf: Droste, 1950), 355–86; Richard Nürnberger, 'Imperialismus, Sozialismus und Christentum bei Friedrich Naumann', *HZ* 170 (1950), 525–48; Theodor Heuss, *Friedrich Naumann. Der Mann, das Werk, die Zeit* (Stuttgart: R. Wunderlich, 1949); Dieter Düding, *Der Nationalsoziale Verein 1896–1903. Der gescheiterte Versuch einer parteipolitischen Synthese von Nationalismus, Sozialismus und Liberalismus* (Munich: Oldenbourg, 1972); James J. Sheehan, 'Deutscher Liberalismus im postliberalen Zeitalter 1890–1914', *GG* 4 (1978), 29–98; Konstanze Wegner, *Theodor Barth und die Freisinnige Vereinigung. Studien zur Geschichte des Linksliberalismus im Wilhelminischen Deutschland 1893–1910* (Tübingen: Mohr, 1968); Elisabeth Fehrenbach, *Wandlungen des deutschen Kaisergedankens 1871–1918* (Munich: Oldenbourg, 1969), 200 ff.; Mommsen, *Weber* (note 1), 73 ff., 186 ff.

12. Ernst Deuerlein, 'Die Bekehrung des Zentrums zur nationalen Idee', *Hochland*, 62 (1970), 432–49 (Kopp's letter to Bachem, 4 Feb. 1900: 446–7; emphasis in original); Rudolf Morsey, 'Die deutschen Katholiken und der Nationalstaat zwischen Kulturkampf und erstem Weltkrieg', in *Die deutschen Parteien vor 1918*, ed. Gerhard A. Ritter (Cologne: Kiepenheuer & Witsch, 1973), 270–98 (quote from Bebel: 283); Wilfried Loth, *Katholiken im Kaiserreich. Der politische Katholizismus in der Krise des wilhelminischen Deutschland* (Düsseldorf: Droste, 1984), 38 ff.; David Blackbourn, *Class, Religion and Local Politics in Wilhelmine Germany: The Centre Party in Württemberg before 1914* (New Haven: Yale University Press, 1980), 23 ff.; Olaf Blaschke, *Katholizismus und Antisemitismus im deutschen Kaiserreich* (Göttingen: Vandenhoeck & Ruprecht, 1997), esp. 119 ff. (on the journalism of the 1890s: 125 ff.; on the debate in the Prussian House of Representatives in November 1880: 238 ff.); Uwe Mazura, *Zentrumspartei und Judenfrage 1870/71–1933. Verfassungsstaat und Minderheitenschutz* (Mainz: Matthias-Grünewald-Verlag, 1994); Winfried Becker, 'Die Deutsche Zentrumspartei im Bismarckreich', in *Die Minderheit als Mitte. Die Deutsche Zentrumspartei in der Innenpolitik des Reiches 1871–1933*, ed. id. (Paderborn: Schöningh, 1986), 9–46; Norbert Schlossmacher, 'Der Antiultramontanismus im Wilhelminischen Deutschland', in *Deutscher Katholizismus im Umbruch zur Moderne*, ed. Wilfried Loth (Stuttgart: Kohlhammer, 1991), 164–98; M. Rainer Lepsius, 'Parteiensystem und Sozialstruktur. Zum Problem der Demokratisierung der

deutschen Gesellschaft', in *Demokratie in Deutschland. Soziologisch-historische Konstellationsanalysen* (Göttingen: Vandenhoeck & Ruprecht, 1993), 25–50. For quote from Theodor Mommsen's letter to Lujo Brentano of 3 Jan. 1902 see Lothar Wickert, *Theodor Mommsen*, 4 vols., iv (Frankfurt: Klostermann, 1980), 93. On the *Evangelischer Bund* see Gangolf Hübinger, *Kulturprotestantismus und Politik. Zum Verhältnis von Liberalismus und Protestantismus im wilhelminischen Deutschland* (Tübingen: Mohr, 1994), 52–3 (membership: 53).

13. *Protokoll über die Verhandlungen des Parteitags der Sozialdemokratischen Partei Deutschlands, abgehalten zu Erfurt vom 14. bis 20. Oktober 1891* (Berlin 1891), 169 (Bebel); *Parteiprogramme* (note 10), ed. Mommsen, 344–9 (Engels's critique of the draft of the Erfurt platform), 349–53 (Erfurt platform); Karl Kautsky, *Der Weg zur Macht. Politische Betrachtungen über das Hineinwachsen in die Revolution*, 2nd edn (Berlin: Buchhandlung Vorwärts, 1909), 44–52 (article from the *Neue Zeit*, Dec. 1893; quotes: 44–6), tr. as *The Road to Power: Political Reflections on Growing into the Revolution* (Atlantic Highlands, NJ: Humanities Press, 1996); Dieter Grosser, *Vom monarchischen Konstitutionalismus zur parlamentarischen Demokratie. Die Verfassungspolitik der deutschen Parteien im letzten Jahrzehnt des Kaiserreichs* (The Hague: Nijhoff, 1970), 33–4 (Kautsky to Mehring, 5 July 1893); Ingrid Gilcher-Holtey, *Das Mandat des Intellektuellen. Karl Kautsky und die Sozialdemokratie* (Berlin: Siedler, 1986), 59 ff.; Erich Matthias, 'Kautsky und der Kautskyanismus. Die Funktion der Ideologie in der deutschen Sozialdemokratie vor dem ersten Weltkrieg', *Marxismus-Studien*, 2nd series (Tübingen: Mohr, 1957), 151–97; Lucian Hölscher, *Weltgericht oder Revolution. Protestantische und sozialistische Zukunftsvorstellungen im deutschen Kaiserreich* (Stuttgart: Klett-Cotta, 1989), 231 ff., 307 ff.
14. Eduard Bernstein, *Die Voraussetzungen des Sozialismus und die Aufgaben der Sozialdemokratie* (Stuttgart: J. H. W. Dietz, Nachfolger, 1909), pp. v–vii (to the Stuttgart party congress), pp. viii–ix (to *Vorwärts*, 20 Oct. 1898), 124, 129, 165, 169, 179, 183, 187 (emphasis in original), tr. as *The Preconditions of Socialism* (Cambridge: Cambridge University Press, 1993); Susanne Miller, *Das Problem der Freiheit im Sozialismus. Freiheit, Staat und Revolution in der Programmatik der Sozialdemokratie von Lassalle bis zum Revisionismus-Streit* (Frankfurt: Europäische Verlagsanstalt, 1964), 227 ff.; Peter Gay, *Das Dilemma des Demokratischen Sozialismus. Eduard Bernsteins Auseinandersetzung mit Marx* (Nuremberg: Nest, 1954), orig. *The Dilemma of Democratic Socialism: Eduard Bernstein's Challenge to Marx* (New York: Columbia University Press, 1952); Helmut Hirsch, *Der 'Fabier' Eduard Bernstein. Zur Entwicklungsgeschichte des evolutionären Sozialismus* (Berlin: Dietz, 1977); Francis Ludwig Carsten, *Eduard Bernstein 1850–1932. Eine politische Biographie* (Munich: C. H. Beck, 1993), 81 ff.; id., *August Bebel und die Organisation der Massen* (Berlin: Siedler, 1991), 179 ff.
15. Rosa Luxemburg, *Sozialreform oder Revolution?*, in *Politische Schriften*, 3 vols., ed. Ossip K. Flechtheim (Frankfurt: Europäische Verlagsanstalt, 1966–), i. 47–133 (54, 90, 113–14, 119, 123, 130; emphases in original), tr. as *Reform or Revolution?* (New York: Pathfinder Press, 1973); Karl Kautsky, *Bernstein und das Sozialdemokratische Programm. Eine Antikritik* (Stuttgart: J. H. W Dietz, Nachfolger, 1899; repr. Bonn, 1976, 2nd edn), 43, 183, 191, 193, 195; Friedrich Engels, *Herrn Eugen Dührings Umwälzung der Wissenschaft*, MEW, xx. 1–303, tr. as *Anti-Dühring: Herr Eugen Dühring's Revolution in Science*, MECW, xxv. 1–312; August Bebel, *Die Frau und der Sozialismus* (1878; repr. Bonn: Dietz, 1994), tr. as *Woman under*

Socialism (New York: Schocken Books, 1904, repr. 1971); Peter Nettl, *Rosa Luxemburg* (Cologne, 1967), 54 ff. (orig. New York: Oxford University Press, 1965).

16. *Protokoll über die Verhandlungen des Parteitages der Sozialdemokratischen Partei Deutschland, abgehalten zu Hannover vom 9. bis 14. Oktober 1899* (Berlin: Expedition der Buchhandlung Vorwärts, 1899), 243–4 (Bebel's resolution); *Parteiprogramme* (note 10), ed. Mommsen, 332–44 (Vollmar's speech of 1 June 1891, quotes: 336; emphases in original); Hans Georg Lehmann, *Die Agrarfrage in der Theorie und Praxis der deutschen und internationalen Sozialdemokratie. Vom Marxismus zum Revisionismus und Bolschewismus* (Tübingen: Mohr, 1970); Gerhard A. Ritter and Klaus Tenfelde, *Arbeiter im Deutschen Kaiserreich 1871 bis 1914* (Bonn: J. H. W. Dietz, 1992), esp. 111 ff.; Ritter, *Arbeiterbewegung* (note 3), 128 ff.; Hans Gerd Henke, *Der 'Jude' als Kollektivsymbol in der deutschen Sozialdemokratie 1890–1914* (Mainz: Decaton, 1994); Robert S. Wistrich, *Socialism and the Jews: The Dilemmas of Assimilation in Germany and Austria-Hungary* (London: Associated University Press, 1982); Rosemarie Leuschen-Seppel, *Sozialdemokratie und Antisemitismus im Kaiserreich. Die Auseinandersetzung der Partei mit konservativen und völkischen Strömungen des Antisemitismus 1971–1914* (Bonn: Verlag Neue Gesellschaft, 1978). Quote about anti-Semitism in Ludwig Knorr, *Sozialdemokratischer Katechismus für das arbeitende Volk*, 4th edn (Nuremberg: Wörlein & Co., 1894), 30–1, quoted from Carsten, *Bernstein* (note 14), 56.

17. Julius Braunthal, *Geschichte der Internationale*, 2 vols. (Hanover: Dietz Nachfolger, 1961), i. 263 ff., tr. as *History of the International* (New York: Praeger, 1967); Georges Lefranc, *Le mouvement socialiste sous la troisième république*, i. *1875–1919*, 2nd edn (Paris: Payot, 1977), 105 ff., 196 ff.; Carsten, *Bebel* (note 14), 137 ff.; Huber, *Verfassungsgeschichte*, iv (note 3), 106 ff.

18. Hannelore Horn, *Der Kampf um den Bau des Mittellandkanals* (Cologne: Westdeutscher Verlag, 1964); Puhle, *Interessenpolitik* (note 2), 240 ff.; Theodor Eschenburg, *Das Kaiserreich am Scheidewege. Bassermann, Bülow und der Block* (Berlin: Verlag für Kulturpolitik, 1929); Peter Christian Witt, *Die Finanzpolitik des Deutschen Reiches von 1903 bis 1913. Eine Studie zur Innenpolitik des Wilhelminischen Deutschland* (Lübeck: Matthiesen, 1970), 152 ff.; Gustav Schmidt, *Der europäische Imperialismus* (Munich: Oldenbourg, 1985), 95 ff.; Hildebrand, *Reich* (note 6), 213 ff.; Wehler, *Gesellschaftsgeschichte*, iii (note 1), 1008 ff.; Huber, *Verfassungsgeschichte*, iv (note 3), 287 ff. Quotes from Bernhard Fürst von Bülow, *Denkwürdigkeiten*, 4 vols., ii. *Von der Marokko-Krise bis zum Abschied* (Berlin: Ullstein, 1930), 351 ff. (*Daily Telegraph* interview), 356–7 (on the mood in Germany), tr. as *Memoirs of Prince von Bülow*, 4 vols., ii. *From the Morocco Crisis to Resignation, 1903–1909* (New York: AMS Press, 1931); *Sten. Ber.*, ccxxxiii. 5935 (Bülow, 10 Nov. 1908); *Dokumente zur Deutschen Verfassungsgeschichte*, iii. *Deutsche Verfassungsdokumente (1900–1918)*, 3rd edn, ed. Ernst Rudolf Huber (Stuttgart: Kohlhammer, 1990), 28 (statement on 17 Nov. 1908).

19. Huber, *Verfassungsgeschichte*, iv (note 3), 318 ('threshold' quote); Manfred Rauh, *Die Parlamentarisierung des Deutschen Reiches* (Düsseldorf: Droste, 1977) (theory on the parliamentarization of the German Reich prior to 1914); Thomas Kühne, *Dreiklassenwahlrecht und Wahlkultur in Preussen 1867–1914* (Düsseldorf: Droste, 1994); Barbara Greven-Aschoff, *Die bürgerliche Frauenbewegung in Deutschland 1894–1933* (Göttingen: Vandenhoeck & Ruprecht, 1981), 87 ff.; Angelika Schaser, 'Bürgerliche Frauen auf dem Weg in die linksliberalen Parteien (1908–1933)', *HZ*

263 (1996), 641–80; *'Heraus mit dem Frauenwahlrecht'. Die Kämpfe der Frauen in Deutschland und England um die politische Gleichberechtigung*, ed. Christel Wickert (Pfaffenweiler: Centaurus-Verlagsgesellschaft, 1990). Quotes from the platform of the Progressive People's Party in *Parteiprogramme* (note 10), ed. Mommsen, 173–6; for the election numbers see *Arbeitsbuch* (note 10), ed. Ritter, 140, 146.

20. MEW, xxxiv. 276 (Engels's letter to Johann Philipp Becker of 10 Feb. 1882; here the 'avant-garde' quote), xxxvi. 305–7 (Engels's letter to Vera Zasulich of 23 Apr. 1885; here the remaining quotes; emphasis in original); Friedrich Engels, 'Einleitung zu "Die Klassenkämpfe in Frankreich 1848 bis 1850" von Karl Marx' (1895 edition), MEW, vii., 511–27 (quote: 523); MECW, xlvi. 196–8 (Engels's letter to Johann Philipp Becker of 10 Feb. 1882; here the 'avant-garde' quote), xlvii. 279–81 (Engels's letter to Vera Zasulich of 23 Apr. 1885; here the remaining quotes; emphasis in original); Engels, 'Introduction to Karl Marx's *The Class Struggles in France, 1848 to 1850'*, MECW, xxvii. 506–25; Rosa Luxemburg, *Massenstreik, Partei und Gewerkschaften* (Sept. 1906), in *Politische Schriften*, (note 15), 135–228 (173, 178, 203; emphases in original), tr. as *The Mass Strike: The Political Party and the Trade Unions, and the Junius Pamphlet* (New York: Harper & Row, 1971); *Protokoll über die Verhandlungen des Parteitages der Sozialdemokratischen Partei Deutschlands. Abgehalten zu Bremen vom 18. bis 24. September 1904* (Berlin: Expedition der Buchhandlung Vorwärts, 1904), 193–4 (Bernstein); *Protokoll über die Verhandlungen des Parteitages der Sozialdemokratischen Partei Deutschlands. Abgehalten zu Jena vom 17. bis 23. September 1905* (Berlin: Expedition der Buchhandlung Vorwärts 1905), 142–3 (Bebel's resolution); *Protokoll über die Verhandlungen des Parteitages der Sozialdemokratischen Partei Deutschlands. Abgehalten zu Mannheim vom 23. bis 29. September 1906* (Berlin: Expedition der Buchhandlung Vorwärts, 1906), 137 (resolution of the labor union congress in Cologne), 473 (Mannheim resolution); Peter Lösche, *Der Bolschewismus im Urteil der deutschen Sozialdemokratie 1903–1920* (Berlin: Colloquium Verlag, 1967), 23 ff. (on Luxemburg's critique of Lenin, 1904); Carsten, *Bernstein* (note 14), 115 ff.; Guenther Roth, *The Social Democrats in Imperial Germany: A Study in the Working Class Isolation and National Integration* (Totowa, NJ: Bedminster Press, 1963); Dieter Groh, *Negative Integration und revolutionärer Attentismus. Die deutsche Sozialdemokratie am Vorabend des 1. Weltkriegs* (Frankfurt: Propyläen, 1973); Carl E. Schorske, *Die grosse Spaltung. Die deutsche Sozialdemokratie von 1905 bis 1917* (Berlin: Olle & Wolter, 1981), esp. 123 ff., orig. *German Social Democracy, 1905–1917: The Development of the Great Schism* (Cambridge, MA: Harvard University Press, 1955); Klaus Schönhoven, 'Expansion und Konzentration. Studien zur Entwicklung der Freien Gewerkschaften im Wilhelminischen Kaiserreich 1890 bis 1918', in Klaus Tenfelde et al., *Geschichte der deutschen Gewerkschaften von den Anfängen bis 1945*, ed. Ulrich Borsdorf (Cologne: Bund-Verlag, 1988), 167–278, esp. 236 ff. (figures: 237). On the '*translatio revolutionis*' in Marx see 93–4.

21. Julius Bachem, 'Wir müssen aus dem Turm heraus!', *Historisch-politische Blätter für das katholische Deutschland*, 137 (1906), 376–86 (384 ff.; emphasis in original); *Parteiprogramme* (note 10), ed. Mommsen, 245–6. (Berlin declaration in 1909); Karl Bachem, *Vorgeschichte, Geschichte und Politik der Deutschen Zentrumspartei*, vii (Cologne: J. P. Bachem, 1930), 156 ff.; Loth, *Katholiken* (note 12), 81 ff.

22. Theodor Mommsen, 'Was uns noch retten kann', *Die Nation*, 20 (1902), 163–4; Peter Gilg, *Die Erneuerung des demokratischen Denkens im Wilhelminischen Deutschland.*

Eine ideengeschichtliche Studie zur Wende vom 19. zum 20. Jahrhundert (Wiesbaden: Steiner, 1965), 218 ff.; Siegfried Mielke, *Der Hansa-Bund für Gewerbe, Handel und Industrie 1909–1914. Der gescheiterte Versuch einer antifeudalen Sammlungspolitik* (Göttingen: Vandenhoeck & Ruprecht, 1976), 29 ff.; Elm, *Fortschritt* (note 3); Wegner, *Barth* (note 11), 134 ff.; Donald Warren, *The Red Kingdom of Saxony: Lobbying Grounds for Gustav Stresemann 1901–1909* (The Hague: M. Nijhoff, 1964); Dieter Langewiesche, *Liberalismus in Deutschland* (Frankfurt: Suhrkamp, 1988), 200 ff., tr. as *Liberalism in Germany* (Princeton: Princeton University Press, 1999); the article 'Demokratische Vereinigung 1908–1918', in *Lexikon* (note 2), i, ed. Fricke et al., 496–503 (membership and ballot records: 496); the article 'Fortschrittliche Volkspartei 1910–1918', ibid. ii. 599–609.

23. *Sten. Ber.*, cclix. 898 (Oldenburg, 29 Jan. 1910), cclxviii. 7718 (Hertling, 9 Nov. 1911), 7721–2 (von Heydebrand und der Lasa [Lase], 9 Nov. 1911), 7730 (Bebel, 9 Nov. 1911), 7737 ff. (Bassermann, 9 Nov. 1911); Konrad H. Jarausch, *The Enigmatic Chancellor: Bethmann Hollweg and the Hybris of Imperial Germany* (New Haven: Yale University Press, 1973); Hans-Günther Zmarzlik, *Bethmann Hollweg als Reichskanzler 1909–1914* (Düsseldorf: Droste, 1957), esp. 24 ff.; Stig Förster, *Der doppelte Militarismus. Die deutsche Heeresrüstungspolitik zwischen Status-quo-Sicherung und Aggression 1890–1913* (Stuttgart: F. Steiner, 1985), 208 ff.; Klaus Wernecke, *Der Wille zur Weltgeltung. Aussenpolitik und Öffentlichkeit im Kaiserreich am Vorabend des Ersten Weltkrieges* (Düsseldorf: Droste, 1970), 26 ff. (Bassermann's letter to Kiderlen-Waechter, 24 July 1911: 30), 102 ff. (echo in the press); Thomas Meyer, *'Endlich eine Tat, eine befreiende Tat . . . ' Alfred Kiderlen-Waechters 'Panthersprung nach Agadir' unter dem Druck der öffentlichen Meinung* (Husum: Matthiesen, 1996), 141 ff.; Ralf Forsbach, *Alfred von Kiderlen-Wächter (1852–1912). Ein Diplomatenleben im Kaiserreich*, 2 vols. (Göttingen: Vandenhoeck & Ruprecht, 1997), ii. 411 ff.; Emily Oncken, *Panthersprung nach Agadir. Die deutsche Politik während der Zweiten Marokkokrise von 1911* (Düsseldorf: Droste,1981), esp. 219 ff.; *Flucht in den Krieg? Die Aussenpolitik des kaiserlichen Deutschland*, ed. Gregor Schöllgen (Darmstadt: Wissenschaftliche Buchgesellschaft, 1991); *Bereit zum Krieg. Kriegsmentalität im wilhelminischen Deutschland 1890–1914. Beiträge zur historischen Friedensforschung*, ed. Jost Dülffer and Karl Holl (Göttingen: Vandenhoeck & Ruprecht, 1986); Wolfgang J. Mommsen, *Bürgerstolz und Weltmachtstreben. Deutschland unter Wilhelm II. 1890 bis 1918* (Berlin: Propyläen, 1995), 450 ff.; Volker Ullrich, *Die nervöse Grossmacht 1871–1918. Aufstieg und Untergang des deutschen Kaiserreiches* (Frankfurt: S, Fischer, 1997), 223 ff.; Joachim Radkau, *Das Zeitalter der Nervosität. Deutschland zwischen Bismarck und Hitler* (Munich: Hanser, 1998), 263 ff.; Hildebrand, *Reich* (note 6), 260 ff.; Schmidt, *Imperialismus* (note 6), 100 ff.; Chickering, *We Men* (note 7), 262 ff.; the article 'Alldeutscher Verband', *Lexikon* (note 2), i, ed. Fricke et al., 26–7.

24. Friedrich von Bernhardi, *Deutschland und der nächste Krieg* (Stuttgart: J. G. Cotta, 1912), pp. v, 9, 12–13, 34, 73, 89, 110 ff., 123–4, 275, 293–4, 333 (emphasis in original), tr. as *Germany and the Next War* (New York: Longmans, Green, and Co., 1914); Weber, 'Nationalstaat' (note 1), 569; *Sten. Ber.*, cclxviii. 7728 (Bebel, 9 Nov. 1911); Marilyn Shevin Coetzee, *The German Army League: Popular Nationalism in Wilhelmine Gemany* (New York: Oxford University Press, 1990); Förster, *Militarismus* (note 23), 144 (theory about 'militarism from below'); Eley, *Reshaping* (note 5), 160 ff. (theory about 'populist' nationalism); Wernecke, *Wille* (note 23), 174 ff.; Hans-

Günther Zmarzlik, 'Der Sozialdarwinismus in Deutschland als geschichtliches Problem', *VfZ* (1963), 246–73; Klaus Saul, *Staat, Industrie, Arbeiterbewegung im Kaiserreich. Zur Innen- und Aussenpolitik des Wilhelminischen Deutschland 1903–1914* (Düsseldorf: Droste, 1974), 115 ff.; the article 'Reichsverband gegen die Sozialdemokratie 1904–1918', in *Lexikon* (note 2), iv, ed. Fricke et al., 63–77 (membership: 63); the article 'Deutscher Wehrverein 1912–1935', ibid. ii. 330–41 (membership: 330). For a pre-1914 international comparison of imperialism and nationalism see Georg W. F. Hallgarten, *Imperialismus vor 1914. Die soziologischen Grundlagen der Aussenpolitik europäischer Grossmächte vor dem Ersten Weltkrieg*, 2 vols. (Munich: C. H. Beck, 1963), ii. 209 ff.; Zara S. Steiner, *Britain and the Origins of the First World War* (London: St Martin's Press, 1977); *Nationalist and Racialist Movements in Britain and Germany before 1914*, ed. Paul Kennedy and Anthony Nicholls (Oxford: Macmillan in Association with St Antony's College, 1981); Markus Ingenlath, *Mentale Aufrüstung. Militarisierungstendenzen in Frankreich und Deutschland vor dem Ersten Weltkrieg* (Frankfurt; Campus, 1998); Gerd Krumeich, *Aufrüstung und Innenpolitik in Frankreich vor dem Ersten Weltkrieg. Die Einführung der dreijährigen Dienstpflicht 1913–1914* (Wiesbaden: F. Steiner, 1980), tr. as *Armaments and Politics in France on the Eve of the First World War: The Introduction of Three-Year Conscription, 1913–1914* (Leamington Spa, Warwicks.: Berg, 1984). Quote from Ernst Moritz Arndt from 'Letzter Zug an Gott' (1844), in *Sämmtliche Werke* (Leipzig, n.d., v 128–30.

25. 'Daniel Frymann' [= Heinrich Class], *Wenn ich der Kaiser wär'. Politische Wahrheiten und Notwendigkeiten*, 5th edn (Leipzig: Dieterich, 1914), 30 ff., 67, 74, 103, 111, 135, 149 ff., 179, 227, 254, 256, 259–60; Paul de Lagarde, *Deutsche Schriften*, 3rd edn (Munich: J. F. Lehmann, 1937); *Rembrandt als Erzieher. Von einem Deutschen* (Julius Langbehn), (Leipzig: C. L. Hirschfeld, 1890; 3rd edn, 1891), 3; Houston Stewart Chamberlain, *Die Grundlagen des Neunzehnten Jahrhunderts*, 2 vols., unabridged popular edition (Munich: F. Bruckmann, n.d.); orig. *Foundations of the Nineteenth Century* (New York: H. Fertig, 1910); Fritz Stern, *Kulturpessimismus als politische Gefahr* (Bern: Scherz, 1963) esp. 25 ff., 127 ff., orig. *The Politics of Cultural Despair: A Study in the Rise of the Germanic Ideology* (Berkeley: University of California Press, 1961); Lamar Cecil, 'Wilhelm II. und die Juden im Wilhelminischen Deutschland 1890–1914', in *Die Juden im wilhelminischen Deutschland 1890–1914*, ed. Werner E. Mosse (Tübingen: Mohr, 1976), 313–47; Norbert Kampe, *Studenten und Judenfrage im Deutschen Kaiserreich. Die Entstehung einer akademischen Trägerschicht des Antisemitismus* (Göttingen: Vandenhoeck & Ruprecht, 1988); Notker Hammerstein, *Antisemitismus und deutsche Universitäten 1871–1933* (Frankfurt: Campus, 1995), 64 ff.; Konrad Jarausch, *Deutsche Studenten 1800–1970* (Frankfurt: Suhrkamp, 1984), 82 ff.; Michael Peters, *Der Alldeutsche Verband am Vorabend des Ersten Weltkrieges (1908–1914)* (Frankfurt: P. Lang, 1992), 165 ff.

26. Werner Jochmann, 'Antisemitismus im Deutschen Kaiserreich', in *Gesellschaftskrise und Judenfeindschaft in Deutschland 1870–1945* (Hamburg: Christians, 1988), 30–98 (on Gebsattel esp. 87 ff.); Hartmut Pogge von Strandmann, 'Staatsstreichpläne, Alldeutsche und Bethmann Hollweg', in id. and Immanuel Geiss, *Die Erforderlichkeit des Unmöglichen. Deutschland am Vorabend des ersten Weltkriegs* (Frankfurt: Europäische Verlagsanstalt, 1965), 7–45 (38: Wilhelm II); Walter Laqueur, *Die deutsche Jugendbewegung. Eine historische Studie*, 2nd edn (Cologne: Wissenschaft & Politik,

1983), 89 ff.; Werner E. Mosse, 'Die Juden in Wirtschaft und Gesellschaft', in *Juden* (note 25), ed. id., 57–113; Peter Pulzer, 'Die jüdische Beteiligung an der Politik', ibid. 143–239 (figures for Berlin: 189); id., 'Rechtliche Gleichstellung und öffentliches Leben', in *Deutsch-jüdische Geschichte in der Neuzeit*, 4 vols., iii. *Umstrittene Integration 1871–1918*, ed. Michael A. Meyer (Munich: C. H. Beck, 1997), 151–92; id., 'Die Wiederkehr des alten Hasses', ibid. 193–248; id., 'Die Reaktion auf den Antisemitismus', ibid. 249–77; Jacob Toury, *Die politischen Orientierungen der Juden in Deutschland. Von Jena bis Weimar* (Tübingen: Mohr, 1966), 202 ff.; Hadassa Ben-Itto, *Die Protokolle der Weisen von Zion. Anatomie einer Fälschung* (Berlin: Aufbau-Verlag, 1998); Michael Bönisch, 'Die "Hammer"-Bewegung', in *Handbuch* (note 10), 341–65; the article 'Reichshammerbund 1910/12–1920', in *Lexikon* (note 2), ed. Fricke et al., iii. 681–83; the article 'Verein zur Abwehr des Antisemitismus (Abwehrverein) 1890–1933', ibid. iv. 375–8 (membership: 375); the article 'Zionistische Vereinigung für Deutschland 1897/98–1938/39', ibid. iv. 636–41; the article 'Reichsdeutscher Mittelstandsverband 1911–1920', ibid. iii. 657–62 (membership: 657); Puhle, *Interessenpolitik* (note 2), 162 ff.; Stegmann, *Erben* (note 4), 352 ff.; Heinrich August Winkler, *Mittelstand, Demokratie und Nationalsozialismus. Die politische Entwicklung von Handwerk und Kleinhandel in der Weimarer Republik* (Cologne: Kiepenheuer & Witsch, 1972), 52–3 (quotes on the 'Cartel of the Productive Estates').

27. *Schulthess' Europäischer Geschichtskalender*, NS 29 (1913) (Munich: C. H. Beck, 1915), 331–2 (Thieme, 18 Oct. 1913); *Sten. Ber.*, cclxxxix. 4552 (Müller-Meiningen, Apr. 1913); Nipperdey, 'Nationalidee' (note 9), 153 (Arndt), 163 ff. (dedication, monument); Hardtwig, 'Bürgertum' (note 9), 218; Stefan-Ludwig Hoffmann, 'Sakraler Monumentalismus um 1900. Das Leipziger Völkerschlachtdenkmal', in *Der politische Totenkult. Kriegerdenkmäler in der Moderne*, ed. Reinhart Koselleck and Michael Jeismann (Munich: Fink, 1994), 249–80; id., 'Mythos und Geschichte. Leipziger Gedenkfeiern der Völkerschlacht im 19. und frühen 20. Jahrhundert', in *Nation und Emotion. Deutschland und Frankreich im Vergleich. 19. und 20. Jahrhundert*, ed. Étienne François et al. (Göttingen: Vandenhoeck & Ruprecht, 1995), 111–32; Steffen Poser, 'Die Jahrhundertfeier der Völkerschlacht und die Einweihung des Völkerschlachtdenkmals zu Leipzig 1913', *Feste und Feiern. Zum Wandel städtischer Festkultur in Leipzig*, ed. Katrin Keller (Leipzig: Edition Leipzig, 1994), 196–213; Wolfram Siemann, 'Krieg und Frieden in historischen Gedenkfeiern des Jahres 1913', *Festkultur* (note 9), ed. Düding et al., 298–320 (299: Rathenau); Ute Schneider, *Politische Festkultur im 19. Jahrhundert. Die Rheinprovinz von der französischen Zeit bis zum Ende des Ersten Weltkrieges (1806–1918)* (Essen: Klartext, 1995), 319 ff.; Dietrich Schäfer, 'Rede zur Erinnerung an die Erhebung der deutschen Nation im Jahre 1813', in *Aufsätze, Vorträge und Reden*, ii (Jena: G. Fischer, 1913), 438–59 (459); *Die Wandervogelzeit. Quellenschriften zur deutschen Jugendbewegung 1896–1919*, ii, ed. Werner Kindt (Düsseldorf: Diederichs, 1968), 501–5 (Wyneken, 12 Oct. 1913: 501); Rüdiger vom Bruch, 'Krieg und Frieden. Zur Frage der Militarisierung deutscher Hochschullehrer und Universitäten im späten Kaiserreich', in *Bereit zum Krieg. Kriegsmentalität im wilhelminischen Deutschland 1890–1914*, ed. Jost Dülffer and Karl Holl (Göttingen: Vandenhoeck & Ruprecht, 1986), 74–98; George L. Mosse, *Nationalisierung* (note 9), 83 ff.

28. Witt, *Finanzpolitik* (note 18), 356 ff.; Groh, *Integration* (note 20), 434 ff.; Wernecke, *Wille* (note 23), 180 ff. (208 ff.: on the 'racial war'; 210: quotes from *Germania* of 8

Mar. 1912); Krumeich, *Aufrüstung* (note 24), 1 ff., 130 ff.; Mommsen, *Bürgerstolz* (note 23), 482 ff.; Schmidt, *Imperialismus* (note 6), 101 ff., 197 ff.; Gregor Schöllgen, *Das Zeitalter des Imperialismus* (Munich: Oldenbourg, 1986), 68 ff.; *Der Kaiser . . . Aufzeichnungen des Chefs des Marinekabinetts Admiral Georg Alexander von Müller über die Ära Wilhelms II.* (Göttingen: Musterschmidt, 1965), 124–5 (conversation on 8 Dec 1912); Fritz Fischer, *Krieg der Illusionen. Die deutsche Politik von 1911 bis 1914* (Düsseldorf: Droste, 1969), 232 ff. (conversation on 8 Dec 1912), 270–1 (William II to Ballin, 15 Dec 1912; emphases in original), tr. as *War of Illusions: German Policies from 1911 to 1914* (New York: Norton, 1975).

29. *Sten. Ber.*, ccxc 5763 (Delbrück, 25 June 1913); Dieter Gosewinkel, 'Die Staatsangehörigkeit als Institution des Nationalstaats. Zur Entstehung des Reichs- und Staatsangehörigkeitsgesetzes von 1913', in *Offene Staatlichkeit. Festschrift für Ernst-Wolfgang Böckenförde*, ed. Rolf Grawert et al. (Berlin: Duncker & Humblot, 1995), 359–78; Roger Brubaker, *Staats-Bürger: Deutschland und Frankreich im historischen Vergleich* (Hamburg: Junius, 1994), origi. *Citizenship and Nationahood in France and Germany* (Cambridge, MA: Harvard University Press, 1992); Mommsen, *Bürgerstolz* (note 23), 434 ff.; Huber, *Verfassungsgeschichte*, iv (note 3), 581 ff.; Hans-Ulrich Wehler, 'Symbol des halbabsolutistischen Herrschaftssystems: Der Fall Zabern von 1913/14 als Verfassungskrise des Wilhelminischen Kaiserreichs', in *Krisenherde* (note 7), 65–84; David Schoenbaum, *Zabern 1913: Consensus Politics in Imperial Germany* (London: Allen & Unwin, 1982).

30. Kurt Riezler, *Tagebücher—Aufsätze—Dokumente*, ed. and introd. Karl Dietrich Erdmann (Göttingen: Vandenhoeck & Ruprecht, 1972), 185 (Bethmann Hollweg, 14 July 1914); Wolfgang Steglich, *Die Friedenspolitik der Mittelmächte 1917/18*, i (Wiesbaden: F. Steiner, 1964), 418 (Bethmann Hollweg to Conrad Haussmann, 1917); *Julikrise und Kriegsausbruch 1914*, ed. and introd. Immanuel Geiss, 2 vols. (Hanover: Verlag für Literatur und Zeitgeschehen, 1963–4), ii. 184–5 (Wilhelm II to State Secretary von Jagow, Foreign Office, 28 July 1914), 380–1 (Bethmann Hollweg to ambassador von Tschirschky in Vienna, 30 July 1914), 439–40 (Moltke, Berchtold, 31 July 1914), tr. as *July 1914: The Outbreak of the First World War. Selected Documents* (New York: Scribner, 1967); George F. Kennan, *Bismarcks europäisches System in der Auflösung. Die französisch-russische Annäherung 1875 bis 1890* (Frankfurt: Propyläen, 1981), 12, orig. *The Decline of Bismarck's European Order: Franco-Russian Relations, 1875–1890* (Princeton: Princeton University Press, 1979), 3; Fischer, *Krieg* (note 28), 663 ff. (724: Müller's journal, 1. Aug. 1914); Wolfgang J. Mommsen, 'Innenpolitische Bestimmungsfaktoren der deutschen Aussenpolitik vor 1914', in *Der autoritäre Nationalstaat. Verfassung, Gesellschaft und Kultur im deutschen Kaiserreich* (Frankfurt: Fischer Taschenbuch, 1990), 316–57; id., 'Der Topos vom unvermeidlichen Krieg: Aussenpolitik und öffentliche Meinung im Deutschen Reich im letzten Jahrzehnt vor 1914', ibid. 380–406; id., *Imperial Germany 1867–1918: Politics, Culture, and Society in an Authoritarian State* (London: Edward Arnold, 1995); id., *Bürgerstolz* (note 23), 535 ff.; Dieter Groh, ' "Je eher, desto besser!" Innenpolitische Faktoren für die Präventivkriegsbereitschaft des Deutschen Reiches 1913/14', *Politische Vierteljahresschrift* [*PVS*], 13 (1972), 501–2; Krumeich, *Aufrüstung* (note 24), 243 ff.; Dietrich Geyer, *Der russische Imperialismus. Studien über den Zusammenhang von innerer u. auswärtiger Politik 1860–1914* (Göttingen: Vandenhoeck & Ruprecht, 1977), 220 ff., tr. as *Russian Imperialism: The Interaction of Domestic and Foreign Policy, 1860–1914*

(New Haven: Yale University Press, 1987); *Der Erste Weltkrieg. Wirkung, Wahrnehmung, Analyse*, ed. Wolfgang Michalka (Munich: Piper, 1994); James Joll, *The Origins of the First World War* (London: Longman, 1984); *Der Erste Weltkrieg. Ursachen, Entstehung und Kriegsziele*, ed. Wolfgang Schieder (Cologne: Kiepenheuer & Witsch, 1969); Niall Ferguson, *Der falsche Krieg. Der Erste Weltkrieg und das 20. Jahrhundert* (Stuttgart: Deutscher Taschebuch Verlag, 1999), 188 ff., orig. *The Pity of War* (London: Allen Lane, 1998). On the 'duel mentality' see Ute Frevert, *Ehrenmänner. Das Duell in der bürgerlichen Gesellschaft* (Munich: Deutscher Taschenbuch Verlag, 1991), esp. 233 ff., tr. as *Men of Honour: A Social and Cultural History of the Duel* (Cambridge: Polity Press, 1995); Norbert Elias, 'Die satisfaktionsfähige Gesellschaft', in *Studien über die deutschen Machtkämpfe und Habitusentwicklung im 19. und 20. Jahrhundert* (Frankfurt: Suhrkamp, 1989), 61–158.

31. Braunthal, *Geschichte* (note 17), i. 340 ff. (Stuttgart congress, 1907; Bebel: 342–3), 349 ff. (Basel congress, 1912); *Sten. Ber.*, cccvi. 1–2 (Wilhelm II, 4 Aug 1914), 7 (Bethmann Hollweg, 4 Aug 1914), 8–9. (Haase, 4 Aug. 1914); *Die Reichstagsfraktion der deutschen Sozialdemokratie 1898 bis 1918*, 2 vols., ed. Erich Matthias and Eberhard Pikart, part 2 (Düsseldorf: Droste, 1966), 3–4 (session of 3–4 Apr. 1914); *Das Kriegstagebuch des Reichstagsabgeordneten Eduard David 1914 bis 1918*, ed. Susanne Miller with Erich Matthias (Düsseldorf: Droste, 1966), 4–13 (entries from 1 Aug. to 4 Aug. 1914); Wilhelm Dittmann, *Erinnerungen*, ed. and introd. Jürgen Rojahn, 3 vols. (Frankfurt: Campus, 1995), ii. 241 ff.; Wolfgang Kruse, *Krieg und nationale Integration. Eine Neuinterpretation des sozialdemokratischen Burgfriedensschlusses 1914/15* (Essen: Klartext, 1993), 42 ff. (51: party leadership's communication to the press on 19 July 1914); Groh, *Integration* (note 16), 634; Susanne Miller, *Burgfrieden und Klassenkampf. Die deutsche Sozialdemokratie im Ersten Weltkrieg* (Düsseldorf: Droste, 1974), 31 ff. (on the fraction meeting on 3 Aug. 1914: 61 ff.); Gottfried Schramm, '1914: Sozialdemokraten am Scheideweg', in *Wendepunkte deutscher Geschichte 1848–1990*, ed. Carola Stern and Heinrich August Winkler (Frankfurt: Fischer Taschenbuch, 1994), 71–97; Jürgen Rojahn, 'Arbeiterbewegung und Kriegsbegeisterung: Die deutsche Sozialdemokratie 1870–1914', in *Kriegsbegeisterung und mentale Kriegsvorbereitung. Interdisziplinäre Studien*, ed. Marcel van der Linden and Gottfried Mergner (Berlin: Duncker & Humblot, 1991), 57–72; Thomas Raithel, *Das 'Wunder' der inneren Einheit. Studien zur deutschen und französischen Öffentlichkeit des Ersten Weltkrieges* (Bonn: Bouvier, 1996); Christian Geinitz, *Kriegsfurcht und Kampfbereitschaft. Das Augusterlebnis in Freiburg. Eine Studie zum Kriegsbeginn 1914* (Essen: Klartext, 1998); Benjamin Ziemann, *Front und Heimat. Ländliche Kriegserfahrungen im südlichen Bayern 1914–1923* (Essen: Klartext, 1997); Ernst Rudolf Huber, *Deutsche Verfassungsgeschichte seit 1789*, v. *Weltkrieg, Revolution und Reichserneuerung 1914–1919* (Stuttgart: Kohlhammer, 1978), 27 ff. Lenin quote from W. I. Lenin, 'Der Krieg und die russische Sozialdemokratie', in *Werke* (Berlin: Dietz, 1950), xxi. 11–21 (20), tr. as 'The War and Russian Social Democracy', in *Collected Works* (New York: International Publishers, 1927), 25–34.

32. Ernst von Dryander, *Erinnerungen aus meinem Leben* (Bielefeld: Velhagen & Klasing, 1922), 276; Arlie J. Hoover, *The Gospel of Nationalism: German Patriotic Preaching from Napoleon to Versailles* (Stuttgart: F. Steiner, 1986), 53 (Lehmann); Wilhelm Pressel, *Die Kriegspredigt 1914–1918 in der evangelischen Kirche Deutschlands* (Göttingen: Vandenhoeck & Ruprecht, 1967), 204 (Dibelius); Karl Hammer,

Deutsche Kriegstheologie (1870–1918) (Munich: Kösel-Verlag, 1971), 242 (Rade), 266 (Poertner), 241–2 (Faulhaber); Otto Seeber, 'Kriegstheologie und Kriegspredigten in der Evangelischen Kirche Deutschlands im Ersten und Zweiten Weltkrieg', in *Kriegsbegeisterung* (note 31), ed. von der Linden and Mergner, 233–58; Gunter Brakelmann, 'Konfessionalismus und Nationalismus', *Bochumer Beiträge zur Nationalismusdebatte*, ed. Bernd Faulenbach et al. (Essen: Klartext, 1997), 36–50; *Die protestantischen Kirchen Europas im Ersten Weltkrieg. Ein Quellen- und Arbeitsbuch*, ed. Gerhard Besier (Göttingen: Vandenhoeck & Ruprecht, 1984); Heinrich Missalla, *'Gott mit uns': Die deutsche katholische Kriegspredigt 1914–1918* (Munich: Kösel-Verlag, 1968), 85, 89 (Peters); Richard van Dülmen, 'Der deutsche Katholizismus und der Erste Weltkrieg', *Francia*, 2 (1974), 347–76. The Bible quote 'If God is for us . . . ' from Romans 8: 31; 'Give to Caesar what is Caesar's . . . ' from Matthew 22: 21. On Arndt's 'German God' see above, p. 57.

33. *Aufrufe und Reden deutscher Professoren im Ersten Weltkrieg*, ed. and introd. Klaus Böhme (Stuttgart: Reclam, 1975), 47–9 ('Aufruf an die Kulturwelt'); Jürgen von Ungern-Sternberg and Wolfgang von Ungern-Sternberg, *Der Aufruf 'An die Kulturwelt'. Das Manifest der 93 und die Anfänge der Kriegspropaganda im Ersten Weltkrieg* (Stuttgart: F. Steiner, 1996); Johann Plenge, *Der Krieg und die Volkswirtschaft*, 2nd edn (Münster: Borgemeyer & Co., 1915), 173–4; id., *1789 und 1914. Die symbolischen Jahre in der Geschichte des politischen Geistes* (Berlin: J. Springer, 1916), 82; Rudolf Kjellén, *Die Ideen von 1914—Eine weltgeschichtliche Perspektive* (Leipzig: S. Hirzel, 1915), esp. 146; Max Scheler, *Der Genius des Krieges und der deutsche Krieg* (Leipzig: Verlag der Weissen Bücher, 1915), 54, 73–4, 100, 150; Paul Lensch, *Die deutsche Sozialdemokratie in ihrer grossen Krisis* (Hamburg: Auer & Co., 1916), 7 ff. (9: 'world war means world revolution!'); id., *Drei Jahre Weltrevolution* (Berlin: S. Fischer, 1917), esp. 44 ff., 86 ff., 172 ff.; Werner Sombart, *Händler und Helden. Patriotische Besinnungen* (Munich: Duncker & Humblot, 1915), 84–5, 116, 121, 142–3; Thomas Mann, 'Gedanken im Kriege' (1914), in *Gesammelte Werke in dreizehn Bänden* (Frankfurt: Fischer Taschenbuch Verlag, 1990), xiii. 527–45; id., 'Friedrich und die grosse Koalition', ibid. ii. 76–135; id., *Betrachtungen eines Unpolitischen* (1918), ibid. xii. 1–589 (1, 587); id., 'Leiden und Grösse Richard Wagners' (lecture in Munich, 10 Feb. 1933), ibid. ix. 363–426 (419); id., *Reflections of a Nonpolitical Man* (New York: F. Ungar, 1983); id., *Freud, Goethe, Wagner* (New York: A. A. Knopf, 1937); Johannes Burkhardt, 'Kriegsgrund Geschichte? 1870, 1813, 1756—historische Argumente und Orientierungen bei Ausbruch des Ersten Weltkrieges', in id. et al., *Lange und kurze Wege in den Ersten Weltkrieg. Vier Augsburger Beiträge zur Kriegsursachenforschung* (Munich: Ernst Vögel, 1996), 9–86; Klaus von See, *Die Ideen von 1789 und die Ideen von 1914. Völkisches Denken in Deutschland zwischen Französischer Revolution und Erstem Weltkrieg* (Frankfurt: Athenaion, 1975), 108 ff.; Reinhard Rürup, 'Der "Geist von 1914" in Deutschland. Kriegsbegeisterung und Ideologisierung des Krieges im Ersten Weltkrieg', in *Ansichten vom Krieg. Vergleichende Studien zum Ersten Weltkrieg in Literatur und Gesellschaft*, ed. Bernd Hüppauf (Königstein: Forum Academicum, 1984), 1–30; Wolfgang Kruse, 'Die Kriegsbegeisterung im Deutschen Reich zu Beginn des Ersten Weltkrieges', in *Kriegsbegeisterung* (note 31), ed. van der Linden and Mergner, 73–87; Christoph Jahr, ' "Das Krämervolk der eitlen Briten." Das deutsche Englandbild im Ersten Weltkrieg', in *Feindbilder* (note 10), ed. id. et al., 115–42; Robert Sigel, *Die*

Lensch-Cunow-Haenisch-Gruppe. Eine Studie zum rechten Flügel der SPD im Ersten Weltkrieg (Berlin: Duncker & Humblot, 1976); Hans Kohn, *Wege und Irrwege. Vom Geist des deutschen Bürgertums* (Düsseldorf: Droste, 1962), 308 ff., orig. *The Mind of Germany: The Education of a Nation* (New York: Scribner, 1960); Ludwig Dehio, 'Gedanken über die deutsche Sendung 1900–1918', in *Deutschland und die Weltpolitik im 20. Jahrhundert* (Munich: Oldenbourg, 1955), 71–106; Hermann Lübbe, *Politische Philosophie in Deutschland. Studien zu ihrer Geschichte* (Stuttgart: B. Schwabe 1963), 173 ff.; Bernd Faulenbach, *Ideologie des deutschen Weges. Die deutsche Geschichte in der Historiographie zwischen Kaiserreich und Nationalsozialismus* (Munich: C. H. Beck, 1980), 122 ff.; Helmut Fries, *Die grosse Katharsis. Der Erste Weltkrieg in der Sicht deutscher Dichter und Gelehrter*, 2 vols. (Konstanz: Verlag am Hockgraben, 1994); Wolfgang J. Mommsen, 'Der Geist von 1914. Das Programm eines politischen "Sonderwegs" der Deutschen', in *Nationalstaat* (note 30), 407–21; *Kultur und Krieg. Die Rolle der Intellektuellen, Künstler und Schriftsteller im Ersten Weltkrieg*, ed. id. (Munich: Oldenbourg, 1996); Klaus Vondung, 'Deutsche Apokalypse 1914', in *Das wilhelminische Bildungsbürgertum. Zur Sozialgeschichte seiner Ideen*, ed. id. (Göttingen: Vandenhoeck & Ruprecht, 1976), 153–71; id., *Die Apokalypse in Deutschland* (Munich: Deutscher Taschenbuch Verlag, 1988), 189 ff., orig. *The Apocalypse in Germany* (Columbia, MO: University of Missouri Press, 2000). On the distribution of the concept of the '*Volksgemeinschaft*' see Gunther Mai, ' "Verteidigungskrieg". Staatliche Selbstbehauptung, nationale Solidarität und soziale Befreiung in Deutschland in der Zeit des Ersten Weltkrieges (1900–1925)', in *Weltkrieg* (note 30), ed. Michalka, 583–607. Quote from Heinrich von Treitschke from id., *Politik. Vorlesungen, gehalten an der Universität zu Berlin*, 2 vols. (Leipzig: S. Hirzel, 1899–1900), ii. 362.

34. Heinrich Class, *Wider den Strom. Vom Werden und Wachsen der nationalen Opposition im alten Reich* (Leipzig: K. F. Koehler, 1932), 341 ff.; *Ursachen und Folgen. Vom deutschen Zusammenbruch 1918 und 1945 bis zur staatlichen Neuordnung Deutschlands in der Gegenwart*, ed. Herbert Michaelis and Ernst Schraepler (Berlin: Dokumenten-Verlag, 1958-II), i. 351–68 (petition of the six economic organizations to the chancellor on 20 May 1915 (358: 'Germanization'); confidential memorandum from German university teachers and officials to the chancellor on 20 June 1915; message from the SPD party and fraction leadership to the chancellor on 25 June 1915); Hans Delbrück, 'Der Kanzlerwechsel.—Die Friedensresolution.—Lloyd Georges Antwort', *Preussische Jahrbücher*, 169 (1917), 302–19 (306–7: Wolff's memorandum); Fritz Fischer, *Griff nach der Weltmacht. Die Kriegszielpolitik des kaiserlichen Deutschland 1914/18*, 3rd edn (Düsseldorf: Droste, 1964), 123 ff. (Bethmann Hollweg), 120 ff. (Class, Erzberger, Thyssen), tr. as *Germany's Aims in the First World War* (New York: W. W. Norton, 1967); Klaus Schwabe, 'Ursprung und Verbreitung des alldeutschen Annexionismus in der deutschen Professorenschaft im Ersten Weltkrieg', *VfZ* 14 (1966), 105–38 (quote: 131, numbers and names: 127, 132); id., *Wissenschaft und Kriegsmoral. Die deutschen Hochschullehrer und die politischen Grundfragen des Ersten Weltkrieges* (Göttingen: Musterschmidt Verlag, 1969), 19 ff.; Annelise Thimme, *Hans Delbrück als Kritiker der Wilhelminischen Epoche* (Düsseldorf: Droste, 1955), 116 ff.; Heinz Hagenlücke, *Deutsche Vaterlandspartei. Die nationale Rechte am Ende des Kaiserreiches* (Düsseldorf: Droste, 1997), 49 ff.; Friedrich Naumann, *Mitteleuropa* (Berlin: G. Reimer, 1915), 31, 40–2, 101; Egmont Zechlin, *Die deutsche Politik und die Juden im Ersten Weltkrieg* (Göttingen: Vandenhoeck & Ruprecht, 1969), 516 ff.

(518–19: Liebig, 525: Erzberger, 550: Oppenheimer); Werner Jochmann, 'Die Ausbreitung des Antisemitismus in Deutschland 1914–1923', in *Gesellschaftskrise* (note 26), 99–170; George L. Mosse, 'The Jews and the German War Experience 1914–1918', Leo Baeck Memorial Lecture 21 (New York: Leo Baeck Institute, 1977); Jürgen Kocka, *Klassengesellschaft im Krieg. Deutsche Sozialgeschichte 1914–1918*, 2nd edn (Göttingen: Vandenhoeck & Ruprecht, 1978), esp. 96 ff., tr. as *Facing Total War: German Society, 1914–1918* (Cambridge, MA: Harvard University Press, 1984); Peter Graf Kielmansegg, *Deutschland und der Erste Weltkrieg*, 2nd edn (Stuttgart: Klett-Cotta, 1980), 129 ff., 385 ff.; Jarausch, *Chancellor* (note 23), 349 ('policy of the diagonal').

35. Miller, *Burgfrieden* (note 31), 75 ff., 156 ff., 283 ff.; Braunthal, *Geschichte* (note 17), ii. 50 ff. (64–5: Kienthal resolutions); Huber, *Verfassungsgeschichte*, v (note 31), 101 ff., 154 ff.; Hartwin Spenkuch, *Das Preussische Herrenhaus. Adel und Bürgertum in der Ersten Kammer des Landtags 1854–1918* (Düsseldorf: Droste, 1998), 124 ff.; Fischer, *Griff* (note 34), 512 ff.; Gerald D. Feldman, *Armee, Industrie und Arbeiterschaft in Deutschland 1914–1918* (Berlin: J. H. W. Dietz, 1985), 169 ff., 243 ff.; orig. *Army, Industry, and Labor in Germany, 1914–1918* (Princeton: Princeton University Press, 1966); Arthur Rosenberg, *Entstehung der Weimarer Republik* (1928; repr. Frankfurt: Europäische Verlagsanstalt, 1961), 160 ff.; Klaus Epstein, *Matthias Erzberger und das Dilemma der deutschen Demokratie* (Berlin: Verlag Annedore Leber, 1962), 186 ff., orig. *Matthias Erzberger and the Dilemma of German Democracy* (Princeton: Princeton University Press, 1959).

36. *Der Interfraktionelle Ausschuss 1917/18*, 2 parts, ed. Erich Matthias (Düsseldorf: Droste, 1959), part 1, 3–118 (July crisis), 213–602 (from Michaelis to Hertling); Max Weber, 'Die Lehren der deutschen Kanzlerkrisis', in *Gesammelte politische Schriften*, ed. Johannes Winckelmann, 2nd edn (Tübingen: Mohr, 1958), 211–16 (213–14, 216); Georg Michaelis, *Für Volk und Staat* (Berlin: Furche-Verlag, 1922), 321; *Sten. Ber.*, cccx. 3572 (Michaelis, 19 July 1917); *Parteiprogramme* (note 10), ed. Mommsen, 417–20 (founding manifesto of the German Fatherland Party, 2 Sept. 1917), 420–1 (manifesto of the People's Federation for Liberty and Fatherland, 14 Nov. 1917); Hagenlücke, *Vaterlandspartei* (note 34), 143–4 (foundation, social structure), 180 (membership), 192 ff. (war goals), 362 ff. (People's Federation); the article 'Volksbund für Freiheit und Vaterland, 1917–1920', in *Lexikon*, iv (note 2), ed. Fricke et al., 414–19 (membership: 414); Stegmann, *Erben* (note 4), 497 ff.; Fischer, *Griff* (note 34), 425 ff.; Ursula Ratz, *Zwischen Arbeitsgemeinschaft und Koalition. Bürgerliche Sozialreformer und Gewerkschaften im Ersten Weltkrieg* (Munich: K. G. Saur, 1994), 307 ff.; Günter Brakelmann, *Der deutsche Protestantismus im Epochenjahr 1917* (Witten: Luther-Verlag, 1974); Huber, *Verfassungsgeschichte*, v (note 31), 372 ff. (argument about the 'breakthrough to parliamentary government' in November 1917).

37. *Sten. Ber.*, cccvi. 6–7 (Bethmann Hollweg, 4 Aug. 1914); Karl Kautsky, 'Die Diktatur des Proletariats' (1918), in *Die Diktatur des Proletariats / W. I. Lenin, Die proletarische Revolution und der Renegat Kautsky / Karl Kautsky, Terrorismus und Kommunismus* (Berlin: Dietz, 1990), 7–87 (33, 36–7 39; emphasis in original); Clara Zetkin, *Mit Entschiedenheit für das Werk der Bolschewiki! Aus einem Brief an eine Konferenz des Reichsausschusses und der Frauenkonferenz der USPD* (early summer 1919), in *Ausgewählte Reden und Schriften*, 3 vols., ii (Berlin: Dietz, 1960), 8–40 (26); Rosa Luxemburg, 'Die russische Revolution' (1918), in *Schriften* (note 20), iii. 106–41 (128 ff., quote: 134), tr. as '*The Russian Revolution*' and '*Leninism or Marxism?*

(Ann Arbor: University of Michigan Press, 1961); *Lenins Rückkehr nach Russland. Die deutschen Akten*, ed. Werner Hahlweg (Leiden: E. J. Brill, 1957); Winfried B. Scharlau and Zbyněk A. Zeman, *Freibeuter der Revolution. Parvus-Helphand. Eine politische Biographie* (Cologne: Verlag Wissenschaft und Politik, 1964); *Deutschland und die Russische Revolution*, ed. Helmut Neubauer (Stuttgart: Kohlhammer, 1968); Lösche, *Bolschewismus* (note 20), 160 ff.; Jürgen Zarusky, *Die deutschen Sozialdemokraten und das sowjetische Modell. Ideologische Auseinandersetzung und aussenpolitische Konzeption* (Munich: Oldenbourg, 1992), 39 ff.; Uli Schöler, *'Despotischer Sozialismus' oder 'Staatssklaverei'. Die theoretische Verarbeitung der sowjetrussischen Entwicklung in der Sozialdemokratie Deutschlands und Österreichs 1917–1919*, 2 vols., i (Münster: Lit., 1990), 84 ff.; *Deutschland und die Russische Revolution*, ed. Gerd Koenen and Lew Kopelew (Munich: W. Fink, 1998); Manfred Hildermeier, *Die Russische Revolution 1905–1921* (Frankfurt: Suhrkamp, 1989), 229 ff.; Dietrich Geyer, *Die Russische Revolution. Historische Probleme und Perspektiven*, 2nd edn (Göttingen: Vandenhoeck und Ruprecht, 1977), 107 ff., tr. as *The Russian Revolution* (New York: St Martin's Press, 1987); Helmut Altrichter, *Russland 1917. Ein Land auf der Suche nach sich selbst* (Paderborn: Schöningh, 1997). On Bismarck in 1866 see Otto Pflanze, *Bismarck. Der Reichskanzler* (Munich: C. H. Beck, 1998), 313 ff., orig. *Bismarck and the Development of Germany: The Period of Unification, 1815–1871* (Princeton: Princeton University Press, 1990).

38. Winfried Baumgart, *Deutsche Ostpolitik 1918. Von Brest-Litowsk bis zum Ende des Ersten Weltkrieges* (Vienna: Oldenbourg, 1966); Georg von Rauch, 'Sowjetrussland von der Oktoberrevolution bis zum Sturz Chruschtschows 1917–1964', *Europa im Zeitalter der Weltmächte* (= *Handbuch der europäischen Geschichte*, ed. Theodor Schieder, vii/1), ed. Theodor Schieder (Stuttgart: Klett-Cotta, 1979), 481–521 (numbers: 485); Fischer, *Griff* (note 34), 627 ff.; Hildebrand, *Reich* (note 6), 363 ff.; Huber, *Verfassungsgeschichte*, v (note 31), 432 ff. (January strike), 447 ff. (Reichstag debate, 25–6 Feb. 1918); Miller, *Burgfrieden* (note 31), 358 ff.; Rosenberg, *Entstehung* (note 35), 183 ff. (187, 189); Pressel, *Kriegspredigt* (note 32), 305–6 (Doehring, 3 Feb. 1918); *Sten. Ber.*, cccxi. 4, 171 (Heydebrand, 26 Feb. 1918); Dittmann, *Erinnerungen* (note 31), ii. 527 ff.

39. Arno J. Mayer, *Political Origins of the New Diplomacy, 1917–1918*, 2nd edn (New York: Vintage Books, 1970), 329 ff.; Klaus Schwabe, *Deutsche Revolution und Wilson-Friede. Die amerikanische und die deutsche Friedensstrategie zwischen Ideologie und Machtpolitik 1918/19* (Düsseldorf: Droste, 1971), 17 ff.; Hagenlücke, *Vaterlandspartei* (note 34), 195 ff.; Huber, *Verfassungsgeschichte*, v (note 31), 428 ff., 500–1; Kielmansegg, *Deutschland* (note 34), 629 ff.; Erich Ludendorff, *Meine Kriegserinnerungen 1914–1918* (Berlin: E. S. Mittler und Sohn, 1919), 547 ff. (547, 551); id., *Ludendorff's Own Story, August 1914-November 1918* (New York: Harper, 1919); Karl-Ludwig Ay, *Die Entstehung einer Revolution. Die Volksstimmung in Bayern während des Ersten Weltkrieges* (Berlin: Duncker & Humblot, 1968), 101 (Brettreich); Ernst Troeltsch, *Spektator-Briefe. Aufsätze über die deutsche Revolution und die Weltpolitik 1918/22* (Tübingen: Mohr, 1924), 10; *Reichstagsfraktion* (note 31), 458 (Geck); Wilhelm Deist, 'Der militärische Zusammenbruch des Kaiserreiches. Zur Realität der "Dolchstosslegende" ', in *Das Unrechtsregime. Internationale Forschungen über den Nationalsozialismus*, I, ed. Ursula Büttner (Hamburg: Christians, 1986), 101–29; id., 'Verdeckter Militärstreik im

Kriegsjahr 1918?', in *Der Krieg des kleinen Mannes. Eine Militärgeschichte von unten*, ed. Wolfram Wette (Munich: Piper, 1992), 146–68; Wolfgang Kruse, 'Krieg und Klassenheer. Zur Revolutionierung der deutschen Armee im Ersten Weltkrieg', *GG* 22 (1996), 530–61; Christoph Jahr, *Gewöhnliche Soldaten. Desertion und Deserteure im deutschen und britischen Heer 1914–1918* (Göttingen: Vandenhoeck & Ruprecht, 1998). Wilson first made the statement 'The world must be made safe for democracy' for the first time on 22 Jan. 1917 in a speech to the American Congress. August Heckscher, *Woodrow Wilson* (New York: Scribner, 1991), 440.

40. *Reichstagsfraktion* (note 31), 417–460 (session on 23 Sept. 1918; 442: Ebert); *Interfraktioneller Ausschuss* (note 36), part 2, 668–9 (memorandum of 21 Sept. 1918), 710 ff. (28 Sept. 1918); Albrecht von Thaer, *Generalstabsdienst an der Front und in der OHL. Aus Briefen und Tagebuchaufzeichnungen 1915–1919*, ed. Siegfried A. Kaehler (Göttingen: Vandenhoeck & Ruprecht, 1958), 234–5 (Ludendorff, 1 Oct. 1918); Friedrich von Payer, *Von Bethmann Hollweg bis Ebert. Erinnerungen und Bilder* (Frankfurt: Frankfurter Societäts-Druckerei, 1923), 82; Karl Kautsky, *Terrorismus und Kommunismus. Ein Beitrag zur Naturgeschichte der Revolution* (1919), in *Diktatur* (note 37), 177–347 (233 ff.); W. I. Lenin, 'Das sozialistische Vaterland in Gefahr!' (appeal from the council of the people's commissars, 21 Feb. 1918), in *Werke* (note 31), xxvii. 15–16, tr. as 'The Socialist Fatherland is in Danger!', in *Collected Works* (note 31), xxvii. 30–3; Stegmann, *Erben* (note 4), 515 (Class, 3 Oct. 1918); Jochmann, 'Ausbreitung' (note 34), 118–19, 388 (Gebsattel/Class, 15 Oct. 1918), 120–1 (Class, 19–20 Oct. 1918); Huber, *Verfassungsgeschichte*, v (note 31), 521. Quote from Kleist from *Germania an ihre Kinder*, referring to Napoleon: 'Strike him dead! On Judgement Day | your reasons won't be questioned', Heinrich von Kleist, *Sämtliche Werke und Briefe*, i, 2nd edn (Munich: C. Hanser, 1994), 27.
41. Huber, *Verfassungsgeschichte*, v (note 31), 551 ff. (continuance of the war 'with the utmost determination': 577); Troeltsch, *Spektator-Briefe* (note 39), 21; Wolfgang Sauer, 'Das Scheitern der parlamentarischen Monarchie', in *Vom Kaiserreich zur Weimarer Republik*, ed. Eberhard Kolb (Cologne: Kiepenheuer & Witsch, 1972), 77–99 (84); *Die Weizsäcker-Papiere 1900–1932*, ed. Leonidas E. Hill (Berlin: Propyläen, 1982), 309 (journal entry, 28 Oct. 1918); Leonidas E. Hill, 'Signal zur Konterrevolution? Der Plan zum Vorstoss der deutschen Hochseeflotte am 30. Oktober 1918', *VfZ* 36 (1988), 114–29; Wilhelm Deist, 'Die Politik der Seekriegsleitung und die Rebellion der Flotte Ende Oktober 1918', *VfZ* 14 (1966), 325–43; Gerhard Paul Gross, *Die Seekriegsführung der Kaiserlichen Marine im Jahre 1918* (Frankfurt: P. Lang, 1989), 390 ff.
42. Dirk Dähnhardt, *Revolution in Kiel. Der Übergang vom Kaiserreich zur Weimarer Republik 1918/19* (Neumünster: K. Wachholtz, 1978); *Die deutsche Revolution 1918–1919. Dokumente*, ed. Gerhard A. Ritter and Susanne Miller, 2nd edn (Hamburg: Hoffmann und Kampe, 1975), 41–64 (58–9: Brunswick, Munich; 62 ff.: Cologne), 68 ff. (Groener, 8 Nov. 1918); Prinz Max von Baden, *Erinnerungen und Dokumente*, ed. Golo Mann and Andreas Burckhardt (new edn, Stuttgart: Klett, 1968), 584 (*Vorwärts*, 5 Nov. 1918), 567 (Ebert, 7 Nov. 918), 588 (Prussian ministry of war, 8 Nov. 1918; emphases in original); Heinrich August Winkler, *Von der Revolution zur Stabilisierung. Arbeiter und Arbeiterbewegung in der Weimarer Republik 1918–1924*, 2nd edn (Berlin: J. H. W. Dietz, 1985), 27 ff.

43. Prinz Max, *Erinnerungen* (note 42), 579–80; *Reichstagsfraktion* (note 31), ii. 513–14 (ultimatum of 7 Nov. 1918); *Die Regierung des Prinzen Max von Baden*, ed. Erich Matthias and Rudolf Morsey (Düsseldorf: Droste, 1962), 579 (7 Nov. 1918), 583–612 (talks over the SPD demands, 8. Nov. 1918), 609–10 (women's suffrage: 8 Nov. 1918); *Schulthess' Europäischer Geschichtskalender*, NS 34th year, 1918, part 1 (Munich: C. H. Beck, 1922), 422–31 (SPD announcements and report in the *B[erliner] Z[eitung] am Mittag*); Reinhold Patemann, *Der Kampf um die preussische Wahlreform im Ersten Weltkrieg* (Düsseldorf: Droste, 1964), 202 ff.; Huber, *Verfassungsgeschichte*, v (note 31), 600 ff.; Winkler, *Revolution* (note 42), 40 ff.
44. Prinz Max, *Erinnerungen* (note 42), 596 ff.; *Die Regierung der Volksbeauftragten 1918/19*, 2 vols., ed. Susanne Miller and Heinrich Potthoff (Düsseldorf: Droste, 1969), i. 3–8 (9 Nov. 1918); *Revolution* (note 42), ed. Ritter and Miller, 64 ff. (9 Nov. 1918, 79–80: Ebert's declarations on 9 Nov. 1918, 86–92: formation of the government and assembly in the Zirkus Busch, 9–10 Nov. 1918); Philipp Scheidemann, *Der Zusammenbruch* (Berlin: Verlag für Sozialwissenschaft, 1921), 174–6 (2 Oct. 1918); id., *Memoiren eines Sozialdemokraten*, 2 vols. (Dresden: C. Reissner 1928), ii. 311 ff.; id., *The Making of New Germany: The Memoirs of Philipp Scheidemann* (New York: D. Appleton and Co., 1929); Manfred Jessen-Klingenberg, 'Die Ausrufung der Republik durch Philipp Scheidemann am 9. 11. 1918', *GWU* 19 (1968), 649–56; Georg Kotowski, *Friedrich Ebert. Eine politische Biographie*, i *Der Aufstieg eines deutschen Arbeiterführers 1871 bis 1917* (Wiesbaden: F. Steiner, 1963); Winkler, *Revolution* (note 42), 45 ff.
45. Richard Müller, *Vom Kaiserreich zur Republik*, 2 vols., ii *Die Novemberrevolution* (Vienna: Malik-Verlag, 1925), 17 (*Berliner Tageblatt*, 10 Nov. 1918); Troeltsch, *Spektator-Briefe* (note 39), 24; Pressel, *Kriegspredigt* (note 32), 308–9 (Doehring, 27 Oct. 1918); Martin Greschat, *Der deutsche Protestantismus im Revolutionsjahr 1918–1919* (Witten: Luther-Verlag, 1974); Max Weber, *Wirtschaft und Gesellschaft*, study edn, ed. Johannes Winckelmann, pt 1 (Cologne: Kiepenheuer & Witsch, 1964), 27, 197 (emphases in original), tr. as *Economy and Society: An Outline of Interpretive Sociology* (New York: Bedminster Press, 1968); Heinrich August Winkler, 'Vom Kaiserreich zur Republik. Der historische Ort der Revolution von 1918/19', in *Streitfragen der deutschen Geschichte. Essays zum 19. und 20. Jahrhundert* (Munich: C. H. Beck, 1997), 52–70.

CHAPTER 7. THE IMPAIRED REPUBLIC 1918–1933

1. Modris Eksteins, *Tanz über Gräben. Die Geburt der Moderne und der Erste Weltkrieg* (Reinbek b. Hamburg: Rowohlt, 1990); esp. 213 ff.; orig. *Rites of Spring: The Great War and the Birth of the Modern Age* (Boston: Houghton Mifflin, 1989), *Kriegserlebnis. Der Erste Weltkrieg in der literarischen Gestaltung und symbolischen Deutung der Nationen*, ed. Klaus Vondung (Göttingen: Vandenhoeck & Ruprecht, 1980); *Kriegserfahrungen. Studien zur Sozial- und Mentalitätsgeschichte des Ersten Weltkriegs*, ed. Gerhard Hirschfeld et al. (Essen: Klartext, 1997); *Keiner fühlt sich hier mehr als Mensch . . . Erlebnis und Wirkung des Ersten Weltkriegs*, ed. id. et al. (Essen: Klartext, 1993); *Eine Welt von Feinden. Der Grosse Krieg 1914–1918*, ed. Wolfgang Kruse (Frankfurt: Fischer Taschenbuch Verlag, 1997); *Krieg im Frieden. Die umkämpfte Erinnerung an den Ersten Weltkrieg*, ed. Bernd Ulrich and Benjamin Ziemann (Frankfurt: Fischer Taschenbuch Verlag, 1997).

2. Susanne Miller, 'Das Ringen um "die einzige grossdeutsche Republik". Die Sozialdemokratie in Österreich und im Deutschen Reich zur Anschlussfrage 1918/19', *AfS* 11 (1971), 1–67; Alfred D. Low, *Die Anschlussbewegung in Österreich und Deutschland, 1918–1919, und die Pariser Friedenskonferenz* (Vienna: W. Braumüller, 1975), 7 ff.; Peter Borowsky, 'Die "bolschewistische Gefahr" und die Ostpolitik der Volksbeauftragten in der Revolution 1918/19', in *Industrielle Gesellschaft und politisches System. Beiträge zur politischen Sozialgeschichte. Festschrift für Fritz Fischer*, ed. Dirk Stegmann et al. (Bonn: Verlag Neue Gesellschaft, 1978), 389–403; Henning Köhler, *Novemberrevolution und Frankreich. Die französische Deutschland-Politik 1918–1919* (Düsseldorf: Droste, 1980); Eberhard Kolb, 'Internationale Rahmenbedingungen einer demokratischen Neuordnung in Deutschland 1918/19', in *Umbrüche deutscher Geschichte 1866/71. 1918/19. 1929/33* (Munich: Oldenbourg, 1993), 261–87; Richard Löwenthal, 'Die deutsche Sozialdemokratie in Weimar und heute. Zur Problematik der "versäumten" demokratischen Revolution', in *Gesellschaftswandel und Kulturkrise. Zukunftsprobleme der westlichen Demokratien* (Frankfurt: Fischer Taschenbuch Verlag, 1979), 197–211; id., *Social Change and Cultural Crisis* (New York: Columbia University Press, 1984); Eduard Bernstein, *Die deutsche Revolution von 1918/19. Geschichte der Entstehung und ersten Arbeitsperiode der deutschen Republik*, (1921), ed. and introd. Heinrich August Winkler, annotated Teresa Löwe (Bonn: J. H. W. Dietz, 1998), 65 (Liebknecht), 237–8.
3. Susanne Miller, *Die Bürde der Macht. Die deutsche Sozialdemokratie 1918–1920* (Düsseldorf: Droste, 1978), 104 ff. (Hilferding: 107); Wolfgang Elben, *Das Problem der Kontinuität in der deutschen Revolution. Die Politik der Staatssekretäre und der militärischen Führung vom November 1918 bis Februar 1919* (Düsseldorf: Droste, 1965); Wolfgang Runge, *Politik und Beamtentum im Parteienstaat. Die Demokratisierung der politischen Beamten in Preussen zwischen 1918 und 1933* (Stuttgart: Klett, 1965); Ulrich Kluge, *Soldatenräte und Revolution. Studien zur Militärpolitik in Deutschland 1918/19* (Göttingen: Vandenhoeck & Ruprecht, 1975), 206 ff.; Eberhard Kolb, *Die Arbeiterräte in der deutschen Innenpolitik 1918–1919* (Düsseldorf: Droste, 1962), 359 ff.; Gerald D. Feldman and Irmgard Steinisch, *Industrie und Gewerkschaften 1918–1924. Die überforderte Zentralarbeitsgemeinschaft* (Stuttgart: Deutsche Verlags-Anstalt, 1985); Jens Flemming, *Landwirtschaftliche Interessen und Demokratie. Ländliche Gesellschaft, Agrarverbände und Staat 1890–1925* (Bonn: Verlag Neue Gesellschaft, 1978), 252 ff.; Stephanie Merkenich, *Grüne Front gegen Weimar. Reichslandbund und agrarischer Lobbyismus 1918–1933* (Düsseldorf: Droste, 1998); Heinrich August Winkler, *Von der Revolution zur Stabilisierung. Arbeiter und Arbeiterbewegung in der Weimarer Republik, 1918–1924*, 2nd edn (Berlin: J. H. W. Dietz, 1985), 68 ff. Quote from Ebert in *Sten. Ber.*, cccxxvi. 2–3 (6 Feb. 1919); quote from Rosa Luxemburg in ead., 'Die Nationalversammlung', in *Gesammelte Werke*, iv (Berlin: Dietz, 1974), 407–10 (408).
4. *Allgemeiner Kongress der Arbeiter- und Soldatenräte Deutschlands. Vom 16. bis 21. Dezember 1918 im Abgeordnetenhaus zu Berlin* (Berlin: Zentralrat der Sozialistischen Republik Deutschlands, 1919), 209–24 (Cohen-Reuss), 226–36 (Däumig), 282, 288, 230 (motions and ballots on the council system and the date for elections), 127–43, 180–91 (the military question), 252, 288–300, 309 (Central Council); Winkler, *Revolution* (note 3), 100 ff. (121–2: Liebknecht); Miller, *Bürde* (note 3), 112 ff.; Kolb, *Arbeiterräte* (note 3), 197 ff.; Kluge, *Soldatenräte* (note 3), 250 ff.; Arthur Rosenberg, *Geschichte der Weimarer Republik*, (1935; repr. Frankfurt: Europäische Verlagsanstalt,

1961), 50 ff. (52); Hagen Schulze, *Freikorps und Republik 1918–1920* (Boppard: H. Boldt, 1969), 22 ff.; Robert G. L. Waite, *Vanguard of Nazism: The Free Corps Movement in Postwar Germany 1918–1923* (Cambridge, MA: Harvard University Press, 1952; repr. New York: W. W. Norton, 1969), 13 ff.; Wolfram Wette, *Gustav Noske. Eine politische Biographie* (Düsseldorf: Droste, 1987), 281 ff.

5. *Deutsche Parteiprogramme*, ed. Wilhelm Mommsen (Munich: Isar Verlag, 1960), 481–6 (manifesto and platform of the German Center Party, 30 Dec. 1918), 519–31 (DVP platform, 18 Dec. 1918); *Die deutsche Revolution 1918–1919. Dokumente*, ed. Gerhard A. Ritter and Susanne Miller, 2nd edn (Hamburg: Hoffmann & Campe, 1975), 296–8 (founding manifesto of the DNVP, 24 Nov. 1918), 300 (DNVP election statement, 22 Dec. 1918), 311–13 (founding manifesto of the DDP, 16 Nov. 1918); *Nationalliberalismus in der Weimarer Republik. Die Führungsgremien der Deutschen Volkspartei 1918–1933*, 1 vol. in 2 pts, ed. Eberhard Kolb and Ludwig Richter (Düsseldorf: Droste, 1999), pt 1, 5 ff.; Rudolf Morsey, *Die Deutsche Zentrumspartei 1917–1923* (Düsseldorf: Droste, 1966), 110 ff.; Lothar Albertin, *Liberalismus und Demokratie am Anfang der Weimarer Republik. Eine vergleichende Analyse der Deutschen Demokratischen Partei und der Deutschen Volkspartei* (Düsseldorf: Droste, 1972); Wolfgang Hartenstein, *Die Anfänge der Deutschen Volkspartei 1918–1920* (Düsseldorf: Droste, 1962); Larry Eugene Jones, *German Liberalism and the Dissolution of the Weimar Party System, 1918–1933* (Chapel Hill: University of North Carolina Press, 1988); Werner Liebe, *Die Deutschnationale Volkspartei 1918–1924* (Düsseldorf: Droste, 1956); Annelise Thimme, *Flucht in den Mythos. Die Deutschnationale Volkspartei und die Niederlage von 1918* (Göttingen: Vandenhoeck & Ruprecht, 1969); Christian F. Trippe, *Konservative Verfassungspolitik 1918–1923. Die DNVP als Opposition in Reich und Ländern* (Düsseldorf: Droste, 1995), 23 ff.; Ernst Rudolf Huber, *Deutsche Verfassungsgeschichte seit 1789*, v. *Weltkrieg, Revolution und Reichserneuerung 1914–1919* (Stuttgart: Kohhammer,1978), 953 ff.; Heinrich August Winkler, *Weimar 1918–1933. Die Geschichte der ersten deutschen Demokratie*, 3rd edn (Munich: C. H. Beck, 1998), 62 ff.

6. Gerhard A. Ritter, 'Kontinuität und Umformung des deutschen Rätesystems 1918–1920', in *Arbeiterbewegung, Parteien und Parlamentarismus* (Göttingen: Vandenhoeck & Ruprecht, 1976), 116–57; Winkler, *Revolution* (note 3), 135 ff.; id., 'Der überforderte Liberalismus. Zum Ort der Revolution von 1848/49 in der deutschen Geschichte', in *Revolution in Deutschland und Europa 1848/49*, ed. Wolfgang Hardtwig (Göttingen: Vandenhoeck & Ruprecht, 1998), 185–206 (esp. 201 ff.); Dieter Langewiesche, *1848 und 1918—zwei deutsche Revolutionen* (Bonn: Friedrich-Ebert-Stiftung, 1998).

7. Bernstein, *Revolution* (note 2), 198 (emphases in original); *Die Regierung der Volksbeauftragten*, introd. Erich Matthias, ed. Susanne Miller with Heinrich Potthoff (Düsseldorf: Droste, 1969), ii. 225, 228 (Ebert and Scheidemann in the session on 14 Jan. 1919); Peter von Oertzen, *Betriebsräte in der Novemberrevolution* (Düsseldorf: Droste, 1963), 109 ff.; Allan Mitchell, *Revolution in Bayern 1918/19. Die Eisner-Regierung und die Räterepublik* (Munich: C. H. Beck, 1967), 236 ff. orig. *Revolution in Bavaria, 1918–1919: The Eisner Regime and the Soviet Republic* (Princeton: Princeton University Press, 1965); David Clay Large, *Hitlers München. Aufstieg und Fall der Hauptstadt der Bewegung* (Munich: C. H. Beck, 1998), 118 ff., orig. *Where Ghosts Walked: Munich's Road to the Third Reich* (New York: W. W. Norton, 1997); Trude

Maurer, *Ostjuden in Deutschland 1918–1933* (Hamburg: Christians, 1986), 148 ff.; Winkler, *Weimar* (note 5), 69 ff. (76: Noske's declaration on 9 Mar. 1919; 79: Munich declaration on 6–7 Apr. 1919).

8. *Die Deutsche Nationalversammlung im Jahre 1919 in ihrer Arbeit für den Aufbau des neuen deutschen Volksstaats*, ed. Eduard Heilfron, iv (Berlin: Norddeutsche Buchdruckerei und Verlagsanstalt, 1919), 2646 (Scheidemann), 2650 (Hirsch), 2716 (Fehrenbach); *Protokoll über die Verhandlungen des Parteitags der Sozialdemokratischen Partei Deutschlands, abgehalten in Weimar vom 10. bis 15. Juni 1919. Bericht über die 2. Frauenkonferenz, abgehalten in Weimar am 15. und 16. Juni 1919* (Berlin: J. H. W. Dietz, 1919; repr. Glashütten: D. Auvermann, 1973), 242–7 (Bernstein), 281 (Scheidemann), 277–8 (Bernstein, quote here); Jürgen C. Hess, *'Das ganze Deutschland soll es sein!' Demokratischer Nationalismus in der Weimarer Republik, am Beispiel der Deutschen Demokratischen Partei* (Stuttgart: Klett-Cotta, 1978), 76 ff.; Ulrich Heinemann, *Die verdrängte Niederlage. Politische Öffentlichkeit und Kriegsschuldfrage in der Weimarer Republik* (Göttingen: Vandenhoeck & Ruprecht, 1983); Hagen Schulze, *Weimar. Deutschland 1917–1933* (Berlin: Severin und Siedler, 1982), 189 ff.; Klaus Hildebrand, *Das vergangene Reich. Deutsche Aussenpolitik von Bismarck bis Hitler 1871–1945* (Stuttgart: Deutsche Verlags-Anstalt, 1995), 383 ff.; Winkler, *Weimar* (note 5), 87 ff.; Huber, *Verfassungsgeschichte*, v (note 5), 1152 ff.; id., *Deutsche Verfassungsgeschichte seit 1789*, vii. *Ausbau, Schutz und Untergang der Weimarer Republik* (Stuttgart: Kohlhammer, 1984), 37–8 (Hindenburg, 18 Nov. 1919). On the Austria protocol of 22 Sept. 1919 see *Dokumente zur deutschen Verfassungsgeschichte*, iv. *Deutsche Verfassungsdokumente 1918–1933*, ed. id., 3rd edn (Stuttgart: Kohlhammer, 1991), 180. For the text of the peace conditions see *Treaty of Peace between the Allied and Associated Powers and Germany and Protocol Signed at Versailles, June 28, 1919* (Paris: Imprimerie nationale, 1919); the official German translation is *Die Friedensbedingungen der Alliierten und Assoziierten Regierungen* (Berlin: R. Hobbing, 1919).

9. Hugo Preuss, 'Volksstaat oder verkehrter Obrigkeitsstaat?', in *Staat, Recht und Freiheit. Aus 40 Jahren deutscher Politik und Geschichte* (Hildesheim: G. Olms, 1964), 365–8; *Die SPD-Fraktion in der Nationalversammlung 1919–1920*, introd. Heinrich Potthoff, ed. Heinrich Potthoff and Hermann Weber (Düsseldorf: Droste, 1986), 43 (Molkenbuhr); *Sten. Ber.*, cccxxvi. 374 (Fischer, 28 Feb. 1919); ibid., cccxxix. 219 (David); Carl Schmitt, *Verfassungslehre* (Berlin: Duncker & Humblot, 1928; repr. 1957), 111–12 ('provisional dictatorship of the president'); Ludwig Richter, *Kirche und Schule in den Beratungen der Weimarer Nationalversammlung* (Düsseldorf: Droste, 1996); Reinhard Rürup, 'Kontinuität und Grundlagen der Weimarer Verfassung', in *Vom Kaiserreich zur Weimarer Republik*, ed. Eberhard Kolb (Cologne: Kiepenheuer & Witsch, 1972), 218–43; Heinrich Potthoff, 'Das Weimarer Verfassungswerk und die deutsche Linke,' *AfS* 12 (1972), 433–83; Reinhard Schiffers, *Elemente direkter Demokratie im Weimarer Regierungssystem* (Düsseldorf: Droste, 1971), 117 ff.; Dieter Grimm, *Die Bedeutung der Weimarer Verfassung in der deutschen Verfassungsgeschichte* (Heidelberg: Stiftung Reichspräsident-Friedrich-Ebert-Gedenkstätte, 1990); Karl Dietrich Bracher, *Die Auflösung der Weimarer Republik. Eine Studie zum Problem des Machtverfalls in der Demokratie*, 4th edn (Villingen: Ring-Verlag, 1964), 21 ff.; Hagen Schulze, 'Das Scheitern der Weimarer Republik als Problem der Forschung', in *Weimar. Selbstpreisgabe einer Demokratie. Eine Bilanz heute*, ed. Karl Dietrich

Erdmann and Hagen Schulze (Düsseldorf: Droste, 1980), 23–41 (on the 'presidential reserve constitution': 30); Hans Mommsen, *Die verspielte Freiheit. Der Weg der Republik von Weimar in den Untergang von 1918 bis 1933* (Berlin: Propyläen, 1989), esp. 70; id., *The Rise and Fall of Weimar Democracy* (Chapel Hill: University of North Carolina Press, 1996); Huber, *Verfassungsgeschichte*, v (note 5), 1178 ff.; Winkler, *Weimar* (note 5), 99 ff.

10. Klaus Epstein, *Matthias Erzberger und das Dilemma der deutschen Demokratie* (Berlin: Verlag Annedore Leber, 1962), 369 ff., orig. *Matthias Erzberger and the Dilemma of German Democracy* (Princeton: Princeton University Press, 1959); Carl Ludwig Holtfrerich, *Die deutsche Inflation 1914–1923. Ursachen und Wirkungen in internationaler Perspektive* (Berlin: de Gruyter, 1981), 115 ff., tr. as *The German Inflation, 1914–1923: Causes and Effects in International Perspective* (Berlin, New York: De Gruyter, 1986); Gerald D. Feldman, *The Great Disorder: Politics, Economics, and Society in the German Inflation, 1914–1923* (Oxford: Oxford University Press, 1993), 25 ff.
11. Johannes Erger, *Der Kapp-Lüttwitz-Putsch. Ein Beitrag zur deutschen Innenpolitik 1919/20* (Düsseldorf: Droste, 1967), 15 ff.; Heinrich Potthoff, *Gewerkschaften und Politik zwischen Revolution und Inflation* (Düsseldorf: Droste, 1979), 267 ff.; Miller, *Bürde* (note 3), 377 ff.; Winkler, *Revolution* (note 3), 295 ff.; id., *Weimar* (note 5), 118 ff. (declarations from 13 to 15 Mar. 1920: 122–4, Ehrhardt Brigade and trade union demands of 18 Mar.: 127); Gerald D. Feldman, Eberhard Kolb, and Reinhard Rürup, 'Die Massenbewegungen der Arbeiterschaft in Deutschland am Ende des Ersten Weltkriegs', *PVS* 18 (1978), 353–439; Wolfgang J. Mommsen, 'Die deutsche Revolution von 1918–1920. Politische Revolution und soziale Protestbewegung', *GG* 44 (1978), 362–91; Huber, *Verfassungsgeschichte*, vii (note 8), 44 ff.; Wette, *Noske* (note 4), 627 ff. On the DVP declaration of 13 Mar. 1920 see *Nationalliberalismus* (note 5), pt 1, 247–50.
12. Ernst Laubach, *Die Politik der Kabinette Wirth 1921/22* (Lübeck: Matthiesen, 1968), 9 ff.; Heinrich Küppers, *Joseph Wirth. Parlamentarier, Minister und Kanzler der Weimarer Republik* (Stuttgart: Steiner, 1997), 104 ff.; Ulrike Hörster-Philipps, *Joseph Wirth 1879–1956. Eine politische Biographie* (Paderborn: Schöningh, 1998), 98 ff.; Gerhard Schulz, *Zwischen Demokratie und Diktatur. Verfassungspolitik und Reichsreform in der Weimarer Republik*, i. *Die Periode der Konsolidierung und der Revision des Bismarckschen Reichsaufbaus 1919–1930* (Berlin: de Gruyter, 1963), 320 ff.; Huber, *Verfassungsgeschichte*, vii (note 8), 25 ff., 169 ff.; Winkler, *Weimar* (note 5), 154 ff.; Norbert Elias, 'Die Zersetzung des staatlichen Gewaltmonopols in der Weimarer Republik', in *Studien über die Deutschen. Machtkämpfe und Habitusentwicklung im 19. u. 20. Jahrhundert* (Frankfurt: Suhrkamp, 1989), 282–94; id., 'Kriegsbejahende Literatur in der Weimarer Republik (Ernst Jünger)', ibid. 274–81; James M. Diehl, *Paramilitary Politics in Weimar Germany* (Bloomington: University of Indiana Press, 1977); Bernd Weisbrod, 'Gewalt in der Politik. Zur politischen Kultur in Deutschland zwischen den beiden Weltkriegen', *GWU* 43 (1992), 391–405; Rolf Geissler, *Dekadenz und Heroismus. Zeitroman und völkisch-nationalsozialistische Literaturkritik* (Stuttgart: Deutsche Verlags-Anstalt, 1964). On Max Weber's analysis see id., *Wirtschaft und Gesellschaft*, study edition, ed. Johannes Winckelmann, pt 1 (Cologne 1964), 39 (pt 1, ch. 1, § 17), 197 (pt 1, ch. 3, § 13), tr. as *Economy and Society: An Outline of Interpretive Sociology* (New York: Bedminster Press, 1968).

13. *Akten der Reichskanzlei. Weimarer Republik* [*AdR*]. *Die Kabinette Wirth I und II. 10. Mai 1921 bis 26. Oktober 1921, 26. Oktober 1921 bis 22. November 1922*, 2 vols., i. *Mai 1921 bis März 1922*, ed. Ingrid Schulze-Bidlingmaier (Boppard: H. Boldt, 1973), 7–13 (Schmidt's memorandum of 19 May 1921), 88–90 (cabinet session on 24, June 1921); Ludwig Thoma, *Sämtliche Beiträge aus dem 'Miesbacher Anzeiger' 1920/21*, ed. and comm. Wilhelm Volkert (Munich: Piper, 1989), 278, 286, 341; Epstein, *Erzberger* (note 10), 428 ff. (*Oletzkoer Zeitung* and *Kreuz-Zeitung*: 433); Gotthard Jasper, *Der Schutz der Republik. Studien zur staatlichen Sicherung der Demokratie in der Weimarer Republik 1922–1930* (Tübingen: Mohr, 1963), 34 ff. (36: *Berliner Lokalanzeiger*); Schulz, *Demokratie* (note 12), 364 ff.; Laubach, *Politik* (note 12), 263 ff.; Huber, *Verfassungsgeschichte*, vii (note 8), 206 ff.; Winkler, *Weimar* (note 5), 160 ff.
14. Sigrid Koch-Baumgarten, *Aufstand der Avantgarde. Die Märzaktion der KPD 1921* (Frankfurt: Campus,1986); Martin Walsdorff, *Westorientierung und Ostpolitik. Stresemanns Russlandpolitik in der Locarno-Ära* (Bremen: Schünemann, 1972), 31 (Wirth quotes); Francis L. Carsten, *Reichswehr und Politik 1918–1933* (Cologne: Kiepenheuer & Witsch, 1964), 78–9 (Seeckt quote), tr. as *The Reichswehr and Politics, 1918–1933* (Oxford: Clarendon Press, 1966); Theodor Schieder, *Die Probleme des Rapallo-Vertrags. Eine Studie über die deutsch-russischen Beziehungen 1922–1926* (Cologne: Westdeutscher Verlag, 1956); Hermann Graml, 'Die Rapallopolitik im Urteil der westdeutschen Forschung', *VfZ* 18 (1970), 366–91; Manfred Zeidler, *Reichswehr und Rote Armee 1920–1933* (Munich: Oldenbourg, 1993); Peter Krüger, *Die Aussenpolitik der Republik von Weimar* (Darmstadt: Wissenschaftliche Buchgesellschaft, 1985), 166 ff.; Hildebrand, *Reich* (note 8), 422 ff.; Küppers, *Wirth* (note 12), 154 ff.; Winkler, *Revolution* (note 3), 459 ff. (Breitscheid quote: 464); id., *Weimar* (note 5), 166 ff.
15. Harry Graf Kessler, *Walther Rathenau. Sein Leben und Werk* (Wiesbaden: Rheinische Verlags-Anstalt, 1928), tr. as *Walther Rathenau: His Life and Work* (New York: H. Fertig, 1969); Ernst Schulin, *Walther Rathenau. Repräsentant, Kritiker und Opfer seiner Zeit* (Göttingen: Musterschmidt, 1979); Martin Sabrow, *Der Rathenaumord. Rekonstruktion einer Verschwörung gegen die Republik von Weimar* (Munich: Oldenbourg, 1994); Winkler, *Weimar* (note 5), 174 ff.; Huber, *Verfassungsgeschichte*, vii (note 8), 249 ff.; Laubach, *Politik* (note 12), 263 ff.; Jasper, *Schutz* (note 13), 56 ff. (196 ff.: quotes on the judiciary); Christoph Gusy, *Weimar—die wehrlose Republik? Verfassungsschutzrecht und Verfassungsschutz in der Weimarer Republik* (Tübingen: Mohr, 1991), 134 ff.; Uwe Lohalm, *Völkischer Radikalismus. Die Geschichte des Deutschvölkischen Schutz- und Trutzbundes 1919–1923* (Hamburg: Leibnitz-Verlag, 1970); the article 'Deutschvölkischer Schutz- und Trutzbund 1919–1922', in *Lexikon zur Parteiengeschichte. Die bürgerlichen und kleinbürgerlichen Parteien und Verbände in Deutschland (1789–1945)*, 4 vols., ed. Dieter Fricke et al. (Leipzig: VEB Bibliographisches Institut Leipzig, 1983-), ii. 562–8 (membership: 562); Bernd Hüppauf, 'Schlachtenmythen und die Konstruktion des "Neuen Menschen"', *Keiner fühlt sich* (note 1), ed. Hirschfeld et al., 43–84 (on the Langemarck myth). Quote from Wirth in *Sten. Ber.*, ccclvi. 8058.
16. Heinrich August Winkler, 'Die deutsche Gesellschaft der Weimarer Republik und der Antisemitismus', in *Die Juden als Minderheit in der Geschichte*, ed. Bernd Martin and Ernst Schulin (Munich: Deutscher Taschenbuch Verlag, 1981), 271–89 (numbers: 274–5); Werner Jochmann, 'Die Ausbreitung des Antisemitismus in Deutschland

1914–1923', in *Gesellschaftskrise und Judenfeindschaft in Deutschland 1870–1945* (Hamburg: Christians, 1988), 99–170; Donald L. Niewyk, *The Jews in Weimar Germany* (Manchester: Manchester University Press, 1980); Dirk Walter, *Antisemitische Kriminalität und Gewalt. Judenfeindschaft in der Weimarer Republik* (Bonn: Dietz, 1999), 52 ff.; Maurer, *Ostjuden* (note 7); Ulrich Herbert, *Best. Biographische Studien über Radikalismus, Weltanschauung und Vernunft 1903–1989*, 2nd edn (Bonn: Dietz, 1996), 51 ff. (on the battle of the German *Hochschulring* against the 'foreign people' of the Jews: 63); Michael H. Kater, *Studentenschaft und Rechtsradikalismus in Deutschland 1918–1933. Eine sozialgeschichtliche Studie zur Bildungskrise in der Weimarer Republik* (Hamburg: Hoffmann und Campe, 1975); Konrad H. Jarausch, *Deutsche Studenten 1800–1970* (Frankfurt: Suhrkamp, 1984), 117 ff.; Jonathan R. C. Wright, *'Über den Parteien'. Die politische Haltung der evangelischen Kirchenführer 1918–1933* (Göttingen: Vandenhoeck & Ruprecht, 1977), 66, 84, 66 (political position of the Evangelical church in general), 84 (Rathenau's murder), orig. *'Above Parties': The Political Attitudes of the German Protestant Church Leadership 1918–1933* (London: Oxford University Press, 1974); Kurt Nowak, *Evangelische Kirche und Weimarer Republik. Zum politischen Weg des deutschen Protestantismus zwischen 1918 und 1922* (Weimar: H. Böhlaus Nachfolger, 1981), 117 ff. (quotes on Rathenau's murder: 118); id., *Geschichte des Christentums in Deutschland. Religion, Politik und Gesellschaft vom Ende der Aufklärung bis zur Mitte des 20. Jahrhunderts* (Munich: C. H. Beck, 1995), 205 ff.; Heinrich Lutz, *Demokratie im Zwielicht. Der Weg der deutschen Katholiken aus dem Kaiserreich in die Republik 1914–1925* (Munich: Kösel-Verlag, 1963); Heinz Hürten, *Deutsche Katholiken 1918–1945* (Paderborn: Schöningh, 1992); Morsey, *Zentrumspartei* (note 5), 401 ff. On the Munich Catholic congress see *Schulthess' Europäischer Geschichtskalender, NS* 38, 1922 (Munich: C. H. Beck, 1927), pt 1, 106–8. Quote from the Würzburg constitution of the German Students' Association from Ernst Rudolf Huber, *Deutsche Verfassungsgeschichte seit 1789*, vi. *Die Weimarer Reichsverfassung* (Stuttgart: Kohlhammer, 1981), 1011.

17. Liebe, *Deutschnationale Volkspartei* (note 5), 62 ff. (quote from Henning: 159); Large, *München* (note 7), 162 ff.; Winkler, *Revolution* (note 3), 434 ff. (Görlitz party congress), 468 ff. (USPD split in 1920), 486 ff. (reunion of MSPD and USPD); id., *Weimar* (note 5), 178 ff.; *Parteiprogramme* (note 5), ed. Mommsen, 453–8 (Görlitz platform of the SPD), 461–9 (Heidelberg platform); Laubach, *Politik* (note 12), 296 ff. (commission of experts and reparations note); Huber, *Verfassungsgeschichte*, vii (note 8), 258 ff.; Gerald D. Feldman, *Hugo Stinnes. Biographie eines Industriellen 1870–1924* (Munich: C. H. Beck, 1998), 741 ff.; Peter Wulf, *Hugo Stinnes. Wirtschaft und Politik 1918–1924* (Stuttgart: Klett-Cotta. 1979), 317 ff.; Alfred Kastning, *Die deutsche Sozialdemokratie zwischen Koalition und Opposition 1919–1923* (Paderborn: Schöningh, 1970), 110 ff.
18. Jacques Bariéty, *Les relations franco-allemandes après la première guerre mondiale* (Paris: Éditions Pedone, 1977), 91 ff.; *Die Ruhrkrise 1923. Wendepunkt der internationalen Beziehungen nach dem Ersten Weltkrieg*, ed. Klaus Schwabe (Paderborn: Schöningh, 1984); Hermann J. Rupieper, *The Cuno Government and Reparations 1922–1923: Politics and Economics* (The Hague: Nijhoff, 1979), 13 ff.; Winkler, *Weimar* (note 5), 186 ff; Laubach, *Politik* (note 12), 262, 263 ('first bread, then reparations'); *Dokumente und Materialien zur Geschichte der deutschen Arbeiterbewegung* [*DuM*], vii/2 (Berlin: Dietz, 1966), 210–13 (KPD declaration of 22 Jan. 1923); Hitler,

Sämtliche Aufzeichnungen 1905–1924, ed. Eberhard Jäckel with Axel Kuhn (Stuttgart: Deutsche Verlags-Anstalt, 1980), 785–6 (declaration on 12 Jan 1923).

19. *Protokoll der Konferenz der Erweiterten Exekutive der Kommunistischen Internationale. Moskau, 12.–23. Juni 1923* (Hamburg: C. Hoym Nachfolger L. Cahnbley, 1923; repr. Milan: Feltrinelli, 1967), 240–5; Otto-Ernst Schüddekopf, *Linke Leute von rechts. Die nationalrevolutionären Minderheiten und der Kommunismus in der Weimarer Republik* (Stuttgart: Kohlhammer 1960), 139 ff.; Louis Dupeux, *'Nationalbolschewismus' in Deutschland 1919–1933. Kommunistische Strategie und konservative Dynamik* (Munich: C. H. Beck, 1985), 178 ff., French orig. *National bolchevisme: stratégie communiste et dynamique conservatrice* (Paris: H. Champion, 1979); Marie-Luise Goldbach, *Karl Radek und die deutsch-sowjetischen Beziehungen 1918–1923* (Bonn: Verlag Neue Gesellschaft, 1973), 121 ff.; Werner T. Angress, *Die Kampfzeit der KPD 1921–1923* (Düsseldorf; Droste, 1973), 374 ff., orig. *Stillborn Revolution: The Communist Bid for Power in Germany, 1921–1923* (Princeton: Princeton University Press, 1963); Rosenberg, *Geschichte* (note 4), 136 ff.; Kastning, *Sozialdemokratie* (note 17), 114 ff.; Günter Arns, 'Die Linke in der SPD-Reichstagsfraktion im Herbst 1923', *VfZ* 22 (1974), 191–203; Winkler, *Revolution* (note 3), 561 ff.; id., *Weimar* (note 5), 190 ff. (on inflation figures: 193, on the KPD: 200, SPD demands: 203).
20. *AdR. Die Kabinette Stresemann I u. II. 13. August bis 6. Oktober 1923, 6. Oktober bis 30. November 1923*, 2 vols., ed. Karl Dietrich Erdmann and Martin Vogt (Boppard: Boldt, 1978), ii. 1215–16 (Seeckt to Wiedfeldt); Angress, *Kampfzeit* (note 19), 426 ff.; Winkler, *Revolution* (note 3), 619 ff.; id., *Weimar* (note 5), 209 ff. (*Völkischer Beobachter*: 211, Severing and Löbe 31 Oct. 1923: 228–9, on Hilferding's theories concerning the 'political wage' and 'organized capitalism': 328–9); Huber, *Verfassungsgeschichte*, vii (note 8), 330 ff.; Maurer, *Ostjuden* (note 7), 405 ff.; Reiner Pommerin, 'Die Ausweisung von "Ostjuden" aus Bayern 1923. Ein Beitrag zum Krisenjahr der Weimarer Republik', *VfZ* 34 (1986), 311–40; Gerald D. Feldman, 'Bayern und Sachsen in der Hyperinflation 1922/23', *HZ* 238 (1984), 569–609; Heinz Hürten, *Reichswehr und Ausnahmezustand. Ein Beitrag zur Verfassungsproblematik der Weimarer Republik in ihrem ersten Jahrfünft* (Opladen: Westdeutscher Verlag, 1977), 33–4; *Der Hitler-Putsch. Bayerische Dokumente zum 8./9. November 1923*, ed. Ernst Deuerlein (Stuttgart: Deutsche Verlags-Anstalt, 1968); Harold J. Gordon, Jr., *Hitler-Putsch 1923. Machtkampf in Bayern 1923–24* (Frankfurt: Bernard und Graefe, 1971), orig. *Hitler and the Beer Hall Putsch* (Princeton: Princeton University Press, 1972); Hanns-Hubert Hofmann, *Der Hitlerputsch. Krisenjahre deutscher Geschichte 1920–1924* (Munich: Nymphenburger Verlagshandlung, 1961).
21. *AdR, Kabinette Stresemann* (note 20), ii. 1059 (Adenauer, 13 Nov. 1923); Gustav Stresemann, *Vermächtnis. Der Nachlass in drei Bänden*, i (Berlin: Ullstein, 1932), 245 (Stresemann, 23 Nov. 1923), tr. as *Gustav Stresemann: His Diaries, Letters, and Papers* (New York: AMS Press, 1935). Karl Dietrich Erdmann, *Adenauer in der Rheinlandpolitik nach dem Ersten Weltkrieg* (Stuttgart: Klett, 1966), 71 ff.; Henning Köhler, *Adenauer. Eine politische Biographie* (Berlin: Propyläen, 1994), 154 ff.; Hans Peter Schwarz, *Adenauer. Der Aufstieg: 1876–1952* (Stuttgart: Deutsche Verlags-Anstalt 1986), 258 ff., tr. as *Konrad Adenauer: A German Politician and Statesman in a Period of War, Revolution, and Reconstruction* (Providence, RI: Berghahn Books, 1995); *Das Krisenjahr 1923. Militär und Innenpolitik 1922–1924*, ed. Heinz Hürten (Düsseldorf: Droste, 1980); Krüger, *Aussenpolitik* (note 14), 263 ff.; Bariéty, *Relations*

(note 18), 263 ff.; Huber, *Verfassungsgeschichte*, vii (note 8), 420 ff.; Winkler, *Weimar* (note 5), 236 ff. (enabling act of 8 Dec. 1923: 247, worker numbers: 245–6). Quote from Franz Eulenburg from id., 'Die sozialen Wirkungen der Währungsverhältnisse', *Jahrbücher zur Nationalökonomie u. Statistik*, 122 (1924), 748–94 (789).

22. *Deutscher Geschichtskalender 40* (1924), i. (internal events), ed. Friedrich Purlitz (Leipzig: Felix Meiner, n.d.), 296–9 (verdict in the Hitler case); *Der Hitler-Prozess 1924. Wortlaut der Hauptverhandlung vor dem Volksgericht München I*, ed. and comm. Lothar Gruchmann and Reinhard Weber with Otto Gritschneder (Munich: K. G. Saur, 1997–); Bernd Steger, 'Der Hitlerprozess u. Bayerns Verhältnis zum Reich 1923/24', *VfZ* 25 (1977), 441–66; Otto Gritschneder, *Bewährungsfrist für den Terroristen Adolf H. Der Hitler-Putsch und die bayerische Justiz* (Munich: C. H. Beck, 1990); Werner Link, *Die amerikanische Stabilisierungspolitik in Deutschland 1921–1932* (Düsseldorf: Droste, 1970), 201 ff.; Eckhard Wandel, *Die Bedeutung der Vereinigten Staaten von Amerika für das deutsche Reparationsproblem 1924–1929* (Tübingen: Mohr, 1971); Adam B. Ulam, *Expansion and Coexistence: The History of Soviet Foreign Policy, 1917–1967*, 3rd edn (New York: Praeger, 1969), 154 ff.; Winkler, *Revolution* (note 3), 725 ff.

23. *Sozialdemokratischer Parteitag 1924. Protokoll mit dem Bericht der Frauenkonferenz* (Berlin: J. H. W. Dietz, 1924; repr. Glashütten: D. Auvermann, 1974), 83 (Müller; emphasis in original), 99 (Dissmann), 139 (ballot), 204 (Müller's motion); Peter Haungs, *Reichspräsident und parlamentarische Kabinettsregierung. Eine Studie zum Regierungssystem der Weimarer Republik in den Jahren 1924 bis 1926* (Cologne: Westdeutscher Verlag, 1968), 74 ff.; Liebe, *Deutschnationale Volkspartei* (note 5), 76 ff.; Krüger, *Aussenpolitik* (note 14), 237 ff.; Huber, *Verfassungsgeschichte*, vii (note 8), 495 ff.; Winkler, *Weimar* (note 5), 261 ff. (May elections: 261–2, economic figures: 268, December elections: 271–2).

24. Adolf von Harnack, 'Brief an Friedrich Ebert', *Berliner Tageblatt*, 27 Dec. 1924; Erich Eyck, *Geschichte der Weimarer Republik*, 2 vols., 4th edn (Erlenbach-Zurich: E. Rentsch Verlag, 1962), i. 436 ff.; Wolfgang Birkenfeld, 'Der Rufmord am Reichspräsidenten. Zu Grenzformen des politischen Kampfes gegen die frühe Weimarer Republik', *AfS* 5 (1965), 453–500; Günter Arns, 'Friedrich Ebert als Reichspräsident', in *Beiträge zur Geschichte der Weimarer Republik*, ed. Theodor Schieder, *HZ*, suppl 1 (Munich: Oldenbourg, 1981), 1–3; Waldemar Besson, *Friedrich Ebert. Verdienst und Grenze* (Göttingen: Musterschmidt, 1963); Hans Mommsen, 'Friedrich Ebert als Reichspräsident', in *Arbeiterbewegung und Nationale Frage* (Göttingen: Vandenhoeck & Ruprecht, 1979), 296–317; Winkler, *Weimar* (note 5), 276 ff. (quotes about Ebert: 277; the emphasis in the *Vorwärts* quote of 28 Feb. 1925 is in the original).

25. *DuM* viii. 130–3 (KPD declaration of 11 Apr. 1925); 'Hindenburg, President by the Grace of Thälmann' ('Hindenburg von Thälmanns Gnaden') *Vorwärts*, 169, 27 Apr. 1925; 'Der Präsident der Minderheit', ibid. 197, 27 Apr. 1925; 'Es lebe die Republik!', *Frankfurter Zeitung*, 309, 27 Apr. 1925; Ernst Feder, 'Der Retter', *Berliner Tageblatt*, 198, 28 Apr. 1925; Heinrich Mann, 'Geistige Führer zur Reichspräsidentenwahl', *Deutsche Einheit* 7 (1925), 633–5; Harry Graf Kessler, *Tagebücher 1918–1937* (Frankfurt: Insel, 1961), 441–2, tr. as *Berlin in Lights: The Diaries of Count Harry Kessler, 1918–1937* (London: Weidenfeld and Nicolson, 1971); Noel D. Cary, 'The Making of the Reich President, 1925: German Conservatism and the Nomination of

Paul von Hindenburg', *CEH* 23 (1990), 179–204; Peter Fritzsche, *Rehearsals for Fascism: Populism and Political Mobilization in Weimar Germany* (New York: Oxford University Press, 1990), 154 ff.; John Zeender, 'The German Catholics and the Presidential Elections of 1925', *JMH* 35 (1963), 366–81; Karl Holl, 'Konfessionalität. Konfessionalismus und demokratische Republik. Zu einigen Aspekten der Reichspräsidentenwahl von 1925', *VfZ* 17 (1969), 254–75; Ulrich von Hehl, *Wilhelm Marx 1863–1946. Eine politische Biographie* (Mainz: Matthias-Grünewald-Verlag, 1987), 335 ff.; Andreas Dorpalen, *Hindenburg in der Geschichte der Weimarer Republik* (Berlin: A. Leber, 1966), 68 ff., orig. *Hindenburg and the Weimar Republic* (Princeton: Princeton University Press, 1964); John W. Wheeler-Bennett, *Der hölzerne Titan. Paul von Hindenburg* (Tübingen: Mohr, 1969), orig. *Hindenburg: The Wooden Titan* (London: St Martin's Press, 1967); Nowak, *Kirche* (note 16), 160 ff.; Heinrich August Winkler, *Der Schein der Normalität. Arbeiter und Arbeiterbewegung in der Weimarer Republik 1924–1930*, 2nd edn (Berlin: J. H. W. Dietz, 1987), 239 ff.; in *Weimar* (note 5), 278 ff.

26. Kurt Tucholsky, 'Berlin und die Provinz', in *Gesammelte Werke*, ii. *1925–1928* (Reinbek: Rowohlt, 1960), 1072–75; Martin Heidegger, *Sein und Zeit* (1927), 8th edn (Tübingen: Niemeyer, 1957), 127, tr. as *Being and Time* (New York: Harper, 1962); Carl Schmitt, *Die geistesgeschichtliche Lage des heutigen Parlamentarismus* (1923), 2nd edn (Berlin: Duncker & Humblot, 1926), 8, tr. as *The Crisis of Parliamentary Democracy* (Cambridge, MA: MIT Press, 1985); id., *Verfassungslehre* (note 9), 350–1; Hans Freyer, *Revolution von rechts* (Jena: E. Diederichs, 1931); Oswald Spengler, *Preussentum und Sozialismus* (Munich: Beck, 1920), 97–8 (emphases in original); Adolf Hitler, 'Warum musste ein 8. November kommen?' (April 1924), in *Aufzeichnungen* (note 18), 1216–27 (1226; emphasis in original); Armin Mohler, *Die Konservative Revolution in Deutschland 1918–1932. Grundriss ihrer Weltanschauungen* (Stuttgart: F. Vorwerk, 1950); Rolf-Peter Sieferle, *Die Konservative Revolution. Fünf biographische Skizzen* (Frankfurt: Fischer Taschenbuch, 1995); Stefan Breuer, *Anatomie der Konservativen Revolution* (Darmstadt: Wissenschaftliche Buchgesellschaft, 1993); Raimund von dem Bussche, *Konservatismus in der Weimarer Republik. Die Politisierung des Unpolitischen* (Heidelberg: C. Winter, 1998); Kurt Sontheimer, *Antidemokratisches Denken in der Weimarer Republik. Die politischen Ideen des deutschen Nationalismus zwischen 1918 und 1933* (Munich: Nymphenburger Verlagshandlung, 1962); Christian Graf v. Krockow, *Die Entscheidung. Eine Untersuchung über Ernst Jünger, Carl Schmitt und Martin Heidegger* (Stuttgart: F. Enke, 1958); Detlef Felken, *Oswald Spengler. Konservativer Denker zwischen Kaiserreich und Diktatur* (Munich: C. H. Beck, 1988), 25 ff.; Peter Gay, *Die Republik der Aussenseiter. Geist und Kultur in der Weimarer Zeit: 1918–1933* (Frankfurt: S. Fischer, 1970); 23 (quote), orig. *Weimar Culture: The Outsider as Insider* (New York: Harper & Row, 1968); Walter Laqueur, *Weimar. Die Kultur der Republik* (Frankfurt: Ullstein, 1976), orig. *Weimar: A Cultural History, 1918–1933* (London: Weidenfeld & Nicolson, 1974); Detlev J. K. Peukert, *Die Weimarer Republik. Krisenjahre der Klassischen Moderne* (Frankfurt: Suhrkamp, 1987); Friedhelm Kröll, *Das Bauhaus 1919–1933* (Düsseldorf: Bertelsmann-Universitätsverlag, 1974).

27. Theodore S. Hamerow, *Die Attentäter. Der 20. Juli—von der Kollaboration zum Widerstand* (Munich: C. H. Beck, 1999), 85 (Dibelius); orig. *On the Road to the Wolf's Lair: German Resistance to Hitler* (Cambridge, MA: Belknap Press of Harvard University Press, 1997); *Der Grosse Herder*, 4th edn, i (Freiburg: Herder, 1926), 725;

Victor Klemperer, *Leben sammeln, nicht fragen wozu und warum. Tagebücher 1925–1932* (Berlin: Aufbau-Verlag, 1996), 281 (entry for 11 July 1926 on Hiddensee); Kurt Tucholsky, 'Gefühlskritik', in *Werke* (note 26), i. 827–8; id., 'Feldfrüchte,' ibid., ii. 508–9.; Thomas Mann, 'Von deutscher Republik' (1922), in *Gesammelte Werke in dreizehn Bänden*, (= *Reden u. Aufsätze*, ii) (Frankfurt: Fischer Taschenbuch Verlag, 1965), 9–52; *Kampf um München als Kulturzentrum. Sechs Vorträge von Thomas Mann, Heinrich Mann, Leo Weismantel, Walter Courvoisier and Paul Renner. Mit einem Vorwort von Thomas Mann* (Munich: R. Pflaum, 1926), 9; Friedrich Meinecke, 'Republik, Bürgertum und Jugend' (1925), in *Werke*, ii. *Politische Schriften u. Reden* (Darmstadt: Siegfried-Toech-Mittler, 1958), 369–83 (376); id., 'Die deutschen Universitäten und der heutige Staat' (1926), ibid. 402–13 (410, 413); Istvan Déak, *Weimar Germany's Left-Wing Intellectuals: A Political History of the 'Weltbühne' and its Circle* (Berkeley: University of California Press, 1968); Winkler, *Gesellschaft* (note 16), 171 ff.; id., *Weimar* (note 5), 285 ff.

28. *Akten zur Deutschen Auswärtigen Politik 1918–1945. Aus dem Archiv des Auswärtigen Amts. Serie B: 1925–1933*, ii/1. *Dezember 1925 bis Juni 1926. Deutschlands Beziehungen zur Sowjet-Union, zu Polen, Danzig und den Baltischen Staaten* (Göttingen: Vandenhoeck & Ruprecht, 1967), 363–5 (Stresemann, 19 Apr. 1926); *Documents on German Foreign Policy, 1918–1945, from the Archives of the German Foreign Ministry* (Washington: U.S. Govt. Print. Off., 1949–); 'Der Sieg des Friedens', *Vorwärts*, 250, Oct. 17 1925; Jon Jacobson, *Locarno Diplomacy. Germany and the West 1925–1929* (Princeton: Princeton University Press, 1972); Klaus Megerle, *Deutsche Aussenpolitik 1925. Ansatz zu aktivem Revisionismus* (Bern: Herbert Lang, 1974); Jürgen Spenz, *Die diplomatische Vorgeschichte des Beitritts Deutschlands zum Völkerbund 1924–1926. Ein Beitrag zur Aussenpolitik der Weimarer Republik* (Göttingen: Musterschmidt, 1960), 33 ff.; Helmut Lippelt, ' "Politische Sanierung". Zur deutschen Politik gegenüber Polen 1925/26', *VfZ* 19 (1972), 323–73; Krüger, *Aussenpolitik* (note 14), 269 ff.

29. Henry A. Turner, Jr., *Stresemann—Republikaner aus Vernunft* (Berlin: Leber, 1968), 217 ff., orig. *Streseman and the Politics of the Weimar Republic* (Princeton: Princeton University Press, 1963); Klaus E. Rieseberg, 'Die SPD in der "Locarno-Krise" Oktober/November 1925', *VfZ* 30 (1982), 130–61; Ulrich Schüren, *Der Volksentscheid zur Fürstenenteignung 1926. Die Vermögensauseinandersetzungen mit den depossedierten Landesherren als Problem der deutschen Innenpolitik unter besonderer Berücksichtigung der Verhältnisse in Preussen* (Düsseldorf: Droste, 1978); Michael Stürmer, *Koalition und Opposition in der Weimarer Republik 1924–1928* (Düsseldorf: Droste, 1967), 132 ff.; Carsten, *Reichswehr* (note 14), 276 ff.; Huber, *Verfassungsgeschichte*, vii (note 8), 576 ff.; Winkler, *Schein* (note 25), 246 ff.; id., *Weimar* (note 5), 306 ff. For Scheidemann's speech on 16 Dec. 1926, see *Sten. Ber.*, cccxci. 8576–86.

30. Huber, *Verfassungsgeschichte*, vi (note 16), 1013 ff. ('Keudell case'); Stürmer, *Koalition* (note 29), 213 ff.; Haungs, *Reichspräsident* (note 23), 208 ff.; Ludwig Preller, *Sozialpolitik in der Weimarer Republik*, 2nd edn (Düsseldorf: Droste, 1978), 350 ff.; Peter Lewek, *Arbeitslosigkeit und Arbeitslosenversicherung in der Weimarer Republik 1918–1927* (Stuttgart: F. Steiner, 1992), 287 ff.; Gerhard A. Ritter, *Der Sozialstaat. Entstehung und Entwicklung im internationalen Vergleich* (Munich: Oldenbourg, 1989), 110 ff.; Wolfram Fischer, *Deutsche Wirtschaftspolitik 1918–1945*, 3rd edn

(Opladen: C. W. Leske, 1968), 43–4; Ellen L. Evans, *The German Center Party 1870–1933: A Study in Political Catholicism* (Carbondale: Southern Illinois University Press, 1981), 217 ff.; Karsten Ruppert, *Im Dienst am Staat von Weimar. Das Zentrum als regierende Partei in der Weimarer Demokratie 1923–1930* (Düsseldorf: Droste, 1992), 287 ff.; Günter Grünthal, *Reichsschulgesetz und Zentrumspartei in der Weimarer Republik* (Düsseldorf: Droste, 1968), 196 ff.; Wolfgang Wacker, *Der Bau des Panzerschiffes «A» und der Reichstag* (Tübingen: Mohr, 1959), 33 ff.; Wolfgang Horn, *Führerideologie und Parteiorganisation in der NSDAP (1919–1933)* (Düsseldorf: Droste, 1972), 209 ff. On the reinterpretation of the NSDAP platform see the article 'Nationalsozialistische Deutsche Arbeiterpartei (NSDAP) 1919–1945', in *Lexikon* (note 15), iii, ed. Fricke et al., 460–523 (481).

31. Wacker, *Bau* (note 30), 90 ff. (*Vossische Zeitung*, 137–8); Rudolf Heberle, *Landbevölkerung und Nationalsozialismus. Eine soziologische Untersuchung der politischen Willensbildung in Schleswig-Holstein 1918–1932* (Stuttgart: Deutsche Verlags-Anstalt, 1963), 48 ff.; Martin Vogt, *Die Entstehung des Youngplans dargestellt vom Reichsarchiv 1931–1933* (Boppard: H. Boldt, 1970); Hermann Weber, *Die Wandlung des deutschen Kommunismus. Die Stalinisierung der KPD in der Weimarer Republik*, 2 vols. (Frankfurt: Europäische Verlagsanstalt, 1969), i. 195 ff.; Siegfried Bahne, ' "Sozialfaschismus" in Deutschland. Zur Geschichte eines politischen Begriffs', *International Review of Social History*, 10 (1965), 211–45; Andreas Wirsching, *Vom Weltkrieg zum Bürgerkrieg? Extremismus in Deutschland und Frankreich 1918–1933/39. Berlin und Paris im Vergleich* (Munich: Oldenbourg, 1999), 361 ff.; Thomas Weingartner, *Stalin und der Aufstieg Hitlers. Die Deutschlandpolitik der Sowjetunion und der Kommunistischen Internationale 1929–1934* (Berlin: de Gruyter, 1970), 70 ff.; Thomas Kurz, *'Blutmai'. Sozialdemokraten und Kommunisten im Brennpunkt der Berliner Ereignisse von 1929* (Bonn: Dietz, 1988); Léon Schirmann, *Blutmai Berlin 1929. Dichtungen und Wahrheit* (Berlin: Dietz, 1992); Winkler, *Schein* (note 25), 521 ff.; id., *Weimar* (note 5), 334 ff. (election results, formation of the government, battleship), 346 (Paris negotiations), 349 ff. (KPD; quotes from the Wedding party congress and unemployment figures: 351–2), 352 ff. (social policy, Stresemann's death).

32. Otmar Jung, 'Plebiszitärer Durchbruch 1929? Zur Bedeutung von Volksbegehren und Volksentscheid gegen den Young-Plan für die NSDAP', *GG* 15 (1989), 489–510; id., *Direkte Demokratie in der Weimarer Republik. Die Fälle 'Aufwertung,' 'Fürstenenteignung', 'Panzerkreuzerverbot' und 'Young-Plan'* (Frankfurt: Campus, 1989), 109 ff.; Friedrich Freiherr Hiller von Gaertringen, 'Die Deutschnationale Volkspartei', in *Das Ende der Parteien 1933*, ed. Erich Matthias and Rudolf Morsey (Düsseldorf: Droste, 1960), 543–652 (544 ff.); John A. Leopold, *Alfred Hugenberg: The Radical Nationalist Campaign against the Weimar Republic* (New Haven: Yale University Press, 1981), 55 ff.; Gerhard Stoltenberg, *Die politischen Stimmungen im schleswig-holsteinischen Landvolk 1918–1933* (Düsseldorf: Droste, 1962), 125 ff.; Anselm Faust, *Der Nationalsozialistische Deutsche Studentenbund. Studenten und Nationalsozialismus in der Weimarer Republik*, 2 vols. (Düsseldorf: Droste, 1973); Kater, *Studentenschaft* (note 16), 147 ff., 218–19, 288 (student numbers); Bracher, *Auflösung* (note 9), 147–8 (AStAelections); Fischer, *Wirtschaftspolitik* (note 30), 43 ff. (economic figures); Preller, *Sozialpolitik* (note 30), 166–7 (unemployment figures); Ilse Maurer, *Reichsfinanzen und Grosse Koalition. Zur Geschichte des Reichskabinett Müller (1928–1930)* (Bern: Lang, 1973), 101 ff.; Rosemarie Leuschen-Seppel, *Zwischen*

Staatsverantwortung und Klasseninteresse. Die Wirtschafts- und Finanzpolitik der SPD zur Zeit der Weimarer Republik unter besonderer Berücksichtigung der Mittelphase 1924–1928/29 (Bonn: Verlag Neue Gesellschaft, 1981), 217 ff.; Winkler, *Weimar* (note 5), 354 ff. ('liberty law': 355, election returns: 356, Hilferding: 360).

33. *Aufstieg oder Niedergang? Deutsche Wirtschafts- und Finanzreform 1929. Eine Denkschrift des Präsidiums des Reichsverbandes der Deutschen Industrie* (Berlin, 1929), 45–6.; Michael Grübler, *Die Spitzenverbände der Wirtschaft und das erste Kabinett Brüning. Vom Ende der Grossen Koalition 1929/30 bis zum Vorabend der Bankenkrise 1931* (Düsseldorf: Droste, 1982), 49 ff.; Erasmus Jonas, *Die Volkskonservativen 1928–1933. Entwicklung, Struktur, Standort und staatspolitische Zielsetzung* (Düsseldorf: Droste, 1965), 186–8 (Hindenburg-Westarp talks, 18 Mar. 1929); Andreas Rödder, 'Dichtung und Wahrheit. Der Quellenwert von Heinrich Brünings Memoiren und seine Kanzlerschaft', *HZ* 265 (1997), 77–116; *Politik und Wirtschaft in der Krise 1930–1932. Quellen zur Ära Brüning*, introd. Gerhard Schulz, ed. Ilse Maurer and Udo Wengst with Jürgen Heideking, 2 vols. (Düsseldorf: Droste, 1980), i. 15–18 (Hindenburg–Westarp talks, 15 Jan. 1930), 61–2 (Hindenburg–Brüning interview, 1. Mar. 1930), 87–8 (letter of the delegate Gilsa [DVP] to the general director of the Good Hope Steel and Iron Works, Paul Reusch, 18 Mar. 1930), 94–5 (Meissner to Schleicher, 19 Jan. 1930; all emphases in the original); Johannes Hürter, *Wilhelm Groener. Reichswehrminister am Ende der Weimarer Republik (1928–1932)* (Munich: Oldenbourg, 1993), 240 ff.; Winkler, *Weimar* (note 5), 364 ff. (Young ballot: 368).

34. 'Eine unheilvolle Entscheidung', *Frankfurter Zeitung*, 232–4, 28 Mar. 1930; Rudolf Hilferding, 'Der Austritt aus der Regierung', *Die Gesellschaft*, 7 (1930/I), 385–92 (386); Winkler, *Schein* (note 25), 797 ff.; id., *Weimar* (note 5), 369 ff.

35. *Sten. Ber.*, cdxxviii. 6401 (Breitscheid, 16 July 1930); *Der deutsche Kommunismus. Dokumente*, ed. Hermann Weber (Cologne: Kiepenheuer & Witsch, 1963), 58–65 ('programmatic declaration'); Larry E. Jones, 'Sammlung oder Zersplitterung? Die Bestrebungen zur Bildung einer neuen Mittelpartei in der Endphase der Weimarer Republik 1930–1933', *VfZ* 25 (1977), 265–304; id., *Liberalism* (note 5), 374 ff.; Huber, *Verfassungsgeschichte*, vii (note 8), 749 ff.; Heinrich August Winkler, *Der Weg in die Katastrophe. Arbeiter und Arbeiterbewegung in der Weimarer Republik 1930–1933*, 2nd edn (Berlin: J. H. W. Dietz Nachfolger, 1990), 123 ff.; id., *Weimar* (note 5), 375 ff.

36. Theodor Geiger, 'Die Panik im Mittelstand', *Die Arbeit* 7 (1930), 637–54; Jürgen W. Falter, *Hitlers Wähler* (Munich: C. H. Beck, 1991), 98 ff. (electoral currents); Thomas Childers, *The Nazi Voter: The Social Foundations of Fascism in Germany, 1919–1933* (Chapel Hill: University of North Carolina Press, 1983), 119 ff.; Richard F. Hamilton, *Who Voted for Hitler?* (Princeton: Princeton University Press, 1982), 309 ff.; Jerzy Holzer, *Parteien und Massen. Die politische Krise in Deutschland 1928–1930* (Wiesbaden: Steiner, 1975), 64 ff.; M. Rainer Lepsius, *Extremer Nationalismus. Strukturbedingungen vor der nationalsozialistischen Machtergreifung* (Stuttgart: Kohlhammer, 1964); Siegfried Weichlein, *Sozialmilieus und politische Kultur in der Weimarer Republik. Lebenswelt, Vereinskultur, Politik in Hessen* (Göttingen: Vandenhoeck & Ruprecht, 1996); *Politische Teilkulturen zwischen Integration und Polarisierung. Zur politischen Kultur in der Weimarer Republik*, ed. Detlef Lehnert and Klaus Megerle (Opladen: Westdeutscher Verlag, 1990); Heinrich August Winkler, *Mittelstand, Demokratie und Nationalsozialismus. Die politische Entwicklung von*

Handwerk und Kleinhandel in der Weimarer Republik (Cologne: Kiepenheuer & Witsch, 1972), 157 ff.; id., *Weg* (note 35), 189 ff.; id., *Weimar* (note 5), 388 ff. The NSDAP platform in *Parteiprogramme* (note 5), ed. Mommsen, 547–50.

37. Thomas Mann, 'Deutsche Ansprache. Ein Appell an die Vernunft', in *Werke* (note 27), xi (= *Reden und Aufsätze*, iii), 870–90 (889–90); 'Braun zur politischen Lage', *Vorwärts*, 433, 16 Sept. 1930; Max Seydewitz, 'Der Sieg der Verzweiflung', *Klassenkampf*, 4/18 (1930), 545–50 (15 Sept.); 'Für Republik und Arbeiterrecht. Entschliessung der sozialdemokratischen Reichstagsfraktion,' *Vorwärts*, 465, 4 Oct. 1930; *Sten. Ber.*, cdxliv. 64 (Strasser, 17 Oct. 1930), 72 (Pieck, 17 Oct. 1930); 'Ferien vom Reichstag', *Vorwärts*, 583, 13. Dec. 1930; 'E. H. [Ernst Heilmann], Frick und Flick', *Das Freie Wort* 2/49 (1930), 1–4 (7 Dec.); 'Erziehung zur Demokratie', *Vorwärts*, 591, 18 Dec. 1930; Huber, *Verfassungsgeschichte*, vii (note 8), 685 ff. (Reichswehr case in Ulm); Winkler, *Weg* (note 35), 207 ff.; id., *Weimar* (note 5), 391 ff.

38. *Sozialdemokratischer Parteitag in Leipzig 1931 vom 31. März bis 5. Juni im Volkshaus. Protokoll* (Berlin: J. H. W. Dietz, 1931), 114 (Sollmann); 'Mahnruf an die Partei,' *Klassenkampf*, 5/13 (1931–2), 384–5 (7 Jan.); Rudolf Hilferding, 'In Krisennot', *Die Gesellschaft* 8 (1931/II), 1–8 (1); Karl-Erich Born, *Die deutsche Bankenkrise 1931. Finanzen und Politik* (Munich: Piper, 1967), 64 ff.; Harold James, *The Reichsbank and Public Finance in Germany 1924–1933: A Study of the Politics of Economics during the Great Depression* (Frankfurt: F. Knapp, 1985), 173 ff.; Gerhard Schulz, *Von Brüning zu Hitler. Der Wandel des politischen Systems in Deutschland 1930–1933* (Berlin: de Gruyter, 1992), 384 ff.; Andreas Rödder, *Stresemanns Erbe: Julius Curtius und die deutsche Aussenpolitik 1929–1931* (Paderborn: Schöningh, 1996), 186 ff.; Winkler, *Weg* (note 35), 288 ff.; id., *Weimar* (note 5), 408 ff.

39. 'Es geht ums Ganze', *Vorwärts*, 478, 12 Oct. 1931; 'Die Harzburger Inflationsfront', ibid. 479, 13 Oct. 1931; 'Schlagt Hitler!', ibid. 97, 27 Feb. 1932; *Das Deutsche Reich von 1918 bis heute. Jg. 1932*, ed. Cuno Horkenbach (Berlin: Verlag für Presse, Wirtschaft und Politik, 1933), 43–57 (Hindenburg commitee, Kyffhäuser Union, Goebbels on the presidential election); *Sten. Ber.*, cdxlvi. 2250 (Goebbels), 2254 (Schumacher); *Schulthess' Europäischer Geschichtskalender*, 73 (1932) (Munich: Beck, 1933), 58–9 (Brüning's speech); Knut Borchardt, 'Das Gewicht der Inflationsangst in den wirtschaftspolitischen Entscheidungsprozessen während der Weltwirtschaftskrise', in *Die Nachwirkungen der Inflation auf die deutsche Geschichte 1924–1933*, ed. Gerald D. Feldman (Munich: Oldenbourg, 1985), 233–60; Thilo Vogelsang, *Reichswehr, Staat und NSDAP. Beiträge zur deutschen Geschichte 1930–1933* (Stuttgart: Deutsche Verlags-Anstalt, 1962), 147 ff.; Volker R. Berghahn, *Der Stahlhelm. Bund der Frontsoldaten 1918–1935* (Düsseldorf: Droste, 1966), 195 ff.; id., 'Die Harzburger Front und die Kandidatur Hindenburgs für die Präsidentschaftswahlen 1932', *VfZ* 13 (1965), 64–82; Rudolf Morsey, 'Hitler als braunschweigischer Regierungsrat', *VfZ* 8 (1960), 419–48; Hagen Schulze, *Otto Braun oder Preussens demokratische Sendung. Eine Biographie* (Frankfurt: Propyläen, 1977), 719–20; Huber, *Verfassungsgeschichte*, vii (note 8), 925 ff.; Winkler, *Weg* (note 35), 511 ff.; id., *Weimar* (note 5), 444 ff. (Thälmann: 445).

40. Ernst Thälmann, 'Letzter Appell', *Rote Fahne*, 75, 8 Apr. 1932; 'An alle deutschen Arbeiter', ibid. 89, 26 Apr. 1932; 'Kampfmai gegen Hunger, Krieg, Faschismus,' ibid. 93, 30 Apr. 1932; Horkenbach, *1932* (note 39), 76–85 (Stahlhelm and DNVP positions); 'Landtagsschluss!', *Der Abend. Spätausgabe des Vorwärts*, 171, 12

Apr 1932; Jürgen W. Falter, 'The Two Hindenburg Elections of 1925 und 1932: A Total Reversal of Voter Coalitions', *CEH* 23 (1990), 225–41; Horst Möller, *Parlamentarismus in Preussen 1919–1932* (Düsseldorf: Droste, 1985), 386 ff.; Dietrich Orlow, *Weimar Prussia 1925–1933: The Illusion of Strength* (Pittsburgh: University of Pittsburg Press, 1991), 68–9; Hans-Peter Ehni, *Bollwerk Preussen? Preussen-Regierung, Reich-Länder-Problem und Sozialdemokratie 1928–1932* (Bonn: Verlag Neue Gesellschaft, 1975), 244 ff.; Richard Breitman, *German Socialism and Weimar Democracy* (Chapel Hill: University of North Carolina Press, 1981), 178 ff.; Siegfried Bahne, *Die KPD und das Ende von Weimar. Das Scheitern einer Politik 1928–1932* (Frankfurt: Campus, 1976), 23 ff.; *Die Generallinie. Rundschreiben des Zentralkomitees der KPD an die Bezirke 1929–1933*, introd. Hermann Weber with Johann Wachtler (Düsseldorf: Droste, 1981), pp. xlvi ff.; Peter Longerich, *Die braunen Bataillone. Geschichte der SA* (Munich: C. H. Beck, 1989), 153 ff.; Weingartner, *Stalin* (note 31), 119 ff.; Winkler, *Weg* (note 35), 385 ff. (1931Prussian referendum), 491 ff. (Stalin, Nov 1931), 528 ff. (second presidential ballot), 545 ff. (*Landtag* elections on 24 Apr. 1932); id., *Weimar* (note 5), 449 ff. (SA ban); Huber, *Verfassungsgeschichte*, vii (note 8), 938 ff.

41. Sten. Ber., cdxlvi. 2545–50 (Groener,. 10 May 1932), 2593–602 (Brüning, 11 May 1932); *Die Tagebücher von Joseph Goebbels. Sämtliche Fragmente*, ed. Elke Fröhlich, part 1, *Aufzeichnungen 1924–1941*, ii. *1 Jan. 1931–31 Dec. 1936* (Munich: K. G. Saur, 1987), 166–7; *Politik* (note 33), ii. 1486–99 (settlement measure; letters to Hindenburg; 1486–7: Gayl's letter of 24 May 1932); *AdR. Die Kabinette Brüning I und II. 30. März bis 10. Oktober 1931, 10. Oktober 1931 bis 1. Juni 1932*, 3 vols., ed. Tilman Koops (Boppard: H. Boldt, 1982–1990), iii. 2578–9 (resolution of the German Nationalist fraction); Heinrich Brüning, *Memoiren 1918–1934* (Stuttgart 1970), 597 ff.; Werner Conze, 'Zum Sturz Brünings', *VfZ* 1 (1953), 261–88; Heinrich Muth, 'Agrarpolitik und Parteipolitik im Frühjahr 1931', in *Staat, Wirtschaft und Politik in der Weimarer Republik. Festschrift für Heinrich Brüning*, ed. Ferdinand A. Hermens and Theodor Schieder (Berlin: Duncker & Humblot, 1967), 317–60; Udo Wengst, 'Schlange-Schöningen, Ostsiedlung und die Demission der Regierung Brüning', *GWU* 30 (1979), 538–51; Merkenich, *Grüne Front* (note 3), 310 ff.; Schulz, *Brüning* (note 38), 859 ff.; Huber, *Verfassungsgeschichte*, vii (note 8), 956 ff.; Winkler, *Weg* (note 35), 560 ff.; id., *Weimar* (note 5), 461 ff.
42. *Sten. Ber.*, cdxlvi. 2331 (Brüning, 24 Feb. 1932); Knut Borchardt, 'Zwangslagen und Handlungsspielräume in der grossen Weltwirtschaftskrise der frühen dreissiger Jahre: Zur Revision des überlieferten Geschichtsbildes', in *Wachstum, Krisen, Handlungsspielräume der Wirtschaftspolitik. Studien zur Wirtschaftsgeschichte des 19. u. 20. Jahrhunderts* (Göttingen: Vandenhoeck & Ruprecht, 1982), 165–82; id., *Perspectives on Modern German Economic History and Policy* (Cambridge: Cambridge University Press, 1991); Carl-Ludwig Holtfrerich, 'Alternativen zu Brünings Wirtschaftspolitik in der Weltwirtschaftskrise?', *HZ* 235 (1982), 605–31; Harold James, 'Gab es eine Alternative zur Wirtschaftspolitik Brünings?', *VSWG* 70 (1983), 523–41; Gottfried Plumpe, 'Wirtschaftspolitik in der Weltwirtschaftskrise. Realität u. Alternativen', *GG* 11 (1985), 326–57; Peter-Christian Witt, 'Finanzpolitik als Verfassungs- und Gesellschaftspolitik des Deutschen Reiches 1930–1932', *GG* 8 (1982), 386–414; *Economic Crisis and Political Collapse: The Weimar Republic 1924–1933*, ed. Jürgen Baron von Kruedener (New York: Berg, 1990); Josef Becker,

'Heinrich Brüning und das Scheitern der "konservativen Alternative," ' *APZ* 22 (1980), 3–17; Udo Wengst, 'Heinrich Brüning und die "konservative Alternative". Kritische Anmerkungen zu neuen Thesen über die Endphase der Weimarer Republik', ibid. 50, 19–26; Josef Becker, 'Geschichtsschreibung im historischen Optativ? Zum Problem der Alternativen im Prozess der Auflösung einer Republik wider Willen', ibid. 27–36; Rudolf Morsey, *Zur Entstehung, Authentizität und Kritik von Brünings 'Memoiren 1918–1934'* (Opladen: Westdeutscher Verlag, 1974); William L. Patch, *Heinrich Brüning and the Dissolution of the Weimar Republic* (Cambridge: Cambridge University Press, 1999); Rödder, 'Dichtung' (note 33), 77–8; Winkler, *Weimar* (note 5), 472 ff.

43. 'Das Kabinett der Barone', *Der Abend. Spätausgabe des Vorwärts*, 254, 1 June 1932; *Generallinie* (note 40), 526–34 (circular from the KPD secretariat, 14 July 1932); A.G. [Arkadij Gurland], 'Tolerierungsscherben—und was weiter?', *Marxistische Tribüne*, 2/12 (1932), 351–6 (352–3; (15 June; emphases in original); Joachim Petzold, *Franz von Papen. Ein deutsches Verhängnis* (Berlin: Buchverlag Union, 1995); Johann Wilhelm Brügel and Norbert Frei, 'Berliner Tagebuch 1932–1934. Aufzeichnungen des tschechoslowakischen Diplomaten Camill Hoffmann', *VfZ* 36 (1988), 131–83 (148–9: on the anti-National Socialist aspect of the *Preussenschlag*); Ludwig Dierske, 'War eine Abwehr des "Preussenschlags" vom 20. 7. 1932 möglich?', *Zeitschrift für Politik*, 17 (1970), 197–245; Thomas Alexander, *Carl Severing, Sozialdemokrat aus Westfalen mit preussischen Tugenden* (Bielefeld: Wetfalen Verlag, 1992), 189 ff.; Léon Schirmann, *Altonaer Blutsonntag, 17. Juli 1932. Dichtungen und Wahrheit* (Hamburg: Ergebnisse, 1994); Huber, *Verfassungsgeschichte*, vii (note 8), 977 ff.; Winkler, *Weg* (note 35), 611 ff. (on contacts between Gayl and Severing: 630–1); id., *Weimar* (note 5), 477 ff. (figures on the violence: 490). For the unemployment figures, see Preller, *Sozialpolitik* (note 30), 166–7.

44. *AdR. Das Kabinett von Papen. 1. Juni 1932 bis 3. Dezember 1932*, 2 vols., ed. Karl-Heinz Minuth (Boppard: H. Boldt, 1989), i. 377–86 (ministers' meeting on 10 Aug. 1932), 386–91 (negotiations on 13 Aug. 1932), 474–9 (Neudeck meeting, 30 Aug. 1932), 491–500 (meeting of the acting Prussian government, 2 Sept. 1932); Walther Hubatsch, *Hindenburg und der Staat. Aus den Papieren des Generalfeldmarschalls und Reichspräsidenten von 1878 bis 1934* (Berlin: Musterschmidt, 1966), 335–8: Meissner's notes, 11 Aug. 1932); Horkenbach 1932 (note 39), 284 (Gayl, 11 Aug. 1932); Hitler, *Reden, Schriften, Anordnungen. Februar 1925 bis Januar 1933*, v. *Von der Reichspräsidentenwahl bis zur Machtergreifung April 1932–Januar 1933*, part 1, *April 1932–September 1932*, ed. and comm. Klaus A. Lankheit (Munich: K. G. Saur, 1996), 300–3 (talks on 13 Aug. 1932), 317 (telegram of 22 Aug. 1932), 318–20 (declaration on 23 Aug. 1932); *Preussen contra Reich vor dem Staatsgerichtshof in Leipzig vom 10. bis 14. u. vom 17. Oktober 1932* (Berlin: J. H. W. Dietz, 1933), 44 (quote from the article 'Die Juden sind schuld' by Goebbels); 'Begnadigung zu Zuchthaus?', *Frankfurter Zeitung*, 629/30, 24 Aug. 1932; Falter, *Wähler* (note 36), 34 ff.; Richard Bessel, 'The Potempa Murder', *CEH* 10 (1977), 241–54; id., *Political Violence and the Rise of Nazism: The Storm-Troopers in Eastern Germany 1925–1934* (New Haven: Yale University Press, 1984), 157–8; Paul Kluke, 'Der Fall Potempa', *VfZ* 5 (1957), 279–97; Thilo Vogelsang, 'Zur Politik Schleichers gegenüber der NSDAP 1932', ibid. 6 (1958), 86–118 (esp. 89–90); id., *Reichswehr* (note 39), 256 ff.; Huber,

Verfassungsgeschichte, vii (note 8), 1048 ff.; Winkler, *Weg* (note 35), 681 ff.; id., *Weimar* (note 5), 505 ff.

45. *AdR, Kabinett Papen* (note 44), ii. 474–9 (Neudeck meeeting, 30 Aug. 1932; emphasis in original); Carl Schmitt, *Legalität und Legitimität* (Berlin: Duncker & Humblot, 1932), esp. 88 ff., tr. as *Legality and Legitimacy* (Durham, NC: Duke University Press, 2004); id., *Der Hüter der Verfassung* (Tübingen: Mohr, 1931), 132 ff.; Johannes Heckel, 'Diktatur, Notverordnungsrecht, Verfassungsnotstand mit besonderer Rücksicht auf das Budgetrecht', *Archiv des öffentlichen Rechts*, NS 22 (1932), 257–338 (260, 310–11); Eberhard Kolb and Wolfram Pyta, 'Die Staatsnotstandsplanung unter den Regierungen Papen und Schleicher', in *Die deutsche Staatskrise 1930–1933. Handlungsspielräume und Alternativen*, ed. Heinrich August Winkler (Munich: Oldenbourg, 1992), 153–79; Dieter Grimm, 'Verfassungserfüllung—Verfassungsbewahrung—Verfassungsauflösung. Positionen der Staatsrechtslehre in der Staatskrise der Weimarer Republik', ibid. 181–97; Heinrich Muth, 'Carl Schmitt in der deutschen Innenpolitik des Sommers 1932', *Beiträge* (note 24), ed. Schieder, 75–147; Joseph W. Benderski, *Carl Schmitt: Theorist for the Reich* (Princeton: Princeton University Press, 1983), 172 ff.; Paul Noack, *Carl Schmitt. Eine Biographie* (Berlin: Propyläen, 1993), 137 ff.; Ernst Rudolf Huber, 'Carl Schmitt in der Reichskrise der Weimarer Endzeit', in *Complexio Oppositorum. Über Carl Schmitt*, ed. Helmut Quaritsch (Berlin: Duncker & Humblot, 1988), 33–50; id., *Verfassungsgeschichte*, vii (note 8), 1073 ff.; Winkler, *Weimar* (note 5), 518 ff.

46. *Sten. Ber.*, cdliv., 1–3 (Zetkin), 13–14 (Torgler), 14–16 (Göring), 17–21 (ballot); *AdR, Kabinett v. Papen* (note 44), ii. 546–61 (Papen's radio address, 12 Sept. 1932), 576–85 (ministers' meeting, 14 Sept. 1932), 593–600 (ministers' meeting, 17 Sept. 1932), 754–64 (Papen's Munich speech, 12 Oct. 1932); Walther Schotte, *Der neue Staat* (Berlin: Neufeld & Henius, 1932); Edgar J. Jung, *Die Herrschaft der Minderwertigen, ihr Zerfall und ihre Ablösung durch ein Neues Reich*, 2nd edn (Berlin: Verlag Deutsche Rundschau, 1930), tr. as *Die Herrschaft der Minderwertigen = The Rule of the Inferior* (Lewiston, NY: E. Mellen Press, 1995); Wilhelm Stapel, *Der christliche Staatsmann. Eine Theologie des Nationalismus*, 2nd edn (Hamburg: Hanseatische Verlagsanstalt, 1932), 255; Walter Gerhart [Waldemar Gurian], *Um des Reiches Zukunft. Nationale Wiedergeburt oder politische Reaktion?* (Freiburg: Herder & Co., 1932), 121, 123; Klaus Breuning, *Die Vision des Reiches. Deutscher Katholizismus zwischen Demokratie und Diktatur (1929–1934)* (Munich: Hueber, 1969); Bernd Faulenbach, *Ideologie des deutschen Weges. Die deutsche Geschichte in der Historiographie zwischen Kaiserreich und Nationalsozialismus* (Munich: C. H. Beck, 1980), 35 ff.; Willi Oberkrome, *Volksgeschichte. Methodische Innovation und völkische Ideologisierung in der deutschen Geschichtswissenschaft 1918–1945* (Göttingen: Vandenhoeck & Ruprecht, 1993), 22 ff.; Hans Mommsen, 'Regierung ohne Parteien. Konservative Pläne zum Verfassungsumbau am Ende der Weimarer Republik', in *Staatskrise* (note 45), ed. Winkler, 1–18; Klaus Fritzsche, *Politische Romantik und Gegenrevolution. Das Beispiel des 'Tat-Kreises'* (Frankfurt: Suhrkamp, 1976); Ebbo Demant, *Von Schleicher zu Springer. Hans Zehrer als politischer Publizist* (Mainz: Hase und Koehler, 1971), 84 ff.; Sontheimer, *Denken* (note 26), 180 ff.

47. *Preussen* (note 44), 492–517; 'Was bedeutet das Urteil?', *Vorwärts*, 504, 25 Oct. 1932 (emphases in original); Goebbels, *Tagebücher* (note 41), 270; *Schulthess 1932* (note 39), 194–6 (Papen's address); Ehni, *Bollwerk* (note 40), 271 ff.; Schulze, *Braun*

(note 39), 763 ff.; Schulz, *Brüning* (note 38), 1000 ff.; Klaus Rainer Röhl, *Nähe zum Gegner. Kommunisten und Nationalsozialisten im Berliner BVG-Streik von 1932* (Frankfurt: Campus, 1994); Huber, *Verfassungsgeschichte*, vii (note 8), 1128 ff.; Winkler, *Weg* (note 35), 765 ff.; id., *Weimar* (note 5), 529 ff.

48. *Anpassung oder Widerstand? Aus den Akten des Parteivorstands der deutschen Sozialdemokratie 1932/33*, ed. Hagen Schulze (Bonn: Neue Gesellschaft, 1975), 55 (Böchel), 71 (Wels); 'Wahlsieg der KPD im Feuer der Streikkämpfe', *Inprekorr*, 12 (1932), 94 3025–7 (11 Jan.); 'Die *Prawda* zu den Ereignissen der Reichstagswahlen in Deutschland', ibid. 3027–8; Stefan Altevogt, 'Bürgerkriegsangst am Ende der Weimarer Republik, Juni 1931 bis Januar 1933', master's thesis, Humboldt University, Berlin, 1996, 80 (*Vossische Zeitung*, 8 Nov. 1932); Bernd Sösemann, *Das Ende der Weimarer Republik in der Kritik demokratischer Publizisten. Theodor Wolff, Ernst Feder, Julius Elbau, Leopold Schwarzschild* (Berlin: Colloquium-Verlag, 1976), 162 ff.; Goebbels, *Tagebücher* (note 41), 276–7. (entry for 10 Nov. 1932).

49. Horkenbach 1932 (note 39), 374 (Papen's announcement of 8 Nov. 1932); *Schulthess 1932* (note 39), 198 (Papen with Hindenburg, 10 Nov. 1932); *AdR, Kabinett Papen* (note 44), ii. 901–7 (ministers' meeting, 9 Nov. 1932), 937–8 (Keppler to Schröder, 13 Nov. 1932); Eberhard Czichon, *Wer verhalf Hitler zur Macht? Zum Anteil der deutschen Industrie an der Zerstörung der Weimarer Republik* (Cologne: Pahl-Rugenstein, 1967), 64–72 (on the letter to Hindenburg; for the text itself, see 69–71), 73 (D Scholz on the meeting of the Langnam Association); Henry A. Turner, Jr., *Die Grossunternehmer und der Aufstieg Hitlers* (Berlin: Siedler, 1985), 358 ff., orig. *German Big Business and the Rise of Hitler* (Oxford: Oxford University Press, 1985); Reinhard Neebe, *Grossindustrie, Staat und NSDAP 1930–1933. Paul Silverberg und der Reichsverband der Deutschen Industrie in der Krise der Weimarer Republik* (Göttingen: Vandenhoeck & Ruprecht, 1981), 167–8; Heinrich Muth, 'Das "Kölner Gespräch" am 4. Januar 1933', *GWU* 37 (1986), 463–80, 529–41; Petzold, *Papen* (note 43), 119 ff.; Winkler, *Weimar* (note 5), 538 ff.

50. *AdR, Kabinett Papen* (note 44), ii. 956–63 (ministers' meeting, 17 Nov. 1932), 984–6 (Hindenburg–Hitler talks, 19 Nov. 1932), 988–92 (Hindenburg–Hitler talks, 21 Nov. 1932), 998–1000 (Meissner to Hitler, 24 Nov. 1932), 1012–22 (ministers' meeting, 25 Nov. 1932), 1025–7 (notes by retired State Secretary Hans Schäffer on the Hindenburg–Papen–Schleicher talks, 26 Nov. 1932, with extracts from the journal of Schwerin von Krosigk); *Die Gewerkschaften in der Endphase in der Republik 1930–1933*, ed. Peter Zahn with Detlev Brunner (= *Quellen zur Geschichte der deutschen Gewerkschaftsbewegung im 20. Jahrhundert*, iv) (Cologne: Bund-Verlag, 1988), 766–70 (Schleicher–Leipart–Eggert talks, 28 Nov. 1932); *Archiv der sozialen Demokratie, Bonn, ADGB-Restakten, NB 112: Verhandlungen mit der Reichsregierung* (Breitscheid's notes on his talk with Schleicher, 28 Nov. 1932; here also Schleicher's report on his talk with Hindenburg on 26 Nov); Richard Breitman, 'German Socialism and General Schleicher,' *CEH* 9 (1976), 352–88 (esp. 367 ff.); Winkler, *Weg* (note 35), 793 ff.; id., *Weimar* (note 5), 543 ff.

51. Theodor Leipart, *Die Kulturaufgaben der Gewerkschaften. Vortrag in der Aula der Bundesschule in Bernau am 14. Oktober 1932* (Berlin: Verlagsgesellschaft des Allgemeinen Deutschen Gewerkschaftsbundes, 1932), 3, 16–20; Ernst Jünger, *Der Arbeiter. Herrschaft und Gestalt* (Hamburg: Hanseatische Verlagsanstalt, 1932); 'Papen nicht!', *Vorwärts*, 562, 29 Nov. 1932; 'Sturm in den Betrieben', ibid.; 'Alarmierende

Gerüchte', ibid. (all emphases in the original); Peter Zahn, 'Gewerkschaften in der Krise. Zur Politik des ADGB in der Ära der Präsidialkabinette 1930 bis 1933', in *Solidarität und Menschenwürde. Etappen der deutschen Gewerkschaftsgeschichte von den Anfängen bis zur Gegenwart*, ed. Erich Matthias and Klaus Schönhoven (Bonn: Verlag Neue Gesellschaft, 1984), 233–53 (the effect of the Bernau speech: esp. 251–2); Axel Schildt, *Militärdiktatur mit Massenbasis? Die Querfrontkonzeption der Reichswehrführung um General von Schleicher am Ende der Weimarer Republik* (Frankfurt: Campus, 1981), 109 ff.; Peter Hayes, ' "A Question Mark with Epaulettes"? Kurt von Schleicher and Weimar Politics', *JMH* 52 (1980), 35–65; Winkler, *Weg* (note 35), 746 ff.; id., *Weimar* (note 5), 550 ff.

52. *AdR, Kabinett Papen* (note 44), ii. 1035–6 (ministers' conference, 2 Dec. 1932), 1036–8 (Krosigk's journal notes for 2 Dec. 1932), 1039–40 (ministers' conference, 2 Dec. 1932); Franz von Papen, *Der Wahrheit eine Gasse* (Munich: P. List, 1952), 243–52 (Hindenburg quote: 250); id., *Vom Scheitern einer Demokratie 1930–1933* (Mainz: Hase & Koehler, 1968), 308–14: Wolfram Pyta, 'Vorbereitungen für den militärischen Ausnahmezustand unter Papen/Schleicher', *MGM* 51 (1992), 385–428; Vogelsang, *Reichswehr* (note 39), 332 ff., 482 ff.; Huber, *Verfassungsgeschichte*, vii (note 8), 1154 ff.; Winkler, *Weimar* (note 5), 553 ff.
53. Goebbels, *Tagebücher* (note 41), 299 (entry for 10 Dec. 1932); Thilo Vogelsang, 'Neue Dokumente zur Geschichte der Reichswehr 1930–1933', *VfZ* 2 (1954), 397–436 (Schleicher's speech: 426–8); *AdR. Das Kabinett von Schleicher. 3. Dezember 1932 bis 30. Januar 1933*, ed. Anton Golecki (Boppard: H. Boldt, 1986), 101–17 (Schleicher's inaugural address); Udo Kissenkötter, *Gregor Strasser und die NSDAP* (Stuttgart: Deutsche Verlags-Anstalt, 1978), 170 ff.; Huber, *Verfassungsgeschichte*, vii (note 8), 1162 ff.; Winkler, *Weg* (note 35), 810 ff.; id., *Weimar* (note 5), 557 ff. (557–8: press reaction to Schleicher's appointment, 559–60: Reichstag session, 562: Imbusch, Leipart).
54. *Schulthess' Europäischer Geschichtskalender*, 74 (1933) (Munich: C. H. Beck, 1934), 5–6 (Cologne talks), 7–8 (Schleicher–Papen meeting, 9 Jan. 1933); Otto Meissner, *Staatssekretär unter Ebert–Hindenburg–Hitler* (Hamburg: Hoffmann und Kampe, 1951), 261–2.; Kissenkötter, *Strasser* (note 53), 191–2; Muth, 'Gespräch' (note 49), 529 ff.; Goebbels, *Tagebücher* (note 41), 331–2; Hans Otto Meissner and Harry Wilde, *Die Machtergreifung. Ein Bericht über die Technik des nationalsozialistischen Staatsstreichs* (Stuttgart: Cotta, 1958), 148 ff.; Henry A. Turner, Jr., *Hitlers Weg zur Macht. Der Januar 1933* (Munich: Luchterhand, 1996), 44 ff., orig. *Hitler's Thirty Days to Power: January 1933* (Reading, MA: Addison-Wesley, 1996); id., *Grossunternehmer* (note 49), 378 ff.; Neebe, *Grossindustrie* (note 49), 171 ff.; Czichon, *Wer verhalf* (note 49), 77 ff.; Petzold, *Papen* (note 43), 134 ff.; Winkler, *Weimar* (note 5), 567 ff.
55. *Schulthess 1933* (note 54), 5 (advisory committee, 4 Jan. 1933), 11–14 (conflict between government and National Land League); *AdR, Kabinett Schleicher* (note 53), 206–20 (National Land League, Darré emphases in original); 'Reichstag erst am 24. Januar', *Vorwärts*, 7, 1 May 1933 (Breitscheid); Horst Gies, 'NSDAP und landwirtschaftliche Organisation in der Endphase der Weimarer Republik', *VfZ* 15 (1967), 341–76; Bert Hoppe, 'Von Schleicher zu Hitler. Dokumente zum Konflikt zwischen dem Reichslandbund und der Regierung Schleicher in den letzten Wochen der Weimarer Republik,' ibid. 45 (1997), 629–57; Merkenich, *Grüne Front* (note 3), 315 ff.; Dieter Gessner, *Agrarverbände in der Weimarer Republik. Wirtschaftliche und soziale*

Voraussetzungen agrarkonservativer Politik vor 1933 (Düsseldorf: Droste, 1976), 242 ff.; Jutta Ciolek-Kümper, *Wahlkampf in Lippe. Die Wahlkampfpropaganda der NSDAP zur Landtagswahl am 15. Januar 1933* (Munich: Verlag Dokumantation, 1976).

56. *AdR, Kabinett Schleicher* (note 53), 230–43 (ministers' conference, 16 Jan. 1933), 297–300 (Simpfendörfer to Schleicher, 24. Jan. 1933); Vogelsang, *Reichswehr* (note 39), 482–4 (Sperr); Schmitt, *Verfassungslehre* (note 9), 345; Ernst Fraenkel, 'Verfassungsreform und Sozialdemokratie', *Die Gesellschaft*, 9 (1932/II), 484–500 (492, 494); Wolfram Pyta, 'Verfassungsumbau, Staatsnotstand und Querfront: Schleichers Versuche zur Fernhaltung Hitlers von der Reichskanzlerschaft August 1932 bis Januar 1933', in *Gestaltungskraft des Politischen. Festschrift f. Eberhard Kolb*, ed. id. and Ludwig Richter (Berlin: Duncker & Humblot, 1998), 173–97; id., 'Konstitutionelle Demokratie statt monarchischer Restauration. Die verfassungspolitische Konzeption Schleichers in der Weimarer Staatskrise', *VfZ* 47 (1999), 417–41; Huber, *Verfassungsgeschichte*, vii (note 8), 1227 ff.; Winkler, *Weg* (note 35), 802 ff., 835 ff.; id., *Weimar* (note 5), 574 ff.

57. 'Warnung an Schleicher. Breitscheid über seine Pläne,' *Vorwärts*, 33, 20 Jan. 1933; 'Staatsstreich-Pläne', ibid. 41, 25 Jan. 1933; Siegfried Aufhäuser, 'Reichstag arbeite!', ibid.; *Schulthess 1933* (note 54), 21–4 (*Osthilfe* scandal), 21 (Hitler's talks with Hugenberg and Papen), 25–6 (DNVP statement); *AdR, Kabinett Schleicher* (note 53), 282–3 (DNVP communiqué to Schleicher), 284–5 (Hindenburg's reception of Schleicher), 304–5 (Kaas' letter to Schleicher); *Die Deutschnationalen und die Zerstörung der Weimarer Republik. Aus dem Tagebuch von Reinhold Quaatz 1928–1933*, ed. Hermann Weiss and Paul Hoser (Munich: Oldenbourg, 1989), 223–7; Joachim von Ribbentrop, *Zwischen London und Moskau. Erinnerungen und letzte Aufzeichnungen* (Leoni: Druffel-Verlag, 1953), 37 ff., tr. as *The Ribbentrop Memoirs* (London: Weidenfeld and Nicolson, 1954); Wolfgang Wessling, 'Hindenburg, Neudeck und die deutsche Wirtschaft', *VSWG* 64 (1977), 41–73; Noack, *Schmitt* (note 45), 155 ff.; Huber, *Verfassungsgeschichte*, vii (note 8), 1240 ff.; Winkler, *Weg* (note 35), 837; id., *Weimar* (note 5), 578 ff.

58. *AdR, Kabinett Schleicher* (note 53), 306–10 (ministers' conference, 28 Jan. 1933), 310–11 (Hindenburg's reception of Schleicher, 28 Jan. 1933), 313 (Kastl's and Hamm's letter to Meissner, 28 Jan. 1933), 314 (letter of the trade union associations to Hindenburg, 28 Jan. 1933); *Schulthess 1933* (note 54), 28–30 (Schleicher's resignation, Papen's exploratory talks); 'Schleicher zurückgetreten', *Vorwärts*, 48, 28 Jan. 1933; 'Das rote Berlin marschiert!', ibid. 49, 29 Jan. 1933 (all emphases in the original); Ribbentrop, *Zwischen London* (note 57), 40–1; Vogelsang, *Reichswehr* (note 39), 382 ff.; Huber, *Verfassungsgeschichte*, vii (note 8), 1251 ff.; Winkler, *Weg* (note 35), 849 ff.; id., *Weimar* (note 5), 584 ff.

59. *Anpassung* (note 48), 131–36 (session of the SPD party executive on 30 Jan. 1933), 145–6 (Breitscheid in the party committee, 31 Jan. 1933); 'Nichtangriffspakt!', *Vorwärts*, 42, 25 Jan. 1933; 'Arbeitendes Volk! Republikaner!', ibid. 51, 31 Jan. 1933; 'SPD-"Nichtangriffspakt" gegen die Werktätigen!', *Rote Fahne*, 22, 26 Jan. 1933; *Die Antifaschistische Aktion. Dokumentation u. Chronik Mai 1932 bis Januar 1933*, ed. and introd. Heinz Karl and Erika Kücklich (Berlin: Dietz, 1965), 354–6; *AdR. Die Regierung Hitler*, pt 1, *1933/34*, i. *30. Januar 1933 bis 31. August 1935*, ed. Karl-Heinz Minuth (Boppard: H. Boldt, 1983), 5–10 (ministers' conference on 31 Jan. and 1 Feb. 1933); *Schulthess 1933* (note 54), 32–7 (Hitler' talks with the Center); *Die Protokolle*

der Reichstagsfraktion und des Fraktionsvorstands der Deutschen Zentrumspartei 1926–1933, ed. Rudolf Morsey (Mainz: Matthias-Grünewald-Verlag, 1969), 611–15 (sessions of the fraction and fraction leadership on 31 Jan and 1 Feb. 1933); Rudolf Morsey, 'Hitlers Verhandlungen mit der Zentrumsführung am 31. Januar 1933. Dokumentation', *VfZ* 9 (1961), 182–94; id., 'Die Deutsche Zentrumspartei', in Matthias and Morsey, *Ende* (note 32), 281–453 (esp. 339 ff.); Winkler, *Weg* (note 35), 305 ff. (on the Comintern's March 1931 argument about the SPD as the 'main social pillar of the bourgeoisie'), 858 ff.; id., *Weimar* (note 5), 593 ff.

60. Hitler, *Reden*, v, pt 1 (note 44), 335 (4 Sept. 1932), 353 (15 Sept. 1932); Schmitt, *Legalität* (note 45), 50; Fraenkel, 'Verfassungsreform' (note 56), 491; Weber, *Wirtschaft* (note 12), i. 23 (part 1, ch. 1, § 5), 157 (part 1, ch. 3, § 1); Huber, *Verfassungsgeschichte*, vii (note 8), 1264 ff.; Winkler, *Weg* (note 35), 861 ff.; id., *Weimar* (note 5), 595 ff.

LOOKING AHEAD

1. Adolf Hitler, *Monologe im Führerhauptquartier 1941–1944. Die Aufzeichnungen Heinrich Heims*, ed. Werner Jochmann (Hamburg: A. Knaus, 1980), 155 (17–18 Dec. 1941).
2. Hermann Oncken, 'Die Wiedergeburt der grossdeutschen Idee' (1920), in *Nation und Geschichte. Reden und Aufsätze 1919–1935* (Berlin: G. Grote'sche Verlagsbuchhandlung, 1935), 45–70 (61, 62, 64; emphasis in original); Bernd Faulenbach, *Ideologie des deutschen Weges. Die deutsche Geschichte in der Historiographie zwischen Kaiserreich und Nationalsozialismus* (Munich: C. H. Beck, 1980), 67 ff.; Stanley Suval, 'Overcoming "Kleindeutschland": The Politics of Historical Mythmaking in the Weimar Republic', *CEH* 2 (1969), 312–30; the article 'Österreichisch-deutscher Volksbund 1920–1933', in *Lexikon zur Parteiengeschichte. Die bürgerlichen und kleinbürgerlichen Parteien und Verbände in Deutschland (1789–1945)*, ed. Dieter Fricke et al., 4 vols. (Leipzig: VEB Bibliographisches Institut Leipzig, 1983–), iii. 3, 566–68; Karl Rohe, *Das Reichsbanner Schwarz Rot Gold. Ein Beitrag zur Geschichte und Struktur der politischen Kampfverbände zur Zeit der Weimarer Republik* (Düsseldorf: Droste, 1966), 227 ff.; Heinrich August Winkler, *Der Schein der Normalität. Arbeiter und Arbeiterbewegung in der Weimarer Republik 1924–1930*, 2nd edn (Berlin: J. H. W. Dietz, 1987), 378 ff. (Schützinger quote: 382).
3. Giselher Wirsing, *Zwischeneuropa und die deutsche Zukunft* (Jena: E. Diederichs, 1932); Reinhard Frommelt, *Paneuropa oder Mitteleuropa. Einigungsbestrebungen im Kalkül deutscher Wirtschaft und Politik 1925–1933* (Stuttgart: Deutsche Verlags-Anstalt, 1977); Alan S. Milward, 'Der deutsche Handel und der Welthandel 1925–1939', in *Industrielles System und politische Entwicklung in der Weimarer Republik*, ed. Hans Mommsen et al. (Düsseldorf: Droste, 1974), 472–84; Dörte Doering, 'Deutsch-österreichische Aussenhandelsverflechtung während der Weltwirtschaftskrise', ibid. 514–30. On the projected German-Austrian customs union see above p.444; on the *jungkonservativ* ideology of the Reich, see p.466.
4. The article 'Verein für das Deutschtum im Ausland 1881–1945', in *Lexikon* (note 2), iv, ed. Fricke et al., 282–97; Norbert Krekeler, *Revisionsanspruch und geheime Ostpolitik der Weimarer Republik. Die Subventionierung der deutschen Minderheit in Polen 1919 –1933* (Stuttgart: Deutsche Verlags-Anstalt, 1973); Michael Fahlbusch,

Wissenschaft im Dienst der nationalsozialistischen Politik? Die 'Volksdeutschen Forschungsgemeinschaften' von 1931–1945 (Baden-Baden: Nomos, 1999), 65 ff.

5. Hitler, Reden, Schriften, Anordnungen. Februar 1925 bis Januar 1933, v. *Von der Reichspräsidentenwahl* bis zur Machtergreifung April 1932–Januar 1933, part 1, April 1932–September 1932, ed. and comm. Klaus A. Lankheit (Munich: K. G. Saur, 1996), 31 ('Reich' quote from the Elbing speech on 5 Apr. 1932); Frank-Lothar Kroll, *Utopie als Ideologie. Geschichtsdenken und politisches Handeln im Dritten Reich* (Paderborn: Schöningh, 1998), 65 ff.; Herfried Münkler, 'Das Reich als politische Macht und politischer Mythos', in *Reich—Nation—Europa. Modelle politischer Ordnung* (Weinheim: Beltz Athenaeum, 1996), 11–59; Jean F. Neurohr, *Der Mythos vom Dritten Reich. Zur Geistesgeschichte des Nationalsozialismus* (Stuttgart: Cotta, 1957); Klaus Schreiner, ' "Wann kommt der Retter Deutschlands?" Formen und Funktionen von politischem Messianismus in der Weimarer Republik', *Saeculum*, 49 (1998), 107–60; Dirk Walter, *Antisemitische Kriminalität und Gewalt. Judenfeindschaft in der Weimarer Republik* (Bonn: Dietz, 1999), 209 ff.

Index